D0822634

P[THE]OWER

NEW TESTAMENT
REVEALING JEWISH ROOTS

Fourth Edition
A TRANSLATION OF THE 1993 4th EDITION
UNITED BIBLE SOCIETY GREEK TEXT

WILLIAM J. MORFORD

Copyright © 2003 by William J Morford

Published in The United States of America by
True Potential Publishing, Inc.
PO Box 904 Travelers Rest, SC 29690
http://tppress.com

4th Edition, This Printing 2011

Originally published by Shalom Ministries, Inc.
1st Printing October, 2003
2nd Printing September, 2004
3rd Printing July, 2005
4th Printing November, 2006
5th Printing January 2007
6th Printing June 2007

The Power New Testament text may be quoted in any form (written, visual, electronic or audio) up to an inclusive of five hundred (500) words, without express written permission of the publisher, True Potential Publishing, providing the words quoted do not amount to a completed book of the New Testament and do not comprise twenty-five percent or more of the total text in which they are quoted.
Notice of copyright must appear as follows on either the title page or the copyright page of the work in which The Power New Testament is quoted: "Scripture taken from The Power New Testament, copyright © 2003 William J. Morford. Used by permission of True Potential Publishing, Inc."
When quotations from The Power New Testament are used in nonsaleable media such as church bulletins, orders of service, newsletters, projections or similar media, a complete copyright notice is not required, but "The Power New Testament" must appear at the end of eeach quotation.
Permission requests for commercial and non-commercial use that exceed the above guidelines must be obtained, in writing from True Potential Publishing, Inc. PO Box 904 Travelers Rest, SC 29690. www.thepowernewtestament.com

ISBN 978-1-935769-08-8
Library of Congress Control Number: 2011922020

Printed in the USA

The Power New Testament and other True Potential books can be purchased in bulk by churches, ministries and other organizations for evangelical, educational or business promotional use. For information please write Special Markets Department PO Box 904 Travelers Rest, SC 29690 or send your request via e-mail to: info@tppress.com.

www.thepowernewtestament.com

~ CONTENTS ~

FRONT COVER: The Hebrew letters spell Ehyeh, the word spoken by God to Moses in Exodus 3:14 when He said "'I AM Who I AM.' (Ehyeh Asher Ehyeh) and He said, 'Thus shall you say to the children of Israel, "The Lord God of your fathers, I AM (Ehyeh), has sent me to you.'"

"To the Israelites in bondage, the meaning would be; 'Although He has not yet displayed His power towards you, He will do so; He is eternal and will certainly redeem you.'" A number of modern Jewish translations say, "'I will be what I will be;' meaning 'no words can sum up all that He will be to His people, but His everlasting faithfulness and unchanging mercy will more and more manifest themselves in the guidance of Israel.'" (The Pentateuch and Haftorahs, Edited by Dr. J. H. Hertz, C. H., Late Chief Rabbi of the British Empire)

COVER DESIGN: Dr. William L. Pettiford III

~ ACKNOWLEDGMENT ~

This, the Fourth Edition, also the seventh printing of The Power New Testament, is greatly expanded from the first six printings. The Fourth Edition has more than 1,700 footnotes and a 105 page Glossary. Although William J. Morford was responsible for the translation of the Greek text, a number of others contributed to the completion and accuracy of the work.

Rabbi Eliezer Ben-Yehuda, now of Synagogue Beth El in Ponte Vedra, Florida, spent many hours with me to bring understanding and Jewishness to numerous passages that are often glossed over or even misunderstood. Rabbi Ben-Yehuda is a Conservative Jewish rabbi who patiently answered many questions and revealed a number of Hebrew idioms and Jewish customs. He has a thorough knowledge of the New Testament, so he made a considerable contribution to this volume.

Two Biblical scholars assisted with this translation. They are:

> Arnold Gause, Ph.D., a Greek scholar of Columbia, SC, who tutored Rev. Morford for two years, then continued to give advice.

> Henry M. Evans, Ph.D., of Monroe, Louisiana, who for a period of six months met with Rev. Morford nearly every week, reviewing difficult passages, sharing books from his personal library, and giving encouragement and advice.

A very dedicated friend, Dr. Waldo Nickel, reviewed the first printing, word for word, comparing The Power New Testament with more than twenty other translations, making voluminous notes and suggestions. Many of those suggestions have been used, making this 4th Edition even more readable than the earlier editions.

Several people helped by commenting at different stages in the preparation of the First Edition of this translation. Special thanks go to: Pastor Kathy Tolleson who proof read the entire manuscript; Rev. Shirley Wine, who commented on Matthew and several Epistles, and several others who made appropriate comments from less intensive scrutiny; and most of all I thank my wife, Jeanie, for all the time she gave to this project, discussing various passages and proofing many times. Jeanie went to be with the Lord in February, 2006.

i

~ PREFACE ~

The goal of The Power New Testament is to bring a greater understanding of and appreciation for the Jewish roots of Christianity. This translation is part of an ongoing study to learn more about Who God is and to find the deeper meanings of Scripture. Because Jesus was, and still is (Hebrews 13:8), Jewish, as was every apostle, and every author of the New Testament, it was necessary to study much more than just the Greek language to do an accurate translation. This involves Hebrew language studies and the teachings of Jewish scholars to come as close as possible to what the Hebrew Scriptures meant to the New Testament authors. It is also important to learn about Hebrew idioms that are intact in the Greek text. A number of Bible scholars believe that at least the Gospels of Matthew, Mark, and Luke were originally written in Hebrew, partly because there are so many Hebrew idioms and so much Hebrew grammar in the Greek text. Whether or not those or other books of the New Testament were originally in Hebrew will not be explored here, but this translation makes every effort to translate those Hebrew expressions properly. Another goal of this translation is to point out Jewish customs that have often been missed and to explain the meanings of various customs.

Throughout the text of The Power New Testament there are over 1,700 footnotes. There is also a seventy page Glossary to describe various first century Jewish customs and to explain Hebrew Scriptures, such as Leviticus 14, which on the surface is about cleansing a leper, but has a much deeper meaning. Read about it in Gossip/Slander in Glossary.

Many Jewish sources were studied. Among those were the Talmud, Mishna, Midrash, and Zohar, but the full list includes many modern Jewish commentaries that draw upon those four, but also quote numerous ancient and more recent sources. Those studies bring real depth to the subjects in the Glossary, but even more importantly that study gives insight into the thinking of Jesus and the Apostles, especially the New Testament authors. It is important for those of us reading in the twenty-first century to understand what a word or expression meant to those who wrote the passages in the first century.

The Greek text used for this translation is the United Bible Societies' Fourth

Edition, published in 1993. The editors used a scientific method called Textual Criticism to determine which of the more than five thousand ancient manuscripts of the New Testament were closest to what the authors wrote in the first century. This method is similar to what the editors of the ancient Greek classics use to determine the most accurate copies of those writings.

Until the first Greek text of the New Testament was printed in 1550, all copies were made by hand, so there was no standard text. A mistake or addition would therefore be passed on as other copies were made of a particular manuscript. What developed from that system were several families of manuscripts, each based geographically. Among those families of texts, one was called Alexandrian, from Egypt, another Caesarean, from Caesarea of Israel, and another was called Byzantine, which was the family of texts taken to England and western Europe by the Roman Church. See Manuscript in Glossary.

Because over the centuries there were many additions to the texts, as the textual scholars have identified them, they have been dropped from some translations or simply identified as added text, but still translated. This translation leaves out completely all passages positively identified by the editors as additions. That makes it possible for you to read a text without the intrusion of material that was not written by the author. The common practice is to translate those passages and just add footnotes to identify them as additions.

In some instances it is necessary to add a word or two for a passage to read properly in English. When that is done, the added words are in italics, so you will know that they were added.

Some words have been translated differently because the traditional translation conveys something not intended by the author. One of those words is the Greek word Ekklesia, which means a gathering of citizens called out from their homes into some public place. Implicit in Ekklesia is a summoning, so this is not just a collection of people, but people called out to a public meeting for a particular purpose. Ekklesia is commonly translated church, but because of our association of church with both a building and an organization, in this translation, Ekklesia is translated congregation.

The Greek word Nomos has nearly always been translated Law, even when used for the Hebrew word Torah. Torah does not mean Law, but Teaching or Instruction. When you see Torah in this translation, do not think Law, but of the Loving God teaching His children, offering an outline to guide them for a better way of life. See Torah in Glossary.

The word for High Priest is capitalized when it refers to the one who occupies that office, or a former High Priest. The word also is used to refer to members of that family, whether or not they are in office at the time. It is often used in the plural, and then is not capitalized. Some translations use "chief priests" for these situations, but this translation uses "high priests" in these cases.

This translation has as its goal to be a very readable text that flows from one book to another while preserving much of the Jewish flavor, especially the Jewishness of Jesus, and much of the power that is in the Greek and Hebrew expressions. The people who have worked on this translation all believe that by the laying on of hands we have all the gifts of the Spirit of the Living God, the King of the Universe, and that God is the same today as when He created the universe, and He will remain the same for eternity.

The editors of the Greek text cite many Old Testament Scriptures throughout the text, so the majority of Scripture references given in the text are from the Greek text used for this translation. All of the references from the Apocrypha are from the Greek text and are given here for those who use the Roman Catholic Bible.

There was no punctuation, nor were chapter or verse numbers in the original manuscripts. Even the present Greek text does not have quotation marks, but proper placement of the marks is taken from the context of a passage. See Manuscript in Glossary. See Chapter and Verse Numbers in Glossary.

~ ACCORDING TO MATTHEW ~

The Genealogy of Jesus Messiah

(Lk 3:23-38)

1.1. A scroll of *the* genealogy of Jesus Messiah, Son of David,[1] Son of Abraham.

1:2. Abraham begat Isaac, Isaac begat Jacob, and Jacob begat Judah and his brothers. 3. And Judah begat Perez and Zerach by Tamar, and Perez begat Hezron, and Hezron begat Ram, 4. and Ram begat Amminadab, and Amminadab begat Nashon, and Nashon begat Salmon, 5. and Salmon begat Boaz by Rahab, and Boaz begat Obed by Ruth, and Obed begat Jesse, 6. and Jesse begat David the king.

And David begat Solomon by the *wife* of Urriah, 7. and Solomon begat Rehoboam, and Rehoboam begat Abijah, and Abijah begat Asa, 8. and Asa begat Jehoshafat, and Jehoshafat begat Joram, and Joram begat Uzziah, 9. and Uzziah begat Jotham, and Jotham begat Ahaz, and Ahaz begat Hezekiah, 10. and Hezekiah begat Manasseh, and Manasseh begat Amon, and Amon begat Josiah, 11. and Josiah begat Jeconiah and his brothers in the time of the Babylonian captivity.

1:12. After the Babylonian captivity Jeconiah begat Shealtiel, ·and Shealtiel begat Zerubbabel, 13. and Zerubbabel begat Abiud, and Abiud begat Eliakim, and Eliakim begat Azor, 14. and Azor begat Sadok, and Sadok begat Achim, and Achim begat Elihud, 15. and Elihud begat Eliazar, and Eliazar begat Matthan, and Matthan begat Jacob, 16. and Jacob begat Joseph,[2] the husband of Mary, of whom[3] was born Jesus, the One called Messiah.

1:17. Therefore all the generations from Abraham to David *are* fourteen generations, and from David until the Babylonian captivity *are* fourteen

---

1   (v.1) See Son of David/Son of Joseph in Glossary.

2   (v.16) Joseph did not father Jesus, so Matthew could not continue saying "begat." For insight to this name. See Son of David/Son of Joseph in Glossary. See Genealogy of Jesus in Glossary.

3   (v.16) The word 'whom' in Greek is feminine, referring specifically to Mary. Some say this makes the lineage that of Mary, but it really is only saying that she gave birth to Him. See both Book Order and Genealogy of Jesus in Glossary.

generations, and from the Babylonian captivity until the Messiah *are* fourteen generations.

The Birth of Jesus Messiah

(Lk 2:1-7)

1:18. And Jesus Messiah was born in this manner. While His mother Mary was betrothed[1] to Joseph, before they came together she was found to have been made pregnant by *the* Holy Spirit. 19. And Joseph her husband, being righteous and not wanting to expose her *publicly*, wanted to secretly divorce her. 20. And when he was considering these things, behold an angel of *the* Lord appeared to him in a dream saying, "Joseph, son of David, you must not be afraid to take Mary to yourself for your wife: for the One being formed in her is by *the* Holy Spirit. 21. And she will give birth to a Son, and you will call his name Jesus:[2] for He will save His people from their sins." 22. And all this had happened so that what was spoken by the Lord through the prophet would be fulfilled, saying,

23. "Behold the virgin will be pregnant and will bear a son,
        and they will call His name Emanuel." (Is 7:14)

which is translated "God with us." 24. And after Joseph rose from his sleep he did as the angel of *the* Lord commanded him and he took his wife, 25. but he did not know her until she gave birth to a son: and he called His name Jesus.

The Visit of the Astrologers

2.1. And after Jesus was born in Bethlehem[3] of Judea in *the* days of Herod the king, behold astrologers from *the* east arrived in Jerusalem 2. saying, "Where is the One Who has been born King of the Jewish People? For we saw His star in the east and we came to pay homage[4] to Him." 3. And when King Herod heard, he was disturbed and all Jerusalem[5] with him, 4. and gathering all the high priests and scribes of the people he inquired from them where the Messiah was to be born. 5. And they said to him, "In Bethlehem of Judea: for thus it has been written through the prophet:

6. 'And you Bethlehem,' country of Judea,
        'you are' by no means 'least among the princes of Judea:

---

1   (v.18) The Jewish marriage began when the ketubah, the marriage contract was signed. Later the ceremony would be performed and the marriage consummated. In Jewish law they were married, not betrothed, at the signing of the ketubah. See Wedding in Glossary.
2   (v.21) Jesus is the English spelling of Iesous, the Greek form of Yeshua, His Hebrew name, which means Deliverer or Savior. See Jesus in Glossary.
3   (v.1) Bethlehem is the Greek spelling of the Hebrew name, Beit-Lekhem, meaning House of Bread. In what more appropriate place could He have been born, the One Who said, "for the bread of God is that which descends from heaven and gives life to the world." (Jn 6:33)
4   (v.2) To pay homage meant to kneel on one knee, bowing down to the ground. See Pay Homage in Glossary.
5   (v.3) Herod and many in Jerusalem were Hellenists, whose power and wealth was based on Roman authority. See Hellenists in Glossary.

for out of you will come a ruler,
> who will shepherd My people Israel.'" (Mic 5:2)

2:7. Then Herod, having secretly called the astrologers, ascertained from them the time of the revealing of *the* star, 8. and sending them into Bethlehem he said, "When you go you must inquire carefully concerning the child: as soon as you would find *Him*, you must report to me right away, then when I come I will pay homage to Him." 9. And those who heard the king went. And lo! The star, which they saw in the east, led them forth, until *it* came *and* stood over where the child was. 10. And when they saw the star they rejoiced *with* extremely great joy. 11. Then when they came into the house[1] they saw the child with Mary His mother, and having fallen *to their knees* they paid homage to Him, then, having opened their treasure boxes, they brought gifts to Him, gold and frankincense[2] and myrrh. 12. And since they had been warned in a dream not to return to Herod, they returned to their country by another way.

The Flight to Egypt

2:13. And after they went away, behold, an angel of *the* Lord revealed to Joseph in a dream saying, "When you get up, you must immediately take the child and His mother and flee into Egypt and you must be there until whenever I tell you: for Herod is going to seek the child to kill Him." 14. Then after he got up he took the child and His mother in *the* night and he went away into Egypt, 15. and he was there until the death of Herod: so that the word of the Lord by the prophet would be fulfilled saying, "I called My Son out of Egypt." (Ho 11.1)

The Slaying of the Infants

2:16. Then after Herod saw that he was tricked by the astrologers he became exceedingly angry, and he sent and killed all the male children in Bethlehem and in all the regions of it from two years old and below, according to the time which he ascertained from the astrologers. 17. Then that spoken by Jeremiah the prophet was fulfilled saying,

18.   "A voice was heard in Rama,
> weeping and" much "mourning:
Rachel weeping *for* her children,
> and she was not to be comforted, because they were not."[3]
> (Jr 31:15)

The Return from Egypt

2:19. Then, after Herod died, behold an angel of the Lord revealed by a dream to Joseph in Egypt 20. saying, "When you get up you must immediately take the child and His mother and go to Israel: for those who were seeking the

---

1   (v.11) That they were in a house, not the cave/barn where He was born indicates that some time had passed since His birth.

2   (v.11) Frankincense is the emblem of devotion.

3   (v.18) "They were not" is an idiom meaning they were dead. See Death in Glossary.

life of the child have died." 21. And when he got up he took the child and His mother and entered the land of Israel. 22. Then, when he heard that Archelos was reigning in Judea instead of his father Herod, he was afraid to go back there: and because he was warned in a dream he returned to the region of Galilee, 23. and when he came he dwelt in a city called Nazareth: thus was the word through the prophet fulfilled that He will be called *of* Nazareth. (Is 11:1[1])

The Preaching of John the Baptist[2]

(Mt 1:1-8, Lk 3:1-9, 15-17, Jn 1:19-28)

3.1. And in those days John the Baptist was coming forth, preaching in the wilderness of Judea 2. and saying, "You must continually repent: for the kingdom of the heavens[3] has come near." 3. For this is what was spoken through Isaiah the prophet saying,

"A voice crying in the wilderness:
'You must right now prepare the way of *the* Lord,
     you must continually make His paths straight.'" (Is 40:3)

4. And this John was wearing his cloak *made* from camel hairs and a leather belt around his waist, and his food was locust *beans* and wild honey. 5. At that time Jerusalem and all Judea and the whole region around the Jordan were going out to him, 6. and, as they were confessing their sins, they were being baptized by him[4] in the Jordan River.

3:7. When he saw many Pharisees and Sadducees coming for his baptism he said to them, "Offspring of vipers, who warned you to flee from the coming wrath? 8. Therefore you must immediately make fruit worthy of repentance 9. and you must now not think to say among yourselves, 'We have Abraham *as our* father.' For I say to you that God is able to raise children for Abraham from these stones. 10. And now the ax is laid to the root of the trees: therefore every tree *that* does not produce good fruit is being cut down and cast into a fire. 11. I am indeed baptizing[5] you in water for repentance, but One Who is coming after me is stronger than I, I am not worthy to carry away His sandals: this One will baptize you in *the* Holy Spirit and in fire: 12. Whose winnowing fork is in His hand and He will clean out His threshing floor and gather His wheat into the barn, but He will burn up the chaff in an inextinguishable fire."

---

1   (v.23) The connection to Galilee is from the word natser, referring to the shoot, branch of Jesse. Nazareth is Natseret in Hebrew.
2   (Caption) The word Baptist comes from the Greek word baptidzo, meaning to immerse. See Baptize in Glossary.
3   (v.2) Kingdom of the heavens was an expression that often, as in this case, referred to God. The plural heavens was used because heavens is always plural in Hebrew, having seven levels. See Heavens in Glossary.
4   (v.6) John stood on the bank preaching and those who repented went into the river for self-immersion. See Baptize in Glossary.
5   (v.11) The Greek word baptidzo means to immerse, which had been a Jewish custom for purification for more than 1,000 years. See Baptize in Glossary.

The Baptism of Jesus

(Mk 1:9-11, Lk 3:21,22)

3:13. Then Jesus came from Galilee across the Jordan to John to be baptized by him. 14. But John was going to prevent Him saying, "I need to be baptized by You, so would You come to me?" 15. And when Jesus answered He said to him, "You must allow it now, for so it is fitting for us to fulfill all righteousness." Then he permitted Him. 16. And after Jesus was baptized He immediately rose from the water: and behold the heavens opened up to Him, and he saw the Spirit of God descending like a dove and coming upon Him: 17. and there was a voice from the heavens saying, "This is My beloved Son, with Whom I am well pleased."

The Temptation of Jesus

(Mk 1:12,13, Lk 4:1-13)

4.1. Then Jesus was led into the wilderness by the Spirit to be tested by the devil. 2. And after He fasted forty days and forty nights, He was then hungry. 3. And when the one who was testing, *the devil*, came, he said to Him, "If You are *the* Son of God, You must now say that these stones would become bread." 4. But when He answered, *Jesus* said, "It has been written,

'Man will not live on bread alone,
> but upon every word going out
>> through *the* mouth of God.'" (Dt 8:3)

5. Then the devil took Him to the holy city and placed Him on the pinnacle of the temple 6. and said to Him, "If You are *the* Son of God, You must throw Yourself down at once for it has been written that

'He will give orders to His angels concerning you
> and they will take you up in their hands,
so that you would not strike your foot against a stone.'" (Ps 91:11,12)

7. Jesus said to him, "Again it has been written, 'You will[1] not test *the* Lord your God.'" (Dt 6:16) 8. Again the devil took Him to an exceedingly high mountain and showed Him all the kingdoms of the world and their glory 9. and said to Him, "I will give all these things to You, if after You fall *on Your knees* You would pay homage to me." 10. Then Jesus said to him, "You must immediately go back where you came from, Satan:[2] for it has been written,

'You will worship *the* Lord your God
> and you will serve only Him.'" (Dt 6:13)

11. Then the devil left Him, and behold angels came and were ministering to Him.

---

1   (v.7) The future tense is frequently translated as a command. See Future Tense in Glossary.

2   (v.10) See Satan in Glossary.

The Beginning of the Galilean Ministry

(Mk 1:14,15, Lk 4:14,15)

4:12. And when He heard that John was arrested He returned to Galilee. 13. And after He left Nazareth, He went *and* stayed in Capernaum,[1] by the lake in *the* region of Zebulun and Naftali: 14. in order that what was spoken through the prophet Isaiah would be fulfilled saying,

15.　　　"Land of Zebulun and land of Naftali,
　　　　　　way of the lake, beyond the Jordan,
　　　　　　　　Galilee of the heathens,
16.　　　the people who dwell in darkness
　　　　　　saw a great light,
　　　and to those who dwell in *the* land and darkness of death
　　　　　a light rose for them." (Is 9:1,2)

4:17. From then *on* Jesus began to preach and to say, "You must continuously repent:[2] for the kingdom of the heavens has come near."

The Calling of Four Fishermen

(Mk 1:16-20, Lk 5:1-11)

4:18. And while He was walking by the lake of Galilee He saw two brothers, Simon, the one called Peter, and Andrew his brother, casting a net into the lake: for they were fishermen. 19. And He said to them, "You must come after Me, and I will make you fishers of men." 20. And immediately, having left their nets, they followed Him. 21. Then, having gone from there, He saw two other brothers, Jacob,[3] the *son* of Zebedee, and John his brother mending their nets in the boat with Zebedee their father, and He called them. 22. And they followed Him immediately, leaving the boat and their father.

Ministering to a Great Multitude

(Lk 6:17-19)

4:23. Then He was going about in all Galilee teaching in their synagogues and proclaiming the Good News of the kingdom[4] and healing every disease and every sickness among the people. 24. And His reputation spread through all Syria: and they brought to Him all those having various evils[5] *and* various diseases and

---

1　　　(v.13) Capernaum is the Latin spelling of the Hebrew name Kafer Na-um. Kafer means town or village and Na-um means pleasant.
2　　　(v.17) The tense used in the Greek tells us to walk in repentance every day, even though we know we have been sanctified and made righteous by the blood of the Lamb. This is because we have not been perfected, but are to strive to be better today than we were yesterday, as we become more like Him. See Eph 5:1.
3　　　(v.21) The Greek text has Iakob, which is written Jacob in English.
4　　　(v.23) His teaching here is about the Father, the kingdom being a reference to the Deity and His love.
5　　　(v.24) The Greek word kakos literally means evil.

being tormented and being possessed by demons and being moonstruck[1] and paralytics, and He healed them. 25. And huge crowds followed Him from Galilee and Dekapolis[2] and Jerusalem and Judea and the other side of the Jordan.

The Sermon on the Mount

(Mt 5:1-7:29)

5.1. And when He saw the crowds He went up on the mountain, and after He sat down His disciples came to Him: 2. then opening His mouth He taught them saying,

The Beatitudes

(Lk 6:20-23)

3.   "Blessed[3] are the repentant,[4]
                because theirs is the kingdom of the heavens. (Is 61.1)
4.   Blessed are those who mourn,
                because they will be comforted. (Is 61:2,3)
5.   Blessed are the humble[5]
                because they will inherit the Earth. (Ps 37:11)
6.   Blessed are those who hunger and thirst for righteousness, (Jn 6:53)
                because they will be filled, satisfied.[6]
                (Nu 25:11, Ps 4:7, Ho 10:12, Mt 6:33)
7.   Blessed are those who forgive,[7]
                because they will be forgiven. (2Sa 22:26)
8.   Blessed are the pure in heart,
                because they will see God. (2Sa 22:27, Ps 24:3,4)
9.   Blessed are the peacemakers, (Ps 37:37, Is 32:17)
                because they will be called 'children of God.'
10.   Blessed are those who press on for the sake of righteousness,
                because theirs is the kingdom of the heavens.[8]
                (Pr 21:21, Mt 11:12)
11.   Blessed are you when they would revile you and they would persecute

---

1   (v.24) Epileptics
2   (v.25) Ten cities, nine east of the Jordan plus Beit-Sh'an west of the Jordan, declared "Free Cities" by Rome. Beit-Sh'an is still a thriving city, just west of the Jordan River, about twenty-five miles south of Tiberias. See Dekapolis in Glossary.
3   (v.3) The Greek word translated Blessed throughout the Beatitudes is Makarios, blessed and happy.
4   (v.3) Literally this is poor in spirit which is a Hebrew idiom for repentant.
5   (v.5) Humble refers to the faithful remnant. See Humble in Glossary.
6   (v.6) Righteousness is action, doing the perfect will of God, so this is hungering to do His perfect will. See Righteousness in Glossary.
7   (v.7) Literally this says to be merciful, which is a Hebrew idiom meaning to be forgiving. See Sin, Forgiveness of in Glossary.
8   (v.10) This means to walk in all the promises of God. The word heavens is always plural in Hebrew because there are seven levels of heaven in the Tanach, the OT. See Heavens in Glossary.

you and they would say all *manner of* evil against you falsely because of Me. (2Chr 36:16) 12. You must continually rejoice and be extremely joyful, because your reward *is* great in the heavens: for in this way they persecuted the prophets, the ones who were before you."

Salt and Light

(Mk 9:50, Lk 14:34,35)

5:13. "You are the salt[1] of the Earth: but if the salt would become tasteless, in what *way* will it become salt again? It is no longer still good except to be thrown outside to be trampled by men. 14. You are the light of the world. A city laid out on a mountain is not able to be hidden: 15. and they do not light a lamp and place it under a peck measure but upon the lamp stand, and it gives light for all those in the house. 16. Your light must now shine like this before *all* mankind, so that they would see your good deeds[2] and they would glorify your Father, the One in the heavens."

Teaching about the Torah[3]

5:17. "Do not think that I came to annul, to bring an incorrect interpretation to, the Torah or the Prophets:[4] I did not come to annul but to bring *spiritual* abundance,[5] for the Torah to be obeyed as it should be and God's promises to receive fulfillment. 18. For truly I say to you: until the sky and the Earth would pass away, **not** one yod[6] or one vav[7] could **ever** pass away from the Torah, until everything would come to pass. (Lk 16:17) 19. Therefore, whoever would break one of the least of these commandments, and would teach people this way, will be called least in the kingdom of the heavens: but whoever would do *the commandments* and would teach *them*, will be called great in the kingdom of the heavens. 20. For I say to you that unless your righteousness would be present in abundance more than *that of* the scribes and Pharisees, you could **not** enter the kingdom of the heavens."

Teaching about Anger

5:21. "You heard that it was said to the ancients, 'Do not murder:' (Ex 20:13) and whoever would murder, that one would be guilty in the judgment. 22. And I say to you that everyone who is angry with his brother will be guilty in

1   (v.13) Salt is a preservative and speaks of permanence, see the Covenant of Salt, Nu 18:18,19.
2   (v.16) Mitsvot, see Mitsvah in Glossary.
3   (Caption) This is a reference to the first five books of the Bible. See Torah in Glossary.
4   (v.17) The Prophetic books are Jsh, Jd, 1 & 2 Sam, 1 & 2Ki, Is through Mal excluding Dn, which is one of the Writings in the Tanach.
5   (v.17) The abundance must be spiritual because Jesus said "You must continually understand and guard yourselves from all covetousness, because someone's life is not abundant from his possessions." (Mt 6:19-21, Lk 12:15)
6   (v.18) The yod is the smallest letter of the Hebrew alphabet. See Yod in Glossary.
7   (v.18) The vav is the second smallest letter of the Hebrew alphabet. The yod and the vav are called "soft letters" because they can be left out of a word and the word not be considered misspelled. See Yod in Glossary.

the judgment. And whoever would say to his brother 'Empty-headed,'[1] that one is guilty to the Sanhedrin: whoever would say, 'Stupid' is guilty in the Gehenna[2] of the fire. 23. If therefore you would present your gift at the altar and there you would remember that your brother has something against you, 24. you must right away leave your gift there in front of the altar and go. You must first become reconciled with your brother,[3] and then, after you come *back*, present your gift. 25. You must quickly be of a peaceable spirit with your opponent *at law, even* while you are with him on the way, lest the opponent would hand you over to the judge, and the judge to the jailer, and you would be cast into prison: 26. truly I say to you, you would **not** come out from there, until you would have given your last penny."

Teaching about Adultery

5:27. "You heard that it was said, 'You will not commit adultery.'[4] (Ex 20:14) 28. But I am saying to you that everyone who looks at a woman with desire *for* her has already committed adultery *with* her in his heart.[5] 29. And if your right eye causes you to sin, you must tear it out at once and cast it from you: for it is more profitable for you that one of your members would be lost and that your whole body would not be cast into Gehenna.[6] 30. And if your right hand causes you to sin, cut it off and cast it from you: for it is more profitable for you that one of your members would be lost but your whole body would not go over into Gehenna."

Teaching about Divorce

(Mt 19:9, Mk 10:11,12, Lk 16:18)

5:31. "And it was said, 'Whoever would divorce his wife, must immediately give her a certificate of divorce.' (Dt 24:1) 32. But I am saying to you that everyone who divorces his wife except for grounds of immorality makes her to be an adulteress, and whoever would marry a divorced woman is committing adultery."

Teaching about Pledges

5:33. "Again you heard that it was said to the ancients, 'You will not swear falsely,[7] (Nu 30:3) and you will keep your oaths to the Lord.' (Dt 23:22) 34. But I say to you not to swear at all: neither by heaven, because it is *the* throne of God, 35. nor by the Earth, because it is His footstool, nor by Jerusalem, because it is a city of the great King, 36. nor by your head may you swear, because you are not able to make one hair white or black. 37. But your word must consistently

---

1	(v.22) The text has Raka, a Hebrew word meaning empty-headed.
2	(v.22) See Gehenna in Glossary.
3	(v.24) See Sin, Forgiveness of in Glossary.
4	(v.27) See Future Tense in Glossary.
5	(v.28) This was in accordance with rabbinic teaching in Jesus' day.
6	(v.29) See Gehenna in Glossary.
7	(v.33) See Future Tense in Glossary.

be definitely yes, *or* definitely no:[1] and what goes beyond these is from the evil one." (Lv 19:12, Nu 30:2, Dt 23:21,22, Ecc 5:4, Ps 76:11, Jas 5:12)

Teaching about Retaliation

(Lk 6:29,30)

5:38. "You heard that it was said, 'An eye for an eye and a tooth for a tooth.'[2] (Ex 21:24, Lv 24:20, Dt 19:21) 39. But I say to you to not stand against the evil person: but who strikes you in your right cheek, you must at once also turn the other to him: 40. and to the one who wishes to sue you and to take your tunic, you must also let him have your cloak: 41. and who will force you one mile,[3] you must now go two with him. 42. And to the one who asks you, you must give, and do not resist the one wanting to borrow from you."

Love for Enemies

(Lk 6:27,28, 32-36)

5:43. "You heard that it was said, 'You will love your neighbor' (Lv 19:18) and you will hate your enemy.[4] 44. But I am saying to you, you must love your enemies and you must pray for those who persecute you, (Pr 24:17,18) 45. so that you would become children of your Father, the One in *the* heavens, because He makes His sun rise on evil and good and rains on *the* righteous and unrighteous. 46. For if you would love those who love you, what reward do you have? Do not even the tax collectors do this? 47. And if you would respect only your brothers, what are you doing *that is* remarkable? Do not even the heathens do this? 48. Therefore you must be perfect as your heavenly Father is perfect."

Teaching about Almsgiving

6.1. "And you must regularly pay close attention not to do your righteousness[5] in front of people in order to be seen by them: otherwise you do not have a reward from your Father, the One in the heavens.

6:2. "Therefore when you would do charitable giving,[6] do not trumpet before yourself, as the hypocrites are doing in the synagogues and in the alleys, *for* in this way they have received praise by people: truly I say to you, they are receiving their reward. 3. But when you make a charitable gift your left hand must not know what your right hand is doing, 4. so that your charitable giving would be in secret: then your Father, the One Who sees in secret, will give back to you."

---

1   (v.37) These are literally "Yes yes and no no." See Double Yes in Glossary.
2   (v.38) This does not mean you are to take out the eye of someone who has knocked out an eye. See Torah in Glossary.
3   (v.41) This is a Roman mile, one thousand paces.
4   (v.43) "Hate your enemy" was from heathens, since it is not found in the Tanach (OT), oral law, or Rabbinic writing.
5   (v.1) Doing righteousness is doing good deeds. See Mitsvah in Glossary.
6   (v.2) Tsedekah, see both Mitsvah and Righteousness in Glossary.

Teaching about Prayer

(Lk 11:2-4)

6:5. "And when you would pray, you must not be like the hypocrites, because they love to pray in the synagogues and standing on the street corners, so that they would be revealed to people: truly I say to you, they are receiving their reward. 6. But when you would pray, you must go into your secret room and after you lock your door pray to your Father, to the One in secret: then your Father, the One Who sees in secret, will reward you. 7. And when you pray, you should not babble as the heathens, for they think that they will be heard because of their many words. 8. Therefore you should not be like them: for your Father knows what need you have before you ask Him. 9. Therefore you must be praying in this way:

'Our Father,[1] Who is in the heavens:
    Your name must at once be made holy:
10.   Your kingdom must now come:
    Your will must be done right now,
        as in heaven also on Earth:
11.   You must now give us today the things necessary for our existence:[2]
12.   You must right now forgive our sins for us, in the same manner as
        we have completed forgiving everyone of everything, big
        and little, against us:[3]
13.   And do not lead us into temptation,[4]
    but You must now rescue us from the evil one.'[5]

14. For if you would forgive *all other* people their transgressions, your heavenly Father will also forgive you: 15. but if you would not forgive *all other* people, neither will your Father forgive your sins."[6] (Col 3:13)

Teaching about Fasting

6:16. "And when you would fast, do not become sad, gloomy like the hypocrites, for they render their faces so that fasting would be revealed to people: truly I say to you, they are receiving their reward. 17. But when you fast you must anoint your head and wash your face, 18. so that you would not reveal fasting to men but to your Father in secret: then your Father, the One Who sees in secret, will reward you."

---

1   (v.9) Our Father was a common opening for prayer, based on Is 63:16 and Ho 11:1.
2   (v.11) The Greek word translated "necessary for our existence" is found only in Mt 6:11 and Lk 11:3. The meaning is not certain. See Daily Bread in Glossary.
3   (v.12) We can only speak this way to God, saying "You must.." as Jesus is teaching, when we have covenant relationship with Him. See Sin, Forgiveness of in Glossary.
4   (v.13) This could also be translated trial.
5   (v.13) The Doxology in some translations of the Lord's Prayer was added in the fifth century. See Lord's Prayer in Glossary for understanding of this prayer.
6   (v.14 & v.15) This admonition is a basic requirement for a relationship with God. See Sin, Forgiveness of in Glossary.

Treasure in Heaven

(Lk 12:33,34)

6:19. "Do not gather treasures on the Earth for yourselves, where moth and rust are destroying and where thieves break in and steal: (Sir[1] 29:11) 20. but build up treasures for yourselves in heaven, where neither moth nor rust destroys and where thieves do not break in and do not steal: 21. for where your treasure is, there also will your heart be."

The Light of the Body

(Lk 11:34-36)

6:22. "The eye is the lamp of the body. Therefore if your eye would be healthy, your whole body will be light: 23. but if your eye would be evil,[2] your whole body will be darkness. Therefore if the light which *is* in you is dark, how great *must* the darkness *be*." (Pr 22:9, 28:22)

God and Wealth

(Lk 16:13)

6:24. "No one is able to serve two masters: for he will hate the one and will love the other, or he will be devoted to one and he will despise the other. You are not able to serve God and wealth."

Care and Anxiety

(Lk 12:22-34)

6:25. "Because of this I say to you, stop being anxious for your life, what you would eat or what you would drink, or what you would put on your body. No indeed! Is life not more than food and the body *more than* clothing? 26. You must consider the birds of the sky that do not sow and do not harvest and do not gather into a storehouse, and your heavenly Father feeds them: are you not worth more than they? 27. And who of you if you are anxious is able to add one single hour upon his age? 28. And concerning clothing, why are you anxious? You must observe the lilies of the field, how they grow: they do not labor and they do not spin: 29. but I say to you that Solomon in all his glory did not dress himself as one of these. 30. And if God clothes the grass of the field this way, *which* is *here* today and tomorrow is cast into a furnace, *will He* not much more *clothe* you, little faiths? 31. Therefore you should not be anxious saying, 'What could we eat?' or, 'What could we drink?' or, 'What should we wear?' 32. For the heathens are striving for all these things: for indeed your heavenly Father knows that you need all these things. 33. But you must continually seek first the kingdom of God and His righteousness, then all these things will be provided for you. 34.

---

1   (v.19) The book of Sirach, from the Apocrypha. See Appendix for the listing of Apocryphal references.

2   (v.23) An evil eye is a Hebrew idiom for stingy or greedy. See Dt 15:9, Pr 23:6, 7 and 28:22.

Therefore do not be anxious for tomorrow, for tomorrow will be anxious of itself: *each day's* trouble *is* enough for that day."

Judging Others

(Lk 6:37,38, 41,42)

7.1. "Do not judge, so that you would not be judged: 2. for in which judgment you judge, you will be judged, and in the measure in which you measure, it will be measured to you. (Ro 14:10-13) 3. Then why are you looking at the speck in your brother's eye, but you do not perceive the beam in your eye? 4. Or how will you say to your brother, 'You must let me cast the speck from your eye,' and there is this beam in your eye? 5. Hypocrite! First you must cast the beam from your eye, and then you will see clearly to cast out the speck from your brother's eye. 6. Do not give the sacred things to the dogs and do not cast your pearls before the swine, lest they will trample them with their feet, then when they turn they will tear you *to pieces*."

Ask, Seek, Knock

(Lk 11:9-13)

7:7. "You must regularly ask and it will be given to you, you must continually seek and you will find, you must knock habitually and it will be opened to you: 8. for everyone who asks takes, and the one who seeks finds, and it will be opened for the one who knocks. 9. Or what man is there of you, who *when* his son will ask for bread, will give him a stone?[1] 10. Or then will ask for a fish will give over to him a snake? 11. Therefore if you, being evil yourselves, know how to give good gifts to your children, how much more your Father, the One in the Heavens, will give good things to those who ask Him. 12. Therefore everything that you would want that people would do to you, in this way you must also do to them: for this is the Torah and the Prophets."[2]

The Narrow Gate

(Lk 13:24)

7:13. "You must immediately enter through the narrow gate: because wide is the gate and broad is the way leading into destruction and many are those who enter through it: 14. how narrow the gate is, and the way that leads to life is constricted, *and* few are those who find it."

A Tree Known by Its Fruit

(Lk 6:43,44)

7:15. "You must consistently beware of the false prophets, who are

---

1   (v.9) The Greek construction here and in v. 10 anticipates a negative answer.
2   (v.12) The Torah and the Prophets refers to the first five books of the Bible plus Jsh, Jd, 1 & 2 Sam, 1 & 2Ki, Is through Mal except for Dn. The expression can also refer to the entire OT. See Torah in Glossary.

coming to you in sheep's clothing, but within they are ravenous wolves. 16. You will recognize *people* by their fruit. Does anyone gather grapes from thorn bushes or figs from thistles?[1] 17. In this way every good tree produces good fruit, but the rotten tree produces evil fruit. 18. A good tree is not able to produce evil fruit, nor a rotten tree to produce good fruit. 19. Every tree not producing good fruit is cut down and thrown into a fire. 20. Consequently you will indeed know them on account of their fruit."

I Never Knew You

(Lk 13:25-27)

7:21. "Not everyone who says to Me, 'Lord. Lord!'[2] will enter the kingdom of the heavens,[3] but the one who does the will of My Father, the One in the heavens. 22. Many will say to Me in that Day, 'Lord. Lord! Did we not prophesy in Your name? And we cast out demons in Your name, and we did many miracles in Your name?' 23. And then I will declare to them that 'I never knew you: you working without Torah[4] must continually depart from Me.'"

The Two Foundations

(Lk 6:47-49)

7:24. "For everyone who hears these words of Mine, and does them, will become like a prudent man who built his house upon the rock: 25. and the rain came down and the rivers came *up* and the winds blew and they beat upon that house but it did not fall, for it has been founded upon the rock. 26. And everyone who hears these words of Mine and does not do them will be like a foolish man, who built his house upon the sand: 27. and the rain came down and the rivers came *up*, and the winds blew and they beat upon that house, and it fell and its fall was great."

7:28. And it happened when Jesus finished these words, the crowds were amazed by His teaching: 29. for He was teaching them as one having authority and not like their scribes.

The Cleansing of a Leper[5]

(Mk 1:40-45, Lk 5:12-16)

8.1. And when He went down from the mountain huge crowds followed Him. 2. And behold when a leper came he was kneeling before Him saying,

---

1   (v.16) The Greek construction shows that a negative response is anticipated.
2   (v.21) This is a desperate call, to be sure of getting the Lord's attention. See Double Name in Glossary.
3   (v.21) Heavens is plural because in the Hebrew Scriptures seven levels of heaven are identified. See Heavens in Glossary.
4   (v.23) Without Torah means to fail to do the things taught in the Torah, the first five books of the Bible.
5   (Caption) The disease called leprosy in the Bible is not the same as modern leprosy. See Leprosy in Glossary.

"Lord, if You would be willing, You are able to cleanse me." 3. Then as He stretched His hand He touched[1] him saying, "I am willing. You must instantly be cleansed." And his leprosy was immediately cleansed. 4. Then Jesus said to him, "You must see that you would not tell anyone, but you must now go, show yourself to the priest and present the offering which Moses commanded, in testimony to them."

The Healing of a Centurion's Servant

(Lk 7:1-10, Jn 4:43-54)

8:5. And when He came into Capernaum[2] a centurion came to Him, begging Him 6. and saying, "Lord, my child[3] has been smitten in the house by paralysis, fearfully tormented." 7. Then He said to him, "When I come I will heal him." 8. Then the centurion said, "Lord, I am not worthy that You should come under my roof, but You must only say a word, and my child will be healed. 9. For I also am a man under authority, having soldiers under myself, and I say to this one, 'You must go,' and he goes, and to another, 'You must come,' and he comes, and to my servant, 'You must do this,' and he does." 10. Then when Jesus heard He was amazed and said to those following, "Truly I say to you, I have not before found so much faith in Israel. 11. I say to you that many will come from east and west and will recline with Abraham, Isaac, and Jacob in the kingdom of the heavens,[4] 12. and the sons of the kingdom will be cast out into the outer darkness: there will be weeping and gnashing of teeth in that place." 13. Then Jesus said to the centurion, "You must now go. As you believed, it must instantly be for you." And his child was healed in that hour.

The Healing of Many People

(Mk 1:29-34, Lk 4:38-41)

8:14. Then after Jesus came into Peter's house He saw that his mother-in-law was in bed and suffering with a fever: 15. and He touched her hand, and the fever left her, and she got up and was serving Him. 16. And when it became evening they brought to Him many *who* were demon possessed: and He cast out the spirits with a word and He healed all who had evil, 17. thus was fulfilled that spoken through Isaiah the prophet saying,

> "He took our sicknesses
> and He bore our diseases." (Is 53:4)

---

1   (v.3) Anyone touching a leper would be unclean, but Jesus gives evidence of His Deity because He cleansed the leper, and the leper did not make Him unclean. "Seven days you shall make an atonement for the altar, and sanctify it; and it shall be an altar most holy; whatever touches the altar shall be holy." (Ex 29:37)

2   (v.5) Capernaum is the Latin spelling of the Hebrew name Kafer Na-um. Kafer means town or village and Na-um means pleasant.

3   (v.6) This indicates a male child, referred to in Lk 7:2 as a slave. Most likely he was a young indentured servant.

4   (v.11) The Hebrew word for heaven is always plural. See Heavens in Glossary.

The Would-be Followers of Jesus
(Lk 9:57-62)

8:18. And when Jesus saw a crowd around Him He ordered[1] *them* to go over to the other side *of the lake*. 19. And having approached, one of *the* scribes said to Him, "Teacher, I will follow You wherever You would go." 20. Then Jesus said to him, "The foxes have dens and the birds of the sky *have* nests, but the Son of Man does not have anywhere He could lay His head." 21. And another of His disciples said to Him, "Lord, You must allow me to leave first and to bury my father." 22. But Jesus said to him, "You must follow Me now and you must let the *spiritually* dead bury their own dead."

The Calming of a Storm
(Mk 4:35-41, Lk 8:22-25)

8:23. When He went into the boat His disciples followed Him. 24. And behold a great storm came on the lake, so the boat was covered by the waves, but He was sleeping. 25. And then they came *and* woke Him saying, "Lord, You must immediately save *us*, we are lost." 26. Then He said to them, "Little faiths, why are you cowards?" Then after He got up He rebuked the winds and the lake, and a great calm came. 27. And the men marveled saying, "What sort is this that even the winds and the lake will obey Him?"

The Healing of the Gadarene Demoniacs
(Mk 5:1-20, Lk 8:26-39)

8:28. Then after He came to the other side in the territory of the Gadarenes, two demon possessed men met Him when they came out from the tombs. *They were* greatly savage, so that no one was able to come through that way. 29. And behold they cried out saying, "What do You have to do with us, Son of God? Did You come here to torment us before *our* time?" 30. And there was a herd of many swine feeding a considerable distance from them. 31. And the demons were begging Him saying, "If You cast us out, You must right away send us into the herd of swine." 32. Then He said to them, "You must now go." And when they came out they went into the swine: and behold the whole herd rushed down the steep bank into the lake and they died in the waters. 33. And the herdsmen fled, then having come into the city they reported everything and what happened with the demon possessed *men*. 34. Then behold all the city came out for the purpose of meeting Jesus and when they saw Him they begged that He would go from their territory.

The Healing of a Paralytic
(Mk 2:1-12, Lk 5:17-26)

9.1. Then after He got in the boat He crossed over and came into His

---

1   (v.18) The Greek word keleuo, translated 'ordered,' is used only for someone of rank issuing an order.

own city. 2. And behold they were bringing Him a paralytic *who* was lying on a stretcher. And when Jesus saw their faith He said to the paralytic, "You must be courageous, child, your sins are forgiven." 3. And behold some of the scribes said among themselves, "This One is blaspheming." 4. Then since Jesus knew their thoughts He said, "Why are you thinking evil in your hearts? 5. For what is easier, to say, 'Your sins are forgiven,' or to say, 'You must rise and you must continually walk?' 6. But so that you would see that the Son of Man has authority upon the Earth to forgive sins"[1] - then He said to the paralytic, "When you get up you must take your stretcher and immediately go into your house." 7. Then after he got up he went into his house. 8. And when the crowds saw *this*, they feared and praised God; the One Who gave authority such as this to mankind.

The Calling of Matthew

(Mk 2:13-17, Lk 5:27-32)

9:9. Then when Jesus went away from there He saw a man, called Matthew, sitting in the tax office, and He said to him, "You must follow Me faithfully." So after he got up, he followed Him.[2] 10. And it happened while He was reclining in his house, then there were many tax collectors and sinners *who* came and they were reclining[3] *at the table* with Jesus and His disciples. 11. And when the Pharisees saw *them* they were saying to His disciples, "Why does your Teacher eat with the tax collectors and sinners?" 12. Then since He heard He said, "The strong have no need of a physician, but those who have evil.[4] 13. But when you go what you must learn is, 'I desire mercy and not sacrifice:' (Ho 6:6) for I did not come to call *the* righteous but *the* sinners."

The Question about Fasting

(Mk 2:18-22, Lk 5:33-39)

9:14. After that the disciples of John came to Him saying, "Why are we and the Pharisees fasting much, but Your disciples do not fast?" 15. And Jesus said to them, "Are the sons of the bridegroom able to mourn as long as the bridegroom is with them? But days will come when the bridegroom would be taken from them, and then they will fast. 16. And no one puts a patch of new cloth on an old garment: for the patch pulls from his garment and becomes a worse tear. 17. And no one puts new wine into old wine skins: otherwise the wine skins burst and the wine spills out and the wine skins are lost: but they put new wine into new wine skins, and both are preserved."

---

1   (v.6) It is interesting that Jesus says He has authority to forgive sins, yet His statement to the paralytic is "Your sins are forgiven," something we can say to any repentant person.

2   (v.9) As a tax collector, Matthew would have been wealthy, upper class. He left everything to become a disciple and follow Jesus.

3   (v.10) Reclining to eat had been a Jewish custom for some time, because reclining was a sign of freedom, that they were no longer Egyptian slaves. See Reclining in Glossary.

4   (v.12) The Greek word kakos literally means evil though it is often translated "sick."

The Ruler's Daughter and The Woman Who Touched Jesus' Prayer Shawl

(Mk 5:21-43, Lk 8:40-56)

9:18. After He said these things to them, behold, one leader *who* came knelt at His feet saying that, "My daughter is now dying: but after You come You must lay Your hand upon her, and she will live." 19. Then, after he got up, Jesus and His disciples followed him. 20. And there was a woman, *who* was suffering with a hemorrhage for twelve years, when she came *up* behind *Him* she touched the fringe[1] of His prayer shawl: 21. for she was saying within herself "If only I could touch His prayer shawl[2] I will be delivered." 22. And when Jesus turned around and saw her He said, "Be of good cheer, daughter: your faith has delivered you."[3] And the woman was delivered from that moment. 23. Then after Jesus came to the house of the leader and when He saw the flute players and the troubled crowd 24. He was saying, "You must go away now, for the girl is not dead but she is sleeping." Then they were laughing at Him. 25. And after the crowd was thrown out, He entered *and* took hold of her hand, and the girl got up. 26. Then this report came out into that whole country.

The Healing of Two Blind Men

9:27. And as He was going away from there two blind *men* followed Jesus, crying out and saying, "You must now have mercy on us, Son of David."[4] 28. And after He went into the house the blind *men* came to Him, and Jesus said to them, "Do you believe that I am able to do this?" They said to Him, "Indeed, Lord." 29. Then He touched their eyes saying, "According to your faith it must now be for you." 30. And their eyes were opened. Then Jesus warned them sternly, saying, "You must see *to it* that no one knows." 31. But after they left, they spread this in that whole country.

The Healing of a Mute Person

9:32. And while they were coming out behold they brought to Him a man *who* had a deaf and mute demon. 33. Then after He cast out the demon the mute man spoke. And the crowds were amazed saying, "Never has this been known in Israel." 34. But the Pharisees were saying, "He casts out demons by the prince of the demons."

The Compassion of Jesus

9:35. And Jesus was going around all the cities and the villages teaching in their synagogues and proclaiming the Good News of the kingdom and healing every disease and every sickness. 36. And when He saw the crowds He was

---

1   (v.20) The corner fringe of the prayer shawl, called tsitsit in Hebrew, represents all the commands and promises of God. See Prayer Shawl in Glossary.
2   (v.21) The prayer shawl worn by an anointed man of God was known to have an anointing for healing. See Prayer Shawl in Glossary.
3   (v.22) See Lk 8:47 and its footnote for more detail.
4   (v.27) See Son of David/Son of Joseph in Glossary.

sympathetic concerning them, because they were weary and laying down like sheep *that* did not have a shepherd. 37. Then He said to His disciples, "On one hand the harvest *is* great, but on the other hand the workers *are* few: 38. so you *all* must immediately appeal to the Lord of the Harvest so that He would send out workers into His harvest." (Rev 14:15)

The Mission of the Twelve

(Mk 3:13-19, Lk 6:12-16)

10.1. Then after He summoned His twelve disciples He gave them authority over unclean spirits, so that they could cast them out and heal every disease and every sickness. 2. And the names of the twelve apostles were these, first Simon, the one called Peter, and Andrew his brother, and Jacob[1] the *son* of Zebedee, and John his brother, 3. Philip and Bartholomew, Thomas and Matthew the tax collector, Jacob the *son* of Alpheus, and Thaddaeus, 4. Simon the Zealot, and Judas from Iscariot, the one who gave Him over.

The Commissioning of the Twelve

(Mk 6:7-13, Lk 9:1-6)

10:5. Jesus sent these twelve, after He commanded them, saying, "On the way do not go to *the* heathens and do not enter a Samaritan city: 6. but you must rather go regularly to the lost sheep of *the* house of Israel. 7. And while you are going you must preach, saying that 'The kingdom of the heavens[2] has come near.' 8. You must continually heal sicknesses, raise *the* dead, cleanse lepers,[3] cast out demons: you took freely, you must now give freely. 9. You can acquire neither gold nor silver nor copper in your belts, 10. nor a knapsack for *the* way nor two tunics nor sandals nor a staff: for the worker is worthy of his food. 11. In whatever city or town you would enter you must at once examine *to determine* who in it is worthy: remain there *in that house* until whenever you would leave. 12. And when you enter a house you must immediately greet it: 13. then if the house would be worthy, your peace must come upon it: but if it would not be worthy, your peace must return to you. 14. And whoever would not take you *in* and would not listen to your message, when you come outside the house or that city you must right away shake off the dust from your feet. 15. Truly I say to you, it will be more bearable in *the* region of Sodom and Gomorra on Judgment Day than in that city."

Coming Persecutions

(Mk 13:9-13, Lk 21:12-17)

10:16. "Behold I am sending you as sheep in *the* midst of wolves: therefore you must become as prudent as serpents and as innocent as doves. 17. And you

---

1   (v.2) The name in the Greek text is Iakob, which is Jacob in English.
2   (v.7) Heavens is always plural in Hebrew. See Heavens in Glossary.
3   (v.8) This is not the disease known as leprosy today. See Leprosy in Glossary.

must be on guard from men: for they will give you over to sanhedrins[1] and they will scourge you in their public gatherings:[2] 18. and you will be led before rulers and even kings because of Me, in witness to them and to the heathens. 19. And when they would arrest you, do not be anxious how or what you would say: for what you should say will be given to you at that moment: 20. for you will not be those speaking but *it will be* the Spirit of your Father, the One Who speaks through you. 21. And a brother will betray a brother into death and a father a child, and children will rise up in rebellion against parents and they will put them to death. 22. And you will be hated by all because of My name: but the one who has persevered to *the* end will be saved. 23. And when they would persecute you in this city, you must flee to another: for truly I say to you, you would not finish the cities of Israel until the Son of Man would come.[3]

10:24. "For a disciple is not above his teacher and a servant is not above his master. 25. *It is* sufficient for the disciple that he would become like his teacher and the servant like his master. If they called the master of the house Beelzebub, how much more those of his household."

Whom to Fear

(Lk 12:2-7)

10:26. "However you should not fear them: for there is nothing which has been concealed which will not be revealed and no secret which will not be known. 27. What I am saying to you in the darkness, you must now say in the light, and what you are hearing in your ear you must immediately proclaim on your roofs.[4] 28. And do not be afraid of those who kill the body, but they are not able to kill *eternal* life: but you must rather fear the One able to destroy both life and body in Gehenna.[5] 29. Do not two sparrows sell for a sixteenth of a denarius? And not one of them will fall on the Earth without the knowledge and consent of your Father. 30. And of you, even all the hairs of *your* head are numbered. 31. Therefore stop being afraid! You are worth more than many sparrows."

Confessing Messiah before Men

(Lk 12:8,9)

10:32. "Therefore everyone who will confess Me in front of people, then I will confess him before My Father, the One in the heavens: 33. but whoever would deny Me before people, then I will deny him before My Father, the One in

---

1   (v.17) Sanhedrins are community councils responsible for maintaining law and order and deciding local issues.

2   (v.17) While this word could be translated synagogues, "a gathering of people" is the primary meaning and no one would be scourged in a synagogue. Lk 4:28 tells of Jesus being driven from the city when the congregation was enraged. See Congregation in Glossary.

3   (v.23) Every generation is to believe that it is in the end times. See Coming of Messiah in Glossary.

4   (v.27) Houses and public buildings in ancient Israel had flat roofs that were often used for storage and other purposes, such as the prophet's room built for Elisha.

5   (v.28) See Gehenna in Glossary.

the heavens."

Not Peace, but a Sword

(Lk 12:51-53, 14:26,27)

10:34. "Do not think that I have come to bring peace upon the Earth: I did not come to bring peace but war. 35. For I came to set one against another

'a man against his father
>> and a daughter against her mother
> and a daughter-in-law against her mother-in-law,
36. and a man's enemies *will be* of his household.' (Mic 7:6)

37. The one who loves father or mother more than Me is not worthy of Me, and the one who loves a son or daughter more than Me is not worthy of Me: 38. and who does not take his cross[1] and follow behind Me, is not worthy of Me. 39. The one who has found his life will destroy it, and the one who has lost his life for My sake will find it."

Rewards

(Mk 9:41)

10:40. "The one who receives you is receiving Me, and the one who receives Me is receiving the One Who sent Me. 41. The one who receives a prophet in *the* name of a prophet[2] will take a prophet's reward, and the one who receives a righteous *person* in *the* name of a righteous *person* will take a righteous person's reward. 42. And whoever would give a cold drink to one of the least of these, only in *the* name of a disciple,[3] truly I say to you, would **not** lose his reward."

11.1. And it was when Jesus finished directing His twelve disciples, He went from there to teach and to preach in their cities.

The Messengers from John the Baptist

(Lk 7:18-35)

11:2. And when John, in the prison, heard about the works of the Messiah, after he sent his disciples, 3. they said to Him, "Are You the One Who is coming or should we be looking for another?" 4. And Jesus said to them, "When you go you must report to John what you are hearing and seeing: 5. blind are regaining sight and lame are walking, lepers[4] are being cleansed and deaf are hearing, and dead are being raised and *the* repentant[5] are being brought the Good News: 6. and blessed is whoever would not be caused to fall away because of Me." 7. And after they left, Jesus began to talk to the crowds about John, "What did you go out

---

1   (v.38) This is a prophetic call by Jesus, noting how He would later be killed.
2   (v.41) Because he is called a prophet.
3   (v.42) Because he is called a disciple.
4   (v.5) This is not the disease called leprosy today. See Leprosy in Glossary.
5   (v.5) Literally, the poor

into the desert to see? A reed being shaken by a wind? 8. But what did you come out to see? A man dressed in soft clothes? Behold those wearing soft clothes are in the houses of kings. 9. But what did you come out to see? A prophet? Indeed I say to you, even more than a prophet. 10. This is concerning whom it has been written,

> 'Behold I am sending My messenger ahead of You,
> who will prepare Your way before You'. (Ex 23:20, Mal 3:1)

11. Truly I say to you: there has not been born of women greater than John the Baptist: but the least in the kingdom of the heavens is greater than he. 12. From the days of John the Baptist until now the kingdom of the heavens is taken by violence, and shares in the heavenly kingdom are sought for with the most ardent zeal and the most intense exertion and violent men are seizing it, each one claiming eagerly for himself. (Lk 16:16) 13. For all the Prophets and the Torah[1] prophesied until John: 14. and if you want to accept *it*, he is Elijah, the one who was going to come. (Mal 4:5) 15. The one who has ears must continually listen.

11:16. "But what is this generation like? It is like children sitting in the markets calling out to the others 17. saying,

> 'We played the flute for you and you did not dance,
> we sang a lament and you did not mourn.'

18. John came neither eating nor drinking, and they are saying 'He has a demon.' 19. The Son of Man came eating and drinking,[2] and they are saying, 'Look, *the* man is a glutton and a wine-bibber, a friend of tax collectors and sinners.' But wisdom was made right[3] by her works."

Woes to Unrepentant Cities

(Lk 10:13-15)

11:20. Then He began to denounce, because they did not repent, the cities in which most of His miracles were done. 21. "Woe to you, Chorazin, woe to you, Bethsaida:[4] because if the miracles happening in you were done in Tyre and Sidon, they would long ago have repented in sack cloth and ashes. 22. Nevertheless I say to you, it will be more bearable in Tyre and Sidon on Judgment Day than in you. 23. And you, Capernaum,[5]

> 'will you be lifted up as far as heaven?[6]
> you will be cast down as far as Hades:' (Is 14:13,15)

---

1   (v.13) The Prophets are the books Jsh, Jd, 1 & 2 Sa, 1 & 2Ki, Is through Mal, but not Dn. See Prophets and Book Order in Glossary.
2   (v.19) This is the Greek word pinao, for drinking any liquid, not just wine.
3   (v.19) Justified
4   (v.21) Bethsaida is the Greek spelling of Beit-Tside, which means House or Place of Fishing (literally hunting, but used for both fishing and hunting) in Hebrew.
5   (v.23) Capernaum is the Latin spelling of the Hebrew name Kafer Na-um. Kafer means town or village and Na-um means pleasant.
6   (v.23) The Greek construction anticipates a negative answer.

because if the miracles that been done in you had been done in Sodom, it *would have* remained until this day. 24. Nevertheless I say to you that on Judgment Day it will be more bearable in the land of Sodom than in you."

Come to Me and Rest

(Lk 10:21,22)

11:25. At that time Jesus said, "I praise You, Father, Master of Heaven and Earth,[1] because You hid these things from *the* wise and intelligent and You revealed them to babies: 26. indeed, Father, because in this way it was well pleasing before You. 27. Everything has been given to Me by My Father, and no one understands the Son except the Father, and no one understands the Father except the Son and to whomever the Son would wish to reveal.[2] 28. Come to Me all those who work and are burdened, and I will give you rest.[3] 29. You must immediately take My yoke[4] upon you and you must now learn from Me, because I am gentle and humble in My heart, and you will find rest in your lives: 30. for My yoke is pleasant and My burden is insignificant."[5]

Plucking Grain on Sabbath

(Mk 2:23-28, Lk 6:1-5)

12.1. In that time Jesus went through the grain fields on the Sabbaths:[6] and His disciples hungered[7] and began to pick grains and to eat. 2. And when the Pharisees saw *them*, they said to Him, "Look! Your disciples are doing what is not permitted to do on a Sabbath." 3. And He said to them, "Have you not read what David did when he and those with him hungered, 4. how he entered the house of God and they ate the Bread of the Presence, (1Sa 21:7) which was not lawful for him to eat and not for those with him, except for the priests only? 5. Or have you not read in the Torah[8] that on the Sabbaths[9] the priests in the temple desecrate the Sabbath and are innocent? 6. And I say to you that *One* greater than

---

1   (v.25) 'Master of Heaven and Earth' was in Jesus' day and is today a frequent reference to God in the opening salutation of a Jewish prayer.

2   (v.27) Apparently Jesus chose not to reveal Himself to some major Jewish teachers, such as Gamaliel under whom Paul studied (Acts 22:3). See Acts 5:33.

3   (v.28) This rest and the one in v. 29 are temporary rests, just a break from work. See Rest in Glossary.

4   (v.29) Rabbis say the Lord's yoke means total spiritual surrender. See Dt 6:5, Mt 22:36,37. See Yoke in Glossary.

5   (v.30) This could be stated "light as a feather" because it is a weight that is not detectable when you bear it.

6   (v.1) This could well be during the Feast of Weeks, because the plural of Sabbath was used for "weeks" and the Feast of Weeks was the season of the wheat harvest. To harvest a crop is work and is not to be done on a Sabbath, but plucking a handful of grain is not work. During the Sabbath year people could gather a day's needs. See Sabbath in Glossary.

7   (v.1) Oral law permits breaking commandments for humanitarian reasons, such as hunger.

8   (v.5) First five books of the Bible; see Torah in Glossary.

9   (v.5) This means that on every Sabbath priests desecrated the Sabbath in carrying out their priestly duties.

the temple is here. 7. And if you had understood what is *written,* 'I desire mercy and not sacrifice,' (Hos 6:6) you would not condemn the innocent. 8. For the Son of Man is Lord of the Sabbath."

The Man with a Withered Hand

(Mk 3:1-6, Lk 6:6-11)

12:9. Then going from there He came into their synagogue: 10. and there was a man *who* had a withered hand. Then they asked Him saying, "Is it permitted to heal on the Sabbaths?" so that they could accuse Him. 11. And He said to them, "What man is among you who will have one sheep and if this would fall into a pit on the Sabbaths, would not take hold himself and will pull it out? 12. By how much is a man worth more than a sheep. Thus it is permitted to do good on the Sabbaths." 13. Then He said to the man, "You must immediately stretch out your hand." And he stretched and it was restored sound as the other. 14. After the Pharisees left they formed a plan against Him, how they could kill Him.

The Chosen Servant

12:15. But, because Jesus knew *that,* He went away from there. And huge crowds followed Him, and He healed them all 16. and He admonished them that they should not make it known, 17. so that what was spoken by Isaiah the prophet would be fulfilled, saying,

18.   "Behold My child whom I chose,
             My beloved in Whom My being takes delight:
    I will put My Spirit upon Him,
             and He will proclaim justice to the heathens.
19.   And He will not quarrel and will not cry out,
             and no one will hear His voice in the streets.
20.   A bent reed He will not break,
             and He will not put out a smoking wick,
    until He would force justice into victory.
21.   And heathens will hope in His name." (Is 42:1-4)

Jesus and Beelzebub

(Mk 3: 20-30, Lk 11:14-23, 12:10)

12:22. Then a blind and deaf demonized *man* was brought to Him, and He healed him, so that the deaf one spoke and saw. 23. And all the crowds were amazed and were saying, "Is this not the Son of David?"[1] 24. And when the Pharisees heard they said, "This One does not cast out demons except by Beelzebub, leader of the demons." 25. And because He knew their thoughts He

---

1   (v.23) The people think of the Son of David as the reigning Messiah. See Son of David/ Son of Joseph in Glossary.

said to them, "Every kingdom divided against itself is made desolate and not one city or house divided against itself will stand. 26. And if Satan[1] casts out Satan, he is divided against himself: therefore how will his kingdom stand? 27. And if I cast out demons by means of Beelzebub, by whose *authority* are your sons casting *them* out? Because of this they will be your judges. 28. But if I cast out demons by *the* Spirit of God, then the kingdom of God has come upon you. 29. Or how is someone able to enter the house of the strong one and to steal his property, unless he would first bind the strong one? And then he will thoroughly plunder his house. 30. The one who is not with Me is against Me, and the one who does not gather with Me is scattering. 31. Because of this I say to you, every sin and blasphemy will be forgiven to mankind, but the blasphemy of the Spirit will not be forgiven. 32. And if someone would speak a word against the Son of Man, it will be forgiven him: but whoever would speak against the Holy Spirit, it will not be forgiven to him either in this age or in the one coming."

A Tree and Its Fruits

(Lk 6:43-45)

12:33. "You must make the tree good and its fruit good, or you must make the tree rotten and its fruit rotten: for the tree will be known by its fruit. 34. Children of vipers, how are you, since you are evil, able to speak good things? For the mouth speaks from the abundance of the heart. 35. The good man casts out good from his good treasure box and the evil man casts out evil from his evil treasure box. 36. And I say to you that every idle word which men will speak will be paid back with regard to his account on Judgment Day: 37. for you[2] will be justified, declared righteous, because of your words, and you will be condemned because of your words." (Lv 19:16, Ps 5:5-7, 52:2-5, Pr 6:2, 10:11, 18:20, 21, Ecc 5:5, 10:12)

The Demand for a Sign

(Mk 8:11,12, Lk 11:29-32)

12:38. Then some of the scribes and Pharisees answered Him saying, "Teacher, we want to see a sign from You." 39. And He said to them, "An evil and adulterous generation seeks a sign, but a sign will not be given to it except the sign of the prophet Jonah. 40. For as 'Jonah was in the belly of the monster three days and three nights' (Jonah 1:17) so also the Son of Man will be in the heart of the Earth three days and three nights.[3] 41. Ninevite men will rise in judgment with this generation and they will condemn it, since they repented because of the preaching by Jonah and behold *One* greater than Jonah *is* here. 42. *The* Queen

---

1   (v.26) See Satan in Glossary.
2   (v.37) Each 'you' in this verse is singular. See Gossip/Slander in Glossary.
3   (v.40) This is the only time the expression "three days and three nights" is used in reference to Jesus' resurrection. Two verses, Mt 16:4 and Lk 11:29, refer to the "sign of Jonah." The following verses say "on the third day:" Mt 16:21, 17:23, 20:19, 27:64, Lk 9:22, 18:33, 24:7,46. See Preparation Day in Glossary.

of *the* South[1] will rise in the judgment with this generation and will condemn it, because she came from the ends of the Earth to hear the wisdom of Solomon, and behold *One* greater than Solomon is here."

The Return of the Unclean Spirit

(Lk 11:24-26)

12:43. "When the unclean spirit would come out from a person, it comes through dry places seeking rest but does not find *it*. 44. Then it says, 'I will return to my house from which I came out:' then when it comes it finds *the house* empty, having been swept and decorated. 45. Then it goes and takes with itself seven other spirits more evil than itself and after they enter they dwell there: and the last *state* of that person becomes worse than the first. And so it will be with this evil generation."

The Mother and Brothers of Jesus

(Mk 3:31-35, Lk 8:19-21)

12:46. While He was still speaking to the crowds, behold His mother and brothers had been standing outside seeking to speak with Him. 47. And someone said to Him, "See, Your mother and Your brothers have been standing outside seeking to speak with You."[2] 48. And He said to the one speaking to Him, "Who is My mother and who are My brothers?" 49. Then stretching out His hand to His disciples He said, "Behold My mother and My brothers. 50. For whoever would do the will of My Father, the One in *the* heavens, this one is My brother and sister and mother." (Ps 22:22, He 2:12)

The Parable of the Sower

(Mk 4:1-9, Lk 8:4-8)

13.1. In that day, after He left the house, Jesus was sitting by the lake: 2. and immense crowds were gathered to Him, so that He got in a boat *and* sat down, and the entire crowd stood on the shore. 3. And He told them many things in parables saying, "Behold the sower of the *seed* came out to sow. 4. And while he was sowing some indeed fell by the way, and when the birds came they devoured them. 5. But some fell upon the rocky *ground* where it did not have much *soil*, and it sprang up right away because it had no depth of soil: 6. and when the sun rose it was burned, and because it did not have a root it was withered. 7. But some fell upon thorns, and the thorns came up and choked them. 8. But some fell upon good ground, and gave fruit, on the one hand a hundred *times*, on another sixty, and another thirty. 9. The one who has ears must listen continually."

---

1   (v.42) The Queen of Sheba
2   (v.47) This verse is omitted from some early manuscripts.

The Purpose of the Parables

(Mk 4:10-12, Lk 8:9,10)

13:10. Then when the disciples came they said to Him, "Why are You speaking to them in parables?" 11. And He said to them, "Because it has been given to you to know the mysteries of the kingdom of the heavens,[1] but it has not been given to those. 12. For who has, it will be given to him and he will have great abundance: but who does not have, even what he does have will be taken from him. 13. I am speaking to them in parables because of this, because although they see, they do not see, and although they hear, they do not hear, and they do not understand, 14. and the prophecy of Isaiah is fulfilled to them, the one saying,

> 'To perceive by hearing, you will hear and you will **not** understand,
>> and seeing you will see and will **not** see *or understand*,
15.   For the heart of this people has been made dull,
>> and they heard in their ears *with* difficulty,
>>> and they closed their eyes
>>> lest they would see with their eyes
>> and they would hear with their ears
> and they would understand in their heart and they would return
>> and I would heal them.' (Is 6:9,10)

16. And blessed are your eyes because they see and your ears because they hear: 17. For truly I say to you that many prophets and righteous *people* desired to see what you are seeing but they did not see, and to hear what you are hearing but they did not hear."

The Parable of the Sower Explained

(Mk 4:13-20, Lk 8:11-15)

13:18. "Therefore you must now hear the parable of the sower. 19. For everyone who hears the message of the kingdom and does not understand, the evil one comes and snatches away what was sown in his heart, this one is what is sown by the way. 20. And the one sown upon the stony ground, this is the one who hears the message and immediately takes it with joy, 21. but it does not have a root in itself, but it is temporary, and when affliction or persecution comes because of the message, he is immediately caused to fall away. 22. And the one sown among the thorns, this is the one who hears the message, and the anxiety of the age and the deceitfulness of wealth (Mt 6:24) choke the message and it becomes useless. 23. And the one sown upon the good ground, this is the one who hears the message and understands, who indeed bears fruit[2] and makes on

---

1   (v.11) "Kingdom of the heavens" can refer to God. Heavens is always plural in Hebrew because in Hebrew there are seven levels of heaven. See Heavens and Kingdom in Glossary.
2   (v.23) In Mt 7:16 Jesus says we will be recognized by our fruit, by the way we live.

the one hand one hundred *times*, and on another sixty and another thirty."

The Parable of the Weeds among the Wheat

13:24. He put another parable before them saying, "The kingdom of the heavens is like a man sowing good seed in his field. 25. Then while the men slept his enemy came and sowed darnel[1] in the midst of the wheat and he left. 26. And when the crop sprouted and made fruit, then the darnel was also revealed. 27. And when the servants of the landowner came they said to him, 'Master, did you not sow good seed in your field? Therefore from where has *the* darnel *come*?' 28. And he said to them, 'A hostile man did this.' Then the servants said to him, 'Do you therefore want us to gather them when we leave?' 29. And he said, 'No, lest when you pull up the darnel you would uproot the wheat along with them. 30. You must now allow *them* both to grow together until the harvest, then in *the* time of the harvest I will say to the reapers, "You must now first gather the darnel and bind them in bundles to burn them up, then gather the wheat into my storehouse."'"

The Parables of the Mustard Seed and the Leaven

(Mk 4:30-32, Lk 13:18-21)

13:31. He put another parable before them saying, "The kingdom of the heavens is like a mustard seed, which when a man took he sowed in his field: 32. which is on the one hand the smallest of all the seeds, but when it would grow is more than the vegetables and becomes a tree, so that the birds of the sky come and they make nests in its branches."

13:33. He told another parable to them: "The kingdom of the heavens[2] is like yeast,[3] which when a woman took, she put *it* into three measures of wheat flour until the whole of it was leavened."

The Use of Parables

(Mk 4:33,34)

13:34. Jesus said these things in parables to the crowds and was saying nothing to them apart from a parable, 35. thus that spoken through the prophet would be fulfilled saying,

> "I will open My mouth in parables,
> I will proclaim *things that* have been concealed
> from *the* beginning of *the* universe." (Ps 78:2)

The Parable of the Weeds Explained

13:36. Then after He dismissed the crowds He came into the house. And

---

1 (v.25) Darnel was a weed that resembled wheat, but was not an edible grain.
2 (v.33) "Kingdom of the heavens" can refer to God. Heavens is always plural in Hebrew because in Hebrew there are seven levels of heaven. See both Heavens and Kingdom in Glossary.
3 (v.33) Yeast, which is usually symbolic of sin, is here used to refer to heaven, saying that good behavior, Godliness, leads others by example to imitate good behavior.

His disciples came to Him saying, "You must now explain for us the parable of the darnel of the field." 37. And when He answered He said, "The sower of the good seed is the Son of Man, 38. and the field is the world, and these good seeds are the sons of the kingdom: and the darnel are the sons of the evil one, 39. and the devil is the enemy who sows them, and the harvest is the end of the age, and the harvesters are angels. 40. Therefore just as the darnel is gathered and consumed in fire, so will it be in the end of the age: 41. the Son of Man will send His angels and they will gather from His kingdom all those drawn into error and those who were doing wickedness[1] 42. and they will cast them into the oven of the fire: in that place there will be weeping and gnashing of teeth. 43. Then the righteous ones will shine like the sun in the kingdom of their Father. The one who has ears must continually listen."

Three Parables

13:44. "The kingdom of the heavens is like a treasure box hidden in the field, which when a man found he hid, then out of his joy, went and sold all that he had and bought that field.

13:45. "Again the kingdom of the heavens is like a merchant seeking good pearls: 46. and when he found one very precious pearl, he left *and* sold everything that he had and he bought it.

13:47. "Again the kingdom of the heavens is like a fishnet[2] cast into the lake gathering from every kind *of fish*: 48. which when it was filled, after they pulled *it* up on the shore and sat down, they gathered the good into a vessel, but they cast the bad[3] outside. 49. And so it will be in the end of the age: the angels will come out and they will separate the evil ones from the midst of the righteous 50. and they will cast them into the fiery furnace: there will be weeping and gnashing of teeth in that place."

Treasures New and Old

13:51. "Do you understand all these things?" They said to Him, "Yes indeed!" 52. And He said to them, "Because of this every scribe who becomes a disciple in the kingdom of the heavens[4] is like a man, a landlord, who casts out from his treasure box new and old."[5]

---

1 (v.41) This could be stated "doing without Torah," not doing what is taught in Scripture.

2 (v.47) This net is a drag net, a very large net with stone weights to fish commercially in deep water. See Fish Nets in Glossary.

3 (v.49) The bad fish were those that were not fit to eat because they did not have both scales and fins.

4 (v.52) "Kingdom of the heavens" can refer to God. Heavens is always plural in Hebrew because in Hebrew there are seven levels of heaven. See both Heavens and Kingdom in Glossary.

5 (v.52) New refers to being fresh as opposed to being stale. Both fresh interpretation and established principles must be taught.

The Rejection of Jesus at Nazareth

(Mk 6:1-6, Lk 4:16-30)

13:53. And it happened that when Jesus finished these parables, He went away from there. 54. Then when He came into His hometown He taught them in their synagogue, so that they were amazed and said, "From where *do* this wisdom, and the miracles, in this One, *come*? 55. Is this not the carpenter's Son? Is not His mother called Mary and His brothers Jacob and Joseph and Simon and Judas? 56. And are not all His sisters with us? Therefore from where in this One *are* all these things?" 57. And they were offended because of Him. But Jesus said to them, "A prophet is not without honor except in his hometown and in his household." 58. And He did not do many miracles there because of their unbelief.[1]

The Death of John the Baptist

(Mk 6:14-29, Lk 9:7-9)

14.1. In that time Herod the Tetrarch heard of the fame of Jesus, 2. and he said to his servants, "This is John the Baptist: he rose from the dead and because of this the miracles are operating in him." 3. For after Herod arrested John he bound him and put him away in prison because *his wife* Herodiah *had been* the wife of Philip his brother: 4. for John was saying to him, "It is not permitted for you to have her." 5. And while he wanted to kill him he was afraid of the crowd, because they held him as a prophet. 6. And when it was a birthday celebration of Herod, the daughter of Herodiah danced in their midst and pleased Herod, 7. then with an oath he promised to give her whatever she would ask. 8. And she, urged by her mother, said, "You must immediately give me the head of John the Baptist here upon a plate." 9. Then although the king was saddened, because of the oaths and those who were reclining together with *him*, he commanded *it* to be given, 10. so then he sent *and* beheaded John in the prison. 11. And his head was brought on a platter and was given to the girl, and she brought *it* to her mother. 12. Then after his disciples came they took the body and they buried it and when they came to Jesus they reported *what happened*.

The Feeding of the Five Thousand

(Mk 6:30-44, Lk 9:10-17, Jn 6:1-14)

14:13. And after Jesus heard He went away from there in a boat to a wilderness place by Himself: but when the crowds heard they followed Him by land from the cities.[2] 14. And when He came out He saw an enormous crowd and had sympathy on them and He healed their sick ones. 15. And when it was evening the disciples came to Him saying, "The place is wilderness and the hour has now come: You must dismiss the crowds immediately so that after they leave

---

1   (v.58) The only place where He is referref to as not having the power is in Nazereth. See Mk 6:5 and Lk 5:17.
2   (v.13) See Location of the Feeding of the Five Thousand in Glossary.

for the towns they could buy food for themselves." 16. And Jesus said to them, "They do not need to leave. You must now give them *something* to eat." 17. But they said to Him, "We do not have *anything* here except five loaves and two fish," 18. Then He said, "Bring them here to Me." 19. And after He ordered the crowds to recline on the grass, having taken the five loaves and the two fish, He looked up into the sky *and* praised God, then when He broke the bread He gave *it* to the disciples, and the disciples *gave it* to the crowds. 20. And all ate and were satisfied, and they took up twelve baskets[1] full of left over broken pieces. (2Ki 4:42-44) 21. And those who were eating were about five thousand men, not counting women and children.

Walking on the Water

(Mk 6:45-52, Jn 6:15-21)

14:22. Then He at once compelled the disciples to embark in the boat and go before Him to the other side, until He could dismiss the crowds. 23. And after He sent the crowds away, He went up on the mountain by Himself to pray. And when evening came only He was there. 24. And now the wind was hindering the boat many stadia[2] distant from the shore, being harassed by the waves, for the wind was against *it*. 25. Then in the fourth watch[3] of the night He came to them as He walked on the lake. 26. But, when the disciples saw Him walking on the lake, they were disturbed saying that "It is a ghost," and they cried out from fear. 27. And Jesus spoke to them at once saying, "You must be courageous! I AM! Stop being afraid!" 28. And answering Him Peter said, "Lord, if it is You, You must right now order me to come to You on the waters." 29. And He said, "You must now come!" And when Peter came down from the boat he walked on the waters and came toward Jesus. 30. But when he saw the strong wind he was afraid, and as he began to sink he cried out saying, "Lord, You must now rescue me!" 31. And immediately Jesus, stretching out His hand, took his *hand* and said to him, "Little faith, why did you doubt?" 32. Then when they got up in the boat the wind stopped. 33. And those in the boat paid homage[4] to Him saying, "Truly You are *the* Son of God."

The Healing of the Sick at Gennesaret

(Mk 6:53-56)

14:34. Then after they crossed they came to shore in Gennesaret.[5] 35. And when they recognized Him the men of that place sent into that whole neighboring region and they brought to Him all those who had evil[6] 36. and they were begging

---

1   (v.20) The basket is smaller than the hamper used in the feeding of the four thousand.

2   (v.24) One stadion is about 200 yards.

3   (v.25) This is Roman time, between 3:00 AM and 6:00 AM. See Day in Glossary.

4   (v.32) To pay homage is to kneel and touch the forehead to the ground or deck of the boat in this case. See Pay Homage in Glossary.

5   (v.34) Gennesaret is a plain on the northwest side of the lake of Galilee, near Capernaum. The plain is very fertile, about three miles long by one mile wide and is named in Mk 6:53.

6   (v.35) The Greek word kakos literally means evil, but is used to refer to any affliction,

Him to just touch the tsitsit[1] of His prayer shawl: and they who touched were rescued.[2]

The Tradition of the Elders

(Mk 7:1-23)

15.1. Then Pharisees and scribes from Jerusalem came to Jesus saying, 2. "Why are Your disciples breaking the tradition of the elders? For they are not washing their hands when they eat a meal." 3. And Jesus said to them, "Then why are you breaking the commandment of God because of your tradition? 4. For God said, 'Honor *your* father and mother,' (Ex 20:12) and 'The one who speaks evil of father or mother must end in death.' (Ex 21:17) 5. But you say, 'Whoever would say to his father or mother, "Whatever gift from me *that* would have helped you *has been devoted to God*."' 6. He will **not** honor his father: so you made void the word of God because of your tradition. 7. Hypocrites, Isaiah rightly prophesied about you saying,

8.   'This people honors Me with their lips,
            but their hearts are far distant away from Me:
9.   and they are worshipping Me in vain
            teaching teachings[3] *that are* commandments of men.'" (Is 29:13)

15:10. Then after He summoned the crowd He said to them, "You must listen and understand: 11. that what *is* entering the mouth does not defile a person but that going out from the mouth.[4] This defiles the person." 12. Then the disciples, having come to Him, said, "Do You know that when the Pharisees heard the statement they were offended?" 13. And He said, "Every plant which My Heavenly Father did not plant will be uprooted. 14. You must leave them: they are blind guides of blind: and if blind would guide blind, both will fall into a pit." 15. And Peter said to Him, "You must now explain this parable to us." 16. And He said, "Are you even now senseless? 17. Do you not understand that everything that enters the mouth *and* the stomach comes out and is thrown out in a latrine? 18. But the things that go out from the mouth come out from the heart, and these things defile the person.[5] 19. For out of the heart come evil thoughts, murders, adulteries, immoralities, thefts, false witnesses, blasphemies. 20. These things are the things that defile a person but to eat with unwashed hands does not defile a person."

---

blindness, deafness, paralysis, disease, etc.
1   (v.36) This is the corner fringe of a prayer shawl. See Prayer Shawl in Glossary.
2   (v.36) The word used here is diasodzo, meaning, "brought safely through."
3   (v.9) Doctrines
4   (v.11) Eating foods forbidden in Scripture will not cause you to lose your eternal life, but we now know a diet excessive in the forbidden foods will shorten your life span on Earth, as will ignoring Acts 15:20 and OT warnings, and by overeating.
5   (v.18) Jesus is saying that we do not lose eternal life by what we eat. See note on v.11.

The Canaanite[1] Woman's Faith

(Mk 7:24-30)

15:21. Then when He came out from there Jesus went into the regions of Tyre and Sidon. 22. And there was a Canaanite woman from those regions, when she came out she cried out saying, "You must have mercy[2] on me right now, Lord, Son of David:[3] my daughter has an evil spirit." 23. But He did not answer a word to her. And when His disciples drew near *to Him* they were asking Him saying, "You must send her away, because she is crying out behind us." 24. And when He answered He said, "I was not sent except to the lost sheep of *the* house of Israel." 25. But the one who had come was kneeling before Him saying, "Lord, You must help me." 26. And He said, "It is not good to take the children's bread and cast *it* to the little dogs."[4] 27. Then she said, "Indeed Lord, for even the dogs are eating from the scraps falling from the table of their masters." 28. Then Jesus said to her, "O Woman, your faith is great: it must now be to you as you wish." And her daughter was healed from that moment.

The Healing of Many People

15:29. And when He departed from there Jesus came by the lake of Galilee, and after He went up on the mountain He was sitting there. 30. And immense crowds came to Him, having with themselves lame, blind, deformed, deaf, and many others and they laid them down at His feet, and He healed them: 31. so to amaze the crowd when it saw deaf speaking, deformed healthy, and lame walking and blind seeing: and they gave glory to the God of Israel.

The Feeding of the Four Thousand

(Mk 8:1-10)

15:32. And after Jesus summoned His disciples He said, "I feel sorry for the crowd, because they have already been staying with Me three days and they do not have anything they could eat: and I do not want to release them hungry lest they would become weary on the way." 33. Then the disciples said to Him, "From where in a wilderness can we get so much food so as to feed so great a crowd?" 34. And Jesus said to them, "How much food do you have?" And they said, "Seven *loaves* and a few fish." 35. Then after He instructed the crowd to recline on the ground 36. He took the seven loaves and the fish and after He gave thanks He broke *them* and was giving *them* to the disciples, and the disciples *gave them* to the crowds. 37. Then they all ate and were satisfied. And they took

---

1   (Caption) The term Canaanite refers to anyone from west of the Jordan River. Her home is more closely defined in Mk 7:26 as Syrophoenecian, from the northern coastal area of Canaan.

2   (v.22) Asking for mercy was an idiom for asking for forgiveness. The people understood that sickness was caused by sin.

3   (v.22) See Son of David/Son of Joseph in Glossary.

4   (v.26) Probably only puppies could get under the tables, which were generally low with the diners reclining on cushions.

up the leftovers, seven hampers[1] full of the pieces. (2Ki 4:42-44) 38. And those who ate were four thousand men[2] not counting women and children. 39. And after He dismissed the crowds He embarked in the boat and came to the region of Magadan.

The Demand for a Sign

(Mk 8:11-13, Lk 12:54-56)

16.1. Then the Pharisees and Sadducees came testing *Him*. They demanded He show them a sign from heaven. 2. And He said to them, "When it becomes evening you say, 'Fair weather, for the sky is fiery *red*:' 3. then early, 'Today *will be* bad weather,' for the gloomy sky becomes red. On the one hand you know how to judge the appearance of the sky, but on the other hand are you not able *to judge* the signs of the times? 4. An evil and adulterous generation demands a sign, but a sign will not be given to it except the sign *of* Jonah." Then departing from them He went away.

The Leaven of the Pharisees and Sadducees

(Mk 8:14-21)

16:5. And when the disciples went to the other side they forgot to take bread. 6. And Jesus said to them, "You must watch out and pay attention on account of the leaven of the Pharisees and Sadducees."[3] 7. And they were discussing among themselves saying that "We did not take bread." 8. But since Jesus knew He said, "What are you discussing among yourselves, little faiths, that you do not have bread? 9. Do you not yet understand, and do you not remember the five loaves of the five thousand and how many baskets you took? 10. And not the seven loaves of the four thousand and how many hampers[4] you took? 11. How do you not understand that I did not speak to you about bread? But you must pay attention to, be wary of, the leaven of the Pharisees and Sadducees." 12. Then they understood that He did not say to be wary of the leaven of the bread but from the teaching of the Pharisees and Sadducees.

Peter's Declaration about Jesus

(Mk 8:27-30, Lk 9:18-21)

16:13. And after Jesus came into the region of Caesarea Philippi *He was* asking His disciples saying, "Who do people say that the Son of Man is?" 14. And they said, "Some indeed John the Baptist, and others Elijah, and others Jeremiah or one of the prophets." 15. He said to them, "And who do you say I am?" 16. And Simon Peter said, "You are the Messiah, the Son of the Living

---

1   (v.37) The hamper was large, being used in Acts 9:25 to describe Paul's being lowered through the Damascus city wall. See Mt 16:10, Mk 8:8, 20.

2   (v.38) See Census in Glossary.

3   (v.6) The leaven of Pharisees is legalism, the leaven of Sadducees is Hellenism, apostasy. See Hellenism in Glossary.

4   (v.10) See note on v.37.

God." 17. And Jesus said to him, "Blessed are you, Simon Bar-Jonah, because, not flesh and blood, but My Father, the One in the heavens,[1] revealed *this* to you. 18. And I am saying to you that you are Peter, and upon this rock I will build My congregation[2] and gates of Hades will not prevail against *the congregation*. 19. I will give you the keys of the kingdom of the heavens, and whatever you would bind[3] upon the Earth will *already* have been bound in the heavens *with ongoing effect*, and whatever you would loose[4] upon the Earth will *already* have been loosed in the heavens *with ongoing effect*."[5] 20. Then He was commanding the disciples that they should not say that He was the Messiah.

Jesus foretells His Death and Resurrection[6]

(Mk 8:31-9:1, Lk 9:22-27)

16:21. From then *on* Jesus began to show His disciples that it was necessary for Him to go away to Jerusalem and to suffer greatly from the elders and high priests and scribes and to be killed, then to be raised on the third day. 22. Then Peter, after he took Him aside, began to reprove Him saying, "God forbid, Lord! This will **not** happen to You." 23. And He, turning about, said to Peter, "You must go behind Me,[7] Satan![8] You are tempting Me, because you are not thinking the things of God but the things of men." 24. Then Jesus said to His disciples, "If someone wants to come after Me he must deny himself and he must immediately take his cross and he must continually follow Me. 25. For whoever would want to save his life will lose it: and whoever would lose his life for My sake will find it. 26. For what will a man profit if he would gain the whole world but would forfeit his very being? Or what will a man give in place of his life? 27. For the Son of Man is going to come in the glory of His Father with His angels, and then He will give back to each according to his actions.[9] 28. Truly I say to you that there are some of those who are standing here who will **not** taste death until they would see the Son of Man coming with His kingdom."[10]

The Transfiguration of Jesus

(Mk 9:2-13, Lk 9:28-36)

17.1. Then after six days Jesus took Peter and Jacob and John his

---

1   (v.17) Heavens is always plural in Hebrew and the Hebrew Scriptures name seven levels of heaven. See Heavens in Glossary.

2   (v.18) Although often translated "church," no Greek word meaning church is used in the NT. See Congregation in Glossary.

3   (v.19) To Bind is a Hebrew idiom meaning forbid. Binding and loosing here refer specifically to the judicial applications for all the dietary, Sabbath, and other regulations, including civil law, and extend to the spiritual realm as well.

4   (v.19) Loose is a Hebrew idiom meaning permit.

5   (v.19) The italicized words are added to express the tense used here by the Greek text.

6   (Caption) See Resurrection in Glossary.

7   (v.23) The word translated go is hupago, which means to go back where you came from.

8   (v.23) See Satan in Glossary.

9   (v.27) See Jas 2:14. See both Mitsvah and Righteousness in Glossary.

10   (v.28) Even Jesus was expecting His Messianic reign momentarily. See Mt 24:36.

brother and brought them up on a high mountain by themselves. 2. And He was transformed before them, and His face shone like the sun, and His garments became white[1] as the light. 3. And behold Moses and Elijah were seen by them conversing with Him. 4. And Peter said to Jesus, "Lord, it is good for us to be here: if You are willing, I will make three booths, one for You and one for Moses and one for Elijah. 5. While he was still speaking, behold a radiant cloud overshadowed them, and there was a voice from the cloud saying, "This is My beloved Son, with Whom I have been well pleased: you must habitually listen to Him." 6. And when the disciples heard they fell upon their faces and they were exceedingly afraid. 7. Then Jesus came and after He touched them He said, "You must get up at once and you must stop being afraid." 8. And when they opened their eyes they saw no one except only Jesus Himself.

17:9. Then while they were coming down the mountain Jesus ordered them saying, "Do not tell what you saw until the Son of Man would be risen from *the* dead." 10. Then the disciples asked Him saying, "Then why are the scribes saying that it is necessary for Elijah to come first?" 11. And He said, "Elijah is indeed coming and will restore all things: 12. but I say to you that Elijah has already come, but they did not recognize him and they did with him what they wanted: so also the Son of Man is going to suffer under them." 13. Then the disciples understood that He spoke to them about John the Baptist.

The Healing of a Boy with a Demon

(Mk 9:14-29, Lk 9:37-43a)

17:14. And when they came to the crowd a man came to Him, kneeling down to Him 15. and saying, "Lord, You must have mercy[2] on my son, because he is epileptic and suffers severely: for often he falls into the fire and often into the water. 16. And I brought him to Your disciples, but they were not able to heal him." 17. And Jesus responded, "O unbelieving and perverted generation, how long will I be with you? Until when will I endure you? You must bring him here to Me." 18. Then Jesus rebuked it and the demon came out from him and the child was healed from that moment. 19. Then, when the disciples came to Jesus privately, they said, "Why were we not able to cast it out?" 20. And He said to them, "Because of your little faith: for truly I am saying to you, if you should have faith like a mustard seed, you will say to this mountain, 'You must immediately go from this place to that place,' and it will go: then nothing will be impossible for you."[3]

---

1   (v.2) White garments represent being in a state of spiritual preparedness, from Ecc 9:8, "Let your garments be always white; and let your head lack no ointment."

2   (v.15) Asking for mercy was an idiom meaning to ask for forgiveness. The people understood that sickness was caused by sin.

3   (v.20) V. 21 is omitted because it was not in the earliest manuscripts.

Jesus again Foretells His Death and Resurrection[1]

(Mk 9: 30-32, Lk 9:43b-45)

17:22. And when they gathered in Galilee Jesus said to them, "The Son of Man is going to be given over into *the* hands of men, 23. and they will kill Him, and on the third day He will be raised." (Mt 16:21) Then they were exceedingly grieved.

Payment of the Temple Tax

17:24. And after they came into Capernaum[2] those who were collecting the two drachma[3] then said to Peter, "Does not your Teacher pay the two drachmas?" (Ex 30:13, 38:26) 25. He said, "Indeed." And, after he came into the house, Jesus spoke first to him saying, "What do you think, Simon? From whom are the kings of the Earth taking a tax or head tax? From their sons or from the others?" 26. And then he said, "From the others," Jesus said to him, "Consequently the sons are indeed free. 27. But so that we would not offend them, on going to *the* lake, you must right away cast a hook and take the first fish coming up, and when you open its mouth you will find a coin: taking that you must at once give *it* to them for Me and you."

The Greatest in the Kingdom

(Mk 9:33-37, Lk 9:46-48)

18.1. In that hour the disciples came to Jesus saying, "Who is the greatest in the kingdom of the heavens?"[4] 2. And after He called a child to Himself, He stood him in their midst 3. and He said, "Truly I say to you, unless you would change and become like the children, you could **not** enter the kingdom of the heavens. 4. Therefore whoever will humble himself like this child, this one is the greatest in the kingdom of the heavens. 5. And whoever would receive one such child in My name, receives Me."

Temptation to Sin

(Mk 9:42-48, Lk 17:1,2)

18:6. "Whoever would cause one of the least of these who believe in Me to sin, it is better for him that a millstone worked by a donkey[5] would be hung around his neck and he would be drowned in the open sea. 7. Woe to the world for those who cause sin: for it is necessary for the temptation to sin to come, but woe to the man by whom the temptation comes. 8. And if your hand or your foot

---

1   (Caption) See Resurrection in Glossary.

2   (v.24) Capernaum is the Latin spelling of the Hebrew name Kafer Na-um. Kafer means town or village and Na-um means pleasant.

3   (v.24) This is the half-shekel temple tax from Ex 30:13, 38:26.

4   (v.1) Heavens is always plural in Hebrew and the Hebrew Scriptures name seven levels of heaven. See Heavens in Glossary.

5   (v.6) It was necessary for Jesus to state that the stone was one worked by a donkey because households often had smaller six to ten pound stones for grinding small quantities of grain.

causes you to sin, you must immediately cut it off and cast *it* from you: it is better for you to enter life[1] crippled or lame, rather than having two hands and two feet to have been cast into the eternal fire. 9. And if your eye causes you to sin, you must immediately pluck it out and cast it from you: it is better for you to enter life one-eyed rather than having two eyes to have been cast into the Gehenna[2] of fire."

The Parable of the Lost Sheep

(Lk 15:3-7)

18:10. "You must continually see that you do not despise one of the least of these *children*: for I say to you that their angels in *the* heavens, for the sake of all *children*, do see the face of My Father, the One in *the* heavens.[3] 12. What do you think? If it would happen to some man *who has* one hundred sheep and one of them would go astray, will he not leave the ninety-nine on the mountains and then go seek the one that strayed? 13. Then if he happens to find it, truly I say to you that he rejoices over it more than over the ninety-nine, those that have not strayed. 14. Thus it is a desire before your Father, the One in *the* heavens, that not one of the least of these would be lost."

A Brother Who Sins

(Lk 17:3)

18:15. "And if your brother sins against you, you must go, you must show him the error between you and him alone. If he listens to you, you have gained your brother: (Lv 19:17) 16. but if he would not listen, you must take with you yet one or two, so that 'by a mouth of two or three witnesses every word would stand:' (Dt 19:35) 17. and if he refuses to listen to them, you must speak at once to the congregation:[4] then if he refuses to listen to the congregation, he must be to you even as the heathen and the tax collector.

18:18. "Truly I say to you: whatever you would bind[5] upon the Earth will already have been bound in heaven *with ongoing effect*, and whatever you would loose[6] upon the Earth will already have been loosed in heaven *with ongoing effect.*[7] 19. Again truly I say to you that if two of you on the Earth would agree concerning any matter, whatever would be asked, it would happen for them before My Father, the One in *the* heavens. 20. For where there are two or three *who* have gathered together in My name, there I am in their midst."

1   (v.8) Jesus several times refers to what we call death as entering life, a clear reference to the wonderful eternal life that awaits us.
2   (v.9) See Gehenna in Glossary.
3   (v.10) V. 11 is omitted because it was not in the earliest manuscripts.
4   (v.17) Although often translated "church," no Greek word meaning church is used in the NT. See Congregation in Glossary.
5   (v.18) To bind is a Hebrew idiom meaning to forbid. Binding and loosing refer specifically to the dietary, Sabbath, and other regulations, including civil law, as well as to spiritual things.
6   (v.18) To loose is a Hebrew idiom meaning to permit.
7   (v.18) The tenses here mean that the effect of the binding or loosing goes on forever.

The Parable of the Unforgiving Servant

18:21. Then when Peter came he said to Him, "Lord, how often will my brother sin against me and I shall forgive him?[1] As many as seven times?" 22. Jesus said to him, "I do not say to you until seven times but until seventy times seven. 23. Because of this the kingdom of the heavens has been made like a man, a king, who wanted to settle accounts with his servants. 24. And when he began to settle, one debtor of ten thousand talents[2] was brought to him. 25. But, when he did not have *it* to repay, the master ordered him and *his* wife and children and all that he had to be sold *at once*, and to be repaid. 26. Then the servant fell prostrated before him, saying, 'You must now be patient on my account, and I will pay you back everything.' 27. Then having pity, the master of that servant released him and forgave the loan to him. 28. And when that servant came out he found one of his fellow servants, who owed him a hundred denarii,[3] and having taken hold of him he was choking *him* saying, 'You must right now pay what you owe.' 29. Then his fellow servant, falling *to his knees*, begged him saying, 'You must be patient with me, and I will repay you.' 30. But he was not willing and when he left he cast him into prison until he would pay the debt. 31. Therefore when his fellow servants saw what was happening they were exceedingly grieved and having come to their master they made known everything that happened. 32. Then, having summoned him, his master said to him, 'Evil servant, I forgave you all that debt because you begged me: 33. so was it not necessary for you to be merciful to your fellow servant, as I was merciful[4] to you?' 34. And his master, being filled with wrath, gave him over to the jailers until he could pay back all that was owed. 35. So also My Father, the One in the heavens, will do to you, if you, each one, would not forgive his brother from your hearts."

Teaching about Divorce

(Mk 10:1-12)

19.1. And it happened when Jesus finished these teachings, He went away from Galilee and He came into the district of Judea on the other side of the Jordan. 2. And great crowds followed Him and He healed them there.

19:3. And Pharisees came to Him, testing Him, and saying, "Is it permitted for a man to divorce his wife for any reason?" 4. And He said, "Have you not read that the One Who Created, from *the* beginning 'He made them male and female?'" (Gn 1:27) 5. Then He said, "'Because of this a man[5] will leave father and mother and will be joined together with his wife,[6] and the two will be

---

1   (v.21) See Sin, Forgiveness of in Glossary.
2   (v.24) One talent, weighing 75 lb., equaled 6,000 drachmas or denarii, with 300 denarii about a year's wages. With one talent being 20 years' wages, 10,000 talents is a truly awesome sum.
3   (v.28) Several months' wages
4   (v.33) To be merciful is to forgive: this could also be translated "as I forgave the debt.."
5   (v.5) The word used here is anthropos and can appropriately be translated "person."
6   (v.5) Both husband and wife need to leave their parents and join together. In ancient

in one flesh.' (Gn 2:24) 6. Thus they are not two but one flesh. Therefore what God united man must not divide." 7. They said to Him, "Then why did Moses command 'to give a certificate of divorce and to divorce her?'" (Dt 24:1) 8. He said to them that "Moses on account of your hardness of heart permitted you to divorce your wives, but from *the* beginning it has not been so. 9. But I say to you that whosoever would divorce his wife not on account of fornication[1] and would marry another is committing adultery." 10. His disciples said to Him, "If the case of the man with the wife is thus, it is not profitable to marry." 11. And He said to them, "Not all grasp this message but for whom it has been given. 12. For there are eunuchs who were born so from a mother's womb, and there are eunuchs who have been made eunuchs by men, and there are eunuchs who have made themselves eunuchs because of the kingdom of the heavens. The one who is able to grasp, must grasp *this truth*."

Little Children Blessed

(Mk 10:13-16, Lk 18:15-17)

19:13. Then children were brought to Him so that He could place hands on them and pray: but the disciples rebuked them. 14. But Jesus said, "You must at once permit the children, and you must not forbid them to come to Me, for the kingdom of the heavens is of such as these." 15. Then after He placed His hands on them He went away from there.

The Rich Young Man

(Mk 10:17-31, Lk 18:18-30)

19:16. And behold one *who* came to Him said, "Teacher, what good must I do so that I would have eternal life?" 17. And He said to him, "Why do you ask Me concerning the good? *Only* One is good: and if you desire to enter life,[2] you must keep the commandments."[3] 18. He said to Him, "Which ones?" And Jesus said, "You will not murder, You will not commit adultery, You will not steal, You will not bear false testimony, 19. Honor *your* father and mother, and You must love your neighbor as yourself." 20. The young man said to Him, "I did keep all these: what yet do I lack?" 21. Jesus said to him, "If you want to be perfect[4] you must immediately go, sell your possessions, then give *that* to the poor, and you will have treasure in *the* heavens, then come, you must habitually follow Me." 22. But after the young man heard the statement he left grieving: for he had abundant property.

Israeli society the wife would join the husband's family. A modern interpretation of this verse would say, "A person will leave father and mother and will join together with his (or her) spouse." Gn 2:24 says a man will leave his parents when he marries. See Wedding in Glossary.

1   (v.9) Any immorality

2   (v.17) Jesus several times refers to what we call death as entering life, a clear reference to the wonderful eternal life that awaits us.

3   (v.17) These commandments are those in the first five books of the Bible, summarized in verses 18, 19.

4   (v.21) Fully developed in a moral sense

19:23. Then Jesus said to His disciples, "Truly I say to you that *only* with difficulty will a rich person enter the kingdom of the heavens.[1] 24. And again I say to you, it is easier for a camel to go through the eye of a needle[2] than a rich person to enter the kingdom of God." 25. And when the disciples heard they were greatly amazed saying, "Then who is able to be saved?" 26. And Jesus, looking at them, said, "With people this is impossible, but with God all things *are* possible." (Gn 18:14, Jr 32:17, 27, Job 42:2) 27. Then Peter said to Him, "Behold we have left everything and we followed You: what then is for us?" 28. And Jesus said to them, "Truly I say to you that you who follow Me, in the restoration of all things[3] when the Son of Man would sit upon *the* Throne of His Glory,[4] then you will be seated upon twelve thrones judging the twelve tribes of Israel. (Dn 7:9,10) 29. And all who left houses or brothers or sisters or father or mother or children or fields for the sake of My name, will take a hundred times as much and will inherit eternal life. 30. And many first will be last and last *will be* first."

The Workers in the Vineyard

20.1. "For the kingdom of the heavens[5] is like a man, master of a house, who came out early in *the* morning to hire workers for his vineyard. 2. Then, after the workers agreed on a denarius *for* the day, he sent them into his vineyard. (Tob 5:5) 3. And when he came out about *the* third hour,[6] he saw others standing in the market unemployed 4. and he said to those, 'You also go into the vineyard, and I will give you whatever would be just.' 5. And they went. And when he came out again *at* about *the* sixth and ninth[7] hours he did likewise. 6. Then when he came out about the eleventh[8] hour, he found others standing and he said to them, 'Why have you stood here unemployed the whole day?' 7. They said to him, 'Because no one hired us.' He said to them, 'Go into the vineyard yourselves.' 8. Then when it was evening the master of the vineyard said to his foreman, 'You must now call the workers and pay them the wage beginning from the last until the first.' 9. And those *who* came about the eleventh hour took one denarius. 10. Then when the first came they thought that they would take more: but they took the one denarius also for themselves. 11. And after they took they were complaining against the master 12. saying, 'Those last ones did one hour

---

1   (v.23) This statement is contrary to the teachings of the Pharisees, who said that obedience to the legalistic rules, traditions, would be rewarded with wealth in this life, parallel to the present day faith prosperity teachings. See Wealth in Glossary.

2   (v.24) The eye of a needle also refers to a small door in a city gate to let someone in or out when the gate was shut. A camel could get through only after having its saddle and packs taken off, then kneeling to go through. See Lk 14:33.

3   (v.28) Resurrection life

4   (v.28) The throne of the King of the Universe is made of Glory. Jr 14:21 speaks of the Throne of Your Glory and Jewish commentary has many references to Throne of Glory. Mt 25:31 has Throne of His Glory.

5   (v.1) Heavens is always plural in Hebrew and the Hebrew Scriptures name seven levels of heaven. As used here the phrase refers to God. See Heavens in Glossary.

6   (v.3) 9:00 AM

7   (v.5) Noon and 3:00 PM

8   (v.6) 5:00 PM

of work, and you made them equal to us, who bore the weight of the day and the burning heat.' 13. And he, responding, said to one of them, 'Friend, I am not doing you wrong: did you not agree with me for a denarius? 14. You must now take yours and go. And I desire in this to give to the last as also to you. 15. Or *is* it not permitted for me to do what I wish with what *is* mine? Or is your eye evil[1] because I am good?' 16. In this way the last will be first and the first will be last."

A Third Time Jesus Foretells His Death and Resurrection[2]

(Mk 10:32-34, Lk 18:31-34)

20:17. Then while Jesus was going up to Jerusalem He took the twelve disciples by themselves and on the way He said to them, 18. "Behold we are going up to Jerusalem, and the Son of Man will be given over to the high priests and scribes, and they will condemn Him to death 19. and they will give Him over to the heathens to ridicule and to scourge and to crucify *Him*, and on the third day He will be raised."

The Request of Jacob and John

(Mk 10:35-45)

20:20. Then the mother of the sons of Zebedee came to Him with her sons. While she was paying homage[3] to Him she was asking something from Him. 21. And He said to her, "What do you want?" She said to Him, "You must now say that these two sons of mine would sit one on Your right and one on Your left in Your kingdom." 22. And Jesus said, "You do not know what you are asking. Are you able to drink the cup which I am going to drink?" They said to Him, "We are able." 23. He said to them, "Indeed you will drink My cup, but to sit on My right and on *My* left this is not Mine to give, but for whom it has been prepared by My Father." 24. Then after the ten heard they were indignant concerning the two brothers. 25. And Jesus, having summoned them, said, "You know that leaders of the heathens lord it over them and the great ones exercise authority over them. 26. It will not be like this among you, but whoever among you would desire to become great will be your minister,[4] 27. and whoever among you would desire to be first will be your servant:[5] 28. just as the Son of Man did not come to be served but to serve and to give His life a ransom for many."

The Healing of the Two Blind People

(Mk 10:46-52, Lk 18:35-43)

20:29. Then when they went from Jericho a huge crowd followed Him.

---

1   (v.15) Having an evil eye means to be greedy. See Dt 15:9, Pr 23:6, 7 and 28:22.
2   (Caption) See Resurrection in Glossary.
3   (v.20) To pay homage means to greet a superior by kneeling and touching the forehead to the ground. See Pay Homage in Glossary.
4   (v.26) Or servant, see Servant in Glossary.
5   (v.27) Or slave, see Servant in Glossary.

30. And behold when two blind people sitting by the way heard that Jesus was passing by, they cried out saying, "You must immediately have mercy on us! Lord! Son of David!¹ 31. Then the crowd rebuked them so that they would be quiet: but they cried out more saying, "You must now have mercy on us! Lord! Son of David!" 32. And after Jesus stopped He called them and said, "What do you want Me to do for you?" 33. They said to Him, "Lord, that our eyes would open." 34. And Jesus, having compassion, touched their eyes,² and they immediately regained *their* sight and they followed Him.

The Triumphal Entry into Jerusalem
(Mk 11:1-11, Lk 19:28-38, Jn 12:12-19)

21.1. And when they approached Jerusalem and came into Bethphage³ at the Mount of Olives, then Jesus sent two disciples 2. saying to them, "Go into the village opposite you, and you will immediately find a donkey⁴ tied and a colt with it: after you loosen *them* lead *them* to Me. 3. And if someone would say something to you, you will say that 'The Lord has need of them: and He will send them *back* immediately.'" 4. And this happened so that what was said by the prophet would be fulfilled saying,

5.   "You must say to the daughter of Zion,
      Behold your king is coming to you
           humble and mounted upon a donkey
               even upon a colt, a son of a donkey." (Zch 9:9)

6. And then the disciples went and did just as Jesus directed them. 7. They led the donkey and the colt and they placed their cloaks⁵ upon them, and He sat on them. 8. And the very large crowd spread out their cloaks⁶ on the road, and others were cutting off branches from the trees and were strewing *them* on the road. 9. And the crowds going before Him and those who were following were crying out saying,

      "Hoshea-na⁷ Son of David:⁸
           Blessed be the One Who comes in *the* name of *the* Lord:
      Hoshea-na in the highest." (Ps 118:25,26)

10. Then when He entered Jerusalem the whole city was stirred up saying, "Who

---

1   (v.30) When they said "Son of David" they were speaking of the reigning Messiah.
2   (v.34) This word for eyes, omma, (used only here and in Mk 8:23) also means "eyes of the soul."
3   (v.1) Bethphage is the Greek spelling of the Hebrew Beit-Pag, meaning Place of Unripe Figs, which was close to Bethany.
4   (v.2) See Donkey in Glossary.
5   (v.7) Most, if not all, of these cloaks were prayer shawls.
6   (v.8) These too would have included prayer shawls.
7   (v.9) This is the Hebrew that they would have been speaking. It means Salvation now! Or Deliverance now! It is usually written Hosanna, the Greek spelling, although it has no meaning in Greek. This was a traditional celebration on the sixth day of Succot. See Hosanna in Glossary.
8   (v.9) See Son of David/Son of Joseph in Glossary.

is this?" 11. And the crowds were saying, "This is the prophet Jesus, the One from Nazareth of Galilee."

The Cleansing of the Temple

(Mk 11:15-19, Lk 19:45-48, Jn 2:13-22)

21:12. Then Jesus entered the temple and He threw out all those who were selling and buying in the temple, and He overturned the tables of the moneychangers and the chairs of those who were selling doves, 13. and He said to them, "It has been written,

'My house will be called a house of prayer,' (Is 56:7, 60:7)

'but you are making it a den of robbers.'" (Jr 7:11)

21:14. And *the* blind and lame came to Him in the temple, and He healed them. 15. And when the high priests and the scribes saw the miracles that He did and the children who were crying out in the temple and saying, "Hoshea-na to the Son of David,"[1] they were indignant 16. and they said to Him, "Do You hear what they are saying?" And Jesus said to them, "Indeed. And did you never read that 'I prepared praise out of *the* mouths of infants and *those* nursing?'" (Ps 8:2) 17. Then leaving them He went outside the city to Bethany[2] and He found lodging there.

The Cursing of the Fig Tree

(Mk 11:12-14, 20-24)

21:18. And when He returned to the city early in the morning He was hungry. 19. And, when He saw one fig tree on the way, He came up to it and found nothing on it except only leaves, and He said to it, "Fruit could no longer ever come from you." And the fig tree immediately withered. 20. Then when the disciples saw *that* they marveled saying, "How did the fig tree wither immediately?" 21. And Jesus said to them, "Truly I say to you, if you would have faith and you would not doubt, not only will you do what *was done* with the fig tree, but even if you would say to this mountain, 'You must be removed at once and you must immediately be cast into the sea,' it will happen: 22. And everything you will ask in prayer, when you believe, you will receive." (Mk 11:23)

The Authority of Jesus Questioned

(Mk 11:27-33, Lk 20:1-8)

21:23. Then when He came into the temple the high priests and the elders of the people came up while He was teaching, saying, "By what authority are You doing these things?" And "Who gave You this authority?" 24. And Jesus said to them, "And I will ask you one question, whatever you would say to Me

---

1   (v.15) See note on v.9.
2   (v.17) Bethany is the Greek spelling of Beit-Anyah, meaning House of Sighing in Hebrew.

then I will tell you by what authority I do these things: 25. from where was the baptism of John? From heaven or from men?" And they were discussing among themselves saying, "If we would say, 'From heaven,' He will say to us, 'Then why did you not believe him?' 26. And if we would say, 'From men,' we are afraid of the crowd, for they all consider John as a prophet." 27. Then answering Jesus, they said, "We do not know." And He said to them, "Then I am not telling you by what authority I am doing these things."

The Parable of the Two Sons

21:28. "And what does it seem to you? A man had two children. And having come to the first he said, 'Child, you must immediately go today *and* work in the vineyard.' 29. and when he answered he said, 'I do not want to,' but later because he repented he went. 30. When he went to the other he said likewise. But when he answered he said, 'I *will*, sir,' but he did not go. 31. Who of the two did the will of the father?" They said "The first." Jesus said to them, "Truly I say to you that the tax collectors and prostitutes are going into the kingdom of God before you.[1] 32. For John came to you in a way of righteousness, and you did not believe him: but the tax collectors and prostitutes did believe in him: and although you saw later, you did not repent of it to believe him."

The Parable of the Vineyard and the Tenants[2]
(Mk 12:1-12, Lk 20:9-19)

21:33. "You must now listen to another parable. A man who was master of a house planted a vineyard and put a fence around it and dug a wine press in it and built a tower, then he leased it to farmers and he went away to a foreign country. 34. And when the time of the fruit was near, he sent his servants to the farmers to take his fruit. 35. And the farmers, having taken his servants, beat some, and others they killed, and others they stoned. 36. Again he sent other servants greater in number than the first, and they did likewise to them. 37. Then later he sent his son to them saying, 'They will respect my son.' 38. But when the farmers saw the son they said among themselves, 'This is the heir: come let us kill him, then we would have his inheritance,' 39. and when they took him they cast *him* outside the vineyard and they killed *him*. 40. Then when the master of the vineyard would come, what will he do to those farmers?" 41. They said to Him, "He will destroy those badly evil *people* and he will lease the vineyard to other farmers, who will pay to him the fruits in their time." 42. Jesus said to them, "And then have you never read in the Scriptures,

'A stone which the builders rejected,
    this became a cornerstone:

---

1   (v.31) Their answer is correct, but the high priests and elders are like the second son, who spoke the right words, but did not do the will of the Father. See Mt 23:3.
2   (Caption) Each of these parables about the vineyard uses the picture of greedy farmers to speak of the High Priest and other Jewish leaders.

this was done by *the* Lord

and is it a wonder in our eyes.'? (Psalm 118:22,23)

43. Because of this I say to you that the kingdom of God will be taken from you and it will be given to a people making its fruits. 44. And the one who falls upon this stone will be dashed to pieces: and on whomever it would fall, it will crush him."

21:45. And when the high priests[1] and the Pharisees heard His parables they knew that He was speaking about them: 46. then although they were seeking to arrest Him they were afraid of the crowds, since *the crowds* considered Him as a prophet.

The Parable of the Marriage Feast

(Lk 14:15-24)

22.1. Then when He answered, Jesus again spoke to them in parables saying, 2. "The kingdom of the heavens[2] is like a man, a king, who made a marriage feast for his son.[3] 3. And he sent his servants to call those invited to the feast, but they did not want to come. 4. Again he sent other servants saying, 'You must say to those invited, "Behold I have prepared my meal, since my bulls and fattened calves have been killed, indeed everything *is* prepared: come to the marriage feast."' 5. But they, who did not care, left, one on the one hand to his own field, and another to his business: 6. then after the rest seized his servants they insulted and they killed *them*. 7. And the king was angered and having sent his soldiers he destroyed those murderers, and he set their city on fire. 8. Then he said to his servants, 'On one hand the feast is prepared, but on the other those who have been invited were not worthy: 9. therefore you must go on the streets of the way and whomever you would find you must invite to the feast.' 10. And those servants went out on the roads *and* they gathered together all those whom they found, both evil and good: then the feast was filled *with those* reclining.[4] 11. But when the king entered to see those who were reclining, he saw there a man not wearing a wedding garment, 12. and he said to him, 'Friend, how did you enter here not having a wedding garment?' But he was silent. 13. Then the king said to his servants, 'After you bind his feet and hands you must cast him into the furthest darkness: in that place there will be weeping and gnashing of the teeth.' 14. For many are invited, but few are chosen."[5]

1   (v.45) The high priests were Sadducees. See Hellenists in Glossary.
2   (v.1) Heavens is always plural in Hebrew, and often in the Greek. In Hebrew Scripture there are seven levels of heaven, which is why Paul referred to the third heaven in 2 Cor 12:2. See Heavens in Glossary.
3   (v.2) See Wedding in Glossary.
4   (v.10) This is a reference to dining. Reclining at a meal was a symbol of being free. See Reclining in Glossary.
5   (v.14) "Many are invited but few are chosen" has several possible interpretations. Among the possibilities are these three: it could be related to Mt 7:21, "Not everyone who says to Me, 'Lord. Lord!' will enter the kingdom of the heavens," or it could be a reference to kingdom living here on Earth before THE kingdom comes, because few are able to live the abundant life He has

Paying Taxes to Caesar
(Mk 12:13-17, Lk 20:20-26)

22:15. Then after the Pharisees went they plotted how they could trap Him with a question. 16. And they were sending their disciples to Him with the Herodians[1] saying, "Teacher, we know that You are true and You are teaching the way of God in truth and You do not court anyone's favor: for You do not look at who someone is. 17. Therefore You must tell us what You think: is it lawful to pay a tax to Caesar or not?" 18. But Jesus, because He knew their evil *intent*, said, "Hypocrites! Why are you testing Me? 19. You must show Me the coin of the tax." And they brought Him a denarius. 20. Then He said to them, "Whose image and inscription *is* it?" 21. And they said to Him, "Caesar's." Then He said to them, "Therefore you must pay to Caesar what *are* Caesar's and to God what *are* God's." 22. And when they heard they were amazed, then, having given up, they left Him.

The Question about the Resurrection[2]
(Mk 12:18-27, Lk 20:27-40)

22:23. In that day Sadducees, *who* said there was no resurrection, came to Him and they asked Him 24. saying, "Teacher, Moses said, 'If someone would die not having children, his brother will marry his wife and he will raise his brother's seed.' (Dt 25:5) 25. And there were beside us seven brothers: and the first married one died, and since he did not have an heir he left his wife to his brother: 26. then likewise the second and the third until the seventh. 27. And last of all the wife died. 28. Therefore in the resurrection of the seven, whose wife will she be? For they all had her." 29. Then Jesus said to them, "You are misled, since you do not know either the Scriptures or the power of God: 30. for in the resurrection they neither marry nor are given in marriage, but they will be like angels in heaven. 31. And concerning the resurrection of the dead did you not read what was spoken to you by God saying, 32. 'I AM[3] the God of Abraham and the God of Isaac and the God of Jacob?' (Ex 3:6) He is not the God of *the* dead but *the* living." (4 Macc 7:19) 33. And when the crowds heard *that* they were amazed by His teaching.

The Great Commandment
(Mk 12:28-34, Lk 10:25-28)

22:34. But when the Pharisees heard that He silenced the Sadducees they gathered together against Him, 35. and one of them, a teacher of Torah,[4] testing

made available to us. The word 'chosen' is the problem. Chosen by whom? By one's self? Could 'eklektoi', the word translated chosen here take on the meaning of excellent or preeminent as in 2 Jn 1 and 13? Then it would read, "Many are called but few are excellent (worthy?)."

1   (v.16) Herodians were Hellenists and would have included Sadducees. See Hellenists in Glossary.
2   (Caption) See Resurrection in Glossary.
3   (v.32) This is the great I AM, Anokhi in the Hebrew text. See Anokhi in Glossary.
4   (v.35) Torah means teaching, instruction and refers to the first five books of the Bible.

Him asked, 36. "Teacher, which is the greatest commandment in the Torah?" 37. And He said to him, "'You will love *the* Lord your God with your whole heart and with your whole being' (Dt 6:5) and with your whole mind: 38. this is the greatest and first commandment. 39. And *the* second *is* like it, 'You will love your neighbor as yourself.' (Lv 19:18) 40. The whole Torah and the Prophets[1] are hanging on these two commandments."

The Question about David's Son

(Mk 12:35-37, Lk 20:41-44)

22:41. And, when the Pharisees gathered, Jesus asked them 42. saying, "What do you think about the Messiah? Whose son is He?" They said to Him, "David's." 43. He said to them, "Then how does David in *the* Spirit call Him Lord saying,

44.   '*The* Lord said to my Lord,
         You must sit at My right hand,[2]
                until I would place Your enemies beneath Your feet?'[3]

    (Ps 110:1)

45. Therefore if David calls Him Lord, how is He his son?" 46. And no one was able to answer Him a word, and no one had any courage from that day to ask Him anything.

The Denouncing of the Scribes and Pharisees

(Mk 12:38-40, Lk 11:37-52, 20:45-47)

23.1. Then Jesus spoke to the crowds and to His disciples 2. saying, "The scribes and the Pharisees sit on Moses' chair *in the synagogues*.[4] 3. Therefore everything which they would say to you, you must do and you must keep, but you must not do according to their works: for they are saying but not doing. 4. And they bind a heavy, hard to be borne burden and they place *it* upon the shoulders of people, but they are not willing to lift a finger to help. 5. And they do all their works in order to be seen by people: for they make their phylactaries[5] broad and they make their fringes[6] long, 6. and they love the place of honor[7] in the banquets

---

See Torah in Glossary.

1   (v.40) The Torah and the Prophets refers to the first five books of the Bible plus Jsh, Jd, 1 & 2 Sam, 1 & 2Ki, Is through Mal except for Dn. The expression can also refer to the entire Bible. See Prophets in Glossary.

2   (v.44) "At the right hand" is a Hebrew idiom that speaks of power and strength, from Ex 15:6. See Right Hand in Glossary.

3   (v.44) See Footstool in Glossary.

4   (v.2) This is the place of honor, evidence of the occupant's knowledge and authority. See Reclining in Glossary.

5   (v.5) Boxes, containing certain Scriptures, that are tied on the upper arm and the forehead.

6   (v.5) This is the corner fringe on the prayer shawl. See Prayer Shawl in Glossary.

7   (v.6) The place of honor was referred to as Abraham's lap. See Reclining in Glossary.

and the best seats[1] in the synagogues 7. and the greetings in the markets and to be called 'Rabbi' by the people. 8. But you should not be called, 'Rabbi:' for One is your Teacher, and you are all brothers. 9. And do not call *anyone* on the Earth your father, for One is your heavenly Father. 10. And you should not be called teacher, because One, the Messiah, is your Teacher. 11. And the greatest of you will be your servant/minister. 12. But who will exalt himself will be humbled and who will be humble will be exalted.

23:13. "And woe to you, hypocrite scribes and Pharisees, because you are closing the kingdom of the heavens in the sight of people: for you are not entering and you do not permit those who *would* enter to come in.

23:15. "Woe to you hypocrite scribes and Pharisees, because you go about the sea and the land to make one proselyte, and when it would happen you make him a son of Gehenna[2] two fold more than yourselves.

23:16. "Woe to you blind guides, those who say, 'Whoever would swear by the sanctuary, it is nothing: but whoever would swear by the gold of the sanctuary is obligated *to pay or to do.*' 17. Fools and blind ones, for which is greater, the gold, or the sanctuary which has sanctified the gold? 18. And 'Whoever would swear by the altar, it is nothing: but whoever would swear by the gift above it, is obligated.' 19. Blind ones, for which is greater, the gift or the altar which sanctifies the gift?[3] 20. Therefore the one who swears by the altar swears on it and on everything above it: 21. and the one who has sworn by the sanctuary swears on it and on the One Who inhabits it, 22. and the one who has sworn on heaven swears on the throne of God and on the One Who sits on it.

23:23. "Woe to you, hypocrite scribes and Pharisees, because you tithe[4] the mint and the dill and the cumin but you have canceled the more important things of the Torah, justice and mercy and faith: but it was necessary to do these things[5] but not to cancel those things. 24. Blind guides, those who strain the gnat, but swallow the camel.

23:25. "Woe to you, hypocrite scribes and Pharisees, because you clean the outside of the cup and the dish, but inside they are filled with greed and self-indulgence. 26. Blind Pharisees, first you must cleanse the inside of the cup, so that the outside would also become pure.[6]

23:27. "Woe to you, hypocrite scribes and Pharisees, because you are like graves *that* have been whitewashed, which on the outside are indeed shining beautiful, but on the inside they are filled with dead bones and everything unclean.

---

1   (v.6) This is a reference to Moses' chair, a place of honor in every synagogue.
2   (v.15) For Hebrew Gehinnom, Valley of Hinnom. See Gehenna in Glossary.
3   (v.19) The altar sanctifies whatever or whoever touches it. See Ex 29:37.
4   (v.23) See Tithe in Glossary.
5   (v.23) It is necessary to tithe all income, all your increase.
6   (v.26) Cleanse yourself on the inside, your thoughts and motives, so your actions will be pure. You will be known by your fruit. See Mt 7:15-20 & 12:33-37, and Mk 6:43-45.

28. So also on the one hand you shine on the outside in righteousness to men, but on the other hand inside you are full of hypocrisy and without Torah.

23:29. "Woe to you, hypocrite scribes and Pharisees, because you are building the sepulchers of the prophets and you decorate the graves of the righteous, 30. and you say, 'If we were in the days of our fathers, we would not be sharers with them in the blood of the prophets.' 31. So you testify for yourselves that you are sons of those who murdered the prophets. 32. And you must now fulfill the measure of your fathers. 33. Snakes, offspring of vipers, how would you flee from the judgment of Gehenna?[1] 34. Because of this, behold, I am sending prophets and learned and scribes to you: *some* of them you will kill and you will crucify and *some* of them you will scourge in your gatherings[2] and you will pursue *them* from city to city: 35. so would come upon you all *the* righteous blood being shed upon the earth from the blood of the righteous Abel until the blood of Zechariah son of Barachiah, whom you murdered between the sanctuary and the altar. 36. Truly I say to you, all these things will come upon this generation."

The Lament over Jerusalem

(Lk 13:34,35)

23:37. "Jerusalem. Jerusalem! The one who kills the prophets and stones those who have been sent to her, how often did I desire to gather your children, just as a hen gathers her chicks under her wings, but you did not want *Me to*. 38. Behold your house is abandoned, a desolate place for you. (Tob 14:4) 39. For I say to you, you would **not** see Me again until you would say, 'Blessed is He Who comes in *the* name of *the* Lord.'" (Ps 118:26)

The Destruction of the Temple Foretold

(Mk 13:1,2, Lk 21:5,6)

24.1. Then, after Jesus came out from the temple, He was departing, and His disciples came to show Him the buildings of the temple. 2. And He said to them, "Do you not see all these things? Truly I say to you, there will **not** be a stone here left upon a stone which will not be thrown down."

The Beginning of Woes

(Mk 13:3-13, Lk 21:7-19)

24:3. After He sat down upon the Mount of Olives the disciples came to Him privately saying, "You must now tell us when these things will be" and

---

1   (v.33) See Gehenna in Glossary.
2   (v.34) While this word could be translated synagogues, "a gathering of people" is the primary meaning and no one would be scourged in a synagogue. Lk 4:28 tells of Jesus being driven from the city when the congregation was enraged. The gathering would have been related to the Sanhedrin, which was the local court. See Congregation in Glossary.

"What will be the sign of Your coming[1] and *the* end of the age?" 4. And Jesus said to them, "See that no one would lead you astray: 5. for many will come in My name saying, 'I am the Messiah,' and they will deceive many. 6. And you will be going to hear of wars and reports of wars: see that you are not frightened: for it is necessary to happen, but it is not yet the end. 7. For heathen will rise against heathen and kingdom against kingdom and there will be famines and earthquakes in various regions: 8. and all these things *are the* beginning of labor in birthing. 9. Then they will give you over to affliction and they will kill you, and you will be hated by all the heathens because of My name. 10. And then many will be caused to fall away and they will give over others and they will hate others: 11. and many false prophets will be raised and they will lead many astray: 12. and because of the increase of lawlessness the love of many will grow cold. 13. But the one who remains to *the* end, this one will be saved. 14. Then this Good News of the kingdom will be proclaimed in the whole inhabited world in witness to all the heathens, and then the end will come."

The Great Tribulation

(Mk 13:14-23, Lk 21:20-24)

24:15. "Therefore when you would see the abomination of the devastation placed in a holy place, which was foretold by Daniel the prophet, (Dn 9:27,11:31,12:11, 1Macc 1:54, 6:7) the one who reads must faithfully consider, 16. at that time those in Judea must flee to the mountains, 17. the one on the roof must not go down to take anything from his house, 18. and the one in the field must not return to take his prayer shawl. 19. And woe to those who are pregnant and to those who are nursing *their babies* in those days. 20. But you must pray that your flight would not be of winter and not on a Sabbath. 21. For then there will be great affliction such as has not happened from *the* beginning of the world until now and would **never** happen *again*. 22. And unless these days were shortened, not any flesh would be saved: but because of the elect those days will be shortened. 23. At that time if someone would say to you, 'Behold here is the Messiah,' or 'Here,' do not believe *it*: 24. for false messiahs and false prophets will be raised and they will give great signs and wonders in order to lead astray, if possible, even the elect. 25. Behold, I have told you beforehand. 26. Therefore if they would say to you, 'Behold, He is in the desert,' do not come out: 'Behold, He is in the inner rooms,' do not believe *it*: 27. for as the lightning comes out from *the* east and shines until *the* west, so will be the coming of the Son of Man: 28. wherever the corpse would be, there the eagles will be gathered."

The Coming of the Son of Man

(Mk 13:24-27, Lk 21:25-28)

29.   "'But immediately after the affliction of those days

---

1   (v.3) See Coming of Messiah in Glossary.

the sun will be darkened,
    and the moon will not give its light,
and the stars will fall from the sky,
    and the powers of the heavens[1] will be shaken.'
(Is 13:10, Eze 32:7)

30. And then the sign of the Son of Man will be revealed in the sky, and then all the tribes of the Earth will be cut off and they will see 'the Son of Man coming upon the clouds of the sky' (Zch 12:10,14) with power and great glory. 31. Then He will send His angels with a great trumpet[2] call, and they will gather His chosen ones from out of the four winds as far as the uttermost parts of *the* heavens."

The Lesson of the Fig Tree

(Mk 13:28-31, Lk 21:29-33)

24:32. "But you learned the parable from the fig tree: now when its branch would become tender and it would put forth its leaves, you know that summer is near: 33. so then you, when you would see all these things, you know that He is near *the* doors. 34. Truly I say to you that this generation would **not** pass until all these things would happen. 35. The sky and Earth will pass away, but My words would **never** pass away."

The Unknown Day and Hour

(Mk 13:32-37, Lk 17:26-30, 34-36)

24:36. "But no one knows about that Day and hour,[3] and neither *do* the angels of the heavens nor the Son, except the Father only. 37. For just as the days of Noah, so will be the coming of the Son of Man. 38. For as *people* were among them in those days before the flood, eating and drinking, marrying and being given in marriage, until it was *the* day Noah came into the ark, 39. but they did not know until the flood came and it took up everything, so will the coming of the Son of Man also be. 40. Then two will be in the field, one is taken to *Him*[4] and one is left: 41. two women will be grinding in the mill, one is taken and one is left. 42. Therefore you must steadily be watchful, because you do not know what sort of day your Lord is coming. 43. But you know that if the house owner had known what sort of watch, *when*, the thief was coming, he would have been watchful and would not have allowed his house to be broken into. 44. Because of this then you must always be prepared, because you must not continually think of the time the Son of Man is coming."[5]

---

1   (v.29) Heavens is always plural in Hebrew, and often in Greek. See Heavens in Glossary.
2   (v.31) The word translated trumpet could just as well be translated shofar, which would mean Judgment Day. See both Shofar and Yom Kippur in Glossary. See Re 20:4, 11-14.
3   (v.40) Each generation is to believe that He is coming soon, but no one knows when. See Coming of Messiah in Glossary.
4   (v.40) The Greek word paralambano used here and in v. 41 speaks of a bride being taken to her bridegroom. See Jn 14:3.
5   (v.44) We are to be focused on Him and what He would have us do, and not focused on

The Faithful or the Unfaithful Servant

(Lk 12:41-48)

24:45. "Who then is the faithful and wise servant whom the owner appointed over his household servants to give them food in due season? 46. Blessed is that servant whom when his master comes will find him doing thus: 47. truly I say to you that he will place him over all his possessions. 48. But if that evil servant would say in his heart, 'My lord lingers,' 49 and he would begin to beat his fellow servants, and he would eat and he would drink[1] with the drunkards, 50. the master of that servant will come in a day in which he does not expect and in a moment which he does not know, 51. and he will punish him severely and his lot will place him with the hypocrites: there will be weeping and gnashing of teeth in that place."

The Parable of the Ten Maidens

25.1. "Then the kingdom of the heavens[2] will be like ten virgins, who, having taken their lamps, came out to meet the bridegroom.[3] 2. And five of them were foolish and five *were* wise. 3. For when the foolish took their lamps, they did not take olive oil[4] with them. 4. But the wise took olive oil in the containers with their own lamps. 5. And when the bridegroom[5] delayed they all grew drowsy and they were sleeping. 6. Then in the middle of the night there had come a cry, 'Behold the bridegroom, you must come out to meet him!' 7. Then all those virgins rose and trimmed their own lamps. 8. And the foolish said to the wise, 'You must now give us from your olive oil, because our lamps are going out.' 9. But the wise ones answered saying, 'Then there would **not** be enough for us and for you: you must rather go to the sellers and buy *oil* for yourselves.' 10. And while they were gone to buy *it*, the bridegroom came, and the prepared ones entered the bridal chamber with him and the door was locked. 11. And later the remaining virgins came saying, 'Lord. Lord! You must open to us now!' 12 But he said, 'Truly I say to you, I do not know you.' 13. Therefore you must habitually be watchful, because you do not know the Day or the hour."[6]

The Parable of the Talents

(Lk 19:11-27)

25:14. "For as a man *was* about to go on a journey he called his own servants and turned his property over to them, 15. and to one in the first place

---

when He is coming. See Coming of Messiah in Glossary.
1   (v.49) This Greek word, pin-e, translated drink, just means to drink, without identifying what is drunk. There is another Greek word for drinking any intoxicant, which is methu-o.
2   (v.1) In Hebrew the word heavens is always plural. See Heavens in Glossary.
3   (v.1) See Wedding in Glossary.
4   (v.3) In the Talmud, olive oil symbolizes knowledge of Torah, which provides spiritual illumination. Oil is also the symbol of joy, from Is 51:3, so it is called the oil of gladness.
5   (v.5) See Wedding in Glossary.
6   (v.13) Hour could also be translated "the time or season."

he gave five talents[1] and to one he gave two, and to one, one, to each according to his own ability, then he went on the journey. Immediately 16. after he left, the one who took the five talents worked with them and gained another five: 17. likewise, the one *with* two gained another two. 18. But then the one who took the one went, dug in *the* ground and hid his master's money. 19. And after a long time the master of those servants came and settled accounts with them. 20. And after he came *back*, the one who took five talents brought another five talents saying, 'Lord, you gave me five talents: look, I gained another five talents.' 21. His master said to him, 'Well done! Good and faithful servant, you were faithful over little, I will place you over much: you must enter your master's joy.' 22. And then the one *with* the two talents, as he approached said, 'Lord, you gave me two talents: see, I gained another two talents.' 23. His master said to him, 'Well done! Good and faithful servant, you were faithful over little, I will set you over much: you must enter your master's joy.' 24. And then when the one who took one talent approached he said, 'Lord, I knew that you were a hard man, reaping where you did not sow and gathering from where you did not scatter, 25. and since I was afraid, I went and hid your talent in the ground: see, you have what *is* yours.' 26. But his master said to him, 'Evil and lazy servant, *so* you had known that I harvest where I had not sown and I gather from where I did not scatter? 27. Therefore it was necessary for you to have put my money with the moneychangers, so when I came I *would have* received whatever *was* mine with interest. 28. Therefore you must take the talent away from him and give *it* to the one who has the ten talents: 29. for it will be given to the one who has everything, and he will abound, but the one who does not have, even what he does have will be taken from him. 30. So you must cast the worthless servant out into the farthest darkness: in that place there will be weeping and gnashing of teeth.'"

The Judgment of the Multitudes

25:31. "And when the Son of Man would come in His glory and all the angels with Him, (Dt 33:2, Zch 14:5) then He will sit upon *the* Throne of His Glory:[2] 32. and all the multitudes will be gathered in front of Him, and He will separate them from one another, as the shepherd separates the sheep from the goats, 33. then indeed He will place the sheep on His right hand,[3] but the goats on His left. 34. Then the King will say to those on His right hand, 'Come, the blessed of My Father, you must now inherit what has been prepared for you *in the* kingdom from the foundation of the world. 35. For I was hungry and you gave Me to eat, I was thirsty and you gave Me to drink, I was a stranger and you

---

1 (v.15) One talent, weighing 75 lb., equaled 6,000 drachmas or denarii, with 300 denarii about a year's wages.
2 (v.31) The throne of the King of the Universe is made of Glory. Jr 14:21 speaks of the Throne of Your Glory and Jewish commentary has many references to Throne of Glory. Mt 19:28 also has Throne of His Glory.
3 (v.33) The right hand here is a symbol of God's salvation, from Ps 20:6, while the left symbolizes calamity and judgment. See Right Hand in Glossary.

took Me in, 36. and *I was* poorly clothed and you clothed[1] Me, I was sick and you visited Me, I was in prison and you came to Me.' 37. Then the righteous will answer Him saying, 'Lord, when did we see You hungry and we fed *You*, or thirsty and we gave *You something* to drink? 38. And when did we see You a stranger and we took You in, or poorly clothed and we clothed *You*? 39. And when did we see You sick or in prison and we came to You?' 40. Then the King will say to them, 'Truly I say to you, in so much as you did *anything* for one of these, the least of My brothers, you did *it* for Me.'[2] (Is. 58:6-10)

25:41. "Then He will also say to those on His left, 'You, the ones who have been cursed, must continually go from Me into the eternal fire prepared for the devil and his angels. 42. For I was hungry and you did not give Me *anything* to eat, I was thirsty and you did not give Me a drink, 43. I was a stranger and you did not take Me in, poorly clothed and you did not clothe Me, sick and in prison and you did not visit Me.' 44. Then they also answered saying to Him, 'Lord, when did we see You hungry or thirsty or a stranger or poorly clothed or sick or in jail and we did not serve You?' 45. Then He will answer them saying, 'Truly I say to you, in so much as you did not do *something* for one of the least of these, you did not do *it* for Me.' 46. And they will go into eternal punishment, but the righteous into eternal life."

The Plot to Kill Jesus

(Mk 14:1,2, Lk 22:1,2, Jn 11:45-53)

26.1. Then it happened when Jesus finished all these statements, He said to His disciples, 2. "You know that after two days Passover is coming, and the Son of Man is to be given over to be crucified." 3. Then the high priests and the elders of the people were gathered in the court of the High Priest named Caiaphas 4. and they consulted among themselves so that they could arrest Jesus in secret, then they could kill *Him*: 5. but they were saying, "Not during the feast," so that there would not be turmoil among the people.

The Anointing at Bethany

(Mk 14:3-9, Jn 12:1-8)

26:6. And while Jesus was in Bethany[3] in *the* house of Simon the leper,[4] 7. a woman having a flask of very expensive ointment came to Him, and she poured *it* over His head while He was reclining. 8. And, when the disciples saw *that*, they were indignant saying, "Why is this waste?" 9. For she was able to sell this for much and to give *it* to *the* poor. 10. And since Jesus knew *what they were saying* He said to them, "Why do you cause trouble for the woman? For she did

---

1   (v.36) The Greek word for clothed refers to the outer garment or prayer shawl.

2   (v.40) This passage gives the real heart of God, "To love your neighbor as yourself." (Lv 19:18)

3   (v.6) Bethany is the Greek spelling of Beit-Anyah, meaning House of Sighing in Hebrew.

4   (v.6) This is not the disease called leprosy today. See Leprosy in Glossary.

a good deed[1] for Me: 11. for you always have the poor with you (Dt 15:11), but you do not always have Me: 12. for when she poured this ointment on My body, she did *it* to prepare Me for burial. 13. Truly I say to you, wherever in the whole world this Good News would be proclaimed, then what she did will be spoken in her memory."

Judas' Agreement to Give Jesus Over to the High Priests

(Mk 14:10,11, Lk 22:3-6)

26:14. Then when one of the twelve, the one called Judas, from Iscariot, went to the high priests 15. he said, "What do you want to give me, so I will give Him over to you?" And they paid thirty pieces of silver to him. (Zch 11:13) 16. And from then on he was seeking an opportune moment so that he could give Him over.

The Seder[2] with the Disciples

(Mk 14:12-21, Lk 22:7-14, 21-23, Jn 13:21-30)

26:17. And *before*[3] the Feast of Unleavened Bread the disciples came to Jesus saying, "Where do You want us to prepare for You to eat the Seder?" 18. And He said, "You must go into the city to a certain man and you must say to him, 'The Teacher says, "My time is near, I will celebrate the Seder with My disciples *at your house*."' 19. Then the disciples did as Jesus directed them and they prepared the Seder. 20. And when it was evening He reclined with the twelve.[4] 21. Then, while they were eating, He said, "Truly I say to you that one of you will give Me over." 22. Then, becoming extremely sad, they began, each one, to say to Him, "It is not I, Lord?" 23. And He said, "The one who is dipping his hand in the bowl with Me will give Me over. (Ps 41:9) 24. Indeed the Son of Man is going just as it has been written about Him, but woe to that man through whom the Son of Man is given over: it *would* be better for him if that man would not have been born." 25. And answering, Judas, the one who was betraying Him said, "It is not I, Rabbi?" He said to him, "You said *it* yourself."

The Seder

(Mk 14:22-26, Lk 22:15-20, 1Cor 11:23-25)

26:26. And as they were *about to* eat, Jesus, after He took bread and praised God, broke *it* and when He gave *it* to the disciples He said, "You must take *this and* you must now eat, this is My body." 27. Then having taken a cup, after He gave thanks He gave *the cup* to them saying, "You must all drink from

---

1   (v.10) Mitsvah, see Mitsvah in Glossary.
2   (Caption) This is the Passover meal. See Seder in Glossary.
3   (v.17) The Greek text literally says, "at the beginning of" but had the Passover begun it would have been too late, the meal has to be prepared before the Feast.
4   (v.20) Reclining at any meal is a symbol of freedom from the Egyptian bondage, which is the theme of the Seder. See Reclining in Glossary.

this, 28. for this is My blood of the covenant, which is being poured out[1] on behalf of many for forgiveness of sins. 29. And I say to you, I will **not** drink from this fruit of the vine from now until that day when I drink this with you anew in My Father's kingdom." 30. Then after singing the Hallel[2] they went out to the Mount of Olives.

Peter's Denial Foretold

(Mk 14:27-31, Lk 22:31-34, Jn 13:36-38)

26:31. Then Jesus said to them, "You all will be caused to sin this night because of Me, for it has been written,

'I will strike the Shepherd,

and the sheep of the flock will be scattered.' (Zch 13:7)

32. But after My resurrection[3] I will meet you in Galilee." 33. And Peter said to Him, "If all will be caused to sin because of You, I will never be caused to sin." 34. Jesus said to him, "Truly I say to you that on this night before a cock crows you will deny Me three times." 35. Peter said to Him, "Even if it would be necessary *for* me to die with You I will **not** deny You." And all the disciples said likewise.

The Prayer in Gethsemane

(Mk 14:32-42, Lk 22:39-46)

26:36. Then Jesus came with them into a place called Gethsemane and He said to the disciples, "You must stay here while I go, I will pray there." 37. And, having taken Peter and the two sons of Zebedee, He began to be sad and distressed. 38. And He said to them, "My very being is deeply grieved even to death: you must remain here and be watchful with Me." (Ps 42:5,11 & 43:5) 39. Then when He went a little way He fell on His face praying and saying, "My Father, if it is possible, this cup must pass from Me: nevertheless not as I desire Myself but as You *desire*." 40. Then He came to the disciples and He found them sleeping, and He said to Peter, "So, were you not strong enough to be watchful one hour with Me? 41. You must incessantly be watchful and pray, so that you would not enter a trial: the spirit *is* indeed willing but the flesh *is* weak." 42. Again after He left a second *time* He prayed saying, "My Father, if it is not possible to pass this unless I would drink *it*, Your will must now be done." 43. Then when He came again He found them sleeping, for their eyes were heavy. 44. And leaving them again, after He left, He prayed a third *time* saying this message once more. 45. Then He came to the disciples and said to them, "You

---

1   (v.28) The use of the present tense indicates that His blood is still being poured out today.

2   (v.30) Ps 113 through 118, which are still sung toward the close of a Seder. See Hallel in Glossary.

3   (v.32) See Resurrection in Glossary.

must sleep and from now on you must take *your* rest:[1] *but* see the hour has come near and the Son of Man is being given over into *the* hands of sinners. 46. You must get up *so* we could go: behold the one who is giving Me over has come near."

The Betrayal and Arrest of Jesus

(Mk 14:43-50, Lk 22:47-53, Jn 18:3-12)

26:47. And while He was still speaking, behold Judas, one of the twelve, came, and a large crowd *was* with him, with small swords and clubs, from the high priests and elders of the people. 48. And the one who was giving Him over gave a sign to them saying, "Whomever I would kiss is He, you must arrest Him at once." 49. Then immediately coming to Jesus he said, "Hail, Rabbi," and he kissed Him. 50. And Jesus said to him, "Friend, do that for which you have come." Then, having come, they put *their* hands on Jesus and they arrested Him. 51. And behold one of those with Jesus drew out his sword in his hand and striking the servant of the High Priest he cut off his ear. 52. Then Jesus said to him, "You must return your sword into its place: for all those who take a sword will die by means of a sword. 53. Or do you think that I am not able to call for My Father, and He will at once place at My disposal more than twelve legions[2] of angels? 54. Then how would the Scriptures be fulfilled that this is necessary to happen?" 55. In that instant Jesus said to the crowds, "Did you come upon Me to seize Me with swords and clubs as upon a robber? I was sitting day by day in the temple teaching and you did not arrest Me." 56. But this all happened so that the writings of the prophets would be fulfilled. Then all the disciples were fleeing, leaving Him.

Jesus before the Council

(Mk 14:53-65, Lk 22:54,55, 63-71, Jn 18:13,14, 19-24)

26:57. And those who arrested Jesus led Him to Caiaphas the High Priest, where the scribes and the elders were gathered. 58. And Peter was following Him from a great distance as far as the courtyard of the High Priest, and after he entered he was sitting inside with the servants to see the outcome. 59. And the high priests and the whole Sanhedrin were seeking false witnesses against Jesus so they could put Him to death, 60. but they did not find many false witnesses coming forward. But later two *who* came forward 61. said, "This One said, 'I am able to destroy the sanctuary of God and to build *it* in three days.'" 62. Then when he got up, the High Priest said to Him, "And are You not answering what these are testifying against You?" 63. But Jesus kept silent. And the High Priest said to Him, "I charge You under oath according to the Living God that You should tell us if You are the Messiah, the Son of God." 64. Jesus said to him, "You said *it*. Nevertheless I say to you,

---

1   (v.45) This is the short, coffee break rest. See Rest in Glossary.
2   (v.53) A legion at full strength was 6,826 men.

From now *on* you will see 'the Son of Man
  sitting on the right hand[1] of the Power (Psalm 110:1)
  and coming upon the clouds of the sky.'" (Dn 7:13)

65. Then the High Priest tore his garments saying, "He blasphemed. What further need do we have for witnesses? Behold now, you heard the blasphemy: 66. what does it seem to you?" And those answering said, "He is deserving of death." 67. Then they spit in His face and they struck Him with their fists, and they slapped *Him* 68. saying, "You must prophesy to us, Messiah, who is the one who is hitting You?"

Peter's Denial of Jesus

(Mk 14:66-72, Lk 22:56-62, Jn 18:15-18, 25-27)

26:69. And Peter was sitting outside in the courtyard: and one maid came to him saying, "And you were with Jesus of Galilee." 70. But he was denying *it* before all saying, "I do not know what you are saying." 71. Then when he went out into the gateway another *maid* saw him, and said to those there, "This one was with Jesus of Nazareth." 72. And again he denied with an oath "I do not know the Man." 73. And after a little while, as those who were standing *around* approached, they said to Peter, "Truly then you are *one* of them, for even your dialect gives you away." 74. Then he began to curse and to swear, "I do not know the Man." And immediately a cock crowed. 75. Then Peter remembered the remark Jesus had spoken that "Before a cock crows you will deny Me three times." And going outside he wept bitterly.

Jesus Brought before Pilate

(Mk 15:1, Lk 23:1,2, Jn 18:28-32)

27.1. And when it was early morning all the high priests and the elders of the people formed a plan regarding Jesus, to put Him to death: 2. and after they bound Him they brought *Him* and they gave *Him* over to Pilate the governor.

The Death of Judas

(Ac 1:18,19)

27:3. Then after Judas, the one who gave Him over, saw that He was condemned; because he changed his mind he returned the thirty pieces of silver to the high priests and elders 4. saying, "I sinned when I betrayed innocent blood." But they said, "What is *that* to us? See to that yourself!" 5. Then he withdrew after he threw the silver into the sanctuary, and after he left he hanged himself. 6. And after they took the silver the high priests said, "It is not proper to cast these *coins* into korban,[2] since it is *the* price of blood." 7. And after they

---

1   (v.64) The right hand is a symbol of power, from Ex 15:6. See Right Hand in Glossary.
2   (v.6) Offering to God. See Korban in Glossary.

took counsel they bought with these[1] the field of the potter for burying strangers. 8. On this account that field is called "Field of Blood" until today. 9. Then the word through Jeremiah the prophet was fulfilled saying, "And they took the thirty pieces of silver, the price which had been set for Him, which they set by the children of Israel, 10. and they gave it for the field of the potter, according *as the* Lord directed me." (Jr 32:6-9 & Zch 11:12,13)

Jesus Questioned by Pilate

(Mk 15:2-5, Lk 23:3-5, Jn 18:33-38)

27:11. And Jesus stood before the governor: and the governor asked Him saying, "Are You the King of the Jewish nation?" And Jesus said, "You are saying *it*." 12. And during His being accused by the high priests and elders He did not answer. 13. Then Pilate said to Him, "Do You not hear how many things they are testifying against You?" 14. But He did **not** answer him with even one word, so to exceedingly astonish the governor. (Is 53:7)

Jesus Sentenced to Die

(Mk 15:6-15, Lk 23:13-25, Jn 18:39-19:16)

27:15. And at *the* feast, *Passover*, the governor was accustomed to set one prisoner free, whom they wanted, to the crowd. 16. But they then had a notorious prisoner named Barabbas.[2] 17. Therefore when they had gathered, Pilate said to them, "Whom do you want me to pardon for you, the Barabbas or Jesus the One called Messiah?" 18. For he had known that they gave Him over because of jealousy. 19. And while he was sitting upon the judicial bench, his wife sent *a message* to him saying, "*Have* nothing *to do* with that Righteous One: for I suffered much today in a dream because of Him." 20. But the high priests and the elders[3] persuaded the crowds so that they would ask for Barabbas, and they would kill Jesus. 21. And when he answered, the governor said to them, "Which of the two do you want me to set free for you?" And they said, "Barabbas." 22. Pilate said to them, "Then what should I do with Jesus, the One called Messiah?" All said, "He must be crucified!" 23. But he said, "For what evil did He do?" And they were crying out even more saying, "He must be crucified!" 24. And when Pilate saw that it was not benefiting, but was becoming more turmoil, having taken water he washed *his* hands in sight of the crowd saying, "I am innocent from this blood: you see to it." (Dt 21:6-9, Ps 26:6, Susana 46 Theodotion) 25. Then all the people said, "His blood *will be* upon us and upon our children." (Eze 33:5) 26. Then he released Barabbas to them, and after he scourged Jesus he gave *Him* over so that He could be crucified.

---

1   (v.7) Acts 1:18 says that Judas bought the field, but who bought it is less important than that it was purchased with the thirty pieces of silver.
2   (v.16 & v.17) Several ancient manuscripts have the name Jesus Barabbas.
3   (v.20) See Hellenists in Glossary.

The Soldiers Mocked Jesus
(Mk 15:16-20, Jn 19:2,3)

27:27. Then, when the governor's soldiers took Jesus into the praetorium,[1] they gathered the whole cohort[2] around Him. 28. And after they stripped Him they put a scarlet cloak on Him, 29. and having woven a crown from thorns they placed *it* upon His head and a reed in His right hand, and falling on their knees before Him, they mocked Him saying, "Hail, King of the Jewish People." 30. Then after they spit on Him they took the reed and beat on His head. 31. And when they had mocked Him, they stripped the cloak *from* Him and they dressed Him *with* His garments and they led Him away to be crucified.

The Crucifixion of Jesus
(Mk 15:21-32, Lk 23:26-43, Jn 19:17-27)

27:32. And as they were coming out they found a Cyrene man named Simon. They pressed this one into service so that he would carry His cross. 33. And then they came to a place called Golgotha, which is called "Place of *the* Skull," 34. they gave Him wine mixed with gall to drink: and when He tasted *it* He did not want to drink. (Ps 69:21) 35. And after they crucified Him they divided His garments, casting lots, (Ps 22:18) 36. and then they sat there keeping watch over Him. 37. And they placed above His head the charge that had been written *against* Him: "This is Jesus, the King of the Jewish People." 38. Then two robbers were crucified with Him, one on *the* right and one on *the* left. (Is 53:12) 39. And those who were going by were blaspheming Him, shaking their heads (Ps 22:17, 109:25, Lam 2:15) 40. and saying, "The One Who destroys the sanctuary and builds it in three days, You must immediately save Yourself, if You are *the* Son of God, then You must right now come down from the cross." 41. Likewise also the high priests, mocking with the scribes and elders, were saying, 42. "He saved others, He is not able to save Himself: *if* He is King of Israel, He must now come down from the cross and we will believe in Him. 43. He had trusted God, *God* must now rescue Him if He wants Him: for He said that 'I am *the* Son of God.'" (Ps 22:8, Wisdom 2:18-20) 44. And also the robbers crucified with Him were reviling Him.

The Death of Jesus
(Mk 15:33-41, Lk 23:44-49, Jn 19:28-30)

27:45. And it became dark upon all the Earth from the sixth hour until the ninth hour.[3] (Amos 8:9) 46. And about the ninth hour Jesus cried out in a loud voice saying *in Hebrew*, "Eli! Eli! L'mah sh'vaktani?" This is, "My God! My God! Why have You utterly forsaken Me?" (Ps 22:1) 47. But when some of those who stood there heard they were saying "This One is calling for Elijah."

1   (v.27) Governor's residence
2   (v.27) About 600 men
3   (v.45) Noon to 3:00 PM

48. Then immediately one of them ran and took a sponge filled with sour wine, then having pressed *it* on a reed was giving *it to* Him to drink. (Ps 69:21) 49. And the rest were saying, "You must stop! We should see if Elijah is coming to save Him." 50. And after Jesus again cried out in a loud voice His spirit left *Him*. 51. Then behold the veil of the sanctuary was split in two from top to bottom and the earth quaked and stones were split, 52. and the graves were opened and many bodies of the sleeping[1] saints[2] were raised. 53. Then when they came out of the graves, after His resurrection,[3] they entered the holy city and they appeared to many. 54. And after the centurion, and those who were keeping watch over Jesus with him, saw the earthquake and the things that happened, they became very greatly fearful, saying, "Truly He was *the* Son of God." 55. And many women, who followed Jesus from Galilee to minister to Him, were there to see from afar: 56. among whom were Mary Magdalene, and Mary the mother of Jacob and Joseph, and the mother of the sons of Zebedee.

The Burial of Jesus
(Mk 15:42-47, Lk 23:50-56, Jn 19:38-42)

27:57. And when it was late,[4] a rich man from Arimathea, named Joseph, who was also discipled by Jesus, came: 58. after he went to Pilate, he asked for the body of Jesus. Then Pilate ordered *it* to be given *to him*. 59. And, after he took the body, Joseph wrapped it in clean linen 60. and placed it in his new grave, which he cut in the rock, then after he rolled a great stone in the door of the tomb he left. 61. And Mary Magdalene and the other Mary were there sitting opposite the tomb.

The Guard at the Tomb

27:62. And the next day, which was after the preparation[5] *for the Sabbath*, the high priests and the Pharisees were gathered to Pilate 63. saying, "Sir, we remembered that that deceiver said *while* still living, 'After three days I will rise.' 64. Therefore you must immediately order the tomb to be guarded until the third day, so when His disciples come they could not steal Him so they could say to the people, 'He was raised from the dead,' and the last deception will be worse than the first." 65. Pilate said to them, "You have a guard: go, as you know you will have your guard." 66. And then after they left they guarded the tomb, by having sealed the stone with a guard.

The Resurrection of Jesus
(Mk 16:1-8, Lk 24:1-12, Jn 20:1-10)

---

1   (v.52) One of a number of references to what we call death as sleep. See Death in Glossary.
2   (v.52) Who were these saints? Notice their release came immediately after the death of Jesus' body, before His resurrection.
3   (v.53) See Resurrection in Glossary.
4   (v.57) After 3:00 PM
5   (V.62) See Preparation Day in Glossary.

28.1. And after Sabbaths,[1] on the First Day of the Week at dawn, Mary Magdalene and the other Mary came to see the tomb. 2. And behold there was a great earthquake: for *there was* an angel of the Lord, *who* descended from heaven, and after he came he rolled the stone away and was sitting upon it. 3. And his appearance was like lightning and his clothing white[2] as snow. 4. And those who were guarding trembled from fear of him and became as dead. 5. And the angel said to the women, "You must not be afraid, for I know that you are seeking the crucified Jesus: 6. He is not here, for He has risen just as He said: come. See the place where He was laid. 7. And go quickly, you must tell His disciples, 'He has risen from the dead, and behold He is going before you into Galilee, for you will see Him there:' behold I told you." 8. Then they left quickly from the tomb with fear and great joy, and were running to report to His disciples. 9. And behold Jesus met *the women* saying, "Greetings." And they, who had approached *Him*, took hold of His feet and they paid homage[3] to Him. 10. Then Jesus said to them, "You must not be afraid: you must go, report to My brothers so they would go into Galilee, they will see Me there."

The Report of the Guard

28:11. And after they left, behold, some of the guards, having gone into the city, reported to the high priests everything that happened. 12. And gathering with the elders they formed a plan and taking silver coins they gave *them* to the soldiers 13. saying, "You must say, 'When His disciples came in the night they stole Him while we were sleeping.' 14. And if this is heard by the governor, we will persuade him. We will keep you out of trouble." 15. And those who took the silver did as they were taught. And this word was spread widely by Jewish people until today, this very day.

The Commissioning of the Disciples

(Lk 24:36-49, Jn 20:19-23, Ac 1:6-8)

28:16. And the eleven disciples went into Galilee to the mountain which Jesus appointed to them, 17. and when they saw Him they paid homage *to Him* but they doubted. 18. Then when Jesus came He spoke to them, saying, "All authority[4] has been given to Me in heaven and upon the Earth. 19. Therefore when you go, you must now make disciples[5] of all the heathens, 20. teaching them to keep all the things that I have been commanding you: and behold I AM with you all the days until the end of the age."

---

1   (v.1) Sabbaths is plural because it denotes a feast day, and is a Sabbath, the first day of Unleavened Bread. See Lv 23:7.

2   (v.3) White garments represent being in a state of spiritual preparedness, from Ecc 9:8, "Let your garments be always white; and let your head lack no ointment."

3   (v.9) See Pay Homage in Glossary.

4   (v.18) Including authority over death, Is 25:8, Ho 13:14, 1Cor 15:54, 55.

5   (v.19) See Matthew 28:19 in Glossary.

~ ACCORDING TO MARK[1] ~

The Preaching of John the Baptist
(Mt 3:1-12, Lk 3:1-9, 15-17, Jn 1:19-28)

1.1. *The* beginning of the Good News of Jesus Messiah Son of God. 2. Just as it has been written by the prophet Isaiah,

> "Behold I send My messenger[2] before You,
> > who will prepare Your way:" (Ex 23:20, Mal 3:1)

3.   "a voice crying out in the wilderness,
> > 'You must immediately prepare the way of *the* Lord,
> > you must make His paths straight,'" (Is 40:3)

4. John the Baptist was in the wilderness, proclaiming a baptism[3] of repentance for forgiveness of sins. 5. And all the country of Judea and all the *people* from Jerusalem were going out to him, and, confessing their sins, they were being baptized by him[4] in the Jordan River. 6. And John was wearing *clothing woven of* camel's hair and a leather belt around his waist and eating locust *beans* and wild honey. 7. And he was preaching saying, "The One stronger than I is coming after me, I am not worthy to bend down to loose the thongs of His sandals. 8. I baptized you in water, but He will baptize you in *the* Holy Spirit."

The Baptism of Jesus
(Mt 3:13-17, Lk 3:21-22)

1:9. And it happened in those days Jesus came from Nazareth of Galilee and was baptized in the Jordan by John. 10. And immediately while He was rising straight from the water he saw the heavens being split and the Spirit descending upon Him as a dove: 11. and there was a voice from out of the heavens, "You are My beloved Son, in You I take delight."

---

1   (Title) Written about 50-60 AD, Mark, is very basic, factual, getting right to the meat, not presenting background information like Luke and Matthew. In Scriptural interpretation this is the literal reading. This book would be the most appropriate first gospel of the New Testament. See Book Order in Glossary.
2   (v.2) This could also be translated 'angel.'
3   (v.4) Baptism was and still is Jewish and calls for total immersion. See Baptize in Glossary.
4   (v.5) John stood on the bank of the river and as people repented they went into the water and immersed. See Baptize in Glossary.

64

The Temptation of Jesus

(Mt 4:1-11, Lk 4:1-13)

1:12. And the Spirit immediately led Him out into the desert. 13. And He was in the desert forty days being tested by Satan,[1] and He was with the wild animals, and the angels were ministering to Him.

The Beginning of the Galilean Ministry

(Mt 4:12-17, Lk 4:14,15)

1:14. And after John was arrested Jesus came into Galilee proclaiming the Good News of God 15. and saying that "The time has been fulfilled and the kingdom of God has drawn near: you must continually repent and believe in the Good News."

The Calling of Four Fishermen

(Mt 4:18-22, Lk 5:1-11)

1:16. Then while He was passing beside the lake of Galilee He saw Simon, and Andrew, Simon's brother, casting *a net* in the lake: for they were fishermen. 17. And Jesus said to them, "Come, follow Me, and I will make you become fishers of men." 18. And immediately leaving their nets they followed Him. 19. And after He went a little way He saw Jacob[2] the *son* of Zebedee and his brother John, and they *were* in the boat mending their nets. 20. And He immediately called them. And leaving their father Zebedee in the boat with the hired hands they followed Him.[3]

The Man with an Unclean Spirit

(Lk 4:31-37)

1:21. And they went into Capernaum:[4] and immediately on the Sabbaths, when He entered the synagogue, He was teaching.[5] 22. And they were amazed at His teaching: for He was teaching them in a manner as having authority and not like the scribes. 23. And straightway in their synagogue was a man with an unclean spirit and he cried out 24. saying, "What has this to do with You, Jesus of Nazareth? Did You come to destroy us? I know Who You are, the Holy One of God." 25. And Jesus rebuked him saying, "You must now hold your peace and you must come out of him at once!" 26. And the unclean spirit collapsed him, then calling out in a loud voice it came out of him. 27. And they were all amazed, so they discussed among themselves saying, "Who is this? A new teaching, with

---

1   (v.13) See Satan in Glossary.
2   (v.19) The name in the Greek text is Iakob, which is Jacob in English. See Jacob in Glossary.
3   (v.20) Literally, 'went after Him,' which is an idiom meaning they became His disciples.
4   (v.21) Capernaum is the Latin spelling of the Hebrew name Kafer Na-um. Kafer means town or village and Na-um means pleasant.
5   (v.21) Right away He started teaching in a synagogue every Sabbath. See Sabbath in Glossary.

authority: and He commands the unclean spirits, and they obey Him." 28. Then the report about Him came out immediately everywhere in all of the Galilee.

The Healing of Many People

(Mt 8:14-17, Lk 4:38-41)

1:29. And immediately when they came out from the synagogue they went into Simon and Andrew's house with Jacob and John. 30. And Simon's mother-in-law was lying down, suffering with a fever, and right away they told Him about her. 31. And when He came *over* and took her hand He raised her: then the fever left her and she was serving them. 32. Then as it became evening, when the sun went down, *ending the Sabbath*, they brought to Him all those who had evil[1] and those who were demon possessed: 33. and the whole city was gathered at the door. 34. And He healed many having evil and various diseases and He cast out many demons and He was not allowing the demons to speak, since they knew Him.

A Preaching Tour

(Lk 4:42-44)

1:35. And very early morning *while it was* still very dark, when He got up He came out and went into an isolated place and He was praying there. 36. And Simon and those with him searched for Him, 37. and they found Him and said to Him that "Everybody is looking for You." 38. And He said to them, "We should go elsewhere to neighboring market towns, so that I could also preach there: indeed I came for this." 39. And He went preaching and casting out demons in their synagogues in all Galilee.

The Cleansing of a Leper[2]

(Mt 8:1-4, Lk 5:12-16)

1:40. And a leper came to Him begging Him and kneeling down and saying to Him, "If You are willing, You are able to cleanse me." 41. And having pity, as He stretched out His hand He touched[3] *him* and said to him, "I am willing, be cleansed immediately:" 42. and the leprosy went from him instantly, and he was cleansed. 43. Then, warning him sternly, He immediately sent him away 44. and said to him, "See that you tell nothing to anybody, but you must go, you must show yourself to the priest, and you must offer on behalf of your cleansing what Moses commanded, in witness to them." (Lv 14:2-32) 45. But when he left he began to proclaim openly many times and to spread the word abroad, so that no longer was He able to come openly into a city, but He was outside in wilderness places: and they were coming to Him from all directions.

---

1   (v.32) The Greek word kakos, meaning evil, is commonly translated sickness.

2   (Caption) This is not the disease called leprosy today. See Leprosy in Glossary.

3   (v.41) Touching a leper would have made anyone else unclean, but Jesus' touch cleansed the leper. See Cleanse in Glossary.

The Healing of a Paralytic

(Mt 9:1-8, Lk 5:17-26)

2.1. Then, after He again went into Capernaum[1] for some days, it was heard that He was in a house. 2. And many gathered so that *there was* no longer room, not even *for* those by the door, and He was speaking the Word to them. 3. And they came to Him carrying a paralytic *who* was brought by four *men*. 4. And not being able to bring him through the crowd they removed the roof where He was, and then they dug out so they could lower the pallet on which the paralytic was lying. 5. And when Jesus saw their faith He said to the paralytic, "Child, your sins are forgiven." [2] 6. And some of the scribes were sitting there and pondering in their hearts, 7. "What is this He is saying in this way? It is blasphemy: who is able to forgive sins except One, God?" 8. Then immediately Jesus, because He knew in His spirit that they were reasoning among themselves this way, said to them, "What *are* all these things you are pondering in your hearts? 9. What is easier, to say to the paralytic, 'Your sins are forgiven?' or to say 'You must rise at once and take your pallet and you must walk?' 10. So that you would have known that the Son of Man has authority to forgive sins here on the Earth" - He said to the paralytic, 11. "I say to you, you must now rise! You must immediately take your pallet and you must go to your house." 12. And he rose and immediately, having taken the pallet, he came out before all, thus all were astounded and glorified God saying that "Never have we seen this."

The Calling of Levi

(Mt 9:9-13, Lk 5:27-32)

2:13. And He went out again beside the lake: and the whole crowd was coming to Him, and He was teaching them. 14. And as He was passing by He saw Levi[3] *son* of Alpheus sitting in the tax office, and He said to him, "You must now follow Me." So he got up and he followed Him. 15. And *so* it was *that while* He was reclining in his house, even many tax collectors and sinners were reclining together, *eating* with Jesus and His disciples:[4] for indeed many were following Him. 16. And when the scribes of the Pharisees[5] saw that He was eating with the sinners and tax collectors they were saying to His disciples, "Why is He eating with the tax collectors and sinners?" 17. And having heard them Jesus said to them, "Those in good health have no need of a physician but the ones who have

---

1　　(v.1) Capernaum is the Latin spelling of the Hebrew name Kafer Na-um. Kafer means town or village and Na-um means pleasant.

2　　(v.5) It is interesting that Jesus says He has authority to forgive sins, yet His statement to the paralytic is "Your sins are forgiven," something we can say to any repentant person.

3　　(v.14) Levi was also called Matthew.

4　　(v.15) That Jesus, twelve disciples, and many tax collectors and sinners could recline together at Matthew's table shows how large his home was. They could be seen by the Pharisees because they were in the courtyard of the house.

5　　(v.16) Many priests and scribes were Pharisees, not Hellenists. See Hellenists in Glossary.

evil:[1] I did not come to call *the* righteous but sinners."

The Question about Fasting

(Mt 9:14-17, Lk 5:33-39)

2:18. And the disciples of John and the Pharisees were fasting. And they came and said to Him, "Why are the disciples of John and the disciples of the Pharisees fasting, but Your disciples are not fasting?" 19. Then Jesus said to them, "Are *the* sons of the bridegroom able to fast while the bridegroom is with them? While they have the bridegroom with them they are not able to fast. 20. But days will come when the bridegroom is taken from them, and then they will fast in that day.

2:21. "No one sews a new piece of cloth on an old garment: otherwise, the patch raises from itself, the new from the old, and *the* tear becomes worse. 22. And no one puts new wine in old wine skins: otherwise the wine will burst the wineskin and the wine and the wine skins are lost: but new wine *is put* in new wine skins."

Plucking Grain on the Sabbath

(Mt 12:1-8, Lk 6:1-5)

2:23. Then it happened on Sabbaths,[2] He was going through grain fields, and His disciples began *along the* way to pick the kernels of grain. 24. And the Pharisees were saying to Him, "Do you see they are doing something on Sabbaths which is not permitted?" 25. And He said to them, "Haven't you ever read what David did when he had a need and he and those with him were hungry,[3] 26. how he entered the house of God in the time of Abiathar *the* high priest and ate the breads of the presence, which is not permitted except *for* the priests to eat, and he even gave *it* to those who were with him?" 27. And He was saying to them, "The Sabbath was made because of man and not man because of the Sabbath. 28. So the Son of Man is Lord also of the Sabbath."

The Man with a Withered Hand

(Mt 12:9-14, Lk 6:6-11)

3.1. And He entered the synagogue again. And a man *who* had a withered hand was there. 2. And they were watching Him closely, *to see* if He would heal him on Sabbaths,[4] so that they could accuse Him. 3. And He said to the man who had the withered hand, "You must get up *and stand* in the middle *of the congregation*." 4. Then He said to them, "Is it proper to do good on Sabbaths, or to do evil, to save a life or to kill?" But they were silent. 5. Then looking around

---

1   (v.17) This Greek word, kakos, meaning evil, is commonly translated sickness.
2   (v.23) The plural of Sabbath can mean: any feast day, weeks, or more than one Sabbath. See Sabbath in Glossary.
3   (v.25) Oral law permits breaking commandments for humanitarian reasons, such as hunger.
4   (v.2) Same as the above comment on v. 25.

at them with anger, being grieved by the callousness of their hearts, He said to the man, "Stretch out your hand." And he did stretch *it* out and his hand was restored. 6. And right away after the Pharisees came out they were deliberating against Him with the Herodians,[1] how they could kill Him.

A Multitude at the Lakeside

3:7. And Jesus left for the lake with His disciples, and a great multitude from Galilee followed, also from Judea 8. and from Jerusalem and from Idumea[2] and across the Jordan and around Tyre and Sidon, a great multitude came to Him when they heard what He was doing. 9. And He said to His disciples that a small boat should be waiting continually for Him because of the crowd, so that they would not press hard upon Him: 10. for He healed many, so that they pressed in to Him so that they, as many as were afflicted,[3] could touch Him. 11. And the unclean spirits, whenever they noticed Him, fell down before Him and were crying out saying, "You are the Son of God." 12. And He was commanding many of them that they should not make Him known.

The Choosing of the Twelve

(Mt 10:1-4, Lk 6:12-16)

3:13. Then He went up on the mountain and called forth whom He wanted, and they came with Him. 14. And He made twelve whom He also called apostles so that they would be with Him and so that He could send them out to preach 15. and to have authority to cast out the demons: 16. and He made the twelve, and He put *the* name Peter on Simon, 17. and Jacob the *son* of Zebedee and John the brother of Jacob and He named them the B'nei-Regesh,[4] which is Sons of Thunder: 18. and Andrew and Philip and Bartholomew and Matthew and Thomas and Jacob the *son* of Alpheus and Thaddeus and Simon the Zealot 19. and Judas Iscariot, who also gave Him over.

Jesus and Beelzebub

(Mt 12:22, Lk 11:14-23, 12:10)

3:20. And they came into a house: and the crowd came together again,[5] so they were not able to eat a meal. 21. And having heard *the commotion*, those *disciples* with Him came out to take hold of Him: for they were saying that He was out of His senses. 22. And the scribes, who had come down from Jerusalem, were saying, "He has Beelzebub" and, "He is casting out demons by the ruler of the demons." 23. And then He summoned them and He was speaking to them

---

1   (v.6) Herodians were Hellenists and would have included Sadducees. See Hellenists in Glossary.
2   (v.8) Idumea is the Greek spelling of Edom.
3   (v.10) Literally scourged as God disciplines His people, who believed that sickness was a result of sin.
4   (v.17) The Hebrew name: the Greek spelling is Boanerges
5   (v.20) This is a crowd of common people gathered outside the home. The disciples come to get Him.

in parables. "How is Satan[1] able to cast out Satan? 24. And if a kingdom would be divided against itself, that kingdom is not able to stand. 25. And if a house would be divided against itself, that house will not be able to stand. 26. And if Satan rose against himself and was divided, he could not stand but has *his* end. 27. But no one is able, when he comes into the house of the strong *man*, to steal his goods, unless first he would bind the strong *man*, and then he could plunder his house. 28. Truly I say to you that all of the sins by the sons of men will be forgiven, even blasphemies, no matter how great they would blaspheme: 29. but whoever would blaspheme against the Holy Spirit does not ever have forgiveness, but he is guilty of eternal sin." 30. *He said this* because they were continually saying, "He has an unclean spirit."

The Mother and Brothers of Jesus

(Mt 12:46-50, Lk 8:19-21)

3:31. And His mother and His brothers came and, as they stood firm outside, they sent to Him, summoning Him. 32. And a crowd was sitting around Him, and they were saying to Him, "Behold, Your mother and Your brothers and Your sisters are outside looking for You." 33. And answering them He said, "Who are My mother and My brothers?" 34. And looking around He said *to* those who were sitting all around Him, "Behold My mother and My brothers. 35. For whoever would do the will of God, this one is My brother and sister and mother." (Ps 22:22, He 2:17)

The Parable of the Sower

(Mt 13:1-9, Lk 8:4-8)

4.1. And again He began to teach by the lake: and a very great crowd gathered to Him, so that He embarked to sit in a small boat on the lake, and all the crowd was beside the lake on the shore. 2. And He taught them in many parables and was saying to them in His teaching, 3. "Listen. Behold, the one who sows seeds came out to sow. 4. And it indeed happened while he was sowing, some fell beside the way, and the birds came and ate it. 5. And other *seed* fell on rocky ground where it did not have much soil, and it sprang up immediately because it did not have a depth of soil: 6. then when the sun rose it was scorched, and because it did not have a root it withered. 7. And other *seed* fell among the thorns, and the thorns came up and they were choking it, and it did not give fruit. 8. And others fell on the good soil and when it came up it was giving fruit and increasing and it was bearing, one thirty, and one sixty, and *another* one hundred *times*." 9. And He was saying, "Who has ears to hear must continually listen."

The Purpose of the Parables

(Mt 13:10-17, Lk 8:9,10)

4:10. And when He happened to be alone, those around Him with the

---

1   (v.23) See Satan in Glossary.

twelve were asking Him *about* the parables.   11. And He was saying to them, "To you has been given the mystery of the kingdom of God: but to those outside everything is in parables, 12. so that

'When they look they would look but they would not see,
and when they would listen they would hear but they would not understand,
lest at any time they would turn back, *repent,* and it would be forgiven them.'" (Is 6:9,10)

The Parable of the Sower Explained

(Mt 13:18-23, Lk 8:11-15)

4:13. And He said to them, "You do not understand this parable, then how will you understand all the parables? 14. The one who sows is sowing the Word. 15. And these are those beside the way: and where the Word is sown and when they would hear, Satan[1] comes immediately and takes away the Word which was sown in them. 16. And these are those sown on the rocky ground, when those would hear the Word they take it instantly with joy 17. and they do not have a root in themselves, but they endure for a season, then when oppression or persecution comes because of the Word they are immediately caused to sin. 18. And others are those sown among the thorns: these are those who heard the Word, 19. but the cares of the age and the deceitfulness of wealth and the desires for the rest of the things that remain, when they come in they choke the Word and it becomes unfruitful. 20. And there are those which are sown on the good soil, who hear the Word and receive and bear fruit, one thirty, and one sixty, and *another* one hundred *times*."

A Light under a Bushel

(Lk 8:16-18)

4:21. And He was saying to them, "Is the lamp brought so that it would be placed under the peck measure or under the bed? Has it not been placed on the lamp stand? 22. For it is not hidden except that it would be revealed and nothing became hidden except so that it would come to open view. 23. Whoever has ears to hear must listen steadily."

4:24. And He was saying to them, "Beware of what you hear. In the measure with which you are measuring it will be measured to you and it will be added to you. 25. For the one who has, it will be given to him: and who does not have, even what he does have will be taken from him."

The Parable of the Growing Seed

4:26. And He was saying, "In this manner the kingdom of God is like a man *who* would cast a seed on the earth 27. and he would sleep and would rise

---

1   (v.15) See Satan in Glossary.

night and day, and, while he does not understand how, the seed would sprout and would grow tall. 28. The earth bears fruit of itself, first a stem, then the spike of grain, then full of wheat in the spike. 29. When the fruit might be ripe, he immediately sends the sickle because the harvest is at hand."

The Parable of the Mustard Seed

(Mt 13:31,32, Lk 13:18,19)

4:30. And He was saying, "How would we liken the kingdom of God or with whom should we stand in this parable? 31. *It is* like a mustard seed, which when it would be sown upon the ground, *it is* smaller than all the seeds on the earth, 32. and when it would be sown, it comes up and becomes greater than all the vegetables and makes large branches, so that the birds of *the* sky *are* able to dwell under its shade."

The Use of Parables

(Mt 13:34,35)

4:33. And He was speaking the Word to them with many parables such as these so far as they were able to understand: 34. and He was not speaking to them without a parable, but privately He was explaining everything to His own disciples.

The Calming of a Storm

(Mt 8:23-27, Lk 8:22-25)

4:35. And He said to them on that day, after it became evening,[1] "Let us go across to the other side." 36. And after they sent the crowd away, they took Him, as He was in the boat,[2] and other boats were with Him. 37. And a great windstorm came up with a strong wind and the waves beat upon the boat, so that now the boat was filled *with water*. 38. And He was in the stern sleeping on a cushion. And they roused Him and were saying to Him, "Teacher, does it not concern You that we are perishing?" 39. And when He woke up He rebuked the wind and said to the lake, "You must be silent, you must be muzzled." Then the wind ceased and there was a great calm. 40. And He said to them, "Why are you timid?[3] Do you not yet have faith?" 41. And they feared intensely and were saying to one another, "Who then is this that even the wind and the lake obey Him?"

The Healing of the Gerasene Demoniac

(Mt 8:28-34, Lk 8:26-39)

5.1. And they came to the other side of the lake in the region of the Gerasenes. 2. And when He got off the boat, immediately a man with an unclean spirit *who came* from the tombs met Him. 3. He was living in the tombs, and not

---

1   (v.35) This would be between 3:00 PM and 6:00 PM. See Day in Glossary.

2   (v.36) Apparently He was already sitting in a boat while speaking as in Mt 13:2.

3   (v.40) The word used here speaks of timidity, for not taking authority as Jesus did.

even chains or anything was able to bind him 4. because many times he had been bound in fetters and chains but the chains were torn by him and the fetters were smashed, and no one was strong enough to subdue him: 5. and through all night and day in the tombs and in the vicinity he was crying out and cutting himself with stones. 6. And when he saw Jesus from afar he ran and fell down and paid homage[1] to Him 7. and crying in a loud voice he said, "What do You want with me, Jesus, Son of the Most High God? I implore You by God, do not torment me." 8. For He was saying to him, "Unclean spirit, you must immediately come out from the man." 9. And He was asking him, "What *is* your name?" And he said to Him, "My name is Legion,[2] because we are many." 10. And he urged Him repeatedly that He would not send him outside the country.

5:11. And there was a large herd of pigs feeding beside the hill: 12. and *the unclean spirits* were begging Him saying, "You must now send us into the pigs, so that we could enter them." 13. And He permitted them. And after the unclean spirits left they entered the pigs, and the herd, about two thousand, rushed down the steep slope into the lake and they were drowning in the lake. 14. And those who were tending them fled and were reporting in the city and in the fields: and *the people* came to see what it was that happened, 15. and they were coming to Jesus and when they saw the demon-possessed *man* sitting dressed and of sound mind, the one who had the legion, then they were afraid. 16. And the ones who saw were telling them how it happened to the demon-possessed *man* and about the pigs. 17. And they began to beg Him to leave from their district. 18. And when He got into the boat, the demon-possessed man was begging Him that he could be with Him. 19. But He did not allow him, but said to him, "You must now go into your home with your kin and you must report to them what the Lord has done for you and *that* He was merciful to you." 20. And he left and began to proclaim openly in the Ten Cities[3] what Jesus did for him, and everybody was amazed.

The Daughter of Jairus and The Woman Who Touched Jesus' Prayer Shawl

(Mt 9:18-26, Lk 8:40-56)

5:21. And when Jesus crossed back over to the other side in the boat, a large crowd gathered around Him, and He was beside the lake. 22. And one of the synagogue leaders, named Jairus, came *seeking Jesus* and when he saw Him he fell at His feet 23. and begged Him repeatedly saying that "My little daughter is at the point of death, so if You come You could lay hands on her so she would be saved and would live." 24. And He left with him.

And a huge crowd was following Him and pressing upon Him. 25. And

---

1   (v.6) He got down on one knee, touching his forehead to the ground. See Pay Homage in Glossary.

2   (v.9) In Jesus' day a legion was 6,826 troops at full strength.

3   (v.20) See Dekapolis in Glossary.

a woman who had a flow of blood *for* twelve years 26. and suffered much under many physicians and spent everything beyond her *means* and was not helped but rather became worse: 27. having heard about Jesus, as she came from behind the crowd she touched *the fringe of* His prayer shawl:[1] 28. for she was saying "If I could just touch His prayer shawl I will be saved." 29. And immediately the flow of her blood dried and she knew that *her* body was healed from the plague. 30. And immediately Jesus perceived in Himself *that* the power left Him. Turning in the crowd He was saying, "Who touched My prayer shawl?" 31. And His disciples were saying to Him, "You see the crowd pressing around You and You say, 'Who touched Me?'" 32. And He was looking around to see the one who did this. 33. And the woman, *who* was afraid and trembling, since she knew what happened to her, came and fell down before Him and told Him all the truth. 34. And He said to her, "Daughter, your faith has saved you: you must continually go in peace. You are cured from your affliction."[2]

5:35. While He was still speaking they came from *the home of* the synagogue leader, saying that "Your daughter has died: why are you still bothering the teacher?" 36. But when Jesus overheard the message being spoken, He said to the leader, "You must stop being afraid, you must only continually believe." 37. And He did not allow anyone to accompany Him except Peter and Jacob and John, the brother of Jacob. 38. Then they came to the house of the leader, and He saw turmoil and crying and much wailing, 39. and when He entered He said to them, "Why are you distressed and weeping? The child did not die but is sleeping." 40. And they were laughing at Him. And, after He threw *them* all out He took along the father and the mother of the child and the ones with Him and they went in where the child was. 41. And when He took the hand of the child He said to her, "Prayer shawl rise!"[3] 42. Then immediately the girl rose and walked: for she was twelve years old. And they were right then greatly astonished. 43. And He gave them strict orders so that no one might know this, and He said to give her *something* to eat.

The Rejection of Jesus at Nazareth

(Mt 13:53-58, Lk 4:16-30)

6.1. And He went out from there and came into His hometown and His disciples followed Him. 2. And when *the* Sabbath came He began to teach in the synagogue, and many, when they heard, were amazed saying, "Where did He *get* this *authority and knowledge*, and what wisdom *has been* given to this One, and powers such as these *that* come through His hands? 3. Is this not the carpenter,

1   (v.27) The fringe is the tsitsit on the prayer shawl. See Prayer Shawl in Glossary.
2   (v.34) See Lk 8:47 and its footnote for more detail on this miracle.
3   (v.41) The Greek text says "Talita coum!" then includes a statement saying "which is translated 'Girl, I say to you, rise.'" This purports to be a translation of "Talita coum!" and must have been added by a well-intentioned copier who did not understand, mistaking talitha, the Greek spelling of talit, for the Aramaic talyiata, meaning young woman. "Talita coum" is Hebrew for "Prayer shawl rise!" See Prayer Shawl in Glossary.

the son of Mary and brother of Jacob, and Joey[1] and Judas and Simon? And are not His sisters here with us?" And they were offended by Him. 4. And Jesus was saying to them "A prophet is not without honor except in his home town and among his relatives and in his house." 5. And He was not able to do anything powerful there, except He healed a few sick when He laid hands on *them*.[2] 6. And He was amazed because of their unbelief.

The Mission of the Twelve

(Mt 10:1, 5-15, Lk 9:1-6)

And He was going through villages all around teaching. 7. And He summoned the twelve and began to send them two *by* two and He gave them authority over the unclean spirits, 8. and He ordered them that they should take nothing for the journey except a staff only, not bread, not a knapsack, not a copper coin in a belt, 9. but when they put on sandals, then *He said,* "You are not to wear two tunics." 10. And He was saying to them, "Whenever you would enter a house, remain there until whenever you would leave from *that town.* 11. And that place which would not receive you, and would not listen to you, when you leave from there you must shake the dust *from* under your feet in witness to them." 12. And after they left they were preaching so that *the people* would repent, 13. and they were casting out many demons, and they were anointing many with olive oil[3] as they were healing *the* sick.

The Death of John the Baptist

(Mt 14:1-12, Lk 9:7-9)

6:14. And King Herod heard, for His name became known, and they were saying that John the Baptist had risen from *the* dead and because of this the miracles were working in Him. 15. But others were saying that "He is Elijah:" and others were saying, *"He is* a prophet as one of the prophets." 16. And when Herod heard he was saying, "John whom I beheaded, this one has risen." 17. For Herod had sent *and* arrested John and bound him in prison because of Herodiah *who had been* the wife of Philip his brother, because *Herod* married her: 18. for John was saying to Herod "It is not permitted for you to have the wife of your brother." (Lv. 18:16) 19. And Herodiah had a grudge against him and wanted to kill him, but she was not able: 20. for Herod was fearing John, since he knew him *to be* a righteous and holy man, and he was protecting him, and as he heard him much he was uncertain, but he listened to him gladly. 21. And a suitable day came when Herod for his birthday celebration made a banquet for his courtiers and the military leaders and the leading people of Galilee. 22. And when his

---

1   (v.3) The Greek text has the name Iosetos, a nickname for Joseph, with Yossi the Hebrew and Joey the English equivalent. See Mk 15:40, 47.

2   (v.5) The only place where He is referred to as not having the power is in Nazereth. See Mt 13:58 and Lk 5:17.

3   (v.13) In the Talmud, olive oil symbolizes knowledge of Torah, which provides spiritual illumination. Oil is also the symbol of joy, from Is 51:3, so it is called the oil of gladness.

stepdaughter by Herodiah came in and danced she pleased Herod and those reclining. The king said to the maiden, "You must ask me whatever you would wish, and I will give *it* to you:" 23. and he swore insistently to her, "Whatever you would ask, I will give unto half of my kingdom." 24. Then after she left she said to her mother, "What should I ask?" And she said, "The head of John the Baptist." 25. Then as she immediately entered eagerly to the king she asked, saying, "I want that you would right now give me the head of John the Baptist on a platter." 26. Then the king became very sorrowful but, because of the oaths and those who were reclining, he did not want to refuse her. 27. And so the king immediately sent an executioner, *and* commanded to bring his head. And after he went he beheaded him in the prison 28. and brought his head on a platter and gave it to the girl, and the girl gave it to her mother. 29. Then when they heard, his disciples came and took his corpse and placed it in a tomb.

The Feeding of the Five Thousand
(Mt 14:13-21, Lk 9:10-17, Jn 6:1-14)

6:30. And the apostles gathered to Jesus and reported to Him everything that they did and that they taught. 31. And He said to them, "Come privately to a deserted place and rest[1] a little." For many were coming and going and they did not have an opportunity to eat. 32. And they departed covertly in the boat to a desolate place.[2] 33. But many saw them going and from all the cities they found out and ran together and went there by land ahead of them. 34. And He saw a vast crowd coming and He had pity on them, because they were like sheep that did not have a shepherd, and He began to teach them many things. (Judith 11:19) 35. And now after many hours passed, when His disciples came to Him they were saying that "The place is wilderness and now it is late: 36. You must dismiss them right away, so that as they go into the surrounding hamlets and villages they could buy for themselves something to eat." 37. But He said to them, "You must now give them *something* to eat." And they were saying to Him, "If we go, should we buy two hundred denarii of bread to give them *something* to eat?" 38. And He said to them, "How much bread do you have? You must go see." And since they knew they said, "Five *loaves* and two fish." 39. Then He commanded them, all parties, to recline upon the green grass. 40. And they reclined by groups of a hundred and of fifty. 41. And having taken the five loaves and the two fish, after He looked up into the sky He praised *God* and broke the loaves and was giving *them* to His disciples so that they could set *the food* before them, and He divided the two fish to all. 42. And all ate and they were filled, (2Ki 4:42-44) 43. and they removed pieces, twelve baskets[3] full, even from the fish. 44. And those who ate the food were five thousand men.[4]

1　　(v.31) This is a brief, temporary rest. See Rest in Glossary.
2　　(v.31) See Location of the Feeding of the Five Thousand in Glossary.
3　　(v.43) The basket is smaller than the hamper used in the feeding of the four thousand.
4　　(v.44) See Census in Glossary.

Walking on the Water

(Mt 14:22-33, Jn 6:15-21)

6:45. And He immediately compelled His disciples to embark in the boat and to go before *Him* to the other side to Bethsaida,[1] while He dismissed the crowd. 46. And when He took leave from them He went to the mountain to pray. 47. And when it became evening the boat was in the middle of the lake, and only He *was* on the land. 48. Then when He saw them being harassed in rowing, for the wind was against them, about the fourth watch of the night,[2] He came to them walking on the lake and He wanted to pass by them. 49. But when they saw Him walking on the lake they thought that He was a ghost, and they cried out: 50. for they all saw Him and they were disturbed. But He immediately spoke with them and said to them, "Be cheerful! I AM! Stop being afraid!" 51. And He went up to them in the boat and the wind ceased, and they were very amazed among themselves from *this* extraordinary thing: 52. for they did not understand about the bread, but it was because their heart had been hardened.

The Healing of the Sick in Gennesaret

(Mt 14:34-36)

6:53. Then after they crossed to the shore they came into Gennesaret[3] and entered the harbor. 54. And when they came off the boat, immediately recognizing Him 55. they were running about that whole region, and they began to bring upon their mattresses those who had evil[4] wherever they heard that He was. 56. And wherever He went in villages or in cities or in hamlets, they placed the sick in the markets and were begging Him that they could just touch the fringe of His prayer shawl:[5] and as many as were touching it were being delivered.

The Tradition of the Elders

(Mt 15:1-20)

7.1. And Pharisees and some of the scribes, having come from Jerusalem, gathered to Him. 2. And having seen some of His disciples, that they were eating meals with common, that is unwashed, hands 3. - for the Pharisees and all the Jewish people if they cannot wash *their* hands with *the* fist, *using the clenched fist to scrub the open hand*, they do not eat, since they carefully keep the tradition

---

1   (v.45) Bethsaida is the Greek spelling of Beit-Tside, which means House or Place of Fishing (literally hunting, but also used for fishing) in Hebrew. This is the Beit-Tsaida on the west side of the lake. See Location of the Feeding of the Five Thousand in Glossary.

2   (v.48) 3:00-6:00 AM, Roman time

3   (v.53) Gennesaret is a plain on the northwest side of the lake, near Capernaum. Apparently they were blown off course since they were headed for Bethsaida, verse 45. See Mt 14:34.

4   (v.55) The Greek word kakos, meaning evil, speaks of any sickness, weakness, or any other demonic influence.

5   (v.56) The corner fringe, tsitsit, on a prayer shawl represents all the commandments and promises of God. On an anointed man of God that fringe held all the power of God. See Prayer Shawl in Glossary.

of the elders, 4. and *when they come* from a market, unless they could immerse[1] themselves they do not eat, and then there are many other traditions which they accepted to keep, immersing[2] cups and pitchers and kettles and lids - 5. and the Pharisees and the scribes would ask Him, "Why are Your disciples not walking according to the tradition of the elders, but they are eating a meal with unwashed hands?" 6. And He said to them, "Isaiah rightly prophesied about you hypocrites, as it has been written that

'This people honors Me with their lips
      but their hearts are far away *and* distant from Me:
7.   In vain are they worshipping Me
      when they teach *for* instruction *the* commandments of men.'
      (Is 29:13)

8. Having canceled the commandment of God you are holding the tradition of men." 9. And He was saying to them, "You are just rejecting the commandment of God, so that you could establish your tradition. 10. For Moses said, 'Honor your father and your mother,' (Ex 20:12) and 'The one who speaks evil *of* father or mother surely dies.' (Ex 21:17) 11. But you are saying, 'If a man would say to father or mother, "Korban,"[3] which is "Gift *to God*," whatever you would have received from me,'[4] 12. And you no longer permit him to do anything for his father or his mother, 13. so you make void the Word of God by your tradition[5] which you had passed on: and you are doing many things such as these."

7:14. And again after He summoned the crowd He was saying to them, "You must all listen to Me and understand. 15. There is nothing outside of a person *that* goes into him that is able to defile him, but the things which go out from a person are the things that defile *him*." (Ro 14:17, 1Jn 5:17)[6][7] 17. And when He entered *the* house from the crowd, His disciples were asking Him about the parable. 18. And He said to them, "Are you too without understanding? Do you not perceive that everything from the outside, which goes into a person, is not able to defile him 19. because it is not going into his heart but into his stomach, after *the stomach* cleanses all the food, then it goes out into the latrine?" 20. And He was saying, "That going out from a person defiles *him*.[8] 21. For the evil

---

1   (v.4) The Greek word used here is baptidzo, the same word from which we get the word baptize. See Baptize in Glossary.

2   (v.4) The word used here is baptidzo and is commonly translated wash.

3   (v.11) Korban speaks of drawing near to God when you make an offering. See Korban in Glossary.

4   (v.11) This means that when you neglected your parents you used the excuse that you gave to the Lord.

5   (v.13) Jesus emphasized keeping the Scriptural commands, and not using our traditions. See Mt 5:18.

6   (v.15) Salvation is not lost by what someone eats, but ignoring God's instructions (Torah) concerning foods may well shorten his life.

7   (v.15) V. 16 is omitted because it was not in the earliest manuscripts.

8   (v.20) Jesus is saying that we do not lose eternal life by what we eat, but we do know that our life on Earth is shortened by what we eat, ignoring Acts 15:20 and OT warnings, and by

purposes within go out from the hearts of people, immoralities,[1] stealing, murder, 22. adultery, covetousness, evil, deceit, sensuality, stinginess,[2] blasphemy, pride, foolishness: 23. all these evils within go out and defile the person."

The Syrophoenecian[3] Woman's Faith

(Mt 15:21-28)

7:24. Then when He got up from there He left for the territory of Tyre, and when He entered a house, He did not want anyone to know, but He was not able to escape notice: 25. but right away when a woman heard about Him, whose little daughter had an unclean spirit, as she came, she fell at His feet: 26. and the woman was Greek, Syrophoenecian by birth: and she was asking Him to cast out the demon from her daughter. 27. But He was saying to her, "You must first permit the children[4] to be filled, for it is not good to take the bread of the children and to throw *it* to the little dogs." 28. And she answered and said to Him, "Lord: even the little dogs[5] underneath the table are eating from the children's crumbs." 29. And He said to her, "Because of this answer, go, the demon has come out from your daughter." 30. Then when she went into her house she found the child thrown upon the bed and the demon gone.

A Deaf and Mute Man Healed

7:31. And again when He came out from the territory of Tyre He came through Sidon to the lake of Galilee through the territories of the Ten Cities.[6] 32. And they were bringing a deaf and speech-impaired *man* to Him and they were begging Him to lay His hand on him. 33. And after He took him privately aside from the crowd, He cast His fingers into his ears, and after He spit[7] He touched his tongue, 34. and then He looked up into the sky, sighed and was saying to him *in Hebrew*, "Hippatach,"[8] (Is 61:1) that is "You must right now be opened." 35. And immediately his hearing did open and the bondage of his tongue was loosed and he was speaking correctly. 36. And He ordered them that they would say nothing: the more He ordered them, the more they were proclaiming openly. 37. And they were astonished beyond all measure saying, "He has done all these things well, *for* He even makes the deaf to hear and the mutes to speak."

---

overeating.

1   (v.21) Immoralities consist of all forms of idolatry, including heresy.

2   (v.22) Literally 'evil eye' which is a Hebrew idiom for being greedy or stingy.

3   (Caption) Syriophoenecia was the northwestern corner of Canaan, on the Mediterranean Sea.

4   (v.27) The children are the children of Israel.

5   (v.28) Little dogs are puppies and only very small dogs could be under most tables. The standard table was low and diners reclined on cushions.

6   (v.31) Ten cities, nine east of the Jordan plus Beit-Sh'an, were declared "Free Cities" by Rome. These cities are all south and/or east of the lake, while Tyre and Sidon are northwest of the lake, about fifty miles away. See Dekapolis in Glossary.

7   (v.33) The spittle of the first-born son of the father was believed to have healing power.

8   (v.34) This is the word in the Hebrew Scripture of Is 61:1 "to open the prison.." It refers specifically to opening eyes and ears, both physical and spiritual.

The Feeding of the Four Thousand

(Mt 15:32-39)

8.1. In those days there was again a large crowd and since they did not have anything they could eat, after He summoned the disciples He said to them, 2. "I feel sorry for the crowd, because now they have been staying with Me three days and they do not have anything they could eat: 3. and if I will dismiss them hungry to their houses, they will give out on the way: and some of them have come from afar." 4. And His disciples answered Him that "From where in a wilderness will anyone be able to satisfy these *people* here with loaves *of bread*?" 5. And He asked them, "How many loaves do you have?" And they said "Seven." 6. And He instructed the crowd to recline on the ground: then taking the seven loaves, after He gave thanks He broke *them* and gave *them* to His disciples so that they could set *the bread* before *the people*, and they did set *it* before the crowd. 7. And they had a few little fish: and after He praised God for them He said to also set these before *them*. 8. And they ate and were satisfied, and they took up seven hampers[1] of scraps of crumbs. (2Ki 4:42-44) 9. And there were about four thousand. And He dismissed them. 10. Then, having immediately embarked in the boat with His disciples, He came into the province of Dalmanuta.[2]

The Demand for a Sign

(Mt 16:1-4)

8:11. And the Pharisees came out and began to dispute with Him, seeking a sign from heaven from Him, testing Him. 12. And sighing deeply in His spirit He said, "What sign does this generation seek? Truly I ask you, will a *further* sign be given to this generation?" 13. And after He dismissed them, having embarked again, He left for the other side.

The Leaven of the Pharisees and of Herod

(Mt 16:5-12)

8:14. And they forgot to take bread, except one loaf they had in the boat with them. 15. And He ordered them saying, "You must continually take care, you must continually beware of the leaven of the Pharisees and the leaven of Herod."[3] 16. And they were discussing with one another that *it was because* they did not have bread. 17. And since He knew, He said to them, "Why are you discussing that you do not have bread? Do you not yet consider and not understand? Have you hardened your heart? 18. Although you have eyes do you not see and ears do you not hear? And do you not remember, 19. when I broke the five loaves for the five thousand how many baskets full of crumbs did you take?" They said to Him,

---

1   (v.8 & v.20) The hamper was quite large, being used in Acts 9:25 describing Paul's being lowered through the Damascus city wall. See Mt 16:10.
2   (v.10) Dalmanuta is on the west side of the lake, just north of Tiberias.
3   (v.15) The leaven of Pharisees is legalism, the leaven of Herod is Hellenism. See Hellenism in Glossary.

"Twelve." 20. "When the seven *loaves* among the four thousand, how many hampers[1] full of broken *pieces* did you take?" And they said to Him, "Seven." 21. And He was saying to them, "Do you not yet understand?"

The Healing of a Blind Man at Bethsaida

8:22. And they came into Bethsaida.[2] And they brought to Him a blind *man* and begged Him that He would touch him. 23. Then taking the hand of the blind *man*, He led him outside the village and having spit[3] in his eyes,[4] after He placed His hands on him, He was asking him, "Do you see anything?" 24. And when he looked up he was saying, "I see men that *are* as trees I see walking." 25. Then He again laid hands upon his eyes, and he stared straight ahead and he was restored and he was looking at everything clearly. 26. And He sent him to his house saying, "And do not enter the village."

Peter's Declaration about Jesus

(Mt 16:13-20, Lk 9:18-21)

8:27. And Jesus and His disciples came out to the villages of Caesarea Philippi:[5] and on the way He was asking His disciples, saying to them, "Who do people say that I am?" 28. And they spoke to Him saying, "John the Baptist, and others, Elijah, and others that *You are* one of the prophets." 29. Then He asked them, "Who do you say I am?" Peter answering said to Him, "You are the Messiah." 30. And He warned them so that they would not say anything about this.

Jesus Foretells His Death and Resurrection[6]

(Mt 16:21-28, Lk 9:22-27)

8:31. And He began to teach them that it was necessary for the Son of Man to suffer many things, and to be rejected after testing by the elders and the high priests and the scribes, and to be killed, and after three days to be raised: 32. and He was speaking the message openly. And Peter, after he took Him aside, began to reprove Him. 33. And when He turned around, as He saw His disciples, He rebuked Peter and said, "You must return to where you came from, Satan,[7] because you do not think the things of God but the things of men." 34. Then after He summoned the crowd *along* with His disciples He said to them, "If someone wishes to follow after Me, he must immediately deny himself and take up his

---

1 (v.20) Hampers were quite large. Paul was lowered through the Damascus city wall in a hamper, Acts 9:25.
2 (v.22) Bethsaida is the Greek spelling of Beit-Tside, which means House or Place of Fishing (literally hunting, but also used for fishing) in Hebrew.
3 (v.23) The spittle of a man who was the first-born son of his father was known to have healing power. See Mt 20:34.
4 (v.23) The word translated eyes is omma, which means both natural and spiritual eyes, used only here and in Mt 20:34.
5 (v.27) Caesarea Philippi is over thirty miles north of Bethsaida, a great distance to walk.
6 (Caption) See Resurrection in Glossary.
7 (v.33) See Satan in Glossary.

81

cross[1] and he must constantly follow Me. 35. For whoever would wish to save his life will lose it: and whosoever will lose his life because of Me and the Good News, he will save it. 36. For what does it profit a man to gain the whole world and to forfeit his very being? 37. For what might a man give in exchange for his life? 38. For whoever would be ashamed of Me and My words in this adulterous and sinful generation, then the Son of Man will be ashamed of him, when He would come in the glory of His Father with the holy angels."[2] (Mt 25:31, 1Thes 3:13, Jude 14, Re 19:14)

9.1. And He was saying to them, "Truly I say to you that there are some of those who stand here who would **not** in any way taste death until they would see the kingdom of God when it comes in power."

The Transfiguration of Jesus
(Mt 17:1-13, Lk 9:28-36)

9:2. Then after six days Jesus took Peter and Jacob and John and led them to a high mountain privately, alone. And He was transformed before them, 3. and His garments became shining very white, such as no bleach upon the Earth is able to whiten in this way. 4. And Elijah was seen by them with Moses and they were speaking together with Jesus. 5. And Peter said to Jesus, "Rabbi, it is good for us to be here, so we could make three booths, one for You and one for Moses and one for Elijah." 6. For he did not know what He would answer, for they became terrified. 7. And it happened a cloud overshadowed them and there was a voice from the cloud, "This is My beloved Son, you must habitually listen to Him." 8. Then suddenly, when they looked around, they no longer saw anyone but only Jesus with them.

9:9. Then while they were coming down from the mountain He gave orders to them that they should not discuss what they saw, except at the time that the Son of Man would have risen from *the* dead. 10. And they kept the word to themselves, *not* discussing what that was *until* He rose from *the* dead. (See Lk 9:36) 11. And they were asking Him, saying that, "Why do the scribes say that it is necessary *for* Elijah to come first?" 12. And He said to them, "Indeed when Elijah came first he restored everything:[3] and how has it been written *that* in the time of the Son of Man that He would suffer many things and would be treated with contempt? (Ps 22:1-18, Is 53:3) 13. But I say to you that even Elijah has come, (Mal 4:5,6) and they did to him what they wanted, just as it has been written before him."

The Healing of a Boy with an Unclean Spirit
(Mt 17:14-20, Lk 9:37-43a)

9:14. And when they came to the *rest of the* disciples they saw a large

---

1   (v.34) This is a prophetic word by Jesus, noting how He would be killed.
2   (v.38) This is Judgment Day. See Re 20:4, 11-14.
3   (v.12) See Mt 17:10-13.

crowd around them and scribes carrying on a discussion with them. 15. And immediately when the whole crowd saw Him they were thoroughly amazed and as they were running up they were greeting Him. 16. And He asked them, "What are you discussing with them?" 17. And one from the crowd answered Him, "Teacher, I brought my son to You because he has a mute spirit. 18. And wherever it would seize him it throws him down and he foams at the mouth and he gnashes his teeth and is stiff: and I asked Your disciples to cast it out, but they were not able."[1] 19. And answering them He said, "O unbelieving generation, until when will I be with you? How long am I to endure you? Bring him to Me." 20. And they brought him to Him. And when it saw Him the spirit immediately convulsed him, and then he fell on the ground, *and* he was rolling, foaming *at the mouth*. 21. And He asked his father, "How long a time has it been *like* this with him?" And he said, "From childhood: 22. and it also frequently threw him into a fire and into water so that it could kill him: but if You are able, You must now help us, if You have pity on us." 23. And Jesus said to him, "If you would be able *to believe*, all things *are* possible to the one who believes." 24. Immediately crying out, the father of the child was saying, "I believe: You must continually help my unbelief." 25. And when Jesus saw that the crowd was running together, He rebuked the unclean spirit by saying to it, "Mute and deaf spirit, I command you, you must come out from him at once and never again can you enter into him." 26. And after it cried out and *the boy* had many convulsions it left: and he became as dead, so that many of those said that he died. 27. But Jesus, when He took hold of his hand, raised him, and he got up. 28. And when He entered *the* house His disciples asked Him privately, "Why were we not able to cast it out?" 29. And He said to them, "This kind is in no way able to come out except in prayer."[2]

Jesus Again Foretells His Death and Resurrection[3]
(Mt 17:22,23, Lk 9:43b-45)

9:30. And after they came out from there they were passing through the Galilee, and He did not want that anyone might know: 31. for He was teaching His disciples and was saying to them that "The Son of Man is being given into *the* hands of men, and they will kill Him and, when He is killed, after three days He will rise." 32. But they did not understand the statement, and they were afraid to ask Him.

Who is the Greatest
(Mt 18:1-5, Lk 9:46-48)

9:33. And they came into Capernaum.[4] And while He was in the house

---

1   (v.18) Or strong enough
2   (v.29) Other texts say "prayer and fasting." The editors of the Greek text believe the phrase "and fasting" was added. "And fasting" has been found on a fragment from the 3rd century, and may well have been in the original. It has Biblical support, in Is 58:6.
3   (Caption) See Resurrection in Glossary.
4   (v.33) Capernaum is the Latin spelling of the Hebrew name Kafer Na-um. Kafer means

He was asking them, "What were you discussing on the way?" 34. But they were being silent: for with one another on the way they discussed who *was* greater. 35. And after He sat down He summoned the twelve and said to them, "Whoever wishes to be first, will be last of all and a servant of all." 36. And taking a child He placed him in *the* middle of them and after He took him into *His* arms He said to them, 37. "Whoever would receive one of these children in My name, receives Me: and whoever would receive Me, does not receive Me but the One Who sent Me."

He Who is Not against Us is for Us

(Lk 9:49,50)

9:38. John said to Him, "Teacher, we saw someone casting out demons in Your name and we stopped him, because he was not following[1] us." 39. But Jesus said, "Stop hindering him! For no one who will do a miracle in My name is then able quickly to speak evil of Me. 40. For they who are not against us, are for us. 41. For whoever would give you a cup of water to drink in *My* name because you are from Messiah, truly I say to you that he would **not** *in any way* lose his reward."

Temptation to Sin

(Mt 18:6-9, Lk 17:1,2)

9:42. "And whoever would cause one of the least of these who believe in Me to sin, it is better for him if a millstone turned by a donkey[2] were placed around his neck and he were cast into the sea. 43. And if your hand would cause you to sin, you must immediately cut it off: it is expedient *for* you to enter life[3] crippled rather than, having two hands, to go into Gehenna,[4] into the unquenchable fire.[5] 45. And if your foot would cause you to sin, you must immediately cut it off: it is better for you to enter life lame rather than having two feet to have been thrown into Gehenna.[6] 47. And if your eye would cause you to sin, you must immediately cast it out: it is *more* profitable for you to enter the kingdom of God with one eye rather than having two eyes to have been cast into Gehenna,[7] 48. where their worms do not die and the fire is not put out. (Is 66:24) 49. For everyone will be salted with fire. 50. Salt is good: but if the salt would become salt-less, with what will you season? You have salt[8] in yourselves and you must

---

town or village and Na-um means pleasant.
1   (v.38) This means that this person is not a disciple of Jesus.
2   (v.42) The millstone turned by a donkey is an important distinction because many households had one or more small hand-sized stones for grinding small quantities of grain.
3   (v.43) Jesus several times refers to what we call death as entering life, a clear reference to the wonderful eternal life that awaits us.
4   (v.43) See Gehenna in Glossary.
5   (v.43) V. 44 is omitted because it was not in the earliest manuscripts.
6   (v.45) V. 46 is omitted because it was not in the earliest manuscripts.
7   (v.47) Gehinnom in Hebrew, Valley of Hinnom, see Gehenna in Glossary.
8   (v.49) Salt is a preservative and speaks of permanence, the meaning of the Covenant of Salt, Nu 18:18,19.

continually live in peace with one another."

Teaching about Divorce

(Mt 19:1-12)

10.1. Then when He went up from there He came into the territories of Judea and beyond the Jordan, and again crowds were going with Him and He was yet again teaching them as He was accustomed. 2. And Pharisees *who* came were asking Him if it was permitted for a husband to divorce a wife, testing Him. 3. And He said to them, "What did Moses command you?" 4. And they said, "Moses permitted 'To write a certificate of divorce and to divorce.'" 5. And Jesus said to them, "On account of your hardness of heart he wrote this precept for you. 6. But from *the* beginning of creation 'He made them male and female:' (Gn 1:27, 5:2) 7. because of this 'a man will leave behind his father and mother and will be united with his wife, 8. and the two will be in one flesh:' (Gn 2:24) so that no longer are they two, but one flesh. 9. Therefore what God joined together man must not divide." 10. And again in the house the disciples were asking Him about this. 11. And He said to them, "Whoever would dismiss his wife and would marry another commits adultery on account of her: 12. and if she, having divorced her husband, would marry another she commits adultery."

Little Children Blessed

(Mt 19:13-15, Lk 18:15-17)

10:13. And they were bringing children before Him so that He would touch them: but the disciples rebuked them. 14. And, when Jesus saw *that*, He was indignant and said to them, "You must allow the children to come to Me, you must stop hindering them, for the kingdom of God is of such as these. 15. Truly I say to you, whoever would not receive the kingdom of God as a child, could **not** enter it." 16. Then, after He took *them* into His arms, He blessed them, laying hands on them.

The Rich Man

(Mt 19:16-30, Lk 18:18-30)

10:17. And while He was going out on a journey, one *who* ran up to Him, after he fell on his knees, was asking Him, "Good Teacher, what shall I do so that I will inherit eternal life?" 18. And Jesus said to him, "Why do you call Me good? No one is good except One, God. 19. You know the commandments: 'Do not murder, do not commit adultery, do not steal, do not bear false witness,' do not defraud, 'honor your father and mother.'" (Ex 20:12-16) 20. But he said to Him, "Teacher, I have kept all these things from my youth." 21. And Jesus, looking at him, loved him and said to him, "One thing fails you: you must go, sell what you have, and give *it* to the poor, and you will have treasure in heaven, then come, you must continually follow Me." 22. But being shocked at the message, he left grieving: for he had many possessions.

10:23. Then Jesus, looking around, said to His disciples, "How difficult it will be for those who have riches[1] to enter the kingdom of God." 24. And the disciples were amazed[2] at His words. And Jesus again answering said to them, "Children, how difficult it is to enter the kingdom of God: 25. it is easier for a camel to go through the hole of the needle than for a rich man to enter the kingdom of God."[3] 26. And they were very much amazed, saying among themselves, "Then who is able to be saved?" 27. Looking around at them Jesus said, "With men *it is* impossible, but not with God: for all things *are* possible in the power of God." (Gn 18:14, Jr 32:17, 27, Job 42:2) 28. Peter began to say to Him, "See, we left everything and have followed You." 29. Jesus said, "Truly I say to you, there is no one who left house or brothers or sisters or mother or father or children or farms because of Me and because of the Good News, 30. who would not take one hundred times as much now in this time, houses and brothers and sisters and mothers and children and farms, with persecutions, and in the coming age eternal life. 31. And many first will be last and the last *will be* first." (Mt 20:16, Lk 13:30)

A Third Time Jesus Foretells His Death and Resurrection[4]

(Mt 20:17-19, Lk 18:31-34)

10:32. And they were on the road going up to Jerusalem, and Jesus was going before them, and they were amazed, and those who were following were afraid. And again taking aside the twelve He began to tell them what was going to happen to Him 33. that "Behold we are going up to Jerusalem, and the Son of Man will be given over to the high priests and the scribes, and they will condemn Him to death and they will give Him over to the heathens 34. and *the heathens* will mock Him and spit upon Him and they will scourge Him and they will kill *Him*, and after three days He will rise."

The Request of Jacob and John

(Mt 20:20-28)

10:35. And Jacob and John, the sons of Zebedee, came up to Him, saying to Him, "Teacher, we wish that if we would ask You *something*, You would do *it* for us." 36. And He said to them, "What do you want Me to do for you?" 37. And they said to Him, "You must now grant to us that we could sit one on Your right and one on *Your* left in Your glory." 38. And Jesus said to them, "You do not know what you are asking. Are you able to drink the cup which I am drinking

---

1   (v.23) This contradicted the commonly accepted belief that prosperity was an appropriate reward for obedience to Torah and traditions such as the legalism of the Pharisees. We have similar prosperity teachings today.

2   (v.24) Pharisees taught that keeping tradition was rewarded with wealth.

3   (v.25) The hole, or eye, of a needle was also used to refer to the small door in the gate of a city that could let people in or out when the gate was closed. A camel could go through only by removing the saddle and any load it was carrying, then by kneeling down to squeeze through the door. See Lk 14:33.

4   (Caption) See Resurrection in Glossary.

or to be baptized in the baptism *with* which I am baptized?" 39. And they said to Him, "We are able." And Jesus said to them, "The cup which I am drinking you will drink and *in* the baptism which I am baptized, you will be baptized, 40. but to sit on My right or left is not for Me to give, but for whom it has been prepared." 41. And when they heard, the ten *other disciples* began to be disturbed about Jacob and John. 42. And after He summoned them Jesus said to them, "You know that those who are considered to lead the heathens are lording over them and *that* the great ones of them tyrannize them. 43. But it is not so among you, but whoever would wish to become great among you will be your servant,[1] 44. and whoever among you would wish to be first will be servant[2] of all: 45. for also the Son of Man did not come to be served but to serve and to give His life as a ransom in exchange for many."

The Healing of Blind Bartimaeus
(Mt 20:29-34, Lk 18:35-43)

10:46. And they came to Jericho. And as He and His disciples and a large crowd were going out from Jericho a blind beggar, Bartimaeus, the son of Timaeus, was sitting beside the road. 47. And when he heard it was Jesus of Nazareth he began to cry out and to say, "Son of David![3] Jesus! You must right now have mercy on me!"[4] 48. And many were rebuking him so that he would be silent: but he was crying out much more, "Son of David, You must right now have mercy on me!" 49. Having stopped, Jesus said, "Call him." And they summoned the blind *man* saying to him, "Be cheerful! Rise, He is calling you." 50. And as he threw off his *official beggar's* cloak,[5] *and* jumped up, he came to Jesus. 51. And responding to him Jesus said, "What do you want Me to do for you?" And the blind *man* said to Him, "My Rabbi, that I would regain my sight." 52. And Jesus said to him, "You must now go, your faith has delivered you." And immediately he regained his sight and was following Him on the way.

The Triumphal Entry into Jerusalem
(Mt 21:1-11, Lk 19:28-40, Jn 12:12-19)

11.1. And when they were drawing near to Jerusalem, in Bethphage[6] and Bethany[7] beside the Mount of Olives, He sent two of His disciples 2. and said to them, "You must go to the town opposite you, and immediately when you enter

1   (v.43) This is diakonos and can mean servant, minister, or deacon. See Servant in Glossary.

2   (v.44) This is doulos and means either servant or slave. See Servant in Glossary.

3   (v.47) See Son of David/Son of Joseph in Glossary.

4   (v.47) 'Have mercy on me' is a Hebrew idiom asking for forgiveness, since he believed his blindness was punishment for sin.

5   (v.50) Everyone begging was required to get approval from a priest, who gave a special cloak signifying that the beggar was authorized. Throwing off this cloak showed his faith that he would be healed and no longer had a need for that cloak.

6   (v.1) Bethphage is the Greek spelling of the Hebrew Beit-Pag, meaning Place of Unripe Figs, which was close to Bethany.

7   (v.1) Bethany is the Greek spelling of Beit-Anyah, meaning House of Sighing in Hebrew.

it you will find a colt[1] tied upon which no one ever before of men has sat: loose it and bring *it*. 3. And if someone would say to you, 'Why are you doing this?' Say 'The Lord has need of it, and He is sending it straight back to this place.'" 4. And they left and found a colt tied to a gate outside on the street and they loosed it. 5. And some of those standing there were saying to them, "What are you doing loosing the colt?" 6. And they said to them just as Jesus said, and they permitted them. 7. And they brought the colt to Jesus and laid their prayer shawls on it, and He sat on it. 8. And many spread their garments[2] on the road, and others who had cut spreads of leaves from the fields *spread those*. 9. And those who were leading and those who were following were crying out,

"Hoshea-na:[3]
Blessed is He Who comes in the Name of the Lord:"
(Ps 118:25,26)

10.   "Blessed is the coming kingdom of our father David: Hoshea-na in the highest."

11. And He entered Jerusalem and after He had looked around at all the things in the temple, since it was now a late hour, He went to Bethany with the twelve.

The Cursing of the Fig Tree

(Mt 21:18,19)

11:12. And the next day when they came out from Bethany He was hungry. 13. And when He saw a fig tree from afar, *which* had leaves, He came *to see* if perhaps He would find some *fruit* on it, then when He came upon it He found nothing except leaves: for it was not *the* season of figs. 14. And He said to it, "Nevermore may anyone eat fruit from you." And His disciples were listening.

The Cleansing of the Temple

(Mt 21:12-17, Lk 19:45-48, Jn 2:13-22)

11:15. Then they came into Jerusalem. And entering the temple He began to throw out those who were selling and those who were buying in the temple, and He overturned the tables of the money-changers and the chairs of those who were selling doves, 16. and He was not allowing anyone to carry goods through the temple. 17. And He was teaching and was saying to them, "Has it not been written that,

'My house will be called a house of prayer for all the nations'? (Is 56:7)

'but you have made it a den of robbers.'" (Jr 7:11)

---

1   (v.2) This is the foal of a donkey. See Donkey in Glossary.

2   (v.8) These were probably prayer shawls because the men would have been wearing prayer shawls and they knew that they were welcoming the Messianic reign.

3   (v.9) Hoshea-na means "Deliver us now!" or "Save us now!" They thought Messiah had come to take the throne, throw out the Romans and begin the Messianic reign. See Hosanna in Glossary.

18. And the high priests and the scribes heard and they were seeking how they could destroy Him: for they were afraid of Him, because the whole crowd was amazed over His teaching. 19. And when it was late, they went outside the city.

The Lesson from the Withered Fig Tree

(Mt 21:20-22)

11:20. And in the morning when they passed by they saw the fig tree withered from *the* roots. 21. And Peter, remembering, said to Him, "Rabbi, look! The fig tree which You had cursed has become withered." 22. And Jesus said to them, "You must have faith in God. 23. Truly I say to you that whoever would say to this mountain, 'You must immediately be removed and you must immediately be cast into the sea,' and would not doubt in his heart but would believe that what he is saying is happening, it shall be to him. 24. Because of this I say to you, you must continually pray for everything, then *for* whatever you are asking, believe that you have taken *it*, and it will be *there* for you. 25. And when you are standing praying, forgive whatever you have against anyone,[1] in order that your Father Who is in the heavens would forgive you your trespasses."[2]

The Authority of Jesus Questioned

(Mt 21:23-27, Lk 20:1-8)

11:27. And they came again into Jerusalem. And while He was walking in the temple the high priests and the scribes and the elders came to Him 28. and they were saying to Him, "By what kind of authority are You doing these things?" Or "Who gave You this authority so that You could do these things?" 29. Then Jesus said to them, "I will ask you one question, and you must answer Me, then I will tell you with what authority I am doing these things. 30. The baptism of John, was it out of heaven or from men? You must answer Me right now!" 31. And they were discussing among themselves saying, "If we would say, 'From heaven,' He will say, 'Then why did you not believe him?' 32. But if we would say, 'From men?'" - they were fearing the crowd: for all were maintaining *that* John really was a prophet. 33. And answering Jesus they said, "We do not know." And Jesus said to them, "Then I am not telling you by what sort of authority I am doing these things."

The Parable of the Vineyard and the Tenants[3]

(Mt 21:33-46, Lk 20:9-19)

12.1. And He began to speak to them in parables, "A man planted a vineyard and placed a fence around *it* and he dug a pit for the wine press and he built a tower and he leased it to tenant farmers and he went away. 2. And in

---

1   (v.26) See Sin, Forgiveness of in Glossary
2   (v.25) V. 26 is omitted because it was not in the earliest manuscripts.
3   (Caption) Each of these parables about the vineyard uses the picture of greedy farmers to speak of the High Priest and other Jewish leaders.

time he sent a servant to the farmers to take *his share* of the fruit of the vineyard from the farmers: 3. and then they took *and* beat him and sent *him away* empty. 4. And he again sent another servant to them: and they beat that one on the head and dishonored *him*. 5. Then he sent another: and that one they killed, and many others, on the one hand beating some and on the other hand killing others. 6. Yet he had one beloved son: he sent him last to them saying that 'They will respect my son.' 7. And those farmers said to themselves, 'This is the heir: come, we should kill him, then the inheritance will be ours.' 8. And when they took *him* they killed him and cast him outside the vineyard. 9. What then will the owner of the vineyard do? He will come and will kill the farmers and he will give the vineyard to others. 10. And did you not read this Scripture,

'A Stone which the builders rejected,
> this became *the* cornerstone:

11.   This happened from *the* Lord and it is
> marvelous in our eyes?'" (Ps 118:22,23)

12:12. And they were seeking to lay hold of Him, for they knew that He said the parable to them, but they feared the crowd. And after they dismissed Him they went away.

Paying Taxes to Caesar
(Mt 22:15-22, Lk 20:20-26)

12:13. And they were sending some of the Pharisees and Herodians[1] to Him so that they could catch Him in a teaching. 14. And when they came they said to Him, "Teacher, we know that You are honest and it is not a care to You concerning anything: for You do not look into a face[2] of men but You are teaching on *the* true way of God: is it permitted to pay a tax to Caesar or not? Should we pay or should we not pay?" 15. And because He knew their hypocrisy, He said to them, "Why do you test Me? Bring Me a denarius so that I could see." 16. And they brought *it*. And He said to them, "Whose likeness and inscription *is* this?" And they said to Him, "Caesar's." 17. Then Jesus said to them, "You must give back to Caesar what *things are* Caesar's, and to God what *are* God's." And they were greatly amazed concerning Him.

The Question about Resurrection[3]
(Mt 22:23-33, Lk 20:27-40)

12:18. And Sadducees came to Him, who were saying *there was* not to be a resurrection, and they were questioning Him saying, 19. "Teacher, Moses wrote for us that 'If some brother would die and would leave a wife but would not leave a child, that his brother would take the wife and would raise up a seed

---

1   (v.13) Herodians were Hellenists and would have included Sadducees. See Hellenists in Glossary.

2   (v.14) This is an idiom for not showing partiality. See Acts 10:34.

3   (Caption) See Resurrection in Glossary.

for his brother.' (Dt 25:5) 20. There were seven brothers: and the first took a wife and when he died he did not leave a seed.[1] 21. And the second took her and he died not leaving a seed: and the third likewise: 22. and the seven did not leave a seed. Then last of all the wife died. 23. In the resurrection when they would rise of which one of them will she be a wife? For seven had her *as* wife." 24. And Jesus said to them, "Are you not led astray by this, since you know neither the Scriptures nor the power of God? 25. For when they would rise from the dead they neither marry nor are given in marriage, but they will be as angels in the heavens. 26. And concerning that the dead rise, did you not read in the book of Moses in the case of the bush, where God spoke to him, saying, 'I *AM*[2] the God of Abraham and the God of Isaac and the God of Jacob?' (Ex 3:6) 27. He is not God of *the* dead but of *the* living: you are much deceived."

The Great Commandment

(Mt 22:34-40, Lk 10:25-28)

12:28. Then when one of the scribes came, having heard of their questioning, since he saw that He answered them well, he asked Him, "What commandment is the most important of all?" 29. Jesus answered him that "First is, 'Hear O Israel, *the* Lord *is* our God, *the* Lord is One, 30. and you shall love the Lord your God out of your whole heart and out of your whole being and out from your whole understanding and out from your whole strength.' (Dt 6:4,5) 31. This *is* second, 'You will love your neighbor as yourself.' (Lv 19:18) There is not another commandment greater than these." 32. And the scribe said to Him, "Quite right! Teacher, You said in truth that 'He is One and there is not another except Him:' (Is 45:21) 33. and to love Him out of his whole heart and out of his whole mind and out of his whole strength and to love his neighbor as himself is greater than all burnt offerings and sacrifices." (1Sam 15:22, Ho 6:6) 34. And when Jesus saw that he answered wisely He said to him, "You are not far from the kingdom of God." And no one dared to question Him any more.

The Question about David's Son

(Mt 22:41-46, Lk 20:41-44)

12:35. And while teaching in the temple Jesus was saying, "How do the scribes say that the Messiah is a son of David?[3] 36. David himself said by the Holy Spirit,

> '*The* Lord said to my Lord,
> Sit at My right hand,[4]
>   until I place Your enemies under Your feet.'[5] (Ps 110:1)

---

1   (v.20) Son
2   (v.26) The great I AM, Anokhi in Hebrew: See Anokhi in Glossary.
3   (v.35) See Son of David/Son of Joseph in Glossary.
4   (v.36) "At the right hand" is a Hebrew idiom that speaks of power and strength, from Ex 15:6. See Right Hand in Glossary.
5   (v.36) See Footstool in Glossary.

37. David himself calls Him Lord, so how is He his son?" And the huge crowd heard Him gladly.

The Denouncing of the Scribes

(Mt 23:1-36, Lk 20:45-47)

12:38. And in His teaching He was saying, "Be wary of the scribes who want to walk in long flowing robes[1] and *receive* greetings in the markets 39. and chief seats in the synagogues and chief places at the tables in the banquets, 40. *they are* those who consume the houses of the widows, and *who* pray long for appearance's sake: they will take greater judgment."

The Widow's Offering

(Lk 21:1-4)

12:41. And after He sat down opposite the treasury He was watching how the crowd cast copper coin into the treasury. And many rich were casting much: 42. and when she came one poor widow cast two small copper coins, which is about a quarter of a cent. 43. Then after He summoned the disciples He said to them, "Truly I say to you that this poor widow cast more than all those when they cast into the treasury: 44. for they all cast from their abundance, but she cast from her need all that she had her whole life."

The Destruction of the Temple Foretold

(Mt 24:1,2, Lk 21:5,6)

13.1. And as He left from the temple one of His disciples said to Him, "Teacher, see how great *the* stones *are* and how great *the* buildings *are*." 2. And Jesus said to him, "Do you see these great buildings? **Not** a stone would be left here upon a stone which would **not** be cast down."

The Beginning of Woes

(Mt 24:3-14, Lk 21:7-19)

13:3. And as He sat upon the Mount of Olives opposite the temple, Peter and Jacob and John and Andrew were asking Him privately, 4. "You must tell us, when will these things be and by what sign? When would all these things be going to come to pass?" 5. And Jesus began to say to them, "See that no one would mislead you: 6. many will come in My name saying that *they are* 'I AM' and they will deceive many. 7. And when you would hear of wars and rumors of wars, you must not be frightened: it must happen, but *it is* not yet the end. 8. For people will rise against people[2] and kingdom against kingdom, there will be earthquakes throughout places, there will be famines: these things *are the*

---

1   (v.38) Flowing robes are an indication of high rank.
2   (v.8) While frequently translated nation against nation, people is more appropriate as we now see in Uganda, Bosnia, Indonesia, China, Ireland, and other places where citizens are attacked and imprisoned because of different beliefs or ethnic heritage.

beginning of labor. 9. And you must watch out for yourselves: they will give you over to councils and you will be beaten in public gatherings[1] and you will stand before governors and kings in witness to them because of Me. 10. But first it is necessary for the Good News to be preached among all the heathens. 11. And when they would lead you, arresting *you*, do not be anxious about what you would say, but you must speak whatever you would be given in that moment: for you are not the ones speaking, but the Holy Spirit. 12. And a brother will hand over a brother into death and a father a child, and children will rise up against parents and will put them to death. 13. And you will be hated by all because of My name. But the one who remains to the end will be delivered."[2]

The Great Tribulation
(Mt 24:15-28, Lk 21:20-24)

13:14. "When you would see the abomination of the desolation placed where it must not *be*, the one who reads must understand that those in Judea must flee to the mountains, 15. and the one on the roof must not go down and enter to take anything from his house, 16. and the one in the field must not turn back to the things behind to take his cloak.[3] 17. And woe to those who are pregnant and to those who are nursing in those days. 18. And you must pray that it would not happen in winter: 19. for those days will have affliction such as has not happened from *the* beginning of creation, which God created until now, and it would **not** happen *again*. 20. And unless *the* Lord shortened the days, no flesh would be saved: but because of the chosen, whom He selected, He shortened the days. 21. And then if someone would say to you, 'Behold! Here *is* the Messiah!' 'Look! There!' You must not believe: 22. for false messiahs and false prophets will be raised up and they will give signs and wonders in order to lead astray, if possible, the elect. 23. But you must see: I have told you everything ahead of time."

The Coming of the Son of Man
(Mt 24:29-31, Lk 21:25-28)

13:24. "But in those days after that affliction
the sun will be darkened,
　　　　and the moon will not give its light,
25.　　and the stars will be falling from the sky,
　　　　and the powers that are in the heavens will be shaken.
　　　　(Is 13:10, 34:4, Ez 32:7,8, Jl 2:10,31, 3:15)

1　　　(v.9) While this Greek word, "sunagoga" could be translated synagogues, "a gathering of people" is the primary meaning of the word, and no one would be scourged in a synagogue. Lk 4:28 tells of Jesus being driven from the city when the congregation was enraged. The gathering would have been related to the Sanhedrin, which was the local court. See Lk 21:12. See Congregation in Glossary.

2　　　(v.13) Or saved

3　　　(v.16) The cloak would have been a prayer shawl. To leave a cloak behind would not have been anywhere near as significant as a man leaving his prayer shawl.

26. And then they will see 'The Son of Man coming in clouds' with great power and glory. (Dn 7:13) 27. And then He will send the angels and gather His elect out from the four winds from *the* end of *the* Earth to *the* extremity of heaven."

The Lesson of the Fig Tree

(Mt 24:32-35, LK 21:29-33)

13:28. "But you learned from the parable of the fig tree: when its branch would already be tender and the leaves would grow out, you know that summer is near: 29. in this way also you, when you would see these things happening, you know that it is near at *the* doors. 30. Truly I say to you that this generation would **not** pass until all these things would happen. 31. The sky and Earth will pass away, but My words will **not ever** pass away."

The Unknown Day and Hour

(Mt 24:36-44)

13:32. "But concerning that Day and the hour no one knows, not even the angels in heaven and not the Son, only the Father. 33. You must watch out! You must continually be alert: for you do not know when the time is. 34. As a man went away to a foreign country, having left his house, after he gave authority to his servants for each *to do* his work, then he commanded the doorkeeper that he should be watchful. 35. Therefore you must constantly be watchful: for you do not know when the master of the house is coming, either evening or midnight or when the cock crows or morning, 36. *so that* if he comes suddenly he would not find you sleeping. 37. And I say this to you, I say to all *of you*, you must be continually watchful."

The Plot to Kill Jesus

(Mt 26:1-5, Lk 22:1,2, Jn 11:45-53)

14.1. And it was two days before Passover and the *Feast of* Unleavened Bread. And the high priests and the scribes were seeking in treachery, how, after they arrested Him, they would kill *Him*: 2. but they were saying, "Not during the Feast, lest there will be an uproar of the people."

The Anointing at Bethany

(Mt 26:6-13, Jn 12:1-8)

14:3. And when He was in Bethany[1] in the house of Simon the leper,[2] while He was reclining, a woman came *who* had an alabaster flask of genuine costly nard perfume, *and* after she broke the flask she poured *the perfume* on His

---

1   (v.3) Bethany is the Greek spelling of Beit-Anyah, meaning House of Sighing in Hebrew.
2   (v.3) Simon is a former leper who has been cleansed, or people could not have come into his home. See Cleanse in Glossary. This is not the disease called leprosy today. See Leprosy in Glossary.

head. 4. And some among them were indignant, "For what *reason* has this waste of ointment been made? 5. For it was possible *for* this perfume to have been sold for more than three hundred denarii[1] and to have been given to the poor:" and they were scolding her. 6. But Jesus said "You must permit her: why are you causing trouble for her? She was doing a good deed[2] for Me. 7. For you always have the poor with you (Dt 15:11) and whenever you would want you are able to do well for them, but you do not always have Me. 8. She did what she was able: she took it upon herself to anoint My body in preparation for burial. 9. And truly I say to you, wherever the Good News would be proclaimed in the whole world, then what she did will be spoken in her memory."

Judas' Agreement to Betray Jesus

(Mt 26:14-16, Lk 22:3-6)

14:10. And Judas Iscariot, one of the twelve, went to the high priests so that he might hand Him over to them. 11. And when they heard they rejoiced and they promised to give him money. Then he was seeking how he might conveniently hand Him over.

The Seder[3] with the Disciples

(Mt 26:17-25, Lk 22:7-14, 21-23, Jn 13:21-30)

14:12. And *before*[4] the first day of the Feast of Unleavened Bread, when they killed the Passover, (Lk 22:7) His disciples said to Him, "After we leave, where do You want us to prepare so that You could eat the Seder?" 13. And He sent two of His disciples and He said to them, "You must go into the city, and a man carrying an earthen vessel of water will meet you: you must follow him 14. and wherever he would enter you must say to the master of the house that 'The Teacher says, "Where is My dining room where I could eat the Seder with My disciples?"' 15. And he will show you a large upper room furnished *and* ready: and there you must prepare for us." 16. And the disciples left and came into the city and found just as He said to them and they prepared the Seder. 17. And when it became evening He came with the twelve. 18. And while they were reclining and eating Jesus said, "Truly I say to you that one of you who is eating with Me will give Me over." 19. They began to be distressed and to say to Him one by one, "It is not I?" 20. And He said to them, "One of the twelve, the one who is dipping with Me into the bowl. 21. Because on the one hand the Son of Man goes just as it has been written concerning Him, but on the other hand, woe to that man through whom the Son of Man is given over: *it would be* better for him if that man would not have been born."

---

1 (v.5) About a year's wages
2 (v.6) Mitsvah, see Mitsvah in Glossary.
3 (Caption) The Passover meal. See Seder in Glossary.
4 (v.12) The Greek text actually says "on the first day" which cannot be since the Passover lamb has to be killed before the start of Unleavened Bread. See Preparation Day in Glossary.

The Seder

(Mt 26:26-30, Lk 22:15-20, 1Cor 11:23-25)

14:22. And when they ate, after He took bread *and* praised God, He broke *it* and He gave *it* to them, then said, "You must take *this*, this is My body." 23. And having taken a cup, after giving thanks He gave *it* to them, and they all drank from it. 24. And He said to them "This is My blood of the covenant which is being poured out on behalf of many. (Ex 24:8, Zch 9:11) 25. Truly I say to you that **never again** am I drinking from the fruit of the vine until that day when I drink it new in the kingdom of God." 26. And after they sang *the Hallel*[1] they went to the Mount of Olives.

Peter's Denial Foretold

(Mt 26:31-35, Lk 22:31-34, Jn 13:36-38)

14:27. And Jesus said to them "You all will fall away, for it has been written,

'I will smite the shepherd,[2]
and the sheep will be scattered.' (Zch 13:7)

28. But, after I am raised up, I shall go before you into Galilee." 29. And Peter said to Him, "Even if all will fall away, I *will* not." 30. And Jesus said to him, "Truly I say to you that today, this night, before a cock crows twice, you will deny Me three times." 31. And he said with great emphasis, "If it would be necessary for me to die with You, I will **not** deny You." And then all were saying likewise.

The Prayer in Gethsemane

(Mt 26:36-46, Lk 22:39-46)

14:32. And they came into a place which is named Gethsemane and He said to His disciples, "You must sit here while I am praying." 33. And He took Peter and Jacob and John with Him and He began to be distressed and to be troubled 34. and He said to them, "My inner being is deeply grieved even to death, *so that I almost died*: you must remain here and you must be continually watchful." 35. And then He went ahead a little *and* fell on the ground and was praying that, if it were possible, the hour would pass away from Him, 36. and He was saying "Abba, Father, in You all things *are* possible: You must take this cup away from Me: but not what I want but what You *want*." 37. And He came and found them sleeping, and He said to Peter, "Simon, are you sleeping? Are you not strong enough to be watchful for one hour? 38. You must faithfully be watchful and you must continually pray, so that you would not come into temptation: the spirit *is* indeed willing but the flesh *is* weak." 39. And again, when He left He prayed, saying the same message. 40. And when He came again He found them

---

1   (v.26) Singing the Hallel, Ps 113-118, is part of the Seder. See Hallel in Glossary.
2   (v.27) For a description of the Shepherd, see Son of David/Son of Joseph in Glossary.

sleeping, for their eyes were burdened and they had not known what they should answer Him. 41. And He came the third *time* and He said to them, "You must sleep. From now on you must also rest:[1] it is received in full: the hour has come, behold, the Son of Man is being given over into the hands of the sinners. 42. Get up, let us go: behold, the one who is giving Me over has drawn near."

The Betrayal and Arrest of Jesus

(Mt 26:47-56, Lk 22:47-53, Jn 18:3-12)

14:43. And immediately, while He was still speaking, Judas, one of the twelve, arrived and with him a crowd with swords[2] and clubs beside the high priests and the scribes and the elders. 44. And the one who betrayed Him gave them a signal, saying, "Whomever I would kiss is He, you must seize Him and you must lead *Him* away securely." 45. And immediately after he came, as he was approaching he said to Him, "Rabbi," and he kissed Him: 46. and they put their hands on Him and arrested Him. 47. And when one of those who were present drew his sword, he struck the servant of the high priest and took off his ear. 48. And Jesus said to them, "Did you come out as upon a robber with swords and clubs to arrest Me? 49. Day by day I was with you in the temple teaching and you did not arrest Me: but so that the Scriptures would be fulfilled." 50. And all, having left Him, fled.

The Young Man Who Fled

14:51. And *there was* a young man, wearing a linen tunic over *his* poorly dressed body, who was following Him, and they seized him: 52. but having left the tunic he fled poorly dressed.[3]

Jesus before the Council

(Mt 26:57-68, Lk 22:54,55, 63-71, Jn 18:13,14, 19-24)

14:53. And they led Jesus away to the High Priest, and all the high priests and the elders and the scribes gathered together. 54. And Peter followed Him from afar as far as inside the courtyard of the High Priest and he was sitting together with the servants and warming himself by the fire. 55. And the high priests and the whole Sanhedrin were seeking testimony against Jesus to put Him to death, but they were not able to find any: 56. for many were bearing false witness against Him, but the witnesses were not in agreement. 57. And when some stood up they were testifying falsely against Him saying 58. that "We heard Him saying, 'I will destroy this sanctuary made with hands and during three days I will build another not made by hands'" 59. but their testimony was just not in agreement. 60. And the High Priest, when he got up in the middle, asked Jesus, saying, "Are You not answering anything that these are testifying against You?"

---

1   (v.41) This rest is a short break.
2   (v.43) These are the small personal swords.
3   (v.52) In the Hebrew idiom this would be in undergarments because wearing only a loincloth was called "being naked."

61. And He was silent and did not answer anything. Again the High Priest was asking Him and said to Him, "Are You the Messiah, the Son of the Blessed?" 62. And Jesus said, "I AM,

> and 'You will see the Son of Man
> sitting at the right hand[1] of the Power (Ps 110:1)
> and coming with the clouds of the sky.'" (Dn 7:13)

63. And the High Priest, as he tore his clothes said, "Why do we still have need of witnesses? 64. You heard the blasphemy: what does it seem to you?" And they all condemned Him guilty, to be *put to* death. 65. And some began to spit on Him and to cover His face and to beat Him and to say to Him, "You must prophesy," and the servants slapped Him.

Peter's Denial of Jesus

(Mt 26:69-75, Lk 22:56-62, Jn 18:15-18, 25-27)

14:66. And while Peter was below in the courtyard one of the maids of the High Priest came 67. and as she saw Peter warming himself, after she looked at him, she said, "And you were with Jesus of Nazareth." 68. But he denied *it*, saying, "I neither know nor understand what you are saying." And he went outside into the gateway and a rooster crowed.[2] 69. And when the maid saw him she again began to say to those present that "This is *one* of them." 70. And he was again denying *it*. And after a little while those present were saying again to Peter, "Truly you are from them, for you too are from Galilee." 71. But he began to bind with an oath and to swear that "I do not know this man *of* Whom you speak." 72. And immediately a cock crowed a second *time*.[3] Then Peter was reminded of the statement just as Jesus told him that "Before a cock crows twice you will deny Me three times:" and putting his mind to *Jesus' word* he was weeping.

Jesus before Pilate

(Mt 27:1,2, 11-14, Lk 23:1-5, Jn 18:28-38)

15.1. And, as soon as morning came, the high priests, as they had made a plan with the elders and scribes and *the* whole Sanhedrin, having bound Jesus, they led *Him* and gave *Him* over to Pilate. 2. And Pilate asked Him, "Are You King of the Jewish People?" And He said to him, "You are saying *it*." 3. And the high priests were accusing Him of many things. 4. And Pilate again was asking Him saying, "Do You not answer anything? See how much they are accusing You." 5. But Jesus did not respond in any way, so to amaze Pilate.

---

1 (v.62) "At the right hand" is a Hebrew idiom that speaks of power and strength, from Ex 15:6. See Right Hand in Glossary.

2 (v.68) "and a rooster crowed" is not in the oldest nearly complete manuscript, Alef, as well as others.

3 (v.72) The "cock crowed a second time" is not in Alef, the oldest nearly complete manuscript, and other manuscripts.

Jesus Sentenced to Die

(Mt 27:15-26, Lk 23:13-25, Jn 18:39-19:16)

15:6. And in accordance with *the* feast he was to free for them one prisoner for whom they were asking. 7. And one called Barabbas was with the rebels, a prisoner who had committed murder in the insurrection. 8. And when the crowd went up they began to ask *for a prisoner* just as *Pilate* was *used to* doing for them. 9. And Pilate asked them saying, "Do you want me to free the King of the Jewish People for you?" 10. For he knew that the high priests had given Him over because of envy. 11. But the high priests stirred up the crowd[1] more so that he would set Barabbas free for them. 12. And Pilate, asking again, was saying to them, "Therefore whom do you say? What do you want me to do *with* the King of the Jewish People?" 13. And again they were crying out, "You must crucify Him now!" 14. And Pilate was saying to them, "What evil did He do?" But they cried out more, "You must crucify Him!" 15. And Pilate, wishing to satisfy the crowd, freed Barabbas to them, and after he scourged *Him* he gave Jesus over so that He could be crucified.

The Soldiers Mock Jesus

(Mt 27:27-31, Jn 19:2,3)

15:16. And the soldiers led Him inside the courtyard which is the governor's residence, and they summoned the whole cohort.[2] 17. And they put a purple garment[3] on Him, then placed a thorny woven crown on Him: 18. and they began to greet Him, "Hail, King of the Jewish People!" 19. And they were striking His head with a reed and spitting on Him and as they knelt they were paying homage to Him. 20. And when they *had* mocked Him, they stripped Him of *the* purple garment and they placed His own garments on Him. And they led Him away so that they could crucify Him.

The Crucifixion of Jesus

(Mt 27:32-44, Lk 23:26-43, Jn 19:17-27)

15:21. And they forced a certain Simon, a Cyrenean passing by, coming from a field, the father of Alexander and Rufus, to carry His cross. 22. And they brought Him to the place Golgotha, which is translated "Place of the Skull." 23. And they were giving Him wine mixed with myrrh: which He did not take. 24. And they crucified Him

"And they divided His garments
casting lots over them, who would take which." (Ps 22:18)

25. And it was the third hour[4] and they crucified Him. 26. And the inscription of

---

1   (v.11) The high priests and this crowd were all Hellenists. See Hellenists in Glossary.
2   (v.16) About 600 men
3   (v.17) Purple signifies royalty.
4   (v.25) 9:00 AM

His charge was written, "The King of the Jewish People." 27. And they crucified two robbers with Him, one on *His* right and one on His left.[1] 29. And those who went by were blaspheming Him, moving their heads and saying, "Ha, the One Who is tearing down the sanctuary[2] and building *it* in three days, 30. You must save Yourself by coming down from the cross." 31. Likewise also the high priests were saying, as they were mocking with one another *along* with the scribes, "He saved others, He is not able to save Himself: 32. the Messiah, the King of Israel, must now come down from the cross, so that we would see and we would believe." And those who were crucified with Him were reproaching Him.

The Death of Jesus

(Mt 27:45-56, Lk 23:44-49, Jn 19:28-30)

15:33. And when it was the sixth hour[3] it became dark upon the whole Earth until *the* ninth hour.[4] 34. And at the ninth hour Jesus cried out, *in Hebrew*, in a loud voice, "Elohi. Elohi! L'mah azavtani?"[5] (Ps 22:1) Which is translated "My God, My God, why have You utterly forsaken Me?" 35. And when some of those who were standing by heard they were saying, "Behold He is calling Elijah." 36. And someone, having run up, then having filled a sponge with wine vinegar, after he placed *it* on a reed, was giving it *to Him* to drink, *someone else* saying, "Wait, let us see if Elijah is coming to take *Him* down." 37. Then Jesus, as He uttered a loud cry, expired. 38. And the veil of the sanctuary was split in two from top to bottom. 39. And when the centurion, who was standing by opposite Him, saw that He expired in this way he said, "Truly this man was the Son of God." 40. And some women were looking on from afar, among whom were also Mary Magdalene, and Mary, the mother of Jacob the small and Joey,[6] and Salome. 41. When those *women* were in Galilee they were following[7] Him and were serving[8] Him, and *there were also* many other women who came up to Jerusalem with Him.

The Burial of Jesus

(Mt 27:57-61, Lk 23:50-56, Jn 19:38-42)

15:42. And now when it became evening, since it was the day of preparation,[9] that is the day before a Sabbath, 43. Joseph from Arimathea, a

---

1   (v.27) V. 28 is omitted because it is not in the oldest manuscripts.
2   (v.29) The sanctuary contains both the Holy Place and the Holy of Holies. See Sanctuary in Glossary.
3   (v.33) Noon
4   (v.33) 3:00 PM
5   (v.34) Azavtani is the correct English spelling of the Hebrew word used in Ps 22. The Greek text uses the Greek spelling of the Hebrew word, which in English is sh'vaktani or s'vaktani.
6   (v.40) The Greek text has the name Iosetos, a nickname for Joseph, with Yossi the Hebrew and Joey the English equivalent. (See Mk 6:3)
7   (v.41) This means they were His disciples.
8   (v.41) This could be translated "..ministering with Him."
9   (v.42) See Preparation Day in Glossary.

prominent member of the Sanhedrin who also was anticipating the kingdom of God, summoned up courage and went to Pilate and asked for the body of Jesus. 44. And Pilate wondered if He had already died and after he summoned the centurion he asked him if He was already dead: 45. and when he knew from the centurion, he gave the corpse to Joseph. 46. And since he had bought linen, when he took Him down, he wrapped *Him* in linen and placed Him in a tomb, which was hewn out of rock, and he rolled up a stone across the door of the tomb. 47. And Mary Magdalene and Mary *mother of* Joey[1] were watching where He was placed.

The Resurrection[2] of Jesus

(Mt 28:1-8, Lk 24:1-12, Jn 20:1-10)

16.1. And, after the Sabbath passed, Mary Magdalene and Mary, *mother of* Jacob, and Salome bought spices so that when they came they could anoint Him.[3] 2. And very early in the morning on the First Day of the Week,[4] they came to the tomb *as* the sun was rising. 3. And they were saying among themselves, "Who will roll away the stone from the door of the tomb for us?" 4. And when they looked up they saw that the stone had been rolled away: for it was extremely large. 5. And after they entered the tomb they saw a young man sitting on the right side wearing a white robe,[5] and they were distressed. 6. And he said to them, "Stop being distressed! You are seeking Jesus of Nazareth, the One Who was crucified: He is risen, He is not here: see the place where they put Him. 7. But you must now go, say to His disciples and to Peter, that 'He is to go before you into Galilee: you will see Him there just as He told you.'" 8. And after they went out they fled from the tomb, for they were quite beside themselves trembling with amazement: and they did not say anything: for they were afraid.[6]

---

1   (v.47) See note for v. 40, above.

2   (Caption) See Resurrection in Glossary.

3   (v.1) Their bringing spices is unusual because women would never anoint a man's corpse, nor would men anoint a woman's. See Jn 19:38-40, which says that Nicodemus brought 100 pounds of spices when he and Joseph prepared the body.

4   (v.2) First Day of the Week is the Hebrew expression for Sunday.

5   (v.5) White garments represent being in a state of spiritual preparedness, from Ecc 9:8, "Let your garments be always white; and let your head lack no ointment."

6   (v.8) The earliest manuscripts of the Book of Mark end here.

~ ACCORDING TO LUKE[1] ~

Dedication to Theophilus[2]

1.1. Since many set their hands to organize a narrative concerning the matters that have been accomplished among us, 2. just as the eye-witnesses *with Him* from the beginning gave over to us *who were* then becoming servants of the message, 3. and it seemed to me, after I carefully investigated everything successively from the beginning, that I should write to you, most excellent Theopholis, 4. so that you would understand the certainty about the things which you were instructed.

The Birth of John the Baptist Foretold

1:5. In the days of King Herod of Judea there was a certain priest named Zechariah from *the* division Abijah,[3] and his wife *was* of the daughters of Aaron and her name *was* Elizabeth.[4] 6. And they both were righteous before God, going blameless in all the commandments and requirements of the Lord. 7. But there was not a child for them because Elizabeth was barren, and both were advanced in their days. 8. And he was in the office of the priest in the succession of his division before God, 9. according to the custom of the service, appointed to burn incense when he entered the sanctuary[5] of the Lord, 10. and all the multitude of people was outside, praying at the hour of the incense.[6] 11. And an angel of the Lord appeared to him, standing by the right of the altar of incense. 12. And when

---

1   (Title) Written about 59-63 AD, the book of Luke uses many medical terms. There are more healings, not just more technical terms in Luke than in any other Gospel. Luke also includes more allusions and more incidents or events, but there is less detail in any one incident than in Matthew. Compare the Beatitudes and the Lord's Prayer in Luke and in Matthew to see this. His style of writing concentrates on facts. See Book Order in Glossary.

2   (Caption) Theopholis means 'loves God' in Greek. Whether this letter is to a person named Theopholis or to believers is not clear, but the prevailing view is that it is to a person.

3   (v.5) Abijah was one of twenty-four divisions of the Aaronic priesthood. See Division of Abijah in Glossary.

4   (v.5) Elizabeth is taken from the Greek spelling of the Hebrew name Elisheva, which was also the name of Aaron's wife.

5   (v.9) The Greek word naos, meaning sanctuary, is often translated temple, but sanctuary is correct. See Sanctuary in Glossary.

6   (v.10) The hour of incense refers to one of the two times each day that incense was burned in the Holy Place. Ex 30:7, 8 order the burning of the incense in the morning when the priest dresses the lamps and afternoon when he lights the lamps.

Zechariah saw *him* he was disturbed and fear fell upon him. 13. And the angel said to him, "Do not fear, Zechariah, because your entreaty has been listened to and your wife Elizabeth will bear a son to you and you will call his name John. 14. And for you there will be joy and gladness and many will rejoice over his birth. 15. For he will be great before the Lord, and he should **not** drink wine or strong drink, and he will be filled with *the* Holy Spirit while he is still in his mother's womb, 16. and he will return many of the children of Israel to *the* Lord their God. 17. And he will go before Him in *the* spirit and power of Elijah, he will cause *the* hearts of fathers to return to *their* children and *the* disobedient to an understanding of righteousness, to prepare a people being made ready by *the* Lord." (Mal 4:5,6) 18. Then Zechariah said to the angel, "How will I know this? For I am an old man and my wife *is* advanced in her days." 19. And the angel said to him, "I am Gabriel, the one who stands before God, and I was sent to speak to you and to give you this good news: 20. now behold, you will be silent and not able to speak until the day these things happen because you did not believe my words, which will be fulfilled in their time."

1:21. And the people were expecting Zechariah and they were wondering what was delaying him in the sanctuary. 22. But when he came out he was not able to speak to them, and they understood that he had seen a vision in the sanctuary: and he was beckoning to them and was remaining mute. 23. And it happened as the days of his service were completed he went to his house. 24. And after these days Elizabeth his wife conceived and she concealed herself five months saying, 25. "Thus *the* Lord has done for me, in *the* days in which He considered to take away my reproach among men."

The Birth of Jesus Foretold

1:26. And in the sixth month *of her pregnancy* the angel Gabriel was sent down from God to a city of Galilee by the name of Nazareth, 27. to a virgin betrothed to a man by the name of Joseph out of *the* house of David, and the name of the virgin *was* Mary.[1] 28. And when he came to her he said, "Hail, highly favored *one*, the Lord *is* with you." 29. But she was confused over the message and was wondering what sort of greeting this might be. 30. And the angel said to her, "Do not be afraid, Mary, for you have found favor with God. 31. And behold you will conceive in *your* womb and you will bear a Son and will call His name Jesus.[2] 32. This One will be great and He will be called Son of *the* Most High, and *the* Lord God will give Him the throne of David His father, 33. and He will reign over the house of Jacob forever, and His kingdom will not end." 34. And Mary said to the angel, "How will this be, since I have not had intimacy with a husband?" 35. Then the angel said to her, "*The* Holy Spirit will come upon you and power of *the* Most High will cover you: for this reason then

---

1   (v.27) Mary is the English spelling of the Latin Maria. The Greek spelling is Mariam. See Section II in Glossary for more on names.

2   (v.31) See Jesus in Glossary.

the Holy One Who is birthed will be called *the* Son of God. 36. And behold your kin Elizabeth has also conceived a son in her old age and this is her sixth month *from* her being called barren: 37. because with God nothing is impossible." (Gn 18:14 Jr 32:17, 27, Job 42:2) 38. And Mary said, "Behold the servant of *the* Lord: may it be according to your word." Then the angel left from her.

Mary Visits Elizabeth

1:39. And when Mary rose in those days she went with haste into the hill country to a city of Judea, 40. and she entered the house of Zechariah and greeted Elizabeth. 41. Then it happened as Elizabeth heard Mary's greeting, the infant in her womb leaped, and Elizabeth was filled with the Holy Spirit, 42. then she cried out in a great shout and said, "Blessed are you among women and blessed *is* the fruit of your womb. 43. And why *is* this with me that the mother of my Lord would come to me? 44. For behold as the sound of your greeting came into my ears, the infant in my womb leaped in exultation. 45. And blessed *is* she who believed that there will be fulfillment for what has been spoken to her by *the* Lord."

Mary's Song of Praise

1:46. Then Mary said,

47.   "My very being magnifies the Lord,
            and my spirit rejoiced on account of God my Savior,
48.   because He looked upon the humble station of His servant.
            For behold from now *on* all generations will bless me,
49.   because the Almighty did great things for me.
            And His name *is* Holy,
50.   and His mercy *is* for generation after generation
            with those who fear Him.
51.   He did mighty deeds with His arm,
            He scattered *the* proud with their understanding hearts:
52.   He pulled down rulers from thrones
            and He raised up *the* lowly,
53.   He filled *those* who hungered with goods
            and sent away empty *those* who were rich.
54.   He helped His child Israel,
            by remembering mercy,
55.   just as He spoke to our fathers,
            to Abraham and to his seed forever."

56. And Mary remained with her about three months, then she returned to her house.[1]

---

1   (v.56) It was a custom in the Middle East to have complete rest during the first three months of pregnancy.

The Birth of John the Baptist

1:57. And the time for Elizabeth to bear was completed for her and she gave birth to a son. 58. And the neighbors and her kin heard that *the* Lord showed her great mercy, and they were rejoicing with her. 59. And it happened on the eighth day they came to circumcise the boy and they were calling him by the name of his father Zechariah. 60. Then his mother said, "No, but he will be called John." 61. And they said to her "There is no one of your kin who is called by this name." 62. But they were nodding to his father *to see* whatever he might want *him* to be called. 63. Then after he asked for a writing tablet he wrote saying, "His name is John." And all were amazed. 64. Then at once his mouth and his tongue were opened, and he was speaking, praising God. 65. And reverential fear came upon all those who lived around them, and in the whole hill country of Judea they were discussing all these reports, 66. and all those who heard kept saying in their hearts, "So what will this child be?" For indeed the hand of the Lord was with him.

The Prophecy of Zechariah

1:67. Then Zechariah his father was filled with the Holy Spirit and he prophesied saying,

68.   "The Lord God of Israel be praised, (Ps 41:13, 72:12, 106:48)
            because He looked upon and made redemption for His people, (Ps 111:9)

69.   and He raised a horn of salvation for us, (Ps 18:2)
            in *the* house of His child David,

70.   just as He spoke through *the* mouth of His holy prophets
            from the earliest times,

71.   salvation from our enemies and out of *the* hand
            of all those who hate us, (Ps 106:10)

72.   to show mercy with our fathers
            and His holy covenant *is* to be remembered, (Ps 106:45,46)

73.   *the* oath which He swore to our father Abraham, (Ps 105:8,9, Gn 17:7)
            to give to us 74. when without fear we were
                rescued out of *the* hand of enemies (Gn 22:16,17)
        to serve Him 75. in piety and righteousness
            before Him all our days.

76.   And also you, child, will be called 'Prophet of the Most High:'
            for you will go on before *the* Lord to prepare His ways,[1] (Is 40:3, Mal 3:1)

77.   to give knowledge of salvation to His people
            in forgiveness of their sins,

78.   because of the inner kindness of mercies of our God,

---

1   (v.76) To get us ready for His manner of thinking, course of conduct

with which *mercies* the rising sun looks down upon us
from on high, (Mal 4:2)

79.   to bring light to those in darkness and sitting in *the* shadow of death,
        to direct our feet into *the* way of peace." (Is 9:2, 58:8, and
        60:1,2)

1:80. And the child grew and was becoming strong in spirit, and he was in the desert places until *the* day of his commissioning to Israel.

The Birth of Jesus

(Mt 1:18-25)

2.1. And it happened in those days there came out a decree from Caesar Augustus[1] to register all the inhabited world. 2. This first census was while Quirinius was governing Syria. 3. And all were going to be registered, each to his own city. 4. And Joseph went up from Galilee from *the* city of Nazareth[2] to Judea to a city of David, which is called Bethlehem,[3] because he was out of *the* house and clan of David, 5. to be registered with Mary, *who* was big with child, to whom he had become betrothed. 6. And it happened while they were there the days were completed for her to bear the child. 7. And she delivered her son, the Firstborn, and she wrapped Him and she laid Him in a manger,[4] because there was not a place for them in the inn.

The Shepherds and the Angels

2:8. And shepherds were in this field, living out of doors and keeping watch by night over their flock.[5] 9. And an angel of *the* Lord appeared to them and *the* glory of the Lord shone around them, and they feared a great fear. 10. Then the angel said to them, "You must not be afraid, for behold I have good news for you, great joy which will be for all the people, 11. because this day in *the* city of David a Savior was born for you, Who is Messiah, Lord. 12. And this *will be* a sign to you, you will find an infant wrapped and lying in a stall." 13. Then suddenly there were with the angel a great number of *the* heavenly hosts[6] praising God and saying,

14.   "Glory to God in *the* highest
        and on Earth peace *and* good will among men."

---

1   (v.1) Caesar Augustus reigned from 27 BC to 14 AD.
2   (v.4) The Hebrew name is Natseret, meaning shoot or branch, as in Is 11:1.
3   (v.4) Bethlehem is the Greek spelling of the Hebrew name, Beit-Lekhem, meaning House of Bread. In what more appropriate place could He have been born, the One Who said, "for the bread of God is that which descends from heaven and gives life to the world." (Jn 6:33)
4   (v.7) The Hebrew translation of this Greek word means stall, but He likely was placed in a manger (feed box) that was in the stall.
5   (v.8) This makes a December birth date very unlikely, because the shepherds would not have been living in the field. See Division of Abijah in Glossary.
6   (v.13) Literally the "soldiers of heaven" referring to the army that Elisha saw at Dothan (2Ki 6:16, 17) and to the Lord Tsvaot, the Lord of Hosts.

2:15. And it happened as the angels left from them into heaven, the shepherds were saying to one another, "We should now go to Bethlehem so we could see what this report is which the Lord revealed to us." 16. Then hastening they came and they looked for Mary and Joseph and the infant lying in the stall: 17. and after they saw *them* they made known about the message spoken to them concerning this child. 18. And all those who heard were amazed about the things that were told them by the shepherds: 19. and Mary was treasuring all these words, considering *them* in her heart. 20. Then the shepherds returned glorifying and praising God over all that they heard and saw just as it was spoken to them.

2:21. And when *the* eight days were completed to circumcise Him (Lv 12:2,3) His name was called Jesus,[1] being called that by the angel to the one who conceived Him in her womb.

The Presentation of Jesus in the Temple

2:22. And when the days of their purification[2] were completed according to the Torah[3] of Moses, they brought Him up to Jerusalem to present *Him* to the Lord, 23. just as it has been written in *the* Torah of *the* Lord that "Every male opening the womb will be called holy to the Lord," (Ex 13:2, 12, 15) 24. and to give an offering according to that which was said in the Torah of *the* Lord, "A pair of turtledoves, or two young doves."

2:25. And behold a man by the name of Simeon[4] was in Jerusalem and this righteous and devout man was waiting for *the* Comforter of Israel, and *the* Holy Spirit was upon him: 26. and it was revealed to him by the Holy Spirit that he would not see death before he would see the Messiah of *the* Lord. 27. And he came into the temple in the Spirit: and His parents brought in the child Jesus for them to do according to the custom of the Torah concerning Him 28. and he took Him in his arms and praised God and said,

29.　　 "Now You are releasing Your servant, Lord,
　　　　　 in peace according to Your word:
30.　　 because my eyes have seen Your Salvation,
31.　　　　 the One You prepared before *the* face of all the people,
32.　　 a Light in revelation for *the* heathens
　　　　　 and *the* Glory of Your people Israel."

33. And His father and mother were amazed over what was spoken concerning Him. 34. Then Simeon blessed them and said to Mary His mother, "Behold this One is appointed for *the* fall and rising of many in Israel and for a sign *that* is

---

1　　　 (v.19) Y'shua in Hebrew. See Jesus in Glossary.
2　　　 (v.22) Lv 12:2 sets a 7 day period and v.4 sets a 33 day period for a total of 40 days.
3　　　 (v.22) Torah means teaching or instruction. See Torah in Glossary.
4　　　 (v.25) The Hebrew name is Sh'mon, sometimes written in Greek as Simeon, which is the way it is written in 2 Pe 1:1. Other times it is written as Simon. See Names and Section II in Glossary.

opposed 35. - but then for you a sword[1] will pierce your own inner being too, - as thoughts of many hearts would be revealed."

2:36. And Anna[2] was a prophetess, daughter of Phanuel, from *the* tribe of Asher: she had gone forward many days, living with a husband seven years from her virginity[3] 37. and she *was* a widow until eighty-four years. She did not leave the temple, while she was serving night and day in fasting and prayer. 38. And at this time she was standing and giving thanks to God and speaking about Him to all those who were waiting for *the* redemption *of* Jerusalem.

The Return to Nazareth

2:39. And as they completed everything according to the Torah of *the* Lord, they returned to Galilee, to their own city, Nazareth.[4] 40. And the child grew and was becoming strong, being filled with wisdom, and *the* favor of God was upon Him.

The Boy Jesus in the Temple

2:41. And His parents were going to Jerusalem from year to year to the Feast of Passover. 42. And when He was twelve years *old*, they went up for the feast according to their custom *and for His Bar Mitzvah*[5] 43. and when the days were completed, on their return the child Jesus remained in Jerusalem, but His parents did not know *that*. 44. And thinking He was in the caravan they came a day *on the* way[6] and they were searching *for* Him among their relatives and acquaintances, 45. but when they did not find Him they returned to Jerusalem looking for Him. 46. Then it happened after three days they found Him in the temple, sitting in the middle of the teachers and listening to them and questioning[7] them: 47. and all those who heard Him were amazed over His understanding and answers. 48. And when they saw Him they were amazed, and His mother said to Him, "Child, why did You do this to us? Look, Your father and I *were* suffering *while* we were searching for You." 49. Then He said to them, "Why were you seeking Me? Had you not known that it was necessary for Me to be among these of My Father?" 50. And they did not understand the answer that He spoke to them. 51. Then He went down with them and came into Nazareth and was subject to them. And His mother was keeping all the words in her heart. 52. And Jesus was progressing in wisdom and stature and favor before God and men.

---

1   (v.35) This sword is the very heavy sword used by barbarians.
2   (v.36) The Greek text has the name "Hanna," the same as Samuel's mother in 1 Sa.
3   (v.36) Marriage
4   (v.39) Nazareth is Natseret in Hebrew, meaning shoot or branch as in Is 11:1.
5   (v.42) This refers to the service at which a Jewish boy assumes the religious responsibilities of an adult. The present service called Bar Mitzvah was instituted some time after Jesus' death.
6   (v.44) When traveling, the women and children walked in the center of the group, while the men split, with half walking in front and half behind for protection. On the way to Jerusalem He walked with the women and children, but on the return, after His admission to adulthood, He would have walked with the men, so Joseph had assumed He was with the other group of men.
7   (v.46) Many of His answers could have been in the form of questions, still a common form for Torah study.

The Preaching of John the Baptist

(Mt 3:1-12, Mk 1:1-18, Jn 1:19-28)

3.1. And in *the* fifteenth year of the reign of Tiberius Caesar,[1] while Pontius Pilate was governor of Judea, and Herod *was* the tetrarch of Galilee, and Philip his brother *was* the tetrarch of *the* countries of Iturea and Trachonitid, and Lysansias the tetrarch of Abilene, 2. during *the* High Priesthood of Annas and Caiaphas, a message from God came upon John, the son of Zechariah, in the desert. 3. And he came into all the neighboring region of the Jordan preaching *the* baptism of repentance for forgiveness of sins, 4. as it has been written in a scroll of *the* words of Isaiah the prophet,

"A voice crying in the wilderness,
You must immediately prepare the way of *the* Lord,
　　you must continually make His paths straight:
5.　　every ravine will be filled
　　　　and every mountain and hill will be made low,
　　and the crooked will be straight
　　　　and the rough into smooth ways
6.　　and all flesh will see the salvation of God." (Is 40:3-5)

3:7. Therefore he was saying to the crowds that went out to be baptized[2] under him,[3] "Offspring of vipers, who showed to you to flee from the coming wrath? 8. Therefore you must now produce fruit worthy of repentance and do not be led to say among yourselves, 'We have father Abraham.' For I say to you that God is able to raise up children for Abraham from these stones. 9. But the ax is already being laid to the root of the trees: therefore every tree not making good fruit is cut down and cast into a fire." 10. Then the crowds were asking him saying, "Therefore what should we do?" 11. And he was saying to them, "The one who has two tunics must share with the one who has none, and the one who has food must do likewise." 12. And even tax collectors came to be baptized and said to him, "Teacher, what should we do?" 13. And he said to them, "And you must collect no more than what has been ordered to you." 14. And even *those* serving as soldiers were asking him saying, "Now what should we do?" And he said to them, "Do not extort money by violence and do not falsely accuse and you must be satisfied with your pay."

3:15. And the people looked for and considered everything in their hearts concerning John, whether he could be the Messiah. 16. John answered saying to all, "Indeed I baptize you in water: but One mightier than I is coming, I am not worthy to loose the thong of His sandals: He will baptize you in *the* Holy Spirit

---

1　　(v.1) Tiberius Caesar reigned from 14 AD to 37 AD.
2　　(v.7) This is the Greek word baptidzo, meaning to immerse. Immersion for purification had been a Jewish custom for more than 1,000 years by this time. See Baptize in Glossary.
3　　(v.7) Although often translated "baptized by him," it is speaking of the response to his message, because Jewish baptism was and still is self-immersion. See Baptize in Glossary.

and fire: 17. His winnowing shovel *is* in His hand to clean out His threshing floor and to gather the wheat into His storehouse, but He will burn up the chaff in unquenchable fire." 18. Therefore with much other urging he was indeed preaching the Good News to the people. 19. But Herod the Tetrarch, being called to account by him concerning Herodiah his brother's wife and concerning all *the* evils which Herod did, 20. then added this to all those *evils* and locked up John in prison.

The Baptism of Jesus

(Mt 3:13-17, Mk 1:9-11)

3:21. And it was while all the people *were* being baptized,[1] Jesus was also baptized and while He was praying heaven opened 22. and the Holy Spirit descended upon Him in bodily form like a dove, and a voice came out of heaven, "You are My beloved Son, I have been well pleased with You."[2]

The Genealogy of Jesus[3]

(Mt 1:1-17)

3:23. Then Jesus was beginning *His ministry* at about thirty years *old*,[4] being a Son, as it was thought, of Joseph[5] *son* of Eli[6] 24. of Matthat of Levi of Melchi of Jannai of Joseph 25. of Mattathias of Amos of Nahum of Esli of Naggai 26. of Maath of Mattathias of Semein of Josech of Joda 27. of Joanan of Rhesa of Zerubbabel of Shealtiel of Neri 28. of Melchi of Addi of Cosam of Elmadam of Er 29. of Jesus of Eliezer of Jorim of Matthat of Levi 30. of Symeon of Judas of Joseph of Jonam of Eliakim 31. of Maleah of Menna of Mattatha of Nathan of David 32. of Jesse of Obed of Boaz of Salmon of Nahshon 33. of Amminadab of Admin of Arni of Hezron of Perez of Judah 34. of Jacob of Isaac of Abraham of Terah of Nahor 35. of Serug of Reu of Peleg of Eber of Shelah 36. of Cainan of Arpaxad of Shem of Noah of Lamech 37. of Methuselah of Enoch of Jared of Mahalaleel of Cainan 38. of Enos of Seth of Adam of God.

The Temptation of Jesus

(Mt 4:1-11, Mk 1:12,13)

4.1. Now Jesus returned from the Jordan full of *the* Holy Spirit and He was being led in the wilderness by the Spirit 2. being tested by the devil *for* forty days.[7] And He ate nothing in those days and when they were completed

---

1   (v.21) This was according to the Jewish custom of self-immersion for purification. See Baptize in Glossary.
2   (v.22) The tense here means that everything Jesus has done has pleased the Father.
3   (Caption) See Genealogy of Jesus in Glossary.
4   (v.23) Thirty years of age is when an Aaronic priest began ministry. See Nu Ch. 4.
5   (v.23) For insight to this name see Son of David/Son of Joseph in Glossary.
6   (v.23) Some Greek manuscripts have Heli, but the oldest Greek and the Hebrew have Eli.
7   (v.2) Although the text actually says He was tested for forty days, the testing came at the end of the forty days.

He was hungry. 3. Then the devil said to Him, "If You are *the* Son of God, You must speak to this stone so that it would become bread." 4. And Jesus answered him, "It has been written that 'Man will not live on bread alone.'" (Dt 8:3) 5. Then leading Him up he showed Him all the kingdoms of the inhabited world in a moment of time 6. and the devil said to Him, "I will give You authority *over* all this and their glory, because it has been given over to me and I could give it to whomever I wish: 7. therefore if You would worship before me, it will all be Yours." 8. Then Jesus said to him, "It has been written,

> 'You will worship[1] the Lord your God
> and you will serve only Him.'" (Dt 6:13)

9. Then he led Him up into Jerusalem and stood upon the pinnacle of the temple and said to Him, "If You are Son of God, You must immediately throw Yourself down from here: 10. for it has been written that

> 'His angels will be commanded concerning you
> to protect you,' (Ps 91:11)

11. and that

> 'they will take you up in *their* hands,
> lest you would beat your foot against a stone.'" (Ps 91:12)

12. And Jesus said to him that "It has been said, 'You will not test *the* Lord your God.'" (Dt 6:16) 13. Then after the devil finished every test he went away from Him until an opportune season.

The Beginning of the Galilean Ministry

(Mt 4:12-17, Mk 1:14,15)

4:14. Then Jesus returned to Galilee in the power of the Spirit. And news about Him went out throughout the whole region. 15. And He was teaching in their synagogues, being praised by everyone.

The Rejection of Jesus at Nazareth

(Mt 13:53-58, Mk 6:1-6)

4:16. Then He came into Nazareth, which was where He grew up, and He entered the synagogue according to His custom on the day of Sabbaths[2] and He stood up to read. 17. And a scroll[3] of the prophet Isaiah was handed to Him and when He opened the scroll He found the place were it was written,

18.　　"*The* Spirit of *the* Lord *is* upon Me

1　　　(v.8) This is the Greek word proskuneo, meaning bow down to or pay homage to. See Pay Homage in Glossary.

2　　　(v.16) Sabbaths can mean: a feast day, weeks, or more than one Sabbath. See Sabbath in Glossary.

3　　　(v.17 & v.20) Opening a scroll is not nearly as easy as opening a book to a certain page. The scroll, which contains the prophetic books, is unrolled to almost its entire length to reach Is 61, then is rolled up to be placed in its cover for storage. The scrolls are vertical, opening from left to right for Hebrew.

because He has anointed Me
to preach Good News to *the* repentant,[1]
He has sent Me to preach release to captives
and recovery of sight to the blind,[2]
to send release to *the* oppressed,

19.   to preach *the* acceptable year of the Lord." (Is 61:1,2)

20. Then rolling up the scroll, after He gave *it* back to the attendant, He sat down. And the eyes of all in the synagogue were looking attentively at Him. 21. And He began to say to them "Today this Scripture has been fulfilled in your ears." 22. And everyone was speaking well of Him and was amazed by the grace in those words that came out from His mouth, and they were saying, "Is this not a son of Joseph?" 23. Then He said to them, "Certainly you will tell Me this parable, 'Physician, You must now heal Yourself:' what we heard happened in Capernaum[3] You must now do here in Your home town." 24. Then He said, "Truly I say to you that no prophet is welcome in his home town. 25. And in truth I say to you, there were many widows in Israel in the days of Elijah, when the sky was locked for three years and six months, as there was a great famine on all the Earth, 26. but Elijah was sent to not one of them except to a widow woman in Zarephath of Sidon. (1Ki 17:9) 27. And there were many lepers[4] in Israel in the time of Elisha the prophet, but not one of them was cleansed except Naaman the Syrian." (2Ki 5:1-14) 28. And when they heard these things everyone in the synagogue was filled with rage 29. and when they stood up they drove Him outside the city to the brow of the hill on which their city had been built so that *they could* throw Him down: 30. but then He went through the middle of them *and* left.

The Man with an Unclean Spirit

(Mk 1:21-28)

4:31. And He came down to Capernaum, a city of Galilee: and He was teaching them regularly on the Sabbaths: 32. and they were amazed at His teaching, because His message was with authority. 33. And a man having an unclean demon spirit was in the synagogue and *the demon* cried out in a loud voice, 34. "Ah ha! What has this to do with You,[5] Jesus of Nazareth? Did You come to destroy us? I know Who You are, the Holy One of God." 35. Then Jesus commanded it saying, "You must be quiet and you must immediately come out from him," Then, after the demon threw *the man* down in the middle *of them,*

---

1   (v.18) Literally the poor, a Hebrew idiom for repentant.
2   (v.18) This is not the way Is 61:1 is translated in our Bibles, but the Hebrew verb translated "open" in "open the prison.." means to open eyes and/or ears, both physically and spiritually. The Greek spelling of the Hebrew word is hippatach, Mk 7:34.
3   (v.23) Capernaum is the Latin spelling of the Hebrew name Kafer Na-um. Kafer means town or village and Na-um means pleasant.
4   (v.27) This is not the disease called leprosy today. See Leprosy in Glossary.
5   (v.34) Literally, "What to us and to You" is a Hebrew idiom meaning "What does this have to do with you or me?"

it came out from him and did not hurt him at all. 36. And there was amazement upon all and they were discussing with one another saying, "What is this talk that He orders the unclean spirits with authority and power and they come out?" 37. And *the* report concerning Him was going out into every place in the region.

The Healing of Many People

(Mt 8:14-17, Mk 1:29-34)

4:38. And after He got up from the synagogue He entered Simon's house. And Simon's mother-in-law was having a high fever and they were asking Him about her. 39. Then as He stood before her, He commanded the fever and it left her: and then she immediately got up *and* was serving them. 40. And after the sun set *ending the Sabbath* they led to Him as many as were having sickness with various diseases, and as He laid hands on each one of them He was healing them. 41. And then demons came out from many, crying out and saying, "You are the Son of God." But while He was rebuking *them* He was not allowing them to speak, because they had known He was the Messiah.

A Preaching Tour

(Mk 1:35-39)

4:42. And when it became day, when He came out He went to a desolate place: and the crowds were searching for Him and they came until *they found* Him and they prevented Him from going away from them. 43. Then He said to them "It is even necessary for Me to be preaching the Good News about the kingdom of God in different cities, because I was sent on account of this." 44. And He was preaching in the synagogues of Judea.

The Calling of the First Disciples

(Mt 4:18-22, Mk 1:16-20)

5.1. And it happened while He was standing by Lake Gennesaret[1] the crowd pressed in to Him to hear the Word of God 2. and He saw two boats standing to the side of the lake: and the fishermen from them, *who* had gotten out, were washing their nets.[2] 3. And when He got in one of the boats, which was Simon's, He asked him to put out a little way from the shore, and after He sat on the boat He was teaching the crowds. 4. And as He stopped speaking, He said to Simon, "You must now go out into the deep *water* and you must cast your nets at once for a catch." 5. And Simon said, "Master, while working through *the* whole night we took nothing: but upon Your word I will lower the nets." 6. Then when they did this they enclosed *the nets* full of many fish, and their nets were being torn. 7. Then they signaled by a nod to their partners in the other boat,

---

1   (v.1) This lake is called Kinneret in Hebrew, and sometimes lake of Tiberius or of Galilee. See Sea of Galilee in Glossary.
2   (v.2) This net is the small, round net normally used by one person. At twenty feet in diameter it is easy to see why they needed help. See Fish Nets in Glossary.

who came to help them: and they came and they filled both boats so as to *almost* sink them. 8. And when Simon Peter saw he fell down to his knees before Jesus saying, "You must now go from me because I am a sinful man, Lord." 9. For astonishment seized him and all those with him over the catch of the fish, which they took, 10. and likewise also Jacob[1] and John, sons of Zebedee, who were partners with Simon. And Jesus said to Simon, "You must not fear: from now on you will be capturing men." 11. Then after they drew the boats up on the shore, leaving everything, they followed Him.

The Cleansing of a Leper[2]

(Mt 8:1-4, Mk 1:40-45)

5:12. And it happened He was in one of the cities and here was a man full of leprosy: and after he saw Jesus, falling on his face he begged of Him saying, "Lord, if You are willing You are able to cleanse me." 13. And stretching out His hand He touched him[3] saying, "I am willing, you must immediately be cleansed:" and the leprosy left him at once. 14. Then He commanded him to tell no one, "But when you leave you must immediately show yourself to the priest and you must make an offering concerning your cleansing just as Moses commanded, in witness to them." (Lv 14:2-32) 15. And the word was going out more concerning Him, and many crowds were gathering to listen and to be healed from their sicknesses: 16. but He was withdrawing to the wilderness *places* and praying.

The Healing of a Paralytic

(Mt 9:1-8, Mk 2:1-12)

5:17. Then it happened on one of the days that He was teaching, and Pharisees and teachers of Torah were sitting *listening*. They were coming from every region of Galilee and Judea and Jerusalem: and *the* power of *the* Lord was in Him to heal.[4] 18. And there were men bringing a man who was paralyzed. *He was* on a stretcher and they were seeking to bring him in and to place him before Him. 19. Then not finding by what way they could bring him in because of the crowd, after they went up on the roof they let him and his pallet down through the tiles into the middle in front of Jesus. 20. And when He saw their faith He said, "Man, your sins have been forgiven you."[5] 21. Then the scribes and the Pharisees began to discuss saying, "Who is this Who is speaking blasphemy? Who is able to forgive sin except only God?" 22. But Jesus, well knowing their

---

1   (v.10) The name in the Greek text is Iakob, which is spelled Jacob in English.

2   (Caption) This is not the disease called leprosy today. See Leprosy in Glossary.

3   (v.13) Touching a leper would have made anyone else unclean, but Jesus' touch cleansed the leper. See Cleanse in Glossary.

4   (v.17) The only place where He is referref to as not having the power is in Nazereth. See Mt 13:58 and Mk 6:5.

5   (v.20) The common belief was that sickness and physical problems were caused by sin. It is interesting that Jesus says He has authority to forgive sins, yet His statement to the paralytic is "Your sins are forgiven," something we can say to any repentant person.

discussion, said to them, "What are you discussing in your hearts? 23. What is easier, to say 'Your sins are forgiven to you,' or to say, 'You must rise and you must walk?' 24. But so that you would know that the Son of Man has authority upon the Earth to forgive sins" - He said to the paralyzed one, "To you I say, you must rise, and when you take up your pallet you must go into your house right away." 25. Then quickly getting up in front of them, after he took up what he was reclining *on*, he went to his house glorifying God. 26. Then amazement took all and they were glorifying God and they were filled with awe saying, "*What* we have seen today *is* wonderful."

The Calling of Levi

(Mt 9:9-13, Mk 2:13-17)

5:27. And after these things He went out and He saw a tax collector named Levi sitting in the tax office, and He said to him, "You must continually follow Me." 28. Then after he got up, leaving everything behind, he was following Him. 29. And Levi made a great banquet for Him in his house, and there was a large crowd of tax collectors and others *and* they were reclining with them. 30. And the Pharisees and the scribes were complaining of them to His disciples saying, "Why are you eating and drinking with the tax collectors and sinners?" 31. And Jesus said to them, "The healthy do not have need of a physician but those who have evil[1] do: 32. I have not come to call *the* righteous but sinners into repentance."

The Question about Fasting

(Mt 9:14-17, Mk 2:18-22)

5:33. And they said to Him, "The disciples of John and likewise those of the Pharisees are fasting frequently and supplications are being made to God, but those with You are eating and drinking."[2] 34. And Jesus said to them, "Are you able to make the sons of the bridegroom[3] fast while the bridegroom is with them? 35. But days will come, then, when the bridegroom would be taken away from them, they will fast in those days." 36. And He was then telling them a parable that "Also, no one places a patch torn from a new garment upon an old garment: otherwise, even the new will tear and the patch which *was* from the new *garment* will not fit on the old. 37. And no one puts new wine into old skins: otherwise the new wine will burst the skins and it will itself be poured out and the skins will be destroyed. 38. But you must put new wine into new skins. 39. But no one drinking old wants new: for he says 'The old is suitable.'"[4]

---

1   (v.31) The Greek word kakos, meaning evil, is often translated sickness.
2   (v.33) The word for drinking is pino, referring to any drinking, not referring to an intoxi-cant.
3   (v.34) Since all were aware of His claim as Messiah, this is a reference to all His disciples, both male and female. The Greek construction anticipates a negative answer.
4   (v.39) This statement of no one having old wants new is still true as we can see in Church history. In The Eternal Church, Dr. Bill Hamon details the resistance to each new spiritual

Plucking Grain on the Sabbath

(Mt 12:1-8, Mk 2:23-28)

6.1. And He happened to go through grain fields on a Sabbath, and His disciples were picking and eating the grains, rubbing their hands. 2. But some of the Pharisees said, "Why are you doing what is not proper on Sabbaths?"[1] 3. Then Jesus said to them, "Have you not read what David did when he and those who were with him were hungry,[2] 4. how he entered the house of God and having taken the Bread of the Presence, he ate and gave to those with him, that which is not right to eat except only *by* the priests?" 5. Then He was saying to them, "The Son of Man is Lord of the Sabbath."

The Man with the Withered Hand

(Mt 12:9-14, Mk 3:1-6)

6:6. And it happened on another Sabbath He entered the synagogue and taught. And a man was there whose right hand was withered. 7. And the scribes and Pharisees were watching Him closely with evil intent, *to see* if He healed on the Sabbath, so that they would find *something* to accuse Him. 8. But He had known their thoughts, and He said to the man who had the withered hand, "You must rise and now stand in the middle:" then after he rose he stood *there*. 9. And Jesus said to them, "I ask you if it is proper on the Sabbath to do good or to do evil, to save or to destroy life?" 10. Then as He looked around at them all He said to him, "You must immediately stretch out your hand." And he did and his hand was restored. 11. But they were filled with fury and were discussing with one another whatever they might do to Jesus.

The Choosing of the Twelve

(Mt 10:1-4, Mk 3:13-19)

6:12. And it happened in these days He went out to the mountain to pray, and He was spending the night in prayer with God. 13. And when it became day He called His disciples, and *He* chose twelve from them, whom He then called apostles. 14. *They were* Simon, whom He also called Peter,[3] and Andrew his brother, and Jacob[4] and John and Philip and Bartholomew 15. and Matthew and Thomas and Jacob, *son of* Alpheus, and Simon the one called Zealot 16, and Judas, *son of* Jacob, and Judas Iscariot, who became a betrayer.

---

move down through the centuries.
1   (v.2) This could well be during the Feast of Shavuot when the wheat is harvested.
2   (v.3) Oral law permits breaking commandments for humanitarian reasons, such as hunger.
3   (v.14) Actually, he was called by the Hebrew Kaf or Aramaic Kefa. Written in Greek, then Latin, it is in the English Scriptures as Cephas, from the Latin spelling. See Cephas in Glossary.
4   (v.14) This is the English spelling of the Greek word Iakob in this text.

Ministering to a Great Multitude

(Mt 4:23-25)

6:17. Then, when He went down[1] with them, He stood on a flat place, and a great crowd of His disciples, and a great multitude of people, from all of Judea and Jerusalem and the coast of Tyre and Sidon 18. came to hear Him and to be healed from their diseases: and those who were troubled by unclean spirits were being healed,[2] 19. and the whole crowd was seeking to touch Him, because power was coming out from Him and He was healing all.

Blessings and Woes

(Mt 5:1-12)

6:20. Then when He lifted up His eyes to His disciples He was saying, "Blessed are the repentant,[3]
>because the kingdom of God is yours. (Is 61:1)
21.   Blessed are those who hunger now, (Jn 6:53)
>because you will be filled. (Nu 25:11, Ps 4:7, Ho 10:12)
Blessed are those who cry now,
>because you will laugh. (Is 61:2,3)

22. Blessed are you when men would hate you and when they would excommunicate you and they would reproach *you* and they would spurn your name as evil because of the Son of Man: (2Chr 36:16) 23. you must rejoice and you must leap about[4] in that day, for behold your reward *is* great in heaven: for their fathers were doing corresponding things to the prophets.

24.   But woe to you rich,
>because you are now receiving your comfort. (Jas 5:1)
25.   Woe to you, who are satisfied now,
>because you will hunger.
Woe, those who laugh now,
>because you will grieve and you will cry.

26. And woe when all men would speak well about you: for their fathers were doing corresponding things to the false prophets." (Jas 4:4)

Love for Enemies

(Mt 5:38-48, 7:12a)

6:27. "But to you who are listening I say, You must constantly love your enemies, (Pr 25:31) you must do good for those who hate you, 28. you must

---

1   (v.17) Notice that Jesus went down from the hill, that this is a different time and place for this teaching and not another description of the Sermon on the Mount, Mt 5:1-7:28.
2   (v.18) The word used here is therapeuo, to heal, strengthening the connection between deliverance and healing.
3   (v.20) Literally, this is poor, which is a Hebrew idiom for repentant.
4   (v.23) Dance

habitually bless those who curse you, you must continually be praying on behalf of those who abuse you. 29. To the one who strikes you on the cheek you must also offer the other one, and with the one who takes your cloak you should not then refuse your tunic. 30. You must give to everyone who asks you, and from the one who takes your things you must not demand back. 31. And just as you wish that people would do for you, you must do likewise for them. 32. And if you love those who love you, what credit is it to you? For even the sinners would love those who love them. 33. For even if you would do good things for those who do good things to you, what credit is *that* to you? Even the sinners do the same. 34. And if you would lend *to someone* from whom you hope to take *something in pledge*, what sort of credit is it to you? Even sinners lend to sinners in order that they would take something back. 35. But you must love your enemies and you must do good things *to them* and you must lend expecting nothing: then your reward will be great, and you will be children of *the* Most High, because He is kind to the ungrateful and evil. 36. You must become compassionate, even just as your Father is compassionate."

Judging Others

(Mt 7:1-5)

6:37. "And *if you* do not judge, then you would **not** be judged: and *if you* do not condemn, then you would **not** be condemned. You must set free, then you will be set free: 38. you must give, then it will be given to you: they will give a good measure, pressed down, shaken, poured into your bosom: for, in which measure you measure, it will be measured to you in return." 39. And He also told a parable to them: "Is a blind *person* able to lead a blind *person*? Will not both fall into a pit? 40. A disciple is not above a teacher: but after he has been prepared everyone will be like his teacher. 41. And what *is* the chip you see in your brother's eye, but you do not perceive the beam in your own eye? 42. How are you able to say to your brother, 'Brother, you must permit me to remove the chip in your eye,' when you do not see the beam in your own eye? Hypocrite, you must first take the beam out of your eye, and then you will see clearly to remove the chip in your brother's eye."

A Tree Known by Its Fruit

(Mt 7:17-20, 12:34b, 35)

6:43. "For a good tree is not making rotten fruit, and again a rotten tree *is* not making good fruit. 44. For each tree is known by its own fruit: for they do not gather up figs from thorn plants and they do not gather a bunch of grapes from a thorn bush. 45. The good man produces good from the good treasure of his heart, and the evil *man* produces evil from the evil *in his heart*: for his mouth is speaking out from the abundance of *his* heart."

The Two Foundations

(Mt 7:24-27)

6:46. "Why do you call Me, 'Lord. Lord!'[1] and do not do what I say? 47. For everyone who comes to Me and hears My words and does them, I will show you what he is like: 48. he is like a man building a house who dug and made deep and placed *the* foundation upon the rock: and when the flood came the river burst upon that house and it was not able to shake it because it was well built. 49. But the one who heard and did not do is like a man who built a house upon the ground without a foundation, which the river beat against and it immediately collapsed and there was a great ruin of that house."

The Healing of a Centurion's Servant

(Mt 8:5-13, Jn 4:43-54)

7.1. After He finished all His words[2] in the hearing of the people, He entered Capernaum.[3] 2. And a certain servant[4] of a centurion, who was dear to *the centurion*, having evil,[5] was going to die. 3. And when he heard about Jesus he sent elders of the Jewish people to Him asking Him that if He came would He cure his servant. 4. And those who came to Jesus were urging Him earnestly, saying that "This one is worthy for whom You should offer this: 5. for he loves our nation and he built the synagogue for us." 6. And Jesus was going with them. But now when He was not far distant from the house, the centurion sent friends *who* said to Him, "Lord, You must not be bothered, for I am not worthy that You should come under my roof: 7. on this account I was not worthy to come to You myself: but You must say a word, and my child must be healed. 8. For I am also a man under authority, *and in authority,* as I have soldiers under me, and I say to this one, when I order, 'You must now go,' and he goes, and to another, 'You must come,' and he comes, and to my servant, 'You must now do this,' and he does." 9. And when He heard these things Jesus was amazed at him and after He turned to the crowd that was following Him He said, "I say to you, not in Israel have I found so much strong faith." 10. Then when they returned to the house, those who were sent found the servant in good health.

The Raising of a Widow's Son at Nain

7:11. Then it happened on the next *day* He was going into a city called Nain, and His disciples and a great crowd were going together with Him. 12. And as He approached the gate of the city, then behold an only son of his mother,

1   (v.46) The doubling of a salutation indicates emphasis, really needing to get His attention. See Double Name in Glossary.
2   (v.1) This message is rhema, translated words, with the emphasis on speaking, on the sounds. See Logos/Rhema in Glossary.
3   (v.1) Capernaum is the Latin spelling of the Hebrew name Kafer Na-um. Kafer means town or village and Na-um means pleasant.
4   (v.2) This apparently was a young male indentured servant because here in v. 7, and in Matthew and John he is called a child.
5   (v.2) A synonym for being sick

who died, was being carried out, and she was herself a widow, and a crowd of that city was with her. 13. And when He saw her, the Lord had pity upon her and said to her, "Stop crying!" 14. Then when He went over He touched the bier,[1] and those bearing *it* stood still, and He said, "Young man, I say to you, you must rise immediately!" 15. Then the dead *boy* sat up and began to speak, and He gave him to his mother. 16. And reverential fear took all and they were glorifying God saying that "A great prophet has risen among us" and that "God cared for His people." 17. And this message about Him went out in all Judea and in every neighboring region.

The Messengers from John the Baptist

(Mt 11:2-19)

7:18. And his disciples reported about all these things to John. Then having summoned a certain two of his disciples John 19. sent *them* to the Lord saying, "Are You the One Who is coming or should we expect another?" 20. And when they came to Him the men said, "John the Baptist sent us to You saying, 'Are You the One Who is coming or should we expect another?'" 21. In that hour He healed many from sicknesses and torments and evil spirits and He granted to many blind to see. 22. Then He said to them, "When you go you must report to John what you saw and heard: blind are regaining sight, lame are walking, lepers[2] are being cleansed and deaf are hearing, dead are being raised, repentant[3] are receiving the Good News: 23. and blessed is whoever would not be made to stumble because of Me." 24. And after John's messengers left He began to talk to the crowds about John, "What did you come out into the desert to see? A reed being shaken by *the* wind? 25. But what did you come out to see? A man clothed in soft garments? Behold those in glorious and luxurious garments are living delicately in palaces. 26. But what did you come out to see? A prophet? Indeed I say to you, even greater than a prophet. 27. This one is about whom it has been written,

'Behold, I am sending My messenger before Your presence,
who will prepare Your way before You.' (Mal 3:1)

28. I say to you, no man born of women is greater than John, but the least in the kingdom of God is greater than he." 29. And when all the people, even the tax collectors, heard, they acknowledged God's justice by being baptized the baptism of John: 30. but the Pharisees and those learned in Torah rejected the will of God for themselves, not being baptized under him.

7:31. "Therefore to what will I compare the people of this generation and who are they like? 32. They are like the children, those who sit in a market and call to one another, who say,

---

1   (v.14) The bier was a pallet on which the body was placed, then the body was slid from the bier into the grave.

2   (v.22) This is not the disease called leprosy today. See Leprosy in Glossary.

3   (v.22) Literally poor, which is a Hebrew idiom for repentant.

'We played flutes for you and you did not dance,
    we sang a lament and you did not weep.'

33. For John the Baptist has come not eating bread and not drinking wine, and you say, 'He has a demon.' 34. The Son of Man has come eating and drinking, and you say, 'Behold *the* man *is* a glutton and a wine bibber, a friend of tax collectors and sinners.' 35. And wisdom was declared right by all her children."

A Sinful Woman Forgiven

7:36. And a certain one of the Pharisees was asking Him to eat with him, and after He entered the house of the Pharisee He reclined at the table. 37. And behold a certain sinful woman was in the city, and since she knew that He was reclining in the house of the Pharisee, she brought an alabaster flask of ointment, 38. then standing behind by His feet, crying tears, she began to wet His feet and she wiped *them* with the hairs of her head and she was kissing His feet and she was anointing *them* with her ointment. 39. But when the Pharisee saw, the one who invited Him spoke to himself, saying, "If this One were a prophet, He would know what sort of woman *this is* who is touching Him, because she is sinful." 40. Then Jesus said to him, "Simon, I have something to say to you." And he said, "Teacher, You must speak." 41. "There were two debtors to some money lender: the one owed five hundred denarii, but the other fifty. 42. Because they did not have *it* to repay he forgave *them* both. Therefore who of them will love him more?" 43. Simon said, "I assume that to whom he forgave more." And He said to him, "You judged correctly." 44. Then turning to the woman He said to Simon, "Do you see this woman? *When* I entered your house, you did not give water to Me for *My* feet: she wet My feet with her tears and wiped them with her hair. 45. You did not give Me a kiss: but she has not stopped kissing My feet from when I entered. 46. You did not anoint My head with olive oil: but she anointed My feet with perfume. 47. Of which I say again to you, her many sins have been forgiven, because she loved much: but for whom little is forgiven, he loves little." 48. And He said to her, "Your sins are forgiven." 49. Then those who were reclining began to say among themselves, "Who is this Who even forgives sins?" 50. But He said to the woman, "Your faith has saved you: you must continually go in peace."

Some Women Accompany Jesus

8.1. And then it happened He was going through city and town, one after the other, preaching and giving the Good News of the kingdom of God, and the twelve *were* with Him, 2. also some women who had been healed from evil spirits and sicknesses, Mary, the one called Magdalene, from whom seven demons had come out, 3. and Joannah, wife of Chuza, manager of Herod's *household*, and Susanna and many others, who were ministering to them from their possessions.

The Parable of the Sower

(Mt 13:1-9, Mk 4:1-9)

8:4. Then a great crowd gathered and while they were going down with Him to another city He spoke to them through a parable, 5. "The sower of the seed came out *with* his seed. And among what he sowed, *some* on the one hand fell by the way and it was trampled under foot and the birds of the sky ate it up. 6. And other fell upon the rock, and it grew, *then* withered because it did not have moisture. 7. And other fell in the middle of thorn-plants, and grew up *and* thorn-plants choked it. 8. And other fell on good ground and as it grew it made fruit one hundred times as much." After He said these things He called out, "The one who has ears to hear must constantly listen!"

The Purpose of the Parables

(Mt 13:10-17, Mk 4:10-12)

8:9. But His disciples were asking Him what this parable could be. 10. And He said, "It has been given to you to know the mysteries of the kingdom of God, but to the rest in parables, so that

'Seeing they would not see

and hearing they would not understand.'" (Is 6:9,10)

The Parable of the Sower Explained

(Mt 13:18-23, Mk 4:13-20)

8:11. "This is the parable. The seed is the Word of God. 12. Those by the way are those who hear, then the devil comes and takes the word from their hearts, so that they who *may have* believed would not be saved. 13. And those upon the rock, when they would hear they receive the message with joy, but they do not have a root, *so* they believe for a time, then in a time of trial or testing they fall away. 14. And the one that fell among the thorn-plants, these are those who hear, then while they are going, under worries and riches and pleasures of life, they are choked and they do not bear fruit to maturity. 15. But the one in the good soil, these are those with good and upright hearts, as they have listened to the Word and they are bearing fruit with patience."

A Light under a Vessel

(Mk 4:21-25)

8:16. "And no one having lit a lamp conceals it with a dish or places *it* underneath a bed, but places *it* upon a lamp stand, so that those who go in would see the light. 17. For nothing is hidden which will not become visible. What would **not** have been known[1] would then come into open view. 18. Therefore

---

1   (v.17) With the emphasis on what has not been known, this means that all spiritual mysteries will be revealed. These are the things pertaining to the second coming and end times, with

you must continually be careful how you listen: for whoever would have, it will be given to him: and whoever would not have, even what he thinks he has will be taken from him."

The Mother and Brothers of Jesus
(Mt 12:46-50, Mk 3:31-35)

8:19. And His mother and brothers came to Him and they were not able to meet with Him because of the crowd. 20. And it was reported to Him, "Your mother and Your brothers have been standing outside wanting to see You." 21. And He said to them, "My mother and My brothers are these who hear and do the Word of God."

The Calming of a Storm
(Mt 8:23-27, Mk 4:35-41)

8:22. And it happened on one of the days that He and His disciples embarked in a boat and He said to them, "Let us go over to the other side of the lake," and they set out. 23. And He fell asleep while they were sailing. Then a strong gust of wind came down upon the lake and they were being swamped and endangered. 24. And when they went to Him they woke Him saying "Master. Master! We are being destroyed." Then after He got up He rebuked the wind and the wave of the water: then it stopped and it was calm. 25. And He said to them, "Where is your faith?" But being afraid, they were amazed, saying to one another, "Who then is this that even commands the winds and the water, and they obey Him?"

The Healing of the Gerasene Demoniac
(Mt 8:28-34, Mk 5:1-20)

8:26. Then they sailed to the region of the Gerasenes, which is across the *lake of* Galilee. 27. And when He came out on the shore a man from the city, *who* had demons, met *Him*. For a long time he had not worn a garment or *stayed* in a house, but was staying in the tombs.[1] 28. And when he saw Jesus, as he cried out, he fell down before Him and said in a loud voice, "What do You have to do with me, Jesus,[2] Son of the Most High God? I beg You, do not torment me." 29. For He commanded the unclean spirit to come out from the man. For many times it seized him and although he was guarded and bound in chains and fetters, he broke the chains, being driven by the demon into the wilderness areas. 30. And Jesus asked him, "What is your name?" And he said. "Legion,"[3] because many demons went into him. 31. And they were begging Him not to command them to go into the abyss.

many variations and explanations floating around. It also refers to disobedience and sinful behavior that will be exposed on Judgment Day.

1   (v.27) Tombs were caves.
2   (v.28) This is another use of the Hebrew idiom "what to you and to me" as used by Jesus at Cana in Jn 2:4.
3   (v.30) In Jesus' day a legion at full strength was 6826 men.

8:32. And there was a herd of many pigs there feeding on the mountain: and they begged Him to allow them to enter those: and He allowed *the demons to enter the pigs*. 33. And when the demons came out from the man they entered the pigs, then the herd set out down the slope into the lake and was drowned. 34. And when those who were tending saw what happened they fled and reported *that* in the city and in the fields. 35. And they came out to see what happened and they came to Jesus and they found the man from whom the demons came out, sitting by the feet of Jesus, dressed and of sound mind, and they were afraid. 36. And those who saw reported to them how the one who was demon possessed was delivered. 37. Then all the multitude of the region of the Gerasene asked Him to leave from them, because they were being distressed with great fear: then He returned, having embarked in a boat. 38. And the man from whom the demons had come out was begging Him to be with Him: but He released him saying, 39. "You must return to your house and you must continually tell what God did for you." Then he left, proclaiming throughout the whole city what Jesus did for him.

Jairus' Daughter and The Woman Who Touched His Prayer Shawl[1]

(Mt 9:18-26, Mk 5:21-43)

8:40. And on Jesus' return the crowd welcomed Him: for they were all looking for Him. 41. And behold a man named Jairus came and this one was a leader of the synagogue, and he fell at the feet of Jesus, begging Him to come to his house, 42. because his only daughter was about twelve years old and she was about to die.

And while He was going the throngs were crowding together around Him. 43. And a woman *who* was in a flow of blood for twelve years, who having spent *her* whole living on doctors was not able to be healed by anyone, 44. when she came up behind she touched the fringe[2] of His prayer shawl and immediately her flow of blood stopped. 45. Then Jesus said, "Who is the one who touched Me?" But when all denied, Peter said, "Master, the crowds are choking You and pressing in." 46. And Jesus said, "Someone touched Me. For I know power has come out from Me." 47. And when the woman saw that she did not escape notice, she came trembling and as she fell before Him she reported[3] before all the people *what* the reason was she touched Him and as *she spoke* she was healed immediately. 48. And He said to her, "Daughter, your faith has saved you. You must continually go in peace."

8:49. While He was still speaking someone came from *the home* of the synagogue leader saying that "Your daughter has died: you must no longer

---

1   (Caption) The prayer shawl was worn by nearly every Jewish man in those days. See Prayer Shawl in Glossary.

2   (v.44) The fringe, called tsitsit, on the corner of the prayer shawl represented all the commandments and promises of God. See Nu 15:37-41. See Prayer Shawl in Glossary.

3   (v.47) Her testimony, saying things that are not (Ro 4:17) facilitated the miracle.

trouble the teacher." 50. But since Jesus heard He answered him, "Stop being fearful! You must only believe, and she will be rescued." 51. Then after He came into the house He did not permit any to enter with Him except Peter and John and Jacob[1] and the father and the mother of the child. 52. But all *the mourners* were crying and mourning her. And He said, "Stop crying! For she did not die but she is sleeping." 53. Then they were laughing scornfully at Him because they knew that she had died. 54. But He, taking hold of her hand, spoke to her saying, "Child, you must rise." 55. Then her spirit returned and she stood up immediately and He ordered *something* to be given for her to eat. 56. And her parents were astonished: but He ordered them not to tell what had happened.

The Mission of the Twelve

(Mt 10:5-15, Mk 6:7-13)

9.1. And after He summoned the twelve He gave them power and authority over all demons and to heal sicknesses 2. and He sent them to preach the kingdom of God and to heal diseases, 3. and He said to them, "And you must take nothing for the journey, neither staff, nor knapsack, nor bread, nor money, nor for *each* to have two prayer shawls.[2] 4. And whatever house you would enter, you must remain there and you must *come and* go out from there. 5. And as many as would not take you in, when you come out from that city shake the dust from your feet in testimony against them." 6. And after they left they were going through the region bringing the Good News and healing everywhere.

Herod's Anxiety

(Mt 14:1-12, Mk 6:14-29)

9:7. And Herod the Tetrarch heard all that was happening and he was perplexed because it was said by some that John was raised from *the* dead, 8. and by some that Elijah appeared, and others that some prophet of the ancients had risen. 9. But Herod said, "I beheaded John: but Who is this about Whom I hear such things as these?" Then he was seeking to see Him.

The Feeding of the Five Thousand

(Mt 14:13-21, Mk 6:30-44, Jn 6:1-14)

9:10. And when the apostles returned they reported to Him what they did. And then He took them *and* went back *with them* by themselves to a city called Bethsaida.[3] 11. But when the crowds knew they followed Him: and welcoming them, He was speaking to them about the kingdom of God, and those who had need of healing were being healed. 12. And the day began to draw to a close:

1   (v.51) This the first time John is listed before Jacob.
2   (v.3) The prayer shawl was the standard outer garment for men. See Prayer Shawl in Glossary.
3   (v.10) Bethsaida is the Greek spelling of Beit-Tside, which means House or Place of Fishing (literally hunting) in Hebrew. See Location of the Feeding of the Five Thousand in Glossary.

and after the twelve came they said to Him, "You must release the crowd now, so that when they go into the villages and fields around they would find lodging and they could find provision, because we are here in a desolate place." 13. But He said to them, "You must now give them *something* to eat." And they said, "There are not more than five loaves and two fish with us, unless we go to buy food for all these people." 14. For there were about five thousand men.[1] But He said to His disciples, "You must make them sit down in groups of about fifty or more." 15. And they did so and they all reclined. 16. And when He took the five loaves and the two fish, as He looked up into heaven He praised God for them, then He broke *them* in pieces and He was giving *them* to the disciples to set before the crowd. 17. And they ate and they all were satisfied, and the leftovers, twelve baskets[2] of pieces, were taken up by them. (2Ki 4:42-44)

Peter's Declaration about Jesus

(Mt 16:13-19, Mk 8:27-29)

9:18. And it happened while He was praying the disciples were alone with Him, and He asked them saying, "Who do the crowds say that I am?" 19. And they said, "John the Baptist, and others Elijah, and others that some prophet of the ancients has risen." 20. And he said to them, "But who do you say I am?" And Peter said, "The Messiah of God."

Jesus Foretells His Death and Resurrection[3]

(Mt 16:20-28, Mk 8:30-9:1)

9:21. But then He warned *them and* commanded them not to say this 22. saying, "It is necessary for the Son of Man to suffer many things and to be rejected by the elders and high priests and scribes and to be killed and to be raised up on the third day." 23. And He was saying to everyone, "If someone wants to come after Me, he must now deny himself and he must take his cross at once, and day by day he must consistently follow Me. 24. For whoever would want to save his life will lose it: but whoever would lose his life because of Me will save it. 25. For what does a man benefit if he has gained the whole world, but then lost or forfeited himself?[4] 26. For whoever would be ashamed of Me and My messages,[5] the Son of Man will be ashamed of this one when He would come in the glory of Himself and the Father and the holy angels.[6] 27. But I say to you truly, there are some of those who are standing *in* this *place* who will **not** taste death until they would see the kingdom of God."

---

1   (v.14) Nu 1:3 instructs to count only men between the ages of twenty and fifty. See Census in Glossary.

2   (v.17) The basket is smaller than the hamper used in the feeding of the four thousand.

3   (Caption) See Resurrection in Glossary.

4   (v.25) He forfeited his chance for eternal life.

5   (v.26) The Greek word here is logos. See Logos/Rhema in Glossary.

6   (v.26) This is on Judgment Day. See Re 20:4, 11-14.

The Transfiguration of Jesus

(Mt 17:1-8, Mk 9:2-8)

9:28. And it was about eight days after these messages, and taking Peter and John and Jacob He went up to the mountain to pray for Himself.[1] 29. And it happened while He was praying, the appearance of His face *was* different and His cloak[2] *was* white, gleaming like lightning. 30. And behold two men were speaking with Him, who were Moses and Elijah, 31. while those who had been seen in glory were speaking about His death, which He was going to fulfill in Jerusalem. 32. And Peter and those with him were burdened in sleep: but as they kept awake they saw His glory and the two men who had stood with Him. 33. Then it happened while they were being separated from Him, Peter said to Jesus, "Master, it is good for us to be here, now let us make three booths, one for You and one for Moses and one for Elijah," although he had not understood what he was saying. 34. But while he was saying these things a cloud came and covered them: and they were afraid while they entered the cloud. 35. Then a voice came from the cloud saying, "This is My Son, the One Who has been chosen, you must continually listen to Him." 36. And, after the voice came, Jesus was found alone. And they kept silent and no one reported in those days anything that they had seen.

The Healing of a Boy with an Unclean Spirit

(Mt 17:14-18, Mk 9:14-27)

9:37. And it happened the next day when they came down from the mountain a huge crowd met Him. 38. And behold a man from the crowd called out saying, "Teacher, I beg You to look at my son, because he is my only *child*, 39. and behold a spirit takes him and suddenly it cries out and convulses him with foaming at the mouth and it goes away from him with difficulty, wearing him out. 40. And I urged Your disciples to cast it out, but they were not able." 41. And Jesus said, "O unbelieving and perverted generation, how long will I be with you and will I endure you? You must bring your son here at once." 42. But while he was coming the demon threw him down and convulsed *him*: but Jesus rebuked the unclean spirit and healed the child and gave him to his father. 43. And all were amazed at the majesty of God.

Jesus Again Foretells His Death

(Mt 17:22,23, Mk 9:30-32)

And everyone was amazed at everything He was doing. He said to His disciples, 44. "You must now place these words in your ears: for the Son of Man is going to be given over into *the* hands of men." 45. But they did not understand

---

1   (v.28) The mood of the verb indicates that He prayed for His needs, confirmed by Moses and Elijah in verses 30 and 31.
2   (v.29) His prayer shawl

this statement and it was hidden from them so that they could not perceive it, and they were afraid to ask Him about this statement.

Who is the Greatest?

(Mt 18:1-5, Mk 9:33-37)

9:46. And a thought came among them, whoever might be greatest of them. 47. But since Jesus saw the thought of their hearts, after He took hold of a child, He stood him beside Himself 48. and said to them, "Whoever would receive this child in My name, receives Me: and whoever will receive Me, is receiving the One Who sent Me: for the one who is least among you all, this one is great."

He Who is Not against You is for You

(Mk 9:38-40)

9:49. And John said, "Master, we saw someone casting out demons in Your name and we prevented him, because he does not follow with us."[1] 50. And Jesus said to him, "You must not forbid *him*: for whoever is not against you, is for you."

A Samaritan Village Refuses to Receive Jesus

9:51. And it was the days in which His ascension *was* to be fulfilled and He steadfastly set His face to go to Jerusalem. 52. And He sent messengers before Him. And as they went they entered a town of Samaritans in order to prepare for Him: 53. and *the townspeople* did not receive Him because His face was *set steadfastly* going to Jerusalem. 54. When the disciples Jacob and John saw they said, "Lord, do You want us to call fire to come down from the sky and to destroy them?" 55. But then He turned *and* rebuked them. 56. And they went into a different village.

The Would-be Followers of Jesus

(Mt 8:19-22)

9:57. And while they were going on the way someone said to Him, "I will follow You wherever You would go." 58. And Jesus said to him, "The foxes have dens and the birds of the sky *have* nests, but the Son of Man does not have anywhere He could rest His head." 59. And He said to another, "You must continually follow Me." And he said, "Lord, You must first permit me to return to bury my father." 60. But He said to him, "You must permit the dead to bury their own dead, and when you go you must proclaim the kingdom of God far and wide." 61. And another also said, "I will follow You, Lord: but first You must permit me to say good-bye to those in my house." 62. And Jesus said to him, "No one, after he laid *his* hand on a plow and then looked at the things behind is fit for the kingdom of God."

---

1   (v.49) To follow meant to be a disciple. See Disciple in Glossary.

The Mission of the Seventy-two

10.1. And after these things the Lord appointed seventy-two others and sent them up two by two ahead of Him to every city and place to which He was going to come. 2. And He was saying to them, "On the one hand the harvest *is* great, but on the other hand the workers *are* few: therefore you must beg the Lord of the Harvest to send out workers into His harvest. 3. You must go: behold I am sending you as lambs in *the* midst of wolves. 4. Do not carry purse or knapsack, or sandals, and do not greet anyone along the way. 5. And whenever you would enter a house, first say, 'Peace to this house.' 6. And if a son of peace[1] would be there, your peace will rest[2] upon him: but if not it will return upon you. 7. And you must remain in that house eating and drinking whatever *they have* with them: for the worker is worthy of his reward. You must not move out of *that* house to *another* house. 8. And whatever city you would enter and they would receive you, you must eat what has been set before you 9. and you must continually heal the sicknesses in this *city* and you must say to them, 'The kingdom of God has drawn near you.' 10. But whatever city you would enter in which they would not receive you, when you come out into its streets you must immediately say, 11. 'We even wipe the dust on us from your city that clings to our feet: moreover know this, that the kingdom of God has drawn near.' 12. I say to you that Sodom will in that Day be more bearable than in that city."

Woes to Unrepentant Cities

(Mt 11:20-24)

10:13. "Woe to you Chorazin, woe to you Bethsaida:[3] because if the miracles *that* happened among you had happened in Tyre and Sidon they would long ago have repented, sitting in sackcloth and ashes. 14. Nevertheless it will be more bearable for Tyre and Sidon in the judgment than for you. 15. And you, Capernaum,[4]

'Will you be lifted up until heaven?[5]

No, you will descend as far as Hades.'[6] (Is 14:13,15)

16. The one who hears you hears Me, and the one who rejects you is rejecting Me: and the one who rejects Me rejects the One Who sent Me."

---

1   (v.6) The son of peace is a very Godly person, as Mordecai is described in the Midrash Rabbah 10:3, "For Mordecai the Jew was.. seeking the good of his people and speaking peace to all his seed. Of him Scripture says, "Mark the man of integrity and behold the upright; for there is a future for the man of peace." (Ps 37:37)
2   (v.6) The word, epanapauomai, used for rest means to lean upon or to trust in something. In the NT used only here and in Ro 2:17.
3   (v.13) Bethsaida is the Greek spelling of Beit-Tside, which means House or Place of Fishing (literally hunting) in Hebrew.
4   (v.15) Capernaum is the Latin spelling of the Hebrew name Kafer Na-um. Kafer means town or village and Na-um means pleasant.
5   (v.15) This is not a question in Is 14:13. See Memorization in Glossary.
6   (v.15) This is Sheol in the Hebrew text. See Gehenna in Glossary.

The Return of the Seventy-two

10:17. And the seventy-two returned with joy saying, "Lord, even the demons are subject to us in Your name." 18. And He said to them, "I was watching Satan[1] while he was falling as lightning from heaven. (Is 14:12, Rev 9:1) 19. Behold I have given you authority to trample on snakes and scorpions, and upon every power of the enemy, and **nothing** could harm you. 20. But, you must not rejoice in this because the spirits are subject to you, but you must rejoice because your names have been written in the heavens."

The Rejoicing of Jesus

(Mt 11:25-27, 13:16,17)

10:21. At this time He rejoiced in the Holy Spirit and said, "I praise You, Father, Lord of Heaven and Earth, because You concealed these things from *the* wise and understanding and You revealed them to children: indeed, Father, because in this way it was good pleasure before You. 22. All things were given to Me by My Father, and no one knows Who the Son is except the Father, and Who the Father is except the Son and to whomever the Son would wish to reveal." 23. Then, after He turned toward the disciples by themselves, He said, "Blessed *are* the eyes that see what you are seeing. 24. For I say to you that many prophets and kings wanted to see what you are seeing but they did not see, and to hear what you are hearing but they did not hear."

The Good Samaritan

10:25. Then behold some master of Torah[2] stood up testing Him saying, "Teacher, what will I have to have done to inherit eternal life?" 26. And He said to him, "What has been written in the Torah? How do you read *it*?" 27. And he said, "'You will love the Lord your God out of your whole heart and with your whole being and with your whole strength' and with your whole mind, and '*love* your neighbor as yourself.'" (Dt 6:5, Lv 19:18) 28. And He said to him, "You answered correctly: you must do this and you will live *eternally*." 29. But because he wanted to justify himself he said to Jesus, "Who in fact is my neighbor?" 30. When He replied[3] Jesus said, "A certain man went down from Jerusalem to Jericho and fell among robbers, and then they stripped him, and after inflicting wounds went away, leaving *him* half dead. 31. And by chance there was a priest who came down by that way and when he saw him he crossed over to the other side: 32. and likewise also *a man who* was a Levite, as he came by the place, and when he saw *him* he crossed over. 33. And a certain traveling Samaritan came by him and when he saw *him* he was moved with compassion,

---

1   (v.18) See Satan in Glossary.
2   (v.25) Torah means teaching, instruction. See Torah in Glossary.
3   (v.30) This is a parable, a story that Jesus made up. On a tour to Israel our guide pointed out a small building on the road from Jerusalem to Jericho, saying that it was the inn where the man in this parable was taken. We should be careful to stick to facts, not elaborating, making false statements.

34. and then he came *over to him and* bound up his wounds, pouring olive oil[1] and wine, and after he put him on his own animal he led him to an inn and took care of him. 35. Then on the next day when he had to leave he gave two denarii to the innkeeper and said, 'You must take care of him, and whatever in addition you would spend, I will repay to you on my return.' 36. Who of these three does it seem to you had become a neighbor of the one who fell among the robbers?" 37. And he said, "The one who had mercy on him." And Jesus said to him, "You must go and you must do likewise."

Visiting Martha and Mary

10:38. And while they were going He entered a certain village: and a woman named Martha hosted Him. 39. And she had a sister called Mary[2] and after *Mary* seated herself at the feet of the Lord she was listening to His teaching. 40. But Martha was overburdened about so much serving: and standing by she said, "Lord, does it not concern You that my sister leaves only me to serve? Therefore, You must tell her that she should help me." 41. And the Lord said to her, "Martha. Martha![3] You are anxious and troubled concerning many things, 42. but one is a necessity, indeed Mary chose the good part which will not be taken away from her."

Teaching about Prayer

(Mt 6:9-15, 7:7-11)

11.1. Then it happened while He was in a certain place praying, as He finished, one of His disciples said to Him, "Lord, You must now teach us to pray, just as also John taught his disciples." 2. And He said to them, "When you pray you must say,

'Father, Your name must now be sanctified:
    Your kingdom must now come:
3.   You must continually give us day by day the things[4]
    necessary for our existence: [5]
4.   And You must immediately forgive us our sins,
    for we ourselves also forgive everything owing to us:[6]
And do not lead us into a trial.'" [7]

11:5. Then He said to them, "Who of you will have a friend and will go to him at midnight and would say to him, 'Friend, you must now lend me three

---

1   (v.34) In the Talmud, olive oil symbolizes knowledge of Torah, which provides spiritual illumination. Oil is also the symbol of joy, from Is 51:3, so it is called the oil of gladness.
2   (v.39) The name in Greek is Mariam, also in v. 42.
3   (v.41) The name repeated in this instance is a stern rebuke in Hebrew. See Double Name in Glossary.
4   (v.3) The text has bread, but that was an idiom that meant whatever was needed.
5   (v.3) The Greek word translated "necessary for our existence" is found only in Lk 11:3 and Mt 6:11. The meaning is not certain. See Daily Bread in Glossary.
6   (v.4) See Sin, Forgiveness of in Glossary.
7   (v.4) Or temptation

loaves of bread, 6. since my friend came to me from a journey and I do not have anything to set before him:' 7. and answering from inside, he said, 'You must not cause me trouble: the door has already been shut and my children are with me in the bed: I am not able to get up to give *it* to you.' 8. I say to you, even if he will not get up to give to him because he is a friend, but because of his shamelessness, when he gets up, he will give him what he needs. 9. And I say to you, You must continually ask and it will be given to you, you must continually seek and you will find, you must continually knock and it will be opened to you: 10. for everyone who asks takes and the one who seeks finds and for the one who knocks it will be opened. 11. And which of you *if* a son will ask his father for a fish will he then give him a snake instead of a fish? 12. Or also, *if* he will ask for an egg, will he give a scorpion to him? 13. If therefore you, *who* are evil yourselves, know how to give good gifts to your children, how much more the Father from heaven will give *the* Holy Spirit to those who ask Him."[1]

Jesus and Beelzebub

(Mt 12:22-30, Mk 3:20-27)

11:14. Then He was casting out a demon and this one was deaf and mute: and it happened, after the demon came out, the mute person spoke and the crowds were amazed. 15. But some of them said "He is casting out the demons by means of Beelzebub the leader of the demons:" 16. but others, testing, were seeking a sign from heaven from Him. 17. And because He knew their thoughts He said to them, "Every kingdom *that* is divided against itself is laid waste and a house *divided* against a house falls. 18. And if in fact Satan[2] is divided against himself, how will his kingdom stand? *Yet* you say that I cast out demons by Beelzebub. 19. But if I am casting out demons by Beelzebub, by whom are your sons casting *them* out? Because of this they will be your judges. 20. But if I am casting out demons by a finger of God, then the kingdom of God has come upon you. 21. 'When the strong one, since he was equipped, would guard his house, his possessions *would* be in peace: 22. but when *one* stronger than he attacked he would overcome him. He takes his armor from him in which he placed his confidence and they would distribute his booty.' (Ps Solomon 5:4) 23. The one who is not with Me is against Me, and the one who does not gather with Me is scattering."

The Return of the Unclean Spirit

(Mt 12:43-45)

11:24. "When the unclean spirit comes out from a person, it goes through dry places seeking rest,[3] but when it does not find any: then it says, 'I will return to my house from which I came: 25. and when it comes it finds that *its house* has

---

1   (v.13) From this we can conclude that we are to ask the Father to give us the Holy Spirit.
2   (v.18) See Satan in Glossary.
3   (v.24) This word for rest means just a short break, so demons cannot even get a coffee break.

been swept and decorated. 26. So then it goes and takes along seven other spirits more evil than itself and, after it enters, it dwells there: and the last days of that person become worse than the first."

True Blessedness

11:27. And it happened while He was saying these things some woman from the crowd, as she lifted her voice, said to Him, "Blessed *is* the womb which bore You and with whom You nursed." 28. And He said, "On the contrary, blessed are those who hear and observe[1] the Word of God."

The Demand for a Sign

(Mt 12:38-42, Mk 8:12)

11:29. And, when the crowds gathered even more, He began to say, "This generation is an evil generation: it seeks a sign, but no sign will be given it except the sign of Jonah. 30. For just as Jonah was a sign to the Ninevites, so also will the Son of Man be to this generation. 31. *The* queen of *the* South[2] will be raised in judgment with the people of this generation and she will condemn them, because she came from the ends of the Earth to hear the wisdom of Solomon, and behold greater than Solomon *is* here. 32. Ninevite men will rise in judgment with this generation and will condemn it: because they repented because of the preaching of Jonah, and behold greater than Jonah is here."

The Light of the Body

(Mt 5:15, 6:22,23)

11:33. "No one *who* has lit a lamp places *it* in hiding and not under a peck measure but on the lamp stand, so that those who go in would see the light. 34. Your eye is the lamp of your body: when your eye would be sound,[3] then your whole body is full of light: but when it would be evil[4] then your body *is* dark. 35. Therefore you must not ever consider that the light in you is darkness. 36. Then if your whole body is full of light, since it does not have any part which *is* darkness, the whole *body* will be full of light as when the lamp would illuminate you in the gleam of light."

The Denouncing of the Pharisees and Scholars

(Mt 23:1-36, Mk 12:38-40, Lk 20:45-47)

11:37. While He was speaking a Pharisee asked Him to dine with him: and after He entered He reclined. 38. But when the Pharisee saw he wondered because He did not first wash before dinner. 39. And the Lord said to him, "Now you Pharisees clean the outside of the cup and the dish but the inside of you is

---

1   (v.28) This Greek word, fulasso, means to guard, protect, take care not to violate.
2   (v.31) Queen of Sheba
3   (v.34) A good, or sound, eye is a Hebrew idiom for being generous.
4   (v.34) An evil eye is a Hebrew idiom for being stingy, selfish: See Dt 15:9, Pr 23:6, 7 and 28:22.

full of greediness and wickedness. 40. Foolish ones, did not the One Who made the outside also make the inside? 41. Nevertheless, you must now give gifts for the poor of what is inside *you*, then behold all is clean in you. 42. But woe to you Pharisees, because you tithe[1] the mint and the rue and every vegetable but you neglect justice and the love of God: and it was necessary to do these things, *tithe, but* not to neglect the other, *alms*. (Lv 27:30) 43. Woe to you, Pharisees, because you love the chief seat[2] in the synagogues and the greetings in the market places. 44. Woe to you, because you are like unseen graves, and people who walk over *the graves* do not know *it*."

11:45. But when he responded, one of the scholars[3] said to Him, "Teacher, when You say these things You even insult us." 46. Then He said, "And woe to you Torah scholars, because you load people with difficult burdens, then you do not even lift one finger to help with the burdens. 47. Woe to you, because you are building the tombs of the prophets, and your fathers killed them. 48. Now you are witnesses and you approve of the works of your fathers, because they indeed killed them, and indeed you are building *their tombs*. 49. Because of this the wisdom of God also said, 'I am sending prophets and apostles among them, and they will kill *some* of them, and they will persecute *others*,'[4] 50. so that the blood of all the prophets, that which has been shed from the foundation of *the* world, would be required from this generation, 51. from *the* blood of Abel until *the* blood of Zechariah, who was killed between the altar and the house:[5] indeed I say to you, it will be sought out, *required,* from this generation. 52. Woe to you Torah scholars because you took away the key of knowledge: you did not enter and you held back those who were entering." 53. And then when He came out from there the scribes and the Pharisees began to be very hostile and to interrogate Him concerning more things, 54. plotting to catch Him by something He would say.

A Warning against Hypocrisy

12.1. Meanwhile as the crowd of so many thousands gathered, so *they* trampled one another, He began to say to His disciples first, "You must be on guard for yourselves from the leaven of the Pharisees,[6] which is hypocrisy. 2. But there is nothing that has been concealed which will not be revealed and hidden which will not be known. 3. Because what you said in the darkness will

---

1   (v.42) See Tithe in Glossary.
2   (v.43) The chief seat is also called Moses' chair and signifies that its occupant is an acknowledged authority.
3   (v.45) Scholar or Learned in Torah refers to one who teaches the Hebrew Scriptures plus the oral teachings.
4   (v.49) The reference for this quote is not known.
5   (v.51) The word house is used frequently throughout the Bible to refer to either the temple or the sanctuary. In this case it is used for the sanctuary because the altar is next to the sanctuary, and both are in the temple. Luke refers to the temple as the house in Acts 2::2.
6   (v.1) The leaven of the Pharisees is legalism, which not even the Pharisees were able to keep, leading to hypocrisy.

be heard in the light, and what you spoke against others in the inner chambers will be proclaimed from the roofs."

Whom to Fear

(Mt 10:28-31)

12:4. "But I say to you, My friends, do not be afraid of those who kill the body but after these things *they* do not have anything more they can do. 5. But I will show you something you should fear: you must now fear the One Who after He kills has authority to throw *you* into Gehenna.[1] Indeed I say to you, you must now fear Him! 6. Are not five sparrows sold for two assarions?[2] And not one of them is forgotten in the sight of God. 7. But even the hairs of your head have all been counted. You must not be afraid: you are worth more than many sparrows."

Confessing Messiah before Men

(Mt 10:32,33, 12:32, 10:19,20)

12:8. "And I say to you, all, whoever would confess Me before people, then the Son of Man will confess him before the angels of God: 9. but the one who has denied Me before people will be denied before the angels of God. 10. And anyone who will speak a word against the Son of Man, it will be forgiven him: but to the one who has blasphemed against the Holy Spirit, it will not be forgiven. 11. And when they would bring you into the synagogues and *before* the leaders and the authorities, do not be anxious how you would defend yourselves or what you would say: 12. for the Holy Spirit will teach you in this moment what is necessary to say."

The Parable of the Rich Fool

12:13. And someone from the crowd said to Him, "Teacher, You must now tell my brother to divide the inheritance with me." 14. But He said to him, "Sir, who appointed Me a judge or arbitrator over you?" 15. And He said to them, "You must continually understand and guard yourselves from all covetousness, because someone's life is not abundant from his possessions." (Jn 10:10) 16. And He told them a parable, saying, "The field of some rich man was fruitful. 17. And he was deliberating with himself saying, 'What shall I do, because I do not have *a place* where I could gather my fruit?' 18. Then he said, 'I will do this, I will take down my storehouses and I will build bigger. Then I will gather there all the wheat and all my goods 19. and I will say to my very being, "Self, you have many good possessions being stored up for many years *to come*: you must continually rest,[3] you must right now eat, drink, enjoy yourself."' 20. Then God said to him,

---

1   (v.5) See Gehenna in Glossary.
2   (v.6) Pennies
3   (v.19) The Greek word translated rest means a temporary rest, a break. The rich man is not thinking of God's eternal rest, but of one continuous break from work, a permanent vacation. See Rest in Glossary.

'Foolish man, on this night they are demanding back your life from you: but what you have prepared, to whom will it be *given*?' (Sir 11:19) 21. This is *how it will be for* the one who stores up for himself and *does* not *store up* riches in God."

Care and Anxiety

(Mt 6:25-34, 19-21)

12:22. And He said to His disciples, "Because of this I say to you, do not be anxious in life about what you would eat nor with what you would clothe the body. 23. For life is more than food and the body *more* than clothes. 24. You must now consider the ravens because they do not sow and they do not harvest, for whom there is neither storeroom nor barn, and God feeds them: how much more than birds you yourselves are worth. 25. But who of you if you are anxious is able to add a cubit to his stature? 26. And therefore if you are not the least able *to do even this*, why are you anxious about the rest? 27. You must now consider the lilies, how they grow: they neither work nor spin: but I say to you, not even Solomon in all his glory was clothed like one of these. 28. And if God so clothes grass, *which* is in a field today then tomorrow is cast into a furnace, how much more you, little faiths. 29. So you must not be seeking what you could eat and what you could drink and you must stop being anxious: 30. for the heathens of the world are searching for all these things, but your Father knows that you continually have need of these things. 31. But you must habitually seek His kingdom, and these things will be added to you. 32. You, little flock, stop being afraid, because your Father took delight[1] to give you the kingdom. 33. You must sell your possessions and you must now give to the poor: you must now make for yourselves purses that do not wear out, an inexhaustible treasure in the heavens, where no thief comes near and no moth ruins: 34. for where your treasure is, there also will your heart be."[2]

Watchful Servants

(Mt 24:45-51)

12:35. "Your loins must be gird continually and your lamps burning: 36. and you *must be* like people while they are expecting the Lord Himself when He would return from the wedding feast,[3] so that when He comes and when He knocks they would open immediately for Him. 37. Blessed are those servants, whom the Lord will find alert when He comes: truly I say to you that He will gird Himself and He will recline *with* them and when He comes He will serve them. 38. And if He would come in the second or if in the third watch[4] then blessed are those *people* He would find this way. 39. But you know this, that if the master of the house had known what hour the thief was coming, he would not

---

1   (v.32) This is a done deal. The Father has already delighted to give you the kingdom.
2   (v.34) Note the tenses used: God took delight to give (v.32), there your treasure is (v.34).
Enjoy your covenant treasures now!
3   (v.36) See Wedding in Glossary.
4   (v.38) The second watch in Israeli time is from Midnight to 3:00 AM. See Day in Glossary.

have permitted anyone to dig through his house. 40. And you must be prepared because the Son of Man is coming in a time you do not think *He is coming.*"[1]

12:41. And Peter said, "Lord, are You telling this parable to us or also to all?" 42. Then the Lord said, "Who is really the faithful, wise steward, whom the Lord appointed in His service to give the portion *of food* in *the appointed* time? 43. Blessed is that servant whom, when his Lord comes, He will find *him* doing thus. 44. Truly I say to you that He will appoint him over all His possessions. 45. But if that servant would say in his heart, 'My Lord is delayed from coming,' and he would begin to beat the servants and the maids, to eat and even to drink and be drunk, 46. the Lord of that servant will come in a day in which he does not expect, and an hour, which he does not know, then He will punish him severely, and He will place his share with the unbelievers. 47. And that servant, the one who knows the will of his Lord, and who has not prepared or done in accordance with His will, will be beaten much: 48. but the one who has not known and has done *things* worthy of beating will be beaten little. And to everyone to whom much was given, much will be sought from him, and to whom He entrusted much, He will ask him more."

Jesus the Cause of Division
(Mt 10:34-36)

12:49. "I came to cast fire upon the earth, and how I wish it were already kindled. 50. But I have to be baptized[2] *with* a baptism, and somehow I am enduring until that would be completed. 51. Do you think that I have placed Myself near to give peace in the earth? I say to you, 'No,' but dissension. 52. For from now on five in one house will have been divided into opposing parts, three against two and two against three,

53.   'They will be divided father against son,
                and son against father,
        mother against daughter
                and daughter against mother,
        mother-in-law against her *son's* bride
                and bride against the mother-in-law.'" (Mic 7:6)

Discerning the Time
(Mt 16:2,3)

12:54. Then He was saying to the crowds, "When you see the cloud rising in the west, right away you say that 'A storm is coming,' and so it comes: 55. and when a south wind blows, you say that 'It will be burning heat,' and it is. 56. Hypocrites! You know how to examine the face of the earth and of the sky, but how is it you do not know how to examine this time?"

---

1   (v.40) No one knows when He is coming. Each must be ready every minute of every day. See Coming of Messiah in Glossary.
2   (v.50) This is speaking of the ordeal of His trial and crucifixion.

Settling with Your Accuser

(Mt 5:25,26)

12:57. "But why are you not even judging what is *obviously* right for yourselves? 58. For as you are going to a judge with your adversary, on the way you must give pains to be free from him, lest he would drag you away to the judge, and the judge will give you over to the bailiff, and the bailiff cast you into prison. 59. I say to you, you would **not** come out of there, until you would give even the last penny."

Repent or Perish

13.1. And some were present with Him at that very time reporting to Him about the Galileans whose blood Pilate mixed with their sacrifices. 2. Then He said to them, "Do you suppose that those of Galilee were greater sinners than all the others of Galilee, because they have suffered these things? 3. No, I say to you, but unless you would all repent you will likewise be destroyed. 4. Or those eighteen upon whom the tower in Siloam fell and it killed them, do you suppose that they were worse sinners than all the people who were dwelling in Jerusalem? 5. No, I say to you, but unless you would all repent you will likewise be destroyed."

The Parable of the Barren Fig Tree

13:6. And He was saying this in a parable: "Someone had a fig tree planted in his orchard, and he came seeking fruit on it but he did not find any. 7. So he said to the gardener, 'See, for three years I have been coming looking for fruit on this fig tree and I have not found any: so why does it use up the ground? Therefore you must now cut it.' 8. And he said to him, 'Sir, you must permit it just this year, until I will dig around it and I would put fertilizer *on it*, 9. and *see* if indeed it makes fruit in that year: then if it *does* not, you can cut it.'"

The Healing of a Crippled Woman on the Sabbath

13:10. And He was *regularly* teaching in one of the synagogues on the Sabbaths. 11. And behold *there was* a woman *who* had a spirit of sickness eighteen years and she was bent over and not able to stand fully erect. 12. And when Jesus saw her He called *her* out and said to her, "Ma'am, you have been set free from your sickness," 13. and He placed His hands on her: and she was immediately straightened up and was glorifying God. 14. But, angered that Jesus healed on the Sabbath, the synagogue leader was saying to the crowd that "There are six days in which it is necessary to work: therefore you must be healed *by* coming on those *days* and not on the Sabbath day." 15. And when He answered, the Lord then said, "Hypocrites! Does not each of you on the Sabbath loose his cow or donkey from the stall and lead it out *to* give *it* to drink? 16. But this one, *who* is a daughter of Abraham, whom Satan[1] bound eighteen long years, is it not

---

1   (v.16) See Satan in Glossary.

necessary to loose *her* from this bondage *even* on the Sabbath day?" 17. Then, while He was saying these things, all those opposed to Him were put to shame, but the whole crowd was rejoicing over all the splendid things taking place under Him.

The Parables of the Mustard Seed and the Leaven

(Mt 13:31-33, Mk 4:30-32)

13:18. Then He was saying, "What is the kingdom of God like and to what will I compare it? 19. It is like a mustard seed, which when a man took he threw *it* into his garden, then it grew and became a tree, and the birds of the sky lived in its branches."

13:20. Then He said again, "To what will I compare the kingdom of God? 21. It is like leaven, which when a woman took she hid *it* in three measures[1] of meal until *the* whole of it was leavened."

The Narrow Door

(Mt 7:13,14, 21-23)

13:22. Then He was going through city after city, and town after town, teaching and making His way to Jerusalem. 23. And someone said to Him, "Lord, *are* those being saved *just* a few?" But He said to them, 24. "You must continually strive to enter through the narrow door, because many, I say to you, will seek to enter, but they will not be strong enough. 25. Whenever the Master of the house would rise and shut the door and you would begin to stand outside and to knock on the door saying, 'Sir, you must immediately open to us,' then He will say to you, 'I do not know you *or* where you are from.' 26. Then you will begin to say, 'We ate and drank in Your presence and You taught in our streets:' 27. and He will speak, saying to you, 'I do not know you *or* where you are from: you must immediately depart from Me, all you workers of unrighteousness.' 28. There will be weeping and gnashing of teeth there, when you would see Abraham and Isaac and Jacob and all the prophets in the kingdom of God, but you being cast outside. 29. Then they will be present from east and west and from north and south and they will recline in the kingdom of God.[2] 30. And behold those who are first will be last and those who are last will be first."

The Lament over Jerusalem

(Mt 23:37-39)

13:31. In the same hour some Pharisees[3] came to Him saying, "You must come out at once and You must now go from this place because Herod wants to kill You." 32. Then He said to them, "When you go you must say to that

---

1   (v.21) Three measures is about a peck and a half.
2   (v.29) The saints in Heaven will recline to eat. See Reclining in Glossary.
3   (v.31) Although Jesus was upset by the legalism of the Pharisees, He and the Pharisees agreed down the line theologically, so He had friends among them.

fox, 'Behold I am casting out demons and healing. I am finishing today and tomorrow, and the third day I will reach My goal. 33. Nevertheless it is necessary for Me to go today and then tomorrow having to go *on to Jerusalem*, because it is not possible to kill a prophet outside Jerusalem. 34. Jerusalem. Jerusalem! The one who kills the prophets and stones those sent to her, how many times did I want to gather your children just as a hen gathers her brood under her wings, but you did not want *that*. 35. Behold your house is left desolate to you. But I say to you, you would **not** see Me until when He will come *and* you would say, 'Blessed *is* He Who comes in *the* name of *the* Lord.'" (Ps 118:26)

The Healing of the Man with Dropsy

14.1. And it happened, while He went to a house of a certain one of the leaders of the Pharisees on a Sabbath to eat a meal, that they were watching Him closely. 2. And behold a man who was suffering with dropsy *was* in front of Him. 3. And Jesus spoke to the Torah scholars and Pharisees saying, "Is it or is it not permitted to heal on the Sabbath?" 4. But they were silent. Then after He took hold *of him* He healed him and set *him* free. 5. Then He said to them, "A son or ox of any of you will fall into a well, and will any *of you* not immediately pull him up on a Sabbath day?" 6. And they were not able to dispute these things.

A Lesson to Guests and a Host

14:7. Then He was telling a parable to those who were invited, noticing how they chose the places of honor,[1] saying to them, 8. "When you would be invited by someone to wedding feasts you should not recline in the place of honor since *someone* more honored than you could have been invited by him, 9. and then when he comes, the one who invited you will say to you, 'You must now give *your* place to this one,' and then with shame you will begin to take possession of the last place.[2] 10. But when you would have been invited, when you go you must recline in the last place, so that when the one who invited you would come he will say to you, 'Friend, you must go up higher:' then honor will come to you in front of all those who recline[3] with you. 11. For everyone who exalts himself will be humbled and the one who humbles himself will be exalted." 12. And He was saying even to the one who invited Him, "When you would make a breakfast or supper, call neither your friends nor your brothers nor your kin nor rich neighbors, lest they would *also* invite you and it would be repayment to you. 13. But when you would make a banquet you must always invite poor, crippled, lame, blind: 14. then you will be blessed, because they do

---

1   (v.7) The place of honor was also referred to as Abraham's lap. See Reclining in Glossary.

2   (v.9) Pr 25::6,7 "Do not glorify yourself in the presence of the king, and do not stand in the place of the great, for it is better that it should be said to you, 'Come up here.' than that you be demoted before the prince, as your eyes have seen [happen to others]." (Stone Edition ArtScroll Tanach)

3   (v.10) They reclined to eat as a sign that they were free people, not Egyptian slaves. See Reclining in Glossary.

not have *the means* to repay you, for it will be repaid to you in the resurrection[1] of the righteous."

The Parable of the Great Banquet

(Mt 22:1-10)

14:15. And when a certain one of those who were reclining with *Him* heard these things he said to Him, "Blessed is he who will eat a meal in the kingdom of God." 16. But He said to him, "A certain man was making a great dinner, and invited many 17. and sent his servant in the hour of the dinner to say to those invited, 'You must come at once because it is now ready.' 18. And they all began from first to last to excuse themselves. The first said to him 'I bought a field and I have of necessity to go out to see it: I ask you, you must have me excused.' 19. And another said, 'I have bought five yoke of oxen and I am going to check them, I ask you, you must have me excused.' 20. Then another said, 'I married a wife and because of this I am not able to come.' 21. And when he returned the servant reported these things to his master. Then because the master of the house was angered he said to his servant, 'You must immediately go out into the streets and alleys of the city and you must now lead here the poor and *the* crippled and *the* blind and *the* lame.' 22. Then the servant said, 'Lord, what you commanded has been done, but there is even now a place.' 23. Then the master said to the servant, 'You must go out now into the roads and fences[2] and you must compel *them* to come in immediately, so that my house would be full: 24. for I say to you that none of those people invited will taste my dinner.'"[3]

The Cost of Discipleship

(Mt 10:37,38)

14:25. And enormous crowds were going with Him. Then after He turned He said to them, 26. "If anyone comes to Me and does not hate[4] his own father and mother and wife and children and brothers and sisters, yet even his own being, he is not able to be My disciple. 27. Who does not bear his own cross[5] and come behind Me, is not able to be My disciple. 28. For who of you when you want to build a tower, after he sits down *does* not first count the cost, if he has *enough* to complete *it*? 29. So that after he placed *the* foundation, then if he is not able to finish, all those who saw *it* would begin to mock him 30. saying that 'This man began to build and was not able to finish.' 31. Or if some king *is* going to engage a different king in war, does he not first sit down to consider

---

1   (v.14) See Resurrection in Glossary.
2   (v.23) Also translated hedges referring to the division of the fields. The servant was sent outside the city.
3   (v.24) How many of us today are too busy to sup daily with the King of Kings?
4   (v.26) Hate here is a relative term as it is used in OT verses, Dt 21:15, Mal 1:3, and others. The rabbis say these refer to one being loved more than another and are not to be taken as literal hatred.
5   (v.27) This is a prophecy by Jesus, telling how He would be killed.

if he is able to meet with ten thousand the one who is coming against him with twenty thousand? 32. Otherwise, when he is still far off, then he would send his ambassador *and* he would ask for peace. 33. So in this way every one of you who does not renounce all his own possessions is not able to be My disciple."

Tasteless Salt

(Mt 5:13, Mk 9:50)

14:34. "Salt to be sure is good: but if then the salt would become tasteless, with what will it be made savory? 35. It is suitable neither for *the* ground nor for the dung heap; they throw it outside. The one who has ears to hear must always listen."

The Parable of the Lost Sheep

(Mt 18:12-14)

15.1. And all the tax collectors and sinners were coming near to Him to listen to Him. 2. Then the Pharisees and the scribes were complaining, saying that "This One welcomes sinners and He eats with them." 3. But He told them this parable, saying, 4. "A certain man of you has one hundred sheep, and if he has lost one of them, will he not leave the ninety-nine in the wilderness and go after the lost one until he would find it? 5. Then when he finds it he places it upon his shoulders rejoicing. 6. And after he comes into *his* house he calls together *his* friends and neighbors saying to them, 'You must now rejoice with me, because I found my lost sheep.' 7. I say to you that in this way they are rejoicing in heaven over one repenting sinner more than ninety-nine righteous *people* who have no need of repentance."

The Parable of the Lost Coin

15:8. "Or if some woman, if she has ten drachmas *and* would lose one drachma,[1] does she not light a lamp and sweep the house and seek diligently until she would find it? 9. Then after she finds *it* she summons her friends and neighbors saying, 'Would you rejoice with me, because I found the drachma which I lost.' 10. Thus I say to you, there is joy before the angels of God over one sinner *who* repents."

The Parable of the Lost Son

15:11. And He said, "A certain man had two sons. 12. And the younger of them said to his father, 'Father, you must now give me the part of the property that belongs to me.' And he divided the property between them. 13. And after not many days, once he had collected everything, the younger son went on a journey to a far away country and there he squandered his wealth living dissolutely. 14. And, after he spent everything freely, a severe famine came throughout that country, and he began to be lacking. 15. And then he went *and* was joined *with*

---

1   (v.8) One drachma was about a day's wage.

one of the citizens of that country, *who* then sent him into his fields to feed pigs, 16. and he was desiring to be filled with the carob pods which the pigs were eating, but no one was giving him any. 17. And then he came to himself *and* said, 'How many hired hands of my father abound in food, but I am dying here in a famine. 18. When I get up I will go to my father and I will say to him, "Father, I sinned against heaven and before you, 19. I am no longer worthy to be called your son: you must make me as one of your hired hands."' 20. Then after he got up he went to his own father. And while he was still a great distance *away* his father saw him and was sympathetic and then he ran *and* fell upon his neck and kissed him. 21. And his son said to him, 'Father, I sinned against heaven and before you, I am no longer worthy to be called your son.' 22. But *his* father said to his servants, 'Quickly, you must right away bring out the best long robe and you must immediately put *it* on him, then give *him* a ring for his hand and sandals on his feet, 23. and bring the fattened calf,[1] you must now kill *it*, then, after we eat, we could rejoice, 24. because this my son was dead, but he came to life again. He was lost, but has been found,' and they began to rejoice.

15:25. "But his older son was in a field: and when he was coming, as he neared the house, he heard music and dancing, 26. and when he summoned one of the servants[2] he asked whatever these things might be. 27. And he said to him that 'Your brother has come, and your father killed the fattened calf, because he recovered him healthy.' 28. But he was angry and was not wanting to enter and when his father came out he was urging him. 29. And he said to his father, 'Behold how many years I have been serving you and never did I neglect your comment and never did you give me a goat so that I could rejoice with my friends: 30. but when this your son came, who had eaten up your wealth with prostitutes, you killed the fattened bull for him.' 31. And he said to him, 'Child, you have always been with me,[3] and all my things arc yours: 32. but it is necessary to rejoice and to be glad because this your brother was dead and he lives, and though he was lost now he is found.'"

The Parable of the Dishonest Steward

16.1. And then He was saying to the disciples, "A certain man was wealthy, who had a manager, and this *owner* brought charges against him because he was squandering *the owner's* wealth. 2. Then when he called him he said to him, 'What *is* this I hear about you? You must immediately give back the title of your office, for you are not able to still manage.' 3. But the manager said to himself, 'What shall I do, because my employer[4] is taking away the office from me? I am

---

1   (v.23) This is not a very young calf, but a yearling or older.
2   (v.26) Literally this says "one of the children" referring to a young indentured servant. See Servant in Glossary.
3   (v.31) In this parable the older son represents the Jewish people and the younger son the non-Jewish. While mankind left God when Adam and Eve sinned, the Jewish people returned to Him with Abraham and have been with Him ever since.
4   (v.3) In these verses the primary meaning of the Greek word translated employer is

not strong enough to dig, I am ashamed to beg. 4. I know what I shall do, so that when I would be deposed from the office they will receive me into their homes.' 5. Then after he summoned each one of his employer's debtors he said to the first, 'How much do you owe my employer?' 6. And he said, 'A hundred measures[1] of olive oil.' and he said to him, 'You must take your notes and after you sit down you must quickly write fifty *measures*.' 7. Then to another he said, 'And how much do you owe?' And he said, 'A hundred measures[2] of wheat.' He said to him, 'You must take your documents and you must now write eighty.' 8. Then the employer praised the unjust manager; that he did wisely: because the sons of this age are wiser than the sons of the light in their own generation.[3] 9. And I say to you, you must at once make friends for yourselves apart from unrighteous wealth, in order that when it would give out they[4] would take you into the eternal dwellings. 10. The one faithful in the least is also faithful in much, and the one unrighteous in the least is also unrighteous in much. 11. If therefore you were not faithful in unrighteous wealth, who will trust the true *riches* to you? 12. And if you are not faithful in that belonging to another, who will give your *property* to you? 13. And no house servant[5] is able to serve two masters: for he will either hate the one and will love the other, or he will be devoted to the one and he will despise the other. You are not able to serve God and wealth (Mt 6:24)."

The Torah and the Kingdom of God
(Mt 11:12,13)

16:14. The Pharisees were listening to all these things and since they were lovers of money they were sneering at Him.[6] 15. Then He said to them, "You are justifying yourselves before men, but God knows your hearts: because the one who is exalted among men *is* an abomination before God. 16. The Torah and the Prophets[7] *were proclaimed* until John: from then on the kingdom of God is being preached and everyone enters it forcibly. (Mt 11:12) 17. And it is easier for heaven and Earth to pass away than for one vav[8] of the Torah to fall. (Mt 5:18) 18. Every one who divorces his wife and marries another is committing adultery, and the man who marries *her* when she has been divorced from *her* husband is committing adultery."

The Rich Man and Lazarus

16:19. "And there was a certain wealthy man, and he dressed in a purple

---

master or lord.
1   (v.6) 800-900 gallons
2   (v.7) 1,000 bushels
3   (v.8) From this we know that believers are to seek the kingdom, not wealth, Mt 6:33.
4   (v.9) The righteous will welcome you as you enter eternal life.
5   (v.13) See Servant in Glossary.
6   (v.14) The Pharisees taught that prosperity was an earthly reward for righteousness. See Lk 12:15.
7   (v.16) Torah and the Prophets refers to the first five books of the Bible plus Jsh, Jd, 1 & 2 Sam, 1 & 2Ki, and Is through Mal excluding Dn. See Torah in Glossary.
8   (v.17) The vav is the second smallest letter in the Hebrew alphabet. See Yod in Glossary.

garment and fine linen, enjoying himself splendidly day after day. 20. And some poor *man* named Lazarus, covered with sores, had been lying at his gate 21. desiring to be fed from the things that fell from the table of the wealthy one: but even the dogs that came were licking his sores. 22. And it happened the poor man died and was carried away by the angels to the bosom of Abraham:[1] and then the rich man died and was buried. 23. And in Hades, as he was in torment, when he lifted up his eyes he saw Abraham from afar and Lazarus in front of him. 24. Then when he called out he said, 'Father Abraham, you must immediately have mercy on me and you must now send Lazarus so that he could dip the tip of his finger in water and it would cool my tongue, because I am suffering in this flame.' 25. But Abraham said, 'Child, you must remember that you took your good things in your life, and Lazarus likewise the bad things: but now here he is comforted, and you are in great pain. 26. And in all these *distances* between us and you, a great chasm has been established, so that those who wish to cross over from here to you would not be able, and they could not cross from there to us.' 27. And he said, 'Then I ask you, Father, that you would send him to my father's house, 28. for I have five brothers, so that he could warn them, so that they would not come into this place of torture.' 29. But Abraham said, 'They have Moses and the Prophets:[2] they must listen to them now.' 30. But he said, 'No, Father Abraham, but if someone from *the* dead would go to them they will repent.' 31. But he said to him, 'If they do not listen to Moses and the Prophets, then they will not be persuaded if someone would rise from *the* dead.'"

Some Sayings of Jesus

(Mt 18:6,7, 21,22, Mk 9:42)

17.1. Then He said to His disciples, "It is impossible for the stumbling blocks not to come, but woe *to the one* through whom they come: 2. it is better for him if a millstone were placed around his neck and he was thrown into the sea than that he would cause one of the least of these to sin. 3. You must always be on your guard for them. If your brother would sin you must immediately rebuke him, and if he would repent you must forgive him right away.[3] 4. And if he would sin against you seven times in a day and he would return to you seven times saying 'I repent,' you will forgive him."

17:5. Then the apostles said to the Lord, "You must add faith in us." 6. And the Lord said, "If you have faith like a mustard seed, and you would say to this mulberry tree, 'You must be uprooted at once and be planted in the sea:' then it *would* obey you.

17:7. "And who of you if you have a servant plowing or shepherding,

---

1   (v.22) The bosom of Abraham is an idiom referring to the place of honor at a banquet, although here it refers to his being next to Abraham, a partaker of the same blessedness as Abraham in Paradise. See Reclining in Glossary.

2   (v.29) Moses and the Prophets is the same as the Torah and the Prophets.

3   (v.3) See Sin, Forgiveness of in Glossary

who, when he comes in from the field, will say to him, 'Come now, you must recline,' 8. but will he not say to him, 'You must immediately prepare what I will eat and now gird yourself, you must serve me until I would eat and I would drink, then after these things you will eat and you will drink?' 9. Does he thank the servant because he did the things that were ordered?[1] 10. Thus also yourselves, when you would have done all the things ordered to you, you must say that 'We are worthless servants, we have done what we ought to have done.'"

The Cleansing of Ten Lepers[2]

17:11. Then it happened, while He was going to Jerusalem, that He was crossing the border between Samaria and Galilee. 12. And when He came into a certain village ten leprous men met Him. They stood at a distance 13. and they raised *their* voices saying, "Jesus, Master, You must immediately have mercy on us." 14. And when He saw *them* He said to them, "When you go you must show yourselves at once to the priests." (Lv 14:2,3) And it happened while they were going they were cleansed. 15. And one of them, when he saw that he was healed, returned, glorifying God with a loud voice, 16. and he fell on *his* face at His feet, giving thanks to Him: and this one was a Samaritan. 17. And Jesus said, "Were not ten cleansed? Then where are the nine? 18. Were there not found *any* returning to give glory to God except this foreigner?" 19. Then He said to him, "After you rise you must immediately go: your faith has delivered you."

The Coming of the Kingdom

(Mt 24:23-28, 37-41)

17:20. And having been asked by the Pharisees when the kingdom of God is coming He answered them and said, "The kingdom of God does not come by means of, or in company with,[3] close observation,[4] 21. and will they not say, 'Behold it is here,' 'There *it is*,' for behold the kingdom of God is within you."[5] 22. And He said to the disciples, "Days will come when you will desire to see one of the days of the Son of Man and you will not see *it*. 23. Then they will say to you, 'Behold there' or 'Behold here:' you should not go away and you should not pursue. 24. For just as the lightning flash lights from *one place* under the sky to *another place* under the sky, so will be the Son of Man in His Day. 25. But first it is necessary for Him to suffer many things and to be rejected by this generation. 26. And just as it was in the days of Noah, so also it will be in the days of the Son of Man: 27. they were eating, they were drinking, they were marrying, they

---

1   (v.9) The Greek construction anticipates a negative reply.

2   (Caption) This is not the disease called leprosy today. See Leprosy in Glossary.

3   (v.20) The Greek preposition can be translated either 'by means of,' 'in company with,' or just 'with.' Another way of saying it is that watching for Messiah will not bring Him any sooner.

4   (v.20) That is not by watching for it and not by seeking signs, but by doing the will of the Father.

5   (v.21) Or among you. Paul wrote in 1Cor 15:50. "But I say this, brothers, that flesh and blood are not able to inherit the kingdom of God.." The kingdom is spiritual. See Kingdom in Glossary.

were being given in marriage, until that day Noah entered the ark and the flood came and killed everybody. 28. Likewise just as it happened in the days of Lot: they were eating, they were drinking, they were buying, they were selling, they were planting, they were building: 29. but on the day Lot came out from Sodom, it rained fire and brimstone from heaven and killed *them* all. 30. It will be according to these things on the day the Son of Man is revealed. 31. In that Day he who will be on the roof and his property in the house, must not go down to take it, and likewise the one in a field must not return for the things behind. 32. You must continually remember Lot's wife. 33. Whoever would seek to keep his own life safe will lose it, but whoever would lose *it* will preserve it alive. 34. I say to you, on this night two will be on one bed, the one will be taken along, *and* the other will be left: 35. two *women* will be grinding upon this *stone*, the one will be taken along,[1] but the other will be left."[2] 37. And when they answered they said to Him, "When, Lord?" And He said to them, "Where the body *is*, there also the eagles will be gathered."

The Parable of the Widow and the Judge

18.1. And He was telling them a parable that it was always necessary for them to pray and not to lose heart, 2. saying, "A certain judge in some city was not fearing God and not respecting man. 3. And there was a widow in that city and she was coming to him saying, 'You must immediately vindicate me from my opponent in a law suit.' 4. And for some time he was not wanting *to*. But after these things he said to himself, 'Even if I do not fear God and do not respect man, 5. because this widow causes me trouble I will vindicate her, so that in the end she would not wear me out by *her* coming *and brow-beating.*'" 6. And the Lord said, "You must now hear what the unrighteous judge is saying of the injustice: 7. and would God **not** execute justice for His chosen ones, for those who call to Him day and night, and does He *not* also have patience with them? 8. I say to you that He will see to it that justice is done quickly for them. Nevertheless, when the Son of Man comes, will He find faith on the Earth?"[3]

The Parable of the Pharisee and the Tax Collector

18:9. And He told this parable also to some of those who were confident that they were righteous, even treating the rest with contempt: 10. "Two men went up to the temple to pray, the one a Pharisee and the other a tax collector. 11. When the Pharisee stood he was praying *aloud* these things for himself, 'God, I thank You that I am not like the rest of the people, swindlers, unrighteous, adulterers, or even like this tax collector: 12. I fast twice a week, I tithe[4] everything that I acquire.' 13. But then the tax collector stood far off *and* did not want to lift up

---

1   (v.35) This Greek word, paralambano, speaks of the bridegroom taking his bride.

2   (v.35) V. 36 is omitted because it was not in the earliest manuscripts.

3   (v.8) The construction here anticipates a negative answer and expresses anxiety or impatience.

4   (v.12) See Tithe in Glossary.

his eyes to heaven, but he was beating his chest saying, 'God, You must now be merciful to me, the sinner.' 14. I say to you, this one went down to his house having been made righteous by that: because everyone who raises himself will be humbled, but the one who humbles himself will be lifted up."

Little Children Blessed

(Mt 19:13-15, Mk 10:13-16)

18:15. And they were bringing infants to Him so that He could touch them: but when the disciples saw *them* they were rebuking them. 16. But Jesus summoned them saying, "You must now permit the children to come to Me and you must not forbid them, for the kingdom of God is of such as these. 17. Truly I say to you, whoever would not receive the kingdom of God like a child could **not** come into it."

The Rich Ruler

(Mt 19:16-30, Mk 10:17-31)

18:18. Then some official asked Him saying, "Good teacher, what must I do so that I will inherit eternal life?" 19. And Jesus said to him, "Why do you call Me good? No one is good except One, God. 20. You know the commandments: 'Do not commit adultery, do not murder, do not steal, do not bear false witness, honor your father and your mother.'" 21. And he said, "I have kept all these from *my* youth." 22. And when He heard, Jesus said to him, "Yet one thing is lacking for you: you must immediately sell everything which you have and you must right away distribute *the money* to *the* poor and you will have treasure in the heavens, then come, you must continually follow Me." 23. But when he heard these things he became very sad: for he was extremely wealthy.

18:24. And when Jesus saw him become sad He said, "How hard it is for those who have wealth (Lk 16:9) to enter the kingdom of God: 25. for it is easier for a camel to enter through an eye of a needle[1] than a wealthy person[2] to enter the kingdom of God." 26. Then those who heard said, "Then who is able to be saved?" 27. But He said, "The things not possible with people are possible with God." 28. And Peter said, "Behold, we followed You, leaving our own things." 29. And He said to them, "Truly I say to you that there is no one who left home or wife or brothers or parents or children for the sake of the kingdom of God, 30. who would not recover many times more in this time and in the coming age, eternal life."

---

1   (v.25) The eye of a needle was also a reference to the small door in the city gate so someone could get in or out when the gate was shut. A camel could go through only after the saddle and any pack were removed. See Lk 14:33.

2   (v.25) The Pharisees taught that doing righteous deeds, obeying God's teachings would be rewarded in this life, very much like the prosperity message in today's church. See Wealth in Glossary.

A Third Time Jesus Foretells His Death and Resurrection[1]

(Mt 20:17-19, Mk 10:32-34)

18:31. And taking the twelve He said to them, "Behold, we are going up to Jerusalem, and everything which has been written by the prophets for the Son of Man will be fulfilled: 32. for He will be given over to the heathens and He will be mocked and He will be treated shamefully and He will be spit upon 33. and after they scourge *Him* they will kill Him, and on the third day He will be raised." 34. But they did not understand these things and this message was being hidden from them and they did not comprehend what was said.

The Healing of a Blind Beggar near Jericho

(Mt 20:29-34, Mk 10:46-52)

18:35. And it happened while they were approaching Jericho, a certain blind man was sitting by the road, begging. 36. And when he heard the crowd passing through he asked what this might be. 37. And they were reporting to him that "Jesus of Nazareth is coming by." 38. Then he shouted saying, "Jesus, Son of David,[2] You must right now have mercy on me!" 39. Then those who were going before *Him* were ordering him to be quiet, but he cried out much more, "Son of David, You must right now have mercy on me!" 40 And when He stopped, Jesus ordered him to be led to Him. And when he came near He asked him, 41. "What do you want Me to do for you?" And he said, "Lord, that I will recover my sight." 42. Then Jesus said to him, "You must now receive your sight: your faith has delivered you." 43. And he immediately received his sight and he was following Him, glorifying God. And when all the people saw *the miracle* they gave praise to God.

Jesus and Zachaeus

19.1. Having entered Jericho He was going through *it*. 2. And there was a man named Zachaeus, and he was a chief tax collector[3] and he *was* wealthy: 3. and he was seeking to see Who Jesus was but he was not able on account of the crowd, because his stature was short. 4. And as he was running before *them,* in front of *the crowd* he went up in a sycamore fig tree so that he could see Him, because He was going to pass by there. 5. Then as He came to the place, when Jesus looked up He said to him, "Zachaeus, because you have been zealous *for the Lord* you must now get down, for today it is necessary for Me to stay in your house." 6. Then as he made haste he got down and received Him rejoicing. 7. And when all saw they were complaining saying that "He entered to find lodging with a sinful man." 8. And when Zachaeus stood up he said to the Lord, "Behold half of my possessions, Lord, I am giving to the poor, and if I extorted someone I

---

1   (Caption) See Resurrection in Glossary.
2   (v.38) See Son of David/Son of Joseph in Glossary.
3   (v.2) Every tax collector in Israel was very well connected in Israeli society, born to the right family and wealthy to start with.

am repaying fourfold." 9. And Jesus said to him that "Today salvation has come to this house, because this one also is a son of Abraham: 10. for the Son of Man came to seek and to save the lost."

The Parable of the Ten Minas[1]

(Mt 25:14-30)

19:11. And while they were listening to these things He again told them a parable because He was near Jerusalem and they thought that the kingdom of God was going to be revealed at once, *as soon as He reached Jerusalem.* 12. Therefore He said, "A certain man, a nobleman, was going to a far away land to take a kingdom for himself, then to return. 13. And after he called his ten servants he gave ten minas to them and said to them, 'You must do business while I am gone.' 14. But its citizens hated him and they sent ambassadors after him saying, 'We do not want this one to reign over us.' 15. Then it happened when he returned, after he took the kingdom, that he said to summon to him those servants to whom he had given the money, so that he might know what they had earned. 16. And the first one appeared saying, 'Lord, your mina earned ten minas.' 17. Then he said to him, 'Well done! Good servant, because you were faithful in *the* least, you must continually have authority over ten cities.' 18. Then the second came saying, 'Your mina, lord, made five minas.' 19. And he said to this one also, 'Then you must continually be over five cities.' 20. Then the other one came saying, 'Lord, behold your mina, which I have put away in a handkerchief: 21. for I was fearing you, because you are a severe man, you take what you did not put away and you harvest what you did not sow.' 22. He said to him, 'From your mouth I judge you, evil servant. Had you known that I am a severe man, taking out what I did not put in and reaping what I did not sow? 23. Then why did you not give my money on a changer's table? Then when I came I *would have* exacted with interest.' 24. And to those who were standing by he said, 'You must now take the mina from him and you must give *it* at once to the one who has ten minas' 25. - then they said to him, 'Lord, he has ten minas.' - 26. I say to you that to everyone who has it will be given, but from the one who does not have even what he does have will be taken. 27. 'Moreover my enemies, those who do not want me to reign over them, you must right now lead *them* here and you must slaughter them in front of me.'"

The Triumphal Entry into Jerusalem

(Mt 21:1-11, Mk 11:1-11, Jn 12:12-19)

19:28. Then after He said these things He was going before *them*, going up to Jerusalem. 29. And it happened as He neared Bethphage[2] and Bethany[3]

---

1   (Caption) A mina equals 50 shekels or about 100 drachmas or 100 denarii, a few months' wages.

2   (v.29) Bethphage is the Greek spelling of the Hebrew Beit-Pag, meaning Place of Unripe Figs, which was close to Bethany.

3   (v.29) Bethany is the Greek spelling of Beit-Anyah, meaning House of Sighing in Hebrew.

by the mount called Olives, He sent two of the disciples 30. saying, "You must go into the village opposite,[1] when you enter it you will find a colt[2] tied, upon which nobody has ever sat. Then after you loose *it* you must lead it *here*. 31. And if someone asks you, 'Why are you loosing *it*?' You will say thus, that 'The Lord has need of it.'" 32. And when they went, those who were sent found just as He said to them. 33. And while they were loosing the colt its owners said to them, "Why are you loosing the colt?" 34. And they said, "The Lord has need of it." 35. Then they led it to Jesus and after they put their prayer shawls[3] on the colt they put Jesus on *it*. 36. And while He was going they were spreading their prayer shawls on the road.

19:37. And while He was now nearing the slope of the Mount of Olives the multitude of disciples, rejoicing, were all beginning to praise God in a loud voice concerning all *the* miracles which they had seen, 38. saying,

"'Blessed is the One Who comes,
the King in *the* name of the Lord:' (Ps 118:26)
peace in heaven
and glory in *the* highest."

39. Then some of the Pharisees from the crowd said to Him, "Teacher, You must immediately rebuke Your disciples." 40. And answering them He said, "I say to you, if they are silent the stones will cry out." (Hab 2:11)

19:41. Then as He neared, when He saw the city He wept for it 42. saying that "If you even knew in this day the things pertaining to peace: but now it has been hidden from your eyes. 43. Because days will come upon you and your enemies will cast up palisades[4] about you and they will surround you and they will attack you from all sides, 44. then they will dash you and your children with you to the ground, and they will not leave a stone upon a stone among you, because you did not know the time of your visitation."

The Cleansing of the Temple

(Mt 21:12-17, Mk 11:15-19, Jn 2:13-22)

19:45. And when He entered the temple He began to cast out the sellers, 46. saying to them, "It has been written,

'And My house will be a house of prayer,' (Is 56:7)
but you have made it a cave of robbers." (Jr 7:11)

19:47. And He was teaching daily in the temple. And the high priests and the scribes and the leaders of the people were seeking to kill Him, 48. but they did not find what they could do, because all the people were hanging upon

---

1   (v.30) Across the valley
2   (v.30) This is a foal of a donkey. See Donkey in Glossary.
3   (v.35) The Greek word imatia, meaning cloak or outer garment, is used here and in v. 36, and the cloak of a Jewish man was his prayer shawl. See Prayer Shawl in Glossary.
4   (v.43) Siege works

what they were hearing from Him.

The Authority of Jesus Questioned

(Mt 21:23-27, Mk 11:27-33)

20.1. Then it happened on one of the days while He was teaching the people in the temple and proclaiming the Good News, the high priests and the scribes were standing near with the elders 2. and they spoke, saying to Him, "You must immediately tell us by what authority You are doing these things, or who is the one who gave You this authority?" 3. And He said to them, "And I will ask you a question, and you must immediately tell Me: 4. 'Was the baptism of John from heaven or from men?'" 5. Then they were discussing among themselves saying "If we would say, 'From heaven,' He will say, 'Why did you not believe him?' 6. But if we would say, 'From men,' all the people will stone us, for they are persuaded that John was a prophet." 7. Then they answered that they did not know from where. 8. And Jesus said to them, "And I am not telling you by what authority I am doing these things."

The Parable of the Vineyard and the Tenants[1]

(Mt 21:33-46, Mk 12:1-12)

20:9. And He began to tell this parable to the people: "A certain man planted a vineyard, then leased it to farmers and went on a journey for a long time. 10. And in time he sent a servant to the farmers so that they would give him from the fruit of the vineyard: but the farmers, after they beat him, sent *him* out empty-handed. 11. Then he again sent another servant: but after they beat and dishonored that one also, they sent him out empty-handed. 12. And again he sent a third: and after they also wounded this one they threw *him* out. 13. And the master of the vineyard said, 'What shall I do? I will send my beloved son: they will probably respect him.' 14. But when they saw him the farmers were discussing with one another saying, 'This one is the heir: we should kill him, so that the inheritance would be ours.' 15. Then after they threw him outside the vineyard they killed *him*. What therefore will the master of the vineyard do to them? 16. He will come and he will destroy these farmers and he will give the vineyard to others." When they heard they said, "May it not be!" 17. And looking at them He said, "Then why has this been written:

'A stone which the builders rejected,
　　　this has become *the* cornerstone.' (Ps 118:22)

18. Everyone who falls upon that stone will be dashed to pieces: on whomever it would fall, it will crush him." 19. And the scribes and the high priests sought to get their hands on Him in that hour, for they knew that He spoke against them in this parable, but they feared the people.

1　　　(Caption) Each of these parables about the vineyard uses the picture of greedy farmers to speak of the High Priest and other Jewish leaders.

Paying Taxes to Caesar

(Mt 22:15-22, Mk 12:13-17)

20:20. Then because they were watching Him closely they sent spies *who* were pretending to be righteous themselves, so that they could catch Him in something He said, in order to give Him over to the leader and to the authority of the governor. 21. And they asked Him saying, "Teacher, we know that You are speaking and teaching correctly and You do not show favoritism,[1] but You are teaching the way of God in truth: 22. is it proper for us to pay taxes to Caesar or not?" 23. But when He considered their craftiness He said to them, 24. "You must now show Me a denarius: it has whose likeness and inscription on it?" And they said, "Caesar's." 25. And He said to them, "So you must pay to Caesar what *is* Caesar's and to God what *is* God's." 26. And they were not able to lay hold of Him by what He said before the people, so they were silent, amazed at His answer.

The Question about the Resurrection[2]

(Mt 22:23-33, Mk 12:18-27)

20:27. And some of the Sadducees came, those who were saying there was not to be a resurrection. They asked Him 28. saying, "Teacher, Moses wrote for us, if some brother would die, if he had a wife, and this one would be childless, that his brother would take the wife and he would raise up a seed for his brother. 29. Then there were seven brothers: and the first, after he took a wife, died childless: 30. then the second 31. and the third took her, and likewise also the seven did not leave a child when they died. 32. Later the wife died also. 33. Therefore the wife, in the resurrection, whose wife does she become? For seven had her as wife." 34. Then Jesus said to them, "The children of this age are marrying and being given in marriage, 35. and those of that age, and found worthy to reach the resurrection of the dead, neither marry nor are given in marriage: 36. for they are not able to die again, because they are like angels and are children of God, being children of the resurrection. 37. But since the dead are rising, and Moses revealed *this* at the bush, as he said, 'Lord, the God of Abraham and *the* God of Isaac and *the* God of Jacob.' 38. Thus He is not *the* God of *the* dead but of *the* living, for all should be living in Him." (Ex 3:6,15,16) 39. Then some of the scribes said, "Teacher, You said well." 40. For they were no longer daring to ask Him anything.

The Question about David's Son

(Mt 22:41-46, Mk 12:35-37)

20:41. Then He said to them, "How do they say the Messiah is a son of

---

1   (v.21) Literally this is "take the appearance of a man," a Hebrew idiom meaning He is does not play favorites, Dt 10:17.
2   (Caption) See Resurrection in Glossary.

David?[1] 42. For David himself says in a scroll of Psalms,

> '*The* Lord said to my Lord,
> You must be seated at My right hand,[2]

43. until I would make Your enemies a footstool
under Your feet.' (Ps 110:1)

44. So David calls Him Lord, then how is He his son?"

The Denouncing of the Scribes

(Mt 23:1-36, Mk 12:38-40, Lk 11:37-54)

20:45. And then all the people heard *that* He said to His disciples, 46. "Pay attention to the scribes who want to walk in long robes and love greetings in the markets and chief seats in the synagogues and chief places at the dinners, 47. they are devouring the houses of widows and on a pretext they are praying long: they will receive greater judgment."

The Widow's Offering

(Mk 12:41-44)

21.1. And when He looked up He saw those wealthy as they cast their gifts into the treasury. 2. And He saw some poor widow throwing two small coins there, 3. and He said, "Truly I say to you that this poor widow cast more than all: 4. for they all cast from their abundance for their gifts, but she cast from her need everything that she had for life."

The Destruction of the Temple Foretold

(Mt 24:1,2, Mk 13:1,2)

21:5. Then, when some were saying concerning the temple that it had been adorned with beautiful stones and votive offerings,[3] He said, 6. "These things which you see, days will come in which no stone will be left upon another stone which will not be destroyed."

Signs and Persecutions

(Mt 24:3-14, Mk 13:3-13)

21:7. But they asked Him saying, "Teacher, when therefore will these things be and what sign when these things are going to happen?" 8. And He said, "See that you would not be misled: for many will come in My name saying, 'I am He,' and 'The time has drawn near.' Do not go after them. 9. But when you hear *of* wars and insurrections, do not be terrified: for it is necessary for these things to come first, but the end is not right away." 10. Then He was saying to them,

---

1   (v.41) See Son of David/Son of Joseph in Glossary.
2   (v.42) "At the right hand" is a Hebrew idiom that speaks of power and strength, from Ex 15:6. See Right Hand in Glossary.
3   (v.5) A votive offering is something of value given for permanent display in the temple.

"Heathen will rise against heathen[1] and kingdom against kingdom, 11. there will be great earthquakes and in places famines and pestilences, and horrors and there will be great signs, *terrifying portents*, from heaven. 12. But before all these things *happen* they will seize you and they will persecute *you*, handing *you* over in public gatherings and jails, leading *you* before kings and governors because of My name: 13. it will lead you into bearing testimony. 14. However you must place in your hearts not to prepare to defend yourselves: 15. for I will give you *the* ability to speak with persuasion and wisdom, which all those set against you will not be able to oppose or to speak against. 16. And you will be given over even by parents and brothers and relatives and friends, and they will put some of you to death: 17. and you will be hated by all because of My name. 18. But **not** a hair of your head would be lost.[2] 19. In your perseverance you will acquire your *eternal* lives."

The Destruction of Jerusalem Foretold

(Mt 24:15-21, Mk 13:14-19)

21:20. "And when you see Jerusalem being encircled by armies, then you will know that its desolation has drawn near. 21. Then those in Judea must flee to the mountains and those in the midst of her, *Jerusalem,* must go out and those in the regions must not enter her, 22. because these are *the* days of punishment to be fulfilled for everything, which has been written. 23. Woe to those *who* are pregnant and to those *who* are nursing in those days: for there will be great distress upon the Earth, and wrath for this people, 24. and they will fall by *the* edge of a sword and they will be led away captive among all the heathens,[3] and Jerusalem will be trampled by heathens, until the times of the heathens[4] would be fulfilled." (Dn 12:7, Tob 14:5, Ro 11:25, and see note on Ro 11:25)

The Coming of the Son of Man

(Mt 24:29-31, Mk 13:24-27)

21:25. "And there will be signs in *the* sun and moon and stars (Is 13:10, Ez 32:7, Jl 2:30,31) and on the Earth anguish of heathens in bewilderment, *and the* roar and tossing of *the* sea, (Ps 46:2,3 65:7, Is 24:19, Wsd 5:22) 26. then people *will* stop breathing from fear and expectation of things that are coming in the inhabited world, for the powers of the heavens will be shaken. (Hg 2:6,21) 27. And then they will see the Son of Man as He comes in a cloud with power and

---

1   (v.10) Some translate this as nation against nation, but a nation is the same as a kingdom and today we see heathen against heathen in Bosnia, Kosovo, and other places. A heathen is someone who is not Jewish. Today there are few kingdoms as they have been replaced by entities called nations.

2   (v.18) How can you be killed without having a hair disturbed? Eternal life is assured, as seen in v. 19.

3   (v.24) Or nations

4   (v.24) Times or Fullness of the heathens is seen in Ro 11:25 and Gn 48:19, when Jacob blessed Ephraim, the Hebrew literally says "fullness of the heathens" (m'lo goyim) which is translated "group of nations" (NIV) or "multitude of nations" (Amp).

great glory. (Dn 7:13) 28. But when these things begin to happen you must rise up and you must lift up your heads at once, because your redemption, procured by payment of ransom, is drawing near." (En 51:2)

The Lesson of the Fig Tree

(Mt 24:32-35, Mk 13:28-31)

21:29. Then He told this parable to them: "You saw the fig tree and all the trees: 30. when they would now put forth *their leaves*, when you see them for yourselves, you know that summer is already near. 31. And so then you, when you would see these things happening, you must know that the kingdom of God is near. (Lk 17:21) 32. Truly I say to you, that this generation would **not** pass by until all these things would happen. 33. The sky[1] and the Earth will pass away, but My words will **never** pass away."

Exhortation to Watch

21:34. "But you must take heed for yourselves that your hearts would not be carried away in carousing and drunkenness[2] and cares of life, and that Day, *Judgment*, would appear over you, unexpected 35. as a trap: for it will rush in suddenly and forcibly upon all those who inhabit *the* face of the whole Earth. (Is 24:17) 36. And you must continually be watchful at every time *or every season* asking that you would prevail to escape all these things that are going to happen and to stand before the Son of Man."

21:37. And *during* the days He was in the temple teaching, and the nights when He came out He was staying on the mountain called Olives: 38. and all the people rose early on account of Him, to listen to Him in the temple.

The Plot to Kill Jesus

(Mt 26:1-5, 14-16, Mk 14:1,2, 10,11, Jn 11:45-53)

22.1. And the Feast of Unleavened Bread was approaching, the one called Passover. 2. And the high priests and the scribes were seeking how they could kill Him, *but* they were fearing the people. 3. But Satan[3] entered Judas, the one called Iscariot, *who* was of the number of the twelve: 4. and when he left he discussed with the high priests and magistrates how he could give Him over to them. 5. Then they rejoiced and agreed to give him money. 6. And he consented, and he was seeking an opportunity to give Him over without a crowd with them.

---

1   (v.33) The word translated sky could also be translated heaven, but that is misleading. God is eternal and so is His throne. The Earth and the solar system may well pass away but the heavens are eternal.

2   (v.34) The word translated drunkenness refers to use of any intoxicant. See Sorcery in Glossary.

3   (v.3) See Satan in Glossary.

The Preparation of the Seder[1]

(Mt 26:17-25, Mk 14:12-21, Jn 13:21-30)

22:7. And the day of the Feast of Unleavened Bread came, in which it was necessary to kill the Passover: (Mk 14:12) 8. and He sent Peter and John saying, "When you go you must immediately prepare the Passover *meal* for us so that we could eat." 9. And they said to Him, "Where do You want us to prepare *it?*" 10. And He said to them, "Behold, when you have entered the city a man *who* is carrying a jar of water will meet you: you must at once follow him to the house that he enters 11. and you will say to the master of the house, 'The teacher says to you, "Where is the guest room, where I could eat the Seder with My disciples?"' 12. That one will show you a large furnished upper room: you must prepare *it* there right away." 13. After they left they found just as He had told them and they prepared the Seder.

The Last Seder

(Mt 26:26-30, Mk 14:22-26, 1Cor 11:23-25)

22:14. Then when the hour came, He and the apostles with Him reclined.[2] 15. And He said to them, "I have greatly desired *with* a longing to eat this Seder with you before I suffer: 16. for I say to you that I would **not** eat it *again* until this would be fulfilled in the kingdom of God." 17. Then having taken a cup,[3] after He gave thanks, He said, "You must take this and you must immediately share *it* among yourselves: 18. for I say to you, that from now on I am **not** drinking from this product of the vine until the kingdom of God would come." 19. Then having taken bread, after He gave thanks, He broke *it* and gave *it* to them saying, "This is My body which is being given on your behalf: you must continually do this in My remembrance." 20. Then likewise the cup after they ate,[4] saying, "This *is* the cup of the New[5] Covenant (Jr 31:31-34[6]) in My blood which is being poured out on your behalf. 21. Nevertheless, behold, the hand of the one who is giving Me over *is* with Mine on the table. 22. The Son of Man is indeed going to that which has been appointed, but woe to that man through whom He is given over." 23. Then they began to argue among themselves who of them might consequently be the one who is going to do this.

The Dispute about Greatness

22:24. And there was a dispute among them, which of them seemed to be

1   (Caption) Seder is the name of the Passover meal. See Seder in Glossary.
2   (v.14) They reclined as a reminder that they were free, not slaves in Egypt. See Reclining in Glossary.
3   (v.17) The first cup at a Seder, called The Kiddush, meaning sanctification, sanctifies the table for the evening.
4   (v.20) At a Seder a total of four or five cups are served. See Seder in Glossary.
5   (v.20) Both the Greek word used here and the Hebrew word in Jr 31 have a basic meaning of renew, building on the previous covenants. See New Covenant in Glossary.
6   (v.20) In v. 33 the Hebrew word for sin is khatah, meaning sin committed in error, carelessly. See Sin in Glossary.

greater. 25. But He said to them, "The kings of the heathens are lording *it* over them and those who have authority over them are called benefactors. 26. But you are not thus, but the greatest among you must continually become like the younger, and the one who rules like the one who serves. 27. For who is greater, the one who reclines or the one who serves? Is it not the one who reclines? But I AM in your midst as the One Who serves. 28. And you are the ones who have stood by with Me in My afflictions: 29. and I am assigning to you, just as My Father assigned a kingdom to Me, 30. so that you would eat and you would drink at My table in My kingdom, and you will be seated upon thrones judging the twelve tribes of Israel."

Peter's Denial Foretold

(Mt 26:31-35, Mk 14:27-31, Jn 13:36-38)

22:31. "Simon. Simon![1] Behold Satan[2] demanded to sift you *all*[3] like wheat: 32. but I asked concerning you[4] that your faith would not fail: and you, when you have returned[5] must at once strengthen your brothers." 33. And he said to Him, "Lord, I am ready to go with You even to prison and to death." 34. But He said, "I say to you, Peter, a cock will not crow this very day until you would three times deny knowing Me."

Purse, Bag and Sword

22:35. Then He said to them, "When I sent you without purse and knapsack and sandals, did you lack anything?" And they said, "Nothing." 36. And He said to them, "But now the one who has a purse must take *it*, and likewise a knapsack, and the one who does not have must sell his clothing right away and must immediately buy a sword.[6] 37. For I say to you that this which has been written must be fulfilled in Me, 'And He was counted with *the* lawless:'[7] (Is 53:12) for in fact the purpose pertaining to Me has come." 38. But they said, "Lord, behold, here *are* two swords." And He said to them, "*That* is adequate."

The Prayer on the Mount of Olives

(Mt 26:36-46, Mk 14:32-42)

22:39. And when He came out, He was going according to custom to the Mount of Olives, and then the disciples followed Him. 40. And, when He came to the place, He said to them, "You must continually pray not to come into trials." 41. Then He withdrew about a stone's throw from them, and having knelt, He was praying 42. saying, "Father, if You are willing You must now take this cup

---

1	(v.31) The salutation doubled is very strong, demanding immediate attention. See Double Name in Glossary.
2	(v.31) See Satan in Glossary.
3	(v.31) This "you" is plural.
4	(v.32) This "you" is singular, referring to Simon.
5	(v.32) Repented
6	(v.36) The reference here is to the small, curved, personal sword.
7	(v.37) The word translated lawless refers to intentional sin. See Sin in Glossary.

from Me: nevertheless not My will, but Yours must continually be done."[1] 45. Then after He rose from the prayer *and* came to the disciples, He found them sleeping from the grief, 46. and He said to them, "Why are you sleeping? After you get up you must pray persistently, so that you would not enter a trial."

The Betrayal and Arrest of Jesus

(Mt 26:47-56, Mk 14:43-50, Jn 18:3-11)

22:47. While He was still speaking, behold a crowd *came to them*, and the one called Judas, one of the twelve, was going before them and he approached Jesus to kiss Him. 48. But Jesus said to him, "Judas, are you betraying the Son of Man with a kiss?" 49. When those who were with Him saw *this* they said, "Lord, shall we strike with a sword?" 50. Then one of them, *Peter*, struck the servant of the High Priest, and cut off his right ear. 51. And Jesus said, "You must now permit this:" and then, as He touched his ear, He healed him. 52. And Jesus said to those present before Him, the high priests and soldiers of the temple and elders, "Have you come out with swords and clubs as against a robber?[2] 53. Day after day, while I was with you in the temple you did not lay your hands on Me, but this is your hour and the authority of the darkness."

Peter's Denial of Jesus

(Mt 26:57,58, 69-75, Mk 14:53,54, 66-72, Jn 18:12-18, 25-27)

22:54. And having seized Him they led *Him* and brought *Him* to the house of the High Priest: and Peter was following at a distance.[3] 55. Then after they kindled a fire in the middle of the courtyard, when they sat together Peter was sitting in the midst of them. 56. And when she saw him, a maid who was sitting toward the light, after she looked at him intently, said, "And this one was with Him." 57. But he denied *it*, saying, "I do not know Him, ma'am." 58. Then after a short time when another saw him he said, "And you are *one* of them." But Peter said, "Man, I am not." 59. Then after about one hour went by another one insisted, saying, "In truth then this one was with Him, for he is also of Galilee." 60. But Peter said, "Man, I do not know what you are talking about." And immediately, while he was still speaking, a cock crowed. 61. Then, when He turned, the Lord looked at Peter, and Peter was reminded of the word of the Lord as He said to him that "Before a cock crows this very day[4] you will deny Me three times." 62. Then after he went outside he wept bitterly.

The Mocking and Beating of Jesus

(Mt 26:67,68, Mk 14:65)

22:63. And the men holding Him were mocking *and* beating Him,

---

1   (v.42) Verses 43, 44 are omitted because they were not in the earliest manuscripts.
2   (v.52) This Greek word is also translated revolutionary or insurrectionist.
3   (v.54) John was not with Peter, but another disciple was nearby. See Jn 18:15.
4   (v.61) This is evidence of the Jewish day, since the Jewish day began at sundown, before the Seder meal during which Jesus spoke of Peter's denial.

64. then after they blindfolded *Him* they were asking Him saying, "You must prophesy now, who is the one who hit You?" 65. And they were saying many other blasphemous *things* to Him.

Jesus before the Council

(Mt 26:59-66, Mk 14:55-64, Jn 18:19-24)

22:66. Then as it became daylight the elders of the people were gathered, both high priests and scribes, and they were leading Him away to their Sanhedrin 67. saying, "If You are the Messiah, You must immediately tell us." And He said to them, "If I would tell you, you would **not** believe *Me*: 68. and if I would ask, you would **not** answer. 69. And from now on the Son of Man will be sitting on the right hand[1] of the power of God." (Ps 110:1) 70. And they all said, "Then You are the Son of God?" But He said to them, "You are saying that I AM." 71. And they said, "Then what need of witnesses do we still have? For we ourselves heard from His mouth."

Jesus Brought before Pilate

(Mt 27:1,2, 11-14, Mk 15:1-5, Jn 18:28-38)

23.1. Then after the whole multitude of them got up they led Him to Pilate. 2. And they began to accuse Him saying, "We found this One perverting our nation and forbidding to pay taxes to Caesar and saying He was Messiah, king." 3. And Pilate asked Him saying, "Are You the King of the Jewish People?" And He said to him, "You are saying *it*." 4. And Pilate said to the high priests and the crowds, "I do not find guilt in this man." 5. But they were insisting, saying that "He is inciting the people, teaching throughout *the* whole of Judea, even from Galilee where He began until here."

Jesus before Herod

23:6. And when Pilate heard *that*, he asked if the man was from Galilee, 7. and when he knew that He was from the authority of Herod, he sent Him up to Herod, since he was also in Jerusalem during these days. 8. And when Herod saw Jesus he rejoiced very much, for he was for some length of time wanting to see Him because of what he heard about Him and he hoped to see a sign coming by Him. 9. And he interrogated Him with many questions, but He did not answer him. 10. And the high priests and the scribes had been standing *there* vigorously accusing Him. 11. And then after Herod with his soldiers treated Him with contempt, and after he clothed Him with brilliant raiment, then mocked *Him*, he sent Him back to Pilate. 12. And in this day Herod and Pilate became friends with each other: for before this there was hostility with them.

---

1   (v.69) "At the right hand" is a Hebrew idiom that speaks of power and strength, from Ex 15:6. See Right Hand in Glossary.

Jesus Sentenced to Die

(Mt 27:15-26, Mk 15:6-15, Jn 18:39-19:16)

23:13. And Pilate, having summoned the high priests and the leaders[1] and the people, 14. said to them, "You have brought this man to me as defrauding the people, and see, I, having judged before you, found no guilt of which you accuse against Him. 15. And neither did Herod, for he sent Him back to us, and behold nothing which was done by Him is worthy of death: 16. therefore after I whip *Him* I will release Him."[2] 18. But they were crying out all together saying, "You must raise[3] this One, and you must now free Barabbas for us." 19. He, *Barabbas*, was thrown in jail because of being in some insurrection and murder in the city. 20. And again Pilate called out to them, wanting to free Jesus. 21. But they were shouting saying, "You must crucify, you must crucify Him right now!" 22. And the third time he said to them, "For what evil did He do? I do not find guilt *deserving* of death in Him: therefore after I scourge *Him* I will release Him." 23. But they were pressing upon *him* in loud voices asking *for* Him to be crucified, and their voices prevailed. 24. Then Pilate decided to do their request: 25. and he freed the one who was thrown in jail because of insurrection and murder, for whom they were asking, and he gave Jesus over to their wishes.

The Crucifixion of Jesus

(Mt 27:32-44, Mk 15:21-32, Jn 19:17-27)

23:26. Then as they were leading him away, after they took hold of Simon, a certain Cyrene *who* was coming from a field, they placed the cross on him to carry behind Jesus. 27. And a great multitude of the people, and of women who were mourning and lamenting Him, were following Him. 28. And when He turned to *the women* Jesus said, "Daughters of Jerusalem, you must not be weeping over Me: but weep over yourselves and over your children, 29. because behold days are coming in which they will say, 'Blessed *are* the barren and the wombs which did not bear and breasts which did not nourish.'

30.   Then they will begin 'to say to the mountains,
            You must immediately fall on us,
        and to the hills,
            You must immediately hide us:' (Ho 10:8)

31. because if they do these things in the green tree, what would happen in the dry?"

23:32. And two others, evildoers, were then being led to be executed with Him. 33. And when they came to the place called Skull, they crucified Him and

---

1   (v.13) The high priests and the leaders were Hellenists and most likely the leaders summoned by Pilate were also. See Hellenists in Glossary.

2   (v.16) V. 17 is omitted because it was not in the earliest manuscripts.

3   (v.18) Crucify

the evildoers there, one on His right hand[1] and one on His left. 34. And they cast lots, dividing His garments.[2] 35. And the people stood looking. And they and also the leaders were ridiculing, saying, "He saved others, let Him save Himself, if He is the Messiah, the chosen One of God." 36. And the nearby soldiers also mocked Him, bringing sour wine to Him 37. and saying, "If You are the King of the Jewish People, You must now save Yourself." 38. And it was inscribed over Him, "This *is* the King of the Jewish People."

23:39. Then one of the evil ones who was hanging *there* was blaspheming Him saying, "Are You not the Messiah? You must now save Yourself and us." 40. But the other said, rebuking him, "Do you not yourself fear God, because you are in the same sentence? 41. But we indeed justly, for what we did *is* worthy *of what* we are receiving: but this One did nothing improper." 42. Then he was saying, "Jesus, You must right away remember me when You would enter Your kingdom." 43. Then He said to him, "Truly I say to you, this very day you will be with Me in Paradise."

The Death of Jesus

(Mt 27:45-56, Mk 15:33-41, Jn 19:28-30)

23:44. And it was now about *the* sixth hour and it became dark on the whole Earth until *the* ninth hour[3] 45. as the sun was darkened, and the veil in the middle of the sanctuary was split. 46. And having spoken in a loud voice Jesus said, "Father, into Your hands I entrust My spirit." Then after He said this He breathed out His last. 47. And when the centurion saw what happened he glorified God saying, "Truly this Man was righteous." 48. And all the crowds that came together on this site, when they saw what happened, were returning, *and* beating their chests. 49. But all the known acquaintances of His and the women who had accompanied Him from Galilee had stood from a distance to see these things.

The Burial of Jesus

(Mt 27:57-61, Mk 15:42-47, Jn 19:38-42)

23:50. Then behold, a man named Joseph *who* was a member of the council[4] and a good and righteous man 51. - this one was not agreeing with the resolution and with what they did - from Arimathea, a Jewish city, who was waiting for the kingdom of God, 52. after this one came to Pilate he asked for the body of Jesus 53. and when he took *Him* down he wrapped Him in fine linen and placed Him in a tomb hewn in the rock where no one had lain. 54.

---

1   (v.33) The right hand here is a symbol of God's salvation, from Ps 20:6. The left hand is a symbol of calamity and judgment.
2   (v.34) V. 34a, the sentence "Jesus said, Father forgive them for they do not know what they are doing." is omitted because it was not in the earliest manuscripts.
3   (v.44) From Noon to 3:00 PM
4   (v.50) Sanhedrin

And it was *the* day of preparation[1] for it was approaching the Sabbath. 55. And the women followed, because they, who were traveling together with Him from Galilee, saw the tomb and how His body was placed, 56. and when they returned they prepared spices and ointments.[2]

The Resurrection[3] of Jesus
(Mt 28:1-10, Mk 16:1-8, Jn 20:1-10)

But, since it *was* the Sabbath, they rested according to the commandment. **24**.1. And on the First Day of the Week,[4] they came to the tomb very early, bringing the spices which they prepared.[5] 2. And they found *that* the stone had been rolled away from the tomb, 3. but when they entered they did not find the body of the Lord Jesus. 4. And it happened; while they were at a loss concerning this, then behold two men in radiant clothing stood by them. 5. And because *the women* had been thrown into fear and they were bowing *their* faces to the ground, *the men* said to them, "Why are you seeking the living with the dead: 6. He is not here but He has risen. You must remember when He spoke to you while He was in Galilee 7. saying 'It is necessary for the Son of Man to be given over into *the* hands of sinful men and to be crucified and to be raised on the third day.'" 8. Then they remembered His words. 9. And after they returned from the tomb they reported all these things to the eleven and to all the rest. 10. And they were Mary Magdalene and Joanna and Mary *mother* of Jacob and the rest *of the women* with them. They were telling these things to the apostles, 11. but these words seemed in their sight as nonsense and they did not believe them. 12. But Peter, when he got up, ran to the tomb and when he stooped he saw only the cloth, and he left, wondering to himself what had happened.

The Walk to Emmaus

24:13. Then behold this day two of them were going to a distant village; it was named Emmaus, sixty stadia[6] from Jerusalem. 14. And they were speaking with one another about all these happenings. 15. And it was, while they were speaking and discussing *these things* that Jesus Himself, having approached, was going with them 16. but their eyes were being hindered *so* they did not recognize Him. 17. And He said to them, "What are these accounts which you are exchanging with one another while you are walking?" And they stood still,

---

1   (v.54) The day before a Sabbath when the men immersed for purification before sun-down, which began the Sabbath. See Jn 19:14. See Preparation Day in Glossary.

2   (v.56) "They" are a few of the women who followed Him, named in v. 10 of Chapter 24. Their bringing spices is mysterious because women would never anoint a male corpse and because the body was always prepared before being placed in a tomb. Jn 19:39 says that Nicodemus brought a hundred Roman pounds of myrrh and aloe and the linen with which he and Joseph wrapped the body.

3   (Caption) See Resurrection in Glossary.

4   (v.1) This is the Hebrew expression for Sunday, which begins at sundown Saturday.

5   (v.1) See Note on v.56 above.

6   (v.13) About seven miles

being sad and gloomy. 18. And one named Cleopas[1] said to Him, "Are You the only one living in Jerusalem and not knowing what happened in her during these days?" 19. And He said to them, "Of what sort?" And they said to Him, "The things about Jesus of Nazareth, Who was a man, a prophet powerful in work and in word, in the presence of God and of all the people, 20. how our high priests and our leaders gave Him over in judgment of death and they crucified Him. 21. But we were hoping that He was the One Who was going to redeem Israel:[2] but even with all these things, this third day has passed since these things happened. 22. And even some of our women amazed us, since they came to the tomb early in the morning, 23. and when they did not find His body, they came saying then that in a vision they saw angels, who were saying 'He is alive.' 24. Then some of those with us left for the tomb and also found thus just as the women said, but they did not see Him." 25. But He said to them, "O foolish and slow in heart to believe all that the prophets were saying: 26. for was it not necessary for the Messiah to suffer these things, then to enter His glory?" 27. And beginning with Moses and with all the Prophets He explained to them with all the writings concerning Himself.

24:28. Then they approached the village to which they were going, and He pretended to go farther on. 29. But they urged Him saying, "You must now stay with us because it is toward evening and the day is already over." And He came in to stay with them. 30. And it happened while He reclined with them, when He took the bread He praised God and after He broke *it* He gave *it* to them, 31. and their eyes were opened and they recognized Him: then He became invisible[3] for them. 32. And they said to one another, "Was not our heart burning in us as He was speaking to us on the way, as He was explaining the Scriptures to us?" 33. Then after they got up they returned to Jerusalem[4] the same hour and found the eleven and those gathered with them, 34. saying that truly the Lord had risen and was seen by Simon.[5] 35. And they were recounting the things *discussed by Jesus* on the way and as He was recognized by them while He was breaking the bread.

The Appearance to the Disciples

(Mt 28:16-20, Jn 20:19-23, Ac 1:6-8)

24:36. And while they were saying these things He stood in the midst of them and said to them, "Peace *be* with you." 37. But becoming terrified and

1   (v.18) The Greek spelling of Cleopas is Kleopas, while the spelling of Clopas, Jn 19:25, is Klopa. The "O" in Klopa is an Omega, while the "O" in Kleopas is an Omicron. Both words are in the genitive case, with Klopa masculine, Kleopas feminine. See note for v. 34.

2   (v.21) His disciples expected the ruling Messiah. See "Coming of Messiah" in Glossary.

3   (v.31) See Resurrected Body in Glossary.

4   (v.33) From Emmaus

5   (v.34) This identifies Simon, clarified by Paul in 1Cor 15:5 as Peter, not Simon the Zealot, as one of the disciples walking with Him to Emmaus. V. 18 names Cleopas as the other disciple. While most people assume Cleopas is a man, the Greek spelling has a feminine genitive ending, so some scholars speculate that this could have been Peter's wife on the road to Emmaus with him.

afraid they were thinking that they saw a spirit. 38. Then He said to them, "Why are you disturbed and why are the doubts going up in your heart? 39. You must now look at My hands and My feet because I AM He: you must now touch Me and see, because a spirit does not have flesh and bone just as you see Me having." 40. Then having said this He showed them His hands and feet. 41. But they still did not believe from the joy, and marveling He said to them, "Do you have something here to eat?" 42. And they gave Him a portion of broiled fish: 43. then after He took *it* He ate in front of them.

24:44. And He said to them, "These *are* the messages I told you while I was still with you, that it is necessary for everything to be fulfilled that has been written about Me in the Torah of Moses and in the Prophets and the Psalms."[1] 45. Then He opened their minds and they understood the Scriptures: 46. and He said to them that "Thus it has been written that the Messiah would suffer (Is 53:5, et. al.) and be raised from the dead on the third day (Ho 6:2), 47. and repentance would be preached in His name for forgiveness of sins for all the heathens. Beginning from Jerusalem 48. you *are* witnesses of these things. 49. Then behold, I, Myself, am sending My Father's promise[2] upon you: but you must now stay in the city until you would be clothed in power from on high."

The Ascension of Jesus

(Ac 1:9-11)

24:50. And He led them outside as far as Bethany,[3] then as He raised His hands He blessed them. 51. And it happened while He was blessing them, He went away from them, and He was being brought up into the sky. 52. And after they paid homage to Him they returned to Jerusalem with great joy 53. and they were constantly in the temple praising God.

---

1   (v.44) This includes all Scripture.
2   (v.49) The Baptism of the Holy Spirit, given for the first time in Acts 2:1-12, from Jl 3:1.
3   (v.50) Bethany is the Greek spelling of Beit-Anyah, meaning House of Sighing in Hebrew.

~ ACCORDING TO JOHN[1] ~

The Word Became Flesh

1.1. In *the* beginning was the Word, and the Word was with God, and the Word was God. 2. He was with God in *the* beginning. 3. All things came through Him, and there was not one thing that came into being without His participation. (Wsd 9:1) What had come 4. in Him was life, and the life was the Light of mankind: 5. and the Light shines in the darkness, nevertheless the darkness has not appropriated it (Jn 3:19).[2]

1:6. There was a man *who* was sent from God, his name *was* John: 7. he came in witness so that he could testify concerning the Light, so that all would believe through him. 8. He was not that Light, but *he came* so that he would bear witness concerning the Light. 9. When He came into the world, He was the true Light, He gave light to all mankind. 10. He was in the world, and the world was *made* by Him, but the world did not know Him. 11. He came among His own people, but His own did not receive Him. 12. And so many as did receive Him, He gave them authority to become children of God, to those who believed[3] in His name, 13. they *are* not from blood[4] and not from *the* desire of flesh and not from *the* will of man but were begotten from God.

1:14. And the Word became flesh and lived among us, and we saw His glory, glory in the same manner as *the* only *child* of *the* Father, full of grace and truth. 15. John bore witness concerning Him and cried out saying, "This One was He *of* Whom I said, 'The One Who is coming after Me has been before me, because He is more prominent than I. 16. Because we all took grace upon grace from His fullness: 17. for the Torah[5] was given through Moses, but the grace and

---

1   (Title) Written about 85 AD. John has a style of writing all his own among the New Testament authors. He uses many similes and metaphors, with Jesus as the Way, the Truth, and the Light, the Word, the Bread and the Blood, the Good Shepherd and the Resurrection and the Life. This style is very apparent in the Book of Revelation as well as the Gospel. See John in Book Order in Glossary.

2   (v.5) The forces of darkness still harden themselves against the Light of God's Word.

3   (v.12) Jesus and all who were listening knew that "believe" required action, a change in behavior. Relationship as a child of God is not an intellectual exercise, but real as with an earthly parent. The difference is that our Heavenly Father is perfect.

4   (v.13) Human procreation

5   (v.17) Torah means teaching or instruction. See Torah in Glossary.

the truth came through Jesus Messiah. 18. No one has ever seen God: *the* only *Son of* God, the One Who was in the bosom of the Father. That One declared *Him.*'"

The Testimony of John the Baptist

(Mt 3:1-12, Mk 1:2-8, Lk 3:15-17)

1:19. And this was the testimony of John, when the Jewish *leaders* sent priests and Levites to him from Jerusalem so that they could ask him, "Who are you?" 20. And he confessed and would not deny, but he confessed, "I myself am not the Messiah." 21. And they asked him, "Then who *are you*? Are you Elijah?" And he said, "I am not." "Are you the prophet?" And he answered, "No!" 22. Then they said to him, "Who are you? So that we could give an answer to those who sent us: what do you say about yourself?" 23. He said,

"I am 'a voice crying in the wilderness,

you must now make straight the way of *the* Lord,' (Is 40:3)

just as Isaiah the prophet said." 24. And those who had been sent were from the Pharisees. 25. And they asked him and said to him, "Then why are you baptizing[1] if you are not the Messiah and not Elijah or the prophet?" 26. John answered them saying, "I am baptizing in water: among you stands Whom you do not know, 27. the One Who comes after me, of Whom I myself am not worthy to loosen the strap of His sandal." 28. And these things happened in Bethany,[2] across the Jordan, where John was baptizing.

The Lamb of God

1:29. The next day he saw Jesus coming toward him and he said, "Behold the Lamb of God, the One Who takes away the sin of the world. 30. This is concerning Whom I said, 'A man is coming after me Who was before me, because He is more prominent than I.' 31. And I had not known Him, but, so that He would be revealed to Israel through this, I came baptizing in water." 32. And John testified, saying that "I had seen the Spirit descending from heaven as a dove and it was staying on Him. 33. And I would not have known Him, but the One Who sent me to baptize in water, that One said to me 'Upon whomever you would see the Spirit descending and remaining upon Him, He is the One Who baptizes[3] in *the* Holy Spirit.' 34. And I saw and I had borne witness that this One is the Son of God."

The First Disciples

1:35. The next day John and two of his disciples again stood 36. and when he looked at Jesus walking he said, "You must now behold the Lamb of

---

1   (v.25) Baptism was self-immersion, so John preached and those who responded to his message went into the river, immersing for purification. See Baptize in Glossary.

2   (v.28) Bethany is the Greek spelling of Beit-Anyah, meaning House of Sighing in Hebrew, but note that this is not the Bethany near Jerusalem.

3   (v.33) Immerses, with the present tense meaning He is still immersing people today.

God." 37. And the two disciples heard him speaking and they became disciples of Jesus. 38. And when Jesus turned around and saw them following *Him* He said to them, "Whom are you seeking?" And they said to Him, "Rabbi," which being interpreted says "Teacher," "Where are You staying?" 39. He said to them, "You must come and see." Therefore they came and they saw where He was staying and they stayed with Him that day: it was about *the* tenth hour.[1] 40. Andrew, one of the two who heard from John, was the brother of Simon Peter, and after *that* they followed Him: 41. first he found his own brother Simon, then said to him, "We have found the Meshiach,"[2] which is translated Messiah:[3] 42. he led him to Jesus. When He looked at him Jesus said, "You are Simon the son of John. You shall be called Cephas,"[4] which is interpreted Peter.[5]

The calling of Philip and Nathaniel

1:43. The next day He wanted to come out to Galilee and He found Philip. And Jesus said to him, "You must continually follow Me." 44. And Philip was from Bethsaida,[6] from the city of Andrew and Peter. 45. Philip found Nathaniel and said to him, "We have found about Whom Moses and the Prophets wrote in the Torah,[7] Jesus, son of Joseph, the One from Nazareth." 46. And Nathaniel said to him, "Can anything good come from Nazareth?" Philip said to him, "You must come and see." 47. And Jesus saw Nathaniel coming toward Him and said concerning him, "Behold a true Israeli in whom there is no deceit." 48. And Nathaniel said to Him, "How do You know me?" Jesus answered and said to him, "I saw you while you were under the fig tree before Philip called you." 49. Nathaniel answered Him, "Rabbi, You are the Son of God, You are King of Israel." 50. Jesus answered and said to him, "Do you believe because I said to you that I saw you under the fig tree? You will see better things than these." 51. And He said to him, "Most assuredly I say to you, you will see heaven when it opens and the angels of God are ascending *from* and descending[8] upon the Son of Man."

The Wedding at Cana

2.1. And on Tuesday[9] there was a wedding feast[10] in Cana of Galilee,

---

1   (v.39) 4:00 PM
2   (v.41) This is Hebrew for Messiah or Anointed One. See Christ in Glossary.
3   (v.41) Messiah is the translation of the Greek word Xristos or Christos. See Christ in Glossary.
4   (v.42) Cephas is the Latin spelling of Kefa, an Aramaic word meaning Rock. See Cephas in Glossary.
5   (v.42) A masculine form of the feminine Greek word meaning Rock. In the NT the masculine form is used only for Peter's name.
6   (v.44) Bethsaida is the Greek spelling of Beit-Tside, which in Hebrew means House or Place of Fishing, literally hunting, but including fishing. There were two cities named Bethsaida, this one on the west side of the lake, just south of Capernaum, and the other on the northeast side of the lake, about seven or eight miles from Capernaum.
7   (v.45) This is a reference to the entire Old Testament. See Torah in Glossary.
8   (v.51) To have the angels ascend first means they are on the Earth to start with.
9   (v.1) Literally 'the third day' which is the Hebrew expression for Tuesday.
10   (v.1) See Wedding in Glossary.

and Jesus' mother was there. 2. And Jesus and His disciples were also invited to the feast. 3. And when the wine ran out the mother of Jesus said to Him, "They do not have wine." 4. And Jesus said to her, "Why should that concern Me, ma'am?[1] My appointed time is not yet come." 5. His mother said to the servants, "Whatever He would say to you, you must do right away." 6. And lying there were six stone[2] water pots stored for the rite of purification[3] of the Jewish people, holding up to two or three measures.[4] 7. Jesus said to them, "You must right away fill the jars with water." And they filled them to *the* brim. 8. And He said to them, "You must draw *some* now, then bring *it* to the wedding manager:" and they brought *it*. 9. As the manager tasted the water made into wine, only he did not know how it was *made*, but the servants, those who drew the water knew, the manager called the bridegroom 10. and said to him, "Every man first puts the good wine and then, when they would be drunk, the inferior: you have kept the good wine until now." 11. Jesus did this first of His signs in Cana of Galilee and He revealed His glory, and His disciples believed in Him.

2:12. After this He and His mother and His brothers and His disciples went down to Capernaum[5] and they were remaining there not many days.

The Cleansing of the Temple

(Mt 21:12,13, Mk 11:15-17, Lk 19:45,46)

2:13. And the Passover of the Jewish people was drawing near, and Jesus went up to Jerusalem. 14. And in the temple He found those who were selling cattle and sheep and doves and the moneychangers being seated, 15. and after He made a whip from ropes He cast out of the temple all the sheep and the cattle, and He poured out the coins of the moneychangers and overturned their tables, 16. and to those who were selling doves He said, "You must now take them from this place, you must not make My Father's house a house of market." 17. His disciples remembered that it was written: "The zeal for Your house will consume Me." (Ps 69:9) 18. Therefore the Jewish *leaders* answered and said to Him, "What sign are You showing us *seeing* that You do these things?" 19. Jesus answered and said to them, "You must destroy this sanctuary and in three days I shall raise it." 20. Therefore the Jewish *leaders* said, "This sanctuary was built in forty-six years, and You will raise *it* in three days?" 21. But He was talking about

---

1   (v.4) Literally "what to you and to me," a Hebrew idiom also used in Lk 8:28.
2   (v.6) Stone was used for the water of purification because stone vessels do not become ritually unclean.
3   (v.6) The rite of purification is what we call baptism. Normally, only a synagogue would have a ritual bath, so this wedding was apparently at a synagogue. The water for purification had to be running water, such as from a stream, a spring, or rainwater caught in a cistern. See Baptize in Glossary.
4   (v.6) Twenty to thirty gallons, which means the water weighed at least 150 pounds plus the weight of the stone jar.
5   (v.12) Capernaum is the Latin spelling of the Hebrew name Kafer Na-um. Kafer means town or village and Na-um means pleasant.

the sanctuary of His body.[1] 22. However, when He was raised from *the* dead, His disciples remembered that He said this, and they believed in the Scripture and in the message, which Jesus spoke.

Jesus Knows All Men

2:23. As He was among the Jerusalemites during the Passover feast, many believed in His name, by observing Him *and* the signs that He was doing: 24. but Jesus was not trusting Himself to them because He knew all *men* 25. and because He did not need that anyone would testify about a person: for He knew what was in the person.

Jesus and Nicodemus

3.1. And there was a man of the Pharisees, Nicodemus *was* his name, a leader of the Jewish people: 2. this one came to Him at night and said to Him, "Rabbi, we know that You, a teacher, have come from God: for unless God were with Him no one is able to perform these signs that You do." 3. Jesus answered and said to him, "Most definitely I say to you, unless someone would have been born from above, he is not able to see the kingdom of God." 4. Nicodemus said to Him, "How is a man able to be born when he is in old age? Is he able to enter his mother's womb and be born a second time?"[2] 5. Jesus answered, "Most certainly I say to you, unless someone would have been born out of water[3] and Spirit he is not able to enter the kingdom of God. 6. What has been born of the flesh is flesh, and what has been born of the Spirit is spirit. 7. Do not be astonished that I said to you, 'It is necessary for you to be born from above.' 8. The wind blows where it wishes and you hear its sound, but you do not know where it comes from or where it is going: thus it is with everyone who has been born of the Spirit." 9. Nicodemus answered and said to Him, "How can these things happen?" 10. Jesus answered and said to him, "You are a teacher of Israel and you do not know these things? 11. Most assuredly I say to you that what we know we speak and what we have seen we bear witness, but you do not take our testimony. 12. If I said earthly things to you and you do not believe, how are you to believe if I would say the heavenly things to you? 13. And no one has ascended to heaven[4] except the One Who has descended from heaven, the Son of Man. 14. And just as Moses lifted up the serpent in the wilderness, so also is it necessary for the Son of Man to be lifted up, 15. so that everyone who believes in Him would have eternal life.

3:16. "For God so loved the world, that He gave His only Son, so that every one who believes in Him would not die but would have eternal life. 17. For

---

1   (v.21) The word translated sanctuary is naos, referring specifically to the sanctuary, not the temple. Paul also referred to the body as a sanctuary. See 1Cor 6:19, 2Cor 6:16. See Sanctuary in Glossary.

2   (v.4) The Greek construction anticipates a negative reply.

3   (v.5) Being born of water speaks of baptism but also of Torah, from Ex 14:22 and Is 55:1.

4   (v.13) Since Jesus says He has ascended, He must have been here before.

God did not send His Son into the world so that He would condemn the world, but so that the world would be saved through Him. 18. The one who believes in Him is not condemned: but the one who does not believe has already been condemned, because he has not believed in the name of the only Son of God. 19. Now the judgment is this, that the Light has come into the world and people loved the darkness rather than the Light (Jn 1:5): for their works were evil. 20. For everyone doing wicked things hates the Light and does not come to the Light, so that his deeds would not be exposed. 21. But the one who does truth comes to the Light, so that his works would be revealed because they were worked through God." (Tob 4:6)

Jesus and John the Baptist

3:22. After these things Jesus and His disciples came into the country of Judea and He was staying there with them and He was baptizing.[1] 23. And John was baptizing in *the* Aenon area near Salim, since there was a lot of water there, and they were regularly passing by and being baptized: 24. for John was not yet thrown into prison. 25. Then there was a discussion by the disciples of John with a Jewish man concerning purification. 26. And they came to John and said to him, "Rabbi, the One Who was with you on the other side of the Jordan, *the One* for Whom you have borne witness, behold He is baptizing[2] and all are coming to Him." 27. John answered and said, "A man is not able to take anything unless it would have been given to him from out of heaven. 28. You yourselves are my witness that I said that 'I am not the Messiah, but that I am being sent before that One.' 29. The one who has the bride is the bridegroom: and the friend of the bridegroom *is* the one who stands by, then when he hears his joy he rejoices because of the voice of the bridegroom.[3] Therefore this joy has been fulfilled in me. 30. It is necessary for that One to increase, and for me to decrease."

He Who Comes from Heaven

3:31. "The One who comes from above is over all things: the one who is from the Earth is out of the earth and he speaks from the earth: the One Who comes from heaven is over all: 32. this One bears witness, Who saw and heard, and no one accepts His testimony. 33. The one who accepted His testimony attested that God is true. 34. For He Whom God sent speaks the words of God, for He gives the Spirit without measure. 35. The Father loves the Son and has put all things in His hand. 36. The one who believes[4] in the Son has eternal life: but the one who does not believe in the Son will not see life, but the wrath of God remains upon him."

---

1   (v.22) Immersing according to ancient Jewish custom. See Baptize in Glossary.
2   (v.26) Baptizing meant complete immersion. See Baptize in Glossary.
3   (v.29) See Wedding in Glossary.
4   (v.36) To the Jewish mind believing must be accompanied by action, to help the neighbor whom you must love. (Lv19:18)

The Woman of Samaria

4.1. Then because Jesus knew that the Pharisees heard He was making and was baptizing[1] more disciples than John 2. - and yet Jesus was not Himself baptizing but His disciples *were* - 3. He left from Judea and went again into Galilee. 4. And it was necessary for Him to go through Samaria. 5. Thus He came into a city of Samaria called Shechem near the place that Jacob gave to Joseph his son. (Gn 33:19, 48:22) 6. And *the* well of Jacob was there. Now, since Jesus had grown weary from the journey, He was sitting upon the well: it was about the sixth hour.[2]

4:7. A Samaritan woman came to draw water. Jesus said to her, "You must give Me *something* to drink:" 8. for His disciples had gone away into the city so that they could buy food. 9. Then the Samaritan woman said to Him, "How do You *Who* are Jewish ask to drink from me, being a Samaritan woman?" For Jewish people did not associate with Samaritans. 10. Jesus answered and said to her, "If you knew the gift of God and Who is the One Who says to you, 'You must give Me *something* to drink,' *if* you asked Him then He *would* give you living water." 11. The woman said to Him, "Sir, You do not have a bucket and the well is deep: so from where do You have the living water? 12. Are You greater than our father Jacob, who gave us the well and he and his sons and his animals were drinking from it?"[3] 13. Jesus answered and said to her, "Everyone who drinks from this water will thirst again: 14. whoever would drink from the water[4] which I will give him, will **never** thirst, but the water which I will give him will become in him well water springing up into eternal life." 15. The woman said to him, "Sir, You must now give me this water, so that I would not suffer thirst and would not *have to* draw water in this place."

4:16. He said to her, "You must go, *and* you must now call your husband, and come to this place." 17. The woman answered and said to Him, "I do not have a husband." Jesus said to her, "You said correctly that 'I do not have a husband:' 18. for you have had five husbands and whom you have now is not your husband: you have said this truth." 19. The woman said to Him, "Lord, I see that You are a prophet. 20. Our fathers worshipped on this mountain: and you say that in Jerusalem is the place where it is necessary to worship." 21. Jesus said to her, "You must believe Me, ma'am, that a time is coming when neither on this mountain nor in Jerusalem will you worship the Father. 22. You worship whom you have not known: we are worshipping Whom we do know, because salvation is by the Jewish people.[5] 23. In fact an appointed time is coming and

---

1   (v.1) This is the full immersion as practiced by the Jewish people. See Baptize in Glossary.
2   (v.6) Noon
3   (v.12) The Greek construction here anticipates a negative answer.
4   (v.14) Water is a metaphor for Torah, from Is 55:1 and Ex 14:22.
5   (v.22) The Greek preposition, ek, used here refers to the Jewish people as the origin of salvation, saying that salvation comes out from them.

is now, when the true worshippers will worship the Father in spirit and truth: for the Father is seeking such as these who worship Him. 24. God is spirit, and it is necessary for those who worship Him to worship in spirit and in truth." 25. The woman said to Him, "I know that Meshiach is coming, the One Who is called Messiah: when that One would have come, He tells us all things." 26. Jesus said to her, "I AM, the One Who is speaking to you."

4:27. And on this His disciples came and they were amazed that He was speaking with a *Samaritan* woman:[1] but yet no one said, "What are You seeking or what are You saying with her?" 28. Then the woman left her water pot and went into the city and said to the people, 29. "Come, you must see a man Who told me everything that I have done, is this not the Messiah?" 30. They left from the city and were coming to Him.

4:31. In the meantime the disciples were urging Him saying, "Rabbi, You must now eat." 32. But He said to them, "I have food to eat which you do not know." 33. Therefore the disciples were saying to one another, "Did someone bring Him *something* to eat?" 34. Jesus said to them, "My food is that I would do the will of the One Who sent Me and I would complete His work. 35. Are you not saying that 'It is yet four months and the harvest is coming?' Behold I say to you, you must lift up your eyes and you must see the fields that are white toward harvest. Now 36.[2] the one who reaps takes wages and gathers fruit into eternal life, so that the one who sows would rejoice together with the one who is reaping. 37. For in this the statement is true that "One sows and another reaps." (Mic 6:15) 38. I sent you to harvest what you had not worked: others had worked and you have come into their work."

4:39. And many from that city of Samaria believed in Him because of the word of testimony of the woman that "He told me everything that I did." 40. Then as the Samaritans came to Him, they were asking Him to remain with them: and He stayed there two days. 41. And many more were believing because of His message, 42. and they were saying to the woman "No longer are we believing because of your telling *us, but* because we ourselves have heard and we know that He is truly the Savior of the world."

The Healing of the Official's Son

(Mt 8:5-13, Lk 7:1-10)

4:43. And after two days He went out from there into Galilee: 44. for Jesus Himself testified that a prophet did not have honor in his own hometown. 45. Therefore when He came into Galilee, the Galileans welcomed Him, since they saw everything that He did in Jerusalem during the Feast, for they also went to the Feast.

---

1   (v.27) Speaking with a woman was not extraordinary, but speaking with a Samaritan was.

2   (v.36) See Chapter and Verse Numbers in Glossary.

4:46. Then He came again into Cana of Galilee, where He made the water *into* wine. And the son of a certain king's officer[1] was sick in Capernaum[2]. 47. Who, when he heard that Jesus came from Judea into Galilee he went to Him and was asking Him to come down and heal his son, for *the child* was going to die. 48. Then Jesus said to him, "Unless you would see signs and wonders, you could **not** believe." 49. The king's servant said to Him, "Lord, You must come down before my child dies." 50. Jesus said to him, "You must be going, your son lives." The man believed in the statement, which Jesus said to him and he left. 51. And now while he was going down his servants met him saying that his child lives. 52. Then he inquired from them the hour in which he began to improve: in reply they said, "Yesterday during the seventh hour[3] the fever left him." 53. Then the father knew that *it was* in that hour in which Jesus said to him, "Your son lives," and he and his entire household believed. 54. And moreover this was the second sign Jesus did after He came from Judea into Galilee.

The Healing at the Pool

5.1. After these things there was a feast of the Jewish people and Jesus went up to Jerusalem. 2. And He was among the *people* of Jerusalem at the Sheep Gate pool, the one called in Hebrew Beit-Zata,[4] *which* had five porches. 3. Among those *who* were lying down were a great number of sick, of blind, of lame, of withered.[5] 5. And some man was there thirty-eight years because he had this sickness: 6. when Jesus saw this *man* lying down, knowing that he had already been there a long time, He said to him, "Do you want to become well?" 7. The sick one answered Him, "Lord, I do not have a man so that when the water would be disturbed he could put me into the pool: but while I am coming, another gets down before me." 8. Jesus said to him, "You must immediately get up, you must at once take your pallet and you must continually walk."[6] 9. And immediately the man became well and he took his pallet and he was walking.

But it was a Sabbath on that day. 10. Therefore the Jewish people were saying to the one who had been healed, "It is *the* Sabbath, and it is not permitted[7] for you to take your pallet." 11. And he answered them, "The One Who made me well said to me, 'You must take your pallet and you must walk.'" 12. And they asked him, "Who is the man Who said to you 'You must take *it* and you must

---

1   (v.46) The king's officer is identified in Matthew and Luke as a centurion, who would have been under the Roman emperor, here referred to as king.

2   (v.46) Capernaum is the Latin spelling of the Hebrew name Kafer Na-um. Kafer means town or village and Na-um means pleasant.

3   (v.52) 1:00 PM

4   (v.2) Other manuscripts say Bethesda, which in Hebrew is Beit-Hesed, meaning House of Mercy. Beit-Zata means House of Olives.

5   (v.3) V. 4 is omitted because it was not in the earliest manuscripts.

6   (v.8) This gives a pattern for taking a divine healing: taking it immediately, and then walking continually with it. Do not permit the evil to return. Some healings take time, but the confession and attitude must be of being healed. Walk by faith, not by sight. (2 Cor 5:7)

7   (v.10) Carrying anything was defined by the Pharisees as a burden that could not be carried on a Sabbath. Jesus did not accept that definition. See Sabbath in glossary.

walk?'" 13. And the one who was healed did not know Who it was, for Jesus withdrew since there was a crowd in the place. 14. After these things Jesus found him in the temple and said to him, "Behold you have become well, you must no longer sin, so that it would not become worse for you." 15. The man left and he was reporting to the Jewish *leaders* that Jesus was the One Who made him well. 16. And because of this the Jewish *leaders* were pursuing Jesus, because He was doing these things on a Sabbath. 17. And Jesus was answering them, "My Father until now is working just as I am working:" 18. because of this therefore the Jewish *leaders* were *all* the more seeking to kill Him, for not only was He loosing on the Sabbath, but He was also calling God His own Father, making Himself equal to God.

The Authority of the Son

5:19. Therefore Jesus was answering and was saying to them, "Most assuredly I say to you, the Son is not able to do anything by Himself except what He would see the Father doing: for whatever that One would do, then the Son likewise does these things. 20. For the Father loves the Son and shows Him everything that He does and greater works than these will He show to Him, so that you would be amazed. 21. For just as the Father raises the dead and makes alive, (Dt 32:39, Is 26:19) so also the Son makes alive whom He wishes. 22. For neither does the Father judge anyone, but He has given all judgment to the Son, 23. so that all would honor the Son just as they would honor the Father. The one not honoring the Son does not honor the Father, the One Who sent Him. 24. Most certainly I say to you that the one who listens to My message[1] and believes in the One Who sent Me has eternal life and does not come into judgment, but he has departed from death into life. 25. Most definitely I say to you that a time is coming and now is when the dead will hear the voice of the Son of God, (1Pe 4:6) and those who listen will live. 26. For just as the Father has life in Himself, so also He gave to the Son to have life in Himself. 27. And He gave Him authority to make judgment, because He is *the* Son of Man. 28. Do not be amazed at this, because a time is coming in which all those in the tombs will hear His voice 29. and those who have done good things will go forth into resurrection[2] life, but those who have done evil things into resurrection judgment.[3]

5:30. "I am not able to do anything by Myself: I judge just as I hear, and My judgment is righteous, because I do not seek My will but the will of the One Who sent Me."

Witnesses to Jesus

5:31. "If I testify concerning Myself, My testimony is not true: 32. there is another witnessing about Me, and I know that the testimony is true which he

---

1   (v.24) To listen means to heed, to not just hear, but to change behavior and do what He says.
2   (v.29) See Resurrection in Glossary.
3   (v.29) See Re 20:11-15, Mt 25:31-33.

testifies about Me. 33. You have sent to John, and he has testified the truth: 34. but I do not take the testimony from a person, but I say these things so that you could be saved. 35. That one was the burning and shining lamp, and you desired to rejoice for a moment in his light. 36. And I have a better testimony than John: for the works which the Father has given Me so that I would complete them, these works, which I do, testify concerning Me, that the Father sent Me. 37. And the One Who sent Me, the Father, that One had testified concerning Me. But you have neither heard His voice at any time nor seen His appearance, 38. and you do not have His message remaining in you, because you do not believe in this One Whom He has sent. 39. You must examine the Scriptures, because you think *you* have eternal life in these: and these are those *Scriptures* that testify about Me: 40. and you do not want to come to Me so that you would have *eternal* life.

5:41. "I do not take praise from men, 42. but I have known you that you do not have the love of God in yourselves.[1] 43. I have come in the name of My Father, and you do not accept Me: if another would come in his own name, you will accept that one. 44. How are you able to believe, accepting praise from another, when you are not seeking the glory which *is* from the Only God?[2] 45. Do not think that I will accuse you before the Father: Moses, in whom you have hoped, is the one who accuses you. 46. For if you were believing Moses, then you would believe Me: for that one wrote about Me. (Dt 18:15) 47. And if you do not believe in the writings of that one, how will you believe in My teachings?"[3]

The Feeding of the Five Thousand
(Mt 14:13-21, Mk 6:30-44, Lk 9:10-17)

6.1. After these things Jesus went from Tiberias[4] to the other side of the lake of Galilee. 2. And an enormous crowd was following Him, because they were seeing the signs that He was doing upon the sick. 3. And Jesus went up on the mountain and He was sitting there with His disciples. 4. And the Passover, the Feast of the Jewish people, was near. 5. Therefore, when Jesus lifted up His eyes and saw that a vast crowd was coming toward Him, He said to Philip, "Where could we buy bread so that they could eat?" 6. And He was saying this testing him: for He had known what He was intending to do. 7. Philip answered Him, "Two hundred denarii[5] *worth of* bread is not sufficient so that each of them could take a little." 8. One of His disciples, Andrew, the brother of Simon Peter, said to Him, 9. "There is a boy here who has five barley loaves and two cooked fish: but what are these for so many?" 10. Jesus said, "Make the people recline." And there was a lot of grass in the place. Then they reclined, the number *was*

1   (v.42) Each of us is a priest and must continually spread the love of God as we go.
2   (v.44) God is One as in Dt 6:4.
3   (v.47) This concludes His ministry for this trip to Jerusalem. John does not record His return to Galilee.
4   (v.1) This verse could also be translated "beyond Tiberias" instead of "the other side of .."
See Location of the Feeding of the Five Thousand in Glossary.
5   (v.7) About eight or nine months' wages

about five thousand men.[1] 11. Then Jesus took the bread and after He gave thanks He distributed to those who were reclining, likewise also of the fish, as much as they wanted. 12. And as they were filled, He said to His disciples, "You must gather the leftover broken pieces, so that none would be left." 13. Therefore they gathered and filled twelve baskets[2] of pieces from the five barley loaves, which satisfied those who had eaten. (2Ki 4:42-44) 14. Then after the people saw that He had done a sign they were saying that "This One is truly the Prophet, the One Who is coming into the world." 15. Then, since Jesus knew that they were intending to come and to seize Him so that they could make Him king, He withdrew again to the mountain, by Himself alone.

Walking on the Water

(Mt 14:22-27, Mk 6:45-52)

6:16. And as it became evening His disciples went down to the lake 17. and after they embarked in a boat they were going across the lake to Capernaum.[3] And it was already dark and Jesus had not yet come to them, 18. but now a great wind was blowing, it was stirring up the lake. 19. However, after they had rowed about twenty-five or thirty stadia[4] they saw Jesus walking on the lake, even coming near the boat, and they were afraid. 20. And He said to them, "I AM, you must stop being afraid." 21. Therefore they wanted to take Him into the boat, and immediately the boat was on the shore to which they were going.

Jesus the Bread of Life

6:22. The next day the crowd that had been standing on the other side of the lake understood that there was not another small boat there, except one and that Jesus did not go with His disciples, but only His disciples left in the boat: 23. but small boats came from Tiberias *to* near the place where they ate the bread when the Lord gave thanks. 24. Therefore when the crowd saw that Jesus and His disciples were not there, they embarked in small boats and came into Capernaum[5] seeking Jesus. 25. And when they found Him on the other side of the lake they said to Him, "Rabbi, when did you come here?" 26. Jesus answered them and said, "Most assuredly I say to you, you are not seeking Me because you saw a sign, but because you ate from the bread and ate your fill. 27. Do not work for the food that perishes but the food which remains into eternal life, which the Son of Man will give to you: for the Father God attested this." 28. Therefore they said to Him, "What could we do so that we would do the works of God?" 29. Jesus answered and said to them, "This is the work of God, that you would

---

1   (v.10) Only men were counted because of Nu 1:3. See Census in Glossary.
2   (v.13) The basket is smaller than the hamper used in the feeding of the four thousand.
3   (v.17) Capernaum is the Latin spelling of the Hebrew name Kafer Na-um. Kafer means town or village and Na-um means pleasant.
4   (v.19) Three to three and a half miles
5   (v.24) See note on v. 17.

believe[1] in Whom that One sent." 30. Then they said to him, "Then what sign are You doing, so that we could see and we would believe in You? What work are You doing? 31. Our fathers ate manna in the wilderness, just as it has been written, 'He gave bread from heaven for them to eat.'" (Ex 16:15, Nu 11: 7-9, Ps 78:24) 32. Then Jesus said to them, "Most certainly I say to you, Moses has not given you the bread from heaven, but My Father is giving you the true bread from heaven: 33. for the bread of God is that which descends from heaven and gives life to the world."

6:34. Then they said to Him, "Lord, You must always give us this bread." 35. Jesus said to them, "I am the bread[2] of life: the one who comes to Me would **not** hunger, and the one who believes in Me will **not** ever thirst. 36. But I said to you that you have seen Me and you do not believe. 37. Everyone the Father would give to Me will come to Me, and I could **not** cast outside the one who comes to Me, 38. because I have not descended from heaven so that I would do My will, but the will of the One Who sent Me. 39. This is the will of the One Who sent Me, that I would not lose any of His He has given to Me, but I will raise him on the last Day.[3] 40. For this is the will of My Father, that everyone who sees the Son and believes in Him would have eternal life, and I will raise him on the last Day."

6:41. Therefore the Jewish people were murmuring concerning Him because He said, "I AM the Bread that descends from heaven," 42. and they were saying, "Is this not Jesus, the Son of Joseph, Whose father and mother we know? Now how does He say that 'I have descended from heaven?'" 43. Jesus answered and said to them, "Stop murmuring with one another. 44. No one is able to come to Me unless the Father, the One Who sent Me, would draw him, then I will raise him on the last Day. 45. It has been written in the Prophets, 'And all will be taught by God:' (Is 54:13) everyone who has heard and learned from the Father comes to Me. 46. Not that anyone has seen the Father except the One Who was with God, He has seen the Father. 47. Most assuredly I say to you, the one who believes[4] has eternal life. 48. I AM the Bread of Life. 49. Your fathers ate manna in the wilderness and they died: 50. this One is the Bread that descends from heaven, so that whoever would eat of it would not then die. 51. I AM the Living Bread that descended from out of heaven: if anyone would eat of this Bread he will live forever, and also the Bread which I will give on behalf of the life of the world is My flesh."

6:52. Then the Jewish people were fighting with one another saying, "How is He able to give us His flesh to eat?" 53. Then Jesus said to them, "Most

---

1   (v.29) Jesus' Jewish understanding of 'believe' requires a change of behavior as evidence.

2   (v.35) Bread means not only bread, but all food and clothing, shelter, even spiritual needs.

3   (v.39) Judgment Day. See Re 20:4, 11-14.

4   (v.47) The Hebrew understanding of "believe" requires a change in behavior.

certainly I say to you, unless you would eat the flesh of the Son of Man and you would drink His blood, you do not have life in yourselves. (Mt 5:6) 54. The one who chews My flesh[1] and drinks My blood[2] has eternal life, and I will raise him on the last Day. 55. For My flesh is true food and My blood is true drink. 56. The one who chews My flesh and drinks My blood remains in Me and I in him. 57. Just as the living Father sent Me and I live because of the Father, then the one who chews Me, even that one will live because of Me. 58 This is the Bread which has come down from heaven, not just like the fathers ate and died: the one who chews this Bread will live forever." 59. He said these things teaching in a synagogue in Capernaum.[3]

The Words of Eternal Life

6:60. Then many of His disciples, when they heard *this*, said, "This message is hard: who is able to hear it?" 61. But Jesus, since He knew within Himself that His disciples were murmuring about this, said to them, "Does this give offense *to* you? 62. Then what if you could see the Son of Man going up where He was before? 63. The Spirit is that which gives life, the flesh does not profit anything: the words that I have spoken to you are spirit and they are life. 64. But there are some of you who do not believe." For Jesus knew from *the* beginning there were some who did **not** believe and who was the one who *would* give Him over. 65. And He was saying, "Because of this I have said to you that no one is able to come to Me unless it has been given to him by the Father."[4]

6:66. For this reason many of His disciples left for the things behind *them* and they were no longer walking with Him. 67. Then Jesus said to the twelve, "Now do you want to go?"[5] 68. Simon Peter answered Him, "Lord, to whom will we go? You have *the* words of eternal life, 69. and we have believed and we have known that You are the Holy One of God." 70. Jesus answered them, "Did I not choose you, the twelve? And one of you is a devil." 71. And He was speaking *of* Judas *son of* Simon Iscariot: for this one, one of the twelve, was going to give Him over.

The Unbelief of Jesus' Brothers

7.1. And after these things Jesus was going about in Galilee: for He was not wanting to spend time in Judea, because the Jewish *leaders* were seeking to kill Him. 2. And the Feast of Booths[6] of the Jewish people was near. 3. Therefore

---

1   (v.54) To chew His flesh is to break the Word into small pieces, study, discuss, and meditate on it. See Jr 15:16, Jn 1:14.
2   (v.54) To drink His blood is to swallow, digest the Word of God, translating it into changes in behavior. The life is in the blood (Lv 17:11), in transforming the Word into action. From ancient times rabbis used wine to express covenant, with wine representing blood.
3   (v.59) Capernaum is the Latin spelling of the Hebrew name Kafer Na-um. Kafer means town or village and Na-um means pleasant.
4   (v.65) Ephesians 1:11 says we are chosen by lot. Not one of us has been chosen on merit.
5   (v.67) The Greek construction anticipates a negative reply.
6   (v.2) This is the Feast of Succot, which some English translators have called Taberna-

His brothers said to Him, "You must leave from this place and You must go to Judea, so that Your disciples will see Your works which You do: 4. for no one does anything in secret when he is seeking to be conspicuous. If You must do these things, You must *go where You will* reveal Yourself to the world." 5. For His brothers were not believing in Him. 6. Therefore Jesus said to them, "My appointed time has not yet come, but your time is always ready. 7. The world is not able to hate you, but it does hate Me, because I testify about it that its works are evil. 8. You must go up to the feast: I am not going up to this feast, because My appointed time has not yet been completed."[1] 9. And having said these things He was staying in Galilee.

Jesus at the Feast of Booths[2]

7:10. And as His brothers went up to the feast, then He also went up, not openly, but in secret. 11. Then the Jewish people were seeking Him at the feast and were saying, "Where is that One?" 12. And there was great murmuring about Him among the crowds: indeed some were saying that "He is good," but others were saying, "No, but He would deceive the crowd." 13. Though no one was openly speaking about Him because of fear of the Jewish *leaders*.

7:14. And now, in the middle of the feast, Jesus went up to the temple and He was teaching. 15. Then the Jewish people were amazed saying, "How does He know that which has been written,[3] since He has not been trained?" 16. Then Jesus answered them and said, "My teaching is not Mine, but of the One Who sent Me: 17. if someone would want to do His will, he will know about the teaching, whether it is from God or *if* I am speaking from Myself. 18. The one who speaks from himself is seeking his own glory: but the One who seeks the glory of the One who sent Him, this One is genuine and unrighteousness is not in Him. 19. Has not Moses given you the Torah?[4] And not one of you does the Torah.[5] Why are you seeking to kill Me?" 20. The crowd answered, "You have a demon: who is seeking to kill You?" 21. Jesus answered and said to them, "I did one work and you all are amazed. 22. Because Moses gave you circumcision - not that it is from Moses but from the fathers - and you circumcise a man on the Sabbath. 23. If a man takes circumcision on a Sabbath[6] so that he would not circumvent the Torah of Moses, are you angry with Me, because I made a man's whole body well on a Sabbath? 24. Do not judge according to appearance, but

cles. Succot means booths and each family built a booth of palm fronds to use for a shelter during the feast. See Succot in Glossary.

1   (v.8) The word translated appointed time refers to a predetermined time, here set by God, for Jesus to appear publicly in Jerusalem. The Feast of Succot is one that men were commanded to attend, so it was for His brothers to go, but not God's appointed time for Jesus to go up publicly.

2   (Caption) See Note for v. 2.

3   (v.15) "That which has been written" means Scripture.

4   (v.19) The first five books of the Bible. See Torah in Glossary.

5   (v.19) Doing Torah is summed up in Lv 19:18, "..love your neighbor as yourself."

6   (v.23) This is a reference to circumcising an eight day old infant, Lv 12:3.

judge righteous judgment."

Is This the Messiah?

7:25. Therefore some of those from Jerusalem were saying, "Is this not Whom they are seeking to kill? 26. And behold He is speaking openly and they are saying nothing to Him. Perhaps the authorities truly found out that this One is the Messiah? 27. In fact we know where this One is from: but when the Messiah would come, no one knows where He is from." 28. Then Jesus cried out, teaching in the temple and saying, "And you know Me and you know where I am from: and I have not come for Myself, *to do My will*, but the One Who sent Me is Genuine, Whom you do not acknowledge: 29. I know Him, because I am from Him. He sent Me." 30. Therefore they were seeking to seize Him, but no one laid a hand on Him, because His time had not yet come. 31. And many from the crowd were believing in Him and were saying, "When the Messiah comes will He do more signs than this One has done?"

Officials Sent to Arrest Jesus

7:32. The Pharisees listened while the crowd was murmuring these things about Him, and the high priests and Pharisees sent servants to seize Him. 33. Then Jesus said, "I am with you yet a little time, then I am going to the One Who sent Me. 34. You will seek Me but you will not find Me, and where I AM you are not able to come." 35. Then the Jewish people said among themselves, "Where does this One intend to go that we will not find Him? Does He intend to go into the Diaspora of the Greeks and to teach the Greeks?[1] 36. What is this statement which He said, 'You will seek Me but you will not find Me, and where I am you are not able to come?'"

Rivers of Living Water

7:37. And on the final Sabbath[2] day of the feast Jesus stood and cried out saying, "If anyone would thirst he must continually come to Me and he must continually drink. 38. The one who believes in Me, just as the Scripture said, rivers of living water will flow out from his inner being." (Pr 18:4, Is 58:11) 39. And He said this about the Spirit, which those who believed in Him were about to take: for *the* Spirit was not yet *given*, because Jesus was not yet glorified.

Division among the People

7:40. Then when those of the crowd heard these words they were saying, "This One is truly the prophet:" 41. others were saying, "This One is the Messiah," and they were saying, "What! Does the Messiah come out of Galilee?"[3] 42. "Does not the Scripture say that Messiah comes from the seed of David and

---

1   (v.35) The Greek construction of this question expects a negative answer.
2   (v.37) This is the eighth day, because at the Feast of Booths, Succot, the first day and the eighth day are Sabbaths. See Succot in Glossary.
3   (v.41) The Greek construction here and in verses 48 and 51 anticipates a negative reply.

from the town of Bethlehem[1] where David was?" 43. Consequently there was a division in the crowd because of Him: 44. some of them were wanting to seize Him, but no one put his hands on Him.

The Unbelief of Those in Authority

7:45. Then the servants came to the high priests and Pharisees, and they said to the *servants*, "Why did you not bring Him?" 46. The servants answered, "No man ever spoke in this manner." 47. Then the Pharisees answered them, "Have you not also been deceived? 48. Did any of the leaders or of the Pharisees believe in Him? 49. But this crowd, which does not know the Torah,[2] is accursed." 50. Nicodemus, who came to Him earlier, said to them, being one of them, 51. "Does our Torah judge a man unless it would first hear from him and would know what he was doing?" 52. And they answered and said to him, "Are you, too, from Galilee? You must search and you must see that a prophet is not raised up in Galilee."[3] [4]

Jesus the Light of the World

8.12. So Jesus spoke to them again saying, "I AM the Light of the world: the one who follows Me could **not** walk in darkness, but will have the light of life." 13. Then the Pharisees said to Him, "You are testifying about Yourself: Your testimony is not true." 14. Jesus answered and said to them, "Even if I am testifying about Myself, My testimony is true, because I know where I came from and where I am going: but you do not know where I come from or where I am going.[5] 15. You are judging according to the flesh, I am judging no one. 16. And even if I do judge, My judgment is true, because I am not alone, but *it is* I and *the* Father Who sent Me. 17. And even in your Torah it has been written that two people are the true witness. (Dt 17:6, 19:15) 18. I AM the One who testifies concerning Myself and the Father Who sent Me testifies about Me." 19. Then they were saying to Him, "Where is Your Father?" Jesus answered, "You know neither Me nor My Father: if you had known Me, you *would* also have known My Father." 20. He spoke these words while teaching in the treasury in the temple: but no one seized Him because His time had not yet come.

Where I am Going You Cannot Come

8:21. Then He said again to them, "I am going back and you will seek Me, and you will be dead, *lost*, in your sin: you are not able to come where I

---

1   (v.42) Bethlehem is the Greek spelling of the Hebrew name, Beit-Lekhem, meaning House of Bread. In what more appropriate place could He have been born, the One Who said, "for the bread of God is that which descends from heaven and gives life to the world." (Jn 6:33)

2   (v.49) Torah means teaching and is the name of the first five books of the Bible.

3   (v.52) Mt 2:23 ties Galilee to Messiah with Is 11:1, the connection to Galilee coming from the word natser, referring to the shoot, branch of Jesse. Nazareth is Natseret in Hebrew.

4   (v.52) Verses 7:53-8:11 are omitted because they were not in the earliest manuscripts and were not written by someone who knew Jewish Scriptures. See Adultery in Glossary.

5   (v,14) Both these words "going" mean going back where He came from, heaven.

am going." 22. Therefore the Jewish people were saying, "Will He kill Himself because He says 'Where I am going you are not able to come?'" 23. And He was saying to them, "You are from below, I AM from above: you are from this world, I AM not from this world. 24. Therefore I said to you that you will be dead in your sins: for if you would not believe that I AM, you will be dead in your sins." 25. Therefore they were saying to Him, "Who are You?" Jesus said to them, "And what have I said to you from the beginning? 26. I have much to say and to judge concerning you, but the One Who sent Me is Genuine, and I did hear from Him these things *that* I am saying to the world." 27. He was saying to them that they did not know the Father. 28. Then Jesus said to them, "When you would exalt/lift up[1] the Son of Man, then you will know that I AM, and I do nothing by Myself, but I say these things just as the Father taught Me. 29. And the One Who sent Me is with Me: He has not left Me alone, because I always do things pleasing to Him." 30. After He said these things many believed in Him.

The Truth Will Make You Free

8:31. Therefore Jesus was saying to the Jewish people who believed in Him, "If you would remain[2] in My word, you are truly My disciples 32. and you will know the truth, and the truth will make you free."[3] 33. They answered Him, "We are Abraham's seed and we have never been slaves: how do You say that 'You will become free.'" 34. Jesus answered them, "I most definitely say to you that everyone who commits sin is a slave of sin. 35. And the slave does not stay in the house forever, the son does stay forever. 36. If therefore the Son would set you free, you will truly be free.[4] 37. I know that you are Abraham's seed: but you are seeking to kill Me, because My message does not take hold in you. 38. I am saying what I have seen from the Father: but you are doing[5] what you heard from your father."

Your Father the Devil

8:39. They answered and said to Him, "Abraham is our father." Jesus said to them, "If you are children of Abraham, you must continually be doing the works of Abraham: 40. but now you are seeking to kill Me, a man, I, Who have spoken the truth to you that I heard from God: this Abraham did not do. 41. You are doing the works of your *own* father." Then they said to Him, "We have not been born from immorality:[6] we have one Father, God." 42. Jesus said to them, "If God were your Father you would love Me, for I came out from God and I have come: for I have not come from Myself, but He sent Me. 43. Why do you

---

1   (v.28) This refers both to His being exalted and His being crucified.
2   (v.31) The word translated remain could also be translated live. We are to live in His Word, converting the written Word of God into action, to bring His love to all mankind.
3   (v.32) Freedom from something, from sin, from evil: not freedom to do your will. See Gal 5:13.
4   (v.36) We are free because we are no longer slaves to sin.
5   (v.38) This is "you are saying," instead of "doing" in the oldest manuscripts.
6   (v.41) This refers to any idolatry.

not recognize My manner of speaking?¹ Because you are not able to hear My message. 44. You are from your father the devil and you want to do the desires of your father. That one was a murderer from the beginning and he has not stood in the truth, because truth is not in him. When he would tell a lie, he speaks from his own supply, because he is the father of lies. 45. But because I am speaking the truth, you do not believe Me. 46. Who of you exposes Me concerning sin? If I am speaking truth, why do you not believe Me? 47. The one who is from God hears the words of God: because of this you do not hear, because you are not from God."

Before Abraham was, I AM

8:48. The Jewish people answered and said to Him, "Are we not rightly saying that You are a Samaritan² Yourself and You have a demon?" 49. Jesus answered, "I do not have a demon, but I honor My Father, and you dishonor Me. 50. But I am not seeking My glory: the one who seeks *glory* is also judging. 51. Most assuredly I say to you, whoever would keep My word would **not ever** see death." 52. Then the Jewish people said to Him, "Now we know that You have a demon. Abraham and the prophets died, but You are saying, 'If someone would keep My word, he would **not ever** taste death. 53. Are You greater than our father Abraham, who died?³ And the prophets died. What do You make Yourself?" 54. Jesus answered, "If I will glorify Myself, then it is not My glory: My Father is the One Who glorifies Me, Whom you are saying that 'He is our God,' 55. and you have not known Him, but I do know Him. And if I were to say that I do not know Him, I would be a liar like you: but I do know Him and I keep His Word. 56. Abraham your father rejoiced because he would see My day, and he did see *it* and was joyful." 57. Then the Jewish people said to Him, "You are not yet fifty years old and You have seen Abraham?" 58. Jesus said to them, "I most positively say to you, before Abraham was *born* I AM." 59. Then they took stones so that they could throw *them* at Him. But Jesus was concealed and left the temple.

The Healing of a Man Born Blind

9.1. And when He was passing by He saw a man blind from birth. 2. And His disciples asked Him saying, "Rabbi, who sinned, this one or his parents, that he would have been born blind?" 3. Jesus answered, "Neither he nor his parents sinned, but so that the works of God would be revealed in him. 4. It is necessary for us to perform the works of the One Who sent Me while it is day: night is coming when no one is able to perform.⁴ 5. While I would be in the world, I am *the* Light of the world." 6. After He said these things He spit on the ground and He

1	(v.43) The word translated "manner of speaking" refers to the accent that identifies where the speaker comes from, in this instance to His coming from heaven.
2	(v.48) Samaritan was a derogatory term referring to His not being from Jerusalem.
3	(v.53) The Greek construction here anticipates a negative answer.
4	(v.4) Day speaks of light, while dawn alludes to redemption. Night alludes to exile, separation from God's presence.

made clay from the spittle[1] and He placed this clay upon his eyes 7. and He said to him, "You must go wash in the Pool of Siloam,"[2] the one interpreted "having been sent." Then he went and washed and came *away* seeing. 8. Therefore the neighbors and those who saw him earlier, because he was a beggar, were saying, "Is this not the one who sits and begs?" 9. Some were saying that "This is he," *but* others were saying, "No, but he is like him." That one was saying, "I am *he*." 10. Therefore they were saying to him, "How then were your eyes opened?" 11. That one answered, "The man called Jesus made clay and spread *it* on my eyes and He said to me that 'You must go to Siloam and wash:' then when I went, after I washed I recovered my sight."[3] 12. And they said to him, "Where is that One?" He said, "I do not know."

The Pharisees Investigate the Healing

9:13. They led him, the formerly blind man, to the Pharisees. 14. And it was the Sabbath on the day Jesus made the clay and opened his eyes. 15. Therefore the Pharisees again asked him how he recovered sight. And he said to them, "He placed clay upon my eyes and I washed and I see." 16. Then some of the Pharisees were saying, "This man is not from God, because He is not observing the Sabbath." But others were saying, "How is a man, a sinner, able to do such signs as these?" And there was division among them. 17. However, they again said to the blind *man*, "What do you say about Him, because He opened your eyes?" And he said, "He is a Prophet."

9:18. The Jewish *leaders* then did not believe concerning him that he was blind and received *his* sight until they summoned the parents of the one who recovered sight 19. and they asked them saying, "Is this your son, whom you say was born blind? Then how does he see now?" 20. Then his parents answered and said, "We know that this one is our son and that he was born blind: 21. but how he now sees we do not know, or who opened his eyes we do not know: you must ask him, he is of age, he will speak for himself." 22. His parents said these things because they were afraid of the Jewish *leaders*: for now the Jewish *leaders* agreed that whoever would confess Him *to be* Messiah would be excommunicated. 23. Because of this his parents said that "He is of age, you must ask him."

9:24. Therefore they summoned a second time the man who was blind and said to him, "You must now give glory to God: we know that this man is a sinner." 25. Then he answered, "I do not know if He is a sinner: one thing I do know *is* that although I was blind, now I see." 26. Then they said to him, "What

---

1   (v.6) People believed the spittle of the first-born son of the father was anointed for healing.

2   (v.7) The Hebrew name of the pool is Shiloch. This pool is near the temple mount at the end of Hezekiah's tunnel. It was the source of the water that was used with the ashes of the red heifer for purification.

3   (v.11) How can someone born blind recover sight? Could it be his eyes were perfectly formed in the womb, but by the time of his birth he was blind?

did He do to you? How did He open your eyes?" 27. He answered them, "Now I told you and you did not listen. Why do you want to hear again? Do even you want to become His disciples?" 28. Then they berated him and said, "You are a disciple of that One, but we are disciples of Moses: 29. we know that God had spoken to Moses, but we do not know where this One is from." 30. The man answered and said to them, "Certainly it is wonderful in this, that you do not know where He is from, but He did open my eyes. 31. We know that God does not hear from sinners, but if any would be God fearing, and he would make his desire *known*, He hears this. 32. From the beginning it has not been heard that someone opened eyes of *someone* born blind: 33. if this One were not from God, He would not be able to do anything." 34. They answered and said to him, "You were born wholly in sin[1] and are you teaching us?" And they threw him outside.[2]

Spiritual Blindness

9:35. Jesus heard that they threw him outside, and when He found him He said, "Do you believe in the Son of Man?" 36. That one answered and said, "And Who is He, Lord, so that I could believe in Him?" 37. Jesus said to him, "You have even seen Him. In fact the One Who is speaking with you is that One." 38. And he said, "I believe, Lord:" and he fell down and prostrated himself before Him. 39. And Jesus said, "I came into this world for judgment, so that those who do not see would see and those who see would become blind."

9:40. Those of the Pharisees who were with Him heard these things and said to Him, "Then are we blind?"[3] 41. Jesus said to them, "If you were blind, you would not have sin: but now because you are saying that 'We are seeing,' your sin remains."

The Parable of the Sheepfold

10.1. "Most assuredly I say to you, the one who does not enter through the door into the sheepfold of the sheep, but goes up from another place, that one is a thief and a robber: 2. but the one who enters through the door is *the* shepherd of the sheep. 3. The doorkeeper opens for this one, and the sheep hear his voice and he calls his own sheep by name and he leads them out. 4. When he would bring out all his own sheep, he goes in front of them, and the sheep follow him, because they know his voice: 5. and they will **not** follow a stranger, but they will flee from him, because they do not know the voice of the strangers." 6. Jesus told this proverb to them, but they did not know what it was that He was saying to them.

Jesus the Good Shepherd

10:7. Then Jesus said again, "I most definitely say to you that I AM the

---

1   (v.34) They believed that sin was the cause of his blindness.
2   (v.34) Excommunicated him
3   (v.40) The Greek construction anticipates a negative reply.

Door of the sheep. 8. All who came before Me were thieves and robbers, but the sheep did not hear them. 9. I AM the Door: if someone would enter through Me he will be saved and he will enter and he will go out and he will find pasture. 10. The thief does not come except that he would steal and he would kill and he would destroy: I came so that they would have life and they would have abundance.[1] 11. I AM the Good Shepherd.[2] The Good Shepherd lays down His life on behalf of His sheep: 12. and the hireling, not being a shepherd, whose sheep are not his own, sees the wolf coming and he leaves the sheep and flees - and the wolf seizes and scatters them - 13. because a hireling does not even care in himself about the sheep. 14. I AM the Good Shepherd and I know My *sheep* and My *sheep* know Me, 15. just as the Father knows Me and I know the Father, and I lay down My life on behalf of the sheep. 16. But I also have sheep that are not from this sheepfold:[3] and it is necessary for Me to lead those and they will hear My voice, and they will become one flock,[4] one Shepherd. (Eze 34:23, 37:24) 17. For this reason the Father would love Me, because I am laying down My life so that I could again take it. 18. No one takes this *life* from Me, but I lay this *life* down by Myself, *willingly*. I have authority to lay it down, and I have authority to take it again: I did take this commandment from My Father."

10:19. Again there was division among the Jewish people because of these statements. 20. And many of them were saying, "He has a demon and He is mad: why are you listening to Him?" 21. Others were saying, "These are not the words of one possessed by a demon: is a demon able open eyes of *the* blind?"[5]

Jesus Rejected by the Jewish People

10:22. At that time it was the Feast of Dedication[6] for those in Jerusalem. It was winter, 23. and Jesus was walking in the temple, on Solomon's Porch. 24. Then the Jewish people were circling Him and they were saying to Him, "How long will You keep up the suspense? If You are the Messiah, You must right now tell us plainly." 25. Jesus answered them, "I told you and you do not believe: the works which I am doing in the name of My Father testify these things about Me: 26. but you do not believe, because you are not from My sheep. 27. My sheep hear My voice and I know them and they are following Me, 28. and I am giving them eternal life, and they would **not ever** die and no one is able to seize them from My hand. 29. My Father Who has given *them* to Me is greater than all, and no one is able to seize *them* from the hand of the Father. 30. We, the Father and I, are One."

---

1   (v.10) This is eternal life and spiritual abundance. See Lk 12:15, 14:33. See Life in Glossary.
2   (v.11) See Son of David/Son of Joseph in Glossary.
3   (v.16) A clear reference to the non-Jewish believers, see Eph 2:11-18.
4   (v.16) A joining of Jewish and non-Jewish into one body, see Ro 11 and Is 44:5.
5   (v.21) The Greek construction anticipates a negative reply.
6   (v.22) The Feast of Dedication is Hanukkah, two months after the end of the Feast of Succot. See Hanukkah in Glossary.

10:31. Again the Jewish *leaders* picked up stones so that they could stone Him. 32. Jesus answered them, "I have shown you many good works from the Father: for which of these works do you stone Me?" 33. The Jewish *leaders* answered Him, "We are not stoning You concerning good works but concerning blasphemy, and because You are a man although You are making Yourself God." 34. Jesus answered them, "Has it not been written in your Torah[1] that 'I said, you are gods?' (Ps 82:6) 35. If He called those gods to whom the Word of God came, then the Scripture cannot be done away with. 36. Are you saying *to* the One Whom the Father sanctified and sent into the world, that 'You are blaspheming,' because I said, 'I am a Son of God'? 37. If I do not do the works of My Father, do not believe Me: 38. but if I am doing *the works*, even if you would not believe in Me, believe in the works, so that you would know and you would continue knowing that the Father *is* in Me and I *am* in the Father." 39. Then they were seeking Him again to seize *Him*, but He came out from their hand.

10:40. And He went across the Jordan again, to the place where John was first baptizing and He was staying there. 41. And many came to Him and they were saying that John on the one hand did not do a sign, but on the other hand everything that John said about this One was true. 42. And many there believed in Him.

The Death of Lazarus

11.1. And someone was sick, Lazarus from Bethany,[2] from the town of Mary and her sister Martha. 2. And Mary was the one who anointed the Lord with ointment and wiped His feet with her hair, (Jn 12:3) her brother Lazarus was sick. 3. Therefore the sisters sent to Him saying, "Lord, behold whom You love[3] is sick." 4. When Jesus heard *this* He said, "This sickness is not to death but for the glory of God, so that the Son of God would be glorified through this *sickness*." 5. And Jesus loved[4] Martha and her sister and Lazarus. 6. Therefore as He heard that he was sick, at that time He was indeed staying in that place *where* He was two days, 7. immediately after this He said to the disciples, "We should go to Judea again." 8. The disciples said to Him, "Rabbi, the Jewish *leaders* were just now seeking to stone You, and are You going there again?" 9. Jesus answered, "Are there not twelve hours of daylight? If someone would walk in the day, he does not stumble, because he sees the light of this world: 10. but if someone would walk in the night, he stumbles, because the light is not in *the world*."[5] 11. He said these things, and after this He said to them, "Our friend Lazarus has fallen asleep: but I am going so that I could awaken him." 12. Then the disciples

---

1   (v.34) While the basic meaning of Torah is teaching or instruction and the reference is to the first five books of the Bible, here it refers to the whole Bible. See Torah in Glossary.

2   (v.1) Bethany is the Greek spelling of Beit-Anyah, meaning House of Sighing in Hebrew.

3   (v.3) The verb phileo is used here.

4   (v.5) This time the verb is agapao.

5   (v.10) Day speaks of light, while dawn alludes to redemption. Night alludes to exile, separation from God's presence.

said to Him, "Lord, if he would be sleeping he will be saved." 13. But Jesus had spoken about his death, only they thought that He was talking about the sleep of slumber.[1] 14. Therefore Jesus then said plainly to them, "Lazarus died, 15. and I rejoice for you that I was not there so that you would believe,: but let us go to him." 16. Then Thomas, the one called Twin, said to his fellow disciples, "Let us also go so that we could die with him."

Jesus the Resurrection[2] and the Life

11:17. Then when Jesus came He found *that* he had now *been* in the tomb four days. 18. And Bethany was near Jerusalem, about fifteen stadia.[3] 19. And many of the Jewish people had come to Martha and Mary so that they could console them concerning their brother. 20. Then as Martha heard that Jesus was coming she went to meet Him: and Mary was sitting in the house. 21. Therefore Martha said to Jesus, "Lord, if You had been here my brother would not have died: 22. but now I also know that God will give You whatever You would ask." 23. Jesus said to her, "Your brother will rise." 24. Martha said to Him, "I know that he will rise on the last Day[4] in the resurrection." [5] 25. Jesus said to her, "I AM the Resurrection and the Life: the one who believes in Me, even if he would die, he will live, 26. and everyone who lives and believes in Me would **not ever** die. Do you believe this?" 27. She said to Him, "Certainly Lord, I have believed that You are the Messiah, the Son of God, the One Who was to come into the world."

Jesus Weeps

11:28. And after she said this she left and told Mary her sister secretly, having said, "The Teacher is here and is calling you." 29. And as she heard this she got up quickly and was coming to Him. 30. And Jesus had not yet come into the village, but He was still in the place where Martha met Him. 31. Then the Jewish people, who were then in the house with her, consoling her, when they saw Mary, that she got up quickly and went out, they followed her because they thought that she was going to the tomb so that she could weep there. 32. Then as Mary came where Jesus was, when she saw Him, she fell toward His feet saying to Him, "Lord, if You had been here my brother would not have died." 33. Then as Jesus saw her weeping and those Jewish people who accompanied her weeping, He was deeply moved in the spirit and it troubled Him 34. and He said, "Where have you put him?" They said to Him, "Lord, You must come and see." 35. Jesus wept. 36. Then the Jewish people were saying, "See how He loved[6] him." 37. Some of them said, "Was not this One, Who opened the eyes of the blind, also able to do *something* so that he would not have died?"

1   (v.13) See Death in Glossary.
2   (Caption) See Resurrection in Glossary.
3   (v.18) About two miles
4   (v.24) Judgment Day. See Re 20:4, 11-14.
5   (v.24) See Resurrection in Glossary.
6   (v.36) The verb used here is phileo.

Lazarus Brought to Life

11:38. Jesus then again, being deeply moved within Himself, came to the tomb: and it was a cave and a stone was lying upon it. 39. Jesus said, "You must remove the stone." Martha, the sister of the one who had died, said to Him, "Lord, he already has an odor, for it has been four days." 40. Jesus said to her, "Did I not say that if you would believe you would see the glory of God?" 41. Then they removed the stone. And Jesus looked up and said, "Father, I give You thanks because You heard Me.[1] 42. And I have known that You always hear Me, but I spoke because of the crowd that was standing around, so that they would believe that You sent Me." 43. And after He said these things He cried out in a loud voice, "Lazarus, come outside." 44. The one who died came out, although his feet and hands had been bound with strips of cloth and his face was bound with a face cloth. Jesus said to them, "You must loose him at once and you must allow him to go."

The Plot to Kill Jesus

(Mt 26:1-5, Mk 14:1,2, Lk 22:1,2)

11:45. Therefore many of those Jewish people, who came to Mary and saw what He did, did believe in Him. 46. Some of them went to the Pharisees and told them what Jesus did. 47. Then the high priests and Pharisees assembled *the* Sanhedrin and they were saying, "What *can* we do because this man does many signs? 48. If we in this way allow Him, all will believe in Him and the Romans will come and they will seize both our place[2] and the nation." 49. And one of them, Caiaphas, who was the High Priest of that year, said to them, "You do not know anything, 50. and you do not consider that it profits you that one man should die on behalf of the people so then the whole nation would not be lost." 51. But this *was* not from himself he spoke, but since he was High Priest of that year he prophesied that Jesus was going to die on behalf of the people,[3] 52. and not for the people only but so that also the children of God, those who had been scattered, would gather into one.[4] 53. Then from that day they resolved that they would kill Him.

11:54. Therefore Jesus was no longer walking openly among the Jewish people, but He left from there for the region near the desert, to a city called Ephraim, and He was staying there with the disciples.

11:55. And the Passover of the Jewish people was near, and many went up to Jerusalem from the countryside so that they could purify themselves[5] before

---

1   (v.41) Jesus had already prayed and knew just what He needed to do.

2   (v.48) The temple was Caiaphas' place, which surely would have been lost to Caiaphas and the other Hellenists if the reigning Messiah were to come. See Hellenists in Glossary.

3   (v.51) This refers to all the people of the world. The next statement refers to the return of the Jewish people.

4   (v.52) See Replacement Theology in Glossary.

5   (v.55) They purified themselves as Paul did in Acts 21:24, ending with self-immersion.

the Passover. 56. Therefore they were seeking Jesus and they were saying with one another when they stood in the temple, "What does it seem to you? That He would **not** come to the Feast?" 57. And the high priests and the Pharisees had given orders that if anyone would know where He was he should report *it*, so that they could seize Him.[1]

The Anointing at Bethany

(Mt 26:6-13, Mk 14:3-9)

12.1. Then six days before Passover Jesus came into Bethany,[2] where Lazarus was, whom Jesus raised from the dead. 2. Then they made supper for Him there, and Martha was serving, and Lazarus was one of those who reclined with Him. 3. Then Mary, who took twelve ounces of costly pure nard ointment, anointed the feet of Jesus and wiped off His feet with her hair: and the house was filled from the fragrance of the ointment. 4. And Judas Iscariot, one of His disciples, the one who intended to give Him over, said, 5. "Why was this ointment not sold for three hundred denarii[3] and given to *the* poor?" 6. And he said this, not that he was caring in himself about the poor, but because he was a thief, and since he had the moneybox he was carrying what was offered. 7. Then Jesus said, "You must permit her, so that she could take care of this for the day of My preparation for burial: 8. for you always have the poor with yourselves (Dt 15:11), but you do not always have Me."

The Plot against Lazarus

12:9. The huge crowd of Jewish people knew that He was there and they came not only because of Jesus, but so that they could also see Lazarus whom He raised from *the* dead. 10. And the high priests also wanted to kill Lazarus, 11. because through him many of the Jewish people were going[4] and they were believing in Jesus.

The Triumphal Entry into Jerusalem

(Mt 21:1-11, Mk 11:1-11, Lk 19:28-40)

12:12. The next day *there was* an enormous crowd, which came to the feast. Because they heard that Jesus was coming to Jerusalem 13. they took fronds of palm trees and came out to meet Him and they were crying out,

"Hoshea-na:"[5] (Ps 118:25)

See Baptize in Glossary.

1   (v.57) The cooperation of the high priests and the Pharisees was unusual because the high priests were Hellenists and the Pharisees were very strict followers of the legalistic traditions. Both were threatened by Jesus: the high priests feared His Messianic rule because their power depended on Roman rule, and the Pharisees were threatened because their religious authority was at stake. See Hellenists in Glossary.

2   (v.1) Bethany is the Greek spelling of Beit-Anyah, meaning House of Sighing in Hebrew.

3   (v.5) About a year's pay.

4   (v.11) The Greek word used here implies going back where they came from, returning, that is repentance.

5   (v.13) Hoshea-na means "Deliver us now!" or "Save us now!" See Hosanna in Glossary.

"Blessed is He Who comes in *the* name of the Lord," (Ps 118:26)
"The King of Israel!"[1]

14. And then Jesus found a colt[2] *and* sat upon it, just as it has been written,

15.　"You must not fear, daughter of Zion:
　　Behold your King is coming,
　　　　being seated upon a foal of a donkey." (Zch 9:9)

16. The disciples did not understand these things about Him at first, but when Jesus was glorified, then they remembered that these things had been written for Him and *that* they did these things with Him. 17. Then the crowd, which was with Him when He called Lazarus from the tomb and raised him from the dead, was testifying. 18. Because of this then the crowd went to meet Him, because they heard this One Himself had done the miracle. 19. Then the Pharisees said among themselves, "You see that you are not helping anything: look, the world has gone after Him."

Some Greeks Seek Jesus

12:20. And there were some Greeks among those who went up so that they could worship in the feast: 21. these then came to Philip, the one from Bethsaida[3] of Galilee, and they were asking him saying, "Sir, we want to see Jesus." 22. Philip came and spoke to Andrew, and Andrew and Philip came and told Jesus. 23. And Jesus answered them saying, "The time has come that the Son of Man would be glorified. 24. I most definitely say to you, unless a grain of wheat would die when it falls to the earth, it only remains itself: but if it would die, it brings much fruit. 25. The one who loves his life loses it, and the one who hates his life in this world will keep it in eternal life. 26. If someone would serve Me, he must continually follow Me, and where I AM there also will My servant be: if someone would serve Me the Father will honor him."

The Son of Man Must be Lifted Up/Exalted[4]

12:27. "Now My inner being has been troubled, and what can I say? Father, *will* You save Me from this hour? But *it is* because of this I came into this hour. 28. Father, You must now glorify Your name." And a voice came from heaven, "And I did glorify and I will glorify again." 29. Then when the standing crowd also heard, it was saying that it was thunder, others were saying, "An angel has spoken to Him." 30. Jesus answered and said, "This voice was not for Me but for you. 31. Now is *the* judgment of this world, now the prince of this world

---

1　　(v.13) This crowd, including the disciples, thought He was the reigning Messiah. See Son of David/Son of Joseph in Glossary.
2　　(v.14) This is the foal of a donkey. See Donkey in Glossary.
3　　(v.21) Bethsaida is the Greek spelling of Beit-Tsaida, which means House or Place of Fishing (literally hunting, but also used for fishing) in Hebrew.
4　　(Caption) This refers to both the crucifixion and the need for us to lift up, exalt the risen Lord!

(Jn 14:30) will be cast outside: (Re 20:1-3) 32. and if I would be exalted/lifted[1] up from the earth, I will draw everyone to Myself." 33. And He was saying this, making known by what kind of death He was going to die. 34. Then the crowd answered Him, "We heard from the Torah[2] that the Messiah remains forever, (Is 9:7, Dn 2:44, 7:14) and how do You say that it is necessary *for* the Son of Man to be lifted up? Who is this Son of Man?" 35. Then Jesus said to them, "Yet a short time is the Light among you. You must continually walk while you have the Light, so that darkness would not overtake you: and the one who walks in darkness does not know where he is going. 36. While you have the Light, you must believe in the Light, so that you could become children of Light."

The Unbelief of the Jewish People

Jesus said these things, and after He left He hid from them. 37. But after He had done so many of His signs in front of them they were not believing in Him, 38. so that the word of the prophet Isaiah would be fulfilled which said,

"Lord, who believed in our report?
And was the arm of the Lord revealed to some?" (Is 53:1)
39. Because of this they were not able to believe, because again Isaiah said,
40.　　"He had blinded their eyes
　　　and hardened their hearts,
　　so that they would not see with their eyes
　　　　nor understand with their heart nor would they turn back, *repent,*
　　and I would heal them." (Is 6:10)

41. Isaiah said these things because he saw His glory, and he spoke about Him. 42. Nevertheless many of the leaders believed in Him, but they were not confessing *their belief* because of the Pharisees so that they would not be expelled from the synagogue: 43. for they loved the praise of men more than the glory of God.

Judgment by Jesus' Word

12:44. And Jesus cried out and said, "The one who believes in Me does not believe in Me but in the One Who sent Me, 45. and the one who sees Me sees the One Who sent Me. 46. I have brought light into the world, so that everyone who believes in Me would not remain in the darkness. 47. And if someone would hear My words and would not keep *them*, I do not judge him Myself: for I did not come to judge the world, but so that I would save the world. 48. The one who rejects Me, and does not take My message,[3] has what judges him: that message which I spoke judges him on the last Day. 49. Because I did not speak from

---

1　　　(v.32) This speaks of both His exaltation and His crucifixion.
2　　　(v.34) Torah here refers to the entire Tanach (Hebrew Scriptures). See Torah in Glossary.
3　　　(v.48) This is the plural of rhema, and refers to all His spoken messages. See Logos/ Rhema in Glossary.

Myself, but the Father, the One Who sent Me, gave Me a commandment, what I could say and what I could speak. 50. And I know that His commandment *brings* eternal life. Therefore what I am speaking, just as the Father has spoken to Me, so am I speaking."

Washing the Disciples' Feet

13.1. And Jesus, since He knew before the Feast of Passover that His time *had* come, *He knew* that He would go on from this world to the Father. As He loved His own, those in the world, He loved them to the utmost. 2. And when it was supper,[1] when the devil was now cast into his heart so that Judas Simon Iscariot could give Him over, 3. although He knew that the Father gave all these *sufferings* to Him, into His hands, *in His control,* and that He came out from God and He was going back to God, 4. He got up from supper and He removed His outer garments and taking a towel He tied *it* around Himself. 5. Then He put water in the basin and He began to wash the feet of the disciples and to wipe *their feet* with the towel, which was tied around *Him.* 6. Then He came to Simon Peter: he said to Him, "Lord, are You washing my feet?" 7. Jesus answered and said to him, "What I am doing you do not know now, but you will know later." 8. Peter said to Him, "You can **never** wash my feet." Jesus answered him, "Unless I would wash you, you have no part with Me." 9. Simon Peter said to Him, "Lord, not only my feet but also my hands and my head." 10. Jesus said to him, "The one who has bathed[2] does not have need except to wash his feet,[3] but he is entirely clean: and you are clean, but not all *of you.*" 11. For He knew who was betraying Him: because of this He said, "Not all are clean."

13:12. Therefore when He had washed their feet, and taken His outer garments and reclined again, He said to them, "Do you know what I have done for you? 13. You call Me 'The Teacher' and 'The Lord,' and you say rightly, for I am. 14. Therefore if I, the Lord and the Teacher, washed your feet, then you ought to wash the feet of one another: 15. for I gave you an example so that you would also do just as I did. 16. Most assuredly I say to you, a servant is not greater than his master and one sent[4] is not greater than the one who sent him. 17. If you know these things, blessed[5] are you if you would do them. 18. I am not speaking about all of you: I know whom I selected: but so that the Scripture would be fulfilled, 'The one who ate My bread lifted his heel against Me.' (Ps 41:9) 19. I tell you at this time before it happens, so that when it would happen

---

1   (v.2) He knew beforehand that this Passover meal would be His last chance to minister to them before His death and resurrection.
2   (v.10) This is a reference to immersion for purification, which we call baptism. See Baptize in Glossary.
3   (v.10) This is immersion, baptism, in preparation for them to enter the Holy Place, with their bodies as sanctuaries of the Holy Spirit.
4   (v.16) This could also be translated "..an apostle is not greater than the one who sent him."
5   (v.17) The Greek word translated blessed is makarios, meaning happy as well as blessed.

you would believe that I AM. 20. I most certainly say to you, the one who accepts whomever I will send accepts Me, and the one who accepts Me receives the One Who sent Me."

Jesus Foretells His Betrayal

(Mt 26:20-25, Mk 14:17-21, Lk 22:21-23)

13:21. After He said these things Jesus was troubled in the spirit and testified and said, "Most definitely I say to you that one of you will give Me over." 22. The disciples were looking at one another, being at a loss concerning what He said. 23. One of His disciples, whom Jesus loved,[1] was next to[2] Jesus. 24. Then Simon Peter beckoned to him to ask whoever might be the one about whom He was speaking. 25. So that one, in front of[3] Jesus, said to Him, "Lord, who is it?" 26. Jesus answered, "That one is with whom I will dip the piece of bread and I will give it to him." Then when He dipped the bread He took *it* and gave *it* to Judas Simon Iscariot. 27. And after *he took* the morsel then Satan[4] came into him. Then Jesus said to him, "You must do quickly what you are doing." 28. And not one of those who were reclining knew what He spoke to him about: 29. for some were thinking, since Judas had the moneybox, that Jesus said to him, "You must buy what we need for the feast," or so that he could give it to the poor. 30. Then when he took the morsel, he left immediately. And it was night.

The New Commandment

13:31. Then when he left, Jesus said, "Now the Son of Man has been glorified, and God has been glorified in Him: 32. if God has been glorified in Him then God will glorify Him in Himself, and God will glorify Him immediately. 33. Children, yet a little *while* am I with you: you will seek Me, and just as I said to the Jewish *leaders* that 'Where I go you are not able to come,' and now I tell you. 34. I am giving you a renewed commandment, that you must continually love one another;[5] just as I loved you so also you must love one another. 35. All will know by this, that you are My disciples, if you would have love for one another."

Peter's Denial Foretold

(Mt 26:31-35, Mk 14:27-31, Lk 22:31-34)

13:36. Simon Peter said to Him "Lord, where are You going?" Jesus answered him, "Where I am going you are not now able to follow Me, but you

---

1   (v.23) The Greek word translated love is phileo.
2   (v.23) This is literally "reclining on the chest of" an idiom referring to the person who reclined in front of the person named. See Reclining in Glossary.
3   (v.25) This uses a different word for chest, referring to someone close, possibly across the table.
4   (v.27) See Satan in Glossary.
5   (v.34) The word translated renew is the appropriate translation for this verse. See Lv 19:18.

will follow later." 37. Peter said to Him, "Lord, why am I not able to follow You now? I will lay down my life for Your sake." 38. Jesus answered, "Will you lay down your life for My sake? I say most decidedly to you, a cock will **not** crow until you would deny Me three times."

Jesus the Way to the Father

14.1. "Your heart must not be troubled: you must constantly believe in God and you must faithfully believe in Me. 2. In My Father's house are many dwelling places:[1] and if it were not *so*, would I tell you that I am going to prepare a place for you? (1Ki 8:13) 3. And if I would go, then I will prepare a place for you. I am coming again and I will take[2] you along with Me, so that where I AM you would also be. 4. And you know the way, where I am going." 5. Thomas said to Him, "Lord, we do not know where You are going: how are we able to know the way?" 6. Jesus said to him, "I AM the Way and the Truth and the Life:[3] no one comes to the Father except through Me.[4] 7. If you have known Me, then you will know My Father. And from now on you do know Him and you have been seeing Him." 8. Philip said to Him, "Lord, You must now show us the Father, and it is sufficient for us." 9. Jesus said to him, "I have been with you for so long a time and you have not known Me, Philip? The one who has seen Me has seen the Father: how can you say, 'You must show us the Father?' 10. Do you not believe that I *am* in the Father and the Father is in Me? The words, which I speak to you, I am not speaking from Myself, but the Father *Who* lives in Me does His works. 11. Believe in Me, that I *am* in the Father and the Father *is* in Me: but if not, believe because of these works. 12. Most assuredly I say to you, the one who believes in Me will do the works which I am doing and he will do even greater *things* than these, because I am going to the Father: 13. and whatever you would ask in My name, this I will do, so that the Father would be glorified in the Son: 14. whatever you would ask Me in My name I will do."

The Promise of the Spirit

14:15. "If you love Me, you will keep My commandments: (Wsd 6:18) 16. and I will ask the Father and, so that He would be with you forever, He will give you another Comforter, 17. the Spirit of Truth, Whom the world is not able to accept, because it does not see and does not know Him: you know Him, because He remains beside you and will be inside you. 18. I will not leave you orphans; I am coming with you. 19. Yet a little while and the world will no longer see

---

1   (v.2) While traditionally translated dwelling places or mansion, this is not a building. The primary meaning of the Greek word mon-ai is staying or tarrying. See Dwelling Places in Glossary.

2   (v.3) The verb used here is paralambano which speaks of the bridegroom taking his bride. See Mt 24:40.

3   (v.6) This is eternal life and spiritual abundance. See Lk 12:15, 14:33. See Life in Glossary.

4   (v.6) That is through the Way of Jesus, which is obedience to the Father, doing only what we see the Father doing. It means walking in the spirit of all Scripture, but not being legalistic: focus on the Father, not on the behavior of others with a critical spirit. See Is 43:11.

Me, but you will see Me. Because I live you will also live. 20. In that Day you will know that I *am* in My Father and you *are* in Me and I *am* in you. 21. The one who has My commandments and keeps them, that is the one who loves Me: and the one who loves Me will be loved by My Father, and I will love him and I will reveal Myself to him." 22. Judas, not Iscariot, said to Him, "Lord, then what has happened that You intend to reveal Yourself to us and not to the world?" 23. Jesus answered and said to him, "If someone would continuously love Me, he will keep My Word, and My Father will love him and We will come to him and We will make a dwelling[1] for Ourselves with him. 24. The one who does not love Me does not keep My words: and the message that you hear is not from Me but the Father Who sent Me.

14:25. "I have spoken these things to you while staying with you: 26. but the Comforter, the Holy Spirit, Whom the Father will send in My Name, that One will teach you all things and will remind you *of* everything which I Myself said to you. 27. I am leaving peace with you, I give My peace to you: I am giving to you, not just as the world would give. Your heart must not ever trouble *you* and it must stop being timid. 28. You heard that I said to you, 'I am going where I came from, then I am coming to you.' If you loved Me you would rejoice because I am going to the Father, because the Father is greater than I. 29. And now I have told you before it happens, so that when it would happen you would believe. 30. And I will no longer speak many things with you, for the prince of the world is coming: and he does not have any *part* with Me, 31. but so that the world would know that I love the Father, and just as the Father was commanding Me, this I am doing. You must get up, let us go from here."

Jesus the True Vine

15.1. "I AM the true vine and My Father is the farmer. 2. He removes every branch in Me if it does not bear fruit, and He prunes every branch *that* bears fruit so that it would bear more fruit. 3. You are already pruned because of the Word which I have spoken to you: 4. you must now dwell in Me and I in you. Just as the branch is not able to bear fruit by itself unless it would remain in the vine, so you *could not bear fruit* unless you would dwell continuously in Me. 5. I am the vine, you *are* the branches. The one who dwells in Me and I in him, this one bears much fruit, because apart from Me you are not able to do anything. 6. Unless someone would dwell in Me, he is cast outside like the branch and it withers and they gather it and cast *it* into the fire and it is burned. 7. If you would dwell in Me and My words would dwell in you, whatever you would wish you must immediately ask, and it will be done for you. 8. My Father is glorified in this, so that you would bear much fruit and you will become My disciples. 9. Just as the Father loved Me, and I loved you: you are dwelling in My love. 10. If you would keep My commandments, you will dwell in My love, just as I have kept

---

1   (v.23) While traditionally translated dwelling or home, this is not a building. The primary meaning of the Greek word mon-ai is staying or tarrying. See Dwelling Places in Glossary.

the commandments of My Father and I dwell in His love.

15:11. "I have spoken these things to you so that My joy would be in you and your joy would be made full. 12. This is My commandment, that you would love one another just as I have loved you. 13. No one has greater love than this, that someone would lay down his life on behalf of his friends. 14. You are My friends if you would do whatever I command you. 15. I no longer call you servants,[1] because a servant does not know what his master is doing: but I have called you friends, because everything which I heard from My Father I made known to you. 16. You did not choose Me, but I chose you and I placed you so that you would go and you would bear fruit[2] and your fruit would remain, so that whatever you would ask the Father in My Name He would do for you. 17. I command you these things, so that you *would* love one another."

The World's Hatred

15:18. "If the world hates you, you know that it hated Me before *it hated* you. 19. If you were of the world, the world would love its own: but because you are not of the world, but I chose you from the world, the world hates you because of this. 20. You must continually remember the message, which I spoke to you, 'A servant[3] is not greater than his master.' If they persecuted Me, then they will persecute you: (2Ti 3:12) if they kept My word, then they will keep yours. 21. But they will do all these things to you because of My name, because they have not known the One Who sent Me. 22. If I had not come and spoken to them, they would not have sinned: but now they do not have an excuse concerning their sin. 23. The one who hates Me also hates My Father. 24. If I did not do works among them which no one else had done, they would not have sinned: but now they also have seen and they have also hated both Me and My Father. 25. But so that the statement would be fulfilled which has been written in their Torah[4] that 'They hated Me without reason.' (Ps 35:19, 69:4)

15:26. "When the Comforter[5] would come Whom I will send to you from the Father, the Spirit of Truth, the One who goes out from the Father, that One will testify about Me: 27. and you also are witnessing because you have been with Me from the beginning.

16.1. "I have told you these things so that you would not be led into sin. 2. They will excommunicate you: and a time is coming that anyone who kills you would think he was offering service to God. 3. And they will do these things because they have known neither the Father nor Me. 4. But I have told you these things so that when their time would come you would remember these things that

---

1   (v.15) Or slaves, see Servant in Glossary.
2   (v.16) A person bears fruit by doing the things pleasing to God. See Mt 25:35-41. See Mitsvah in Glossary.
3   (v.20) Or slave
4   (v.25) Torah here refers to the entire Tanach (Hebrew Scriptures). See Torah in Glossary.
5   (v.26) See Jn 14:16, 23.

I told you."

The Work of the Spirit

"I did not say these things to you from the beginning, because I was with you. 5. But now I am going[1] to the One Who sent Me, and none of you can ask Me, 'Where are You going?' 6. But, because I have spoken these things to you, sorrow has filled your hearts. 7. But I am telling you the truth, it is profitable for you that I would leave. For if I would not leave, the Comforter will not come to you: but if I would go back, I will send Him to you. 8. And when that One comes He will expose the world concerning sin and concerning righteousness and concerning judgment: 9. indeed concerning sin, because they do not believe in Me: 10. but concerning righteousness, because I am going back to the Father and you will no longer see Me: 11. and concerning judgment, because the prince of this world has been convicted. (Re 20:1-3)

16:12. "I still have much to say to you, but you are not now able to bear *it*: 13. but when that One[2] would come, the Spirit of Truth, He will guide you in all truth: for He will not speak from Himself, but whatever He will hear He will speak and report the things that are coming to you. 14. That One will glorify Me, because He will take from Me and He will teach you. 15. Whatever things the Father has are Mine: because of this I said that He takes from Me and He will teach you."

Sorrow Will Turn into Joy

16:16. "A little while and you will no longer see Me, and again a little while and you will see Me." 17. Then they of His disciples said to one another, "What is this He is saying to us? 'A little while and you will not see Me, and again a little while and you will see Me?' and, 'Because I am going back to the Father?'" 18. Then they were saying, "What is this that He is saying, 'a little while'? We do not understand what He is saying." 19. Jesus knew that they wanted to ask Him, and He said to them, "Are you seeking with one another about this because I said, 'A little while and you will not see Me, and again a little while and you will see Me?' 20. Most assuredly I say to you that you will weep and you will mourn, but the world will rejoice: you will grieve, but your grief will turn into joy. 21. When a woman would give birth she has distress because her time has come: but when she would bear the child, she no longer remembers the distress because of the joy that a person has been born into the world. 22. And therefore you now indeed have sorrow: but I will see you again, and your heart will rejoice, and no one *will* take your joy from you. 23. And at that time you will not ask Me anything. Most assuredly I say to you, whatever you would ask the Father in My name He will give to you. 24. Until now you did not ask anything in My name: you must continually ask and you will take, so that your joy could

---

1   (v.5) The verb used here is hupago, meaning to go back where the speaker came from.
2   (v.13) The Holy Spirit

be made full."

I Have Overcome the World

16:25. "I have spoken these things to you in figures of speech: a time is coming when I will no longer speak to you in figures of speech, but I will report to you plainly about the Father. 26. In that day you will ask in My name, and I do not say to you that I will ask the Father on your behalf: 27. for the Father Himself loves you, because you have loved[1] Me and you have believed that I came from God. 28. I left from the Father and I have come into the world: I am leaving the world again and I am going back to the Father." 29. His disciples were saying, "See, now You are speaking openly and You are not saying any figures of speech. 30. Now we know that You have known all things and You do not need that someone would question You: by this we believe that You came from God." 31. Jesus answered them, "Do you believe now? 32. Behold, a time is coming and has come so that you would each be scattered *back home* for your own things so that you would leave Me alone: but I am not alone, because the Father is with Me. 33. I have told these things to you so that you would have peace because of Me: in the world you have distress: but be of good courage, I have overcome the world."

The Prayer of Jesus

17.1. Jesus said these things and when He lifted up His eyes to heaven He said, "Father, the time has come: You must now glorify Your Son, so Your Son could glorify You, 2. seeing that You gave Him authority over all flesh, so that He could give eternal life to everyone that You have given to Him. 3. And this is eternal life, that they would know You, the only true God, and Whom You sent, Jesus Messiah. 4. I glorified You on the Earth, when I completed the work which You gave Me to do: 5. and now You must glorify Me, Father, beside Yourself in the glory which I had beside You before the world was *created*.

17:6. "I revealed Your name to the people in the world whom You gave to Me. They were Yours and You gave them to Me and they have kept Your Word. 7. Now they have known that everything that You gave to Me is from You: 8. because I have given to them the words which You gave to Me, and they accepted and they truly knew that I came from beside You, and they believed that You sent Me. 9. I am asking about them, I do not ask for the world but for those You have given Me, because they are Yours, 10. and all My things are Yours and Your things *are* Mine, and I have been glorified in them. 11. And I am no longer in the world, but they are in the world, and I am coming to You. Holy Father, You must guard them[2] by Your name which You have given to Me, so that they would be one just as We *are One*. 12. When I was with them Myself I was guarding them by Your name, which You have given to Me, and I did guard, and not one of them

---

1   (v.27) The words translated 'love' and 'loved' are the Greek word phileo.
2   (v.11) Jesus is praying for the continued unity of believers, a unity lost early in Christianity and still not attained.

was lost, except the son of destruction,[1] so that the Scripture would be fulfilled. 13. And now I am coming to You but I am saying these things in the world so that within themselves they could have My joy that has been made complete. 14. I have given them Your message and the world hated them, because they are not from the world, just as I AM not from the world. 15. I do not ask that You would take them out of the world, but that You would protect them from the evil one. 16. They are not of this world just as I AM not of the world. 17. You must now make them holy by means of the truth: Your Word is truth. 18. Just as You sent Me into the world, I sent them into the world: 19. and I consecrate Myself *to You* on their behalf so that they would also have been consecrated by *the* truth.

17:20. "I do not ask concerning them only, but also concerning those who believe in Me because of the *disciples'* message, 21. so that all would be one, just as You, Father, *are* in Me and I in You, that they also would be in Us, so that the world would believe that You sent Me. 22. And I have given them the glory which You have given to Me, so that they would be one just as We *are* One: 23. I in them and You in Me, so that they would have been brought into unity, so that the world would know that You sent Me and You loved them just as You loved Me. 24. Father, the One Who gave to Me, I want that where I am those would be with Me, so that they would see My glory, which You have given to Me because You loved Me before the foundation of *the* world. 25. Righteous Father, even though the world did not know You, but I did know You, and these knew that You sent Me: 26. and I made Your name known to them and I will make known, so that the love *with* which You loved Me would be in them and I would be in them."

The Betrayal and Arrest of Jesus

(Mt 26:47-56, Mk 14:43-50, Lk 22:47-53)

18.1. After Jesus said these things He came out with His disciples on the other side of the ravine of Kidron where there was a garden, which He and His disciples entered. 2. And Judas, the one who gave Him over, had also known the place, because Jesus often gathered there with His disciples. 3. Then Judas, as he took the cohort[2] and the attendants from the high priests and from the Pharisees, came there with torches and oil lamps and weapons. 4. Then Jesus, since He knew all these things that were coming upon Him, went and said to them, "Whom are you seeking?" 5. They answered Him, "Jesus of Nazareth." He said to them, "I AM." And Judas, the one who was giving Him over, had also stood with them. 6. Then as He said to them, "I AM," they went into those behind and they, *the entire arresting party*, fell to *the* ground.[3] 7. Then again He asked them, "Whom do you seek?" And they said, "Jesus of Nazareth." 8. Jesus answered, "I told you that 'I AM.' Therefore if you are seeking Me, you must let

---

1   (v.12) The one who is destined for destruction.
2   (v.3) A Roman army cohort normally had 600 men.
3   (v.6) They were slain in the spirit by the anointing as the "I AM" spoke.

these go:" 9. so that the word would be fulfilled which said, "I did not lose one of those You have given to Me." 10. Then Simon Peter, since he had a small sword, drew it and struck the servant of the high priest and cut off his right ear: and *the* name of the servant was Malchus. 11. Then Jesus said to Peter, "You must put the sword in its sheath: the Father has given the cup to Me, would I **not** drink it?"

Jesus before the High Priest
(Mt 26:57,58, Mk 14:53,54, Lk 22:54)

18:12. Then the cohort[1] and the commander and the attendants of the Jewish *leaders* seized Jesus and they bound Him 13. and led *Him* to Annas first: for he was father-in-law of Caiaphas, who was High Priest that year. 14. And Caiaphas was the one who advised the Jewish *leaders* that it is profitable *for* one man to die on behalf of the people. (Jn 11:49-51)

Peter's Denial of Jesus
(Mt 26:69,70, Mk 14:66-68, Lk 22:55-57)

18:15. And Simon Peter and another disciple were following Jesus. And that disciple was known by the High Priest[2] and he entered together with Jesus into the courtyard of the High Priest, 16. but Peter had stood outside at the door. Then the other disciple, who was known by the High Priest, came out and spoke to the doorkeeper and she brought Peter in. 17. Then the door-keeping maid said to Peter, "Are you not *one* of the disciples of this man?" He said, "I am not." 18. And, because it was cold, the servants and the attendants, having made a charcoal fire, had been standing and they were warming themselves: and Peter was also standing with them, and warming himself.

The High Priest Questions Jesus
(Mt 26:59-66, Mk 14:55-64, Lk 22:66-71)

18:19. Then the High Priest asked Jesus about His disciples and about His teaching. 20. Jesus answered him, "I have spoken openly to the world, I always taught in a synagogue and in the temple, where all the Jewish people gather, and I spoke nothing whatever in secret. 21. Why are you asking Me? You must ask those who heard what I said to them: see, they know what I said." 22. Then after He said these things one of the attendants standing by hit Jesus saying, "Would you answer the High Priest this way?" 23. Jesus answered him, "If I spoke wrongly, you must testify concerning the evil: but if *I spoke* correctly, why do you beat Me?" 24. Then Annas sent Him bound to Caiaphas the High Priest.

---

1   (v.12) About 600 men
2   (v.15) The other disciple, since he had access to the High Priest's home, was probably someone who was in leadership, like Nicodemus or Joseph of Arimathea. High Priest is capitalized because Annas was the former High Priest.

Peter Denies Jesus Again

(Mt 26:71-75, Mk 14:69-72, Lk 22:58-62)

18:25. And Simon Peter was standing and being warmed. Then they said to him, "Are you not also *one* of His disciples?" He denied *it* and said, "I am not." 26. One of the servants of the High Priest, *who* was a relative of the one whose ear Peter cut off, said, "Did I not see you in the garden with Him?" 27. Then Peter again denied *it*, and immediately a cock crowed.

Jesus before Pilate

(Mt 27:1,2, 11-14, Mk 15:1-5, Lk 23:1-5)

18:28. Then they led Jesus from Caiaphas to the praetorium:[1] it was early: but they did not enter the praetorium, so that they would not be defiled,[2] but could eat the Seder.[3] 29. Then Pilate came outside to them and said, "What accusation do you bring against this man?" 30. And they answered and said to him, "Unless this One was doing evil, we would not have given Him over to you." 31. Then Pilate said to them, "Take Him yourselves and judge Him according to your Torah."[4] The Jewish people said to him, "It is not permitted for us to put anyone to death:" 32. so that the word of Jesus would be fulfilled, which He said indicating by what kind of death He was going to die.[5] 33. Then Pilate entered the praetorium again and called Jesus and said to Him, "Are You the King of the Jewish Nation?" 34. Jesus answered, "Do you say this from yourself or have others told you about Me?" 35. Pilate answered, "Am I Jewish? Your people and the high priests gave You over to me: what did You do?" 36. Jesus answered, "My dominion is not of this world: if My dominion were of this world, My attendants would have been fighting whomever so that I would not be given over to the Jewish *leaders*: but now My kingdom is not from here." 37. Then Pilate said to Him, "Therefore are You a king?" Jesus answered, "You say that I am a king. I have been born for this and have come into the world for this, so that I could bear witness to the truth: everyone who is from the truth hears My voice." 38. Pilate said to Him, "What is truth?"

Jesus Sentenced to Die

(Mt 27:15-31, Mk 15:6-20, Lk 23:13-25)

And having said this he again went to the Jewish *leaders*[6] and said to them, "I find not one reason *to accuse* Him. 39. But it is a custom with you that

---

1   (v.28) Governor's Headquarters

2   (v.28) This does not make sense because if the Seder were a Sabbath they would not have immersed until late in day. See Preparation Day in Glossary.

3   (v.28) The Seder is the Passover meal. See Seder in Glossary.

4   (v.31) Torah means teaching or instruction and generally refers to the first five books of the Bible. See Torah in Glossary.

5   (v.32) He indicated this in Mt 20:19, saying He would be raised.

6   (v.38) The leaders were Hellenists. See Hellenists in Glossary.

I would release one *prisoner* to you in the Passover: therefore do you want that I would release to you the King of the Jewish Nation?" 40. Then they cried again saying, "Not this One, but Barabbas." And Barabbas was a bandit.[1]

19.1. So then Pilate took Jesus and scourged *Him*.[2] 2. And the soldiers, having woven a crown from thorns, placed *it* on His head and they put a purple cloak on Him 3. and they were coming to Him and saying, "Hail, King of the Jewish People:" and they hit Him. 4. And Pilate again came outside and said to them, "See, I am leading Him outside to you, so that you must know that I find in Him no reason *to condemn Him*." 5. Then Jesus came outside, wearing the thorny crown and the purple cloak. And he said to them, "Behold the man." 6. Then when they saw Him the high priests and the attendants cried out saying, "Crucify! Crucify!" Pilate said to them, "Take Him yourselves and you crucify *Him*: for I do not find a crime in Him." 7. The Jewish people answered him, "We have a Torah and according to the Torah He ought to die, because He made Himself Son of God."[3]

19:8. Therefore when Pilate heard this statement, he was more afraid, 9. and came into the praetorium again and said to Jesus, "Where are You from?" But Jesus did not give him an answer. 10. Then Pilate said to Him, "Do You not speak to me? Do You not know that I have authority to release You and I have authority to crucify You?" 11. Jesus answered him, "You would not have any authority over Me unless it was given to you from above: because of this the one who gave Me over to you has greater sin." 12. From this *time* Pilate was seeking to release Him: but the Jewish people cried out saying, "If you would release this One, you are not Caesar's friend: everyone who makes himself king speaks against Caesar."[4]

19:13. Therefore after Pilate heard these remarks he led Jesus outside and sat upon a judicial bench in a place called Lithostrato, and in Hebrew Gab'ta. 14. And it was preparation[5] *day* for Passover; it was about the sixth hour.[6] And he said to the Jewish people, "Behold your king." 15. Then they cried out, "You must take *Him* away! You must take *Him* away! You must now crucify Him." Pilate said to them, "Shall I crucify your king?" The high priests answered, "We have no king except Caesar."[7] 16. Then at that time he gave Him over to them

---

1   (v.40) Some say this means revolutionary or insurrectionist.
2   (v.1) This was a Roman scourging of many strokes, not limited by the Jewish restriction to 39 strokes.
3   (v.7) The Torah, Lv 24:16, says that the person who blasphemes the name of the Lord is to be put to death.
4   (v.12) The office of High Priest was at this time appointed by the Roman government, in this case by Pontius Pilate. The appointment involved paying bribes to the Roman official, Pilate, by Caiaphas. Caiaphas was a politician whose career would have been over with the coming of the reigning Messiah. See Hellenists in Glossary.
5   (v.14) Preparation calls for the men to immerse before the start of Sabbath. See Lk 23:54. See Preparation Day in Glossary.
6   (v.14) Noon
7   (v.15) The high priests during the Roman occupation were Hellenists. See Hellenists in

so that He could be crucified.

The Crucifixion of Jesus

(Mt 27:32-44, Mk 15:21-32, Lk 23:26-43)

Then they took Jesus, 17. and bearing the cross for Himself He went out into the *place* called Place of *the* Skull, the one called in Hebrew Gulgolet, 18. where they crucified Him, and two others with Him, *one* on each side and Jesus in *the* middle. 19. And Pilate also wrote an inscription and placed *it* on the cross: and it was written, "Jesus of Nazareth, the King of the Jewish People." 20. Therefore many of the Jewish people read this inscription, because the place where Jesus was crucified was near the city: and it was written in Hebrew, Roman,[1] and Greek. 21. Then the high priests of the Jewish people were saying to Pilate, "You must not write, 'The King of the Jewish People,' but that 'That One said, "I am King of the Jewish People."'" 22. Pilate answered, "What I have written, I have written."

19:23. Then the soldiers, when they crucified Jesus, took His garments and made four parts, a part to each soldier, and the tunic. But the tunic was seamless,[2] woven from the top throughout. 24. Therefore they said to one another, "We should not divide it, but we should cast lots concerning whose it is *to be*:" so that the Scripture would be fulfilled, the one saying,

"They divided My garments among themselves,

and they cast lots for My clothing." (Ps 22:18)

So then the soldiers did these things. 25. And His mother, and the sister of His mother, Mary *the mother* of Clopas,[3] and Mary Magdalene stood beside Jesus' cross. 26. Then when Jesus saw His mother and the disciple whom He loved standing near, He said to His mother, "Ma'am, see your son." 27. Then He said to the disciple, "Here is your mother." And from that moment the disciple took *His mother* as his own.

The Death of Jesus

(Mt 27:45-56, Mk 15:33-41, Lk 23:44-49)

19:28. After this, Jesus, since He knew that at last everything had been finished, so that the Scripture could be fulfilled, He said, "I thirst." 29. A vessel full of sour wine was lying *near*: then after they placed a sponge full of the sour wine around hyssop they held *it* up to His mouth. 30. Then when He took the

---

Glossary.

1   (v.20) This language later became known as Latin
2   (v.23) The cloak was His prayer shawl, which in those days was a large, poncho-like garment with a hole for the head and fringes on the corners. See Prayer Shawl in Glossary.
3   (v.25) The Greek spelling of Clopas is Klopa, while the spelling of Cleopas, Lk 24:18, is Kleopas. The "O" in Klopa is an Omega, while the "O" in Kleopas is an Omicron. Both words are in the genitive case, with Klopa masculine, Kleopas feminine.

sour wine Jesus said, "It has been completed," and having bowed His head He gave up His spirit.

The Piercing of Jesus' Side

19:31. Then the Jewish people, since it was preparation *day*,[1] so that the bodies would not remain on the cross on the Sabbath, for it was *to be* a great day of that Sabbath,[2] they were asking Pilate that *the soldiers* would break their legs so they could remove *the bodies*. 32. Then the soldiers came and broke the legs of the first and of the other one who was crucified with Him: 33. and when they came to Jesus, as they saw that He was already dead, they did not break His legs, 34. but one of the soldiers pierced *His* side with his spear and immediately blood and water[3] came out. 35. And one who saw has testified, and his testimony is genuine and that one knows that he tells *the* truth, so that you would also believe. 36. And these things happened in order that the Scripture would be fulfilled, "His bones will not be broken." (Ps 34:20) 37. And again another Scripture says, "They will look on Whom they pierced." (Zch 12:10)

The Burial of Jesus

(Mt 27:57-61, Mk 15:42-47, Lk 23:50-56)

19:38. And after these things Joseph, the one from Arimathea, although, because of fear of the Jewish *leaders*, he was a concealed disciple of Jesus, asked Pilate if he could take the body of Jesus: and Pilate did permit *him*. Therefore he came and took His body. 39. And Nicodemus, the one who came to Him on the earlier night, came too, bringing a mixture of myrrh and aloe, about a hundred *Roman* pounds.[4] 40. Then they took the body of Jesus and they bound it in linen cloth with the spices, as is a custom of the Jewish people to prepare for burial. 41. And there was a garden in the place where He was crucified, and a new tomb in the garden, a tomb in which no one had yet been placed.[5] 42. Then, because *it was* the preparation *day*[6] of the Jewish people, since the tomb was near, they placed Jesus there.

---

1   (v.31) The day before a Sabbath, when the men were to immerse for purification.

2   (v.31) This is difficult to understand, because there is a Great Sabbath, Shabbat HaG-adol, which is the Sabbath immediately preceding Pesach. To say "a great day of that Sabbath" is an awkward way to put it, when John could have said "great Sabbath." Could John have meant the Great Sabbath?

3   (v.34) Blood represents life (Lv 17:11, Jn 6:54) while water represents Torah, the Word of God (Ex 14:22, Is 55:1).

4   (v.39) This is equivalent to about seventy-five English pounds, a great quantity used only for royalty. His body had to be prepared by men. A woman could not prepare a man's body nor a man prepare a woman's. Mk 16:1, saying three women brought spices is probably a later addition to the text by someone who did not know Jewish practice.

5   (v.41) Bodies were buried in family tombs, and then after the body had decayed, the bones were placed in a stone box called an ossuary, for permanent storage in that tomb. That way it would make room for another corpse, and a fairly small tomb cut in the rock could easily contain several generations.

6   (v.42) See Preparation Day in Glossary.

The Resurrection[1] of Jesus

(Mt 28:1-10, Lk 24:1-12)

20.1. And on the First Day of the Week[2] Mary Magdalene came to the tomb early, while it was still dark, and saw *that* the stone had been rolled away from the tomb. 2. Then she ran and came to Simon Peter and to the other disciple whom Jesus loved and she said to them, "They took our Lord from the tomb and we do not know where they put Him." 3. Then Peter and the other disciple left and they were coming to the tomb. 4. And the two were running together: and the other disciple quickly ran ahead of Peter and he came to the tomb first, 5. and when he stooped sideways he saw the linen cloths lying, nevertheless he did not enter. 6. Then Simon Peter also came, following him, and he entered the tomb, and saw the cloths lying, 7. and the face cloth, which had been on His head, not lying with the cloths but being folded up separately in one place. 8. Then when he and the other disciple, the one who came to the tomb first, entered, he saw and he believed: 9. for they had not yet understood the Scripture that it was necessary for Him to be raised from *the* dead. (Ps 16:9) 10. Then the disciples went again to those *at their house*.

The Appearance of Jesus to Mary Magdalene

20:11. And Mary stood outside at the tomb weeping. Then as she was weeping, she bent over into the tomb 12. and saw two angels in white, sitting, one at the head and one at the feet, where the body of Jesus had been lying. 13. And those *angels* said to her, "Ma'am, why are you weeping?" She said to them that "They took my Lord, and I do not know where they put Him." 14. After she said these things she turned to those behind and saw Jesus standing but had not recognized that it was Jesus.[3] 15. Jesus said to her, "Ma'am, why are you crying? Whom are you seeking?" Because she thought that He was the gardener she said to Him, "Sir, if you removed Him, you must tell me where you carried Him and I will take Him." 16. Jesus said to her, "Mary." After she turned to that One she said to Him in Hebrew, "Rabbi," which means Teacher. 17. Jesus said to her "Stop touching Me, for I have not yet ascended to the Father: you must go to My brothers and you must say to them, 'I am ascending to My Father and your Father and My God and your God.'" 18. Mary Magdalene came and then announced to the disciples that "I have seen the Lord," and *that* He said these things to her.

The Appearance of Jesus to the Disciples

(Mt 28:16-20, Lk 24:36-49)

20:19. Then when it was late, *from 3:00 to 6:00 PM*, on that day, on the

---

1   (Caption) See Resurrection in Glossary.
2   (v.1) First Day of the Week is the Hebrew name for Sunday, beginning at sundown Saturday to sundown Sunday.
3   (v.14) See Resurrected Body in Glossary.

First Day of the Week,[1] and after the doors were shut where the disciples[2] were because of fear of the Jewish *leaders*, Jesus came and stood in their midst and said to them, "Peace *be* with you." 20. And after He said this He showed them His hands and His side. Then the disciples rejoiced, because they had seen the Lord. 21. Then Jesus said to them again "Peace *be* with you: just as the Father sent Me, so I am sending you." 22. And after He said this He breathed upon *them* and said to them, "You must immediately take *the* Holy Spirit:[3] 23. whomever you would forgive,[4] their sins have been forgiven for them, whomever you would retain *their sins* have been retained."

Jesus and Thomas

20:24. And Thomas, one of the twelve, called Twin, was not with them when Jesus came. 25. Therefore the other disciples were telling him, "We have seen the Lord." But he said to them, "Unless I could see the mark of the nails in His hands and I could put my finger into the mark of the nails and I could put my hand into His side, I will **not** believe." 26. And after eight days[5] His disciples were again inside and Thomas *was* with them. After the doors were closed, Jesus came and He was in the middle *of the room* and said, "Peace to you." 27. Then He said to Thomas, "Put your finger here and see My hands and you must reach out your hand and you must put *it* into My side,[6] and stop being faithless but *have* faith." 28. Thomas answered and said to Him, "My Lord and my God." 29. Jesus said to him, "Because you have seen Me have you believed? Blessed *are* those who have not seen and yet have believed."

The Purpose of the Book

20:30. To be sure Jesus did many other signs in the presence of His disciples, which are not written in this scroll:[7] 31. but these things have been written so that you would believe that Jesus is the Messiah, the Son of God, and so that when you believe you would have *eternal* life in His name.

The Appearance of Jesus to the Seven Disciples

21.1. After these things Jesus revealed Himself again to the disciples at the lake of Tiberias: and He revealed *Himself* like this. 2. Simon Peter and Thomas, the one called Twin, and Nathaniel, the one from Cana of Galilee, and

1   (v.19) The First Day of the Week is the Hebrew expression for Sunday.
2   (v.19) The disciples would have included the eleven apostles, but could also have included others.
3   (v.22) We have to truly seek the baptism of the Holy Spirit. See Take/Receive in Glossary.
4   (v.23) This is not a question of a modern disciple saying "I forgive you." When a disciple discerns that someone has truly repented, the disciple can say as Jesus did, "Your sins are forgiven."
5   (v.26) It is easy to think that after His resurrection Jesus was with the disciples continuously, but He was not. Eight days would have been a long time for them to go without seeing Him.
6   (v.27) See Resurrected Body in Glossary.
7   (v.30) John wrote on a papyrus scroll.

the *sons* of Zebedee and two others of His disciples were together. 3. Simon Peter said to them, "I am going[1] to fish *from now on*."[2] They said to him, "We are coming and we *are* with you."[3] They left and they embarked in the boat, and during that night they caught nothing. 4. And after dawn came Jesus already stood on the shore, though the disciples did not yet know that it was Jesus. 5. Then Jesus said to them, "Children, do you have any fish?"[4] They answered Him, "No." 6. And He said to them, "You must cast the net to the right side of the boat, and you will find *fish*." Then they cast, and they no longer *had the* ability to haul *it* on account of the great number of the fish. 7. Then that disciple whom Jesus loved said to Peter, "It is the Lord." [5] Then after Simon Peter heard that it was the Lord he gird around his outer garment, for he was without his outer garment, and he threw himself into the lake, 8. but the other disciples came in the little boat, for they were not far off from the shore, only about two hundred cubits,[6] dragging the net of fish. 9. Then as they got off on the shore they saw coals lying *there* with fish and bread being laid on *them*. 10. Jesus said to them, "You must now bring *some* of the fish which you just caught." 11. Then Simon Peter went up and hauled the net to the shore, full of a hundred fifty-three big fish: even when there were so many the net was not torn. 12. Jesus said to them, "Come, you must eat breakfast." And not one of *the* disciples was bold enough to ask Him, "Who are You?" since they knew that it was the Lord. 13. Jesus came and took the bread and gave *it* to them, and likewise the roasted fish. 14. This *was* now *the* third time Jesus was revealed to the disciples after He rose from *the* dead.[7]

Jesus and Peter

21:15. Then while they ate breakfast Jesus said to Simon Peter, "Simon *son of* John, do you love Me more than these?" He said to Him, "Indeed Lord, You know that I love You." He said to him, "You must continually feed My lambs." 16. Again He said to him a second time, "Simon, *son of* John, do you love Me?" He said to Him, "Indeed Lord, You have known that I love You." He said to him, "You must continually tend[8] My sheep." 17. He said to him the third time, "Simon *son of* John, do you love Me?" Peter became distressed because He said to him the third time, "Do you love Me?" and he said to Him, "Lord, You know all things, You know that I love You." Jesus said to him, "You

---

1   (v.3) The Greek word here is hupago, meaning to go back were you came from.
2   (v.3) This continuing action is a characteristic of the Greek present tense.
3   (v.3) This meant that they were going back to secular jobs, even while the resurrected Jesus was on the Earth.
4   (v.5) The construction here indicates He anticipates a negative answer to His question.
5   (v.7) It had been some time since His last appearance and the disciples did not know His plan.
6   (v.8) About one hundred yards
7   (v.14) Paul lists three times He was seen by at least all the apostles in 1Cor 15:5-7.
8   (v.16) Tend refers to the ministry of the Good Shepherd. See Son of David/Son of Joseph in Glossary.

must continually feed My sheep. 18. I most certainly say to you, when you were younger, you were girding yourself and you were walking where you wanted: but when you grow old, you will stretch your hands and another will clothe you and will carry *you* where you do not want *to go.*" 19. And He said this indicating by what kind *of* death he will glorify God. And after He said this He said "You must continually follow Me."

Jesus and the Beloved Disciple

21:20. Then Peter turned, *and* saw the disciple following *him*, whom Jesus loved, who also reclined next to Him[1] at the supper and said, "Lord, who is the one who is giving You over?" 21. Therefore when Peter saw him he said to Jesus, "Lord, what *about* him?" 22. Jesus said to him, "If I want him to remain until I come, what *is it* to you? You must steadfastly follow Me." 23. Then this word came out among the brothers that that disciple would not die: but Jesus did not say to him that he would not die but, "If I want him to remain until I come, what *is it* to you?"

21:24. This is the disciple who is testifying concerning these things, and the one who wrote these things, and we know that his testimony is true.

21:25. And there are also many other things which Jesus did, which if everything were written down in one *document*, I do not suppose the world could make room for the books that would be written.

---

1   (v.20) This is literally "upon His chest" which means he reclined next to Him. See Reclining in Glossary.

~ ACTS BY THE APOSTLES[1] ~

The Promise of the Holy Spirit

1.1. Indeed the first narrative I made concerning everything, O Theopholis,[2] which Jesus began to do and also to teach, 2. until that day He was taken up, after He gave orders to the apostles whom He had chosen by the Holy Spirit: 3. to whom He also presented Himself alive, by many convincing proofs, after He suffered, while He appeared to them for forty days and was saying these things about the kingdom of God: 4. and while He was staying with *them*, He ordered them "Do not go away from Jerusalem but wait for the promise of the Father which you heard from Me, 5. for John on the one hand baptized[3] in water, but you on the other hand will be baptized in the Holy Spirit after these not many days."[4]

The Ascension of Jesus

1:6. Therefore indeed those who came asked Him saying, "Lord, are You restoring the kingdom in Israel at this time?"[5] 7. But He said to them, "It is not for you to know *the* times or seasons which the Father set by His own authority, 8. but you will take power when the Holy Spirit comes upon you and you will be My witnesses in Jerusalem and in all Judea and Samaria and to *the* outermost *part* of the earth." 9. And after He said these things, as they were watching, He was lifted up and a cloud bore Him up and away from their eyes. 10. And as they were looking intently into the sky at His going, then there were two men in white clothing[6] *who* stood by them, 11. and they said, "Men of Galilee, why have you stood looking into the sky? This Jesus, Who, as He has been taken up from you into the sky, will come *back* in the same way as you saw Him going into the

---

1   (Title) Written about 63-70 AD.
2   (v.1) Theopholis means 'loves God' in Greek. Whether this letter is to a person named Theopholis or to believers is not clear, but the prevailing view is that it is to a person.
3   (v.5) The word baptize is from the Greek word baptidzo, which means to immerse. See Baptize in Glossary.
4   (v.5) The emphasis is that it will be very soon. It happened ten days after this, His ascension.
5   (v.6) The Apostles expected the start of His reign right then!
6   (v.10) White garments represent being in a state of spiritual preparedness, from Ecc 9:8, "Let your garments be always white; and let your head lack no ointment."

sky."[1]

The Choice of Judas' Successor

1:12. Then they returned to Jerusalem from *the* mountain, called "Olive Grove," which is near Jerusalem, a Sabbath journey away. 13. And when they entered, they went up to the upper room in which they were staying, Peter and John and Jacob[2] and Andrew, Philip and Thomas, Bartholomew and Matthew, Jacob *son of* Alpheus, Simon the Zealot and Judas *son* of Jacob.[3] 14. These were all waiting with one purpose in prayer with *the* women, and Mary the mother of Jesus, and His brothers.

1:15. And in those days,[4] Peter got up in the middle among the believers. It was a crowd of about one hundred twenty people:[5] he said 16. "Men, brothers, the Scripture had to be fulfilled which the Holy Spirit told beforehand by the mouth of David concerning Judas, who became a guide to those arresting Jesus, 17. because he was being numbered among us and received *his* portion of this service[6] by divine allotment. 18. Indeed then he obtained a piece of land[7] by means of *the* wages of his unrighteousness and after he fell headlong *his* middle burst apart[8] and all his inner parts were poured out: 19. and it became known to all those who were living in Jerusalem. Therefore that field was to be called[9] Akeldama, which is Field of Blood. 20. 'For it has been written in the book of Psalms,

'Let his cottage become empty
  and let him not be the one who lives in it,' (Ps 69:25)
and, 'Let another take his *place* as overseer.' (Ps 109:8)

21. Therefore it is necessary for *one of* those men who have come together with us during the whole time in which the Lord Jesus came in and went out from among us,[10] 22. beginning from the baptism[11] of John until the day on which He was taken

---

1   (v.11) When He comes again, "And His feet shall stand on that day upon the Mount of Olives, which is before Jerusalem on the east, and the Mount of Olives shall be split in its midst toward the east and toward the west, and there shall be a very great valley; and half of the mountain shall be moved toward the north, and half of it toward the south." (Zch 14:4)

2   (v.13) The Greek text has Iakob, which is Jacob in English.

3   (v.13) Apparently these eleven stayed in this room.

4   (v.15) This indicates a different time from the previous verses.

5   (v.15) This is not in the upper room, which would not have held 120, but in some public place.

6   (v.17) Or ministry, see Servant in Glossary.

7   (v.18) The middle voice of this verb indicates he obtained the land for himself. How he did this and also threw money into the treasury is a mystery. See Mt 27:3, 7.

8   (v.18) An article in Biblical Archeological Review held that this land was steep and when he hanged himself the rope broke and he fell some distance to the ground, breaking open.

9   (v.19) The Greek text inserts the phrase, "in their own language," which is a later addition.

10   (v.21) See Disciple in Glossary.

11   (v.22) The word baptism is from the Greek word baptisma, which means immersion. Immersion had been a Jewish custom for over 1,000 years by the time of Jesus and was necessary for purification. See Baptize in Glossary.

up from us, a witness of His resurrection,[1] to become one of these *apostles* with us." 23. And they placed two *for selection*, Joseph the one called Barsabbas who was surnamed Justos, and Matthias. 24. And when they prayed they said, "You Lord, because You know *the* hearts of all, show clearly whom You chose, one from these two 25. to take the place of this service and an apostleship from which Judas did turn aside to go into his own place *where he belonged*." 26. And they gave out lots to them and the lot fell on Matthias and he was chosen to be added to the eleven apostles.

The Coming of the Holy Spirit

2.1. And when the day of Shavuot[2] had come they were all in one place together. 2. And a sound came suddenly out of heaven as bringing a violent wind and it filled the whole house[3] where they were sitting 3. and dividing tongues like fire were seen by them and the *flames* sat upon each one of them, 4. and all were filled by the Holy Spirit and began to speak in other languages just as the Spirit was giving them to speak out boldly.

2:5. And there were Jewish people staying in Jerusalem, devout people from all the nations under heaven. 6. And when this sound was made a multitude gathered and was amazed, because while they were speaking, they all were hearing in their own languages. 7. And they were astounded and amazed saying, "Look, are not all those who are speaking from Galilee? 8. Then how do we each hear in our own language with which we were born? 9. Parthians and Medes and Elamites and those who dwell in Mesopotamia, Judea, and even Cappadocia,[4] Pontus, and Asia, 10. Phrygia, and also Pamphylia, Egypt and the parts of Libya around Cyrene, and the visiting Romans, 11. Cretes and Arabs, both Jewish people and proselytes. We hear them speaking the greatness of God in our languages." 12. And all were amazed and perplexed, saying to one another, "What does this mean?" 13. But others, mocking, were saying, "They are drunk because they have been filled with sweet new wine."

Peter's Speech at Shavuot[5]

2:14. But Peter, as he stood up with the eleven, raised his voice and spoke out to them, "Men, Jewish people, and all those who are visiting Jerusalem, let this be known to you and pay attention to my words. 15. For these are not drunk

---

1   (v.22) See Resurrection in Glossary.
2   (v.1) This is the Feast of Weeks, called Pentecost in Greek. See Shavuot in Glossary.
3   (v.2) This is the temple. "The house" is frequently used in Hebrew when speaking of the temple and here the steps of the temple were one of the few places in Jerusalem where thousands could gather, on the steps of Solomon's Porch. The streets were too narrow and the houses too small for such a large crowd. Few houses would have had a room that could hold over one hundred people. Luke also refers to the sanctuary as "the house" in Lk 11:51.
4   (v.9) Cappadocia, an inland region of Asia Minor, is referred to as Gammadim in Eze 27:11.
5   (Caption) Feast of Weeks, called Pentecost in Greek.

as you assume, for it is *the* third hour of the day,[1] 16. but this is that which was spoken through the prophet Joel,

17.   'And it shall be in the last days,' says God,
        'I will pour out My Spirit upon all flesh,
            and your sons and your daughters will prophesy
      and your youths will see visions
            and your elders will dream dreams:
18.   and indeed upon My male servants and upon My female
            servants/ministers[2]
        in those days I will pour out from My Spirit,
            and they will prophesy.
19.   And I shall give wonders in heaven above
        and signs upon the earth below,
            and blood and fire and vapor of smoke.
20.   The sun will be changed into darkness
        and the moon into blood,
            before the great and glorious Day of the Lord is
        manifest.
21.   And it will be that everyone who would call upon the name of *the* Lord
        will be saved.' (Jl 2:28-32)

2:22. "Men of Israel, listen to these words! Jesus *of* Nazareth, a man Who was proven among you by God, in miracles and wonders and signs which God did through Him in your midst, just as you yourselves know, 23. you killed this One, *Who was* given up by the before determined purpose and foreknowledge of God, when you nailed *Him* by lawless hands, 24. Whom God raised up, after He loosed the cords of death, (Ps 18:4, 116:3) because *cords* were not able to hold Him fast under *death*. 25. For David said in respect to this,

    'I foresaw the presence of the Lord before me through everything,
        because He is on my right hand so that I would not be moved.
26.   Because of this My heart rejoiced and My tongue was glad,
        but yet also My flesh will dwell in hope,
27.   because You will not abandon My life to Hades
        and You will not give Your Holy One to see corruption.
28.   You made known to Me *the* ways of life,
        You will fill Me with joy in Your presence.' (Ps 16:8-11)

2:29. "Men, brothers, allow me to say to you with confidence concerning the Patriarch David, that he died and was buried, and his tomb is among us until this day. 30. Therefore since he was a prophet, and knew that God swore to him with an oath "He will cause *One* to sit on His throne from *the* fruit of *David's* loins," (Ps 132:11, 2Sm 7:12,13) 31. since he saw beforehand, he spoke

---

1   (v.15) 9:00 AM, the hour of morning prayer
2   (v.18) These are the sold out to God, fully committed slaves, priests of the Lord.

concerning the resurrection[1] of the Messiah that

> 'neither would He be forsaken in Hades
>> nor' His flesh 'see corruption.' (Ps 16:10)

32. God resurrected this Jesus, of which we all are witnesses: 33. therefore since He has been raised to the right hand of God, and has taken the promise of the Holy Spirit from the Father, He poured this out which also you are seeing and hearing. 34. For David was not raised into the heavens, but he says,

> 'The Lord said to My Lord,
> You must sit at My right hand,[2]

35. until I would have put Your enemies under Your feet.'[3] (Ps 110:1)

36. Therefore assuredly all *the* house of Israel must continually know that God also made Him Lord and Messiah, this Jesus Whom you crucified."

2:37. And when they heard *this* they were pierced *in* their hearts. They said to Peter and the rest of *the* apostles, "What could we do, men, brothers?" 38. And Peter said to them, "You must immediately repent, and each of you must immediately be baptized[4] in the name of Jesus Messiah, for forgiveness of your sins and you will take the gift of the Holy Spirit. 39. For the promise is for you and for your children and for all those in far away *places*, whomever *the* Lord our God will call to Himself." 40. And he charged *them* in many other words and was urging them saying, "You must right now be rescued from this[5] crooked generation." 41. Then indeed, those who accepted his message were baptized[6] and there were added on that day about three thousand lives. 42. And they were continuing steadfastly in the teaching by the apostles and in fellowship, in the breaking of bread and in prayers.

Life among the Believers

2:43. And reverential fear came to everyone, and many wonders and signs were done through the apostles. 44. And all those who believed were together and *shared* all things in common 45. and they sold their possessions and properties and they were dividing *the proceeds* to all to whatever degree anyone had a need: 46. and day-by-day *they were* holding forth of one mind in the temple, and breaking bread from house to house. They were sharing nourishment in joy and simplicity of heart 47. praising God and having favor with all the people. And every day the Lord was adding to those who had been saved.

---

1   (v.31) See Resurrection in Glossary.
2   (v.34) "At the right hand" is a Hebrew idiom that speaks of power and strength. See Right Hand in Glossary.
3   (v.35) This means to eliminate your enemies. See Footstool in Glossary.
4   (v.38) This immersion had been practiced by the Jewish people for over 1,000 years. See Baptize in Glossary.
5   (v.40) This generation refers to every generation, including our own.
6   (v.41) There were so many pools for immersion at the temple that for all these to immerse would have taken about twenty minutes.

The Lame Man Healed at the Gate of the Temple

3.1. And Peter and John were going up to the temple at the ninth hour[1] for prayer. 2. And a certain man, *who* was lame from his mother's womb, was carried, whom they placed every day[2] beside the door of the temple called Beautiful Gate to ask for alms from those going into the temple: 3. who, when he saw Peter and John about to enter the temple, was asking to take money. 4. And Peter with John, when he looked intently at him, said, "Look upon us." 5. And he fixed his attention on them, expecting to take something from them. 6. And Peter said, "I do not have silver and gold for myself, but what I do have, this I give to you: in the name of Jesus Messiah of Nazareth you must rise and you must continually walk." 7. And as he took hold of him by the right hand, he was raising him: and immediately his feet and ankles were strengthened, 8. and leaping up he stood and was walking and entered the temple with them, walking and leaping and praising God: 9. so all the people saw him walking and praising God: 10. and they recognized him because he was the one who was sitting for alms at the Beautiful Gate of the temple and they were filled with astonishment and amazement after that happened to him.

Peter's Speech in Solomon's Portico

3:11. And, when he took hold of Peter and John, all the people, greatly amazed, ran toward them on the portico called Solomon's. 12. And when Peter saw *them* he responded to the people, "People of Israel, why are you amazed over this or why do you look upon this as if we had made him walk by our own power, or godliness? 13. 'The God of Abraham and the God of Isaac and the God of Jacob, the God of our fathers,' (Exodus 3:6,15) honored His child Jesus whom you surely gave over and denied in the presence of Pilate, after he decided to release that One: 14. but you denied the holy and righteous One and asked for a man, a murderer, to be given to you, 15. and you put to death the Author of Life, Whom God raised from *the* dead, of which we are witness. 16. And because of faith in His name, this one whom you see and you know, His name did strengthen, and the faith which *God* gave through Him to *the lame man*, gave this perfect *physical* wholeness in front of all of you. 17. And now, brothers, I know that you acted through ignorance just as also your leaders: 18. and thus God fulfilled what He announced beforehand through *the* mouths of all the prophets that His Messiah *was* to suffer.[3] 19. Therefore you must immediately repent and you must return *to God* at once for your sins to be wiped out,[4] 20. thus times of rest[5] would

---

1 (v.1) 3:00 PM, the time of afternoon prayer

2 (v.2) Having been placed by the gate every day for years means that Jesus walked past him numerous times. Acts 4:22 says the man was over forty years old.

3 (v.18) In Is 53 and others. See Son of David/Son of Joseph in Glossary.

4 (v.19) This Greek word means obliterated, removed, wiped out: the word was also used for the process that dissolved the ink on a parchment so the parchment could be used again. Your sins cannot be found after true repentance. See Sins, Forgiveness of in Glossary.

5 (v.20) This word for rest means to lean on, trust in, speaking of the Messianic reign when people will have the Incarnate God to lean on.

come from the presence of the Lord and He would send to you the One Who was appointed Messiah, Jesus, 21. Whom it was necessary for heaven indeed to take until times of restoration of everything which God spoke through *the* mouths of His holy prophets from eternity. 22. Indeed Moses said that 'The Lord your God will raise for you a prophet like myself from your brothers: you will listen to Him for everything, whatever He would tell' you. (Dt 18:18) 23. 'And it will be every person that would not listen to that prophet will be utterly destroyed from among the people.' (Dt 18:19, Lv 23:29) 24. And in fact all the prophets from Samuel and his successors onward, as many as spoke, also proclaimed these days. 25. You are the sons of the prophets and of the covenant, which God made with your fathers when He said to Abraham, 'And in your seed all the peoples of the earth will be blessed.' (Gn 22:18, 26:4) 26. Then God raised His child for you first. He sent Him, blessing you by turning each *of you* from your depravities."

Peter and John before the Council

4.1. And while they were speaking to the people, the priests and the commander of the temple guard and the Sadducees stood by them. 2. They were greatly disturbed because they taught the people and proclaimed the resurrection[1] from *the* dead in Jesus, 3. so they arrested them and put *them* in prison for the next day in the morning: for it was already evening. 4. And, when many of those *people* heard the Word, they believed and the number of the men[2] was about five thousand.

4:5. And it happened on the next day, their leaders and elders and scribes gathered in Jerusalem, 6. and Annas the High Priest and Caiaphas and John and Alexander and as many as were of the High Priest's family, 7. and having placed them in the middle they asked, "By what power or in what name did you do this?" 8. Then Peter, because he was filled with the Holy Spirit, said to them, "Leaders of the people and elders, 9. if we are judged this day because of a good deed *for* an infirm man by means of which *good deed* this one has been delivered, 10. it must be known to you all and to all the people in Israel that in the name of Jesus Messiah of Nazareth Whom you crucified, Whom God raised from *the* dead, by means of Him, this one stands before you whole. 11. This is

'The stone, the one who has been rejected by' you 'the builders,
the one who became the cornerstone.'(Ps 118:22)

12. And deliverance is **not** in any other, for there is no other name under heaven which was given to mankind by which it is necessary for us to be saved." 13. And when they saw the boldness of Peter and John and understood that they were unlearned[3] and unskilled men, they were astonished and recognized them, because they had been with Jesus, 14. and when they saw the man who was standing with

---

1   (v.2) See Resurrection in Glossary.
2   (v.4) See Census in Glossary.
3   (v.13) Unlearned meant that they had not studied at a rabbinic school. They all had memorized Scripture, which was just part of growing up Jewish.

them, the one who had been healed, there was no way to contradict, *deny the miracle*. 15. And after they commanded them to go outside the Sanhedrin they were conferring with one another 16. saying, "What shall we do with these men? Because indeed a very notable sign has come through them, known, visible to all those who live in Jerusalem and we are not able to deny *it*: 17. but in order that it would not be spread further among the people we should warn them not to speak any longer to anyone in this name." 18. Then after they called them, they warned *them* not to speak and not to teach at all on the name of Jesus. 19. And Peter and John said to them, "You must judge if it is just before God to hear from you, rather than God: 20. for we are not able to speak except what we saw and heard." 21. And after they were threatened further they set them free, for they did not find a way they could punish them, because of the people, because all were glorifying God on account of what happened: 22. for the man, for whom this miracle of healing happened, was more than forty years old.

The Believers Pray for Boldness

4:23. And after being set free they came to their own *place* and reported what the high priests and the elders said to them. 24. And those who heard took one mind and voice and said to God, "Master, You *are* the One Who made heaven and the earth and the sea and everything in them. 25. Our Father, when You spoke by the Holy Spirit through *the* mouth of Your child David,

> 'Why were heathens arrogant
> and peoples did conspire vain things?
26. And the kings of the earth appeared
> and the leaders gathered together against Him
> against the Lord and against His Messiah.' (Ps 2:1,2)

27. For they, both Herod and Pontius Pilate with heathens and people of Israel, truly gathered in this city against Your Holy Child Jesus, Whom You anointed, 28. to do whatever Your hand and Your will predestined to have happened. 29. And now these things, Lord, You must look upon their threats and You must right now give to Your servants to speak Your message with the greatest boldness, 30. while You stretch out Your hand in healing and miracles and wonders to be done through the name of Your holy Child Jesus." 31. And after they made supplication, the place in which they were gathering was shaken, and they were all saturated with the Holy Spirit and they were speaking the Word of God with boldness.

All Things in Common

4:32. And the multitudes of believers were of one heart and mind, and no one was saying *that* his possessions were his own but they were common to them all. 33. And the apostles were giving out testimony of the resurrection[1] of the Lord Jesus in great power; and great favor was on them all. 34. And in fact

---

1   (v.33) See Resurrection in Glossary.

not any among them was needy: for as many as were possessing properties or houses, as they sold *the things*, they brought the prices of the sales 35. and were putting *the money* beside the feet of the apostles, and it was being distributed to each to the degree that any had a need. 36. And Joseph, the one who was called Barnabas by the apostles, which is translated "Son of Encouragement," a Levite, a Cypriot by birth, 37. when he sold a field owned by him he brought the money and placed *it* at the feet of the apostles.

Ananias and Sapphirah

5.1. And a certain man named Ananias, with his wife Sapphirah, sold property 2. and kept back from the payment, while his wife was also fully aware, and then he brought part *and* placed it beside the feet of the apostles. 3. And Peter said, "Ananias, by what means did Satan[1] fill your heart, for you to have lied to the Holy Spirit and to have kept back from the price of the property? 4. While it remained *unsold* was it not remaining yours until you sold it by your authority? Why did you place this deed in your heart? You did not lie to men but to God." 5. And when Ananias heard these words, as he fell down he breathed his last, and great fear came upon all those who heard. 6. Then the young men got up, covered him and after they carried him out, buried *him*.

5:7. And it was about a three hour interval when his wife came in, not knowing what had happened. 8. And Peter declared to her, "You must tell me, if you sold the field for so much?" And she said, "Indeed, so much." 9. And Peter *said* to her, "Why was it agreed between you to test the Spirit of *the* Lord? Behold the feet of those who buried your husband are at the door and they will carry you out." 10. And she fell at once at his feet and expired: and when the young men came in they found her dead and after they carried *her* out, they buried *her* beside her husband, 11. and great fear was upon the whole congregation and upon all those who heard these things.

Many Signs and Wonders Performed

5:12. And many signs and wonders were being done among the people through the hands of the apostles. And they were all together on Solomon's Colonnade, 13. but none of the rest was daring to join with them, but the people were holding them in high esteem. 14. And more believing in the Lord were being added, a multitude of both men and women, 15. so that they even brought the sick out into the streets and placed *them* on stretchers and cots, so that when Peter was passing his shadow would fall on some of them. 16. And the multitude was also gathering from the cities around Jerusalem, bringing *the* sick and *those* troubled by unclean spirits, who were all healed.

Persecution of the Apostles

5:17. Then the High Priest and all those with him, which is the sect of the

---

1   (v.3) See Satan in Glossary.

Sadducees, rose up, filled with jealousy 18. and they arrested the apostles and put them in *the* public prison. 19. But an angel of the Lord, having opened the doors of the jail by night, after he led them out then said, 20. "You must go and when you stand in the temple you must continually speak the words of this *eternal* life to all the people." 21. Then after they heard *this* they entered the temple before dawn and they were teaching. And when the High Priest arrived he and those with him summoned the Sanhedrin, even all the council of elders of the children of Israel, and they sent to the jail to have them brought. 22. But when the attendants arrived they did not find them in the jail. And when they returned they reported 23. saying, "We found the prison secured in every certainty and the guards standing by the doors, but when we opened *the doors*, we found no one inside." 24. And as the captain of the temple guards and the high priests heard these words, they were perplexed about these things, whatever this might be. 25. And then someone approached *and* reported to them that "Behold the men whom you put in prison are standing in the temple and teaching the people." 26. Then when the captain left with the attendants, he was leading them, *but* not with force, because *the attendants and guards* were afraid that the people would stone *them*.

5:27. And having led them *in* they stood among the Sanhedrin. And the High Priest asked them 28. saying, "Did we not give you an order not to teach on this name, and look, you have filled Jerusalem with your teaching and you wish to have brought the blood of this man upon us." 29. And Peter and the apostles said, "It is necessary to obey God rather than men. 30. The God of our fathers raised Jesus *from the dead*, Whom you killed by hanging *Him* on wood: 31. God lifted up this Chief Leader and Savior to His right hand, to give repentance and forgiveness of sins to Israel. 32. And we are witnesses of these events and *so is* the Holy Spirit Whom God gave to those who obey Him."

5:33. And when they heard this, they were infuriated and wanted to kill them. 34. But someone in the council got up, a Pharisee named Gamaliel, a teacher of Torah,[1] held in honor by all the people, *and* he ordered *them* to put the men outside a short time. 35. Then he said to them, "Men of Israel, pay close attention to what you are going to do to these men. 36. For before these days Theudas rose saying that he was somebody, to whom a number of men, about four hundred, attached themselves: who was killed, and all, as many as were won over to him, broke up and became nothing. 37. After this Judas of Galilee rose in the days of the census and he caused people behind him, *his followers*, to revolt: that one also died and all, as many as were won over to him, were scattered. 38. And now I say these things to you, you should go away from these men and let them be: because if it would be from human origin, it will be brought to an end, 39. but if it is from God, you will not be able to stop them, and you would

---

1   (v.34) Torah here refers to the Tanach (Old Testament) and oral teachings. See Torah in Glossary. Saul, who later was called Paul, attended the yeshiva, school, of Gamaliel.

never *want to* be found resisting God." And they were persuaded by him. 40. And after they summoned *and* beat the apostles, they warned *them* not to speak about the name of Jesus and released *them*. 41. Then they indeed went from *the* presence of the council, rejoicing that they were considered worthy to have been dishonored on behalf of the name, 42. and they were not ceasing all day teaching and proclaiming the Good News of Messiah Jesus in the temple and house to house.

The Appointment of the Seven

6.1. And in those days as the disciples were increasing *in number* there was a complaint of the Hellenists[1] against the Hebrews, because their widows were being neglected in the daily service.[2] 2. And when the twelve summoned the multitude of disciples, they said, "It is not pleasing that we have neglected the Word of God to look after tables. 3. And you, brothers, must now provide seven approved men from yourselves, filled with *the* Spirit and wisdom, whom we could appoint for this need, 4. and we shall persist in prayer and in service of the Word." 5. And the request pleased the whole multitude and they chose Stephen, a man full of faith and *the* Holy Spirit, and Philip and Prochoros and Nicanor and Timon and Parmenas and Nicolas, a proselyte *from* Antioch, 6. whom they stood before the apostles, and when they prayed they laid hands on them.

6:7. And the Word of God was spreading and the number of disciples was multiplying greatly in Jerusalem, and a great crowd of priests was submitting in the faith.

The Arrest of Stephen

6:8. And Stephen, full of grace and power, was doing great wonders and signs among the people. 9. But some of those from the synagogue called Freed Slaves, those from Cyrene and Alexandria and those from Cilicia and Asia, rose up disputing with Stephen, 10. but they were not able to resist the wisdom and spirit with which he was speaking. 11. So they incited people by saying that "We have heard him speaking blasphemous words against Moses and God:" 12. and they stirred up the people and the elders and the scribes and so they came upon *him and* seized him suddenly by force and led *him* to the Sanhedrin, 13. and they set up false witnesses saying, "This man does not stop speaking messages against this holy place and the Torah: 14. for we heard him saying that this Jesus of Nazareth will destroy this place and will transform the customs which Moses gave to us." 15. And when all those who were sitting in the council looked intently upon him they saw his face was like a face of an angel.

---

1   (6:1) These were Israelis who were nominally Jewish but had adopted Greek ways. See Hellenists in Glossary.
2   (6:1) The word service refers to the food, clothing, and other necessities provided by the congregation.

Stephen's Speech

7.1. And the High Priest said, "Are these things so?" 2. And he said, "Men, brothers and fathers,[1] you must listen. The God of glory (Ps 29:3) was seen by our father Abraham while he was in Mesopotamia before he dwelt in Haran 3. and He said to him, 'You must now leave your country and your kin, and come[2] into the country wherever I will show you.' (Gn 11:31-12:1) 4. Then when he left the land of the Chaldeans he settled in Haran. From there, after his father died, He resettled him in this land in which you are now living, 5. and He did not give him an inheritance in this *land*, not even a foot of ground, but promised 'to give it to him and to his seed after him for a possession,' (Gn 12:7, 13:15, et al.) although there was not a child for him. 6. And God spoke in this way that 'His seed will be alien in a strange land and they will enslave his *descendants* and they will mistreat *them* for four hundred years: 7. and I will judge the nation wherever they will be enslaved,' said God, 'and after these things they will come out and they will worship Me in this place.' (Gn 15:13,14, Ex 3:12) 8. And He gave him a covenant of circumcision: and so he fathered Isaac and circumcised him on the eighth day, (Gn 17:10-14) and Isaac *fathered* Jacob, and Jacob the twelve patriarchs.

7:9. "And the patriarchs, being jealous, sold Joseph into Egypt. But God was with him 10. and set him free from all his afflictions and gave him favor and wisdom before Pharaoh, king of Egypt, and he appointed him governor over Egypt and over his whole house. 11. And a famine and great affliction came upon all Egypt and Canaan, and our fathers did not find food *for their needs*. 12. But when Jacob heard that there was food in Egypt, he sent our fathers on their first *trip*. 13. And on the second *trip* Joseph was recognized by his brothers and the nationality of Joseph was known by Pharaoh. 14. And then Joseph sent *and* summoned his father Jacob and all the seventy-five living relatives. 15. And Jacob went down into Egypt and he and our fathers died *there*, 16. and *Jacob's body* was transferred to Shechem and they placed *him* in the tomb, which Abraham bought with a price of silver from the sons of Hamor in Shechem.

7:17. "And just as the time was drawing near for the promise which God had made to Abraham, the people increased and multiplied in Egypt 18. until 'a different king rose over Egypt who had not known Joseph.' (Ex 1:7,8) 19. This one, dealing treacherously with our people, mistreated our fathers by making them expose their infants so they could not live. 20. During which time Moses was born and he was acceptable to God: who was cared for in his father's house for three months, 21. and after he was set out the daughter of Pharaoh adopted

---

1   (7:2) Referring only to males does not mean that only males were present. There was no need, as we have in the last few years, to be politically correct, so each statement, such as 'brothers' included sisters without having to say that. Men outnumbered women because men were commanded to attend services while women could be excused to care for children.
2   (v.3) Note that the Lord said to come, not to go because the Lord was going with Abraham, as He goes with each of us today.

him for herself and raised him as a son. 22. And Moses was educated in all *the* wisdom of Egypt, and he was powerful in words and in his deeds.

7:23. "And as he completed forty years of time in this *education*, it rose upon his heart to care for his brothers, the children of Israel. 24. And when he saw one being injured, then by slaying the Egyptian he made vengeance for the one who was treated roughly. 25. And he thought his brothers would understand that God would give them salvation by his hand: but they did not understand. 26. And on the next day he was seen while they were quarreling and he was trying to reconcile them so they would be peaceful saying, 'Men, you are brothers: why are you doing evil to one another?' 27. But the one who was doing evil to his neighbor pushed him aside saying, 'Who appointed you leader and judge over us? 28. Do you want to kill me the same way you killed the Egyptian yesterday?' 29. And Moses fled at this statement and became a stranger in *the* land of Midian, where he fathered two sons.

7:30. "And after forty years were completed 'in the wilderness of the mountain' *of* Sinai 'an angel was seen by him in a flame of a burning bush.' (Ex 3:2,3) 31. And Moses, when he saw the vision, was amazed, and when he approached to look at it, *the* voice of *the* Lord came, 32. 'I AM[1] the God of your fathers, the God of Abraham and Isaac and Jacob.' (Gn 3:6) And Moses, trembling, was not daring to look at it. 33. And the Lord said to him, 'You must now untie the sandals from your feet, for the place upon which you are standing is holy ground. 34. Because I saw, I really saw, the ill-treatment of My people, the one in Egypt, and I heard their groaning, and I came down *for* them to come out: and now come,[2] I am sending you to Egypt.' (Ex 3:4-10) 35. This Moses, whom they rejected when they said, 'Who appointed you leader and judge?' God has also sent this leader and redeemer accompanied by *the* hand of *the* angel of the One Who was seen by him in the bush. 36. He led them out after he made wonders and signs in *the* land of Egypt then in *the* Red Sea and in the wilderness for forty years. 37. This is Moses, the one who said to the children of Israel, 'God will raise a prophet for you from your brothers as *He raised* me.' (Dt 18:15) 38. This is the one who was in the congregation in the wilderness with the angel who spoke to him on Mount Sinai, and with our fathers, who received living words to give to us, 39. to which our fathers did not want to become obedient, but they rejected *them,* and in their hearts turned back to Egypt 40. when they said to Aaron, 'You must right now make gods for us, who will go on before us: for this Moses, who led us out from *the* land of Egypt, we do not know what happened to him.' (Ex 32:1,23) 41. And they made a calf in those days and they brought an offering to the idol and rejoiced in the works of their hands. 42. And God turned *away* and gave them over to serve the host of the sky,[3] just as it has been written

1   (v.32) The great I AM, Anokhi in Hebrew in the verse referenced here. See Anokhi in Glossary.
2   (v.34) Here, too, as in v. 3, the Lord is coming with Moses in his assignment.
3   (v.42) Stars, long the focus of false religions

in *the* scroll of the prophets,

> 'Did you not bring victims and offerings to Me
>> forty years in the wilderness, house of Israel?

43.   And you took up the dwelling of Moloch
>> and the star of your god Rephan,
>>> the images which you made' to worship them,
> 'and I will deport you beyond' Babylon. (Am 5:25-27)

7:44. "Our fathers had the tabernacle of the testimony in the desert, just as the One Who spoke to Moses ordained to make it, according to the pattern which he had seen: (Ex 27:21, Nu 1:50) 45. which also when our fathers received *it*, in turn they brought *it* in with Joshua when they took possession *of the land* of the heathens, whom God expelled from in front of our fathers until the days of David, 46. who found favor before God and he asked to find the dwelling place for *the God of* the descendants of Jacob. 47. And Solomon built a house for Him. 48. But the Most High does not dwell in *that which* has been made by human hands, just as the prophet says,

49.   'Heaven *is* My throne,
>> and the earth *is* the footstool of My feet:
> what kind of house will you build for Me, says *the* Lord,
>> and what is *the* place of My rest?[1]
50.   Did not My hand make all these things?' (Is 66:1,2)

7:51. "Stubborn and uncircumcised hearts and ears, you always oppose the Holy Spirit, your fathers and you alike. 52. Which of the prophets did your fathers not persecute? And they killed those who announced beforehand about the coming of the Righteous One, of Whom now you have become betrayers and murderers, 53. you who took the Torah by ordinances of angels but you did not keep *it*."

The Stoning of Stephen

7:54. And hearing these things infuriated their hearts and they gnashed their teeth over this. 55. But, being filled with the Holy Spirit, when he gazed into heaven he saw *the* glory of God and Jesus standing at the right hand of God 56. and he said, "Behold I see the heavens opened and the Son of Man standing at the right hand of God." 57. And crying out in a loud voice they held together their ears *with their hands* and in one accord rushed upon him 58. and after they threw him outside the city they were stoning *him*. And the witnesses put their prayer shawls beside the feet of a young man called Saul, 59. and they were stoning Stephen *who* then, as he called out, was saying, "Lord Jesus, You must now take my spirit." 60. Then he knelt *and* cried out in a loud voice, "Lord, do

---

1   (v.49) This is God's eternal rest, katapausin.

not place this sin to them." Then after he said this he slept.[1] **8.1.**[2] And Saul was approving of killing him.

Saul Persecutes the Congregation

And there was in that day a great persecution against the congregation in Jerusalem, and all except the apostles were scattered throughout the regions of Judea and Samaria. 2. And devout men buried Stephen and they made great lamenting over him. 3. And Saul was damaging the congregation by entering their houses, dragging away and giving men and women over to prison.

The Gospel Preached in Samaria

8:4. Therefore those who were scattered went through *Judea and Samaria* preaching the Word. 5. And when Philip came down to the city of Samaria he proclaimed the Messiah to them. 6. And the crowds paid attention to those things which were spoken by Philip. Of one mind in this, they listened and saw the signs which he was doing. 7. For then many of them had unclean spirits *and* they, *unclean spirits*, were coming out shouting in a loud voice, and many paralytics and lame were being healed: 8. and there was much joy in that city.

8:9. And a certain man named Simon was amazing the people of Samaria, practicing magic arts in the city and saying that he was someone great, 10. whom all from least to great were following saying, "This one is the power of god called 'Great.'" 11. And they were paying close attention to him because for a long time he had amazed them by his magic arts. 12. But when they believed in Philip's preaching concerning the kingdom of God and the name Jesus Messiah, then both men and women were being baptized.[3] 13. And even Simon himself believed and, after he was baptized, he was attaching himself to Philip, and he was amazed when he saw that there were signs and great miracles.

8:14. And when the apostles in Jerusalem heard that the Samaritans welcomed the Word of God, they sent Peter and John to them, 15. who, when they went down *from Jerusalem*, prayed on their behalf to the end that they would take *the* Holy Spirit: 16. for not yet was it fallen upon any of them, but they were only being baptized in the name of the Lord Jesus. 17. Then *Peter and John* were laying hands on them and they were taking *the* Holy Spirit.[4] 18. And when Simon saw that the Spirit was given by the laying on of the hands of the apostles, he offered them gifts 19. saying, "Now you must immediately give me this authority so that if I would lay hands on someone he would take *the* Holy Spirit." 20. And Peter said to him, "May your silver be destroyed with you because you believe

---

1   (v.60) See Death in Glossary.
2   (v.1) See Chapter and Verse Numbers in Glossary.
3   (v.12) The word baptize is from the Greek word baptidzo, which means to immerse. See Baptize in Glossary.
4   (v.17) The laying on of hands for baptism in the Holy Spirit comes from this. See Acts 19:6. Notice that those prayed for 'took' the Holy Spirit. The baptism of the Holy Spirit must be sought.

the gift of God is acquired by money: 21. neither is there for you any part nor any share in this message, for your heart is not right before God. 22. Therefore you must immediately repent from this evil of yours and ask the Lord if He will really forgive the thought of your heart for you, 23. for I see *that* you are in a gall of bitterness, *extreme wickedness*, and a bond of sin." 24. And Simon said, "You must right now ask the Lord about me in order that nothing which you said would come upon me."

8:25. So then after they had charged and spoken the word of the Lord they were returning to Jerusalem, and they were preaching the Good News *in* many Samaritan towns.

Philip and the Cushite Eunuch

8:26. Then an angel of the Lord spoke to Philip saying, "Rise and go down south on the road that descends from Jerusalem to Gaza." This is wilderness. 27. And when he got up he went. And there was a man, an Ethiopian[1] eunuch, of great authority under Candace queen of *the* Ethiopians, who was over all her royal treasury, who had come in order to worship in Jerusalem 28. and was returning. And while he was sitting in his chariot he was reading the prophet Isaiah. 29. And the Spirit said to Philip, "You must approach and join this one in the chariot." 30. And as he was running up Philip heard him reading Isaiah the prophet and said, "Do you really understand what you are reading?" 31. And he said, "How indeed would I be able unless someone would guide me?" He urged Philip to come up to sit with him. 32. And the portion of the Scripture which he was reading was this:

"As a sheep was led to slaughter
and as a lamb before the one shearing it *is* mute,
in the same way He does not open His mouth.
33.   In His humiliation His justice was taken away:
who will describe His generation?
because His life is taken from the earth." (Is 53:7,8)

8:34. And the eunuch said to Philip, "I beg you, concerning whom is the prophet saying this? Concerning himself or concerning some other?" 35. And Philip then opened his mouth and having begun from this Scripture he proclaimed to him the Good News *about* Jesus. 36. And as they were going along the way, they came upon some water, and the eunuch said, "Look! Water! What prevents me from being baptized?"[2] [3]38. And he ordered the chariot[4] to stop and Philip and

---

1   (v.27) Ethiopian in Hebrew is Cushite.
2   (v.36) Philip's baptizing him was unusual since the general practice for Jewish people was, and still is, self-immersion. The word baptize is from the Greek word baptidzo, which means to immerse. See Baptize in Glossary.
3   (v.36) V. 37 is omitted because it was not in the earliest manuscripts.
4   (v.38) This was a large vehicle, not like a war chariot, but had passenger seats and a driver.

the eunuch both went down into the water, and he baptized him.[1] 39. And when they came up out of the water, *the* Spirit of the Lord took Philip away and the eunuch no longer saw him, then *the eunuch* went on his way rejoicing. 40. And Philip was found in Ashdod:[2] and he was evangelizing, coming through all the cities until he came into Caesarea.

The Conversion of Saul

9.1. And Saul, still breathing threat and murder among the disciples of the Lord, when he went to the High Priest, 2. asked from him letters to the synagogues in Damascus, to the end that if he would find any *who* were of the Way,[3] both men and women, he would lead them bound to Jerusalem. 3. And it happened while he was going *as* he drew near to Damascus, a light from heaven suddenly shone around him 4. and as he fell to the ground he heard a voice saying to him, "Saul. Saul!"[4] Why are you persecuting Me?" 5. And he said, "Who are You, Lord?" And He *said*, "I AM Jesus Whom you are persecuting: 6. but you must now rise and enter the city and it will be told to you what is necessary for you to do." 7. And the men traveling with him had stood speechless, hearing the voice on the one hand but on the other hand not seeing anyone. 8. Then Saul got up from the ground, but when he opened his eyes he was not seeing anything: and taking him by the hand they were leading him to Damascus. 9. And he was without sight three days and he was neither eating nor drinking.

9:10. And there was a certain disciple in Damascus named Ananias, and the Lord said to him in a vision, "Ananias." And he said, "Here I am, Lord." 11. Then the Lord said to him, "When you get up you must be going to the street called Straight and you must at once seek in *the* house of Judas *someone* named Saul of Tarsus: for behold he is praying 12. and he saw in a vision a man named Ananias *who* had entered and after he laid his hands on him then he would regain his sight." 13. But Ananias answered, "Lord, I have heard from many about this man who did evil to Your saints in Jerusalem: 14. and here he has authority from the high priests to bind all those who call on Your name." 15. Then the Lord said to him, "You must be going, because this one is a chosen vessel for Me, to carry My name before heathens and even kings and children of Israel: 16. for I will show him how much it is necessary for him to suffer on behalf of My name." 17. Then Ananias left and entered the house and when he placed his hands on him said, "Saul, brother, the Lord has sent me, Jesus the One Who set upon you on the way while you were coming, so that you would regain your sight and you would be filled with *the* Holy Spirit." 18. And immediately there fell away from

---

1   (v.38) When Philip baptized the eunuch he placed his hand on the eunuch's head to hold him under water, forcing a struggle to come out of the water as a reminder of the dying to self and the new birth, paralleling a newborn baby's struggle in birth.
2   (v.40) Azotus is the Greek name for the Israeli city Ashdod.
3   (v.2) The Way refers to those who are totally committed to God. It was first used in Gn 18:19.
4   (v.4) The doubled name is a strong rebuke. See Double Name in Glossary.

his eyes *something* like scales, and he regained sight and then when he got up he immersed[1] 19. and when he took food he regained strength.

Saul Preaches at Damascus

And he was with the disciples in Damascus some days 20. and right away he preached Jesus in the synagogues, that He was the Son of God. 21. And all those who heard were amazed and were saying, "Is this not the one who devastated those who called on this name in Jerusalem, and has he *not* come here for this, so that after he bound them he could lead *them to* the high priests?" 22. And Saul was becoming stronger and threw the Jewish people living in Damascus into dismay by proving that *Jesus* was the Messiah.

Saul Escapes from the Jewish People

9:23. And when many days had passed, the Jewish *leaders* plotted to kill him: 24. but their plot was known by Saul. And they were even watching the gates both day and night so they could kill him: 25. so his disciples, having taken him by night, let him down, having lowered *him* through the wall in a hamper.[2]

Saul at Jerusalem

9:26. And when he arrived in Jerusalem[3] he was trying to join the disciples, but they were all afraid of him, not believing that he was a disciple. 27. But then Barnabas took hold of him *and* led him to the apostles and he related to them how on the road he saw the Lord and that He spoke to him and how in Damascus he spoke openly in the name of Jesus. 28. And he went in and out among them at Jerusalem, speaking openly in the name of the Lord, 29. and he was speaking and debating with the Hellenists,[4] and they were trying to kill him. 30. But when the brothers found out they led him down to Caesarea and they sent him out to Tarsus.

9:31. Then in fact the congregation throughout the whole of Judea and Galilee and Samaria was having peace, being built up and going in the fear of the Lord and it was being filled *with people* in the comfort of the Holy Spirit.

The Healing of Aeneas

9:32. And it happened *that* Peter was going through all those *cities* to go down also to the saints living in Lud. 33. And he found some man there named Aeneas, who was paralyzed, lying on a pallet for eight years. 34. And Peter said to him, Aeneas, Jesus Messiah is healing you: you must rise and you must immediately take care of your own pallet. And he got up at once. 35. And all

---

1   (v.18) This is immersion for purification, which we call baptism. See Baptize in Glossary.
2   (v.25) A hamper is a very large basket, also used to pick up scraps when the 4,000 were fed in Mt 15:37 and Mk 8:8. This basket is identified in 2 Cor 11:33 as being made of braided ropes.
3   (v.26) Saul went to Jerusalem three years after his Damascus road experience. See Gal 1:18.
4   (v.29) These were Israelis who were nominally Jewish and had adopted Greek ways. See Hellenists in Glossary.

who lived in Lud and Sharon saw him *and* returned to the Lord.

Tabitha Restored to Life

9:36. And in Joppa there was a certain disciple named Tabitha, which when it is translated means Gazelle:[1] she was rich in good deeds[2] and charities that she was doing. 37. And it happened in those days, that she became sick *and* died: and when they had washed her[3] they placed her in an upstairs room. 38. And because Lud was near Joppa, the disciples, having heard that Peter was in *Lud*, sent two men to him urging, "Do not delay to come to us." 39. And then Peter got up *and* went with them: after they arrived they led him up to the upstairs room and all the widows came to him crying and pointing out how many tunics and garments Gazelle used to make when she was with them. 40. Then after he put all those outside and knelt, he prayed and when he turned to the body he said, "Tabitha, you must immediately get up." And she opened her eyes, and when she saw Peter she sat up. 41. And then he gave her a hand *and* stood her up: and, after he called the saints and the widows, he presented her alive. 42. And it became known throughout the whole of Joppa and many believed in the Lord. 43. And it happened he stayed many days in Joppa with a certain tanner, Simon.

Peter and Cornelius

10.1. And a certain man in Caesarea named Cornelius, a centurion from a cohort[4] called Italian, 2. devout and God-Fearing[5] with all in his house, doing many charitable things for the people and praying to God for everything, 3. about the ninth hour of the day[6] saw clearly in a vision an angel of God coming to him and saying to him, "Cornelius." 4. Then, after he looked intently at him, he became terrified *and* said, "What is it, Lord?" And he said to him, "Your prayers and your charities came up as a memorial before God. 5. And now you must send men at once to Joppa[7] and summon a certain Simon who is called Peter: 6. this one is staying with a certain tanner, Simon, with whom he is in a house by *the* sea." 7. And as the angel, the one who was speaking to him, left, then he called two of the household *servants* and a devout soldier of those attached to him 8. and after he described everything to them he sent them to Joppa.

10:9. And the next day, as those traveling were nearing the city, about the sixth hour[8] Peter went up on the roof to pray. 10. And he became very hungry and was wanting to eat. And while they were preparing *a meal* a trance[9] came

---

1   (v.36) The Greek word for gazelle is dorkas.
2   (v.36) Mitsvot, see Mitsvah in Glossary.
3   (v.37) This is still the way the Jewish people prepare a body for burial.
4   (v.1) About 600 men
5   (v.2) God-Fearer was the name given to those non-Jewish believers who were attending a synagogue and learning Judaism, but were not full proselytes.
6   (v.3) 3:00 PM, the time of afternoon prayer
7   (v.5) Caesarea is about fifty miles north of Joppa.
8   (v.9) Noon
9   (v.10) A state of ecstasy, brought about by God, in which consciousness is wholly or partially suspended

over him 11. and he saw heaven opening and something lowering, like a great sheet, being let down by four corners upon the ground, 12. in which were all the four-footed *animals* and reptiles of the earth and birds of the sky. 13. And a voice came to him, "Rise, Peter, you must right now kill and eat." 14. But Peter said, "Certainly not, Lord, because I never ate anything defiled or unclean." (Eze 4:14) 15. And again a second time a voice said to him, "What God has cleansed,[1] you must not declare unclean." 16. And this happened three times, *and* then the object was immediately taken up into the sky.

10:17. And as Peter was greatly perplexed with himself whatever could be *the meaning of* the vision (See Acts 10:28,29, 11:5-12) which he saw. Behold, the men who were sent by Cornelius, as they found out by asking *about* the house of Simon, stood by the gate, 18. and when they called they asked if Simon, the one called Peter, was a guest here. 19. And while Peter was pondering about the vision the Spirit said to him, "Behold three men are seeking you, 20. so after you get up you must go down and you must go with them, not doubting that I have sent them." 21. And when Peter went down he said to the men, "Behold I am *the one* whom you are seeking: what is the reason for which you are here?" 22. And they said, "Cornelius, a centurion, a righteous and God-Fearing[2] man, *who* is well spoken of even by the whole nation of the Jewish people, was directed by a holy angel to summon you to his house and to hear what you have to say." 23. Then, having invited them in, he entertained *them*.

And the next day when he got up he left with them, and some of the brothers from Joppa came with him. 24. Then the day after that he entered Caesarea. And Cornelius was waiting for them, having called together his kin and close friends. 25. And as Peter happened to come, when Cornelius met him he fell at his feet *and* paid homage[3] to him. 26. But Peter raised him saying, "You must get up: for I am also a man." 27. And conversing with him he entered and found many gathered, 28. and he said to them, "You believe that it is contrary to law and justice for a Jewish person to associate with or to approach a foreigner: but God explained to me not to say in any way that a man *is* common or unclean: 29. for this reason then I came without raising any objection when I was sent for. Therefore I ask for what reason did you send for me?" 30. And Cornelius said, "From four days ago to this *very* hour *of* the afternoon I was praying at the ninth hour[4] in my house, and behold a man stood before me in shining clothing 31. and he said, 'Cornelius, your prayer has been heard and your charities have

---

1   (v.15) The critical phrase is, "What God has cleansed," not saying that all things are clean, but only what God has cleansed. The converts were cleansed because of their yearning for more of God, with the later evidence of their baptism in the Holy Spirit.
2   (v.22) God-Fearer was the name given to those non-Jewish believers who were attending synagogue and learning Judaism, but were not full converts to Judaism. In Neh 7:2 God-Fearer is used in reference to Jewish leaders.
3   (v.25) This is going down on one knee and bowing to the ground to a great person. See Pay Homage in Glossary.
4   (v.30) 3:00 PM, the time of afternoon prayer

been remembered before God. 32. Therefore you must now send to Joppa and summon Simon, who is called Peter. He is staying in *the* house by *the* sea, of Simon, a tanner.' 33. Therefore I immediately sent for you, and you did well by coming. Now then we all are present before God to hear everything that has been ordered to you by the Lord."

Peter Speaks in Cornelius' House

10:34. Then when Peter opened his mouth he said, "In truth I understand that God does not show partiality,[1] (Dt 10:17, 2Chr 19:7, Mk 12:14) 35. but in every nation the one who fears Him and works righteousness[2] is acceptable to Him. 36. *The* message, which He sent to the children of Israel, when He proclaimed Good News of peace through Jesus Messiah, this One, is Lord of All. 37. You know the report, what happened throughout the whole of Judea, beginning from Galilee after the baptism[3] which John preached, 38. as God anointed this Jesus, the One from Nazareth, in *the* Holy Spirit and power, Who came through doing good and healing all those who were oppressed by the devil, because God was with Him. 39. And we *are* witnesses of all that He did in both the country of the Jewish people and in Jerusalem. And Whom they killed, by hanging Him on wood. 40. God raised Him on the third day and caused Him to be revealed, 41. not to all the people, but to witnesses chosen beforehand by God, to us, we who ate and drank with Him after He was raised from *the* dead: 42. and He commanded us to preach to the people and to testify earnestly that He is the One Who has been appointed by God *as* Judge of *the* living and *the* dead. 43. All the prophets testify; everyone who believes[4] in Him takes forgiveness of sins through His name." (Is 33:24, Jr 31:34, Dn 9:24)

Pagans Receive the Holy Spirit

10:44. While Peter was still speaking these words the Holy Spirit fell upon all those listening to the message.[5] 45. And the faithful from the circumcision who came with Peter were amazed, because the gift of the Holy Spirit fell even upon the heathens: 46. for they heard them speaking in tongues and glorifying God. Then Peter responded, 47. "No one can deny *the* water, can they, *for* any of these to be baptized, who took the Holy Spirit like we *did?*" 48. And he ordered them to be baptized in the name of Jesus Messiah. Then they asked him to spend some days *with them*.

---

1 (v.34) Literally, "does not look at the face," a Hebrew idiom commonly translated "not a respecter of persons."
2 (v.35) Mitsvot. See both Mitsvah and Righteousness in Glossary.
3 (v.37) The immersion for purification. See Baptize in Glossary.
4 (v.43) To Peter and all those with him belief requires a complete change in behavior.
5 (v.44) God can do anything He wants, any way He wants. This is the only example of this spontaneous, unexpected baptism of the Holy Spirit, as much as anything else to give credible evidence to the apostles of God's acceptance of the non-Jewish converts. When the disciples were waiting for the baptism of the Holy Spirit, they did not know what was going to happen, but they were waiting for something spectacular.

Peter's Report to the Congregation at Jerusalem

11.1. And the apostles, and the brothers who were throughout Judea, heard that even the heathens received the Word of God. 2. And when Peter went up to Jerusalem, those of *the* circumcision disputed with him 3. saying that "You entered with uncircumcised men and you ate with them." 4. And when Peter began he explained to them point by point saying, 5. "I was in *the* city of Joppa praying and I saw in amazement a vision, a vessel being let down from the sky by four corners, something like a great sheet, and it came to me. 6. When I looked intently upon it I observed and I saw the four-footed *creatures* of the earth and the wild beasts and the reptiles and the birds of the sky. 7. And I also heard a voice saying to me, 'When you rise, Peter, you must kill and you must eat right away.' 8. And I said, 'Not me, Lord, because *the* common or unclean never entered my mouth.' 9. Then a voice answered a second time from heaven, 'What God cleansed you must stop declaring defiled!' 10. And this happened three times, *and* then everything was again taken up into the sky. 11. And behold in that instant three men stood by the house in which we were, having been sent to me from Caesarea. 12. And the Spirit said for me to accompany them and not to make a distinction. They and these six brothers came with me and we entered the man's house. 13. And he reported to us how he saw the angel standing in his house saying, 'You must immediately send to Joppa to summon Simon, the one called Peter, 14. who will speak a message to you by which you and all your house would be saved.' 15. And while I was beginning to speak, the Holy Spirit fell upon them just as upon us in *the* beginning. 16. And I remembered the word of the Lord as He was saying, 'John indeed baptized in water, but you will be baptized in *the* Holy Spirit.' 17. Therefore if God gave the same gift to them, as also to us believers in the Lord Jesus Messiah, who was I *to be* able to hinder God?" 18. And when they heard these things they remained silent, then glorified God saying, "So then God also gave the heathens the repentance into life."

The Congregation at Antioch

11:19. Then indeed those who were scattered on account of the persecution that took place against Stephen went as far as Phoenicia and Cyprus and Antioch, but not speaking the Word except only to Jewish people. 20. But some of them were men of Cyprus and Cyrene, who when they came into Antioch were speaking then to the Hellenists[1] preaching the Good News of the Lord Jesus. 21. And *the* hand of *the* Lord was with them, and a great number who believed turned to the Lord. 22. And the report concerning them was heard in the ears of the congregation that was in Jerusalem and they sent out Barnabas to come through as far as Antioch. 23. Who, when he arrived and saw the favor of God, greeted and encouraged all to continue with purpose of heart in devotion to the Lord, 24. for *Barnabas* was a good man and full of *the* Holy Spirit and faith. And

---

1   (v.20) These were Israelis who were nominally Jewish and had adopted Greek ways. See Hellenists in Glossary.

a huge crowd was added to the Lord. 25. Then he came out to Tarsus to look for Saul, 26. and when he found *him* brought *him* to Antioch. And he was then with them a whole year, to meet with the congregation and to teach a great number of people, and in Antioch the disciples *were* first called Christians.

11:27. And in these days prophets came down from Jerusalem to Antioch. 28. And one of them, named Agabus, (Acts 21:10) when he got up, was reporting through the Spirit *that* a great famine will be going on against the whole world, which happened in the time of Claudius.[1] 29. And of the disciples, just as any was prospered, each of them designated to send support for those brothers living in Judea: 30. and they did, sending to the elders by *the* hand of Barnabas and Saul. (Gal 1:18, 2:1)

Jacob[2] Killed and Peter Imprisoned

12.1. And at that time Herod the king arrested any of those from the congregation to abuse *them*. 2. And he killed Jacob, the brother of John, with a sword. 3. And because he saw that it was pleasing to the Jewish *leaders*, he proceeded also to arrest Peter, - and they were the days of Unleavened Bread[3] - 4. whom he placed in jail after he seized *him*, having given *him* over to four squads of soldiers to guard him, since he wanted to bring him before the people after Passover. 5. So indeed Peter was being kept in jail: but there was fervent prayer to God being made by the congregation concerning him.

Peter Delivered from Prison

12:6. But when Herod was going to bring him out, that night Peter was sleeping between two soldiers, bound by two chains, and there were guards by the door, guarding the prison. 7. And behold an angel of *the* Lord stood and a light shone out in the prison: and as he struck Peter's side, he woke him up saying, "You must get up quickly." And his chains fell off from his hands. 8. And the angel said to him, "You must immediately gird yourself and put on your sandals." And so he did. Then he said to him, "You must put on your cloak[4] and follow me." 9. Then after they went out he was following and he was not knowing that what was happening through the angel *was* real: but he was thinking he was seeing a vision. 10. And then they came through *the* first guard then a second *and* they came upon the iron gate leading *one* into the city, which was open to them by itself and after they came out they went down one alley, then immediately the angel left him. 11. And when Peter came to himself he said, "Now I know truly that the Lord sent out His angel and delivered me from Herod's hand and every expectation of the Jewish *leaders*." 12. And when he understood *what was going on* he went to the house of Mary, the mother of John,

---

1   (v.28) Claudius was Emperor from 41-54 AD.
2   (Caption) The Greek text has Iakob, which is Jacob in English. See Jacob in Glossary.
3   (v.3) Passover
4   (v.8) The cloak of every Jewish man was his prayer shawl. See Prayer Shawl in Glossary.

the one called Mark, where many were gathering and praying. 13. And when he knocked on the door of the vestibule a maid named Rhoda came to open, 14. and when she recognized Peter's voice, on account of her joy she did not open the gate, but running in reported that Peter was standing at the gate. 15. But they said to her, "You are mad." But she insisted it was so. And they were saying, "It is his angel." 16. And Peter was continuing to knock: and when they opened they saw him and they were amazed. 17. Then after he made a sign to them with his hand that they should be silent he described to them how the Lord led him out from the jail *and* said, "Report these things to Jacob, *the brother of Jesus*, and to the brothers." Then when he came out he went to a different place.

12:18. And when it became day there was not a little consternation among the soldiers *about* what really became of Peter. 19. And when Herod searched for him and did not find *him*, after he questioned the guards he commanded *them* to be led away for punishment, and going down from Judea he spent time in Caesarea.[1]

The Death of Herod

12:20. And he was very angry with the people of Tyre and Sidon: *who* of one mind were present with him and after they persuaded Blastus, the chamberlain of the king, they were asking peace because their country *was* to be fed from that which belonged to the king. 21. At the appointed time of day Herod put on his royal robe and when he sat on the judicial bench he was delivering an address to them, 22. and the people were crying out, "A voice of a god and not of a man." 23. And immediately an angel of *the* Lord hit him because he did not give the glory to God, and then he became eaten by worms and expired.[2]

12:24. And the message of God was growing and spreading. 25. And Barnabas and Saul returned *to Antioch*, since they had accomplished the ministry[3] to Jerusalem, having taken along John, the one called Mark.

Barnabas and Saul Commissioned

13.1. And there were prophets and teachers among the congregation which was in Antioch, Barnabas and Simon, the one called Black, and Luke the Cyrene, and Menachem, a childhood companion of Herod the tetrarch, and Saul. 2. The Holy Spirit said while they were serving the Lord and fasting, "Now separate right away for Me Barnabas and Saul for the work to which I have called them." 3. Then after they fasted and prayed and laid hands on them they left.

The Apostles Preach in Cyprus

13:4. Then indeed as they were sent out by the Holy Spirit they went down into Seleucia, from there they sailed to Cyprus 5. and while they were

1   (v.19) At this time Caesarea was the capital of Judea, so how could you go from Judea to Caesarea? Only rabbis used the phrase "came down from Judea to Caesarea."
2   (v.23) This was in the year 44 AD. Herod Agrippa I reigned from 37-44 AD.
3   (v.25) The ministry was the delivery of the gift to the congregation in Jerusalem.

in Salamis they were proclaiming the Word of God in the synagogues of the Jewish people. And they had John[1] as a servant. 6. And after they went through the whole island as far as Paphos they found a certain man, a sorcerer, a false prophet, a Jewish man by the name of Bar-Jesus 7. who was with the proconsul Sergius Paulus,[2] an intelligent man. Then after he summoned Barnabas and Saul, he sought diligently to hear the Word of God. 8. But the sorcerer, Elymas, for thus his name was translated, was opposing them, seeking to turn the proconsul away from the faith. 9. And when Saul, or Paul[3], having been filled with *the* Holy Spirit, fixed his eyes on him 10. he said, "O you, full of every deceit and every villainy, a son of *the* devil, enemy of everyone righteous, would you stop perverting the right ways of the Lord? 11. And now behold *the* hand of *the* Lord *is* upon you and you will be blind, not seeing the sun for a time." And immediately mistiness fell upon him, then darkness, and he was seeking someone *to* lead him about by the hand. 12. Then, when the proconsul saw what happened, he believed, being amazed at the teaching of the Lord.

Saul and Barnabas at Antioch of Pisidia

13:13. And when they set sail from Paphos those with Paul came into Perga of Pamphylia, and then John left them *and* returned to Jerusalem. 14. And after they left from Perga they went to Pisidian Antioch, and having entered the synagogue on the day of Sabbaths[4] they sat down. 15. And after the reading from the Torah and the Prophets[5] the synagogue leaders sent for them saying, "Men, brothers, if someone among you has a word of encouragement for the people, speak." 16. Then when Paul got up, he signaled with his hand and said:

"Men of Israel and God-Fearers,[6] you must listen. 17. The God of this People Israel chose our fathers and lifted the people high during the sojourn in *the* land of Egypt and led them out from her with an upraised arm, 18. and in the same way he put up with them forty years in the wilderness 19. and after He conquered seven nations in *the* land of Canaan He distributed their land as an inheritance 20. after about four hundred fifty years *from going to Egypt*. And after these things He gave them judges until Samuel the prophet. 21. And afterward they asked for a king and God gave them Saul son of Kish, a man from *the* tribe of Benjamin, for forty years,[7] 22. and after He removed him He raised David for them as king,

---

1   (v.5) John Mark
2   (v.7) A large stone inscribed "Sergius Paulus, Proconsul" was found a few years ago in a town near Paphos.
3   (v.9) This is the first time the name Paul is used in the New Testament.
4   (v.14) The plural being used here probably indicates that it is one of the feast days. See Sabbath in Glossary.
5   (v.15) This is the first five books of the Bible, plus Jsh, Jd, 1 & 2 Sam, 1 & 2Ki, Is through Mal, but not including Dn. See Prophets in Glossary.
6   (v.16) God-Fearer was the name given to those non-Jewish believers who were attending synagogue and learning Judaism, but were not full proselytes. In Neh 7:2 God-Fearing is used in reference to Jewish leaders.
7   (v.21) The forty years is mysterious because Saul's reign was twenty-one years, from c. 1030-1009 BC.

of whom He also said when He bore testimony, 'I found David the *son* of Jesse, a man according to My heart, who will do all My will.' (1Sam 16:12,13, Ps 89:20, Is 44:28) 23. From the seed of this one, God, according to the promise to Israel, led a savior, Jesus, 24. while John proclaimed *the* baptism[1] of repentance to all the people of Israel before His coming. 25. And as John was fulfilling the course *of life*, he was saying, 'Who do you suppose I am? I am not *He*: but behold after me He is coming of Whom I am not worthy to loose the sandal of His feet.'

13:26. "Men, brothers, sons of the family of Abraham and those God-Fearers[2] among you, the message of this salvation was sent out in us. 27. For those who dwell in Jerusalem and those who lead them because they have not known this One and the voices of the prophets, those who are read every Sabbath, *the leaders* fulfilled *the prophecies* when they condemned *Him*, 28. and although they found nothing deserving of the death penalty they asked Pilate to condemn Him to death. 29. And as they brought to completion everything that was written about Him, taking *Him* down from the cross they placed *Him* in a tomb. 30. But God raised Him out from *the* dead, 31. Who was seen on many days by those who went up with Him from the Galilee to Jerusalem, who now are His witnesses to the people. 32. And we are bringing you the Good News, the promise *that* was made to our fathers, 33. that God has fulfilled this for their children, since He raised Jesus for us as it has also been written in the second Psalm,

> 'You are My Son,
> today I have begotten You.' (Ps 2:7)

34. And that He raised Him from *the* dead, no longer being about to abandon *Him* into decay, just as He has said that

> I shall give 'to You the faithful holy things of David.' (Is 55:3)

35. And therefore in another He says,

> 'You will not give Your Holy One to see decay.' (Ps 16:10)

36. For indeed David, after he served his own generation in the will of God, fell asleep and was placed with his fathers and saw corruption: 37. but *the One* Whom God raised did not see corruption. 38. Therefore let *it* be known to you, men, brothers, that through this One forgiveness of sins is proclaimed to you, and *cleansing* from all things by which you were not able to be put into a right relationship with God by means of the tradition of Moses, 39. everyone who believes[3] in this One is put into a right relationship with God. 40. Therefore you must beware that what was spoken by the prophets would not come,

41.   'Behold, scoffers,

---

1   (v.24) Immersion for purification, which had been a Jewish custom for over 1,000 years. See Baptize in Glossary.
2   (v.26) God-Fearer was the name given to those non-Jewish believers who were attending synagogue and learning Judaism, but were not full proselytes. In Neh 7:2 God-Fearing is used in reference to Jewish leaders.
3   (v.39) The Jewish understanding of "believe" required a change in behavior as evidence.

and marvel and perish,
because I am doing a work in your days,
work which you would **not** in any way
believe if someone would tell you in detail.'" (Hab 1:5)

13:42. And when *Paul and Barnabas* were leaving, they[1] were urging them[2] to speak about these teachings to them the next Sabbath. 43. And after being dismissed from the synagogue many of the Jewish people and the devout proselytes[3] followed Paul and Barnabas, who, as they spoke to them, were persuading them to continue in the grace of God.

13:44. And when the Sabbath came nearly all the city gathered to hear the word of the Lord. 45. And when the Jewish people[4] saw the crowds they were filled with jealousy and were speaking against *him*, blaspheming the things being spoken by Paul. 46. Paul and Barnabas, speaking freely, said, "It was required to speak the Word of God to you first: since you reject it and do not judge yourselves worthy of eternal life, behold, we are turning to the heathens. 47. For so the Lord did order us,

'I have placed you for a light to heathens
for you to be bringing salvation to the very ends of the earth.'"
(Is 49:6)

48. And the heathens, hearing this, were rejoicing and praising the message about the Lord and as many as were believing were being set into eternal life: 49. and the message about the Lord was being spread through the whole country. 50. But the Jewish *leaders* aroused elegant women who were worshipping and the leading men of the city and they stirred up persecution against Paul and Barnabas and they expelled them from their region. 51. And after they shook off the dust from *their* feet they went to Iconium, 52. and the disciples were being filled with joy and *the* Holy Spirit.

Paul and Barnabas at Iconium

14.1. And it happened in Iconium they entered the synagogue of the Jewish people together and spoke in such a way that a great number of the congregation[5] of both Jewish and Greeks believed. 2. But the disbelieving Jewish people aroused and angered the minds of the heathens against the brothers. 3. Yet they indeed stayed for a long time speaking out boldly for the Lord, Who was continually bearing testimony on the message of His grace, giving signs and wonders that came through their hands. 4. And the population of the city was divided, and there were on the one hand those with the Jewish people and on the

---

1   (v.42) Jewish members, God-Fearers, and proselytes in the synagogue.
2   (v.42) Paul and Barnabas
3   (v.43) Proselytes were the full converts to Judaism.
4   (v.45) Those Jewish people who did not accept Paul's message the week before.
5   (v.1) Although often translated "church," no Greek word meaning church is used in the NT. See Congregation in Glossary.

other those with the apostles. 5. So then there was a hostile movement of the heathens, and also Jewish people with their leaders, to do them harm and to stone them. 6. When they became aware they fled down to the cities Lystra and Derbe of Lyconia and the neighboring regions, 7. and there also they were proclaiming the Good News.

Paul and Barnabas at Lystra

14:8. And in Lystra a certain man who never walked, without strength in his feet, was sitting, lame from his mother's womb. 9. He heard Paul speaking: who when *Paul* fixed his eyes on him, since he saw that *the man* had faith to be delivered, 10. he said in a loud voice, "You must get straight up on your feet right now." And he did spring up and he was walking. 11. And when the crowds saw what Paul did they raised up their voices saying in Lyconian, "The gods, having become like men, came down to us," 12. and they were calling Barnabas Zeus, and Paul Hermes, since he was the one leading the speaking. 13. And the priest of Zeus, who was just outside the city *in the temple*, and who brought bulls and wreaths, was, together with the crowds, wanting to sacrifice by the city gate. 14. But when the apostles Barnabas and Paul heard, as they tore their garments, they rushed into the crowd crying out 15. and saying, "Men, why are you doing these things? We also are men with the same nature as you, proclaiming the Good News to you, to turn *you* from these vain things to the living God, Who made heaven and earth and the sea and all the things in them: 16. Who in past generations permitted all heathens to go their own ways: 17. and yet He did not leave Himself without witness, showing kindness, giving you rain from heaven and fruit-bearing seasons *that* satisfy your hearts with food and joy." 18. And by saying these things, with difficulty they restrained the crowds from sacrificing to them.

14:19. But Jewish people came from Antioch and Iconium, and then they persuaded the crowds *to stone Paul*, then after they stoned Paul they were dragging *him* outside the city thinking he had died. 20. But, after the disciples circled him, he got up *and* entered the city.[1] And the next day he went out with Barnabas to Derbe.

The Return to Antioch in Syria

14:21. And, after they preached in that city and made many worthy disciples, they returned to Lystra and to Iconium and to Antioch 22. strengthening the lives of the disciples, encouraging *them* to persevere in the faith, and that it was necessary for us to enter the kingdom of God through many troubles. 23. And, after they appointed elders for them in each congregation, with prayer *and* fasting they committed them to the Lord in Whom they had believed. 24. And having gone through Pisidia they came into Pamphilia 25. and after they gave

---

1   (v.20) Could it be that Paul had died and when the disciples circled him, praying, that he was restored to life? It certainly seems impossible that someone taken for dead could simply get up and walk away. Could he have had the out of body experience described in 2 Cor 12:2?

the message in Perga they went down to Attalia 26. and from there they sailed away to Antioch, where they were *originally* given over by the grace of God for the work that they fulfilled. 27. And when they arrived and gathered the congregation[1] they reported what God had done with them and that He opened a door of faith to the heathens. 28. And they were spending no little time with the disciples.

The Council at Jerusalem

15.1. And some who came down from Judea were teaching the brothers "Unless you would be circumcised in the custom of Moses, (Lv 12:3) you are not able to be saved." 2. But when there was strife and no little debate by Paul and Barnabas with them, they appointed Paul and Barnabas and some others to go up from them to the apostles and elders in Jerusalem concerning this issue. 3. Therefore now when they were sent on their way by the congregation, they were passing through Phoenicia and Samaria, telling in detail the conversion of the heathens and they were giving great joy to all the brothers. 4. And when they arrived in Jerusalem they were welcomed by the congregation and the apostles and the elders, and they were reporting what God did among them. 5. And some of them from the party of the Pharisees, who believed, stood saying that it was necessary to circumcise them and to command *them* to keep the Torah of Moses.

15:6. Both the apostles and the elders were gathered to see about this matter. 7. And after there was ample discussion, when Peter got up he said to them, "Men, brothers, you understand that from the beginning days *of the congregation* among you that God chose that the heathens should hear and believe the message of the Good News by my mouth. 8. And God, Who knows the heart, testified when He gave the Holy Spirit to them just as also to us 9. and nothing differentiates between us and them, since He cleansed their hearts by faith. 10. Now therefore why are you tempting God by placing a yoke on the necks of the disciples, which neither our fathers nor we were strong enough to bear? 11. But we believe that we are saved by the grace of the Lord Jesus, in the same way as also they *are*."

15:12. Then all the multitude stopped speaking and was listening to Barnabas and Paul describing what signs and wonders God did through them among the heathens. 13. And after they were quiet Jacob[2] responded saying, "Men, brothers, you must now listen to me. 14. Simon explained how God first showed His concern to take a people from *the* heathens in His name. 15. And in this the words of the prophets agree just as it has been written,

16.　　'After these things I shall return

1　　(v.27) Although often translated "church," no Greek word meaning church is used in the NT. See Congregation in Glossary.
2　　(v.13) The Greek text has Iakob, which is Jacob in English. This Jacob is Jesus' half brother.

and shall build up again the booth of David[1] that has fallen down
>> and the things that have been destroyed, I will build up its ruins
>> and I will restore it,

17. to the end that the remnants of the *Jewish* people and all the heathens[2]
>> upon whom My name would have been
>> invokedwould seek out the Lord,
> says *the* Lord *Who* does all these things' (Am 9:11,12) 18. known
>> from eternity.

19. On this account I judge *that* we should not cause difficulty for those of the heathens who are turning to God, 20. but to instruct them to abstain from the pollutions of the idols and from immorality[3] and from the *meat* of strangled *animals* and from the blood.[4] 21. For throughout every city from ancient generations Moses has those who preach him, since he is read in the synagogues on every Sabbath."

The Reply of the Council

15:22. Then it seemed best to the apostles and elders, with *the* whole congregation, to send men chosen from *among* them to Antioch, with Paul and Barnabas, Judas called Barsabbas, and Silas, men who were leaders among the brothers, 23. having written by their hand, "The apostles and the elders, brothers to those down in Antioch and Syria and Cilicia, to the brothers[5] from the heathens. Greetings. 24. Since we heard that some *who* came out from us, whom we had not ordered,[6] disturbed you with *their* messages, tearing down your inner beings, 25. it was decided, with our being of one mind, to send chosen men to you with our beloved Barnabas and Paul, 26. men who have given their lives on behalf of the name of our Lord Jesus Messiah. 27. We therefore have sent Judas and Silas and they are reporting the same things by word *of mouth*. 28. For it was considered by the Holy Spirit and by us to place no more burden on you except these necessary things, 29. to abstain from meat offered to idols and from blood and strangled animals and immorality,[7] you will do well to keep yourselves from

---

1   (v.16) Succah in the Hebrew text is not tabernacle, but booth, speaking of the personal booth of the feast of booths. The booth of David represents two things, the restoration of the Davidic kingdom, which will be the Messianic reign, and the sovereignty of David, the establishment of the kingship authority, which is the legitimacy of David's -- and the Messiah's -- reign. That also clearly states the legitimacy of the national sovereignty of the state of Israel.

2   (v.17) Raising the Booth of David is tied to evangelism to the heathen peoples.

3   (v.20) This must be immorality in the broadest sense, including the whole of Jewish Scripture regarding our relationships with one another. That is, judging by Paul's statements in Ro 1:28-32, 9:29-31, 13:9, 1Cor 5:9,10, Gal 5:19-21, Col 3:8,9, 1 Tim 1:8-11, and others.

4   (v.20) In the USA we consume huge quantities of meat with blood in it, going against this prohibition.

5   (v.23) The word Brothers often includes all members of the group, both men and women, as it does here, but in v. 22 brothers refers specifically to males.

6   (v.24) These are apostles who did not report to any controlling authority, people who claimed to report to "God alone" just as we have some of these today.

7   (v.29) See note on immorality for v. 20..

these. Farewell."

15:30. So then, when they were sent, they went down to Antioch, and after they gathered the assembly they delivered the letter. 31. And on reading *it* they rejoiced after the exhortation. 32. Both Judas and Silas, *who* were also prophets, encouraged and strengthened the brothers through a great message, 33. and after they spent time they were released with peace from the brothers to *return* to those who sent them.[1] 35. Paul and Barnabas, also with many others, were remaining in Antioch teaching and proclaiming the Good News, the Word of the Lord.

Paul and Barnabas Separate

15:36. And after some days Paul said to Barnabas, "Now that we have returned we could visit the brothers in every city in which we preached the Word of the Lord *to see* how they are doing." 37. And Barnabas was wanting to take along also the John called Mark: 38. but Paul thought not to take *him* along, since this one deserted them in Pamphilia (Acts 13:13) and did not come with them into this work. 39. And there was a sharp disagreement so that they were separated from one another, and then Barnabas took Mark to sail to Cyprus, 40. and Paul, having chosen Silas, departed after he was commended by the brothers in the grace of the Lord. 41. And he was passing through Syria and Cilicia strengthening the congregations.[2]

Timothy Accompanies Paul and Silas

16.1. And he then went down to Derbe and Lystra. And behold a certain disciple named Timothy was there, son of a Jewish woman, a believer, but a Greek father, 2. who was well spoken of by the brothers in Lystra and Iconium.[3] 3. Paul wanted this one to go on with him, and so he took *him and* circumcised him because of the Jewish people who were in those places: for they all had known that his father was Greek. 4. And as they were passing through the cities, they delivered over to them to keep the decrees which had been judged by the apostles and elders in Jerusalem. 5. So indeed the congregations were strengthening in faith and growing greatly in number day by day.

Paul's Vision of the Man of Macedonia

16:6. And they went through the regions of Phrygia and Galatia because they had been prevented by the Holy Spirit from speaking the Word *of God* in Asia: 7. and when they came down to Mysia they were trying to go into Bithynia, but the Spirit of Jesus did not let them: 8. and after they went through Mysia they went down to Troas. 9. And during the night a vision was seen by Paul, a man of

---

1   (v.33) V. 34 is omitted because it was not in the earliest manuscripts.

2   (v.41) Although often translated "church," no Greek word meaning church is used in the NT. See Congregation in Glossary.

3   (v.2) Lystra and Iconium were about twenty miles apart, a full day's journey in the first century, which shows that synagogues that far apart had enough contact for both synagogues to know Timothy and that Timothy's father was Greek.

Macedonia who was standing and urging him and saying, "You must now come over into Macedonia *and* help us right away." 10. And when he saw in the vision, we[1] immediately left to go out into Macedonia because we concluded that God had called us to evangelize them.

The Conversion of Lydia

16:11. And when we set sail from Troas we ran a straight course to Samothrace, and to Neapolis the next day 12. and from there into Philippi, which is a leading city of that part of Macedonia, a colony *of Rome*. And we were staying in this city some days. 13. So on the day of Sabbaths[2] we came outside the *city* gate by a river, which we thought to be a *place of* prayer, and having sat, we were speaking to those women who had gathered together. 14. And a certain woman named Lydia, a dealer in purple cloth of the city of Thyatira, a worshipper of God,[3] was listening, whose heart the Lord opened to pay close attention to those things being spoken by Paul. 15. And as she and her household were baptized,[4] she urged, saying, "If you have judged me to be faithful in the Lord, come to my home, you must stay there:" and she prevailed on us.

The Imprisonment at Philippi

16:16. And it happened while we were going into prayer, a certain servant girl *who* had a spirit of divination met us, who, acting as seer, was bringing a lot of profit to *her* masters. 17. She, following Paul and us, was crying out saying, "These men are servants of the Most High God, who are proclaiming a way of salvation to you." 18. And she was doing this over many days. And since Paul was disturbed, then, after he turned, he said to the spirit, "I command you in *the* name of Jesus Messiah to come out from her:" and it came out from her at *that* moment. 19. And when her owners saw that the hope of their profit came out, having caught hold of Paul and Silas they dragged *them* into the market place to the officials 20. and bringing them they said to the chief magistrates, "These men, who are Jewish, are agitating our city 21. and they are proclaiming customs which are not lawful for us since they are not for Romans to accept or to do." 22. And the crowd rose up together against them and the magistrates, having torn off their prayer shawls, were commanding *that* they beat *them* with rods, 23. and after they put many strokes on them they threw *them* in jail, having given orders to the jailer to keep *them* under guard. 24. He, when he received such a command, then took *them*, threw them into the inner prison and secured their feet in the shackle.

---

1   (v.10) This is the first time Luke uses the pronoun "we." Perhaps he joined Paul, Silas, and Timothy at Troas.

2   (v.13) This could have been a feast day or an indication that he routinely did this every Sabbath. See Sabbath in Glossary.

3   (v.14) Lydia was Jewish. Apparently she and other Jewish women met here routinely for prayer, keeping their faith strong in corporate worship. Could it be that Philippi did not have a synagogue?

4   (v.15) Immersed for purification according to Jewish custom. See Baptize in Glossary.

16:25. And at midnight while Paul and Silas were praying, they were singing hymns of praise *to* God and the prisoners were listening to them. 26. Then suddenly there was a great earthquake so as to shake the foundations of the prison: and all the doors were immediately opened and the bonds of all were loosed. 27. And as the jailer became aroused and when he saw the doors of the jail were opened, after he drew a sword he was going to kill himself because he thought the prisoners had escaped. 28. But Paul cried out in a loud voice saying, "Do not do *this* evil to yourself, for we are all here." 29. Then after he asked for lights he rushed in and he fell down trembling before Paul and Silas 30. and leading them outside he said, "Sirs, what must I do so that I would be saved?" 31. And they said, "You must believe[1] at once in the Lord Jesus and you and your household will be saved." 32. And they spoke the word of the Lord to him with all those in his house. 33. And then he took them along in that hour of the night *and* he washed their wounds, and immediately he himself and all those of his *household* were baptized[2] 34. and when he led them into the house he set a table before them and he rejoiced with *the* whole family because they had believed in God.

16:35. And when it became day the magistrates sent the policemen saying, "Release those men." 36. And the jailer reported these words to Paul that "The magistrates sent so that you would be released: therefore now as you leave, go in peace." 37. But Paul said to them, "After they beat us publicly without trial, men who are Roman, they threw *us* into jail, and now they throw us out secretly? No indeed, but when they come to us they must lead us out." 38. And the policemen reported these words to the magistrates. And they were afraid when they heard that they were Romans,[3] 39. and so when they came they called *Paul and Silas* and when they led *them* out, they asked *them* to go away from the city. 40. And when they left the jail they went to Lydia and when they saw *her* they encouraged the brothers[4] *who met there*, then they left.

The Uproar in Thessalonica

17.1. And after they traveled through Amphipolis and Apollonis they came into Thessalonica where there was a synagogue of the Jewish people. 2. And according to the custom with Paul, he went in to them and on three Sabbaths spoke to them from the Scriptures, 3. explaining and pointing out that it was necessary for the Messiah to suffer and to be raised from *the* dead and that "The Messiah is this Jesus" Whom I am proclaiming to you. 4. And some of them were persuaded and joined with Paul and Silas, a great many of the Greek worshipers[5]

1 (v.31) Paul's Jewish understanding of "believe" required a change in behavior as evidence.

2 (v.33) Immersed for purification according to Jewish custom. See Baptize in Glossary.

3 (v.38) They were afraid because it was against the law to beat (v.22) or chain (v.24) a Roman citizen who had not been convicted in a fair trial. Paul and Silas could have pressed charges.

4 (v.40) In the Hebrew manner of speaking this refers to all the people who met there.

5 (v.4) Converts to Judaism

and not a few of the leading women. 5. But the Jewish *leaders*, because they were filled with jealousy, then took along some men of the rabble, and when they formed a mob of *those* evil *people* they were setting the city in an uproar. Since *the mob* believed *Paul and Silas were* in the house of Jason they were seeking to lead them out into the mob: 6. and when they did not find them they dragged Jason and some brothers to the city magistrates crying out that "These are the ones who have disturbed the inhabited world and they are present here, 7. whom Jason has welcomed: and all these are acting contrary to the decrees of Caesar, to a different king, by saying Jesus is *king*." 8. And when they heard these things the crowd and the magistrates were stirred up, 9. then, after they took security[1] from Jason and the rest, they set them free.

The Apostles at Berea

17:10. And immediately the brothers sent Paul and Silas away through the night to Berea, *and* when they arrived, they were going into the synagogue of the Jewish people. 11. And these were more noble-minded than those in Thessalonica, who received the message with all willingness, examining the Scriptures day by day *to see* if they might have these things to be so. 12. So indeed many of them did believe, and not a few of the prominent Greek women and men. 13. But when the Jewish people from Thessalonica knew that the Word of God was also being proclaimed in Berea by Paul, they went there also, shaking and stirring up the crowds. 14. And then immediately the brothers sent Paul away to go to the sea, but both Silas and Timothy remained there. 15. And those who brought Paul led *him* as far as Athens, then they went away, since they had taken a request for Silas and Timothy that they should come to him as soon as possible.

Paul at Athens

17:16. And while Paul was waiting for them among the Athenians his spirit was greatly upset when he saw that the city was full of many idols. 17. So then he was discussing in the synagogue with the Jewish people and with those *God-Fearers* who were worshipping, and in the market place day after day with those *he was* meeting by chance. 18. And also some of the Epicurean and Stoic philosophers were meeting with him, and some were saying, "What might this babbler want to say? He even thinks he is an announcer of foreign demons, because he is preaching Jesus and the resurrection."[2] 19. After they took hold of him they led him before the High Council saying, "Can we know what this new teaching *is* that is being spoken of by you? 20. For you are bringing some strange things into our ears: therefore we want to know what these things might mean." 21. And then all the Athenians and foreign visitors had leisure, nothing *to do* other than to hear and to speak what is newer.

---

1 (v.9) Bail
2 (v.18) See Resurrection in Glossary.

17:22. And after he stood in the middle of the Aero Pago, *the High Council*, Paul said, "Men, Athenians, I observe that in every way you are very religious. 23. For as I was going around examining your objects of worship I even found an altar on which was written, 'To an Unknown God.' What then you worship without knowing *it*, I proclaim this to you. 24. The God Who created the world and everything in it, this One, Who is Lord of heaven and earth, does not live in sanctuaries made by human hands. 25. Neither is He served[1] by human hands, as if He needed anything, because He gives life and breath and everything to everyone. 26. From one *man* He made every nation of men to settle upon all *the* face of the earth, after He determined fixed times and the boundaries of their habitations. 27. God is seeking to find whether they would even seek after tokens of Him and find *Him*, and truly He is not far from any one of us. (Ps 145:18, Jr 23:23)

28.   'For in Him we live and move and have our being,'[2] as also some of your own poets have said,

'For we are also the offspring.' (Aratus, *Phaenomena 5*)

29. So, since we are offspring of God we ought not to think that the divine is like gold or silver or stone, a mark of skill, or thought of man. 30. So then, although God has overlooked a time of ignorance, now He is ordering people everywhere to repent for everything 31. because He established a Day in *which* He is going to judge the world in righteousness, by a man Whom He appointed, when He gave assurance to all the faithful by having raised Him out from *the* dead."

17:32. And after they heard of the resurrection of *the* dead, some began mocking, but others said, "We will also hear you again concerning this." 33. In this way Paul went out from their midst. 34. But some people were on his side *and* believed, among whom *were* Dionysius of the High Council and a woman named Damaris and others with them.

Paul at Corinth

18.1. After these things he left from Athens and went to Corinth. 2. And when he found a certain Jewish man named Aquila, a native of Pontus *who* came recently from Italy with Priscilla his wife, because of the order of Claudius to separate all the Jewish people[3] from Rome, *Paul* came to them 3. and because they were in the same trade he was staying with them, and he was working: for they *all* were prayer shawl makers[4] by trade. 4. And he was discussing in

---

1   (v.25) The Greek word translated served is therapeuo, which is usually translated heal. Serve is the primary meaning of therapeuo.

2   (v.28) There are multiple references of secular Greek authors for this quote, one being Epimenedes' de Oraculis, another, Aratus Phaenomena 5, still another Cleanthes.

3   (v.2) In 49 AD the Emperor Claudius forced all the Jewish people living in Rome to leave.

4   (v.3) Prayer shawl making required rabbinic training that all three had. The word ske-nopoioi, translated prayer shawl makers or tent makers, is not found anywhere else in Scripture or secular Greek writing. Jewish men referred to the prayer shawl as a tent or prayer closet because it was placed over the head to shield the eyes while praying. See Prayer Shawl in Glossary.

the synagogue throughout every Sabbath and he was winning over both Jewish people and Greeks.

18:5. After both Silas and Timothy came from Macedonia, Paul was wholly absorbed in preaching, bearing witness to the Jewish people, *that* Jesus was the Messiah. 6. But after they resisted and blasphemed, he shook *his* garments *and* said to them, "Your blood *is* upon your head: I *am* clean from this. From now on I shall go to the heathens."[1] 7. And when he went from there he entered *the* house of someone named Titus Justus, a worshipper *of* God,[2] whose house was next door to the synagogue. 8. And Crispos, the leader of the synagogue, with his whole house, believed in the Lord, and many of the Corinthians, when they heard, were believing and were being baptized.[3] 9. And the Lord said to Paul at night through a vision, "You must not be afraid! But you must be speaking and do not be silent, 10. for I AM with you and no one will be able to lay hold of you to harm you, for many of My people are in this city." 11. And he stayed[4] among them a year and six months teaching the Word of God.

18:12. And while Gallionos[5] was proconsul of Achia the Jewish people, with one mind, rose up against Paul and led him to the judicial bench 13. saying, "This one induces men to worship God contrary to the Torah."[6] 14. When Paul was about to open *his* mouth Gallionos said to the Jewish people, "If indeed it was a wrong or evil crime, O Jewish people, according to reason then I would put up with you, 15. but if on the other hand it is a question concerning doctrine and names according to your Torah, you will see to it: I do not wish to be judge of this." 16. And he drove them away from the court. 17. And then they[7] all laid hold of Sosthenes, the leader of the synagogue, *and* were striking *him* in front of the bench: but none of these things was concerning Gallionos.

Paul's Return to Antioch

18:18. And yet Paul stayed many days, then he said farewell to the brothers,[8] *then* Priscilla and Aquila set sail for Syria with him. *Aquila*, because he was fulfilling a vow, had cut the hair of his head in Cencrae. 19. And they came into Ephesus, and *Paul* left them there, but he, when he went into the synagogue, reasoned with the Jewish people. 20. And when they asked him to remain for a

---

1   (v.6) This statement apparently was specific to the Corinthians, as the statement in Antioch (Acts 13:46) had pertained only to Antioch. See v. 19 of this chapter.

2   (v.7) He was a convert to Judaism.

3   (v.8) Immersed according to Jewish custom. See Baptize in Glossary.

4   (v.11) The word translated stayed literally means sat, other places translated dwelt or inhabited. This is a Hebrew idiom as in Psalm 22:3, which is literally, "enthroned on the praises of Israel" but the KJV has "inhabitest the praises of Israel."

5   (v.12) A fragmented stone found at Delphi has part of a letter from Emperor Claudius to "Gallio, my friend." Claudius reigned from 41-54 AD.

6   (v.13) Torah here refers at least to the first five books of the Bible, but probably also the entire Tanach (Old Testament) and all the oral teachings. See Torah in Glossary.

7   (v.17) It is not clear who "they" are, whether Jewish or Greek. Sosthenes could well be the person in 1Cor 1:1.

8   (v.18) From the Hebrew usage, this refers to both male and female believers.

longer time he did not consent, 21. but after he said farewell he also said, "I will return to you again, God willing," *and* he set sail from Ephesus. 22. And when he arrived in Caesarea, after he went up *to Jerusalem for Passover* and paid respects to the congregation,[1] he went down to Antioch. 23. And after he spent some time he left, going through one place after the other, in the Galatian region and Phrygia, strengthening all the disciples.

Apollos Preaches at Ephesus

18:24. And a certain Jewish man, named Apollos, a native of Alexandria, a learned man *who* was strong in the Scriptures, came to Ephesus. 25. He was teaching the Way of the Lord and being fervent in the spirit. He was speaking and teaching accurately the things about Jesus, although he knew only the baptism[2] of John: 26. and he began to speak boldly in the synagogue. And when they heard him Priscilla and Aquila took him aside and carefully explained the Way of God to him. 27. And when he desired to go to Achia, after the brothers encouraged *him* they wrote to the disciples to accept him, and when he arrived he helped many of those who, through grace, had believed: 28. for he was refuting vigorously with the Jewish people, publicly demonstrating by the Scriptures that Jesus was the Messiah.

Paul at Ephesus

19.1. And it happened while Apollos was in Corinth, after Paul went through the interior parts he went down to Ephesus and found some disciples, 2. and he asked them, "Did you take the Holy Spirit when you believed?" And they *said* to him, "But in fact we did not hear whether there is a Holy Spirit." 3. So he said, "Then in what *name* were you baptized?"[3] And they said, "In John's baptism." 4. Then Paul said, "John did baptize a baptism of repentance to the people, saying that they should believe in the One Who was coming after him, that is in Jesus." 5. And when they heard they were baptized in the name of the Lord Jesus, 6. and when Paul laid his hands upon them[4] the Holy Spirit came upon them, and they were speaking in tongues and they were prophesying. 7. And there were about twelve men.

19:8. And going into the synagogue he was speaking boldly for three months discussing and persuading the things about the kingdom of God. 9. But as some were hardening and disobeying, speaking evil *of* the Way in the presence of the throng, when he left from them he took the disciples,[5] discussing daily in

---

1   (v.22) Although often translated "church," no Greek word meaning church is used in the NT. See Congregation in Glossary.

2   (v.25) Baptism, immersion for purification, had been practiced by the Jewish people for over 1,000 years by this time. What Apollos was teaching was the call to repentance of John. See Baptize in Glossary.

3   (v.3) That is, immersed in water according to Jewish custom.

4   (v.6) The laying on of hands for baptism in the Holy Spirit comes from this. See Acts 8:17.

5   (v.9) This is the first split of a congregation recorded in the NT, justified in this case to

the yeshiva[1] of Turannus. 10. This went on for two years, so that all those who were living in Asia, both Jewish and Greek, heard the message of the Lord.

The Sons of Sceva

19:11. God was doing extraordinary miracles by the hands of Paul, 12. so that even face cloths or aprons were taken away from his skin *and placed* upon those who were sick and their diseases left from them, and the evil spirits departed. 13. And also some of the Jewish exorcists who were going around tried to speak the name of the Lord Jesus over the ones who had evil spirits saying, "I implore you by Jesus Whom Paul preaches." 14. And seven sons of a certain Sceva, a high priest of Judea, were doing this. 15. But when the evil spirit answered it said to them, "Indeed I know Jesus and I am acquainted with Paul, but yourselves, who are you?" 16. And the man in whom was the evil spirit, leaping upon them, was strong, overpowering all of them so that as they were wounded and nearly naked,[2] *they had* to flee away from that house. 17. And this became known to all, both Jewish and Greeks, who were living in Ephesus, and fear fell upon them all and the name of the Lord Jesus was being glorified. 18. And many of those who believed were coming, confessing and reporting their *evil* doings. 19. And many of those who had been practicing magic, after they brought their scrolls *of the magic* they were burning *them* before everyone, and they counted up the value of them and found *it* fifty thousand pieces of silver.[3] 20. In this manner the word of the Lord was increasing mightily and growing in strength.

The Riot at Ephesus

19:21. And as these things were finished, Paul resolved in his spirit to go through Macedonia and Achia, *then* to go to Jerusalem, saying that "After I am there, it is then necessary for me to see Rome." 22. And after he sent two of those who served him, Timothy and Erastus, to Macedonia he stayed a time in Asia.

19:23. And there was at that time a not small commotion concerning the Way. 24. For someone named Demetrius, a silversmith, was making no small profit for himself by making silver shrines of Artemis. 25. And when he gathered those with similar work, he said concerning such things as these, "Men, you must understand that our prosperity is from this business, 26. and you see and hear that not only in Ephesus but in nearly all Asia, this Paul, when he induced by his persuasion, caused a large crowd to change their minds, saying that those *gods* created by *human* hands are not gods *at all*. 27. And not only is this trade in danger of coming into disrepute, but also *the* temple of the great goddess Artemis, to be counted for nothing, and *Artemis*, who is worshipped in all Asia

---

bring people to a deeper walk with the Lord.
1   (v.9) Jewish talmudic college
2   (v.16) The Jewish people were modest and wore underclothes, loincloths, so they would not have been naked, although this is frequently translated as naked.
3   (v.19) About $10,000

and in the civilized world, is even going to suffer the loss of her magnificence."

19:28. And when they heard *this* then they were full of anger. They were crying out saying, "Great is Artemis of *the* Ephesians." 29. And the city was filled with confusion, and they rushed with one mind into the theater, seizing Gaius and Aristarchus of Macedonia, fellow travelers of Paul, by force. 30. And although Paul wanted to go into the mass of people, the disciples did not let him: 31. and then some of the consuls, *who* were friends with him, when they sent to him, *they* were urging *him* not to go into the theater. 32. Then indeed others were crying out something different: for the assembly was confused and did not know why they had gathered. 33. And they brought Alexander out of the crowd, because the Jewish people put him forward: and Alexander, who waved *his* hand, was wanting to defend himself to the crowd. 34. But when they perceived that he was Jewish, one voice came from all for about two hours crying out, "Great is Artemis of Ephesus." 35. And after the city clerk quieted the crowd he said, "Men of Ephesus, who in fact is there who does not know *that* the city of Ephesus is the temple keeper of the great Artemis, also fallen from Zeus? 36. Therefore these things are undeniable. It is proper, now that you have been quieted, to remain so, and in no way to act rashly. 37. For you brought these men, *who are* neither temple robbers nor blasphemers of our goddess. 38. Now then if Demetrius and those craftsmen with him have a ground of action against anyone, court days are in session and there are proconsuls, they could bring court charges against one another. 39. But if you want to know further, it will *have to* be decided in a legal gathering. 40. For we also run a risk of being accused of rebellion concerning this today, and there is no reason which we are able to give to account for this disorderly gathering." And having said these things he dismissed the gathering.

Paul's Journey to Macedonia and Greece

20.1. And after the disturbance was restrained Paul sent for the disciples and exhorted them, *then* after he wished them well he left to go to Macedonia. 2. Then, as he passed through those regions and encouraged them with much advice, he went to Greece, 3. and he stayed three months. After a plot was made against him by the Jewish *leaders* as he was about to sail to Syria, he was of a mind to return through Macedonia. 4. And Sopater, *son* of Purro, a Berean, and Aristarchus and Secundus of Thessalonica, and Gaius of Derbe and Timothy, and Asians Tychikos and Trophimus *all* accompanied him. 5. And these *men* who had gone before were waiting for us in Troas, 6. and we sailed away from Phillipi after the days of Unleavened Bread and after five days we went to them in Troas, where we stayed seven days.

Paul's Farewell Visit to Troas

20:7. And after sundown at the end of the Sabbath, *with a service called Havdalah,*[1] when we gathered to break bread, Paul was speaking with them

---

1   (v.7) The Havdalah service makes the transition from the holy Sabbath to the secular

because he was planning to go on a journey the next day, and he was prolonging the message until midnight. 8. And there were many lamps in the upper room in which we were gathered. 9. And while a certain youth named Eutuchus was sitting in the window, as he became overwhelmed by deep sleep while Paul was discoursing more and more, he fell down from the third story window and was taken away dead. 10. But when Paul went down he fell upon him and after embracing *him* said, "Do not be troubled for his life is in him." 11. And then he went up and broke bread and ate, talking for a long while until dawn, *and* then he left. 12. And they were leading the living child and they were greatly comforted.

The Voyage from Troas to Miletus

20:13. And, since we went on the boat before *Paul*, we set sail to Assos, intending to pick up Paul there: for having thus arranged he was going to travel by land. 14. And as he met us in Assos, after we took him aboard we came into Mitylene, 15. and having sailed from there, the next day we came opposite Chios, and the day after that we came into Samos, and the day after *that* we came into Miletus. 16. For Paul had decided to sail past Ephesus, so that he would not lose time in Asia: for if he hastened it would be possible for him to be in Jerusalem for Shavuot.[1]

Paul Speaks to the Ephesian Elders

20:17. And having sent from Miletus to Ephesus he summoned the elders of the congregation.[2] 18. And when they came to him, he said to them, "You understand, from the first day on which I set foot in Asia, how I was with you all the time, 19. serving the Lord in all humility and tears and trials that came upon me in the plots of the Jewish *leaders*, 20. as I was neither timid about bringing together nor to make known to you and to teach you publicly and from house to house, 21. declaring solemnly to both Jewish people and Greeks, repentance in God and faith in our Lord Jesus. 22. And now behold, I, bound in the spirit, am going to Jerusalem, not knowing what will happen to me *there*, 23. except that the Holy Spirit in city after city is bearing witness to me saying that imprisonment and affliction wait for me.[3] 24. But I do not in any way make life worth anything for myself, if only I finish my course and *my* service[4], which I took from the Lord Jesus, to solemnly proclaim the Good News of the grace of God.

20:25. "And now behold, I know that no longer will you all, among

---

work-a-day world. The service starts two hours after sundown on Saturday evening. The Greek text says "On the first day of the week," the Hebrew expression for Sunday, which starts at sundown on Saturday. See Havdalah in Glossary.

1   (v.16) Shavuot is the Feast of Weeks, called Pentecost in Greek.

2   (v.17) Although often translated "church," no Greek word meaning church is used in the NT. See Congregation in Glossary.

3   (v.23) Paul knew he was in for trouble, but God would bring him through. See Acts 21:7-14.

4   (v.24) Or ministry, see Servant in Glossary.

whom I have gone preaching the kingdom, see my face. 26. For this reason I am testifying to you this very day that I am clean from the blood of all *of you*: 27. for I did not shrink from disclosing every wish of God for you. 28. Be on guard for yourselves and for all the flock, in which the Holy Spirit has placed you *to be* guardians to shepherd the congregation of God, which He purchased with His own blood. 29. I know that savage wolves will enter among you with my departure, not sparing the flock, 30. and men will rise among you, saying perverted things to draw away the disciples after them. 31. On this account you must continually be alert, remembering that period of three years *when* I did not cease for one moment from warning *you* night and day with tears. 32. And now I entrust you to God and to the message of His grace, by which He is able to build *you* up and to give *you* the inheritance among all those who have been sanctified. 33. I have not desired silver or gold or garment: 34. you know that my hands served my needs and for those who were with me. 35. I have shown everything to you because it is necessary by working in this way to help the weak, and to remember the words of the Lord Jesus that He said, 'It is more blessed to give than to receive.'"[1]

20:36. And after he said these things, having knelt, he prayed with them all. 37. And there was great weeping by all and, embracing Paul's neck, they kissed him, 38. especially suffering pain on the word that he had spoken, that they were no longer going to see his face. Then they accompanied him to the boat.

Paul's Journey to Jerusalem

21.1. And so it was we put to sea, after we tore ourselves away from them. Having drawn a straight course we came to Cos, and the next day to Rhodes and from there to Patara. 2. Then having found a boat crossing over to Phoenicia we boarded *and* set sail. 3. And sighting Cyprus we sailed past it *on the* left then were sailing to Syria and went down to Tyre: for it was there the boat was unloading its cargo. 4. And after we searched out the disciples we stayed with them seven days. They were saying to Paul by the spirit not to go up to Jerusalem. 5. And when it happened *that* our time was up, when we came out, we, *even* all the wives and children escorting us for the journey, were going until *we were* outside the city, and, after we knelt on the beach, we prayed. 6. *Then* we parted from one another and embarked in the boat, and they returned to their own *homes*.

21:7. And we, completing the voyage from Tyre, reached Ptolmais and having greeted the brothers we stayed one day with them. 8. And the next day after we left we went into Caesarea and entered the house of Philip the evangelist, who was *one* of the seven *deacons* (Acts 6:5). We were staying with him. 9. And in this *household* there were four prophesying virgin daughters. 10. And while

---

1   (v.35) Could this be a reference to Mt 10:8, "You must continually heal sicknesses, raise the dead, cleanse lepers, cast out demons: you took freely, you must now give freely."

we were staying more days a certain prophet named Agabus (Ac 11:28) came down from Judea,[1] 11. and when he came to us he took Paul's belt, and after he bound his own feet and hands he said, "The Holy Spirit says these *things*, 'The man whose belt this is, the Jewish people in Jerusalem will bind *him* in this manner and will give him over into *the* hands of *the* heathens.'" 12. And as we heard these things, both we and those from Caesarea were begging him not to go up to Jerusalem. 13. Then Paul answered, "What are you doing, weeping and breaking my heart? For I am not only in readiness to be bound, but also to die in Jerusalem on behalf of the name of the Lord Jesus." (Acts 20:23) 14. And when he was not persuaded we fell silent saying, "The Lord's will must continually be done."

21:15. And after these days, having made preparation, we were going up to Jerusalem: 16. and also *some* of the disciples from Caesarea came with us, leading us to *the house of the one* with whom we would be staying, Mnason[2] of Cyprus, a leading disciple.

Paul Visits Jacob[3]

21:17. When we reached Jerusalem the brothers greeted us gladly. 18. The next day Paul went with us to Jacob, and all the elders were present. 19. And greeting them warmly he explained, point by point, what God had done among the heathens through his ministry. 20. And those listening praised God and said to him, "You see, brother, how many thousands of those who believe are among the Jewish people and all are zealous for the Torah: 21. and they were informed about you, that you teach apostasy from Moses to all *the* Jewish people among the heathens, telling them not to circumcise their children and not to walk in the customs *of our fathers*. 22. Therefore what is *to be done*? They will certainly hear that you have come. 23. So you must do this, which we are telling you: there are with us four men having a vow on themselves. 24. Taking them with *you,* you must now take it upon yourself to be purified with them and you must pay for them so that they will shave their heads, and all will know that what was reported about you is not *true* but that you are holding and guarding the Torah. 25. And concerning the believing heathens we wrote instructions to them *that* it seems good to keep themselves from that *meat* offered to idols and blood and strangled *animals* and immorality."[4] 26. Then the next day, Paul, having taken the men, *and* having been purified with them, was entering the temple giving notice of the completion of the days of purification until the offering *could be* offered for each one of them.

---

1   (v.11) Caesarea was the Roman capital of Judea, so how could you go down from Judea to Caesarea? This was an expression used only by rabbis. See Hebraisms in Glossary.

2   (v.16) This name is pronounced M'nason.

3   (Caption) The Greek text has Iakob, which is Jacob in English. See Jacob in Glossary.

4   (v.25) This must be immorality in the broadest sense, including the whole of Jewish Scripture regarding our relationships with one another. Paul's statements attest to this in Ro 9:29-31, 1Cor 5:9,10, Gal 5:19-21, Col 3:8,9, 1 Tim 1:8-11, and others. See Acts 15:20.

Paul Arrested in the Temple

21:27. And when the seven days were completed, as they were going *into the temple*, Jewish men from Asia, when they saw him in the temple, were stirring the whole crowd and they seized him 28. crying out, "Men of Israel, you must help: this is the man, the one who teaches everyone everywhere against our people and the Torah and this place, and what's more he even led Greeks into the temple and he has profaned this holy place." 29. For they had previously seen Trophimus the Ephesian in the city with him, whom they were supposing that Paul led into the temple. 30. And the whole city was aroused, and the people rushed together, then when they took hold of Paul they were dragging him outside the temple and the doors were immediately shut. 31. And while seeking to kill him a report went up to the commander[1] of the cohort that all Jerusalem was in an uproar. 32. He at once took soldiers and a centurion, ran down upon them, and when they saw the commander and the soldiers they stopped beating Paul. 33. Then when the commander came near, he arrested him and ordered *him* to be bound with two chains, *and* then he inquired who he might be and what had been done. 34. But others in the crowd were shouting different things, and since he was not able to know the truth because of the noise he ordered him to be led to the barracks. 35. And when they came to the steps, he was carried by the soldiers because of the violent pressing of the crowd, 36. for the multitude of the people was following, shouting, "You must take him *from among the living.*"

Paul Defends Himself

21:37. And Paul, about to be led into the barracks, said to the commander, "Is it permitted for me to say something to you?" And he said, "Do you know Greek? 38. Are you not the Egyptian who stirred up before these days then led out into the desert the four thousand men of the assassins?" 39. And Paul said, "I am indeed Jewish, a man *from* Tarsus of Cilicia, a citizen of a not insignificant city: and I ask you, you must permit me to speak to the people." 40. And when he allowed, Paul, having stood on the steps, motioned to the people with his hand. Then, when *the crowd* became very quiet, he was calling out in the Hebrew language saying, **22.**1. "Men, brothers and fathers, you must now listen to my defense before you." 2. And when they heard that he called to them in the Hebrew language, they showed even more silence. Then he said, 3. "I am a man, Jewish, born in Tarsus of Cilicia, but having been brought up in this city beside the feet of Gamaliel,[2] instructed according to the precision of our fathers' tradition, being zealous for God, just as you all are today: 4. who did persecute this Way until death, putting both men and women in chains and giving *them* over into jail, 5. in the same way also the High Priest and all the council of elders spoke well of me,

---

1   (v.31) The commander was at the headquarters of the garrison, just outside the north wall of the temple mount.

2   (v.3) This school is referred to in Acts 5:34. Teachings of Gamaliel are still quoted by Jewish scholars.

from whom I even took a letter to the brothers in Damascus *where* I was going, so after they were bound, I would lead those *of the Way* at that place to Jerusalem so that they could be punished."

Paul Tells of His Conversion

22:6. "And it happened to me while I was going and drawing near to Damascus, about noon, suddenly a great light from heaven shown about me, 7. and I fell to the ground and I heard a voice saying to me, 'Saul. Saul! Why are you persecuting Me?' 8. And I answered, 'Who are You, Lord?' And He said to me, 'I AM Jesus the Nazarene,[1] Whom you are persecuting,' 9. and those who were with me did indeed see the light but did not hear[2] the voice of the One Who spoke to me. 10. And I said, 'What should I do, Lord?' And the Lord said to me, 'You must get up *and* go immediately into Damascus and there it will be told to you concerning everything which has been assigned for you to do.' 11. And as I was not able to see on account of the glory of that light, then I was led by the hand by those who accompanied me, *and so* I came into Damascus.

22:12. And a certain Ananias, a devout man according to the Torah, well spoken of by all the Jewish people living there, 13. when he came to me and stood near he said to me, 'Saul, brother, you must immediately receive *your* sight.' And in that moment I received my sight *and looked* at him. 14. And he said, 'The God of our fathers has chosen you to know His will and to see the Righteous One and to hear a voice from His mouth, 15. because you will be a witness for Him to all mankind of what you have seen and heard. 16. And now what are you waiting for? After you call upon His name you must immediately get up to immerse[3] and to wash away your sins.'"

Paul Sent to the Pagans

22:17. "And it happened, when I returned to Jerusalem and while I was praying in the temple, I became entranced, *in a state of ecstasy*, 18. and saw Him saying to me, 'You must hurry and come out quickly from Jerusalem, because they will not accept your testimony about Me.' 19. And I said, 'Lord, they understand that throughout the synagogues I was imprisoning and beating those who believe in You, 20. and, when they were pouring out the blood of your witness Stephen, I was standing by and agreeing and guarding the prayer shawls of those who were killing him.' 21. And He said to me, 'You must be going, because I will send you out far away to *the* heathens.'"

Paul and the Roman Tribune

22:22. And they were listening to him up to this statement, then they were lifting their voices saying, "You must take such a one as this from the earth, for it is not fit for him to live." 23. Then since they were shouting and

---

1   (v.8) Nazarene is the English spelling of the Greek; Natsrati would be the Hebrew.
2   (v.9) Or understand
3   (v.16) Immerse for purification; see Baptize in Glossary.

throwing off *their* cloaks and throwing dust in the air, 24. the commander ordered *the soldiers* to lead him into the barracks, then he said to whip and torture him so that he would find out by this why he was charged as they were crying out to him. 25. And as they were stretching him with the straps, Paul said to the centurion who was standing by, "If a man is a Roman, then is it proper for you to whip *him* without a trial?" 26. And when the centurion heard this he went to the commander *and* reported, saying, "What are you going to do? For this man is a Roman." 27. And after the commander approached *Paul* he said to him, "You must tell me, are you a Roman?" And he said, "Indeed." 28. And the commander responded, "I acquired this citizenship for a large sum of money." And Paul said, "But in fact I was born *Roman*." 29. Then those who intended to give him a hearing *by torturing him,* immediately left him, and even the commander was afraid, recognizing that he was Roman and that he had placed him in chains.[1]

Paul before the Council

22:30. And the next day, since *the commander* wanted to know with certainty what he was accused of by the Jewish *leaders*, he loosed him and ordered *Paul* to accompany *him* to the high priests and all the Sanhedrin, and when he led Paul down he placed *him* before them. **23**.1. And Paul, as he fixed his eyes on the Sanhedrin, said, "Men, brothers, I have lived for God in all good conscience up to this very day." 2. Then the High Priest Ananias ordered those standing by him to strike his mouth. 3. Then Paul said to him, "God is going to strike you, whitewashed wall: and you would sit judging me according to the Torah and you order me to be struck, breaking the Torah?" 4. And those standing by said, "Do you revile the High Priest of God?" 5. And Paul said, "I did not know, brothers, that he was High Priest: for it has been written that 'You will not speak evil of leaders of your people.'" (Ex 22:28)

23:6. And since Paul knew that one part were Sadducees and the other *part* Pharisees he cried out in the Sanhedrin, "Men, brothers, I am a Pharisee, a son of Pharisees, I am myself judged concerning hope and resurrection[2] of *the* dead." 7. And after he said this there was strife with the Pharisees and Sadducees and the multitude was divided. 8. For the Sadducees on the one hand were saying there was not to be a resurrection, and neither an angel nor a spirit, but Pharisees on the other hand were declaring all three things. 9. And there was a great clamor, and when some of the scribes of the sect of the Pharisees got up, they contended sharply, saying, "We find nothing evil in this man: and *what* if a spirit or an angel spoke to him?" 10. And because there was much strife the commander, fearing that Paul would be torn apart by them, ordered the soldiers *who* went down to carry him off from their midst and to bring him into the barracks.

23:11. And the next night as the Lord stood by him He said, "Be cheerful:

---

1 (v.29) It was against Roman law to chain or whip a Roman citizen who had not been tried.
2 (v.6) See Resurrection in Glossary.

for as you solemnly declared the things about Me in Jerusalem, so it is also necessary for you to testify in Rome."

The Plot against Paul's Life

23:12. And when it became day, *some* Jewish people, as they made a plot, bound themselves with an oath saying they would neither eat nor drink until they could kill Paul. 13. And there were more than forty of these who had made this plot, 14. who, having gone to the high priests and the elders, said, "We have bound ourselves with an oath not to eat until we would kill Paul. 15. Therefore now you with the Sanhedrin must inform the commander at once so that he would bring him to you, as though *you are* intending to accurately determine the issues concerning him, and we will be prepared to kill him before he draws near." 16. But when the son of Paul's sister heard *of* the ambush, he went and entered the barracks, *and* told Paul. 17. So then Paul called one of the centurions *and* said, "You must take this young man to the commander, for he has something to report to him." 18. Now then the one who took him led *him* to the commander and said, "The prisoner Paul called me *and* asked *me* to bring this young man to you, because he has something to tell you." 19. Then the commander, having taken his hand and having withdrawn privately asked, "What is it you have to tell me?" 20. And he said, "Jewish *leaders* covenanted to ask you that tomorrow you would bring Paul as if they intended to accurately learn about him by questioning *him*. 21. Therefore do not be persuaded by them, for they will ambush him by their more than forty men, who have bound themselves with an oath to neither eat nor drink until they would have killed him, and now they are prepared, waiting for the promise from you." 22. Then indeed the commander sent the youth away ordering him "Do not speak out that you have made these things known to me."

Paul Sent to Felix the Governor

23:23. And then he summoned a certain two of the centurions *and* said, "Prepare two hundred soldiers and seventy horsemen and two hundred bowmen so they could go to Caesarea by the third hour of the night,[1] 24. to provide pack animals so that Paul, by being mounted, could be brought safely through to Felix the governor," 25. then he wrote a letter having this content: 26. "Claudius Lucias to the Most Excellent Governor Felix, greetings. 27. This man was seized by the Jewish people, and they were intending to kill him by themselves. I, *who* was standing by with the detachment, took him out when I learned that he was a Roman. 28. Wanting to understand the charge by which they were accusing him, I brought him to their Sanhedrin, 29. which I found was accusing him concerning issues of their Torah, and they did not have a charge worthy of death or imprisonment. 30. So when a plot against the man was revealed to me, I immediately sent *him* to you. Then I also ordered the accusers to tell you the things relating to him."

---

1   (v.23) 9:00 PM

23:31. Then indeed as they had been ordered, taking Paul up, the soldiers brought *him* during *the* night to Antipatris,[1] 32. and the next day they let the horsemen leave with him, *while the foot soldiers* returned to the barracks: 33. when they entered Caesarea and delivered the letter to the governor, they also presented Paul to him. 34. And after he read *the letter* and asked what province he was from, when he learned that *he was* from Cilicia, 35. "I will give you a hearing," he said, "when also your accusers would come:" then he ordered him to be guarded in the praetorium of Herod.

The Case against Paul

24.1. And after five days the High Priest Ananias went down with some elders and a certain orator Tertullus, who made a report to the governor concerning Paul. 2. Then after he was called, Tertullus began to accuse *Paul* saying, "Now we have gained much peace through you, and through your foresight reforms have come upon this nation, 3. and also with everyone everywhere we recognize *you*, most excellent Felix, with utmost gratitude. 4. But in order that I not weary you more, I beg you to hear us briefly in your graciousness. 5. For since we have found this man to be a pest, causing strife for all Jewish people throughout the civilized world by the sect of the Nazarites 6. who even tried to desecrate the temple but we seized him,[2] 8. from whom you yourself, after you investigate, will be able to learn about all these things of which we accuse him." 9. And the Jewish people then joined in the attack, alleging these things were so.

Paul Defends Himself before Felix

24:10. Then the governor signified by a nod for him to speak and Paul answered, "Because I know that you have been a judge in this nation for many years, I cheerfully speak these things in my defense, 11. because you are able to ascertain that it is not more than twelve days since I went up from *where* you are to Jerusalem to worship. 12. And they did not find me in the temple, either arguing with anyone, or stirring up among a crowd, or in the synagogues, or throughout the city, 13. and they are not able to prove to you about *these charges* of which they now accuse me. 14. But I confess this to you that regarding the Way, which they call a sect; this is how I worship God the Father, believing all these things according to the Torah and the things that were written in the Prophets,[3] 15. since I have hope in God, which *hope* they also accept, that there is to be a resurrection[4] of both righteous and unrighteous. (Dn 12:2) 16. And in this I always do my best to have a clear conscience before God and men. 17. And then I came, after several years, producing gifts for the poor and offerings for my

---

1   (v.31) Herod the Great built Antipatris on the site of the ancient city Aphek (Afeq on modern maps of Israel) and named it after his father, Antipater. Aphek is named several times in the Old Testament and was destroyed by Nebuchadnezzar in the 6th century BC.

2   (v.6) V. 7 is omitted because it was not in the earliest manuscripts.

3   (v.14) Torah and the Prophets here refers to the entire Jewish Bible. See both Prophets and Torah in Glossary.

4   (v.17) See Resurrection in Glossary.

nation, 18. because of which, after my rites of purification, they found me in the temple, not with a crowd and not with an uproar, 19. but *there were* some Jewish men from Asia, who ought to be present before you and to bring charges if they have anything against me. 20. Let those who *are present* say what wrong they found when I stood before the Sanhedrin, 21. unless *it is* this one statement which I cried out while I stood among them that '*It is* concerning resurrection from *the* dead that I am being judged before you on this day.'"

24:22. And then Felix adjourned, since he knew more accurately the things about the Way, saying, "When Lucias the commander comes down,[1] I shall decide the things against you:" 23. then he ordered the centurion to keep him under guard but to have freedom and not to hinder his own *visitors* from attending him.

Paul Held in Custody

24:24. And after some days when Felix came with his own wife Drusilla, who was Jewish, he sent for Paul and heard him concerning his faith in Messiah Jesus. 25. And when he was speaking about righteousness and self-control and the coming judgment, Felix then became afraid *and* answered, "For the present time, go, and I will call you when I find time," 26. at the same time also hoping that gifts will be given to him by Paul: on this account then he was conversing with him, sending for him often.

24:27. Then after two years passed Felix was succeeded by Porcius Festus, and since he desired to do a favor for the Jewish people, Felix left Paul in prison.

Paul Appeals to Caesar

25.1. Therefore three days after Festus arrived in the province, he went up to Jerusalem from Caesarea, 2. and the high priests and the leaders of the Jewish people informed *him* about Paul and were urging him 3. asking him a favor, that he would bring him to Jerusalem, while they were plotting to kill him along the way. 4. So then Festus answered that Paul was under guard in Caesarea, and he intended to go out quickly himself: 5. therefore "Those among you," he said, "who are able,[2] by going down with me, must accuse him if there is anything wrong with the man."

25:6. After staying not more than eight or ten days with them he went down to Caesarea, *and* the next day when he sat on the judicial bench he ordered Paul to be brought. 7. And when he was present, the Jewish people who had come down from Jerusalem stood around him making many and serious charges which they were not able to prove, 8. while Paul defended himself saying, "Neither in

---

1   (v.22) Lucias would come down from the 3,000-foot elevation of Jerusalem, south of Caesarea.
2   (v.4) In authority, qualified to go

the Torah[1] of the Jewish people nor in the temple nor in Caesarea was I sinning." 9. And Festus, wishing to grant a favor to the Jewish people, answering Paul said, "Do you want to go up to Jerusalem to be judged there by me concerning these things?" 10. But Paul said, "I am standing before Caesar's court, where it is necessary for me to be judged. I have done nothing wrong to the Jewish people, as even you very well know. 11. Then if indeed I am wrong and deserving of death I do not refuse to die: but if there is nothing to these accusations, no one is able to give me to them: I appeal to Caesar."[2] 12. Then Festus, after he consulted with the council, answered, "You have appealed to Caesar, you will go to Caesar."

Paul Brought before Agrippa and Bernice

25:13. And after several days passed, Agrippa the king and Bernice arrived in Caesarea greeting Festus. 14. And as they were remaining there more days, Festus referred the things regarding Paul to the king saying, "Some man is *here, who* has been left bound by Felix, 15. concerning whom, when I was in Jerusalem, the high priests and the elders of the Jewish nation made *these things* known, asking about a sentence of condemnation against him. 16. I answered them that it is not a custom of the Romans to hand over any man before the one who was accused might face his accusers *in* a place where he might defend himself concerning the charge. 17. Therefore when they came here *with me*, then I did not delay any longer sitting on the judicial bench, *and* the next day I ordered the man to be brought: 18. concerning whom, when the accusers stood, not one accusation they were revealing *was* of *the* evils I was expecting, 19. since they *only* had some questions about their own religion with him and concerning a certain Jesus *Who* had died, Whom Paul was alleging to live. 20. And I was at a loss concerning these charges. I asked if he might want to go to Jerusalem to be judged there concerning these things.[3] 21. But after Paul appealed to be kept under guard for the purpose of the decision of Augustus,[4] I called *for* him to be guarded until I could send him up to Caesar." 22. And Agrippa *said* to Festus, "I too have been wanting to hear this man." "Tomorrow," he said, "You will hear him."

25:23. Therefore the next day, when Agrippa and Bernice came with much pomp, and after they entered the hearing room with the commander and prominent men of the city, then Festus ordered *that* Paul should be led *in*. 24. And Festus said, "King Agrippa and all men present with us, you see this one

---

1   (v.8) Torah, meaning teaching, refers specifically to the first five books of the Bible, but can also refer to the entire Tanach (Old Testament) and even the oral teachings. See Torah in Glossary.
2   (v.11) This is to bring about his testimony in Rome, Acts 23:11.
3   (v.20) Why did Festus consider taking Paul to Jerusalem, to be judged again, when he had already determined that Paul had done nothing deserving of death? Apparently it was only to curry favor with the Jewish leaders, but it did serve God's plan. See Acts 19:21, 20:22,23.
4   (v.21) Augustus was a title and not a reference to Caesar Augustus who had died about 40 years earlier.

concerning whom all the multitude of the Jewish community in Jerusalem petitioned me, even calling out here *that* it is necessary for him not to live any longer. 25. But I understand he did nothing *that is* worthy of death, but because he appealed I decided to send *him to the* emperor. 26. Concerning which I have nothing firm to write to the sovereign, on which account I brought him before you *all* and especially to you, King Agrippa, so I would have something I could write of the coming investigation: 27. for sending a prisoner and not to indicate the charges against him seems unreasonable to me."

Paul Defends Himself before Agrippa

26.1. Then Agrippa said to Paul, "I am permitting you to speak about yourself." Then Paul, stretching out a hand, defended himself, 2. "Concerning everything which I am charged by *the* Jewish people, King Agrippa, I consider myself blessed going before you today to make a defense 3. especially your being expert of all the protocol and questions according to Jewish customs, and for which reason I ask *you* to hear me patiently. 4. Indeed then, all Jewish people have known my manner of life since, from *the* beginning of *my* youth, I was among my people and knew all the Jewish people in Jerusalem, 5. *who* have known me for a long time from the past, if they might want to testify, because I lived a Pharisee according to the most precise sect of our religion. 6. And now I stand being judged upon hope of the coming promise *made* to our fathers by God, 7. to which *promise* our twelve tribes hope to attain, serving earnestly night and day, concerning which hope, King, I am accused by *the* Jewish people. 8. Why is it judged unbelievable by you *all* if God raises *the* dead? 9. Indeed then I, myself, *once* considered *it* necessary to do many things against the name of Jesus of Nazareth, 10. and which I did in Jerusalem, and I even shut up many saints in prisons myself by taking authority from the high priests, and I cast a vote condemning them to death. 11. So throughout all the synagogues, often punishing them, I was compelling *them* to blaspheme, and raging at them exceedingly, I was pursuing *them* even to foreign cities."

Paul Tells of His Conversion

26:12. "For this purpose I went to Damascus with authority and a commission from the high priests. 13. Along the way at midday, King, *there was* a light from heaven more brilliant than the sun shining around me and those who were going with me. 14. And after all of us fell to the earth I heard a voice say to me in the Hebrew language, 'Saul. Saul! Why are you persecuting Me? *It is* hard for you to kick against *the* goads.'[1] 15. Then I said, 'Who are You, Lord?' And the Lord said, 'I AM Jesus, Whom you are persecuting. 16. But you must rise and stand upon your feet: for I have appeared to you for this, to appoint you a servant and a witness both of what you saw and of what I will show to you, 17. because I selected you from your people and from the heathens to whom I am

1   (v.14) Iron cattle prods

sending you 18. to open their eyes, to turn *them* back from darkness into light and from the authority of Satan[1] to God, to take them forgiveness of sins and a portion among those who have been consecrated by faith which *is* in Me.'"

Paul's Testimony to Jewish People and Pagans

26:19. "For which reason, King Agrippa, I have not been disobedient to the heavenly vision 20. but first to those in Damascus and then in Jerusalem, and in every region of Judea and to the heathens, bringing a call to repent and to turn back to God, doing works worthy of repentance.[2] 21. Because of all these things, when Jewish people *who* were in the temple seized me, they were trying to kill *me*. 22. Then obtaining help from God, until this day I have stood bearing testimony to both small and great, saying nothing except what the prophets and Moses were saying *is* going to happen. 23. If then Messiah suffered, if *He is* first from resurrection[3] of *the* dead, He is going to proclaim light to both the *Jewish* people and to the heathens."

Paul Appeals to Agrippa to Believe

26:24. And after he defended himself *by* these things, Festus said in a loud voice, "You are mad, Paul: your great learnings are turning you into madness." 25. And Paul said, "I am not mad, most excellent Festus, but I boldly speak out words of truth and rationality. 26. For the king, to whom I am speaking, even boldly, understands about these things for I can not bring myself to believe any of these things has escaped his notice: for this has not been carried on in a corner.[4] 27. King Agrippa, do you believe in the prophets? I know that you believe." 28. But Agrippa *said* to Paul, "*Do not think that* in a short time you are persuading me to declare Messiah."[5] 29. And Paul *answered*, "I would pray to God whether in a short time or in a long time, not only you but also all those hearing me today would become like such as I am except for this imprisonment."

26:30. And the king and the governor and Bernice and those who were sitting with them rose, 31. and after they withdrew, they were speaking to one another saying that, "This man is doing nothing deserving of death or prison." 32. And Agrippa said to Festus, "This man is able to be set free, except he has appealed to Caesar."

Paul Sails for Rome

27.1. As it was decided for us to set sail for Italy, they were then giving Paul and some other prisoners over to a centurion named Julius of Augustus'[6] Cohort. 2. After we went aboard *the* boat Adramutten, intending to sail in it

---

1   (v.18) See Satan in Glossary.
2   (v.20) The NIV has "..prove their repentance by their deeds." See Mitsvah in Glossary.
3   (v.23) See Resurrection in Glossary.
4   (v.26) Done in secret
5   (v.28) Become a Christian
6   (v.1) Augustus in this instance is a title referring to the Emperor, not the name of the Emperor. A cohort had about 600 men.

along the Asian districts, we set sail, Aristarchus of *the city of* Thessalonica, Macedonia, being with us. 3. And the next day we were brought into Sidon, and Julius, treating Paul benevolently, permitted *him* to go to friends to gain care. 4. And when we set sail from there we sailed under the lee of Cyprus because the winds were against *us*, 5. and having sailed the open sea along Cilicia and Pamphylia we came into Myra of Lycia. 6. And from there, when the centurion found an Alexandrine ship sailing to Italy he put us on it. 7. And after we sailed slowly for many days and had difficulty along Cnidus,[1] when the wind did not permit us to approach, we sailed to the leeward of Crete, along Salmone, 8. and sailing past it with difficulty we came into some place called Beautiful Harbor which city was near Lasea.

27:9. But after a long time passed and it was now really dangerous for the voyage, because even the Fast[2] had already gone by, Paul was urging, 10. saying to them, "Men, I see that the voyage is going to be with hardship and great damage, not only for the cargo and the ship, but also our lives." 11. But the centurion was persuaded by the steersman and the ship owner rather than by the things being said by Paul. 12. And then the harbor was not fit for wintering, *so* the majority decided to set sail from there, if at all possible they might be able after they arrived in Phoenix of Crete to winter *there with* a harbor facing from southeast to northeast.

The Storm at Sea

27:13. When the south wind blew gently, supposing they had attained *their* purpose, after they weighed anchor they were sailing past Crete. 14. But not long after, a northeast hurricane called Euraquilo buffeted against it. 15. And because the ship was being dragged away and not able to face the wind, giving over *to the wind*, we were being carried along. 16. And after we sailed under the lee of a little island called Cauda we were scarcely able to get control of the lifeboat, *putting it on deck, while it was normally towed.* 17. After they pulled it on board, for helps they were using *cables* under-girding the ship, and since they were fearful they would drift off course into the Surtis *sandbars*, then the sails and ropes were let down, so that *the winds and waves* were driving us along. 18. And since we were being violently tossed, the next *day* we were throwing the cargo overboard 19. and by the third day they were throwing out the ship's gear by their own hands. 20. And *with* neither sun nor stars showing for many days, while a not small storm was pressing upon us, it was taking away all remaining hope for us to be rescued.

27:21. And since many had gone without eating, Paul then stood in their midst and said, "Men, you ought to have followed my advice not to sail from Crete and to be spared this hardship and the loss. 22. And now I urge you to be

---

1   (v.7) Pronounced C'needus
2   (v.9) The Fast is Yom Kippur, the Day of Atonement, which would be sometime between mid September & mid October. See Yom Kippur in Glossary.

of good cheer: for there is to be no loss of life among you, except the ship *will be destroyed.* 23. For this night an angel from God, to Whom I belong and Whom I serve, stood beside me 24. saying, 'You must not be afraid, Paul, it is necessary for you to stand before Caesar, and behold God has granted to you all those who are sailing with you.' 25. For this reason, men, be of good cheer: for I trust in God that it will be just as it has been spoken to me. 26. And it is necessary for us to run aground on some island."

27:27. And as it was *the* fourteenth night while we were being driven in the Adriatic, during *the* middle of the night the sailors were supposing that we were approaching some dry land. 28. And taking soundings they found twenty fathoms,[1] then when they had gone a little further and again having taken soundings they found fifteen fathoms: 29. and being afraid we would run aground on some rocky place, after they threw four anchors from the stern they were wishing *for it* to become daylight. 30. But the sailors were seeking *a way* to flee from the ship and they were letting down the skiff into the sea in pretense as intending to stretch out anchors from *the* prow. 31. Paul said to the centurion and the soldiers, "If they would not remain on the boat, you will not be able to be rescued." 32. Then the soldiers cut the ropes of the skiff and they let it fall.

27:33. And at the time when it was about to become daylight, Paul was urging all to take food saying, "*It has been* fourteen days today you have been continuing, waiting without eating and having taken nothing. 34. On this account I urge you to take food: for this is the means for your salvation, for not one hair from your head will be lost." 35. And after he said these things he took bread and gave thanks to God in front of all and when he broke *the bread* he began to eat. 36. And then all became cheerful and they took food. 37. And we all were two hundred seventy-six lives on the ship. 38. And when they were filled with food they lightened the ship by throwing the wheat into the sea.

The Shipwreck

27:39. And when it was daylight, they did not know the country, but *they* noticed a certain bay, *which* had a beach on which they wanted to drive the boat, if they were able. 40. And when they removed the anchors, letting *them fall* into the sea, then at the same time they loosened the ropes of the rudder and raised the foresail to the blowing wind, heading toward the beach. 41. But then they struck a sandbar, running the ship aground and the prow having jammed fast, it remained unmoved, but the stern was being broken to pieces by the force of the waves. 42. And the intention of the soldiers was that they would kill the prisoners, *so* no one could escape by swimming away. 43. But the centurion, wanting to save Paul, prevented them from carrying out their plan, *and* he ordered those able to swim to go forth first, throwing themselves overboard to escape to the land, 44. then the rest *followed*, some indeed on a plank, and some on things from the ship. And so

---

1   (v.28) Twenty fathoms is 120 feet, fifteen fathoms is 90 feet.

it was all were saved on the shore.

Paul on the Island of Malta

28.1. And after we were saved we then understood that the island was called Malta. 2. And the natives were granting uncommon hospitality to us, for after they kindled a fire, they accepted us all because it had begun to rain and because of the cold that had set in. 3. And when Paul gathered some quantity of sticks and placed *them* upon the fire, a viper *that* came out from the heat seized his hand. 4. And when the natives saw the beast hanging from his hand, they were saying to one another, "Certainly this man is a murderer, whom, although he was saved from the sea, justice does not permit to live." 5. However, he just shook the beast into the fire and suffered nothing evil, 6. and they were expecting that he would become swollen from it, *and* then suddenly fall down dead. And yet many of them, expecting and watching, when nothing unusual *was* happening to him, they changed *their minds and* were saying he was a god. 7. And among the *farms* around that place was land of the chief of the island, named Poplio, who, having welcomed us *into his home*, showed us hospitality in a friendly manner for three days. 8. And it happened that the father of Poplio was suffering, lying down from a fever and dysentery, for whom Paul, when he came and prayed, laid hands on him *and* healed him. 9. And after this happened the rest *of the people* of the island, those who were sick, were coming to *him* and being healed, 10. and they were rewarding us with much honor and when we put to sea they gave us the things we needed.

Paul Arrives at Rome

28:11. And after three months, we set sail in a ship that wintered on the island, Alexandrine, marked with an image of Dioskuri.[1] 12. And when we put into Syracuse we stayed three days. 13. Going on from there we came into Rhegium. And after one day a south wind came up, *then* on the second *day* we came into Puteoli, 14. where we then found brothers *and* we were encouraged by them to stay seven days:[2] and thus we came into Rome. 15. And when the brothers[3] from there heard things about us they came to a meeting with us *from* as far as Appii Forum[4] and Three Taverns.[5] When Paul saw them he gave thanks to God, *and* took courage.

28:16. When we came into Rome, it was allowed for Paul to stay by

---

1 (v.11) The Dioskuri are Castor and Pollux, twin sons of Zeus and Leda.
2 (v.14) What kind of a prisoner was Paul? Could he delay the ship's departure? Verses 16 and 30 tell of his being in a rented house, with one soldier to guard him. We know he had friends with him, which would certainly be a strange privilege for a prisoner today. While Roman citizens did have privileges, for instance they could not be beaten or placed in chains until they had been tried and convicted, Paul seems to have had extraordinary privileges.
3 (v.15) These were apparently some of those to whom Paul had written the book of Romans.
4 (v.15) Forty-three miles away
5 (v.15) Thirty-three miles away

himself with the soldier guarding him.

Paul Preaches in Rome

28:17. And it happened after three days he summoned those who were leaders of the Jewish people:[1] then when they gathered he was saying to them, "Men, brothers, although I have done nothing against the people or to the customs of our forefathers, I was given over, bound, from Jerusalem into the hands of the Romans, 18. who, after they examined me, wanted to release *me* because there was no reason at all for my death. 19. And when the Jewish *leaders* spoke against *release* I was compelled to appeal to Caesar, not as I have anything to accuse against my people. 20. Because of this, therefore, the reason I summoned you, to see and to speak *to you*, truly, *is that* it is for the sake of the Hope of Israel I am kept a prisoner." 21. And they said to him, "We did not receive letters about you from Judea nor has any of the brothers reported or spoken any evil concerning you. 22. And we desire to hear what you think, for indeed all that is known to us about this faction *is* that it is spoken against everywhere."

28:23. And when they appointed a day for him, *even* more came to him in the lodging place, to whom he explained *things*, declaring the kingdom of God, from morning until evening, solemnly and emphatically, and persuading them about Jesus from both the Torah of Moses and the Prophets.[2] 24. And *some* were indeed persuaded by the teachings, but others were not believing: 25. and being at variance with one another, they were leaving when Paul was saying one *last* statement, "Just as the Holy Spirit spoke to your fathers through Isaiah the prophet 26. saying,

'You must go to this people and you must say,
Listening you will hear and you would **not** understand
    and seeing you will see and you would **not** perceive:
27.   for the heart of this people has become dull
    and they heard with their ears with difficulty
        and they closed their eyes:
           so that they would not ever see with their eyes
    nor would they hear with their ears
nor would they understand with their heart and return,[3]
    so I could heal them.' (Is 6:9,10)

---

1   (v.17) Paul arrived in Rome some time after writing the letter to the Romans, but that letter was not written to Jewish people. It is interesting that Paul summoned Jewish leaders rather than the non-Jewish people to whom he had written.

2   (v.23) Torah, meaning teaching, refers to the first five books of the Bible, while the Prophets refers to Jsh, Jd, 1 & 2 Sam, 1 & 2Ki, Is through Mal, except for Dn. See both Prophets and Torah in Glossary.

3   (v.27) Repent

28. Therefore let it be known to you that He has sent this salvation of God to the heathens: and they will listen."[1]

28:30. And he remained two whole years in his own rented house and was welcoming all those who were going in to him, 31. proclaiming the kingdom of God and teaching the things concerning the Lord Jesus Messiah with all boldness and without hindrance.

---

1   (v.28) V. 29 is omitted because it was not in the earliest manuscripts.

~ ROMANS[1] ~

Salutation

1.1. Paul, a servant[2] of Messiah Jesus, a called apostle, *who* has been set apart to preach *the* Good News of God. 2. This was the promise from the beginning through His prophets in Holy Scripture 3. concerning His Son, the One Who was from a seed of David with regard to *the* flesh, 4. the designated Son of God, in power, according to a spirit of holiness by resurrection[3] of *the* dead, Jesus Messiah our Lord, 5. through Whom we took grace and apostleship in obedience of faith to all the nations for the sake of His name, 6. among whom you too are called by Jesus Messiah, 7. to all the beloved of God who are in Rome, called saints, grace and peace to you from God our Father and Lord Jesus Messiah.

Paul's Desire to Visit Rome

1:8. First, I indeed give thanks to my God through Jesus Messiah concerning you all because your faith is being proclaimed to the whole world. 9. For God is my witness, Whom I serve by my spirit in the Good News of His Son, in the same manner as I am constantly making remembrance of you 10. always in my prayers, asking if somehow now at last I shall be so blessed in the will of God as to come to you. 11. For I long to see you, so that I could share some spiritual gift (ICor 12:6-11) with you to strengthen you, 12. and this is to be encouraged together among you for one another through your faith and also mine. 13. But I do not want you to be ignorant, brothers, because I frequently purposed to come to you,[4] but thus far I have been hindered until now, so that I would have some fruit then among you also just as among the rest of the heathens. 14. And I am a debtor to both Greeks and foreigners, and both wise and foolish, 15. thus I am eager to proclaim the Good News to you and to *all* those in Rome.

---

1   (Title) Written about 57 AD, several years after Thessalonians, and at least two years after Corinthians. Written to former heathens although this was during the first five years of Nero's reign when Jewish people were allowed back in Rome. (See Ro 16:3).

2   (v.1) Or slave, see Servant in Glossary.

3   (v.4) See Resurrection in Glossary.

4   (v.13) Apparently these were not the Jewish leaders he summoned in Acts 28:15, because the message of this letter is primarily to non-Jewish believers.

The Power of the Gospel

1:16. For I am not ashamed of the Gospel, because it is *the* power of God for salvation for everyone who believes, Jewish first and then Greek.[1] 17. For *the* righteousness of God is revealed in this, *coming* out of faith for *greater* faith, just as it has been written, "And the righteous will live by faith." (Hab 2:4)

The Guilt of Mankind

1:18. For *the* wrath of God is revealed from heaven against everything godless and unrighteous of men, of those who hold back the truth by *their* wickedness. 19. For what is known of God is evident among them: for God revealed *Himself* to them. 20. For the unseen things, both His eternal power and divine authority, from His creation of *the* world, are seen clearly, being understood by His works. so they are without excuse. 21. Because, although they knew God, they did not glorify *Him* as God or give thanks, but their thoughts became directed to worthless things and their foolish hearts *and minds* became covered in darkness. 22. Although they claim to be wise they were made foolish 23. and they transformed the glory of the incorruptible God into a likeness of an image of a corruptible man and of birds and four-footed beasts and reptiles.

1:24. For this reason God gave them over in the lusts of their hearts into uncleanness, their bodies to suffer disgrace among themselves: 25. who exchanged the truth of God for the false and worshipped and served the created thing contrary to the Creator, Who is blessed forever, amen. 26. Because of this God gave them over into vile passion of disgrace, and indeed their females exchanged the natural function for that contrary to nature, 27. and likewise also the males who neglected the natural function with the females. They were inflamed in their lustful passion with one another, males performing the unseemly deed with males and receiving the reward which was necessary for their deceit in repayment for their *sin*. 28. And since they did not see fit to have true knowledge of God, God gave them over into an unrighteous mind, to do the shameful things, 29. since they were filled with every unrighteousness, wickedness, avarice, desire to injure, full of envy, murder, contention, deceit, evil habits, whisperers, 30. slanderers,[2] God-haters, insolent, arrogant, braggart, contriving evil, refusing to obey parents, 31. without understanding, covenant breaking, without natural affection, without mercy: 32. who, although they know the ordinances of God thoroughly, because they are practicing such things as these that are worthy of death, not only are they doing them but they are also applauding *others* who do *them*.

---

1   (v.16) Did Paul think the Gospel had more power for a Jewish believer than for a former heathen? Why does he write "Jewish first?" It could be because of the advantage Jewish people had from learning the Jewish Scriptures at a very early age, starting with Leviticus at three to five years old. See Memorization in Glossary. See Ro 2:9, 10.

2   (v.30) See Gossip/Slander in Glossary.

The Righteous Judgment of God

2.1. On this account you are without excuse, O Man, everyone who judges: for by what you are judging the other, you are condemning yourself. For you, the one who judges, are doing the same things. 2. But we know that the judgment of God is according to truth upon those who perpetrate things such as these. 3. And do you take this into account, O Man, the one who judges those who practice such things as these and does them, that you will *not* escape from the judgment of God? 4. Do you despise the riches of His kindness and His forbearance and His patience, being ignorant that the kindness of God leads you into repentance? 5. According to your hardness and *your* unrepentant heart you are storing up for yourself[1] wrath on *the* Day of wrath and *the* revelation of God's righteous judgment 6. Who will reward each according to his works:[2] 7. on the one hand according to *the* steadfast endurance of good work, glory and honor and immortality to those who seek eternal life, 8. but on the other hand to those who are persuaded out of a desire to put themselves forward, and not allowing *themselves* to be persuaded in the truth, then *they will be* in the wrath and fury for *their* unrighteousness. 9. Trouble and affliction upon every person's life, the one who performs evil, and first for a Jewish person,[3] then a Greek: 10. but glory and honor and peace to everyone who does what is good, and first for a Jewish person,[4] then a Greek: 11. for there is no partiality before God. (Dt 10:17) 12. For however many sin without Torah,[5] will also perish without Torah, and however many who sin in Torah, will be judged through Torah: 13. for *it is* not the hearers of Torah *who are* righteous before God, but those who do *the commandments* of Torah will be declared righteous.[6] (Jas 2:14-26) 14. For when heathens, the ones who do not have Torah, would, guided by their natural sense of what is right and proper, do the things of Torah, these who do not have Torah are a Torah to themselves: 15. those who demonstrate *that* the work of the Torah *is* written in their hearts, when their conscience, accusing or even excusing, bears witness *with them* and between one another, as their thoughts *will be* 16. in *the* Day when God judges the hidden things of people through Messiah Jesus according to my gospel.[7]

---

1   (v.5) Every "you" so far in this chapter is singular.
2   (v.6) Mitsvot. See Mitsvah in Glossary.
3   (v.9) This is a reference to the responsibility once someone has been taught Scripture. Jewish children were taught Scripture from three to five years old on up, beginning with Leviticus. See Memorization in Glossary.
4   (v.10) This indicates that those who have studied Scripture longer have greater benefit, God's presence and peace. The more mature believer should have a greater measure of God's gifts, especially peace.
5   (v.12) Torah, which means teaching or instruction, refers specifically to the first five books of the Bible, but can also refer to the entire Jewish Bible and sometimes even the oral teachings. See both Prophets and Torah in Glossary.
6   (v.13) Righteousness is action. It is doing for others, even though we are made righteous by faith. See Righteousness in Glossary.
7   (v.16) This is the gospel the apostles from the congregation in Jerusalem were teaching, not the false apostles.

The Jewish People and the Torah[1]

2:17. But if you would call yourself Jewish and would cause yourself to rest[2] upon Torah and to take pride in God 18. then you know His will and since you are instructed in the Torah, you are testing the things that differ, *holy and profane,*[3] 19. and you have persuaded yourself to be a guide of *the* blind, a light for those in darkness, 20. an instructor of *the* foolish, a teacher of infants, since you have the essence of the knowledge and of the truth in the Torah: 21. then, *why* do you, the one who teaches another, not teach yourself? The one who preaches not to steal, are you stealing? 22. The one who says not to commit adultery, do you commit adultery? The one who detests idols, do you rob temples? 23. You who boast in Torah, you are dishonoring God by violating the Torah: 24. for just as it has been written, "The name of God is being blasphemed among the heathens because of you." (Is 52:5, Ez 36:20) 25. For what does it profit if on the one hand you would practice Torah in circumcision: if on the other hand you would be breaking Torah. Your circumcision has become uncircumcision. 26. Therefore if the uncircumcised one would keep the things established in Torah, will not his uncircumcision be credited to his account as circumcision? 27. And the physically uncircumcised,[4] *who* are keeping the Torah will condemn you, although *you have* Scripture and circumcision, *you are* a violator of Torah. 28. For the Jewish person is not the one to be plainly recognized *by what he wears, his prayer shawl or Kippah,* and neither *is* circumcision *just* openly in the flesh, 29. but one *is* Jewish inwardly, and circumcised in *his* heart (Dt 10:16, Jr 4:4; 9:25) in spirit not letter, whose praise *is* not from people but from God.

3.1. Therefore what *is* the superiority of the Jewish person or the advantage of circumcision? 2. Much in every way; because indeed they were entrusted first with the words[5] of God. 3. So what if some failed to believe? Will their unbelief cancel the faithfulness of God?[6] 4. May it not be! But God must be true, even *if* every man *is* a liar (Ps 116:11), just as it has been written,

> "So that you would be declared righteous by your words
> and you will be victorious when you are being judged."
> (Ps 51:4, Mt 12:37)

---

1 (Caption) Torah, meaning teaching or instruction, refers primarily to the first five books of the Bible, but here it also means the entire Tanach (Old Testament) plus the oral teachings. See both Prophets and Torah in Glossary.

2 (v.17) The word, epanapauomai, used for rest means to lean upon, to trust in something, in this case in the Word of God. In the NT used only here and in Lk 10:6.

3 (v.18) The things that differ are the holy and profane, from an indictment of the priests in Eze 22:26. Each one of us is a priest – we are a kingdom of priests. (Ex 19:6, 1Pe 2:9, Re 1:6, 5:10) The things that differ are defined in Lv 10:9-11.

4 (v.27) The Talmud teaches that non-Jews are subject to the covenant with Noah. Noah's covenant has seven laws: Promote justice, prohibitions of idolatry, immorality, blasphemy, murder, cruelty to animals, and theft. Noah's covenant does not include circumcision. See Dt 10:16, 30:6, Jr 4:4; 9:25, and Eze 44:7 for circumcision of the heart.

5 (v.2) This Greek word, logion, frequently translated oracles, refers to the spoken word of God's promises to the Jewish people; that is, all that God spoke to Moses at Mount Sinai.

6 (v.3) The Greek construction anticipates a negative reply.

5. But if our unrighteousness brings out the righteousness of God, what shall we say? Is God, the One Who inflicts the wrath, unrighteous? I am speaking according to man. 6. God forbid! For otherwise how *could* God judge the world? 7. But *someone says,* "If by my falsehood the truth of God overflows to His glory, why am I still being judged as a sinner?" 8. And just as we are maligned and just as some declare that we say that "Should we do evil, so that the good things could come?" For whom the sentence is just. 9. What then? Are we protecting ourselves? Are we making excuses? By all means no! For we accuse ourselves beforehand, all, both Jewish and Greeks are under sin, 10, just as it has been written that

> "There is not even one righteous person," (Ps 14:3)

11.   "there is no one who has gained insight,
           there is not one seeking God." (Ps 14:2)

12.   "All turned aside together, *and* became depraved:
         there is not one doing goodness,
           there is not even one." (Ecc 7:20)

13.   "Their throat is as a grave which has been opened,
         they were deceiving with their tongues," (Ps 5:9)
  "there is poison of asps under their lips:" (Ps 140:3)

14.   "whose mouth is full of bitterness and a curse," (Ps 10:7)

15.   "Their feet *are* swift to pour out blood,

16.   destruction and misery *are* in their ways,

17.   and they did not know a way of peace." (Is 59:7,8)

18.   "There is no fear of God before their eyes." (Ps 36:1)[1]

19. But we know that what the Torah[2] speaks it says to those in the Torah, so that every mouth should be closed and the entire world would become liable to judgment by God: 20. because no flesh will be justified before Him by works of Torah, for knowledge of sin *is* through Torah.

Righteousness through Faith

3:21. But now without Torah *the* righteousness of God has been revealed in being witnessed by the Torah and the Prophets,[3] 22. and *the* righteousness of God *is* through faith, for all those who believe[4] in Jesus Messiah. For there is no distinction, 23. for all have sinned and come short of the glory of God (1Ki 8:46) 24. being made righteous freely by His grace[5] through the redemption that *is* by means of Messiah Jesus: 25. & 26. Whom God put forth *as* a propitiation through

1   (v.18) This string of quotes shows that Paul had indeed memorized Scripture, as had all the apostles as well as many other Jewish people. See Memorization in Glossary.
2   (v.19) Torah, meaning teaching or instruction, here refers to the Tanach, the Jewish Bible. See Torah in Glossary.
3   (v.21) The Prophets are Jsh, Jd, 1 & 2 Sam, 1 & 2Ki, Is through Mal, but not the Book of Dn. See both Prophets and Torah in Glossary.
4   (v.22) Paul's Jewish understanding of "believe" required action, a change in behavior.
5   (v.24) This is not a contradiction of Ro 2:13. We are made righteous by grace and by faith, but righteousness is action. Righteousness is doing right, being just.

faith by His blood in proof of His righteousness,[1] in God's forbearance, because He had not punished the former sins before the evidence of His righteousness up to the present time. For He is righteous, even making righteous the one who has faith[2] in Jesus.

3:27. Where therefore *is* the boasting? It has been shut out. Through what sort of Torah? Works? No, but through Torah by faith. 28. For we consider a man to be made righteous by faith without works of Torah. 29. Or *is* He God only of Jewish people? And not also of heathens? Indeed also of heathens, 30. since God is One, He will make righteous *the one* circumcised by his faith, and *the one* uncircumcised through his faith.[3] 31. Therefore do we cancel Torah through faith? God forbid! But we cause Torah to stand.

The Example of Abraham

4.1. What therefore shall we say our forefather Abraham found according to flesh? 2. For if Abraham was made righteous by works, he had something to boast about, but not before God. 3. For what does the Scripture say? "And Abraham believed God and it was counted to him as righteousness." (Gn 15:6) 4. But the reward for the one who works is not counted according to grace but according to debt, *what is owed to him*. 5. To the one who does not work but believes in the One Who makes the impious righteous, his faith is counted into righteousness: 6. just as also David said of the blessedness of the man whom God counted righteous without works,

7.   "Blessed *are* the lawless ones who *have been* forgiven
               and whose sins would be covered:
8.   blessed *is* a man for whom *the* Lord would **not** count sin." (Ps 32:1,2)

9. Therefore *is* this blessing upon the circumcised or also the uncircumcised? For we say, "Faith was counted to Abraham as righteousness." (Gn 15:6) 10. Then how was *his faith* counted? In being circumcised or in being uncircumcised? Not in circumcision but in uncircumcision: 11. then, *later*, he took *the* sign of circumcision (Gn 17:10) *as* a seal of the righteousness of *the* faith while *he was still* uncircumcised, *so he could* be a father of all those who believe, though not circumcised, to be counted also with them, the righteous, 12. and father of circumcision not only to those from circumcision but *the* uncircumcised also proceed with them by faith in the footsteps of Abraham our father.

The Promise Realized through Faith

4:13. For the promise, *that* he was the inheritor of *the* world, *was* not through legalism to Abraham or his seed, but through righteousness by faith. 14. For if the heirs *were* from legalism, faith has been made empty and the promise

---

1   (v.25, v.26) God patiently let pass the sins committed prior to Jesus' atoning death.
2   (v.26) To Paul and the other Jewish people, faith must be accompanied by new behavior.
3   (v.30) See 1Cor 7:17-24.

has been destroyed: 15. for legalism produces wrath: but where there is no law, then neither is there transgression. 16. Because of this *it is* by faith, so that through grace the promise is certain for every seed, not only for the one from the Torah but also by faith to Abraham, who is father of us all, 17. just as it has been written that "I have appointed you a father of many nations," (Gn 17:5) before which he believed God, the One Who brings the dead to life (Is 26:19) and calls those things that are not as though they are[1] *and they come into being.* (Is 48:3) 18. Who by hope upon hope, *when the situation appeared to be hopeless,* did *still* believe in it, he became "father of many nations" according to what was said, "So will your seed be," (Gn 15:5) 19. And by faith he considered his own body not weak now, although it was as good as dead, being then about one hundred years old, and *considering* the deadness of Sarah's womb: 20. but because of the promise of God he did not waver in unbelief, but he was strengthened in faith, when he gave glory to God 21. and because he was fully convinced that what He has promised He is also able to do. 22. And for this reason "it was counted to him as righteousness." (Gn 15:6) 23. But it was not written that it was counted to him for his sake only 24. but also for us, to whom it is going to be counted, who believe in the raising from *the* dead of Jesus our Lord, 25. Who was given over because of our sins and raised because of our *need for* righteousness.

Results of Justification[2]

5.1. Therefore, since we have been made righteous by faith, we have peace with God through our Lord Jesus Messiah 2. also through Whom we have had access by faith into this grace in which we stand and we boast in hope of the glory of God. 3. And not only *that*, but we also boast in the afflictions, knowing that affliction brings about perseverance, 4. and patient endurance *brings* tried character, and character *brings* hope. 5. And hope does not disappoint, because the love of God has been poured out in our hearts through *the* Holy Spirit which has been given to us. 6. For, although we are weak, yet Messiah died in *the appointed* time on behalf of *the* ungodly. 7. For very rarely will someone face death on behalf of *the* righteous: for possibly someone also would dare to die on behalf of a good person: 8. but God demonstrates His love for us Himself, because, although we were still sinners, Messiah died on our behalf. 9. Then much more now, because we have been made righteous by His blood, we shall be saved by Him from the wrath. 10. For if while we were enemies *of God* we were reconciled to God through the death of His Son, we shall be saved all the more, since we have been reconciled by means of His life: 11. and not only *that*, but we also rejoice in God through our Lord Jesus Messiah through Whom we took the reconciliation in our time.

---

1   (v.17) See Psalm 57:5-12 to see how David handled a potentially depressing situation.

2   (Caption) Justification means to be declared just or right by what you do. The verb 'to justify' is from the Latin, 'just + faoere (to make)' which is the translation of the Greek 'dikaio.' We are justified, declared righteous by faith, but our actions, not our beliefs, confirm the fact. See Righteousness in Glossary.

Adam and Messiah

5:12. Because of this, just as sin came into the world through one man and death through sin, and thus death passed through all mankind, on account of which all sinned: 13. for until Torah[1] sin was in *the* world, but sin was not being counted, there not being a Torah, 14. and death reigned from Adam until Moses even upon those who have not sinned in the likeness of the transgression of Adam, who is a type of the One Who is coming.

5:15. But the gift is not like the sin: for if many died in the sin of the one, how much more the grace of God and the gift to the many did abound in the grace of the one Man, Jesus Messiah. 16. And the gift *was* not like *that* through *the* one *who* sinned, *Adam*: for indeed judgment in condemnation *was* by means of one *man*, but the gift *brought us* from many misdeeds into righteousness. 17. For if death reigned by the one transgression of the one *man*, how much more those who take the abundance of the grace and the gift of righteousness will reign in life through the One, Jesus Messiah. 18. So then just as through one transgression with respect to all men; *they were* in condemnation, so also through one righteous act, righteousness of life *became available* for all mankind: 19. for just as through the disobedience of the one man the many were declared sinners, in this manner also, through the obedience of the One, the many will be declared righteous. 20. But legalism slipped in,[2] so that transgression would increase: but where sin did abound, grace did super abound, 21. so that just as sin reigned in death, so also grace would reign through righteousness into eternal life through Jesus Messiah our Lord.

Dead to Sin but Alive in Messiah

6.1. Then what shall we say? Shall we remain in sin, so that grace would abound? 2. God forbid! We who died to sin, how shall we still live in it? 3. Or are you ignorant that, we, as many as were baptized[3] in Messiah Jesus, were baptized into His death?[4] 4. Therefore we were buried with Him through immersion into death, so that just as Messiah was raised from *the* dead through the glory of the Father, so also we could walk in newness of life. 5. For if we have become joined together in the likeness of His death, then we shall also be *united with the likeness* of His resurrection:[5] 6. knowing this, that our old *unregenerate* man was

---

1   (v.13) Torah, meaning teaching or instruction, refers specifically to the first five books of the Bible, but can also refer to the entire Bible and even all the oral teaching. See Torah in Glossary.

2   (v.20) This verb means to sneak in or slip in, as experience shows that legalism comes from good motivation, an attempt to define Scripture so all believers agree and understand. See Legalism in Glossary.

3   (v.3) Baptize comes from the Greek word baptidzo, which means immerse. See Baptize in Glossary for this and the next note.

4   (v.3) Jewish baptism by someone calls for the one baptizing to hold under water the head of the one being baptized, to represent dying to self, then in the struggle to rise the one coming out of the water parallels an infant coming out of the amniotic fluid at birth.

5   (v.5) See Resurrection in Glossary.

crucified together *with Him*, so that the body of sin would be condemned, and we are no longer serving sin: 7. for the One Who died has been made righteous apart from sin. 8. Then if we died with Messiah, we are believing that we will also live with Him, 9. because we know that Messiah, Who has been raised out from *the* dead, no longer dies, death no longer rules over Him. 10. Truly therefore He died, He died once for all in sin: but Who lives, lives for God.[1] 11. And in the same way count yourselves to be dead indeed to sin, but living for God in Messiah Jesus.

6:12. Therefore sin must not reign in your mortal body to obey its lustful desires, 13. and you must stop presenting your bodily members to sin as instruments of unrighteousness, but you must immediately present yourselves to God as living, *raised* out from *the* dead, and your members as instruments of righteousness to God. 14. For sin will not rule you: for you are not under legalism but grace.

Slaves of Righteousness

6:15. Then what? Should we sin, because we are not under legalism but under grace? May it not be! 16. Do you not know that you are slaves to whom you submit? *You are* in submission to whom you present yourselves as servants, either to sin, *which leads* into death, or to righteousness. 17. But thanks *be* to God because you were slaves of sin but you obeyed from *your* hearts for which you would be given over a *new* image from *the* teaching, which embodies the sum and substance of *your beliefs*, 18. and since you have been set free from sin you must now be enslaved to righteousness. 19. I am speaking in human terms because of the weakness of your flesh. For just as you would *formerly* present your members *as* slaves to the unclean and without Torah into lawlessness, so now you must present your members to righteousness *as* slaves in holiness. 20. For while you were slaves of sin, you were free with reference to righteousness. 21. Therefore what fruit were you then bearing? Over which you are now ashamed, for the end of those *is* death. 22. But now since you have been set free from sin, and because you are servants of God, you have your fruit into sanctification, and the end *is* eternal life. 23. For the wages of sin *is* death, but the gift of God *is* eternal life in Messiah Jesus our Lord.

An Analogy from Marriage

7.1. Or are you ignorant, brothers, the fact is I am speaking for *those* who know Torah,[2] that the Torah rules the man for as long a time *as* he would live? 2. For the married woman is bound to the living husband by Torah: but if the husband would die, she is released from her husband by the Torah. 3. Consequently then while the husband is living will she not be called an adulteress if she would become *a wife* to another husband: but if her husband would die,

---

1   (v.6) The repetition of the verbs "die" and "live" emphasize His death and resurrection.

2   (v.1) Torah, meaning teaching or instruction, refers to the first five books of the Bible, but can also refer to the whole Bible and the oral teachings. See Torah in Glossary.

she is set free by the Torah, she is not an adulteress when she becomes *a wife* to another husband. 4. So then, my brothers, you also died to legalism through the body of the Messiah, *now* you belong to another, to the One Who has been raised from *the* dead, so that we would bear fruit for God. 5. For when we were in the flesh, the passions of the sins, those through legalism, were working in our members so that we would bear fruit in death: 6. but now we have been released from legalism, since we died to that by which we were bound, so that we serve in newness of spirit and not in oldness of letter.[1]

The Problem of Indwelling Sin

7:7. Then what shall we say? *Is* the Torah sin? God forbid! But I did not know sin except through Torah: for I would not have known coveting except the Torah was saying, "You will not covet." (Ex 20:17) 8. But sin, because it took *the* opportunity through the commandment, was producing every desire in me: so without Torah sin *is* dead. 9. And once I was living without Torah, but, after the commandment came, sin became alive, 10. and the commandment *which* was found in me for *the bringing of* life, this *resulted* in death and I died: 11. for, after sin took an opportunity through the commandment, *sin* deceived me and it killed *me* through this *commandment*. 12. So indeed the Torah[2] *is* holy and the commandment *is* holy and righteous and good.

7:13. Therefore did the good *Torah* become death in me? God forbid! But sin, so that sin would appear, through the good *Torah* in me, when *sin* produced death in me, that sin would become sinful beyond measure through the commandment. 14. For we know that the Torah is spiritual, but I myself am fleshly, since I have been sold as a slave under sin. 15. For I am producing what I do not know: for I do not want this that I am doing, but I hate this, which I am doing. 16. But if I do not want this that I do, I agree with the Torah because *it is* good. 17. But now I no longer am producing this myself but the sin dwelling in me *produces it*. 18. For I know that no good is dwelling in me, that is, in my flesh: for desire *to do good* is present in me, but to produce good *is* not: 19. for I do not do *the* good that I want *to do*, but I do this evil that I do not want *to do*. 20. But if I myself do this that I do not want, I am no longer producing this, but the sin dwelling in me *is producing it*.[3] 21. So I find the Torah, in my wanting to do good things, that evil is present in me: 22. for I rejoice together in the Torah of God with respect to the inner man, 23. but I see another law in my members warring against the Torah of my mind and taking me captive in the law of sin, the

---

1   (v.6) This is an exhortation to live by the Spirit with a pure heart, loving your neighbor as yourself, not going by some list of do's and don'ts that has been drawn up by denominational leaders.

2   (v.12) See footnote of v. 1. See Torah in Glossary.

3   (v.20) To keep verses 13-20 in perspective, see 1Cor 4:16, 11:1, and Phil 3:17 where Paul says to imitate him. The sins he refers to here are those inadvertent things that we all do and say -- or should do or say, but fail to. None of us is perfect, so we too need the attitude Paul has here, to recognize that none of us is perfect, but should still be good examples to others.

one which is in my members. 24. Wretched man that I *am*: who will rescue me from this body of death? 25. But thanks to God *He will* through Jesus Messiah our Lord. So then this - on the one hand in *my* mind I am serving the Torah of God, but on the other hand in the flesh *I serve the* law of sin.

Life in the Spirit

8.1. There is therefore now no condemnation for those in Messiah Jesus: 2. for the Torah of the spirit of life in Messiah Jesus set you free from the law of sin and death. 3. For what was impossible for the law by which it was weak because of the resistance of the flesh, God, when He sent His own Son in a likeness of sinful flesh and, concerning sin, *God* was condemning sin in the flesh, 4. so that the requirement of the Torah could be fulfilled in us, by those who walk not according to *the* flesh but according to *the* Spirit. 5. For those who are flesh are thinking the things of the flesh, but those according to the Spirit *are thinking* the things of the Spirit. 6. For the mind-set, *thoughts and purposes*, of the flesh *is* death, but *the* mind-set of the Spirit *is* life and peace: 7. because the mind-set of the flesh *is* enmity to God, for it is not subject to the Torah[1] of God, nor is it really able *to submit to God*: 8. and those who are in *the* flesh are not able to please God. 9. But you are not in *the* flesh but in *the* Spirit, if indeed *the* Spirit of God dwells in you. But if someone does not have *the* Spirit of Messiah, this one is not His. 10. And if Messiah *is* in you, on the one hand *your* body *is* dead because of sin, but on the other hand *the* spirit *is* alive because of righteousness. 11. And if the Spirit of the One Who raised Jesus from *the* dead dwells in you, the One Who raised Messiah from *the* dead will also make alive your mortal bodies through His Spirit because He abides within you.

8:12. So then, brothers, we are obligated not to live according to *the* flesh, 13. for if you would live according to flesh, you are going to die: but if you are dead to the deeds of the body, you will live by *the* Spirit. 14. For as many as are led by *the* Spirit of God, these are the children of God. 15. For you did not take a spirit of bondage again in fear, but to Whom you took a spirit of adoption as children we cry, "Abba, Father." 16. The Spirit Himself bears witness with our spirit that we are children of God. 17. And if children, then *we are* heirs: indeed heirs of God, and fellow-heirs of Messiah, provided that we suffer together to the end so that we would also be glorified together.

The Glory That is to Be

8:18. For I consider that the sufferings of the present time *are* not comparable to the glory about to be revealed in us. 19. For the anxious and persistent expectation of all creation awaits diligently and patiently the revelation of the children of God, *which is on Judgment Day*. 20. Because creation was subjected to frustration, not voluntarily, but because of the One Who made

---

1   (v.7) See Torah in Glossary.

creation subject, upon hope 21. that also this creation will be set free from the bondage of corruption into the freedom of the glory of the children of God. 22. For we know that all creation groans together and travails together until now: 23. and not only *that*, but also those *of us* who have the first fruits of the spirit, then we are sighing in ourselves diligently and patiently awaiting adoption, the redemption of our body. 24. Because we have been delivered by hope: but hope being seen is not hope: for who hopes for what he sees? 25. But if we hope for what we do not see, we eagerly await through perseverance.

8:26. And likewise also the Spirit helps together with us in our weakness: for we do not know what we should pray according to what is needed, but the Spirit Himself intercedes in unutterable groanings: 27. and the One Who searches our hearts knows what *is in* the mind of the Spirit, because He intercedes with God on behalf of the saints. 28. And we know that, for those who love God, He works all things for good, for those who are called according to His purpose. 29. Because whom He knew beforehand, He appointed ahead of time, because they have the same form of the likeness of His Son, for He was Firstborn among many brothers: (Mt 12:50, 13:55, Mk 6:3, et. al.) 30. and whom He appointed beforehand, He also called: and whom He called, He also made righteous: and these whom He made righteous, He also glorified.

God's Love

8:31. Then what shall we say pertaining to these things? If God *is* for us, who *can be* against us? 32. He in fact did not spare His own Son but gave Him over on behalf of us all, then how will He not freely give us all things with Him? 33. Who will accuse against *the* chosen people of God? God is the righteous One: 34. who is the one who condemns? *Certainly not* Messiah Jesus the One Who died, but rather, has risen, and Who is on the right hand of God, and Who is interceding on our behalf. 35. What will separate us from the love of the Messiah? Affliction or distress or persecution or famine or destitution or peril or *death by* sword? 36. Just as it has been written that

> "Because of You we are put to death the whole day,
>> we were counted as sheep for slaughter." (Ps 44:22)

37. But in all these things we would have a glorious victory through the One Who loved us. 38. For I have been persuaded that neither death nor life nor angels nor rulers nor present *circumstances* nor things coming nor powers 39. nor height nor depth nor any other creation will be able to separate us from the love of God, which is in Messiah Jesus our Lord.

God's Election of Israel

9.1. I am telling *the* truth in Messiah, I am not lying, while my conscience is bearing witness with me by means of *the* Holy Spirit, 2. because grief is great for me and pain *is* unceasing in my heart. 3. For I could wish to be accursed to

God myself, separated from the Messiah on behalf of my brothers, my kinsmen according to *the* flesh, 4. who are Israelis, of whom are the adoption and the glory and the covenants[1] and the giving of the Torah[2] and the worship and the promises, 5. of whom *are* the Fathers[3] and out of whom *is* the Messiah according to the flesh, the One Who is the *only* God over everyone, blessed forever, amen.

9:6. But by no means has the Word of God fallen powerless. For not all those from Israel *are* Israel:[4] 7. because neither are all children *the* seed of Abraham, but, "In Isaac shall your seed be called." (Gn 21:12) 8. That is, these children of God *are* not the children of the flesh, but the children of the promise are looked upon as seed.[5] 9. For this *is* the word of promise, "According to this time I will come and there will be a son for Sarah." (Gn 18:10,14) 10. And not only *that*, but also Rebecca, *who* had *twins* from one conception, *by* Isaac our father. 11. For although they were not yet born and had not done anything good or evil, so that the plan would remain according to the chosen purpose of God, 12. not because of works, but the calling, it was said to her that "The older will serve the younger," (Gn 25:23) 13. just as it has been written,

> "I loved Jacob,
> but I hated Esau."[6] (Mal 1:2,3)

9:14. Then what shall we say? *Is* there injustice by God? May it not be! 15. For He said to Moses,

> "I shall be merciful to whomever I would be merciful
> and I shall have compassion on whomever
> I would have compassion." (Ex 33:19)

16. So then not for desire and not for effort, but by the mercy of God. 17. For the Scripture says to Pharaoh that "I raised you for this reason, so that I could show My power in you and so My name could be proclaimed in all the earth." (Ex 9:16) 18. So then He is merciful on whom He wishes, and He hardens whom He wishes.

God's Wrath and Mercy

9:19. Therefore you will say to me, "Then why does He still blame *us*? For who resisted His will?" 20. O Man, indeed who are you, who answers back to God? That which is molded will not say to the mold, "Why did you make me like this?" 21. Or does the potter not have authority over the clay to make from

---

1   (v.4) Note that Paul uses the plural, covenants, implying that each covenant builds on the previous covenants, but does not replace them.

2   (v.4) Torah, meaning teaching or instruction, refers to the first five books of the Bible, but sometimes refers to the Tanach (Old Testament) and even the oral teachings. See Torah in Glossary.

3   (v.5) Patriarchs

4   (v.6) Not every Israeli is a committed servant of God.

5   (v.8) This word for seed is singular, yet refers to many people. See Gal 3:16, 29.

6   (v.13) The Rabbis say this means that Jacob was loved more than Esau, that this is not literal hatred.

his lump, a vessel on the one hand into honor, or on the other hand into dishonor? 22. And if God, wanting to show anger and to make known His power, bore, with much patience, vessels of wrath *which* were prepared for destruction, 23. so then would He make known the riches of His glory upon vessels of mercy, which He prepared before hand for glory? 24. And whom He called, not only us from *the* Jewish people but also *those* from *the* heathens, 25. as also He says in Hosea,

> "I shall call those not My people, My people
>> and she who has not been loved, *My* beloved:" (Ho 2:23)

26. "And it will be in the place of which He spoke to them, 'You *who are* not My people,
>> there they shall be called children of *the* Living God.'" (Ho 1:10)

27. And Isaiah cries out on behalf of Israel, "Though to her the number of the children of Israel *is* as the sands of the sea, *only* the remnant will be saved: 28. for when He brings the expedited prophecy to pass *the* Lord will do *what has been decreed* upon the earth." (Is 10:22,23) 29. And just as Isaiah spoke beforehand,

> "If the Lord of Hosts had not left a seed in us,
>> we would have become as Sodom
>> and we would be like Gomorrah." (Is 1:9)

Israel and the Gospel

9:30. Then what shall we say? That heathens, those who did not pursue righteousness, did obtain righteousness, but righteousness by means of faith, 31. but Israel, pursuing a Torah *that teaches* righteousness,[1] did not attain *it* in Torah. 32. Why? Because *it was* not from faith but as from works: they stumbled on the stumbling stone, 33. just as it has been written,

> "Behold I place in Zion (Is 28:16) a stumbling stone and a rock causing stumbling, (Is 8:14)
>> and the one who believes upon Him will not be put to shame."
>> (Is 28:16,[2] 54:4)

10.1. Brothers, indeed the desire of my heart and my prayer to God concerning *Israel is* on behalf of their salvation. 2. For I am bearing witness to them because they have zeal for God, but not from *real* knowledge: 3. for since they do not know the righteousness of God but are seeking to make their own righteousness stand, they have not submitted to the righteousness of God: 4. because *the* purpose of Torah *is* Messiah in order *to provide* righteousness for everyone who believes.

---

1   (v.31) We are not saved because we do good works, but we do good works because we have been transformed. See both Righteousness and Mitsvah in Glossary.
2   (v.33) The Greek says "put to shame," but the Hebrew says, "Let the one who believes not expect it soon." A 12th Century rabbi wrote, "He (the believer) will remain steadfast in his faith however long realization may be delayed." See Is 28:16 in Glossary.

Salvation for All

10:5. For Moses wrote of the righteousness *that is* from the Torah that "The man who does these things will live by them." (Lv 18:5) 6. But righteousness *is* from faith, consequently he said, "Do not say in your heart, 'Who will go up to heaven?'" This is to bring Messiah down *to earth*: 7. or, "Who will descend into the abyss?" This is to lead Messiah up from *the* dead. (Dt 9:4, 30:12-14) 8. But what does it say?

"The word is near you
in your mouth and in your heart," (Dt 9:4)

this is the word of faith which we are proclaiming openly. 9. Because if you[1] would confess with your mouth *the* Lord Jesus and you would believe in your heart that God raised Him from *the* dead, you will be saved:[2] 10. for he believes for himself in *his* heart into righteousness, and confesses for himself with *his* mouth into salvation.[3] 11. For the Scripture says, "No one who believes in Him will be put to shame." (Is 28:16[4]) 12. For there is no distinction *between* either Jewish or Greek, for the same One *is* Lord of all, *and He* is rich, *abundantly blessing* all those who call upon Him: 13. for everyone who will call upon the name of *the* Lord will be saved. (Jl 2:32)

10:14. Then how will they call upon Whom they did not believe? And how could they believe what they did not hear? And how could they hear without preaching? 15. And how could they preach unless they would send *preachers*? Just as it has been written, "How beautiful *are* the feet of those who preach the Good News of the good things." (Is 52:7) 16. But they did not all obey the one preaching the Good News. For Isaiah said, "Lord, who believed our report?" (Is 53:1) 17. So then faith *is* from hearing, and hearing through *the* message from Messiah. 18. But I say, Did they **not** hear? Absolutely not,

"Their voice went out into all the earth
and their words into the ends of the inhabited world." (Ps 19:4)

19. But I say, did Israel **not** understand? Moses first said,

"I will provoke you *all* to jealousy by *those* not a nation,
by a foolish nation I shall make you angry." (Dt 32:21)

20. And Isaiah is very bold and says,

"I was found among those who were not seeking Me,
I became visible to those who were not looking for Me." (Is 65:1)

21. But to Israel he said, "I held out My hands the whole day to a disobedient and obstinate people." (Is 65:2)

---

1   (v.9) This is singular.
2   (v.9) The Jewish understanding of belief requires a change in behavior. If I say I love you, but do not give aid when needed, I lied when I said that I loved you. See Mt 7:21, 1Jn 2:4.
3   (v.10) The word translated salvation could also be translated deliverance.
4   (v.11) See Isaiah 28:16 in Glossary.

The Remnant of Israel

11.1. Therefore I ask, did not God reject His people? May it not be! For also I myself am an Isreali, from *the* seed of Abraham, tribe of Benjamin. 2. God did not reject His people whom He knew beforehand. Or do you not know with Elijah what the Scripture says, as he intercedes with God with reference to Israel? 3. Lord, "They killed Your prophets, they tore down Your altars, and only I was left and they are seeking my life." (1Ki 19:10,14) 4. But what does the divine statement say to him? "I reserved seven thousand men for Myself, who did not bend a knee to Baal." (1Ki 19:18) 5. Then, just as also in the present time, a remnant[1] has come into being according to *the* election of grace: 6. and if by grace, *it is* no longer by means of works, because, *if it were*, grace would no longer be grace. 7. Then what? What Israel is seeking, this it did not obtain, but the election did obtain: and the rest grew callous, 8. just as it has been written,

> "God gave them a spirit of stupor,
>> their eyes to not see
>> and their ears to not hear,
> until this very day." (Dt 29:4,[2] Is 29:10, see also Is 6:10a)

9. And David said,

> "Their table[3] must become a snare" and a trap
>> "and into a stumbling block and for a repayment to them,
10.   their eyes must darken so they could not see (Ps 69:22, 23 & 35:8)
>> and their back must now always bend."[4]

The Salvation of the Pagans

11:11. Therefore I say, did they stumble so they would fall *forever*? God forbid! But by their transgression the salvation for the heathens *is* to provoke them to jealousy. (Dt 32:21) 12. And if their transgression *is* riches for *the* world and their loss riches for heathens, how much more *will* their fulfillment *be* riches.

11:13. But I am speaking to you heathens: then as long as I am indeed an apostle for heathens, I honor my ministry, 14. if somehow I could provoke my flesh to jealousy and I could rescue some of them. 15. For if their rejection *of Him means* reconciliation of *the* world, what *is* their acceptance by God if not life out of death? 16. And if the first fruits[5] is holy, the whole batch[6] *is* also: and if the root *is* holy, the branches *are* also.

---

1   (v.5) This remnant is referred to as the Humble in Is 61:1. See Humble in Glossary.

2   (v.8) This is v. 3 in the Tanach.

3   (v.9) The Hebrew is plural, tables, an imprecatory prayer, a curse speaking of the dining tables of those who persecuted David in v. 22.

4   (v.10) The Greek literally says, "You must now always bend their back." a strong request for God to punish them.

5   (v.16) This refers to the first portion of dough that was used for the Bread of the Presence in the Sanctuary.

6   (v.16) Body

11:17. But if some of the branches were broken off, and you,[1] since you are a wild olive, were yourself grafted into them, then you would be a participant for yourself of the richness[2] of the root of the olive tree. 18. Stop boasting of the branches: but, if you do boast, you do not support the root, but the root supports you. 19. Therefore you will say, "Branches were broken off so that I could be grafted in." 20. Just so: they were broken off by unbelief, but you have stood by faith. Do not be proud, but you must continually fear for yourself: 21. for if God did not spare the natural branches, **neither** will He in any way spare you. 22. You must now see the goodness and severity of God: on the one hand severity upon those who fell, but on the other hand goodness of God upon you, if you would remain in the goodness, otherwise you would be cut off. 23. And even these, if they would not remain in unbelief, they will be grafted in: for God is able to graft them in again. 24. For if you were cut off from the naturally wild olive tree and contrary to nature you were grafted into the cultivated olive tree, how much more will these natural *branches* be grafted into their own *cultivated* olive tree.[3]

The Restoration of Israel

11:25. For I do not want you to be ignorant, brothers, of this mystery, lest you become conceited,[4] because dulled perception in part has come upon Israel until the fullness of the heathens[5] would come in[6] (Lk 21:24) 26. and in this way all Israel will be saved, just as it has been written,

"The One Who rescues will come out of Zion,
    He will banish ungodliness from Jacob.
27.   and this *is* the covenant for them with Me,
    when I would take away their sins." (Is 59:20,21)

28. On the one hand regarding the gospel *they are* enemies on account of you, but on the other hand regarding the election *they are* beloved because of the Fathers: 29. for the gifts and the calling[7] of God *are* irrevocable. 30. For just as you yourselves were once disobedient to God, but now you have been shown mercy by their disobedience, 31. then in this way now they have become disobedient, so that also they could now receive mercy themselves because of the mercy shown to you. 32. For God will completely shut up together all those *who are* in disobedience, so that He could be merciful with them all.

11:33. O *the* depth of riches and wisdom and knowledge of God: in the

---

1   (v.17) Every "you" in this paragraph, verses 17-24, is singular, so each one of us is individually grafted into the cultivated, Jewish olive tree. See Is 44:5.
2   (v.17) This literally means to grow fat.
3   (v.24) This is the same olive tree into which you have been grafted.
4   (v.25) Literally, "that you were not wise in the power of relying on your own wisdom."
5   (v.25) Another verse that could well be translated this way is Gn 48:19, when Jacob blesses Ephraim, the Hebrew literally speaks of the "fullness of the heathens" (m'lo goyim) which is translated "group of nations" (NIV) or "multitude of nations" (Amp).
6   (v.25) The heathens are to join with Judaism into one body by means of Messiah Jesus.
7   (v.29) We have multiple gifts, but one calling.

same manner His judgments *are* unfathomable and His ways *are* inscrutable,

34.   "For who knew the mind of *the* Lord?

or who became His councilor?" (Is 40:13, Job 15:8, Jr 23:18)

35.   "or who has given in advance to Him,

so He should repay him?" (Job 41:3)

36. Because all things *are* from Him and through Him and in Him: to Him *be* the glory forever, amen.

The New Life in Messiah

12.1. Therefore I urge you, brothers, through the compassion of God, to present your bodies holy, living offerings, pleasing to God, your spiritual service: 2. and stop being conformed to this age,[1] but you must *from the inside* continually be changed into another form,[2] by the renovation of your mind, to prove what *is* the good and pleasing and perfect will of God for you.

12:3. For I say, through the grace that has been given to me, to everyone who is among you, not to think too highly of yourselves beyond which it is necessary to think,[3] but to think to put a moderate estimate of yourself, in the same manner as God divided to each a measure of faith. 4. For just as we have many members in one body, but all the parts do not have the same function, 5. in this way, we, the many, are one body in Messiah, but each one part of one another. 6. And having different gifts according to the grace given to us, whether prophecy according to the proportion of his faith, 7. or ministry[4] in his service, or the one who teaches in the teaching, 8. or the one who encourages in encouragement: the one who shares,[5] (Eph 4:28) in sincerity *without grudging*, the protector or guardian giving aid in diligent eagerness, the one who is merciful in cheerfulness.

Rules of the Christian Life

12:9. Love must be sincere. Abhorring evil, clinging to the good, 10. devoted to one another in brotherly love, trying to outdo one another in showing respect, 11. in eagerness not sluggishness, fervent in spirit, serving the Lord, 12. rejoicing in hope, persevering in affliction, persisting in prayer, 13. sharing *what you have* in the needs of the saints, pursuing hospitality, 14. you must continually bless those who persecute you, you must continually bless and you must stop cursing. 15. To rejoice with *those who* rejoice, to weep with *those who* weep. 16. Being of the same mind with one another, not being proud but yielding to the lowly *menial tasks*. Do not ever become wise in your own estimation. 17. And

---

1   (v.2) World order
2   (v.2) See Son of David/Son of Joseph in Glossary.
3   (v.3) Each person is to have self-confidence, an assurance of who he is in Messiah.
4   (v.7) The Greek word, diakonia, could also be translated service. See Servant in Glossary.
5   (v.8) The Greek word, metadidous, means to share with someone. It is also used to express imparting knowledge of Scripture, as in Lk 3:11, Ro 1:11.

by not paying back evil against evil, taking thought for good before all mankind: 18. if able from yourselves, living in peace with all mankind: 19. not avenging yourselves, beloved, but you must now give place to the wrath *of God*, for it has been written, "Vengeance *is* Mine, I will repay," (Dt 32:35) says *the* Lord. 20. But "If your enemy hungers, you must continually feed him: if he thirsts, you must continually give him drink: for doing this you will heap coals of fire upon his head." (Pr 25:21,22) 21. I do not overcome evil by *doing* evil but I overcome evil by *doing* good.[1]

Obedience to Rulers[2]

13.1. Every person must continually submit to governing authorities. For there is no authority except under God, and those who are *in authority* are appointed by God. 2. So that the one who resists his authority has opposed the ordinance of God, and the ones who have opposed will bring judgment on themselves. 3. For those who rule are not *to be* feared by the one who works good, but by the *one doing* evil. And you want to be unafraid of authority: whoever does good *things*, then you will have praise from *the authority*: 4. for a servant of God is for *doing* good for you. But if you would do evil, you must fear: for he does not bear the sword without cause: for a servant of God is an avenger to the one who does evil. 5. For this reason *it is* a necessity to be subject, not only because of the wrath but also through conscience. 6. For because of this you must also pay taxes: for magistrates are ministers of God *who* are steadfastly attentive, *serving God* in this itself. 7. You must immediately pay back your debts to all, the tax to whom the tax *is owed*, the customs to whom the customs duties *are owed*, respect to whom respect *is due*, honor to whom honor *is due*.

Brotherly Love

13:8. You must continually **not** owe **anything** to anyone except love to one another: for the one who loves the other has fulfilled Torah.[3] 9. Truly "You shall not commit adultery, You shall not murder, You shall not steal, You shall not covet," (Ex 20:13-15, 17) and if *there is* any other commandment, it is summed up in this word, "You shall love your neighbor as yourself." (Lv 19:18) 10. Love does not work evil to the neighbor: therefore love is fulfillment of Torah.

The Approach of the Day of Messiah

13:11. And this, since we know the season, that *this is* the moment now for you to be raised up from sleep, for now our salvation *is* nearer than when we *first* believed. 12. The night has advanced, and the day has drawn near.

---

1   (12:9-21) These statements relate to Jesus' words in a number of verses. See Mt 5:39, 44, Mk 9:50, Lk 6:28.

2   (Caption) Paul wrote this while Nero was emperor, one of the most cruel, unjust rulers there has ever been.

3   (v.8) Torah, meaning teaching or instruction, refers to the first five books of the Bible. See Torah in Glossary.

Therefore we should put off the works of darkness, and we should put on the weapons of light. 13. In the same manner we should walk decently in daylight, not in carousing and drunkenness,[1] not in sexual excess or in licentiousness, not in strife or in jealousy, 14. but you will become so possessed of the mind of the Lord Jesus Messiah[2] that you will resemble Him and you must not be concerned for desires of the flesh.

Do Not Judge Your Brother

14.1. You must continually take to yourselves the one who is weak in faith, *yet* do not get into quarrels about opinions. 2. Indeed the one believes *it is permissible* to eat all things, but the other who is weak eats vegetables. 3. The one who eats must not ever despise the one who does not eat, and the one who does not eat must not ever judge the one who does eat, for God accepted him. 4. Who are you, the one who judges a house slave belonging to another?[3] He stands or he falls for his own master: but he will stand, for the Lord is able to make him stand. 5. For the one indeed concludes a *certain* day *is* better than *another* day, but the other concludes every day *is* alike: each must be fully convinced in his own mind. 6. The one who sets aside a day sets aside for the Lord: and the one who eats, eats for *the* Lord, truly he gives thanks to God: and the one who does not eat abstains for *the* Lord and he gives thanks to God. 7. Truly no one of us could live within himself and no one dies to *just* himself: 8. for if we would live, we would live for the Lord, and if we would die, then we would die for the Lord. Whether we would live or we would die, we are the Lord's. 9. For Messiah died for this and He became alive again, so that He would be Lord of both *the* dead and *the* living. 10. Then why are you judging your brother? Or then why do you despise your brother? For we will all be brought before the judicial bench of God, 11. for it has been written,

> "As surely as I live, says the Lord, every knee will bend before Me
> and every tongue will openly give praise to God."
> (Is 49:18, 45:23)

12. So then each of us will give an account to God on his own behalf.

Do Not Make Your Brother Stumble

14:13. Therefore we should no longer judge one another (Mt 7:1-6): but rather determine this, not to place a stumbling block or an offense on your brother. 14. And I know I have been persuaded by *the* Lord Jesus that no one thing is defiled in itself, except for the one who counts it to be defiled, *it is* defiled to that one. 15. For if your brother is grieved *by you* because of food,[4] you are no longer

---

1   (v.13) The word translated drunkenness refers to any intoxication. See Sorcery in Glossary.
2   (v.14) To be possessed of or to have the mind of the Lord is to have your spirit so in tune with the Lord that you understand what He means, what He would have you do.
3   (v.4) Each of us is to be a bondservant of the Lord. See Servant in Glossary.
4   (v.15) What you eat.

walking according to love: stop destroying that one, on behalf of whom Messiah died, by your food. 16. Therefore he must stop speaking evil of what is good for you. 17. For the kingdom of God is not food and drink, but righteousness and peace and joy in *the* Holy Spirit: (Mk 7:15, 1Jn 5:17) 18. for the one who serves the Messiah in this manner *is* pleasing to God and approved by men. 19. Consequently then we should pursue the things of peace and the things that build up one another. 20. You must stop destroying the work of God for the sake of food. On the one hand all things are pure, but *it is* evil for the man who eats *to cause another to* stumble. 21. *It is* good not to eat meat and not to drink wine and not *do* anything by which your brother stumbles. 22. You have faith that, with reference to yourself, you must continually have before God. Blessed is the one who does not condemn himself by what he approves: 23. but the one who doubts is condemned if he would eat, because *it is* not from faith: and everything not from faith is sin.

Please Your Fellow Men, Not Yourself

15.1. And we the strong are obligated to support the weaknesses of the powerless and not to please ourselves. 2. Each of us must be pleasing to our neighbor for the purpose of building up for *his* good: 3. for even the Messiah did not please Himself, but just as it has been written, "The reproaches of those who blame you have fallen upon Me." (Ps 69:9) 4. For whatever was written beforehand, was written for our instruction, so that through patience and through the exhortation of the Scriptures we would have hope. 5. And the God of patience and of comfort would give us to set our minds on one another according to Messiah Jesus, 6. so that since you are of one mind you should glorify the God and Father of our Lord, Jesus Messiah, with one voice.

The Gospel for Jewish and Pagans Alike

15:7. On this account take one another to yourselves, just as also the Messiah took you to Himself for *the* glory of God. 8. For I say Messiah has become a servant of circumcision[1] concerning the truth of God, to confirm the promises *given* to the Fathers, 9. and the heathens will give praise concerning *the* mercies of God, just as it has been written,

> "Because of this I will praise You among the heathens
> and I will sing praise to Your name." (Ps 18:49)

10. and it says again,

> "You must now rejoice, heathens, with His people." (Dt 32:43)

11. and again,

> "Praise the Lord, all you heathens
> and all the people would praise Him." (Ps 117:1)

12. and again Isaiah says,

---

1   (v.8) The Jewish people and those circumcised in heart (Lv 26:41, Dt 10:16, 30:6, Jr. 9:25, Eze 44:7)

> "He will be the root[1] of Jesse
> and the One coming to rule heathens,
> heathens will hope upon Him." (Is 11:10)

13. And the God of hope might fill you with every joy and peace when you believe, for you to abound in the hope by *the* power of *the* Holy Spirit.

Paul's Missionary Commission

15:14. And I have been persuaded, my brothers, even myself concerning you, that you also are full of goodness, because you have been filled with all the knowledge, and are able to exhort one another. 15. But I wrote more boldly to you in part as reminding you because of the powers and capabilities given to me by God 16. for me to be a minister of Messiah Jesus to the heathens, ministering the gospel of God as a priest, so that the offering that consists of the heathens *who have come to the Lord* would become acceptable, because *the offering* has been sanctified *with ongoing effect* by *the* Holy Spirit. 17. Therefore I may boast in Messiah Jesus of my relationship with God: 18. for I will not dare to say anything which Messiah did not work out through me for obedience by the heathens, in word and deed, 19. in power of miracles and wonders, in power of *the* Spirit of God: so that I have brought the gospel of the Messiah to fulfillment from Jerusalem and around as far as Illyricum,[2] 20. so in this way considering it an honor to preach the gospel where Messiah was not named *before*, so that I would not build on another's foundation, 21. but as it has been written,

> "They will see to whom nothing about Him was made known,
> and those who have not heard will understand." (Is 52:15)

Paul's Plan to Visit Rome

15:22. On this account I was also being hindered for the most part from coming to you: 23. but now since I no longer have a place *to work* in these districts, and I have desired to come to you for many years,[3] 24. whenever I could go to Spain: I certainly hope to see you when I pass through and to be accompanied there by you, if first I could enjoy your company. 25. But now I am going to Jerusalem, serving the saints. 26. For Macedonia and Achia were well pleased to have made some contribution to the poor among the saints in Jerusalem. 27. Truly they were well pleased and they are indebted to them: for if the heathens shared in their spiritual things, they also ought to serve them in the fleshly *material* things. 28. Therefore when this *mission to Jerusalem* ends and

---

1   (v.12) A Hebrew idiom meaning he will be a descendant of Jesse.
2   (v.19) Illyricum included all of the former Yugoslavia plus Austria and parts of adjoining countries.
3   (v.23) The letter to the Roman Christians was written before Paul had gone to Rome, but when he finally got to Rome a couple of years later, he summoned the Jewish leaders, not those to whom he had written this letter. How did Paul know so many, whom he named in Chapter 16? Perhaps it was through communication with Phoebe, Epaenetus, Junia, and other apostles.

when I seal this fruit[1] to them, I will come back through you to Spain: 29. and I know that when I come to you I will come with *the* full blessing of Messiah.

15:30. And I urge you, brothers, through our Lord Jesus Messiah and through the love of the Spirit, to help me in striving in prayers to God concerning me, 31. so that I would be rescued from those who are disobedient in Judea and that my ministry in Jerusalem would be well received by the saints, 32. that after I come to you in joy through *the* will of God, I will find rest[2] with you. 33. And the God of peace *be* with you all, amen.

Personal Greetings

16.1. And I am introducing our sister Phoebe to you, since she is also a minister of the congregation[3] in Cenchrea,[4] 2. so that you would welcome her in *the* Lord as befitting the saints, and you would stand by her in whatever matter she would have need of you: for she has also become a patroness[5] of many, even of me.

16:3. You must greet Prisca and Aquila,[6] my fellow workers in Messiah Jesus, 4. who risked their own necks for the sake of my life, for whom not only I, but also all the congregations of the heathens are thankful, 5. and *greet* the congregation in their own house.[7] You must greet my esteemed Epaenetus, who is first fruits of Asia in Messiah. 6. You must greet Mary, who labored much, teaching among you. 7. You must greet Andronikus and Junia[8] my kin and my fellow prisoners, who are prominent among the apostles, and they were in Messiah before me. 8. You must greet Ampliatus, my esteemed in *the* Lord. 9. You must greet Urbanus, our fellow worker in Messiah, and my esteemed Stachus. 10. You must greet Appeles, proved in Messiah. You must greet the household of Aristobulus. 11. You must greet Herodion my kin. You must greet those from Narkiss who are in *the* Lord. 12. You must greet Tryphena and Tryphosa, those *women* who are laboring much in teaching in *the* Lord. You must greet the esteemed Persida, *a woman* who labored much in the Lord. 13. You must greet Rufus, the chosen in *the* Lord, and his mother and mine. 14. Greet Asincritus, Phlegon, Hermes, Patrobus, Hermas, and the brothers with them. 15. Greet Philoligon and Julia, Nerea and his sister, and Olympia and all the saints

---

1   (v.28) The donation for the congregation in Jerusalem

2   (v.32) A brief respite from Paul's heavy schedule.

3   (v.1) Although often translated "church," no Greek word meaning church is used in the NT. See Congregation in Glossary.

4   (v.1) Cenchrae was on the west side of the very narrow piece of land connecting northern Greece to southern Greece. Corinth was on the east side, just a short distance away.

5   (v.2) Literally, a woman set over others

6   (v.3) Listing Priscilla first indicates a greater ranking for her in Paul's mind. Paul had met them a few years earlier in Corinth, recorded in Acts 18:2.

7   (v.5) Their living in Rome makes this during the first five years of Nero's reign. Claudius expelled the Jewish people from Rome in 49 AD. Nero succeeded him in 54 AD, permitting them to return, and then five years later expelled them.

8   (v.7) A woman

with them.[1] 16. Greet one another with a holy kiss. All the congregations of the Messiah greet you.

16:17. And I urge you, brothers, to look out for those who make dissensions and draw you away from the true doctrine contrary to the teaching which you learned, and you must continually turn away from them: 18. for such as these are not serving the Lord our Messiah but their own gluttony, and through smooth talk and flattery they could deceive the hearts of the innocents. 19. For your submission has been heard by all: so I rejoice with you, and I want you to be wise in the good things, and pure in respect to evil. 20. And the God of peace will shortly crush Satan[2] under your feet.[3] The grace of our Lord Jesus *be* with you.

16:21. My fellow worker Timothy, and Luke and Jason and Sopater, my relatives, greet you.[4]

22. I, Tertius, the writer of this letter, greet you in *the* Lord. 23. Gaius my host and the whole congregation greet you. Erastus the city treasurer and brother Kouartus greet you.[5]

16:25. And to the one who is able to establish you according to my gospel and the preaching of Jesus Messiah,[6] according to *the* revelation of *the* mystery that was kept hidden for long ages, 26. but *is* now being revealed through the prophetic writings according to the command of the eternal God, Who has been, in faithful obedience, made known to all the heathens, 27. to *the* only wise God, through Jesus Messiah, to Whom *be* the glory forever, amen.

---

1   (v.15) These 15 verses refer to 14 men and 10 women, a higher proportion of women than many might expect, and more than are named in any other letter from Paul. That he knew so many working in ministry there is an indication of the effort of the Jerusalem council to reach the seat of power across the Roman Empire.

2   (v.20) See Satan in Glossary.

3   (v.20) You have been given awesome power. See Footstool in Glossary.

4   (v.21) Paul frequently referred to Timothy as "My fellow worker.." From this I believe v. 21 should be a separate paragraph, while the editors of the Greek text have placed it with the statement of Tertius.

5   (v.23) V. 24 is omitted because it was not in the earliest manuscripts.

6   (v.25) His statement "my gospel" followed by the message of Jesus Messiah, means the gospel of the Jerusalem council, as opposed to the false teachings referred to in other letters. See 2 Cor 4:5.

~ 1 CORINTHIANS[1] ~

Greeting and Thanksgiving

1.1. Paul, a called apostle of Messiah Jesus by *the* will of God, and Brother Sosthenes 2. to the congregation[2] of God, the one that is in Corinth, to those who have been made holy in Messiah Jesus, called saints, with all those who call upon the name of our Lord Jesus Messiah in every place, their *Lord* and ours: 3. grace and peace to you from God our Father and Lord Jesus Messiah.

1:4. I give thanks to My God always concerning you for the grace of God that was given to you in Messiah Jesus, 5. because you were made rich in Him in everything, in every word and in all knowledge, 6. just as the testimony of the Messiah was confirmed in you, 7. so you *are* not to come short in any *spiritual* gift, while you are waiting eagerly for the revelation of our Lord Jesus Messiah: 8. Who will also strengthen you until *the* end, *so you will be* blameless[3] in the Day of Our Lord Jesus Messiah. 9. God *is* faithful, through Whom you were called out into fellowship with His Son Jesus Messiah our Lord.

Divisions in the Congregation

1:10. And I urge you, brothers, by the name of our Lord Jesus Messiah, that you would all say the same things and there would be no division among you, but you would be made complete in the same mind and in the same conviction. 11. For it was shown to me concerning you, my brothers, by those of Chloe's household, that there is some strife among you. 12. But I say this, that each of you says, "I am indeed of Paul," or "I am of Apollos," or "I am of Cephas,"[4] or "I am of Messiah." 13. Has Messiah been divided? Was Paul crucified for you, or were you baptized[5] in the name of Paul? 14. I give thanks to God that I did not baptize any of you except Crispas and Gaius, 15. so that no one could say that

---

1   (Title) Written from Ephesus (16:8) about 55 AD, after Thessalonians, but before Romans.
2   (v.2) Although often translated "church," no Greek word meaning church is used in the NT. See Congregation in Glossary.
3   (v.8) Cannot be called to account, not accused
4   (v.12) Cephas is the Latin spelling of the Aramaic word Kefa. See Cephas in Glossary.
5   (v.13) The Greek verb baptidzo means to immerse, and this was the immersion for purification that had been a Jewish custom for more than 1,000 years. See Baptize in Glossary.

you were baptized in my name. 16. But I also baptized the Stephanus household; I do not know the rest, if I baptized any other one. 17. For Messiah did not send me to baptize but to proclaim the Good News, not *relying* on wisdom in a message, so that the cross of Messiah would not be destroyed.

Messiah the Power and Wisdom of God

1:18. For the message of the cross on the one hand is foolishness to the lost, but on the other hand, to those among us who are saved, it is *the* power of God, 19. for it has been written,

> "I will destroy the wisdom of the wise
>> and I will do away with the understanding of the intelligent."
> (Is 29:14)

20. Where *is* a wise *person*?[1] Where *is* a scribe? Where *is* a debater of this age? Was not God making foolish the wise *people* of the world? 21. For since the world did not know God through its wisdom, in the wisdom of God, God took delight through the preaching of foolishness[2] to save those who believe: 22. and since Jewish people are asking for signs and Greeks are seeking wisdom, 23. but we are proclaiming a crucified Messiah, on the one hand a stumbling block to Jewish people, and on the other hand foolishness to heathens, 24. but to those who are called, to both Jewish and Greeks, *we are proclaiming the* Messiah of God *and proclaiming the* power and wisdom of God: 25. because the foolish thing of God is wiser than men and the weak thing of God *is* stronger than men.

1:26. For you see your call, brothers, that not many *are* wise according to *the* flesh, not many *are* mighty in wealth and influence, not many well born: 27. but God chose the ignorant of the world, so that He would put the wise to shame, and God chose the weak ones of the world, so that He would shame the strong, 28. and God chose the lowly of the world, even those who were despised, even the things that were nothing, so that He would make ineffective the things that were, 29. thus no flesh could boast before God. 30. But because of Him you are in Messiah Jesus, Who became wisdom from God in us, righteousness and also holiness and redemption, 31. so that just as it was has been written, "The one who boasts must always boast in *the* Lord." (Jr 9:24)

Proclaiming Messiah Crucified

2.1. And when I came to you, brothers, I did not come with excellence of word but rather proclaiming to you the mystery of *the* wisdom of God. 2. For I did not judge what I knew in you except Jesus Messiah and this One as having been crucified. 3. And I, in weakness and in fear and in much trembling, have come to you, 4. and my message and my preaching, *are* not in persuasive wise words but in proof of spirit and power, 5. so that your faith would not be in *the*

---

1 (v.20) Each question "Where is.." in this verse anticipates a negative answer.
2 (v.21) To the world system the Gospel message is foolishness.

wisdom of men but in *the* power of God.

The Revelation by God's Spirit

2:6. But we are speaking wisdom among those ready to apprehend divine things, but not *the* wisdom of this age and not of the leaders of this age of those things that are being abolished: 7. but we are speaking wisdom of God, the *wisdom* hidden in a mystery, which God predestined for eternity for our glory, 8. which none of the leaders of this age knew: for if they *had* known, they would not have crucified the Lord of Glory. 9. But just as it has been written,

"'What eye did not see and ear did not hear' (Is 64:4, 52:15)
and did not go up upon *the* heart of man,[1]
what God prepared for those who love Him." (Sir 1:10)

10. But God *has* revealed *them* to us through the Spirit: for the Spirit searches all things, even the deep things of God. 11. For who of men knows the things of a man except the spirit of the man that *is* in him? Thus then no one knows the things of God except the Spirit of God. 12. And we did not take the spirit of the world but the Spirit which *is* from God, so that we would know the things freely given to us by God: 13. and *this is* what we are speaking, not in teachings with words of human wisdom but in teachings of *the* Spirit, *those* thoughts joined together with spiritual *teachings*. 14. But natural man does not accept the things of the Spirit of God: for they are foolishness to him and he is not able to know, because they are discerned spiritually. 15. And the one who discerns all things by the Spirit, then is himself called to account by no one.

16.   For "Who *has* known the mind of *the* Lord,
         who will instruct Him?" (Is 40:13)
But we have *the* mind of Messiah;[2] *we know what He has taught.*

Fellow Workmen for God

3.1. And, brothers, I was not able to speak to you as spiritual *people* but as fleshly, since *you are* infants in Messiah. 2. I gave you milk to drink, not solid food: for you were not yet strong enough *for solid food.* But you are still at the present time not able, 3. for you are still fleshly. For where *there is* jealousy and strife among you, are you not fleshly and walking according to man? 4. For when someone would say, "I am indeed of Paul," and another, "I *am* of Apollos," are you not people? 5. Who therefore is Apollos? And who is Paul? *We are* servants through whom you did believe, and to each as the Lord gave *an assignment.* 6. I planted, Apollos watered, but God caused it to grow: 7. so it is not the one who plants and *it is* not the one who waters *who is anything*, but God *is* the One Who causes growth. 8. The one who plants and also the one who waters are equal,

---

1   (v.9) They could not even be imagined by mankind.
2   (v.16) To have His mind means to be so in tune with His spirit and to know His Torah so well that you understand what He would have you do. See Ro 13:14.

and each will take his own reward according to his own toil: 9. for we are fellow workers of God, you are cultivated fields of God, a building of God.

3:10. According to the grace of God, since it was given to me as a skilled master-builder, I placed a foundation, but another is building. And each must continually see how he is building. 11. For no one is able to place another foundation other than the One being laid, Who is Jesus Messiah. 12. And if someone builds upon the foundation gold, silver, precious stones, wood, grass, straw, 13. the work of each will be clear, for *Judgment* Day will reveal, because it is revealed in fire: and this fire will test what sort the work of each is. 14. If the work of someone, which he built, remains he will take a reward: 15. if the work of someone will burn down, he will suffer loss, but he will be saved, but *it will be* as through fire. 16. Do you not know that you are a sanctuary[1] of God and the Spirit of God dwells in you? 17. If someone corrupts the sanctuary of God, God corrupts this one: for the sanctuary of God is holy, which you are.

3:18. And let no one deceive himself: if someone thinks he is wise in this age, he must become foolish, so that he could become wise. 19. For the wisdom of this world is foolishness before God. For it has been written

"The One who grasps the wise in their cunning:" (Job 5:13)
20. and again,
    "*The* Lord knows the reasonings of the wise
        that they are in vain." (Ps 94:11)

21. So one must not boast about people: for all things are yours, 22. whether Paul, or Apollos, or Cephas,[2] whether world, or life, or death, whether present, or *things* coming: all things *are* yours, 23 and you *are* of Messiah, and Messiah of God.

The Ministry of the Apostles

4.1. Thus people must consider us as servants[3] of Messiah and stewards of mysteries of God. 2. Moreover in this case He is seeking among the stewards, so that someone faithful would be found. 3. And to me it is least, *it just does not matter,* that I would be judged by you or by a human court: in fact I do not judge myself. 4. For although I am no longer conscious of anything against myself, and I am not justified by this, *since I am not without sin* (Ro. 7), the Lord is the One Who judges me. 5. Thus you do not judge ahead of time until whenever the Lord would come, Who also will light the hidden things of the darkness and will reveal the purposes of the hearts: and then the approval will come from God for

1   (v.16) Sanctuary is the correct translation and is a significant point. The temple had a court where sin was welcome and an altar where sin was dealt with. Sin had to be dealt with before entering the sanctuary or the priest who entered was dead! Your body is a sanctuary! See Sanctuary in Glossary.
2   (v.22) Cephas is the Latin spelling of the Aramaic Kefa, meaning Rock. See Cephas in Glossary.
3   (v.1) The Greek word for servant used here refers to a personal attendant, often a soldier or guard for a king or someone in high authority.

each one.

4:6. And these things, brothers, by what I have said of myself and Apollos I have shown you what applies to all Christian teachers, so that you would learn through us "Not *to go* beyond what has been written, *Scripture*," so that you would not be proud on behalf of the one against another. 7. For who is judging you? But what do you have which you did not take? But if you then took, why boast as not having taken? 8. Now you are filled, now you are rich, you reigned apart from us: and I would you did really reign, so that then we could reign with you. 9. For I suppose, God appointed us apostles last as condemned to death, because we became a spectacle to the world both to angels and to mankind. 10. We *are* foolish because of Messiah, but you *are* wise in Messiah: we *are* weak, but you *are* strong: you *are* honored, but we *are* dishonored. 11. Until this very hour then we hunger and we thirst and we are poorly clothed and we are beaten and we are homeless 12. and we labor, working with our own hands: being reviled we bless, we bear with being persecuted, 13. we call for being defamed: we have become a refuse of the world, dirt of all until now.

4:14. I write these things not to shame you but to admonish my dear children. 15. For you could have ten thousand stern disciplinarians in Messiah but not many fathers *disciplining in love*: for I have begotten you in Messiah Jesus through the gospel. 16. Therefore I urge you, you must continually be imitators of me.[1] 17. Because of this I sent Timothy to you, who is my beloved child and faithful in *the* Lord, who will remind you of my ways, those in Messiah Jesus, just as I teach everywhere in every congregation.[2] 18. But since I have not come to you some got puffed up:[3] 19. but I will come quickly to you if the Lord would want, and I will find out not the message of those who are puffed up, but the power: 20. for the kingdom of God is not in speaking but in power. 21. What do you want? Should I come to you with a rod or in love and in a spirit of gentleness?

Judgment against Immorality

5.1. Actually it is heard *there is* sexual immorality among you, and such immorality which *is* not among the heathens, for someone to have his father's wife. 2. And you are proud and should you not rather be sad, that this work which I did could have been taken from among you? 3. For I indeed have already judged the one who did this as if *I* were present, although I am absent in the body, but present in the spirit: 4. when you gather in the name of our Lord Jesus and with my spirit with the power of our Lord Jesus, 5. to give such a one as this over to Satan[4] for destruction of the flesh, so that his spirit could be saved in the Day

1   (v.16) This puts Romans 7:13-20 in perspective. No one is perfect, but we are to lead exemplary lives, to be good examples to others.
2   (v.17) Although often translated "church," no Greek word meaning church is used in the NT. See Congregation in Glossary.
3   (v.18) Proud
4   (v.5) See Satan in Glossary.

of the Lord. 6. Your boasting *is* not good. Do you not know that a little leaven leavens the whole lump of dough? 7. You must immediately cleanse the old leaven, so that you would be a new lump, just as you are unleavened: for also our Passover Messiah was sacrificed. 8. Thus we should celebrate not in old leaven and not in wickedness and evil but in unleavened purity and truth.

5:9. I wrote to you in the letter not to be associated with immoral people, 10. by no means *are you able to avoid contact* with the immoralities of this world or with covetous ones or swindlers or idolaters, for otherwise you would now have to come out of the world. 11. But now I write to you not to be associated if some brother would be called immoral or covetous or idolater or abusive or a drunkard[1] or extortioner, and not to eat with such as this one: 12. for what *allows* me to judge those outside? Are you not judging those inside? 13. But God judges those outside. "You must immediately remove the immoral one from you." (Dt 17:7, 19:19, 22:21,24, 24:7)

Going to Law before Unbelievers

6.1. How dare someone of you having a lawsuit with another, to be judged by the unrighteous and not by the saints?[2] 2. Or do you not know that the saints will judge the world? (Dn 7:22, Wsd 3:8) And if the world is to be judged by you, are you not competent in trivial cases? 3. Do you not know that we will judge angels, let alone ordinary matters? 4. Indeed if you are having lawsuits *over* ordinary matters, do you appoint as judges men who have no standing in the congregation?[3] 5. I am saying *this* to shame you. So, is not one among you wise, who will be able to judge between *one and* his brother? 6. But is brother judged against brother and this by unbelievers? 7. Surely now then these are an utter loss for you that you are having lawsuits with one another. Why not rather be wronged? Why not rather be defrauded? 8. But you are doing wrong and you are defrauding, and this *with* brothers. 9. Or do you not know that *the* unrighteous will not inherit *the* kingdom of God? Stop being deceived: neither fornicators nor idolaters nor adulterers nor effeminate nor homosexuals 10. nor thieves nor covetous people, nor drunkards,[4] nor abusive people, nor swindlers will inherit *the* kingdom of God. 11. And some of you were these things: but you have been washed,[5] but you have been made holy, but you have been made righteous by the name of the Lord Jesus Messiah and by the Spirit of our God.

---

1   (v.11) The Greek word translated drunkard refers to drunkenness from too much of any intoxicant. See Sorcery in Glossary.

2   (v.1) Synagogues had judges in the first century, so Paul was using the pattern with which he was so familiar. See Torah in Glossary.

3   (v.4) Although often translated "church," no Greek word meaning church is used in the NT. See Congregation in Glossary.

4   (v.10 This refers to drunkenness from any intoxicant, but for more on the subject, see Sorcery in Glossary.

5   (v.11) The Greek verb is apolouo, meaning to wash away, which is a reference to baptism.

Glorify God in Your Body

6:12. All things are permitted to me but not all things are profitable: all things are permitted to me but I am not mastered by anything. 13. The foods for the stomach and the stomach for the foods, but God will even do away with this *stomach* and these *foods*. And the body *is* not for immorality but for the Lord, and the Lord *is* for the body: 14. and God even resurrected the Lord and He will resurrect us through His power. 15. Do you not know that your bodies are members of Messiah? So then could the members of Messiah be members of a prostitute? God forbid! 16. Or do you not know that the one who is joined with a prostitute is one with *her* body? For "It will be," it is said, "the two *are* one flesh." (Gn 2:24) 17. But the one who is joined to the Lord is one spirit *with Him*. 18. You must continually flee immorality. Every sin that a man could do is outside *the* body: but of immoralities he sins against his own body. 19. Or do you not know that your body is a sanctuary[1] (Eph 2:21,22) of the Holy Spirit in you, which you have from God, and you do not belong to yourselves? 20. For you were bought with a price: now you must glorify God with your body.

Problems concerning Marriage

7.1. And concerning *the things* of which you wrote, *it is* good for a man not to touch a woman: 2. but because of the *temptation of* immoralities let each have his own wife and let each *woman* have her own husband. 3. The husband must continually surrender *his* obligation to his wife, and likewise also the wife to her husband. 4. The wife does not have power over her own body but the husband *does*, and likewise also the husband does not have power over his own body but the wife *does*. 5. You must continually not deprive one another, except from agreement for a time, so that you could devote yourselves to prayer. Then you should again be continuing *relations* the same way, so that Satan[2] could not test you through your lack of self-control. 6. And I say this by concession not by command. 7. For I want all men to be as even myself:[3] but each has his own gift from God, one in this manner, and another in that.

7:8. And I say for the unmarried and for the widows, it *is* good for them if they would remain as I: 9. but if they do not have self-control, they should marry, for it is better to marry than to be tested. 10. Those who have married I command, not I but the Lord, a wife *is* not to be separated from a husband, 11. - but even if she would be separated, she must remain unmarried or let her reconcile with her husband, - and a husband *is* not to divorce a wife. 12. And for the rest I, not the Lord, say: if some brother has an unbelieving wife and she agrees to live with

---

1   (v.19) The Greek word is naos, which means sanctuary. The temple had an outer court where sinners were welcome and an inner court where sin was dealt with. The priest had to deal with sin before entering the sanctuary or he died on crossing the threshold. See Sanctuary in Glossary.

2   (v.5) See Satan in Glossary.

3   (v.6) That is to remain single. Paul believed the second coming was imminent, Phil 4:5.

him, he must not divorce her: 13. and if some wife has an unbelieving husband and he agrees to live with her, she must not divorce her husband. 14. For the unbelieving husband has been sanctified by the wife and the unbelieving wife has been sanctified by the brother: otherwise your children are unclean, but now they are sanctified. 15. But if the unbelieving one separates, let him separate: the brother or the sister has not been bound as a slave in things such as these: but God has called you in peace. 16. For how do you know, wives, if you will save your husband? Or how do you know, husband, if you will save your wife?

The Life Which the Lord Has Assigned

7:17. Surely to each as the Lord divided, as God has called each, he must continually walk in this manner. And in this way I am ordering in all the congregations. 18. Anyone having been circumcised who has been called, he must not be uncircumcised: anyone uncircumcised who has been called, he must not be circumcised. 19. Circumcision is nothing and uncircumcision[1] is nothing, but keeping the commandments of God *is everything*.[2] 20. Each one must continually remain in this station in which he was called. 21. You were called a slave, you must not think about it: but then if you are able to become free, you must continually be more useful. 22. For the slave who has been called in *the* Lord is a freedman of *the* Lord, likewise the freedman who has been called is a slave of Messiah. 23. You were bought for a price: you must stop being slaves of men. 24. Each in which he was called, brothers, must remain in this before God.

The Unmarried and Widows

7:25. And I do not have a command of the Lord concerning the virgins, but I give an opinion as a faithful one is shown mercy by *the* Lord. 26. Therefore I think this is good because of the present situation, that *it is* good for a man to be *single*.[3] 27. *If* you have been bound to a wife, you must not ever seek divorce: *if* you have been divorced from a wife, stop seeking a wife. 28. But if then you would marry, you are not sinning, and if a virgin would marry, she does not sin: but such as these will have affliction in this life, and I *hope to* spare you *such affliction*. 29. And I say this, brothers, the time is short: from now on, those who have wives should be as those not having 30. and those who are crying as those not crying and those who are rejoicing as those not rejoicing and those who are

---

1   (v.19) The Talmud teaches that non-Jews are subject to the covenant with Noah. Noah's covenant has seven laws: Promote justice, prohibitions of idolatry, immorality, blasphemy, murder, cruelty to animals, and theft. Noah's covenant does not include circumcision.

2   (v.19) The essential circumcision is of the heart, Dt 10:16, 30:6, Jr 4:4; 9:25, and Eze 44:7.

3   (v.26) Paul says this because he believes Messiah is to come soon, shown by his statement in v. 29, "the time is short." Each generation is to act like it is the last generation before the Lord's return, but not to follow Paul's advice here. Jacob wrote in Jas 5:8 "You too must now be patient, you must strengthen your hearts, because the coming of the Lord has drawn near:" 1 Jn 2:18 says, "..it is the last hour.." See Coming of Messiah in Glossary.

buying as if they do not possess, 31. and those who are making use of the good things of this world as those not making full use of *it*: for the present form of this world is passing away. 32. But I want you to be free from anxieties. The unmarried one cares for the things of the Lord, how he could please the Lord: 33. but the one who has married cares for the things of the world, how he could please his wife, 34. and he has been divided. And the unmarried woman and the virgin care for the things of the Lord, so that she could be holy in both the body and the spirit: but the married woman cares for the things of the world, how she could please her husband. 35. And I say this for your own benefit, so that I would not put a noose on you but toward good order and devotion to the Lord without distraction.

7:36. But if someone thinks he is behaving indecently toward his virgin, if she would be past the bloom of youth, then in this way he is obligated to become *her husband*, he must do what she wishes, he does not sin, they must marry. 37. But who has stood steadfast in his heart, not having compulsion, but has power over his own desires and has judged this in his own heart, to keep his virgin, will do well. 38. So also the one who marries his virgin does well but the one who does not marry will do better.[1]

7:39. A wife has been bound for so long a time as her husband would live: but if the husband would sleep,[2] she is free to be married to whom she wishes, only in *the* Lord. 40. And it is more blessed if she would remain *unmarried*, according to my judgment:[3] and I think I have *the* Spirit of God.

Food Offered to Idols

8.1. And concerning meat offered to idols, we know that we all have knowledge. Knowledge makes proud, but love builds up: 2. if anyone thinks he knows something, he has not yet known as he ought to know: 3. but if someone would love God, this *person* is known by Him. 4. Therefore concerning food, of the meat offered to idols, we know that an idol *is* nothing in *the* world and that *there is* no God except One. (Dt. 6:4) 5. For even if indeed there are *some* called gods, whether in heaven or on earth, just as there are many gods and many lords, 6. but to us *there is* one God, the Father from Whom all things *come* and we *are* in Him, and one Lord Jesus Messiah, through Whom all things *are* and we *are* through Him.

8:7. But not everyone has *this* knowledge: and some, being used to the false god up until now, are eating food as offered to idols, and, since their conscience is weak, it is defiled. 8. But food will not place us near God: neither

---

1   (v.38) Paul believed Messiah was about to return, so there was no reason to have more children. See 1Cor 10:11 and Phil 4:5.
2   (v.39) Die, see Death in Glossary.
3   (v.40) Paul said in the 29th verse of this chapter that the time is short, that he expected Messiah's return very soon. Every generation should feel this way, but we must be thankful that few heeded Paul's suggestion not to marry and reproduce.

if we would not eat are we inferior, nor if we would eat are we superior.[1] 9. But watch out *that* somehow this authority of yours would not become a stumbling block to the weak. 10. For if someone would see you, knowing of *your* reclining in a meal offered to idols, then will not the conscience of this weak one be built up to eat the food offered to idols? 11. Thus the one who is weak, the brother for whom Messiah died, is destroyed by your knowledge. 12. And when you sin against your brothers in this manner, by wounding their conscience and making *them* weak, you are sinning against Messiah. 13. Whereupon if food causes my brother to sin, I do **not** eat meat in *this* lifetime, so that I would not cause my brother to sin.

The Rights of an Apostle

9.1. Am I not free? Am I not an apostle? And have I not seen Jesus our Lord? Are you not my work in *the* Lord? 2. If I am not an apostle to others, I most certainly am to you: for you are the seal of my apostleship in *the* Lord.

9:3. My defense to those who are investigating me is this. 4. Do we **not** have authority to eat and to drink? 5. Do we **not** have authority to take around *on apostolic missions* a sister, a wife, as even the rest of the apostles, and the brothers of the Lord, and Cephas?[2] 6. Or *is it* only myself and Barnabas *who* do not have authority to do *that*? 7. Who ever serves as soldiers at their own wages? Who plants a vineyard and does not eat its fruit? Or who tends a flock and does not eat of the milk of the flock? 8. *Is it* according to man I am saying these things, or does not the Torah even say these things? 9. For in the Torah[3] of Moses it has been written, "You shall not muzzle an ox while it is threshing." (Dt 25:4) *Are* oxen more cared about by God?[4] 10. or is He not certainly saying *this* for our sakes *as well*? For it was written for our sakes that the one who is plowing ought to plow on hope and the one who is threshing to partake of it on hope. 11. If we sowed the spiritual things in you, is it a great *thing* if we reap your material things? 12. If others enjoy rights of *support* from you, should we not more?

But we did not make use of this authority, and we were enduring everything, so that we would not give some hindrance to the gospel of the Messiah. 13. Do you not know that those who officiate the temple rites are eating from the *holy* things of the temple, *and* those who serve regularly at the altar have a share in the altar? (Lv 6:16,26[5]) 14. And thus the Lord commanded those who proclaim the gospel to live, *to be provided for,* by the gospel. 15. But I did not make use of any of these things. And I did not write these things, so that, just as it *would*

1   (v.8) Paul is in line with Jesus' statement in Mt 15:11 & Mk 7:15. Eternal life is not lost by what we eat, but earthly lives are shortened by diets too saturated with forbidden foods.
2   (v.5) Cephas is the Latin spelling of the Aramaic word Kefa, meaning Rock. See Cephas in Glossary.
3   (v.9) Torah, meaning teaching or instruction, refers to the first five books of the Bible but can also refer to the whole Tanach (Old Testament), and even the oral teachings. See Torah in Glossary.
4   (v.9) The Greek construction anticipates a negative answer.
5   (v.13) The verse numbers saying this in Lv 6 of the Tanach are: 10,11, and 19.

become for me: for it is better for me to die rather than anyone make my boasting empty. 16. For if I should preach the gospel, it is not boasting for me: for it is a compulsion for me: for woe it is to me if I would not proclaim the gospel. 17. For if I do this willingly, I have a reward: but if unwillingly, I am entrusted with a stewardship: 18. then what is my reward? So that I, while proclaiming the gospel without charge, will give the gospel to them without making full use of my authority in the gospel.

9:19. For although I was free from all things I subjected myself to everyone, so that I would gain more: 20. thus I became to the Jewish people as Jewish, so that I would win Jewish people: to those under legalism as *one* under legalism, although I was not under legalism myself, so that I could win those under legalism: 21. to those without Torah *I became* as without Torah, although I was not without *the* Torah of God, but a subject of Messiah, so that I would win those without Torah: 22. I became weak to the weak, so that I would win the weak: I have become all things to all, so that I would save some of every *gathering*. 23. But I do all things because of the gospel, so that I would become His partner.

9:24. Do you not know that all the runners in a stadium are indeed running, but one takes the prize? So you are running in order that you would lay hold of *the prize*. 25. And everyone who is contending exercises self-control in all things, so then those would take a perishable crown, but we *would take the* imperishable. 26. Hence I then am running not as uncertainly, so I do not box as beating air: 27. but I treat my body roughly and I bring it into subjection, lest somehow I would become disqualified when I preach to others.

Warning against Idolatry

10.1. For I do not want you to be ignorant, brothers, because all our fathers were under the cloud and all went through the sea 2. and all were baptized[1] into Moses in the cloud and in the sea 3. and all ate the same spiritual food 4. and all drank the same spiritual drink: for they drank from a spiritual rock, which *was* following *them*, and the rock[2] was the Messiah. 5. Nevertheless God was not pleased with most of them, and they were laid low in the desert. 6. And these patterns became ours, for we had cravings of a bad nature, just as those people desired bad things. 7. And you must stop being idolaters as some of them *were*, just as it has been written, "The people sat to eat and to drink and they got up to play." (Ex 32:6) 8. But we could not commit adultery, as some of them committed adultery and twenty-three thousand fell in one day. (Nu 25:1) 9. And

1   (v.2) The word baptize comes from the Greek word baptidzo, meaning immerse. See Baptize in Glossary.

2   (v.4) The Greek word translated rock is petra. Petra, meaning rock or large rock, does not convey the depth of the Hebrew words for rock that refer to Messiah. Three Hebrew words speak of God or Messiah as a Rock. They are tsor, referring to a sheer rock cliff; sali, referring to a huge, craggy, rocky cliff; and even (pronounced eh-ven) speaking of a cut stone as used in construction, particularly the cornerstone

we should not ever test the Messiah, in the way that some of them tested and were being destroyed by the snakes. (Nu 25:5,6) 10. And you must not ever grumble, as some of them grumbled and they were destroyed by the destroying angel. (Nu 14:2) 11. And these things typically happened with them, and it was written for our instruction, for whom the ends of the ages have arrived.[1] 12. So thus the one who thinks he has stood must see *that* he would not fall. 13. A trial has not taken you except *what is common to* mankind: but God is faithful, Who will not permit you to be tested beyond what you are able, and therefore He will then in the test make *you* able to patiently bear the way out.[2]

10:14. For which very reason, my beloved, you must habitually flee from idol worship. 15. As to *the* wise I say: you yourselves must constantly judge what I am saying. 16. *When* we are blessing the cup of the blessing, is it not fellowship from the blood of the Messiah? The bread which we break, is it not fellowship with the body of the Messiah? 17. Because *there is* one bread, we many are one body, for we all share from the one loaf. 18. Look at Israel according to flesh: are not those who eat sharers of the offerings of the altar? 19. So what am I saying? That idol worship is anything or that an idol is anything? 20. But that which the heathens are offering, they are offering to demons and not to God: I do not want you to become fellowshippers of the demons. 21. You cannot drink a cup of *the* Lord and a cup of demons, you cannot share a table of *the* Lord and a table of demons. 22. Or do we provoke the Lord to jealousy? Are we stronger than He?[3]

Do All to the Glory of God

10:23. All things are lawful but not all things are profitable: all things are lawful but not all things build up. 24. And no one must seek for himself but for the other. 25. And you are eating everything being sold in a meat market and because of your conscience anxiously questioning nothing: 26. for "The earth and the fullness of it *are* the Lord's." (Ps 24:1) 27. If any of the unbelievers calls you and you want to go, eat everything set before you and do not anxiously question anything because of your conscience. 28. But if someone would say to you, "This is of the temple offering," do not eat that because of that one who reveals *it* and his conscience: 29. but I am not speaking of himself but of the other. For why is my freedom judged by another's conscience? 30. If I share by grace, why am I cursed for what I am giving thanks *to God*? 31. Then whether you are eating or drinking or whatever you are doing, do all things to the glory of God. 32. And you must continually become blameless to Jewish people and to Greeks and to the congregation[4] of God, 33. just as I strive to please everyone

---

1   (v.11) Paul apparently believed his was the generation to welcome the end of time, explaining his writing 1Cor 7:29-38, which is to discourage marriage.
2   (v.13) See Trials in Glossary.
3   (v.22) The Greek construction anticipates a negative answer to the question.
4   (v.32) Although often translated "church," no Greek word meaning church is used in the NT. See Congregation in Glossary.

in every way, as I am not seeking the advantage for myself but for the many, so that they would be saved. **11**.1. You must continually be imitators of me,[1] just as I am of Messiah.

Covering the Head[2] in Worship

11:2. And I praise you because you have remembered everything from me and, just as I gave over to you, you are holding the instructions. 3. I want you to know that the Messiah is the head of every man, and her husband *is the* head of a wife, and God *is the* head of the Messiah. 4. Any man *who* prays or prophesies, if he has *long hair*[3] on his head disgraces his head. 5. But any wife *who* prays or prophesies with her head uncovered[4] disgraces her head: for it is one *and* the same *as* if she had been shaved. 6. Now if the wife is not covered, then she must be sheared: but if *it is* shameful for a wife to be sheared or to be shaved, she must continually be covered. 7. For the husband indeed ought not to cover *his* head *with long hair* since he is *the* image and glory of God: and the wife is *the* glory of *her* husband. 8. For man is not out of woman but woman out of a man, *Adam*: 9. for also man was not created because of the woman but *the* woman because of the man. 10. Because of this the wife ought to have authority upon *her* head because of the *fallen* angels.[5] 11. Nevertheless in *the* Lord *there is* neither a wife without a husband nor a husband without a wife: 12. for just as the wife *is* out of the husband, so also the husband *is* through, *born of*, the woman: and all things from God. 13. You must immediately judge these things for yourselves: is it proper *for* a wife to pray to God uncovered? 14. And does not nature teach you this, that if a man on the one hand *has* long hair it is a disgrace to him,[6] 15. but on the other hand for a woman it is her glory? Because the hair was given to her as an ornament in place of a prayer shawl.[7] 16. But if someone seems to be contentious,[8] we do not have a custom of this kind, *that is being contentious*, and neither do the congregations[9] of God.

Abuses at the Lord's Supper

11:17. But when I give these instructions I do not praise *you*, because you come together, not for the better but for the worse. 18. For indeed to begin

---

1   (v.1) This puts the seventh chapter of Romans in perspective: Paul was not perfect, but was making every effort to take every thought captive and to lead a life that was a good example for others.

2   (Caption) This paragraph is about hair, saying women should have long hair and men short hair, which was the custom throughout the Roman world.

3   (v.4) See v. 14 in this chapter.

4   (v.5) With short hair

5   (v.10) This is a reference to spiritual dangers. The husband must protect his home with prayer.

6   (v.14) The custom throughout the Roman empire was for men to have their hair very short.

7   (v.15) This Greek word is peribolaiou, the same word used to translate Prayer Shawl in the Septuagint, Dt 22:12. See Prayer Shawl in Glossary.

8   (v.16) To be contentious is to want to argue about something.

9   (v.16) See Congregation in Glossary.

with when you gather in a congregation I hear there are divisions among you and I believe it in part. 19. For it is necessary there should even be dissension among you, so that also the proved ones would become revealed to you. 20. Therefore when you come together for this it is not the Lord's supper you eat: 21. for each takes his own supper to eat beforehand, and indeed one is hungry and another is drunk.[1] 22. Do you not have homes in which to eat and to drink? Or do you despise the congregation of God, and do you shame those who do not have *enough*? What could I say to you? Shall I praise you? I do not praise *you* in this.

The Institution of the Lord's Supper

11:23. Now I received from the Lord, which I also gave over to you, that the Lord Jesus, on the night in which He was betrayed, took bread 24. and after He gave thanks[2] He broke *it* and said, "This is My body *being given* on your behalf: you must regularly do this in remembrance of Me." 25. Likewise also the cup after supper[3] saying, "This cup is the New Covenant by means of My blood: you must regularly do this, as often as you would drink *it*, in remembrance of Me." 26. For as often as you would eat this bread and you would drink the cup, you are proclaiming publicly the death of the Lord until He would come.

Partaking of the Supper Unworthily

11:27. Thus whoever would eat the bread or would drink the cup of the Lord unworthily sins against the body and the blood of the Lord. 28. But a man must habitually test himself and he must thus consistently eat from the bread and drink from the cup: 29. for the one who eats and drinks, when he does not *first* discern *that it is* the body of the Lord, is eating and drinking judgment for himself. 30. Because of this many among you *are* weak and sick and many are dying.[4] 31. But if we were judging ourselves correctly, we would not be judged: 32. but we are disciplined, being judged by the Lord, so that we would not be condemned with the world. 33. Thus, my brothers, when you come together to eat you must wait for one another. 34. If someone is hungry he must eat at home, so that you would not come together in judgment. And for the rest, whenever I would come I will set in order.

Spiritual Gifts

12.1. And concerning the spiritual, brothers, I do not want you to be ignorant. 2. Because you know that when you were heathens somehow you were being led away, being led astray to dumb idols. 3. On this account I am making

1   (v.21) This refers to drunkenness from any intoxicant, but for more on the subject, see Sorcery in Glossary.

2   (v.24) The blessing over the bread is made just before eating a meal.

3   (v.25) This is the third cup, taken after eating. The order is like a Seder, but this meal was not a Seder. See Seder in Glossary.

4   (v.30) Literally, this says sleep, a metaphor for what we call death. See Death in Glossary.

known to you that no one says, speaking in *the* Spirit of God, "Curse Jesus," and no one is able to say, "Lord Jesus," except by *the* Holy Spirit.

12:4. And there are varieties of gifts, but the same Spirit: 5. and there are varieties of ministry,[1] but the same Lord: 6. and there are varieties of activities, but the same God, the One Who works all things in all *people*. 7. And to each is given the manifestation of the Spirit toward that which is profitable *for all*. 8. For indeed through the Spirit to one is given a word of wisdom,[2] and to another a word of knowledge[3] according to the same Spirit, 9. to another faith by the same Spirit, and to another gifts of healings by the one Spirit, 10. and to another activities that call forth miracles, and to another prophecy, and to another discernings of spirits (Jn 16:8), *to another to speak* in different kinds of tongues, and to another interpretation of tongues: 11. but the one and the same Spirit operates all these things, distributing His own *gifts* to each, just as He wishes.[4]

One Body with Many Members

12:12. For just as the body is one but has many parts, and all the parts of the body, although there are many, are one body, so also the Messiah: 13. for we also were all baptized[5] by one Spirit into one body, whether Jewish or Greeks or slaves or free, and we all were given one Spirit to drink. 14. Now also the body is not one part but many. 15. If the foot would say, "Because I am not a hand, I am not part of the body," is it not in spite of this still part of the body? 16. And if the ear would say, "I am not an eye, I am not of the body," is it not of the body in spite of this *statement*? 17. If the whole body *were* an eye, how *could it* hear? If *the* whole *body were* a sense of hearing, how *could it* smell? 18. But now God placed the parts, each one of them in the body just as He wished. 19. But if all were one part, how *could there be* a body? 20. And now indeed *there are* many parts, but one body. 21. The eye is not able to say to the hand, "I do not need you," or again the head to the feet, "I do not need you:" 22. but much more the parts of the body *that* seem to be weaker are necessary, 23. and what we think to be insignificant of the body, to these we grant greater honor, and our unseemly *parts* have greater modesty, 24. but our presentable *parts* do not have need *of modesty*. But God united the body, when He gave greater honor to the inferior, 25. so that there would not be division in the body but the parts would have the same care on behalf of one another. 26. Then when one member suffers, all the members suffer together: when one member is glorified, all the members rejoice together.

---

1   (v.4) The Greek word diakonia could just as well be translated service. See Servant in Glossary.

2   (v.8) A word of wisdom tells someone how to act or react in a future situation.

3   (v.8) A word of knowledge gives a fact that is unknown to the speaker, but known to the listener. That could be a name, date, location, event, or some other fact.

4   (v.11) The Holy Spirit can give any gift to anyone at any time.

5   (v.13) The word baptize comes from the Greek word baptidzo, which means immerse. See Baptize in Glossary.

12:27. And you are *the* body of Messiah and members individually. 28. Now God indeed placed them in the congregation.[1] First *He placed* apostles, second prophets, third teachers, then miracles, then gifts of healings, helps,[2] administrations,[3] kinds of tongues. 29. *Are* all apostles? *Are* all prophets? *Are* all teachers? *Are* all miracles? 30. Are all having gifts of healings? Are all speaking in tongues? Are all translating?[4] 31. Then you must continually strive for the better gifts.

Love

And yet I am showing you a better way. **13**.1. If I speak in the tongues of men and of angels, but I do not have love, I have become sounds of brass or a clashing cymbal. 2. Now if I have a gift of prophecy and I would have known all mysteries and all knowledge and if I have all faith so as to move mountains, but I do not have love, I am nothing. 3. And I could give away all my belongings bit by bit *to help the poor* and if I should give over my body so that I could boast[5] in it, but I do not have love, I benefit nothing.

13:4. Love has patience, love is kind, not jealous, love does not boast, it is not proud, 5. it does not dishonor, it does not seek things for itself, it does not become angry, it does not charge evil to another, 6. it does not rejoice over unrighteousness, but rejoices together in truth: 7. it endures all things, it believes all things, it hopes all things, it is steadfast in all things.

13:8. And whether prophecies will be abolished: or tongues will cease: or knowledge will be abolished: love never perishes. 9. We know in part and we prophesy in part: 10. but when the perfect state, that is to be ushered in by the return of Messiah, would come, what *is* in part will be set aside. 11. When I was a child, I was speaking like a child, I was thinking as a child, I was reasoning as a child: when I became a man, I did away with the things of the child. 12. For we are seeing through a mirror dimly, but then face to face: even now I know in part, but then I shall know thoroughly just as I have been known. 13. And now these three remain, faith, hope, love: and the greatest of these *is* love.

Tongues and Prophecy

14.1. You must constantly pursue love, and you must continually be zealous for the spiritual things, and particularly that you would prophesy. 2. For the one who speaks in tongues does not speak to men but to God: for no one understands, but he speaks mysteries in *the* Spirit: 3. but the one who prophesies speaks to men, building up and encouraging and comforting. 4. The one who

---

1   (v.28) Although often translated "church," no Greek word meaning church is used in the NT. See Congregation in Glossary.
2   (v.28) This means care of the poor and the sick.
3   (v.28) Governing, qualities of leadership
4   (v.30) The Greek construction anticipates a negative answer to each of these questions.
5   (v.3) A fifth century manuscript misspelled the word translated Boast, changing the meaning to Burn.

speaks in tongues builds up himself: but the one who prophesies builds up *the* congregation. 5. Now I want you all to speak in tongues, but *even* more that you would prophesy: and the one who prophesies is greater than the one who speaks in tongues unless he would interpret, so that the congregation would be built up.

14:6. Now then, brothers, if I would come to you speaking in tongues, what will I profit you unless I would speak to you in revelation or in knowledge or in prophecy or in teaching? 7. Likewise when lifeless things give a sound, whether a flute or lyre, unless it would give a distinction to the notes, how would it be known *whether* the flute or the lyre was being played? 8. And if a trumpet would give an uncertain note, who will be prepared in war? 9. Thus then, *when* you would give a word through a tongue, unless *it is* clear, how will it be known to the one speaking? For you will be speaking air. 10. Perhaps so many kinds of sounds are in *the* world and **not** capable of conveying meaning: 11. if therefore I would not have known the meaning of the sound, I will be speaking a foreign language and the *other* one speaking a foreign language to me. 12. Thus also since you are zealous of the spiritual, you must constantly seek toward the edification of the congregation so that you would abound. 13. For this reason the one who speaks in tongues must continually pray that he would interpret. 14. For if I would pray in a tongue, my spirit is praying, but my mind is unfruitful. 15. Then what is it? I will pray in the Spirit, and I will pray also in my mind: I will sing in the Spirit, and I will also sing with my mind. 16. For if you would praise God in *the* Spirit, how will the one who takes the place of the unlearned[1] say the "Amen" over thanks given by you? Since he does not know what you are saying: 17. for you on the one hand *it is* good that you give thanks, but on the other hand the other one is not built up. 18. I give thanks to God, I speak in tongues more than all of you: 19. but in a congregation I want to speak five words with my mind, so then I would instruct others, rather than ten thousand words in tongues.

14:20. Brothers, stop being children in your thinking! But you must be infants with evil, and you must become mature in your thinking. 21. It has been written in the Torah that

> "In other tongues
> > and with other lips
> I will speak to this people
> > and thus no one will obey" Me, (Is 28:11,12, Dt 28:49)

says *the* Lord. 22. So tongues are a sign not for the believers but for the unbelievers, and prophecy *is* not for the unbelievers but for the believers. 23. Therefore if the whole congregation would come together at the same *time* and all would speak in tongues, and uninstructed *people* or unbelievers would enter, will they not

---

1   (v.16) This could be either one who does not have the gift of interpretation or one sitting among those who have not been taught in Scripture, in the manner in which seating was segregated in the synagogue.

say that you are mad?[1] 24. But if all would prophesy, and some unbeliever or uninstructed *person* would come in, he is convicted by all, he is called to account by all, 25. the hidden things of his heart become revealed, and so falling on *his* face he will worship God, proclaiming, "God is really among you."

All Things to be Done in Order

14:26. Then what is it, brothers? When you would come together, each one has a Psalm, has a teaching, has a revelation, has *a message in* a tongue, has an interpretation: all things must continually be toward building up *the congregation*. 27. If someone speaks in a tongue, *it should be* by two or at most three then in turn, and one must interpret: 28. but if there would not be an interpreter, he must be silent in *the* congregation, but he must speak to himself and to God. 29. And two or three prophets should speak and the others should consider: 30. and if *something* would be revealed to another who is seated, the first must be silent. 31. For you are all able to prophesy one at a time,[2] so that all could learn and all would be encouraged. 32. And spirits of prophets are subject to prophets, 33. for God is not *a God* of disorder but of peace, as in all the congregations of the saints.[3]

34. The wives must be silent in the congregations: for it is not permitted for them to speak, but they must be subject, just as also Torah (Gn 3:16[4]) says. 35. And if some want to learn, they must ask their own husbands at home: for it is shameful for a wife to speak in a congregation.[5] 36. Or did the Word of God originate with you or did He reach only you?

14:37. If someone thinks he is a prophet or spiritual, he must know what I am writing to you, because it is a command of the Lord: 38. if then someone disregards, he is to be disregarded himself. 39. Thus, my brothers, you must seek continually to prophesy and you must not hinder speaking in tongues:[6] 40. but all things must be done decently and according to order.

---

1   (v.23) V. 23 contradicts v. 22.
2   (v.31) This verse shows that churches are not to put limits on the number of prophecies.
3   (v.33) The editors of the Greek text placed the phrase "As in all the congregations of the saints" with the following verse, but here it is placed in the verse speaking about the proper use of gifts. The reason for this is that Paul mentioned the gifts to varied congregations, but addressed wives speaking in the congregation only to Corinth and to Timothy in Ephesus.
4   (v.34) Gn 3:16 says the wife will be subject to her husband, but Paul could have been referring to traditions. Notice that he only wrote about women to Corinth and Ephesus, while to the Galatian congregations he wrote "For there .. is not one male or female. For you are all one in Messiah Jesus." (Gal 3:28)
5   (v.35) Verses 34 & 35 have variants. Paul wrote about women being quiet or not teaching only to Corinth and Ephesus, (1 Tim 2:11) homes of the fertility goddesses Diana and Artemis, where women dominated and temple prostitution was approved. See the 19th chapter of Acts.
6   (v.39) Speaking in tongues is for today and is to be encouraged within the limits of this chapter, especially verses 27 & 28.

The Resurrection[1] of Messiah

15.1. And I am making known to you, brothers, the Good News which I proclaimed to you, which then you accepted, in which you have also stood, 2. and through which you are being saved, if you hold fast to the kind of message I preached to you, except in case you believed in vain. 3. For I gave over to you at first what also I had accepted, that Messiah died on behalf of our sins according to the Scriptures 4. and that He was buried and that He rose on the third day according to the Scriptures (Ps 16:10, Ho 6:2 Jonah 1:17)[2] 5. and that He was seen by Cephas,[3] then by the twelve:[4] 6. then He was seen by more than five hundred brothers at one time, most of whom are remaining until now, but some fell asleep:[5] 7. then He was seen by Jacob,[6] then by all the apostles: 8. and last of all as in an untimely birth He was seen by me. 9. For I am the least of the apostles, who is not qualified to be called an apostle, because I persecuted the congregation of God: 10. but by *the* grace of God I am what I am, and His grace which is in me did not become ineffective, but I labored more than all of them, not I but the grace of God which is with me. 11. Now whether *it was* I or those, in this way we are proclaiming and so you believed.

The Resurrection[7] of the Dead

15:12. And if it is preached that Messiah rose from the dead, how are some among you saying that there is no resurrection of *the* dead? 13. But if there is not a resurrection of *the* dead, then Messiah has not risen: 14. and if Messiah has not risen, then also our preaching *is* in vain, and your faith *is* in vain: 15. and then we are being found false witnesses of God, because we testified of God that He raised Messiah, Whom, if indeed the dead are not really being raised, He has not risen. 16. For if the dead are not raised, then Messiah has not been raised: 17. and if Messiah has not been raised, your faith is useless, you are still in your sins, 18. and consequently those who sleep[8] in Messiah are lost. 19. If we only have hope in Messiah for this life, we are all miserable people.

15:20. But now Messiah has been raised from *the* dead, first fruits of those who have slept. 21. For since death *is* through a man, then resurrection of *the* dead *is* through a Man. 22. For just as all are dying in Adam, so also will all be made alive in Messiah. 23. But each in his own order: Messiah is first fruits, then those of the Messiah at His coming, 24. then the end, when He would give over the kingdom to God and Father, when every leader and every authority and

---

1   (Caption) See Resurrection in Glossary.
2   (v.4) When Paul wrote this the only Scripture was what Christians call Old Testament. See Mt 12:40, Ac 2:24.
3   (v.5) This was on the road to Emmaus, Lk 24:34. Cephas is the Latin spelling of the Aramaic word Kefa, meaning rock. See Cephas in Glossary.
4   (v.5) See Mt 28:16-20, Lk 24:36-49, Jn 20:19-23, & 20:26-29.
5   (v.6) See Death in Glossary.
6   (v.7) The Greek text has Iakob, which is Jacob in English.
7   (Caption) See Resurrection in Glossary.
8   (v.18 & v.20) Sleep as used here is a Hebrew idiom for death. See Death in Glossary.

every power will be brought to an end. 25. For it is necessary for Him to reign until the time when He would place all His enemies under His feet.[1] 26. Death *is* the last enemy being abolished: 27. for "He subjected all things under His feet." (Ps 8:6) and when He would say that all things have been subjected *it is* clear that the One who subjects all things to *Messiah is Himself* excepted. 28. But when all things would be subject to Him, then also the Son Himself would have been subjected to the One Who subjected all things to Him, so that God would be all in all.

15:29. Because what will those who are baptized[2] on behalf of the dead be doing? If the dead are not actually being raised, then why are they being baptized on their behalf?[3] 30. Why then are we in danger every hour? 31. I die daily, as surely as I may boast in you, brothers, in Messiah Jesus our Lord. 32. If according to man I fought wild beasts in Ephesus, what *was* the profit for me? If the dead are not raised,

"We should eat and we should drink,
for tomorrow we die." (Is 22:13, 56:12)

33. You must stop being deceived:

"Evil associations are corrupting good customs." (Menander, *Thais* 218)

34. You must become righteously sober and stop sinning, for some have ignorance of God, *and* I am speaking to arouse shame in you.

The Resurrection[4] Body

15:35. But some will say, "How are the dead raised?" And "What sort of body is coming?" 36. Foolishness! What you are sowing does not live unless it would die *first*: (Jn 12:24) 37. then what you are sowing, you do not sow what will be the body, but a naked seed. Perhaps it will turn out *to be* wheat or some of the other *grains*: 38. but God would give it a body just as He wished, and to each of the seeds its own body. 39. But not all flesh *is* the same, but *there is* one kind of flesh for people, and another kind of flesh for domestic animals, and another flesh for birds, and another for fishes: 40. then *there are* heavenly bodies, and earthly bodies: another of the splendor of the heavenlies, but another of the earthlies. 41. With another *kind of* splendor for *the* sun, and another *kind of* splendor for *the* moon, and another splendor for *the* stars: for star differs from star in splendor.

15:42. So also the resurrection of the dead. It is sown in corruption, it is raised incorruptible: 43. it is sown in dishonor, it is raised in magnificence: it is

---

1   (v.25) See Footstool in Glossary.
2   (v.29) The word baptize comes from the Greek word baptidzo, meaning immerse. See Baptize in Glossary.
3   (v.29) Apparently Christians stood in for their unsaved dead relatives by being baptized for them.
4   (Caption) See Resurrection in Glossary.

sown in weakness, it is raised in power: 44. a body is sown fleshly, it is raised a spiritual body. If there is a fleshly body, there is also a spiritual.[1] 45. And so it has been written, "The first man was Adam in living life," (Gn 2:7) the last Adam *has become* a life-giving spirit. 46. But the spiritual was not first but the physical, then the spiritual. 47. The first man *is* from dust of *the* earth, the second man out of heaven. 48. What sort of earthly *man*, and such as these earthly *ones*, and what sort of the heavenly *One*, then such as these *born* of the heavenly nature: 49. and just as we bore constantly the image of the earthly, we shall bear constantly also the image[2] of the heavenly One.[3]

15:50. But I say this, brothers, that flesh and blood are not able to inherit *the* kingdom of God, nor does corruption inherit incorruption. 51. Behold I am telling you a mystery: we will not all be asleep *in death*,[4] but we shall all be transformed, 52. in a moment, in a twinkling of an eye, at the last trumpet:[5] for a trumpet will sound and the dead will be raised incorruptible and we will be transformed. 53. For it is necessary to clothe this corruptible *with the* incorruptible and to clothe this mortal *with the* immortal. 54. And when this mortal will be clothed immortal and this corruptible will be clothed incorruptible then the written word will happen,

"Death was swallowed up in victory." (Is 25:8)
55.   "Where, O Death, *is* your victory?
        Where, O Death, *is* your sting?" (Ho 13:14)

56. But sin *is* the sting of death, and the power of sin *is taken from* the Torah:[6] 57. but thanks to God, to the One Who gives us victory through our Lord Jesus Messiah. 58. Thus, my beloved brothers, you must continually be steadfast, immovable, abounding in the work of the Lord always, since you have known that your labor is not without result in *the* Lord.

The Contribution for the Saints

16.1. And concerning the collection for the saints, as I ordered the congregations of Galatia, so also must you now do. 2. On Saturday evening at the Havdalah[7] service each of you must now set aside for himself from *his* treasuries, *from* whatever he would have gained, so that when I would come then collections would not need to be made. 3. And when I would arrive, whomever you would approve, through letters, I will send them to carry your gift to Jerusalem: 4. and if it would be worthwhile for me to go, they will go with me.

---

1   (v.44) See Resurrected Body in Glossary.
2   (v.49) We are to be in His likeness, to continually become more like Him.
3   (v.49) See Resurrected Body in Glossary.
4   (v.51) See Death in Glossary.
5   (v.52) This Greek word, salpiggi, is also translated shofar. See both Shofar and Yom Kippur in Glossary.
6   (v.56) Torah means teaching or instruction. See Torah in Glossary.
7   (v.2) This service starts two hours after sundown Saturday evening to make the transition from the holy Sabbath to the secular workweek. See Havdalah in Glossary.

Plans for Travel

16:5. And I will come to you when I come through Macedonia: for I am coming through Macedonia, 6. and perhaps I could continue with you or even I will spend the winter, so that you could send me wherever I would go. 7. For I do not want to see you just now in passing, since I hope to remain with you some time, if the Lord will permit. 8. And I am staying in Ephesus until Shavuot.[1] 9. For a great and effective door has opened to me, but *there are* many opposed.

16:10. And if Timothy should come *to Corinth*, see *to it*, that he would be without fear among you: for he does the work of the Lord as *do* I: 11. therefore no one should scorn him. But you must now send him on his way in peace, so that he could come to me: for I am expecting him with the brothers.

16:12. And concerning our brother Apollos, I encouraged him much, so that he would come to you with the brothers: and it was not at all *God's* will that he would come now: but he will come when he would have an opportunity.

Final Request and Greetings

16:13. You must constantly be watchful, you must steadily stand firm in the faith, you must habitually conduct yourselves in a courageous way, you must continually increase in strength. 14. Everything you *do* must always be done in love.

16:15. I admonish you, brothers: you know the household of Stephanas, that it is a first fruit[2] of Achia and they placed themselves in service to the saints: 16. and that you would be subject to such as these then who work and toil together in everything. 17. And I rejoice on the arrival of Stephanas and Fortunato and Achaicus, because they filled the gap in your absence: 18. for they refreshed my spirit and yours. Therefore you must give recognition to such as they.

16:19. The congregations of Asia greet you. Aquila and Priscilla greet you warmly in *the* Lord with their house congregation. 20. All the brothers greet you. You must now greet one another with a holy kiss.

16:21. The greeting *is* in my hand, Paul. 22. If someone does not love the Lord, he must now be accursed, *excommunicated, doomed to destruction.* Maran atah![3] 23. The grace of the Lord Jesus *be* with you. 24. My love is with you all in Messiah Jesus.

---

1   (v.8) This is the Feast of Weeks in English, Pentecost in Greek.
2   (v.15) They were the first converts of Achaia, which included Athens and Corinth, the most important areas of Greece.
3   (v.22) The Hebrew "Maran atah" means, "You must come!"

~ 2 CORINTHIANS[1] ~

Salutation

1.1. Paul, an apostle of Messiah Jesus through *the* will of God, and brother Timothy to the congregation[2] of God which is in Corinth, with all those saints who are throughout Achia,[3] 2. grace and peace to you from God our Father and *the* Lord Jesus Messiah.

Paul's Thanksgiving after Affliction

1:3. Blessed be[4] God and Father of our Lord Jesus Messiah, the Father of all compassion and God of every encouragement, 4. the One Who comforts us in our every affliction by enabling us to comfort those in every affliction through the exhortation with which we ourselves are comforted by God. 5. Because just as the suffering of the Messiah abounds in us, so through the Messiah our comfort also abounds. 6. But, if we are afflicted *it is* on behalf of your comfort and salvation: or if we are comforted *it is* on behalf of your comfort, which is being worked in patience by the same sufferings which we are also suffering. 7. And our hope on your behalf *is* firm, since we know that, as you are sharers of the sufferings, so also *are you sharers* of the comforting.

1:8. For we do not want you to be ignorant, brothers, concerning our distress while we were in Asia, because we were burdened beyond measure, beyond ability so we despaired even of living: 9. but we have had the sentence of death on ourselves, so that we could not have trusted in ourselves, but in God, the One Who raises the dead: 10. Who rescued us and will cause us to escape from so great a death, in Whom we have hoped because yet still He will deliver *us*, 11. and, by your joining in helping us with your prayer on our behalf, that thanks could be given by many people for our deliverance from great peril to life.

The Postponement of Paul's Visit

1:12. Now our boasting is this, the witness of our conscience, that we

---

1   (Title) Written about 56 AD, after Thessalonians and 1Corinthians, but before Romans.
2   (v.1) Although often translated "church," no Greek word meaning church is used in the NT. See Congregation in Glossary.
3   (v.1) Achia is a major section of Greece, including Athens and Corinth.
4   (v.3) This is commonly translated "praised," but Blessed is more in keeping with Jewish prayers and is the primary meaning of the Greek word, eulogatos, used here.

have conducted ourselves with sincerity in the world in holiness before God, not with earthly wisdom, but by the grace of God, and far more toward you. 13. For in fact we are not writing to you except what you have read and what you know: and I hope that you will understand fully, 14. then just as you knew us in part, that we are boasting of you just as even you of us on the Day of our Lord Jesus.

1:15. And I wanted the same confidence to come to you earlier so that you would have a second gift of grace, 16. and to come through you *on my way* to Macedonia, then again to come to you from Macedonia and to be sent on my way by you to Judea. 17. So when I wanted this did I then vacillate? Or what I want do I want according to *the* flesh, so that it would be by me definitely yes and definitely no? 18. But God is faithful because our message to you is not Yes then No. 19. For the Son of God, Jesus Messiah, Who *is* in you, since He was proclaimed by us, by me and Silas and Timothy, it did not become Yes and No but it became Yes in Him. 20. For however many promises of God *there are, they are* "Yes, indeed!" in Him: on this account *we* also *say* through Him "Amen, glory to God." 21. And God *is* the One Who establishes us with you in Messiah, and Who has anointed us, 22. and the One Who has sealed us and has given the pledge of the Spirit in our hearts.

1:23. But I call upon God *as* a witness in my spirit, that I did not again come to Corinth, sparing you. 24. Because we are not lording over your faith but we are fellow workers of your joy: for you have stood in faith. **2.**1. For I decided this for myself to not again come to you in sadness. 2. For if I would grieve you, then who *is* the one who cheers me, except the one who has been grieved by me? 3. And I wrote this same thing, so that when I come I would not have grief from whom it was necessary for me to bring joy, confident in you all that my joy is of you all. 4. For from much tribulation and distress *of the* heart I wrote to you through many tears, not so that you would be grieved but especially so that you would know the love which I have for you.

Forgiveness for the Offender

2:5. But if someone has grieved *you, by committing incest*, he has not grieved me, but for part, that I would not say too much, *but he has grieved* you all. 6. Sufficient for such a one *is* this punishment by the majority, 7. so to the contrary rather to pardon and to comfort you, if somehow this one would not be overwhelmed in excessive sorrow. 8. On this account I urge you to confirm *your* love for him: 9. for I also wrote in this, so that I would know your character, if you are obedient in all things. 10. And whom you have forgiven something, I too: for also I have forgiven, if I have forgiven anything, for your sakes in *the* presence of Messiah, 11. so that we would not be taken advantage of by Satan:[1] for we are not ignorant of his purposes.

---

1   (v.11) See Satan in Glossary.

Paul's Anxiety and Relief

2:12. Now when I came to Troas for the purpose of the gospel of the Messiah and a door was opened for me by *the* Lord, 13. I had no rest[1] in my spirit *because* I did not find Titus my brother, but after I said farewell to them, I went out to Macedonia.

2:14. But thanks to God, the One Who always leads us in triumph in the Messiah and in revealing everywhere through us the fragrance of the knowledge of Him: 15. because we are *the* aroma of Messiah to God among those who are saved and among those who are lost to eternal misery, 16. to those on the one hand *it is the* aroma from death into death, but to others *it is the* aroma from life into life. And who *is* adequate for these things? 17. For we are not peddling the Word of God like many *are*, but as from sincerity, but as from God, we are speaking in the presence of Messiah, in the sight of God.

Ministers of the New Covenant

3.1. Are we beginning to commend ourselves again? Or do we need, as *do* some *false apostles*, letters of recommendation to you or from you?[2] 2. You yourselves are our letter, which has been written in our hearts, known and read by all mankind, 3. being revealed because you are a letter from Messiah, being cared for by us, not having been written in ink, but by *the* Spirit of *the* Living God, not on stone tablets but on tablets in fleshy hearts.

3:4. And we have such as this in confidence through the Messiah to God. 5. We are not qualified because of ourselves to reckon anything as from ourselves, but our competence *is* from God, 6. Who also qualified us servants[3] of a new covenant, not of letter but of spirit: for the letter[4] kills but the spirit makes alive.

3:7. But if the ministry[5] *which was* of death, in letters carved on stones, came in glory, so that the children of Israel were not able to look upon the face of Moses because of the radiance, which was to cease, on his face, 8. most surely will *not* the ministry of the Spirit be in more glory? 9. For if the ministry of condemnation *has* glory, the ministry of righteousness abounds in much more glory. 10. For indeed what had been made glorious, *the glow on Moses' face,* is no *longer* glorious in this matter, on account of the surpassing glory *seen on Jesus.* 11. For if that *which was* passing away *is* in the presence of glory, much more *will* the one remain *forever* in glory.

---

1   (v.13) This word means relief from the tension.
2   (v.1) The Greek construction anticipates a negative answer.
3   (v.6) The Greek word diakanos could be translated ministers, servants, or deacons. See Servant in Glossary.
4   (v.6) The letter is a reference to spelling every detail by humans: that is going by legalism and not by the Spirit. See Legalism in Glossary.
5   (v.7) Each word translated "ministry" in this paragraph could just as well be translated "service."

3:12. Therefore since we have such hope as this we proceed with much freedom in speaking 13. and not just as Moses was placing a veil on his face so the children of Israel did not look intently into the end of what was to be done away with, *the glow on his face.* 14. But their minds were hardened. For until the present day the same veil remains on the reading of the old covenant, not having been unveiled because *the veil* is removed by Messiah: 15. but until today whenever Moses would be read, a veil lies upon their hearts: 16. but whenever someone would turn toward *the* Lord, the veil is taken away. 17. And the Lord is Spirit: and where the Spirit of *the* Lord *is, there is* freedom.[1] (Gal 5:13) 18. And we all by raising the veil are transformed from glory to glory just as by *the* Spirit of *the* Lord, to behold for one's self the glory of *the* Lord.

Treasure in Earthen Vessels

4.1. Because of this, since we have this service, just as we have been shown mercy, we do not lose heart 2. but we disowned the hidden things of shame, not walking in cunning and not corrupting the Word of God, but in the disclosure of truth, showing ourselves to everybody's conscience before God. 3. And if indeed our gospel has been covered, it has been hidden to the lost, 4. among whom the god of this age blinded the minds of the unbelievers so the light of the Good News of the glory of Messiah, Who is *the* image of God, did not shine forth. 5. For we are not proclaiming ourselves but Jesus Messiah Lord, and we *are* your servants[2] by means of Jesus. 6. Because God *is* the One Who said, "Light will shine out of darkness," (Gn 1:3, Is 9:2) which shined in our hearts to reveal the knowledge of the glory of God in *the* presence of Jesus Messiah.

4:7. But we have this treasure in clay vessels, so that the extraordinary character of the power would be of God and not out from us: 8. being afflicted in everything but not completely confined, being in doubt but not completely at a loss, 9. being persecuted but not forsaken, being struck down but not being destroyed, 10. always carrying around the death of Jesus in the body, so that indeed the life of Jesus would be revealed in our body.[3] 11. For we, the living, are always given over into death for the sake of Jesus, so that also the life of Jesus would be revealed in our mortal flesh. 12. Thus death works in us, but life in you. 13. And because we have the same spirit of faith according to what has been written, "I believed, on this account I spoke," (Ps 116:10) and we are believing, on account of which we are also speaking, 14. since we have known that the One Who raised the Lord Jesus will also raise us with Jesus, and He will present us together with you *before His Judgment Seat.* 15. For all things *are* for your sakes, so that grace *which* abounds through the very many *saints* would overflow thanksgiving to the glory of God.

---

1   (v.17) The basic meaning of this word is to be free <u>from</u> something, referring first to freedom from sin, no longer being a slave to sin (Jn 8:34), then to deliverance through spiritual warfare.
2   (v.5) Or slaves, see Servant in Glossary.
3   (v.10) This means both each individual body and the collective congregational body.

Living by Faith

4:16. We do not despair on account of this, yet if indeed our outer man is corrupted, then the one within us is being renewed day by day. 17. Truly our affliction for the moment *is* insignificant beyond all measure and proportion into eternal fullness, a weight of glory eternally working out in us, 18. we do not notice what we are seeing but the things we do not see: for the things we see *are* temporary, but the things we do not see *are* eternal.

5.1. For we know that if our earthly house *we live in* of *this* tabernacle[1] would be destroyed, we have a building from God, an eternal house[2] in the heavens not made by *human* hands. 2. For indeed we sigh in this our dwelling, longing to put on, for ourselves, the one[3] from heaven, 3. then indeed, if we have been clothed we will not be found naked.[4] 4. For indeed we, who are in the tent,[5] sigh, being oppressed, because of which we do not wish to be unclothed but to be clothed,[6] so that our mortal *being* would be swallowed up by life. 5. And the One Who has worked this same thing in us *is* God, the One Who gave us the pledge of the Spirit.

5:6. Therefore, since we are always confident, and knowing that when we are at home in the body we are getting away from the Lord: 7. because we are walking by faith, not by sight: 8. but we are confident; we even rather prefer to leave from the body and to be at home with the Lord. 9. For this reason then we strive earnestly, whether when we are at home or when we are away, to be well pleasing to Him. 10. For it is necessary for us all to be revealed before the judgment seat of the Messiah, so that each would receive the things according to what he accomplished with his body, whether good or evil.[7]

The Ministry of Reconciliation

5:11. Therefore, because we have known the fear of the Lord, we persuade people. And we have been revealed to God: and indeed I hope to have been revealed to your consciences. 12. We are not commending ourselves to you again but giving you incentive to boast on our behalf, so that you could have *an answer* for those who boast in front of you, but *are* not *sincere* in *their* hearts. 13. For whether we are out of our senses for God: or we are of sound mind, *we are* for you. 14. For the love of the Messiah impels us, because we have determined this, that One died on behalf of all, therefore all died:[8] 15. He indeed died on

---

1   (v.1) Our bodies
2   (v.1) This is not a physical house, but a place in heaven. See Dwelling Places in Glossary.
3   (v.2) See Resurrected Body in Glossary.
4   (v.3) Without the covering of your heavenly tabernacle.
5   (v.4) That is, we who are alive. The word translated tent is the same word translated tabernacle in v. 1.
6   (v.4) Put on
7   (v.10) This is our good deeds and certain sins. See both Mitsvah and Sin in Glossary.
8   (v.14) Immersed in baptism, dead to self, we are raised in newness of life in Him. See

behalf of all, so that the living would no longer live for themselves but *for Him* because of *His* having died and having been raised on their behalf.

5:16. Thus from now on we know no one according to *the* flesh: if then we had known Messiah according to *the* flesh, nevertheless now we no longer know. 17. So if someone *is* in Messiah, *he is* a new creation: the old things passed away, behold he has become new. 18. And all things *are* from God, the One Who reconciled us to Himself through Messiah and Who gave us the ministry of reconciliation, 19. because God was reconciling *the* universe to Himself by means of Messiah, since He does not reckon their transgressions to them, and because He placed in us the message of reconciliation. 20. Therefore we are ambassadors on behalf of Messiah as God exhorts through us: we beg, in the name of Messiah, *that* you must immediately be reconciled to God. 21. He made the One Who did not know sin *to be* sin on our behalf, so that we ourselves would know *the* righteousness of God by means of Him.

6.1. And working together we also urge you not to receive the grace of God in vain: 2. for He says,

"I hearkened to you in an acceptable time
and I gave aid to you on *the* day of salvation." (Is 49:8)

Behold now *is the* acceptable time, behold now *is the* day of salvation. 3. And in **nothing** giving occasion for taking offense, so that the ministry would not be found at fault, 4. but in all things because we have presented ourselves as servants of God, with much patience, in tribulations, in distresses, in troubles, 5. in beatings, in imprisonments, in disturbances, in laborings, in sleepless nights, often without food, 6. with sincerity, with knowledge, with patience, with goodness, in *the* Holy Spirit, with sincere love, 7. with a message of truth, with *the* power of God: with the weapons of righteousness for offense and for defense, 8. through glory and dishonor, through slander and good report: as impostors and *still* true, 9. as unknown *by the world* but thoroughly known *by the saints*, as being dead but behold we are living, as being chastised by the infliction of evils and calamities but not put to death, 10. as always being grieved but being joyful, as poor but being made very rich, as not having anything but possessing all things.

6:11. Our mouth has opened *speaking freely* to you, Corinthians, our heart has opened wide: 12. you are not restricted in us, but rather you are restricted in your own hearts and inner thoughts: 13. but, like I am speaking to *my* children, widen your hearts in the same way in exchange.

The Sanctuary of the Living God

6:14. You must not ever become unevenly yoked with unbelievers: for would some mix righteousness and iniquity, or some the fellowship in light, with

---

Baptize in Glossary.

darkness? 15. But what agreement *is there* of Messiah with Beliar,[1] or what has a believer in common with an unbeliever? 16. And what agreement *can anyone have* with idols in a sanctuary of God? For we are a sanctuary[2] of *the* living God, just as God said that

> "I will dwell and I will walk among them
> > and I will be their God
> > and they will be My people." (Lv 26:12, Jr 32:38, Eze 37:27)

17. On this account "You must immediately come out from *the* midst of
> > them
> > and you must be separated *from them* at once," says *the* Lord,
> "and you must not ever touch *the* unclean:
> > then I will take you in" (Is 52:11, Eze 20:34,41)

18. and "I will be for a Father to you
> > and" you will be for sons" and daughters "to Me."
> > (2Sm 7:8,14, Is 43:6, Jr 31:9)
> says *the* "Lord of Hosts."[3]

7.1. So since we have these promises, beloved, we should cleanse ourselves from all defilement of flesh and of spirit, bringing about holiness in reverent fear of God.

Paul's Joy at the Congregation's Repentance

7:2. You must immediately make room for us: and we did not do wrong, and neither did we corrupt anyone, nor did we take advantage. 3. I am not saying *this* for *your* condemnation: for I have told you in advance that you are in our hearts to die together and to live together. 4. For myself, *I have* much confidence in you, much boasting by me concerning you: I have been filled with encouragement; in all our affliction I *still* overflow with joy.

7:5. Indeed when we came into Macedonia our flesh had not even had rest[4] but *we were* being afflicted in everything: strife outwardly, fears within. 6. But the One Who comforts the lowly, God, comforted us by the coming of Titus, 7. not only in his coming but also in the comfort by which he was comforted by you, when he reported to us your longing, your mourning, your zeal concerning me so that I rejoiced more. 8. Because even if I did grieve you in my letter, I do not regret *it*: indeed if I were regretting, for I see that the letter, if even for a moment it grieved you, 9. now I rejoice, not because you were grieved but because you were grieved into repentance: for you were grieved according to God, so that you would no longer suffer loss through us. 10. For grief before God,

1   (v.15) Satan
2   (v.16) It is significant that Paul used the word for sanctuary, the Holy Place and Holy of Holies. The temple had the outer court where heathens, with their sin, were welcome. The inner court had the altar where sin was dealt with. See Sanctuary in Glossary.
3   (v.18) Other translators have this "Lord Almighty," but Jewish translators used this Greek word for "Lord of Hosts." See Lord of Hosts in Glossary.
4   (v.5) This means relief from the pressure.

not to be regretted, works repentance into salvation: but grief of the world brings about death. 11. For behold this same thing, to have been grieved according to God brought about so great an eagerness in you, and rather an impatience to clear yourselves, and indignation, then fear, and longing, and zeal, and punishment. You stood together with yourselves in everything *and* have shown that you are blameless in the matter. 12. So if I then wrote to you, not on account of wrong doing and not on account of being wronged, but so your eagerness on our behalf would be revealed by you before God. 13. Because of this we have been encouraged.

But in addition to our encouragement we did far more rather rejoice over the joy of Titus, because his spirit had been refreshed by all of you: 14. because whatever I had boasted to him about you, I was not put to shame, but as everything we said about you *is* true, so also our boasting to Titus became true. 15. And his heart goes out to you so much more by the obedience of you all to us, as you received him with fear and trembling. 16. I am glad that I am confident in you in everything.

Liberal Giving

8.1. And we are making known to you, brothers, the grace of God that was given in the congregations[1] of Macedonia, 2. how that in a great trial of affliction the abundance of their joy and in which their down deep poverty abounded into the wealth of their generosity: 3. *so* that according to ability, I testify, even beyond ability, of their own accord 4. with much urging, when they asked of us the favor to take part in the service[2] to the saints, 5. and not just as we hoped, but through the will of God, they gave themselves first to the Lord then to us: 6. we urged Titus, that just as he began so also he would bring about this grace in you. 7. But even as you are abounding more than enough in all things, in faith and in speaking and in knowledge and in every eagerness and in your love for us, as you also would abound in this grace *of giving*.

8:8. I am not saying in a command, but even proving the sincerity of your love through *showing you* the diligence of others: 9. for you know the merciful kindness of our Lord Jesus Messiah, that although He was rich, He became poor for your sake, so that you would in His poverty now become rich. 10. And I am *only* giving an opinion in this: for this is to your advantage, not only what to do but you even began to want *to send this offering* a year ago. 11. So even now you must right away complete doing *it*, so just as *you are* inclined, so also to finish *what you* have *begun*. 12. For if the willingness to give is there, which is said to be acceptable, *but* not to the degree that he does not have.[3] 13. For not that others

---

1   (v.1) Although often translated "church," no Greek word meaning church is used in the NT. See Congregation in Glossary.
2   (v.4) Donation, ministry, to the believers in Jerusalem.
3   (v.12) Don't give beyond your means.

have rest,[1] *and* you affliction, but from equality:[2] 14. at this time your abundance for those needs, so that *later* then their abundance could come for your needs, so equality could come about, 15. just as it has been written,

"The one who had much did not have too much,
and the one who had little did not have less." (Ex 16:18)

Titus and His Companions

8:16. But thanks *be* to God, the One Who gave this eagerness to Titus' heart on your behalf, 17. because he not only received the urging, but being more eager he came out to you of his own accord. 18. And we sent with him the brother who *is* praised through all the congregations for *his labor in* the Good News, 19. and not only *that*, but, then, he also has been chosen our traveling companion by the congregations, with this gift *that is* being served by us: to the glory of the Lord Himself, and our willingness, 20. now we are trying to avoid this, lest some would find fault with us for this lavish gift which is being distributed by us: 21. for we take into consideration *for us to be* morally good, not only before *the* Lord, but also before mankind. 22. And we sent with them our brother whom we proved to be diligent in many ways, but now *he is* more diligent with much more confidence in you. 23. Whether on behalf of Titus, a sharer with me and a fellow worker among you: or our brothers, *we are* apostles for *the* congregations, glory to Messiah. 24. Therefore the proof of your love and of our boasting concerning you *is* being shown to them before the congregations.

The Offering for the Saints

9.1. For indeed it is unnecessary for me to write to you concerning *this* ministry *gift* to the saints: 2. for I know your willingness which I am boasting about in Macedonia on your behalf, that *you in* Achia prepared from last year and your zeal provoked very many. 3. And I sent the brothers, so that our boasting about you would not be empty in regard to this, so that you would be prepared just as I was saying, 4. how if the Macedonians would come with me then they would find you as we would have boasted, not unprepared, so that I am not saying you *would be unprepared*, in this situation. 5. Therefore I thought it necessary to exhort the brothers, so they would go on before to you and get your previously promised blessing, so this *would* be prepared as a blessing and not as a demand.

9:6. And this, the one who sows[3] sparingly will also reap sparingly, and the one who sows bountifully will also reap bountifully. 7. Each just as he chose in his heart, not reluctantly or from compulsion: for God loves a cheerful giver, 8. And God is able to abound all grace in you, so that in all things always having sufficiency you would abound in every good work, 9. just as it has been written,

---

1   (v.13) This means relief from tension.
2   (v.13) You don't have to carry the whole load.
3   (v.6) See Sowing and Reaping in Glossary.

"He scattered, he gave to the poor,
his righteousness remains forever." (Ps 112:9)

10. But the One Who supplies seed to the sower also provides bread for food and He will increase your seed and will increase the yield of your righteousness. 11. Being made rich in all things for every *demonstration of* generosity. This *generosity served* through us brings about thanksgiving to God: 12. because the ministry of this service is not only filling up the needs of the saints, but even is more than enough through many thanksgivings to God: 13. through the proving of this ministry, glorifying God over the subjection of your confession to the gospel of the Messiah and your sharing in sincerity with them and with everybody, 14. and in their prayer concerning you, longing for you because of the surpassing grace of God upon you. 15. Thanks to God for His indescribable gift.

Paul Defends His Ministry

10.1. I, Paul, urge you, through the gentleness and humility of the Messiah, I indeed in person *am* humble among you, but when I am absent I am bold for you: 2. and I beg that when I am not present, to be bold with confidence, which I consider to be courageous toward some who consider us as walking according to flesh. 3. For though we walk in *the* flesh we are not serving as soldiers according to the flesh, 4. for the weapons of our warfare are not fleshly but powerful in God for *the* tearing down of strongholds, tearing down reasonings 5. even every high thing being lifted up against the knowledge of God, and taking captive every thought in obedience to Messiah, 6. and being ready to punish every disobedience, when your obedience would be achieved.

10:7. You look at things according to outward circumstances. If someone has become confident in himself to be of Messiah, he must continually consider this again on himself, that just as he *is* of Messiah, so also *are* we. 8. For I will not be ashamed if I would boast more than enough about our authority, which the Lord gave for building up, and not for your destruction. 9. So that I would not seem as someone to frighten you by my letters: 10. because, they say, "His letters indeed, *are* severe and strong, but the presence of *Paul's* body *is* weak and his word amounts to nothing." 11. Let such a one consider this, that we are such as these in the message through *our* letters when we were absent. We will also be such as these in deed when we are present.

10:12. For we would not presume to class or to compare ourselves with some of those who recommend themselves, but among themselves, measuring themselves and comparing themselves with themselves, they are not good and upright *with knowledge of things relating to salvation*. 13. Now we will not boast excessively, but according to the measure of the sphere of action which God assigned to us, *which* reaches also even to you. 14. For as we are not overextending ourselves, coming as far as you, for we also reached as far as you with the gospel of the Messiah, 15. not boasting excessively in others' labors, but having hope of your increasing faith magnified superabundantly in you according to our limits 16. to evangelize those beyond you, not to boast in a province, sphere of activity, belonging to another, in *congregations* founded by others. 17. But "The one who boasts must boast in *the* Lord:" (Jr 9:24) 18. for the one who commends himself, that one is not approved, but whom the Lord commends.

Paul and the False Apostles

11.1. I would that you were putting up with a little of my foolishness: but indeed you are putting up with me. 2. Indeed, I am zealous for you, with God's earnest desire, for I gave you in marriage to one Man, to present a chaste virgin to Messiah: 3. and I fear lest somehow, as the snake deceived Eve with his cunning, your thoughts could be corrupted from the simplicity and the sincerity in the Messiah. 4. For if indeed the one who comes is preaching another Jesus whom we did not preach, or you are taking a different spirit which you did not take *from us*, or a different gospel which you did not receive *from us*, but you put up with *it* quite easily. 5. For I consider myself not to be inferior to the super apostles *who were bringing a different message.* 6. And if *I am* also unskilled in speaking, but not in knowledge, but in every way having made known among you in all things.

11:7. Or have I sinned by humbling myself, so that you would be lifted up, because I preached the gospel of God without taking an offering from you? 8. I robbed other congregations,[1] taking support toward your service, 9. and when I was present with you, although I suffered want, I was burdensome to no one: for the brothers supplied *what* I needed when they came from Macedonia, and in everything I kept myself not burdensome for you and I will keep *so.* 10. It is *the* truth of Messiah in me that this boasting will not be stopped in me in the districts of Achia. 11. Why? Because I do not love you? God knows.

11:12. But what I am doing, and I will keep on doing, so that I will cut off the opportunity of those who want opportunity, so that in whom they are boasting they would have been found just like us. 13. For such false apostles as these *are* deceitful workers disguising themselves as apostles of Messiah. 14. And no wonder: for Satan[2] disguises himself as an angel of light.[3] (Is 14:12) 15. Therefore *it is* not great if his servants also are disguised as servants/ministers of righteousness: whose end will be according to their works.

Paul's Sufferings as an Apostle

11:16. Again I say, lest anyone would think me to be a fool: otherwise

---

1   (v.8) Although often translated "church," no Greek word meaning church is used in the NT. See Congregation in Glossary.
2   (v.14) See Satan in Glossary.
3   (v.14) The angel of light is named Lucifer, from the Latin lux for light and ferre to bring. This is another name for Satan. The angel of light also refers to the morning star in Is 14:12, Venus, which was worshipped by the Babylonians, who called it Ishtar.

even if you must take me as a fool, that I also would boast a little. 17. What I am speaking, I am not speaking according to *the* Lord but as in foolishness, in this confidence of boasting. 18. Since many would boast according to flesh, then I myself will boast. 19. For you must gladly endure regularly the foolishness of *those who* are wise. 20. For you must endure if someone enslaves you, if someone devours, if someone takes, if someone is presumptuous, if someone strikes you in *the* face. 21. I must confess my shame, since we have been weak. In whomever any would dare, I say in foolishness, and I myself dare. 22. Are they Hebrew? I also. Are they Israeli? I also. Are they seed of Abraham? I also. 23. Are they servants of Messiah? I am speaking as if I am void of understanding, I more: far more in labors, far more in prisons, exceedingly in beatings, many times close to death. 24. Five times I took forty strokes less one by the Jewish *leaders*, 25. I was beaten with a rod three times, I was stoned once,[1] I suffered shipwreck three times,[2] I have spent a day and a night in the deep sea: 26. in many journeys, in dangers from rivers, in dangers from robbers, in dangers from my people, in dangers from heathens, in dangers in a city, in dangers in a wilderness, in dangers in a sea, in dangers among false brothers, 27. in labor and in hardship, in sleepless nights many times, in famine and in thirst, many times in fasting, in cold and lack of sufficient clothing: 28. apart from *that*, besides the incursion against me day by day, *there is* the care of all the congregations. 29. Are any in weakness and I am not weak? Are any caused to sin and I am not incensed?

11:30. If it is necessary to boast, I will boast the things of my weakness. 31. And God, *the* Father of the Lord Jesus, the One Who is praised forever, knows that I am not lying. 32. In Damascus the governor Areta was surrounding the city of Damascus to seize me, 33. and I was let down in a basket[3] through a window in the wall and I escaped from his hands.

Visions and Revelations

12.1. It is necessary to boast, even though it doesn't help, but I will go on to visions and revelations of *the* Lord. 2. I know a man *who was* in Messiah more than fourteen years ago, whether in *the* body I do not know, God knows, or outside the body I do not know, this one was taken away up to the third heaven.[4] 3. And I know such as this man, whether in *the* body or without *the* body I do not know, God knows, 4. that he was taken away into Paradise and he heard inexpressible words, which are not permissible for a man to speak. 5. I will boast about these things, but I will not boast of myself except in the weaknesses. 6.

---

1   (v.25) The stoning was in Lystra, Acts 14:19.

2   (v.25) This was written before the shipwreck in the 27th Chapter of Acts.

3   (v.33) The only use of this Greek word in the NT, this refers to the type of basket, not the size. This basket was made from braided ropes. In Acts 9:25 Luke uses the same word for hamper as Mt 15:37 and Mk 8:8, after the feeding of the four thousand, giving us a clue to the size of those hampers.

4   (v.2) This could well have been fourteen years after Paul and Barnabas ministered in Lystra, Acts 14:19,20. In the Hebrew Scripture there are seven levels in heaven. See Heavens in Glossary.

For if I would want to boast, I will not be foolish, for I will speak *the* truth: but I am sparing *you*, lest someone would take into account about what he sees in me or hears from me 7. and in the superiority of the revelations. On this account, so that I would not exalt myself, a thorn[1] in the flesh was given to me, a messenger *of* Satan,[2] so that he could strike me, so that I would not exalt myself. 8. I begged the Lord three times about this that it would leave from me. 9. And He spoke to me, "My grace is sufficient for you, for My power is made complete in weakness." Therefore I will gladly boast more in my weaknesses, so that the power of the Messiah would take possession within me. 10. For this reason, on behalf of Messiah, I think it good *to be* in weaknesses, in wrong springing from arrogance, in distress, in persecutions and troubles: for when I would be weak, then I am strong *in spirit*.

Paul's concern for the Corinthian Congregation

12:11. I have become foolish, you forced me. For I ought to have been commended by you: for I am not inferior to the super apostles even if I am nothing. 12. Indeed the signs of the apostle were brought about among you with the greatest perseverance, in signs and in wonders and in miracles. 13. For what is it, that you were worse off more than the rest of the congregations, except that I did not burden you? You must immediately forgive me this unrighteousness. 14. Behold I am ready to come to you this third time, but I will not be burdensome *to you*: for I am not seeking what is yours but you. For the children are not obligated to store up for the parents, but the parents for the children. 15. And I gladly spend *my money* and I will wholly spend myself *physically* on behalf of your lives. If I love you far more, should I be loved less? 16. But it must be, I did not weigh you down: but being clever they took you in deceit. 17. I had not sent any of *the false apostles* to you, did I take advantage of you through this? 18. I urged Titus and I sent the brother with *him* at the same time: and Titus did not take advantage of you did he? Did we not walk in the same spirit? Are not they in the same footprints *as mine*?

12:19. You think *that* for a long time we have been defending ourselves with you. We have been speaking in the presence of God on account of Messiah: and all things, beloved, on behalf of building you up. 20. For I am afraid, how, after I come, I would find you such as I do not want and I would have been found by you in some manner *such as* you do not want: somehow in strife, jealousy, angers, selfish ambitions, slanders,[3] tale-bearings, pride, unruliness: 21. when I come again God would humble me to you and I would weep much over those

---

1   (v.7) There is a great deal of speculation about this thorn. Is it a reference to some physical problem or to troublesome people? There is no way to be certain, but 'painful thorn' is a metaphor for menacing neighbors in Eze 28:24. The Greek word skolops, translated thorn, refers to a sturdy, pointed piece of wood, a pike upon which a body could be impaled. It most likely was not a physical problem.

2   (v.7) See Satan in Glossary.

3   (v.20) See Gossip/Slander in Glossary.

who sinned beforehand and have not repented for the uncleanness and immorality and licentiousness, which they did.

Final Warnings and Greetings

13.1. I am coming to you this third time: "upon *the* mouths of two or three witnesses shall every word stand:" (Dt 19:15) 2. I have told you beforehand and I am telling you plainly beforehand, as when I came the second time and being absent now, to those who sinned formerly and to all the rest, that if I would come into it again I will not spare *you*, 3. since you are demanding a proof that Messiah speaks through me, which is not weakness in you but shows itself powerful in you. 4. For then He was crucified from weakness, but He is living because of *the* power of God. For we also are weak in Him, but we shall live with Him because of *the* power of God in you.

13:5. You must test yourselves *to see* if you are in the faith, you must continually examine yourselves: do you not know that Jesus Messiah *is* in you? Unless indeed, you are disqualified. 6. But I hope that you will know that we are not disqualified. 7. And we pray to God that you would not do any evil, not so that we reveal ourselves proved, but so that you would be doing good things, and as we would be not approved. 8. For we are not enabled any against the truth but on behalf of the truth. 9. For we rejoice when we would be weak, but you would be powerful: and we pray for this, your strengthening, *training, disciplining*. 10. Because of this I write these things while I am absent, so that when I am present I would not act severely, according to the authority which the Lord gave to me to build up and not to tear down.

13:11. Finally, brothers, rejoice, put in order, be encouraged, be in harmony, be at peace, and the God of love and peace will be with you. 12. You must immediately greet one another with a holy kiss. All the saints greet you.

13:13. The grace of the Lord Jesus Messiah and the love of God and the fellowship of the Holy Spirit *be* with you all.

~ GALATIANS[1] ~

Salutation

1.1. Paul, an apostle not from men and not by man, but through Jesus Messiah and God *the* Father, the One Who raised Him from *the* dead, 2. and all the brothers with me, to the congregations[2] of Galatia, 3. grace and peace to you from God our Father and Lord Jesus Messiah 4. the One Who gave Himself on behalf of our sins, so He could deliver us out from the present evil age according to the will of our God and Father, 5. to Whom be the glory forever and ever, amen.

There is No Other Gospel

1:6. I am amazed that you are turning away so quickly to a different gospel from the One Who called you in grace, Messiah, 7. which is not another *gospel*, unless some *deceivers* are troubling you and want to turn around the gospel of the Messiah. 8. But if even we or an angel out of heaven would bring a gospel to you contrary to the one we brought to you, he must be doomed to destruction, *an accursed thing.* 9. As we told beforehand, now I also say again, if anyone brings you a gospel contrary to what you received, he must be accursed, *doomed to destruction.*

1:10. For now do I try to win over men or God? Or do I strive to please people? Yet, if I were pleasing people, I would not be a servant of Messiah.

How Paul Became an Apostle

1:11. For I make known to you, brothers, the gospel which was proclaimed by me that it is not according to man: 12. for neither did I take it from a person nor was I taught *it*, but *I was given it* through a revelation by Jesus Messiah.

1:13. For you have heard about my earlier conduct when in Judea,[3] that I persecuted beyond measure the congregation of God and was destroying it, 14.

---

1   (Title) Written about 48-57 AD.
2   (v.2) Although often translated "church," no Greek word meaning church is used in the NT. See Congregation in Glossary. There were a number of congregations in Galatia because in the first century it was a Roman province in Asia Minor, including the cities of Antioch, Iconium, Lystra, and Derbe. There was another Antioch in Syria, on the Mediterranean coast.
3   (v.13) This Greek word Ioudaismos, normally translated Judaism, means "of or pertaining to Judea." The modern use of the word "Judaism" came centuries later.

and I was advancing in Judaism over many contemporaries in my class, since I was a zealot of the traditions of my ancestors to a much greater degree. 15. But when God chose, the One Who appointed me from my mother's womb and Who called *me* through His grace, 16. to have revealed His Son to me, so that I would proclaim Him to the heathens, I did not immediately consult flesh and blood 17. and I did not go up to Jerusalem to those *who were* apostles before me, but I went to Arabia, then again returned to Damascus.

1:18. Then after three years I went up to Jerusalem to get to know Cephas[1] and I stayed with him fifteen days, 19. but I did not see another of the apostles except Jacob,[2] the brother of the Lord. 20. And *about* which I write to you, behold before God that I am not lying. 21. Then I went through the regions of Syria and Cilicia: 22. but I was not known in person by those congregations of the Jewish people in Messiah. 23. But they were only hearing that "The one formerly persecuting us is now proclaiming the gospel of faith which he was formerly destroying," 24. and they were praising God because of me.

Paul Accepted by the Other Apostles

2.1. Then after fourteen years[3] I again went up to Jerusalem, (Ac 11:30) taking along Barnabas and Titus: 2. and I went up according to a revelation: and I presented the gospel to them which I am proclaiming to the heathens, but privately to those reputed *to be of influence*, lest I would run or did run in vain. 3. But even Titus who *was* with me, although he was Greek, was not compelled to be circumcised: 4. but *the subject came up* because of false brothers, secretly brought in, who did sneak in to spy out our freedom which we have in Messiah Jesus, so they could reduce us to slavery *in legalism*, 5. but to whom we did not yield for an instant to the subjection, so that the truth of the gospel would remain permanently with you. 6. But from those who think they are somebody, - of what sort they were formerly makes no difference to me: God does not show partiality[4] - for those who think *they are something* imparted nothing to me, 7. but on the contrary, when they saw that I had been entrusted the gospel for the uncircumcised, just as Peter with the circumcised, 8. for the One Who worked in Peter in an apostleship for the circumcision also worked in me to the heathens, 9. and since they knew the grace that was given to me, Jacob[5] and Cephas,[6] and John, those who are reputed to be pillars, did pledge mutual fellowship with me and Barnabas, so that we *would go* to the heathens, and they to the circumcision:

1   (v.18) Cephas is the Latin spelling of Kefa, which is an Aramaic word for "Rock." See Cephas in Glossary.
2   (v.19) The Greek text has Iakob, which is Jacob in English. See Jacob in Glossary.
3   (v.1) This could be fourteen years from his Damascus road experience or fourteen years from his Gal 1:18 trip.
4   (v.6) Literally this is "take the appearance of a man," a Hebrew idiom meaning He is does not play favorites, Dt 10:17.
5   (v.9) The Greek text has Iakob, which is Jacob in English.
6   (v.9) Cephas is the Latin spelling of Kefa, which is an Aramaic word for "Rock." See Cephas in Glossary.

10. *they* only *asked* that we would remember the poor, which I was eager to do.

Paul Rebukes Peter at Antioch

2:11. But when Cephas came to Antioch, I resisted him to his face, because he was being accused *by the uncircumcised.* 12. For before some came from Jacob he ate together with the heathens *who had converted*: but when they came, he was withdrawing and separating himself, fearing those from *the* circumcision. 13. And the rest of the Jewish people also played the hypocrite with him, so then even Barnabas was carried away with them in hypocrisy. 14. But when I saw that they were not walking straight with the truth of the gospel, I said to Cephas in front of all, "If you Jewish people are acting like the heathens and do not indeed live like Jewish people *should,* how can you compel the heathens to live like Jewish people *should*?"

Jewish People, Like Pagans, are Saved by Faith

2:15. We *are* natural Jewish people and not sinners from *the* heathens: 16. but, since we know that man is not justified because of works of tradition, *but* only through faith in Jesus Messiah, we too have believed in Messiah Jesus, so that we would be made righteous by faith in Messiah and not by works of legalism, because no one will be made righteous by works of legalism. 17. But if, while we seek to be made righteous in Messiah then are found *to be* sinners, then *is* Messiah a servant of sin? God forbid! 18. For if I build again these things which I destroyed, I have established myself a transgressor. 19. For I died through Torah[1] to legalistic tradition, so that I shall live for God. I have been crucified with Messiah: 20. then I no longer live, but Messiah lives in me: but now *although* I live in *the* flesh, I live by faith in the Son of God, the One Who loves me and has given Himself over on my behalf. 21. I did not cancel the grace of God: for if *I am* in righteousness through legalism, then Messiah died in vain.

Legalism or Faith

3.1. O foolish Galatians, to whom before *your* eyes Jesus Messiah was clearly portrayed as crucified, who bewitched you? 2. Only this *one thing* I wish to learn from you: did you take the Spirit from works of legalism or from hearing in faith? 3. In this way you are foolish, although you began in *the* Spirit, will you now be made complete in *the* flesh? 4. Did you suffer so much in vain? Then you are in vain! 5. Therefore the One Who provides the Spirit for you and works miracles among you, *is it* from works of legalism or from hearing by faith? 6. Just as Abraham "believed in God, and it was counted to him as righteousness." (Gn 15:6)

---

1   (v.19) Torah, meaning teaching or instruction, refers specifically to the first five books of the Bible, but is sometimes used to refer to the entire Tanach (Old Testament), and even to the oral teachings. Here it refers to using the Torah as the basic reference, obeying that rather than the traditions that go beyond Torah. See Torah in Glossary.

3:7. So then you know that those who *are* from faith, these are sons of Abraham. 8. And since the Scripture foresaw that God makes the heathens righteous by faith, He proclaimed in advance to Abraham the Good News that "All the heathens will be blessed in you." (Gn 12:3) 9. So that they are blessed because of faith, with the faith of Abraham. 10. For as many as are from works of legalism, they are under a curse: for it has been written that "Cursed is everyone who does not abide in all those things which have been written in the scroll of the Torah[1] to do them." (Dt 27:26) 11. And that no one is made righteous in God by legalism *is* clear, because "The righteous will live by faith." (Hab 2:4) 12. And legalism is not by faith, but "The one who does these things will live by means of them." (Lv 18:5) 13. Messiah redeemed us from the curse of legalism[2] when He became a curse instead of us, because it has been written, "Cursed *is* everyone who is hung on a tree," (Dt 21:23) 14. So that the blessing of Abraham would come to the heathens by means of Messiah Jesus, so that we could take the promise of the Spirit through faith.

Legalism and the Promise

3:15. Brothers, I am speaking according to man: likewise of man no one sets aside or adds a codicil to a will that has been made valid. 16. And the promises were spoken to Abraham and to his seed. It does not say, "And to the seeds," as upon many but as upon one, "And to your seed,"[3] (Gn 13:15) Who is Messiah. 17. And I say this: when a covenant has been made valid by God, the Torah coming after four hundred thirty years[4] does not invalidate to do away with the promise. 18. For if the inheritance is from *the letter of* Torah, it is no longer from a promise: but God has freely given to Abraham through a promise. 19. Therefore what is the Torah? It was added on account of the transgressions, until the Seed would come for whom it has been promised, since it has been dictated through angels by *the* hand of a Mediator. 20. And the mediator *who represents someone* is not *the* one, *but acts on behalf of another party*, but God is *the* One.

Slaves and Sons

3:21. Therefore is Torah contrary to the promises of God? God forbid! For if Torah was given, that which was able to make alive, in truth righteousness would have been from Torah: 22. but the Scripture has imprisoned everything under the power of sin, so that, through faith in Jesus Messiah, the promise would be given to those who believe.

3:23. And before faith came we were held in custody under tradition, being

---

1   (v.10) Torah here refers to the first five books of the Bible. See Torah in Glossary.
2   (v.13) This could also be translated "curse of Torah" referring to the curses of Dt 28:15-68, from which we have been redeemed.
3   (v.16) The word seed is also singular in Ro 9:7, 8, but there it applies to many.
4   (v.17) This is a reference to the 400 plus years in Egypt before the Torah was given to Moses. Some of the sages said the 400 years were counted from Abraham, others said the 400 years were in Egypt.

kept prisoner against the coming faith *that was* to be revealed, 24. so the Torah has become our custodial guide to Messiah, so that we could be made righteous by faith:[1] 25. and since faith has come we are no longer under custody.

3:26. For you are all children of God through faith in Messiah Jesus: 27. for as many of you as were baptized[2] into Messiah, you have been clothed with Messiah. 28. For there is not one Jewish or Greek, not one slave or free, there is not one male or female. For you are all one in Messiah Jesus. 29. And if you *are* of Messiah, then you are *the* seed of Abraham, heirs according to *the* promise.

4.1. And I say, as long as the heir is a child, he is no different from a servant *although* he is master of all, 2. but he is under guardians and stewards until the day appointed by his father. 3. And just as we, when we were infants, were enslaved under the elements of the world: 4. but when the fullness of time came, God sent forth His Son, Who was *born* of a woman, Who was under Torah,[3] 5. so that He would redeem those under legalism, so that we could take the adoption. 6. And because you are sons, God sent forth the Spirit of His Son into our hearts, crying "Abba, Father." 7. So that you are no longer a servant but a son: and if a son, then an heir through God.

Paul's Concern for the Galatians

4:8. But then indeed, when you did not know God, you served those that were not gods by nature: 9. but since you now know God, or rather are known by God, how do you return again to be subjected to the weak and impoverished principles, *or heavenly bodies*[4] which you want to serve over again? 10. You scrupulously observe days and months and seasons and years.[5] 11. I fear *for* you lest I was toiling among you in vain.

4:12. You must become as I, because also I am as you, brothers, I beg you. And you did not wrong me: 13. and you know that because of weakness of the flesh[6] *when* I proclaimed the gospel to you before, 14. and *that* you did not despise your trial in my flesh, and you did not scorn *me*, but you took hold of me as a messenger of God, as *if I were* Messiah Jesus. 15. Then where *is* your blessing? For I am testifying that if possible you *would* have torn out your eyes *and* you *would* have given *them* to me. 16. So have I become your enemy by telling you *the* truth? 17. They are zealous for you, but *that is* not good, but rather they want to shut you out *from us*, so that you *would* be zealous for them: 18. and *it is* good to be zealous, always with good *intent*, and not only while I am present with you. 19. My children, with whom I again travail until Messiah has been

---

1   (v.20) We are made righteous by faith, but righteousness is action. See Jas 2:14. See Righteousness in Glossary.

2   (v.26) The Greek word baptidzo means immerse. See Baptize in Glossary.

3   (v.4) Jesus was born Jewish, brought up Jewish, and lived by the Torah, never changing it.

4   (v.9) This is a reference to the astrological foundation of their former religion.

5   (v.10) References to astrology

6   (v.13) Sickness

formed in you: 20. and I have purposed to be present with you this moment and to change my tone, because I am perplexed about you.

The Allegory of Hagar and Sarah

4:21. Tell me, you who wish to be under tradition, "Do you not understand the Torah?" 22. For it has been written that Abraham had two sons, one from the slave and one from the free *wife*. 23. But indeed one has been born from the slave according to the flesh, but *the other* one from the free wife through *the* promise. 24. This is being spoken allegorically: for these are two covenants, indeed one from Mount Sinai, born into slavery, who is Hagar. 25. And Hagar is Mount Sinai in Arabia: and now it corresponds to Jerusalem, it puts the yoke of bondage[1] with her children. 26. But the Jerusalem above, who is our mother, is free: 27. for it has been written,

"You must rejoice now, the barren one who has not given birth,
> you must break forth and cry out at once, you who have not
> brought forth:
because many *are* the children of the desolate rather than of the one
> having the husband." (Is 54:1)

28. And you, brothers, you are children of Isaac according to *the* promise. 29. But just as then the one who was born according to the flesh persecuted the one *who was born* according to the Spirit, so also now. 30. But what does the Scripture say? "You must now cast out the slave and her son: for the son of the maid will **not** inherit with the son" of the free *wife*. (Gn 21:10) 31. On this account, brothers, we are not children of a maid but of the free *wife*. **5.**[2]1. Messiah set us free for the freedom *from legalism*: so you must stand *firm* and not be subjected again to a yoke of bondage.

Christian Freedom

5:2. Behold, I, Paul, say to you that if you would be circumcised,[3] Messiah will profit you nothing. 3. And I am testifying again to every circumcised man that he is obligated to do the whole tradition. 4. You, who are made righteous by legalism, have been separated from Messiah, you have fallen away from grace. 5. For we are eagerly awaiting, in *the* Spirit, *the* hope of righteousness by faith. 6. For in Messiah Jesus neither circumcision nor uncircumcision has any strength, but faith working through love.[4]

5:7. You were running well: who kept you from obeying the truth? 8. *That kind of* persuasion *is* not from the One Who calls you. 9. A little leaven leavens the whole lump. 10. I have confidence in you in *the* Lord that you will

---

1   (v.25) The yoke of bondage is legalism.
2   (v.1) See Chapter and Verse in Glossary.
3   (v.2) Paul is telling heathen converts not to be circumcised, but if they do get circumcised they are to adhere to all the legalism of First Century Judaism, as in v. 3.
4   (v.6) See Ignored Commandments in Glossary.

think nothing else: but the one troubling you will bear the judgment, whoever that would be. 11. But myself, brothers, if I still preach circumcision, why am I still persecuted? Then He could set aside the offense of the cross. 12. I would that those who trouble you will also cut themselves off.

5:13. For you have been called in freedom, brothers: only not freedom in the flesh,[1] but you are serving one another through love. (2Cor 3:17) 14. For the whole Torah[2] has found its full expression in one saying, in this "You will love your neighbor as yourself."[3] (Lv 19:18) 15. But if you bite and devour one another, do you not see that you would be consumed by one another!

The Fruit of the Spirit and the Works of the Flesh

5:16. But I say, may you walk in *the* spirit so that you would **not** in any way fulfill *any* desire of *the* flesh. 17. For flesh turns against the spirit, and the spirit against the flesh, these things are opposed to one another, so that you would not do the things you want *to do*. 18. But if you are led by *the* Spirit,[4] you are not under *the* law *of the flesh*. 19. And the works of the flesh are apparent, which are immorality, impurity, licentiousness, 20. idolatry, sorcery,[5] enmity, strife, jealousy, anger, outbreaks of selfishness, dissensions, factions, 21. envy, drunkenness,[6] carousing, and like things. I tell you beforehand, just as I told you before, that the ones who are doing things such as these will not inherit *the* kingdom of God.

5:22. But the fruit of the Spirit is love joy peace, patience kindness goodness, faithfulness 23. gentleness self-control: there is nothing *in* Torah against such as these. 24. But those who belong to Messiah Jesus did crucify their flesh with *its* passions and desires. 25. If we live by *the* Spirit, then we walk, directing our lives by *the* spirit. 26. We should not become boastful, *neither* provoking one another, *nor* envying one another.

Bear One Another's Burdens

6.1. Brothers, if then a man would be overtaken with any sin, you, the spiritual, are to restore such a one as this in a spirit of gentleness, looking out for yourself lest you would also be tempted. 2. Bear the burdens of one another and in this way you will fulfill the Torah[7] of the Messiah. 3. For if anyone thinks he is something and he is not, he deceives himself. 4. And each must continually

---

1   (v.13) Our freedom is spiritual, not a license to do our, or my, thing.
2   (v.14) Torah means teaching or instruction. See Torah in Glossary.
3   (v.14) Rabbi Hillel, a renowned teacher of Torah who lived in Galilee while Jesus was growing up there, taught that loving your neighbor was the most important commandment.
4   (v.18) Pastors are responsible to see that their flocks are taught to live by the Spirit.
5   (v.20) The Greek word translated sorcery is pharmakeia. This refers to taking drugs to cause visions or messages from spirits. See Sorcery in Glossary.
6   (v.21) The word translated drunkenness refers to any intoxication. See Sorcery in Glossary.
7   (v.2) Torah, means teaching or instruction. See Torah in Glossary.

prove his conduct, and then he will have a reason for boasting only to himself, but not to another: 5. for each will bear his own burden. 6. And the one who is being taught the Word must continually share all good things with the one instructing. 7. Do not be deceived, God is not to be mocked. For whatever the man would sow,[1] this also will he reap: 8. because the one who sows into his own flesh will reap corruption from the flesh, but the one who sows into the spirit will reap eternal life from the Spirit. 9. And we should not lose heart doing good, for in its own time we shall reap if we do not give out. 10. So then as we have time, we should do good with all people, and especially with the households of the faithful.

Final Warning and Benediction

6:11. You see I wrote to you in my own hand with such large letters. 12. As many as want to make a good show in *the* flesh, these are compelling you to be circumcised, only so that they would not be persecuted for the cross of the Messiah. 13. For even the ones who are circumcised are not keeping Torah themselves, but they want you to be circumcised, so that they could boast in your flesh. 14. And may it not be for me to boast except in the cross[2] of our Lord Jesus Messiah, through Whom the world has been crucified to me and I to the world. 15. For neither circumcision nor uncircumcision[3] is anything, but a new creation. 16. And as many as will walk by this standard, peace and mercy upon them and upon the Israel of God.

6:17. Finally, let no one cause trouble for me: for I am bearing the marks of Jesus on my body.

6:18. The grace of our Lord Jesus Messiah *be* with your spirit, brothers: amen.

---

1   (v.7) See Sowing and Reaping in Glossary.
2   (v.14) The cross is mentioned several times in this passage, but the cross did not become a Christian symbol until the fourth century, when the Romans stopped using the cross for executions.
3   (v.15) The Talmud teaches that non-Jews are subject to the covenant with Noah. Noah's covenant has seven laws: Promote justice, prohibitions of idolatry, immorality, blasphemy, murder, cruelty to animals, and theft. It does not include circumcision. See Dt 10:16 & 30:6, Jr 4:4; 9:25, and Eze 44:7 for circumcision of the heart.

~ EPHESIANS[1] ~

Salutation

1.1. Paul, an apostle of Messiah Jesus by the will of God, to those saints who are in Ephesus and faithful in Messiah Jesus, 2. grace and peace to you from God our Father and *our* Lord Jesus Messiah.

Spiritual Blessings in Messiah

1:3. Blessed be God and Father of our Lord Jesus Messiah, the One Who blessed us with every spiritual blessing in the heavenlies by Messiah, 4. just as He chose us in Him before *the* foundation of the world, for us to be holy and blameless in His presence in love, 5. because He predestined us into adoption through Jesus Messiah into Himself, according to the good pleasure of His will, 6. into *the* commendation of His glorious grace by which He favored us with the Beloved One. 7. By Whom we have the redemption through His blood, the forgiveness of sins,[2] according to the wealth of His grace 8. from which He furnished richly, abounding to us, wise and understanding in everything, 9. when He made known to us the mystery of His will, according to His good pleasure, which was planned by Him 10. for the arrangement of the fullness of the times *of immaturity*,[3] everything *is* to be brought together in the Messiah, the things over the heavens and the things upon the earth in Him. 11. In Whom our lot is cast[4], since we have been predestined according to *the* purpose of the One Who works all things according to the purpose of His will 12. for us to be a praise of His glory, the ones who were the first to hope in the Messiah. 13. In Whom also yourselves, because you heard the message of truth, the gospel of your salvation, in which also as you believed, you were sealed by the promised Holy Spirit, 14. Who is a down payment of our inheritance, *salvation*, for a redemption of the purchased possession, in praise of His glory.

Paul's Prayer

1:15. And I because of this, since I heard of your faith in the Lord Jesus

---

1   (Title) Written about 60 AD.
2   (v.7) See Sin, Forgiveness of in Glossary.
3   (v.10) When this sinful time has been brought to completion and Satan is bound.
4   (v.11) The meaning of this verb is to appoint by lot. Have we been chosen because we earned it and deserved it? If so, then it is not by grace. See Jn 6:65.

335

and your love for all the saints, 16. I have not ceased giving thanks concerning you, making mention of you in my prayers, 17. in order that the God of our Lord Jesus Messiah, the Father of glory, would have given you a spirit of wisdom and revelation for *your* knowledge of Him, 18. that the eyes of your heart have been enlightened for you to have known what is the hope of His inheritance, the riches of His glory, of His inheritance for the saints, 19. and which exceeds the greatness of His power in us, those who believe, according to the working of the might of His strength. 20. Which He worked in the Messiah when He raised Him from *the* dead and He seated *Him* on His right hand[1] in the heavenlies 21. far above every rule and authority and power and dominion and then He was named above every name, not only in this age, but also in the one that is coming: 22. and He made all things subject under His feet and gave Him authority over everyone in the congregation,[2] 23. which is His body, the extension of the One Who fills everything in every way.

From Death to Life

2.1. And you, because you are dead to your transgressions and to your sins,[3] 2. in which you formerly walked, conforming to the *wicked* age to which this world belongs, according to the prince of the authority of the air, the spirit which is now working in the sons of disobedience: 3. in which we all also formerly lived in the desires of our flesh, doing the desires and the impulses of the flesh, and in nature we were children of wrath, even like the rest: 4. but God, Who is rich in mercy, through His great love *with* which He loved us, 5. and, while we were dead in our sins, He made us alive in Messiah, - you have been saved by grace - 6. and He raised *us* together and caused *us* to sit down together in the heavenlies with Messiah Jesus, 7. so that He could demonstrate in the coming ages the exceeding riches of His grace in kindness for us in Messiah Jesus. 8. For you are saved by grace through faith. And this *is* not from yourselves, *it is* the gift of God: 9. *it is* not from works, so that not anyone could boast. 10. For we are His workmanship, as we have been created in Messiah Jesus for good works[4], which God prepared before hand, so that we would walk in them, *the good works*.[5]

One in Messiah

2:11. On which account remember that formerly you *were* heathens in *the* flesh, the ones who were called uncircumcised by the one who called himself circumcised in *the* flesh by human hands, 12. that you were at that time without

---

1   (v.20) "At the right hand" is a Hebrew idiom that speaks of power and strength, from Ex 15:6. See Right Hand in Glossary.
2   (v.22) Although often translated "church," no Greek word meaning church is used in the NT. See Congregation in Glossary.
3   (v.1) See Sin in glossary.
4   (v.10) Mitsvot, see Mitsvah in Glossary. We are saved by grace, but our behavior has to change.
5   (v.10) The pronoun here refers specifically to good works.

Messiah, having been alienated from the citizenship of Israel and aliens of the promise of the covenants,[1] since you did not have hope and *you were* in the world without God. 13. But now you *are* in Messiah Jesus, you who were formerly far away, you have come near by means of the blood of the Messiah.

2:14. For He is our peace, the One Who has made both things into one[2] and Who has loosed the dividing wall of the fence, cause of the enmity to His flesh, 15. by His nullifying the tradition of the commandments by decrees, so that He could create the two, *Jewish and non-Jewish*, into one new race, establishing peace 16. so He could reconcile both in one body to God through the cross,[3] as *God* killed their enmity[4] by means of *Jesus*. 17. And when He came He proclaimed the Good News *of* peace to you, to those far away, and peace to those near: 18. because through Him we both have the introduction to the Father by means of one Spirit. 19. Therefore then, you are no longer aliens and strangers, but you are fellow citizens of the saints and members of the household of God, 20. building upon the foundation of the apostles and prophets, Messiah Jesus being His cornerstone, 21. in Whom the whole building being constructed is being fit together into a holy sanctuary in *the* Lord, 22. and in Whom you are built together into a habitation of God by *the* Spirit.

Paul's Ministry to the Pagans

3.1. For this reason I, Paul, the prisoner of the Messiah Jesus on behalf of you heathens - 2. and if you heard the plan of the grace of God which was given to me for you, 3. that according to a revelation, the mystery was made known to me, just as I wrote before in brief, 4. by means of which, when you read, you were able to perceive my understanding in the mystery of the Messiah, 5. Who was not made known to the sons of men in different generations, as He has now been revealed to His set apart apostles and prophets by *the Holy* Spirit, 6. *that* the heathens are fellow heirs and members of the same body and sharing with them the promise in Messiah Jesus through the gospel, 7. Whose servant I became according to the gift of the grace of God which was given to me according to the working of His power. 8. To me, the least of all the saints, was given this grace, *first* to preach the inscrutable richness of the Good News of the Messiah to the heathens 9. and, *second*, a plan which *is* to bring to light all of the mystery, which has been hidden from the beginning of time by God, the One Who created everything, 10. so that the many-sided wisdom of God would now be made known, through the congregation,[5] to the rulers and to the authorities in

---

1   (v.12) Notice that Paul uses the plural, covenants, implying that each covenant builds on the previous covenants, in contrast to some translations of Hb 8:13. See Ro 9:4.

2   (v.14) Grafted the Church, the wild olive tree, into the domestic olive tree, Ro 11:17, 18, Jn 10:16

3   (v.16) The cross is mentioned several times in this passage, but the cross did not become a Christian symbol until the fourth century, when the Romans stopped using the cross for executions.

4   (v.16) Heathens versus Jewish people. See Replacement Theology in Glossary.

5   (v.10) Although often translated "church," no Greek word meaning church is used in the

the heavenlies, 11. according to the eternal plan which He made *using* Messiah Jesus our Lord, 12. in Whom we have boldness and access in confidence through faith in Him. 13. For this reason I ask *you* not to lose heart because of my distresses on your behalf, which are an honor *to do* for you.

To Know the Love of Messiah

3:14. On this account I bend my knees to the Father, 15. from Whom every family in *the* heavens and on *the* earth receives its name, 16. so that He would give to you according to the riches of His glory to be strengthened in power by His Spirit *working* in your inner man, 17. to make the Messiah live in your hearts through faith, when you have been rooted and established in love, 18. so that you would be able to seize, with all the consecrated ones, what *is* the breadth and length and height and depth, 19. and to know the love of the Messiah that surpasses our knowledge, so that you would be filled *with* all the fullness of God.

3:20. Now to the One Who is able to do beyond measure far more than we ask or we imagine according to the power which works in us *for our benefit*, 21. to Him be the glory in the congregation and in Messiah Jesus for all generations forever and ever, amen.

The Unity of the Body

4.1. Therefore I, a prisoner of *the* Lord, urge you to walk worthily in the calling to which you have been called, 2. with all humility and gentleness, with patience, and bearing with one another in love, 3. being diligent to keep the unity of the Spirit in the bond of peace: 4. one body and one spirit, just as also you were called in one hope of your calling: 5. one Lord, one faith, one immersion,[1] 6. one God and Father of all, the One over all things and through all things and in all things.

4:7. And the grace was given to each one of us according to the measure of the gift of the Messiah. 8. For this reason it says,

> "When He ascended into the high places He turned the tables on your
> enemies in warfare.[2]
> He gave gifts to mankind."[3] (Ps 68:18)

4:9. And He went up. What is *this ascending*, unless He also descended into the lower parts of the earth? 10. The One Who descended is the same One Who also ascended high above all the heavens,[4] so that all things would be filled

---

NT. See Congregation in Glossary.

1   (v.5) Immersion is the translation of the Greek word baptisma. See Baptize in Glossary.

2   (v.8)The literal is "turned captivity captive" which is a Hebrew idiom for "turn the tables on your enemies in warfare" This idiom is also used in Am 9:14, "V'shavti veyish'vu" in the Hebrew.

3   (v.8) This is from the Greek text, the Hebrew saying, "You (God) took gifts from men," referring to God's taking of Judea and its spiritual advantages, thus making Israel the home of His people forever.

4   (v.10) Heavens is always plural in Hebrew, with seven Hebrew words describing seven

with His presence. 11. And He gave some *to be* apostles, some prophets, and some evangelists, and some pastors and teachers, 12. for the equipping of the saints for *the* work of ministry, for building up the body of the Messiah, 13. until we would all attain in the unity of faith and the knowledge of the Son of God, into a mature person, to *the* measure of the full maturity of the Messiah, 14. so that no longer would we be infants, being tossed about and carried by every wind of teaching in the craftiness of men, in cunning with deceitful scheming, 15. but *that* being truthful in love we would bring to maturity all the things in Him, Who is the Head, Messiah, 16. from Whom the whole body *of Messiah is* being joined together and uniting through every ligament that serves for support, according to working in a measure by each individual part, He is making the body grow, building itself up in love.

The Old Life and the New

4:17. Therefore I say this, and I bear witness in *the* Lord, that you no longer walk as the heathens walk in *the* futility of their minds, 18. since they have been darkened by being in their understanding, because they have been alienated from the life of God through the ignorance which is in them, because of the insensibility of their hearts, 19. who, when they became callous, gave themselves over to licentiousness in practice of every impurity, with a desire to have more. 20. But you did not learn Messiah in this way, 21. if you really heard about Him and were taught by Him, just as truth is in Jesus, 22. you laid aside the old man, according to your former behavior, in accordance with the destruction of your deceitful desires, 23. then to have been renewed in the spirit of your mind 24. and to have put on the new man, the one which has been created corresponding to God in *the* righteousness and holiness of the truth.

Rules for the New Life

4:25. On this account when the falsehood has been put off "You must each speak *the* truth with his neighbor," (Zch 8:16) because we are part of one another. 26. "Be angry but do not sin:" (Ps 4:4) the sun must not set on your anger, 27. so you do not give a place to the devil. 28. The one who steals must no longer steal, but rather let him toil as he works good *things* with his own hands so that he would have *something* to share with the one who has need. (Ro 12:8) 29. An unwholesome[1] word (Mt 12:36,37) must never come out of your mouth, but only what is good for building up, *meeting* their need, so that it would give help to those who are listening. 30. And you must not grieve the Holy Spirit of God, with Whom you became sealed for *the* Day of redemption. 31. Every bitterness and impulsive outburst and anger and clamor and blasphemy with every wickedness must be taken from you at once! 32. And with one another you must continually be kind, compassionate, freely forgiving *others* of your own

---

levels of heaven. See Heavens in Glossary.
1   (v.29) Literally, the Greek word means "rotten."

accord,[1] just as also God granted forgiveness to you in Messiah. **5**.1. Therefore you must continually be imitators of God as beloved children 2. and you must walk constantly in love, just as also the Messiah loved us and gave Himself over on our behalf, an offering and a sacrifice to God for a fragrant aroma. 3. But any immorality or impurity or covetousness must not be named among you, as is fitting for saints, 4. nor foul speaking or foolish talking or low jesting, which things do not belong, but rather thanksgiving. 5. For you know this very well, that anyone who practices immorality or uncleanness or covetousness,[2] who is an idol worshipper, does not have any inheritance in the kingdom of the Messiah and God.

Walk as Children of Light

5:6. Let no one deceive you with empty words! For because of these things the wrath of God comes upon the sons of the disobedient. 7. Therefore you must not ever be participants with them: 8. for you were once darkness, but now *you are* light in *the* Lord: you must continually walk as children of light 9. - for the fruit of the light *is* in every goodness and righteousness and truth - 10. trying to learn what *is* approved by the Lord, 11. and you must not ever participate in the unfruitful works of darkness, but rather even expose *them*. 12. For it is dishonorable even to say the things that are done by them in secret, 13. but all things are exposed, being revealed under the light, 14. for everything is revealed in light. On account of this it says,

"You must wake up, sleeper,
and get up from the dead,
and the Messiah will shine upon you." (Is 26:19, 60:1)

5:15. Therefore look carefully how you walk, not as unwise but as wise, 16. redeeming your time, because the days are evil. 17. Because of this do not be foolish, but you must understand what the will of the Lord *is*. 18. And do not get drunk on wine, in which is debauchery, but you must continually be filled with *the* Spirit, 19. speaking to one another in Psalms and singing praises and spiritual songs, singing praises and playing stringed instruments from your heart to the Lord, 20. giving thanks to our God and Father always for all things in *the* name of our Lord Jesus Messiah.

Wives and Husbands

5:21. Being subject to one another in reverent fear of Messiah, 22. wives to their own husbands as to the Lord, 23. because a husband is head of his wife as also the Messiah *is* head of the congregation,[3] He *is* savior of the body: 24. but as the congregation is subject to the Messiah, so also *should* wives *be subject to their husbands in everything.* 25. Husbands, you must continually love your

1   (v.32) See Sin, Forgiveness of in Glossary.
2   (v.6) The phrase "idol worshipper" refers specifically to covetousness as idol worship.
3   (v.23) Although often translated "church," no Greek word meaning church is used in the NT. See Congregation in Glossary.

wives, just as the Messiah also loved the congregation and gave Himself over on her behalf, 26. so that He would sanctify his *wife, the congregation, the bride*,[1] making *her* pure by washing with the word of Torah,[2] 27. in order that He would present for Himself the glorious congregation, not having spot or wrinkle or any of such things, but so that *His bride* would be holy and without blemish. 28. In this way husbands are obligated to love their own wives as their own bodies. The one who loves his own wife loves himself.[3] 29. For no one ever hated his own flesh but nourishes and cherishes it, just as also the Messiah *nourishes and cherishes* the congregation, 30. because we are members of His body. 31. "For this reason a man will leave his father and his mother and be faithfully devoted to his wife, and the two will be in one flesh." (Gn 2:24) 32. This mystery is great: now I say *this* in Messiah then in respect to the congregation. 33. But then you one by one, each must continually love his own wife just as himself, and that the wife should respect her husband.[4]

Children and Parents

6.1. Children, you must continually obey your parents in *the* Lord: for this is proper. 2. "You must continually honor your father and your mother," which is the first commandment with a promise, 3. "so that it would be well with you and you would be long lived on the earth." (Ex 20:12, Dt 5:16) 4. And fathers, do not provoke your children to anger but bring them up in *the* training and instruction of *the* Lord.

Slaves and Masters

6:5. Slaves,[5] obey your earthly masters with respect and trembling in single-hearted devotion of your heart as to the Messiah, 6. not according to *the* eye as man-pleasers, *as done only when the master is watching*, but, as servants of Messiah, doing the will of God from *your* inner self, 7. serving with enthusiasm as to the Lord, and not to men, 8. each knowing that if any would do good things, he will be repaid by *the* Lord for what he did, whether slave or free. 9. And masters, you must do the same things with them. Stop threatening,[6] knowing that the Lord in *the* heavens is both their *Master* and yours and *there is* no partiality with Him. (Dt 10:17)

The Battle against Evil

6:10. From now on, you must right away become strong in *the* Lord and in the power of His strength. 11. You must continually be clothed with the

---

1   (v.26) The pronoun used here can mean any of these italicized words. Paul may well have meant this double meaning, applying equally to husbands' prayers and Jesus' intercession.

2   (v.26) Water is a metaphor for Torah, from Is 55:1 and Ex 14:22, making this "..washing with the word of Torah." The literal translation is ".. the washing of the water with the Word."

3   (v.28) You cannot love others if you do not love yourself.

4   (v.33) This could possibly be translated "..so that the wife could respect her husband."

5   (v.5) Paul is addressing slaves who were under Greco-Roman law, in which slaves were possessions that an owner could deal with as he pleased, even killing. See Servant in Glossary.

6   (v.9) See note on v. 5.

full armor of God to enable you to stand against the strategies of the devil: 12. because the wrestling for us is not with blood and flesh, but with the rulers, with the powers, with the world rulers of this darkness, with the spiritual *forces* of wickedness in the heavenlies. 13. Because of this you must immediately take up the full armor of God, so that you would be able to resist in the evil day and when you have completely achieved all things, to stand. 14. Therefore you should stand, after you have girded around your waist the belt of truth and have put on the breastplate of righteousness (Is 11:5, 59:17, Wsd 5:18) 15. and have put sandals on your feet in preparation for the gospel of peace, (Is 11:6-10, 52:7, Na 1:15) 16. in all things having taken up the long shield of faith, with which you have been enabled to extinguish all the burning[1] arrows of the evil one: (Ps 7:13) 17. and you must immediately take up the helmet of salvation (Is 59:17) and the sword[2] of the Spirit, which is the Word[3] of God. (Is 11:4, 49:2, Ho 6:5) 18. Through every prayer and entreaty, by praying always in *the* Spirit, and being alert in Him, by means of every perseverance and entreaty concerning all the saints 19. and on my behalf,[4] that a word would be given to me as often as I open my mouth *to speak*, to make known the mystery of the Good News with boldness, 20. concerning which I am an ambassador in chains, so that in this I would have boldness as there is need for me to speak.

Final Greetings

6:21. & 22. And so that you would also know that with regard to me, what I am doing, Tychikus, the beloved brother and faithful minister in *the* Lord, whom I sent to you for this purpose, will make everything known to you, so that you would know the things concerning us and it would comfort your hearts.

6:23. To the brothers (and sisters), peace and love with faith from God *our* Father and *our* Lord Jesus Messiah. 24. Grace *be* with all those who love our Lord Jesus Messiah with never diminishing love.

---

1 (v.16) Burning in the past with the effects still felt today.
2 (v.17) A small sword for personal defense.
3 (v.17) The Greek word is Rhema, specifically referring to the spoken word. See Logos/Rhema in Glossary.
4 (v.19) Paul asked everyone in Ephesus (and probably everyone else) to intercede for him!

~ PHILIPPIANS[1] ~

Salutation

1.1. Paul and Timothy, servants of Messiah Jesus, to all the saints in Messiah Jesus who are in Philipi with elders and deacons, 2. grace and peace to you from God our Father and *our* Lord Jesus Messiah.

Paul's Prayer for the Philippians

1:3. I give thanks to my God over every memory of you 4. always in my every prayer on behalf of you all, making the petition with joy, 5. on account of your sharing in the Good News from the first day until now, 6. because I have been persuaded this same thing, that the One Who began a good work in you will continue on until *the* Day of Messiah Jesus: 7. just as it is right for me to think this on behalf of all of you because I have you on my heart, both in my chains, and in the defense and confirmation of the Good News, as you all are sharers of the grace with me. 8. For God *is* my witness as I long for you all with *the* compassion of Messiah Jesus. 9. And I am praying this, that your love would overflow yet more and more in knowledge and in every perception 10. for you to distinguish between the good and evil things, so that you would be pure and blameless on *the* Day of Messiah, 11. since you have been filled *with the* fruit of righteousness through Jesus Messiah to *the* glory and praise of God.

To Me to Live is Messiah

1:12. And I wish you to know, brothers, that things have turned out in my case for the advancement of the Good News, 13. so that the revelations of my *being in* chains for Messiah came to the whole palace guard and to all the rest, 14. and through my bonds most of the brothers in *the* Lord have been made confident to more exceedingly dare to speak the Word fearlessly.

1:15. Some indeed then, because of envy and strife, but some because of good will, are proclaiming the Messiah: 16. and the latter indeed out of love, since they know that I have been appointed for *the* defense of the gospel, 17. but the former are proclaiming the Messiah publicly from partisanship, not with sincerity, supposing to raise trouble *for me* in my bonds. 18. So what? In

---

1   (Title) Written about 60 AD.

any case, because in every way, and in this time, whether in pretext or in truth, Messiah is proclaimed publicly, and in this I rejoice. But then I will rejoice, 19. for I know that this will turn out for my salvation through your entreaty and *the* support of the Spirit of Jesus Messiah 20. according to my persistent expectation and hope, that I will not be put to shame by anything. But *I will be* in free and fearless confidence as always. And now Messiah will be magnified in my body, whether through *my* life or through *my* death. 21. For to me to live *is* Messiah and to die *is* gain. 22. But if I live in *the* flesh, this *is* for me *the* fruit of *my* labor, and which[1] I will prefer for myself I do not know. 23. And I am hard pressed by the two, since I have the desire to depart *from life* and to be with Messiah, indeed rather much better: 24. but to remain in the flesh *is* a more necessary duty because of you. 25. And because I have believed this, I know that I remain and I am staying beside you all, for your progress and joy in your faith, 26. so that your glorying in Messiah Jesus would overflow in me because of my coming to you again.

1:27. Only you must continually be worthy of being made a citizen of the Good News of the Messiah, so that, whether, because I have come and seen you, or, if I depart, I would hear everything about you, that you have stood in one spirit, one being, contending together *in unity* for the faith of the gospel 28. and not being frightened in anything by those who oppose *you*, which is proof to them of *their* destruction, but for you of salvation, and this from God: 29. because it was given freely to you on behalf of Messiah, not only to believe in Him but also to suffer on His behalf, 30. since we have the same struggle, which sort you saw in me and now you are hearing in me.

Christian Humility and Messiah's Humility

2.1. Therefore if *there is* any admonition in Messiah, if *there is* any consolation of love, if any fellowship of *the* Spirit, if any compassions and mercies, 2. you must make my joy complete, so that you would cherish the same views, since you have this love, of one accord, thinking the same thing, 3. and not according to selfish ambition,[2] and not according to conceit, but in humility esteeming one another more than yourselves, 4. not caring *only* for your own things but even each other's things. 5. For you must live in harmony with yourselves, who *are* also in Messiah Jesus, 6. Who was in *the* form of God, *yet* did not think that this equality with God was to be eagerly clung to or retained, 7. but emptied Himself of His own equality, taking *the* form of a servant,[3] when He came in a likeness of men: and, when He was found in a manner of life as a man, 8. He humbled Himself, becoming obedient until death, even of a death of *the* cross.[4] 9. On this account then God raised Him to the highest rank and He freely

---

1   (v.22) Life or death
2   (v.3) The desire to put yourself forward
3   (v.7) Or slave, see Servant in Glossary.
4   (v.8) The cross did not become a Christian symbol until the fourth century when the

gave Him the name above every name, 10. so that at the name "Jesus!" every knee of *the* heavenlies and *the* earthly and *those* below the earth would bow 11. and every tongue would confess that Jesus Messiah *is* Lord in *the* glory of God *our* Father. (Is 45:23)

Shining as Lights in the World

2:12. Thus, my beloved, just as you always obeyed, not only in my presence but now much more in my absence, you must continually work out your own salvation with fear and trembling: 13. for God is the One Who works in you, both to determine and to work, for *His* good pleasure. 14. You must continually do everything without grumbling or argument, 15. so that you would become blameless and pure, children of God who cannot be censured *in the* midst of a crooked and perverted generation, among whom you are to shine like stars in *the* world,[1] 16. presenting *as lights* a message of life, for my boasting in *the* Day of Messiah, that I did not run in vain and I did not labor in vain. 17. But even if I am poured out as an offering and a service of your faith, I rejoice and I rejoice with you all: 18. and you also rejoice the same way and you must now be glad with me.

Timothy and Epaphroditus

2:19. And I hope in *the* Lord Jesus to send Timothy to you quickly, so that I also *will be* of a cheerful spirit when I know the *news* about you. 20. For I do not have anyone like-minded, who is sincerely anxious *for* the things concerning you: 21. for all those *others* are seeking the things for themselves, not the things of Jesus Messiah. 22. But you know his tried character, because he served with me in the evangelism as a child with *his* father. 23. Therefore indeed I hope to send him at once so I could turn my mind to the things concerning me. 24. I am confident in the Lord that I will come quickly.

2:25. And I thought it necessary to send Epaphroditus to you, my brother and fellow worker and fellow soldier, and your apostle and servant of my need, 26. seeing that he was longing for you all and was not able, because he was sick, *as* you heard. 27. For indeed he was sick almost to death: but God was merciful to him, not to him only but also to me, lest I would have grief upon grief. 28. Therefore I sent him eagerly, so that after you saw him again you would rejoice, and I more free from grief in it. 29. So receive him in *the* Lord with every joy and hold one such as he in high esteem, 30. because he came close to death through the work of Messiah, risking *his* life, so that in your absence he could supply the service to me *that you would have given.*

The True Righteousness

3.1. In addition, my brothers, you must continually rejoice in *the* Lord.

Romans stopped using the cross for executions.

1   (v.15) Just as stars can only be seen in a dark sky, a believer's light is seen in a dark world.

It is indeed not tiresome for me to write the same things to you, but *it is* a safe course for you.

3:2. Watch out for the dogs, watch out for the evil workings, watch out for the mutilation.[1]   3. For we ourselves are the circumcision, those who serve by *the* Spirit of God and who boast in Messiah Jesus and who do not trust in flesh, 4. although I have confidence even in *my* flesh.   If any other thinks he has confidence in *his* flesh, I more: 5. circumcised at eight days *old*, from *the* nation of Israel, tribe of Benjamin, a Hebrew born of Hebrews, according to *the* sect of Pharisees, 6. with respect to zeal persecuting the congregation,[2] regarding righteousness because I was blameless in legalism.   7. But whatever things were for me to gain, I have counted these things a loss because of the Messiah.   8. But no, rather then, I counted everything to be a loss because of the surpassing worth of the knowledge of Messiah Jesus my Lord, for Whose sake I forfeited everything, and I am counting myself, *and those things*, worthless, so that I will gain Messiah's favor 9. to be found by Him, not having my righteousness from legalism, but through faith in Messiah, the righteousness of God *based* on faith, 10. to know Him and the power of His resurrection[3] and the fellowship with His sufferings, when I have been rendered like *Him* in His death, 11. if somehow I should attain to the resurrection from *the* dead.

Pressing toward the Mark

3:12. Not because I have already obtained or I have already been perfected, but I am pursuing, if also I could lay hold of *the victory*, upon which I have come into possession of my inheritance under Messiah Jesus.   13. Brothers, I do not count myself to have *already* obtained *my inheritance*: but one thing, that indeed forgetting what lies behind, and stretching myself out toward the *goal* that lies before *me*, 14. I press on toward *that* goal, the prize that is the object of the upward call of God in Messiah Jesus.   15. Therefore so many as might be mature, we should understand this: and if you think differently, then God will reveal this to you: 16. besides to what we attained, to live by this.[4]

3:17. You must continually be imitators of me, brothers, and you must fix your attention on those who walk in this manner just as you have us *as* an example.[5]   18. For many are walking, the enemies of the cross of the Messiah, of whom I was frequently telling you, and now I am saying *it* even weeping *in grief,* 19. whose end *is* destruction,[6] whose god *is* their stomach and their glory

---

1   (v.2) Circumcision
2   (v.6) Although often translated "church," no Greek word meaning church is used in the NT. See Congregation in Glossary.
3   (v.10) See Resurrection in Glossary.
4   (v.16) To live up to what we have already grasped.
5   (v.17) Paul was still not perfected, see Romans Chapter 7, but this puts that chapter in perspective. We all do and say things we shouldn't, but at the same time we ought to be good examples for others.
6   (v.19) Loss of eternal life

is to their shame, their minds set on earthly pleasures and goods. 20. For our citizenship is in *the* heavens, out from which then we have received for ourselves a Savior, Lord Jesus Messiah, 21. Who will transform our lowly body to the same form as His glorious body through the power that enables Him to subject everything to Himself. **4.**1. So, my esteemed and longed for brothers *and sisters*, my joy and crown, thus you must stand firm in *the* Lord, beloved.

Exhortations

4:2. I urge Euodia and I urge Syntych to be in agreement in *the* Lord. 3. Yes indeed I also ask you *each*, genuinely yoked together, you must each continually help these *women*, who came together with me in the evangelism also with Clement and the rest of *those who* work with me, whose names *are* in *the* Scroll of Life. 4. You must continually rejoice in *the* Lord always: again I say, rejoice! 5. Your gentleness must always be known to all people. The Lord is near. 6. And you must at no point be anxious about anything, but your requests must quickly be made known to God in every prayer and entreaty, with thanksgiving. 7. And the peace of God, which surpasses all understanding, will keep your hearts and your thoughts *and purposes* on Messiah Jesus.

4:8. The rest, brothers, whatever things are true, whatever things *are* honorable, whatever *is* just, whatever *is* pure, whatever *is* pleasing, whatever *is* spoken with good will, if *there is* any moral excellence and any praise, you must continually consider these things for yourselves: 9. and whatever you have learned and you took[1] and you heard and you saw in me, you must faithfully do these things: then the God of peace will be with you.

Acknowledgment of the Philippians' Gift

4:10. And I rejoice in *the* Lord greatly because now then you have revived so as to take thought on my behalf, upon which also you were thinking *about me*, but you were lacking opportunity *to show it*. 11. Not that I am talking on account of a great need, for I learned to be content with what things I have. 12. And I know how to submit myself to want, and I know how to be abundant: in everything and in all things I have learned the secret, both how to be filled and how to be needy and how to be affluent and how to suffer want: 13. I have strength to overcome all things in the One Who strengthens me. 14. Yet you did well, because you were sharers with me in my trouble.

4:15. And you indeed know, Philippians, that in *the* beginning of my evangelism, when I came out from Macedonia, not one congregation shared with me in *the* message of giving and receiving except only you, 16. because indeed in Thessalonica you even sent once then twice for my need. 17. Not that I am seeking the gift, but I do seek for the increasing fruit to your account. 18. But I wholly

---

1   (v.9) The word translated "took" is generally translated "receive" here although its primary meaning is "take." See Take/Receive in Glossary.

receive all things and I overflow: I have been filled now that I have received your *gifts* from Epaphroditus, a sweet smelling odor, an acceptable offering, well-pleasing to God. 19. And my God will fill your every need according to His riches in glory in Messiah Jesus. 20. And to God and our Father *be* the glory forever and ever, amen.

Final Greetings

4:21. You must now greet all the saints in Messiah Jesus. The brothers with me greet you. 22. All the saints, but especially those from Caesar's household, greet you. 23. The grace of the Lord Jesus Messiah *be* with your spirit.

~ COLOSSIANS[1] ~

Salutation

1.1. Paul, an apostle of Messiah Jesus by *the* will of God, and brother Timothy 2. to the saints and believers in Colossae, brothers in Messiah, grace and peace to you from God our Father.

Paul Thanks God for the Colossians

1:3. We always give thanks to God, Father of our Lord Jesus Messiah, when we pray on your behalf, 4. because we have heard of your faith in Messiah Jesus and the love which you have for all the saints 5. because of the hope which is stored up for you in the heavens, which you heard before in the message of truth from the gospel 6. of that at hand in you, just as also in every place in the world *the Gospel* is bearing fruit and causing to grow just as also in you, since the day you heard and you knew the grace of God in truth: 7. just as you learned from Epaphras our beloved fellow servant, who is a faithful servant of the Messiah on your behalf, 8. and the one who has shown us your love by *the* Spirit.

The Person and Work of Messiah

1:9. Because of this also we, from *the* day we heard of it, did not stop praying and asking on your behalf, that you would be filled with the knowledge of His will in all wisdom and understanding in spiritual *things*, 10. to walk worthily of the Lord, desiring to please *Him* in everything, bearing fruit in every good work and growing in the knowledge of God, 11. being strengthened in all power according to the might of His glory, patient and forbearing in everything. With joy 12. giving thanks to the Father, the One Who equips you with adequate power for you to share in the inheritance of the saints in the Light: 13. Who rescued us from the authority of the darkness and transferred *us* to the kingdom of the Son by His love, 14. in Whom we have the redemption, the forgiveness of sins: 15. Who is of *the* image of the invisible God, Firstborn of all creation, 16. because by Him all things were created in the heavens and upon the earth, the visible and the invisible, whether thrones or lordships or leaders or authorities: all things have been created through Him and in Him: 17. and He was *alive* before all things

---

1   (Title) Written about 60 AD.

and all things have come together in Him, 18. and He is the head of the body, of the congregation:[1] Who was in *the* beginning, Firstborn from the dead, so that He would be first in all things, 19. because it pleased *the Father* to have to make all the fullness dwell through Him, 20. and through Him to reconcile all things to Him, because He made peace through the blood of His cross,[2] through Him whether *they be* the things upon the earth or the things in the heavens.

1:21. And although you were formerly alienated and hostile in your way of thinking and feeling because of your evil works, 22. but now He has reconciled *you*, by the body of His flesh, through death, to present you holy and without blemish, and blameless before Him, 23. if indeed you remain in the faith, since you have laid the foundation for yourselves and *are* steadfast and not moving away from the hope of the gospel that you heard, the one that has been preached in all creation to everyone under heaven, of which I, Paul, have become a servant.

Paul's Ministry to the Congregation

1:24. Now I rejoice in my sufferings on your behalf and I make up for His absence *to take on* the afflictions of the Messiah, in my flesh for the sake of His body, which is the congregation, 25. of which I have become a servant according to the divine office of God, the one that was given to me to bring the Word of God to completion in you, 26. the mystery that has been hidden away from the ages, and from the generations - but now it has been revealed to His saints, 27. to whom God desired to make known among the heathens the wealth of the glory of this mystery, which is Messiah in you, the hope of glory: 28. which we are proclaiming, admonishing everyone and teaching everyone in all wisdom, so that we could present every person complete in Messiah: 29. and in which I toil, struggling, according to His working that *which is* being worked in me in power.

2.1. For I want you to know how great a concern I have for you and for those in Laodicea and so many as have not seen my face in *the* flesh, 2. so that their hearts would be comforted, because we have been knitted together in love, and in everything, of *the* wealth of the certainty of the understanding, in knowledge of the mystery of God, of Messiah, 3. in Whom are all the stored up treasures of wisdom and knowledge. 4. I am saying this, so that no one would deceive you with persuasive speech. 5. For if I am absent in the flesh, then I am with you in the spirit, rejoicing and seeing your orderly manner and the steadfastness of your faith in Messiah.

Fullness of Life in Messiah

2:6. As therefore you took the Messiah, Jesus the Lord, to be joined

---

1   (v.18) Although often translated "church," no Greek word meaning church is used in the NT. See Congregation in Glossary.

2   (v.20) The cross did not become a Christian symbol until the fourth century, when the Romans stopped using the cross for executions.

with *you*, you must continually walk with Him, 7. since you have been planted and founded in Him, and made steadfast in the faith just as you were taught, abounding in thanksgiving. 8. See that no one will take you captive through philosophy and empty deceit according to the tradition of men, according to the elements of the world, and not according to Messiah: 9. because in Him all the fullness of Deity dwells bodily, 10. and you must constantly be filled through Him, Who is the Head of every principality and authority. 11. And in Whom you were circumcised with a circumcision, not by human hands in the removal of flesh from the body of flesh, *but* by the circumcision of the Messiah,[1] 12. because you were buried with Him in baptism,[2] by means of Whom you also were raised through your faith in the working of God, the One Who raised Him from *the company of the* dead: 13. and although you were dead in your transgressions and in the uncircumcision of your flesh, He made you alive, together with Himself, when He granted forgiveness of all the transgressions in us. 14. Since *God* wiped away the record against us in the decrees which were set against us, and He took *each decree* away, out from *our* midst, by nailing *the record* to the cross *with Him*: 15. when *God* disarmed[3] the principalities and the authorities He made *them* an example, *exposing them* publicly, when He triumphed over them through Him, *Messiah*.

2:16. Therefore no one must be continually judging you by food and by drink or in part of a feast or new moon or Sabbaths:[4] 17. which are a shadow of the things that are coming, but the reality *is* of the Messiah. 18. Let no one, who has a false humility himself and wants religious worship of angels, rob you of the prize[5] which he has seen in a vision, puffed up without reason by what he saw, groundlessly inflated by his fleshly mind, 19. and if he does not hold fast the Head, from Whom the whole body, *which is* supported and joined together through the joints and bands, grows *only* with divine growth.[6]

The New Life in Messiah

2:20. If you died with Messiah away from the elemental spirits of the world, why are you submitting to rules and regulations as if you were living in *the* world? 21. You should not touch and you should not taste and you should not handle, 22. which are all things that are meant for destruction, because *they are* the precepts and teachings of men, 23. which *rules and regulations* are things indeed *which* have a reputation of wisdom in self-made religion and in having an affected and ostentatious *and* humble opinion of one's self and unsparing severity

---

1   (v.11) Circumcision of the heart, Dt 10:16 & 30:6, Jr 4:4; 9:25, and Eze 44:7.
2   (v.12) The literal meaning of the word translated baptism is immersion. See Baptize in Glossary.
3   (v.15) Literally, "stripped off," which is a reference to the public shaming of high ranking prisoners of war
4   (v.16) Sabbaths here probably refers to every Sabbath. See Sabbath in Glossary.
5   (v.18) Deprive you of your salvation
6   (v.19) God alone causes the body to grow.

of *the* body, not in any honor *to God, but* for the indulgence of the flesh.

3.1. If therefore you were raised together with the Messiah,[1] you are seeking the higher things, where the Messiah is seated at *the* right hand of God: 2. you must continually have in mind the higher things, not the things upon the earth. 3. For you died and your life has been hidden with the Messiah in God: 4. when the Messiah would be revealed, the One *Who is* your life, then also you will be revealed with Him in glory.

3:5. Therefore you must right now put to death the earthly parts, *which are* immorality, uncleanness, passion, evil desires, and covetousness, which is idol worship,[2] 6. because of which[3] the wrath of God is coming upon the sons of the disobedient. 7. Among whom you also once walked, when you were living in these things: 8. but now then you must immediately put everything off from yourself, anger, passion, wickedness, depravity, malice, blasphemy, slander,[4] evil, obscene, abusive speech from your mouth: 9. you must not ever lie to one another, since you stripped off the old man with his deeds 10. and by putting on your new *self*, which is being renewed in knowledge according to *the* image of the One Who created *the universe*, 11. where *there is* not one Greek or Jewish, circumcision or uncircumcision, barbarian, Scythian,[5] slave, free, but then Messiah *is* all things to all those.

3:12. Therefore you must immediately put on, as chosen and beloved saints of God, hearts, inner thoughts of compassion, generosity, humility, gentleness, patience, 13. bearing with one another and forgiving *each other* if any would have a complaint against someone: just as also the Lord forgave you, so also you *must forgive*:[6] (Mt 6:14,15) 14. and upon all of these, love, which is a bond of perfection. 15. And the peace of the Messiah must continually rule in your hearts, into which *peace* you were also called in one body: and you must constantly be grateful. 16. The message of the Messiah must incessantly dwell richly in you, as you teach and admonish *each other* in all wisdom, with Psalms, sacred songs of praise to God, spiritual songs, singing to God with His grace in your hearts: 17. and whatever you would do in word or in deed, *do* all things in *the* name of *the* Lord Jesus, giving thanks to God *the* Father through *Jesus*.

Social Duties of the New Life

3:18. Wives, you must faithfully be subject to your husbands[7] as it is fitting in *the* Lord. 19. Husbands, you must constantly love your wives and you must stop being embittered toward them.

---

1   (v.1) As you rose from being immersed, baptized.
2   (v.5) This refers specifically to covetousness as idol worship.
3   (v.6) This refers to the whole list in v. 5.
4   (v.8) See Gossip/Slander in Glossary.
5   (v.11) Scythians lived in what is now the steppes of Ukraine. They were considered the wildest savages of the Roman world.
6   (v.13) See Sin, Forgiveness of in Glossary
7   (v.18) Ephesians 5:21 says to be subject one to another.

3:20. Children, you must obey your parents without fail in all things, for this is well pleasing to *the* Lord. 21. Fathers, you must not ever provoke your children, so that they would not be discouraged.

3:22. Servants, *employees*, you must regularly obey your *human* masters, *employers*, in everything according to *the* flesh, not in eye-service as man-pleasers, *only when he is looking*, but fearing the Lord with a sincere heart. 23. Which if you would do, you must continually be working from *your* inner being as to the Lord and not for men, 24. because you have known that you will receive the inheritance as your reward. You are serving for the Lord Messiah: 25. because the one who does wrong will be paid back *for* what he did wrong, and there is no partiality *with God*. (Dt 10:17, 1Chr 19:7) **4**.1. Masters, *employers*, you must continually grant justice and fairness to your servants, *employees*, because you know that you too have a Master in heaven.

Exhortation

4:2. You must habitually give attention to prayer, being watchful in *prayer* with thanksgiving, 3. praying also together concerning us, that God would open a door for us to speak the mystery of the message of the Messiah, because of which I have indeed been bound, 4. so that I would reveal the mystery as it is necessary for me to speak. 5. You must continually walk with wisdom toward those outside, making the most of the time. 6. Your message *must* always *be* in grace, seasoned with salt, to know how you need to answer each one.

Final Greetings

4:7. Tychicus, our beloved brother and faithful minister and fellow servant in *the* Lord, will make known everything about me, 8. whom I sent to you because of this same thing, so that you would know the things about us and he would comfort your hearts, 9. with Onesimus[1] our faithful and beloved brother, who is one of you: they will make known to you everything that is done here.

4:10. Aristarchus, my fellow prisoner, greets you. And Mark, (Acts 12:12, 15:39) the cousin of Barnabas, concerning whom you received instructions, if he would come to you, you must immediately welcome him 11. and Jesus, the one called Justus, who are of *the* circumcision, they alone, fellow workers in the kingdom of God, were a comfort to me. 12. Epaphras, *who is* one of you, greets you, a servant of Messiah Jesus, always striving with strenuous zeal on your behalf in his prayers, so that you would stand complete and fully convinced in every desire of God *for you*. 13. For I testify about him that he has done much hard work on your behalf and for those in Laodicea and those in Hierapolis. 14. Luke, the beloved physician, and Demas greet you. 15. You must immediately greet the brothers in Laodicea, and Nympha and the congregation in her house. 16. And when the letter would be read[2] for you, you must right away make *plans*

---

1   (v.9) This is the former slave of Philemon, who was a Colossian.

2   (v.16) This is read because there was no inexpensive way to make copies, but only hand

so that it would be read before the congregation in Laodicea, and that you would read the *one* from Laodicea. 17. And tell Archippo, "You must continually watch out for the ministry which you took in *the* Lord, so that you would fulfill it."

4:18. *I*, Paul, *add this* greeting in my hand. Remember my bonds. Grace *be* with you.

---

copying. See Manuscript in Glossary.

~ 1 THESSALONIANS[1] ~

Salutation

1.1. Paul and Silas and Timothy to the congregation[2] of Thessalonikeon[3] in God *the* Father and Lord Jesus Messiah, grace and peace to you.

The Thessalonians Faith and Example

1:2. We give thanks to God always concerning you all, making mention in our prayers, constantly 3. remembering your work of faith and the labor of love and by patient hope of our Lord Jesus Messiah before our God and Father, 4. because we know your election, brothers, that you have been loved by God, 5. because our gospel did not come to you in word only, but also in power and in *the* Holy Spirit with full conviction, just as you know what sort *of ministers* we were among you for your sake. 6. And you became imitators of us and of the Lord, when you received the word, while in much affliction, with joy from *the* Holy Spirit. 7. Thus you became a pattern for all the believers in Macedonia and in Achia. 8. For the Word of the Lord was caused to ring out from you not only in Macedonia and in Achia, but in every place your faith toward God spoke out, so we have no need to speak it. 9. For they are reporting about us what sort of welcome we had with you, and how you turned toward God from serving the idols to *the* living and true God 10. and to expect His Son from the heavens, Whom He raised from the dead, Jesus, the One Who rescued us from the coming wrath.

Paul's Ministry in Thessalonica

2.1. Indeed you yourselves know, brothers, our visit with you, that it was not in vain, 2. but since we suffered previously and were mistreated, as you know, in Philippi, (Ac 16:19-24) we, because of our God, had the courage to openly tell you the Good News of our God in the face of great opposition. (Ac 17:1-5) 3. For our instruction is not of error and not from impurity and not in

---

1   (Title) Written about 51,52 AD, the letters to the Thessalonians are the earliest of Paul's letters that we have.
2   (v.1) Although often translated "church," no Greek word meaning church is used in the NT. See Congregation in Glossary.
3   (v.1) This is the English spelling of the Greek word. The letter K was changed to C by the Latin text which was used for the early English translations. Thessalonikeon is plural.

deceit, 4. but as we have been tested by God to be entrusted with the Good News, so we are speaking, not as pleasing to people but to God, to the One Who tests our hearts. 5. And indeed we did not ever use flattering words, just as you know, nor with a pretext of satisfying greed, God *is* witness, 6. nor seeking praise from men, either from you or from others, 7. although we are able to wield authority as apostles of Messiah. But we would be gentle in your midst, even as a mother would cherish her own children, 8. so that as we long for you, we resolve to impart to you not only the gospel of God, but also our own lives, because you became beloved to us. 9. Indeed you must continually remember, brothers, our labor and hardship: because working night and day so we would not burden any of you, we proclaimed to you the gospel of the *only* God. 10. You and God *are* witnesses, as in a holy manner, and uprightly and blamelessly, we came to you, to those on the point of believing, 11. just as you know, as each one of you, like a father his own child, 12. exhorting you and encouraging and imploring you to walk worthily of God, the One Who called you into His own kingdom and glory.

2:13. And because of this in fact we on our part, *just as you do*, give thanks to God constantly, because when you learned a message of divine preaching, you received *it* from us not *as* a doctrine of men but, as it truly is, a doctrine of God, Who is working among you who believe. 14. For you became imitators, brothers, of the called out ones of God, those who are in Messiah Jesus in Judea, because you suffered these things even under your own countrymen just as they under the Jewish people, 15. and those who killed the Lord Jesus and the prophets also persecuted us severely and since they were not pleasing to God and because they were hostile to all men, 16. when they hindered us from speaking to the heathens so that they could be saved. In *this manner* they always fill up their sins *to overflowing*. But the wrath *of God* came upon them unexpectedly at last.

Paul's Desire to Visit the Congregation Again

2:17. And we, brothers, since we have been made orphans by separation from you for a season of time, in person not heart, we are all the more eager with great desire to see you in person. 18. Because we have wanted to come to you, indeed I, Paul, did again and again, but Satan[1] has hindered us. 19. Indeed what *is* our hope or joy or crown of boasting before the Lord Jesus at His coming - is it not you? 20. For you are our glory and joy.

3.1. On this account when we could no longer endure it we preferred to be left behind in Athens alone 2. and we sent Timothy, our brother and fellow worker of God in the Good News of the Messiah, to establish and to exhort you on behalf of your faith 3. and no one is to be deceived by these afflictions.[2] For you know that we were appointed for this: 4. for also when we were with you,

---

1   (v.18) See Satan in Glossary.
2   (v.3) See 1 Thes 2:15

we were saying in front of you that we were going to be afflicted, just as in fact then you know it happened. 5. Because of this too, since I could not hold out any longer, I sent to know about your faith, lest somehow the one who tempts did tempt *you*, then our labor would have been useless.

3:6. But now when Timothy came to us from you he brought us good news of your faith and your love and that you always have good remembrance of us, longing to see us just as also we *long to see* you. 7. Because of this, brothers, we, in every distress and in our affliction, were comforted by you through your faith, 8. because now we live if you are steadfast in *the* Lord. 9. For what thanks are we able to give to God concerning you in every joy in which we rejoice before our God because of you, 10. night and day as earnestly as possible, begging in prayer to see your face and to put in proper condition the things of your faith *that are* lacking?

3:11. And the same God and our Father and our Lord Jesus might direct our way to you, removing the things that have hindered us: 12. and the Lord might enrich you and might abound your love for one another and for all just as also we *have love* for you, 13. to establish your hearts blameless in holiness before our God and our Father in the coming of our Lord Jesus with all His holy ones,[1] amen.

A Life Pleasing to God

4.1. For the rest, brothers, we would ask of you and we exhort *you* in *the* Lord Jesus, so that just as you learned from us how it is necessary for you to walk and to please God, and just as you are walking, you would abound more. 2. For you know what instruction we gave to you through the Lord Jesus. 3. For this is *the* will of God, the One Who sanctifies you, that you abstain from immorality. 4. Each of you knows to take a wife for himself (1 Pe 3:7) in holiness and in honor, 5. not in lustful passion like the heathens, the ones who have not known God, 6. not to sin by taking advantage of his brother in a dispute, because *the* Lord is an avenger concerning all these things, just as we also said to you before and we warned *you*. (Ps 94:1, Sir 5:3) 7. For God did not call us to uncleanness but to holiness. 8. For that reason the one who rejects *this warning* is not rejecting man but God, even the One Who gives you His Holy Spirit.

4:9. And you do not need *me* to write to you about brotherly love, for you are taught by God to love one another, 10. for indeed you are doing this for all your brothers *and sisters*, those in all of Macedonia. And we exhort you, brothers *and sisters*, to progress more and more 11. and to aspire to rest[2] and to do your own business and to work with your own hands, just as we instructed you, 12. so that you would walk properly with outsiders[3] and you would have need of

1   (v.13) The holy ones are the heavenly hosts, angels, coming on Judgment Day. See Mt 16:27, 2 Thes 1:10.
2   (v.11) This means to cease from labor.
3   (v.12) Unbelievers

nothing.

The Lord's Coming

4:13. And we do not want you to be ignorant, brothers, concerning those who have fallen asleep,[1] that you would not grieve as the rest of those who do not have hope. 14. For if we believe that Jesus died and rose, so God will also bring with Him those who have fallen asleep by means of Jesus' *redemption*.

4:15. Indeed we say this to you in a word of *the* Lord, that we, those left behind who are living to the coming of the Lord, would **not** precede those who are sleeping: 16. because the Lord Himself will descend from heaven with a command, with a voice of an archangel and with a shofar[2] of God, and the dead in Messiah will rise first, (Rev. 20:4) 17. then we, the living, those who are left behind, will be taken away together with them into the clouds to meet with the Lord in *the* air: (Rev. 20:5) and thus we shall always be with *the* Lord. 18. So you must continually comfort one another with these words.

5.1. And concerning the times and the seasons, brothers, you do not need it to be written to you, 2. for you know accurately that *the* Day of *the* Lord[3] is coming as a thief at night. 3. When *unbelievers* would say, "Peace and safety," (Jr 6:14, 8:11, Eze 13:10) then sudden destruction is standing near just as travail would be in the womb, and they would **not** escape. 4. But you, brothers, are not in darkness, so that the Day would overtake you as a thief: 5. for you are all sons of light and sons of day. We are not of night and not of darkness:[4] 6. we should therefore not sleep as the rest but we should be watchful and we should be sober. 7. For those who are sleeping sleep of night, and those who get drunk get drunk[5] at night: 8. but, since we are of day, we should be sober, putting on a breastplate of faith and of love and *for* a helmet *the* hope of salvation:[6] (Is 59:17, Wsd 5:18) 9. because God did not put us *here* to be subject to wrath but to gain salvation through our Lord Jesus Messiah, 10. the One Who died instead of us, so that whether we would be awake or we would sleep we will live together with Him. 11. On this account you must continually exhort one another and you must steadily build up *one another* one *on* one, just as you are doing.

Final Exhortations and Greetings

5:12. And we are asking you, brothers, to cherish those who labor among you and direct you in *the* Lord and admonish you 13. and to regard them most

---

1   (v.13) See Death in glossary.
2   (v.16) This Greek word, salpiggi, is also translated trumpet, but Shofar is the appropriate translation in this context. See Shofar in Glossary.
3   (v.2) Judgment Day. See Re 20:4, 11-14.
4   (v.5) Day speaks of light, while dawn alludes to redemption. Night alludes to exile, separation from God's presence.
5   (v.7) While this refers to being drunk from too much of any intoxicant, for more on the subject see Sorcery in Glossary.
6   (v.8) See note on v.5.

highly in love because of their work. You must habitually keep the peace among yourselves. 14. And we urge you, brothers, you must regularly admonish the disorderly, you must constantly encourage the discouraged, you must continually help the weak, you must always be patient with all. 15. You must see that no one **ever** repays evil for any evil, but you must always steadily pursue good then for one another and for all.

5:16. Always be rejoicing, 17. you must pray unceasingly, 18. you must continually give thanks in everything: for this *is the* will of God in Messiah Jesus for you. 19. You must habitually not *ever* quench the Spirit, 20. you must continually not ever despise prophecy,[1] 21. but you must constantly prove all things; you must incessantly hold fast the good, 22. you must faithfully keep yourselves away from every form of evil.

5:23. And may the God of Peace Himself purify you *all* completely in all respects, and would He keep your spirit and inner being and body blamelessly whole, with no part unsound, for the coming of our Lord Jesus Messiah. 24. The One Who calls you *is* faithful, Who also will do *what He has said*.

5:25. Brothers *and sisters*, you must also continually pray for us.

5:26. Greet all the brothers[2] with a holy kiss. 27. I solemnly charge you in the name of the Lord to read the letter to the entire congregation.[3]

5:28. The grace of our Lord Jesus Messiah *be* with you.

---

1   (v.20) This is a reference to any of the prophetic gifts.
2   (v.26) The word Brothers refers to all members of the congregation, both male and female.
3   (v.27) The literal translation is brothers, but the Hebrew use refers to the entire congregation.

~ 2 THESSALONIANS[1] ~

Salutation

1.1 Paul and Silvanus[2] and Timothy to the congregation[3] of Thessalonians in God our Father and Lord Jesus Messiah, 2. grace and peace to you from God our Father and *our* Lord Jesus Messiah.

The Judgment at Messiah's Coming

1:3. We must give thanks to God always concerning you, brothers, just as He is worthy, because your faith is increasing bountifully and the love of each one for one another fills all of you, 4. so that we boast of these things in you to the congregations of God concerning your patience and faithfulness in all your persecutions and afflictions which you are enduring, 5. evidence of the righteous judgment of God for you to be considered worthy of the kingdom of God, for which you are now suffering, 6. since it is just for God to repay affliction to those who afflict you 7. and to you, the ones who are *now* being afflicted, grant in turn relief *from persecutions* with us, by means of the revelation of the Lord Jesus from heaven with His powerful angels 8. in flaming fire, giving vengeance to those who have not known God and to those who do not obey the gospel of our Lord Jesus, 9. who will suffer *the* punishment *of* eternal destruction, away from *the* presence of the Lord and from the glory of His strength, 10. when He would come with His holy ones[4] to be glorified and to be marveled *at* in that Day[5] by all who believe, because our testimony was believed by you. 11. And we are always praying on your behalf that our God would judge you worthy of the calling and He would fill you with every delight of goodness and work of faith in power, 12. so that the name of our Lord Jesus would be glorified in you, and you in Him, according to the grace of our God and Lord Jesus Messiah.

---

1   (Title) Written about 51,52 AD.
2   (v.1) Silas
3   (v.1) Although often translated "church," no Greek word meaning church is used in the NT. See Congregation in Glossary.
4   (v.10) The holy ones are the heavenly hosts, angels, coming on Judgment Day. See Mt 16:27, 1 Thes 3:13.
5   (v.10) Judgment Day. See Re 20:4, 11-14.

The Man of Lawlessness/Without Torah

2.1. Concerning the coming of our Lord Jesus Messiah and our assembling with Him we would ask you, brothers, 2. for you not to be quickly shaken in your mind and not to be frightened, either through the spirit or through a word, or through a letter supposedly from us, *saying* that the Day of the Lord has *already* come upon *us*: 3. let no one deceive you in any way. Because when the apostasy would come first, then the man of lawlessness,[1] the son of destruction, would be revealed. 4. *He is* the one who opposes *Torah* and exalts himself upon every Godly saying or object of worship, *and* thus seats himself in the sanctuary of God, proclaiming himself, that he is God. (Eze 28:2) 5. Do you not remember that while I was still with you I was saying these things to you? 6. And you now know Him, the One Who restrains, the One to be revealed in His own time. 7. For the mystery of the one without Torah[2] is already at work: while only He is restraining *him* at the present time until he would come out from among you. 8. And then the one without Torah will be revealed, whom the Lord Jesus will destroy by the breath of His mouth and will abolish by the appearance of His coming, 9. whose coming is through the efficiency of the works of Satan[3] with great power and false signs and wonders 10. and in every unrighteous deception for those who are being destroyed, because they did not accept the love of the truth for them to be saved. 11. And because of this God sends them a working of deception so they would believe in the lie, 12. so that all those would be judged who did **not** believe in the truth, but took pleasure in unrighteousness.

Chosen for Salvation

2:13. And we must give thanks to God always concerning you, brothers, as you have been loved by *the* Lord, because God chose you, first fruits in salvation by means of sanctification of spirit and faith in *the* truth, 14. to which then He called you through our gospel in obtaining *the* glory of our Lord Jesus Messiah. 15. Therefore then, brothers, stand and hold fast the substance of the teachings which you were taught, whether by *the spoken* word or by our letters. 16. And our Lord Jesus Messiah Himself and God our Father, the One Who loved us and by grace gave *us* eternal comfort and good hope, 17. comfort your hearts and *enable you* to stand fast in every work and in a good word.

Pray for Us

3.1. Finally, brothers, concerning us, you must continually pray that the message of the Lord would proceed quickly and be acclaimed, causing the value of the message to become manifest, just as *it did* also with you, 2. and that we would be rescued from evils and from evil men: for faith *is* not for everybody. 3. But the Lord is faithful, Who will strengthen you and will guard *you* from the evil

---

1   (v.3) This can also be translated " the one without Torah."
2   (v.7) The lawless one
3   (v.9) See Satan in Glossary.

one. 4. And we are certain in *the* Lord in your case, because we are instructing and you are doing and you will do *what we suggest.* 5. And may the Lord direct your hearts in the love of God and in the steadfastness of the Messiah.

Warning against Idleness

3:6. And we command you, brothers, in *the* name of our Lord Jesus Messiah that you keep away from every brother walking in an irresponsible manner and not according to the tradition which they took from us. 7. Indeed you know how it is necessary to imitate us, because we were not lazy among you 8. and we were not eating meals from anyone without paying, but in labor and hardship, working night and day to not burden any of you: 9. not that we do not have authority, *a right to be supported,* but so that we would give ourselves *as* an example for you to imitate us.[1] 10. For even when we were with you, we were declaring this to you, that if someone does not want to work then he must not eat. 11. For we hear some among you *are* walking in an irresponsible manner and not working but being busybodies: 12. and we order such as these and exhort *them* in *the* Lord Jesus Messiah, that working in quietness they would eat their own bread. 13. But you, brothers, do not become weary doing what is right. 14. And if anyone does not obey our message in *this* letter, you must take special notice not to associate with him, so that he would be put to shame: 15. and you must continually not consider *him* as an enemy, but admonish *him* as a brother.

Benediction

3:16. And may He, the Lord of peace, give peace to you through everything in every situation. The Lord *be* with all of you. 3:17. The greeting in my hand, Paul, is a sign in every letter: I write in this manner. 18. The grace of our Lord Jesus Messiah *be* with all of you.

---

1   (v.9) See Romans Chapter 7. Although not perfected, he was still a good example for others.

~ 1 TIMOTHY[1] ~

Salutation

1.1. Paul, an apostle of Messiah Jesus, according to a command of God our Savior and Messiah Jesus, our Hope, 2. to Timothy, a true child in faith, grace, mercy, peace from God *the* Father and Messiah Jesus our Lord.

Warning against False Doctrine

1:3. Just as I urged you, remain longer in Ephesus while I go to Macedonia, so that you could command some not to teach a different doctrine 4. and not to pay attention to myths and endless genealogies, which promote useless speculations rather than divine training that is in faith. 5. But the goal of the command is love out of a clean heart and a good conscience and sincere faith, 6. from which, when some missed the mark[2] they turned away to fruitless talk 7. wanting to be teachers of Torah,[3] although they understood neither what they were saying nor about what they were confidently insisting.

1:8. But we know that the Torah *is* good, if someone would use *it* lawfully for himself,[4] 9. as we know this, that Torah is not given for a righteous one, but *one* heedless[5] of Torah and with rebellious ones, impious and sinners, unholy and profane, *who* kill their fathers and mothers, murderers 10. fornicators, homosexuals, kidnappers, liars, perjurers, and any other one *who acts* contrary to sound teaching 11. according to the gospel of the glory of the blessed God, *with* which I was entrusted.

Thankfulness for Mercy

1:12. I have *received* undeserved kindness from Messiah Jesus, the One Who made me strong in our Lord, because He considered me faithful when He

---

1   (Title) Written about 62-65 AD.
2   (v.6) To miss the mark is an Hebraic expression for sin. The verb is astokheo and it is used only in 1 Tim 1:6, 6:21, and 2 Tim 2:18. The noun stokhos means target. See Sin in Glossary.
3   (v.7) Torah means teaching or instruction. See Torah in Glossary.
4   (v.8) Each of us must be responsible only for himself, not constantly correcting others. (Mt 7:3-5, Lk 6:41,42) Other translations leave out "for himself," in v.8, but it is definitely there in the Greek.
5   (v.9) This Greek word refers to intentional sin. See Sin in Glossary.

placed me in ministry[1] 13. although I was formerly a blasphemer and persecutor and arrogant, but I received mercy, because, not knowing, I acted in unbelief: 14. and the grace of our Lord overflowed with faith and love in Messiah Jesus. 15. The statement is faithful and worthy of all approval, that Messiah Jesus came into the world to save sinners, of whom I am foremost.[2] 16. But I received mercy because of this, so that Messiah Jesus would show all patience with me first, for an example for those who were going to believe in Him for eternal life. 17. Now to the Eternal King, Immortal, Invisible, *the* Only God, *be* honor and glory forever and ever, amen.

1:18. I set this command before you, son Timothy, according to the prophecies that went over you earlier, that by them you would fight the good warfare 19. because you have faith and good conscience, which some, when they repudiated *the prophecies*, shipwrecked concerning their faith, 20. of whom are Hymenaeus and Alexander, whom I gave over to Satan,[3] so that they would be disciplined not to blaspheme.

Instructions Concerning Prayer

2.1. So I urge first for everything to be done in supplications, prayers, intercessions, thanksgivings on behalf of all mankind, 2. on behalf of kings and all those who are in authority, so that we would lead a quiet and tranquil life in reverence and in all godliness. 3. This *is* good and acceptable before God our Savior, 4. Who wants all mankind to be saved and to come into true precise and correct knowledge. 5. For there is one God and one Mediator between God and mankind, *the* man Messiah Jesus, 6. the One Who gave Himself, a ransom on behalf of all, His testimony at a suitable time. 7. In which I was placed a preacher and apostle, I am telling *the* truth I am not lying, a teacher of heathens in faith and truth.

2:8. Therefore I desire that men every place would pray, lifting up holy hands without anger or argument. 9. And likewise *I desire* that women would adorn themselves with modesty and decency in modest clothing, not in anything entwined[4] and in gold or pearls or expensive clothing, 10. but through good works,[5] which is fitting for women professing reverence for God. 11. A woman must learn in a quiet manner in all subjection: 12. and I do not permit a wife to teach nor to exercise dominion over a husband, but to be in a quiet manner.[6]

---

1   (v.12) This is the Greek word diakonia and could be translated service. See Servant in Glossary. Read this verse in the context of verses 8-11 & Romans Chapter 7.
2   (v.15) The attitude each of us is to have.
3   (v.20) See Satan in Glossary.
4   (v.9) The Vulgate, Latin NT, says "braided hair" which certainly could have been what Paul was referring to, but possibly there were some with decorative pieces on their dresses.
5   (v.10) V. 9 follows men's attitude in prayer, but v. 10 goes further with mitsvot, see Mitsvah in Glossary.
6   (v.12) Timothy received this letter in Ephesus while he was leading the congregations there. Ephesus was the home of the fertility goddess Artemis, where women dominated and temple prostitution was approved. See the 19th chapter of Acts.

13. For Adam was formed first, then Eve. 14. And Adam was not deceived, but when the wife was deceived she was in transgression: 15. but she will be saved through bearing children, if they would remain in faith and love and holiness with modesty: **3**.1. the word *is* faith.

Qualifications of Elders[1]

If someone aspires to the office of elder, he desires a good work. 2. Therefore it is necessary for an elder to be above reproach, a husband of one wife, temperate, prudent, honorable, hospitable, skillful in teaching, 3. not prone to drinking much wine,[2] not pugnacious, but gentle, peaceable, not greedy, 4. managing his own house well, having *his* children in submission, with all respectfulness 5. for if someone does not know how to manage his own house, how will he take care of a congregation[3] of God? 6. Not newly converted, lest becoming puffed up he would fall into judgment, *like* the devil *did*. 7. And it is also necessary to have a good witness[4] from those outside *the congregation*, so that he would not fall into disgrace and a snare of the devil.

Qualifications of Deacons[5]

3:8. Likewise deacons/ministers *must be* serious, not deceitful, not addicted to much wine, not fond of dishonest gain, 9. keeping in mind the mystery of the faith with a clear conscience. 10. And they must also be proved first, then they must serve if they are blameless. 11. Likewise wives *must be* serious, not slanderous,[6] temperate, faithful in everything. 12. Ministers must be husbands of one wife, managing children and their own households well. 13. For those who have served well acquire for themselves good standing and much confidence in faith in the Messiah, Jesus.

The Mystery of Our Religion

3:14. I write these things to you hoping to come to you quickly: 15. but, if I am delayed, so that you would know how it is necessary to behave in *the* house of God, which is a congregation of *the* living God, a pillar and foundation of the truth. 16. And the mystery that is held and nourished by godliness is undeniably great:

Who was revealed in flesh,
He was proved to be right in spirit,
He was seen by angels,

---

1   (Caption) The Greek word Episkopos is often translated Bishop. Episkopos was the Greek title for the office of Elder, the Hebrew title of leaders. A Jewish Elder was to be at least sixty years old to be eligible for leadership.
2   (V.3) The verb translated "not prone to drinking much wine" can be translated, "abusive."
3   (v.5) Although often translated "church," no Greek word meaning church is used in the NT. See Congregation in Glossary.
4   (v.7) Testimony, reputation
5   (Caption) The Greek word is diakonos. See Servant in Glossary.
6   (v.11) See Gossip/Slander in Glossary.

> He was preached among heathens,
>> He was believed in *the* world,
>>> He was taken up in glory.

Prediction of Apostasy

4.1. And the Spirit expressly says that in the last times some of the faithful will turn their minds to following deceitful spirits and teachings of demons, 2. of liars, *who* have seared their own consciences in hypocrisy, 3. by forbidding to marry, keeping away from food, which God created for the faithful, and for those who know the truth, to receive with thanksgiving. 4. Because everything created by God *is* good and nothing *is* to be rejected after being taken with thanksgiving: 5. for it is sanctified through *the* Word of God and supplication.

A Good Minister of Messiah Jesus

4:6. You will be a good minister of Messiah Jesus when you teach these things to the brothers,[1] bringing *them* up in the words of the faith and of the good teachings which you have understood: 7. but you must continually avoid the profane old womanish myths. And you must continually train yourself toward reverence: 8. for bodily training *is* profitable for a short time, but reverence is profitable forever, since it has *the* promise for life now and for the coming *life*. 9. The message *is* trustworthy and worthy of every approval: 10. for we labor in this and we strive, because we have hoped in the living God, Who is savior of all mankind, especially of *the* faithful.

4:11. And you must continually command and habitually teach these things. 12. One must not despise your youth, but you must constantly be an example for the faithful in word, in conduct, in love, in faith, in purity. 13. Until I come you must steadily occupy yourself with reading, exhortation, *and* teaching. 14. You must not ever neglect the spiritual gift in you, which was given to you through prophecy with *the* laying on of hands by the elders.[2] 15. You must regularly cultivate these *spiritual gifts*; you must continually be among those *people*, so that your progress would be revealed to all. 16. You must continually take pains with yourself and in teaching. You must ceaselessly persevere with them: for by doing this you will save both yourself and those who listen to you.

Duties toward Others

5.1. You should not rebuke an older man but you must continually encourage *him* as *you would your* father, younger men as brothers, 2. older women as mothers, younger women as sisters in all purity.

5:3. You must continually honor widows, those *who are* really widows.

1　　　(v.6) This reference to brothers does not mean men only, but refers to the entire congregation.

2　　　(v.14) It is significant that Paul describes the gift of prophecy, which is for all believers (1Cor 12:4-11), as transferred by the laying on of hands. V. 15 orders cultivation of spiritual gifts.

4. But if some widow has children or grandchildren, *the children* must learn first to show godliness toward their own house and to give recompense to their parents *or grandparents*: for this is acceptable before God. 5. But the widow really *is* one if she has been left alone, and had hoped on God, and remains in entreaties and in prayers night and day. 6. But the one who is living luxuriously has *already* died even while she lives. 7. And you must continually command these things, so that they would be above reproach. 8. And if someone of their own and especially of their household does not care *for a widow*, he would deny the faith and is worse than an unbeliever. 9. A widow must not be enrolled less than sixty years old, a wife of one husband,[1] 10. being witnessed in good deeds,[2] if she brought up children, if she showed hospitality, if she washed feet of saints, if she helped *those who* were afflicted, if she was devoted in every good work. 11. But you must continually refuse younger widows: for when they would feel sensual impulses taking *them* from Messiah, they want to marry. 12. They are subject to condemnation because *the impulses* would nullify the first faith: 13. and besides they are also learning idleness, going about from house to house, and not only idleness, but also *they are* gossips[3] and busybodies, saying what is not proper. 14. Therefore I want younger *widows* to marry, to bear children, to manage a household, to give no opportunity for an opponent to abuse *the congregation*: 15. because some have already turned away to follow Satan.[4] 16. If some faithful woman has a widow *in her family*, she must give aid from her own resources and not continually burden the congregation, so that *the congregation* could help those *who* really *are* widows.

5:17. The elders who have ruled well must always be worthy of double honor, especially those laboring in preaching and in teaching. 18. For the Scripture says, "You will not muzzle an ox while it is threshing." (Dt 25:4) Also, Jesus said, "The worker *is* worthy of his hire." (Mt 10:10, Lk 10:7) 19. You must not accept an accusation against an elder, unless *it is* on the basis of two or three witnesses. (Dt 17:6, 19:15) 20. You must, in front of all, rebuke those who sin, so that also the rest would have respectful fear. 21. I am charging *you*, before God and Messiah Jesus and the chosen messengers,[5] that you would guard these *principles* without pre-judgment, not doing *anything* out of favoritism. 22. You must not ever lay hands quickly on anyone and not share another's sins: you must habitually keep yourself pure. 23. You must no longer drink *only* water, but you must regularly use a little wine because of your stomach and your frequent sicknesses.

5:24. The sins of some people are clear to all, leading *them* into judgment,

---

1   (v.9) This probably means a wife of only one man at a time, since this letter is going to Ephesus, which was matriarchal and polygamous.
2   (v.10) Mitsvot, see Mitsvah in Glossary.
3   (v.13) See Gossip/Slander in Glossary.
4   (v.15) See Satan in Glossary.
5   (v.21) This could be either apostles or angels.

but *the sins* also follow after some: 25. likewise also good works[1] *are* known to all, and those things that otherwise have to be hidden are not able *to be hidden*.

6.1. As many as are slaves under a yoke, they must consistently consider their own masters worthy of every honor, so that the name of God and the teaching would not be blasphemed. 2. But those who have believing masters must continually not look down on *them*, because they are brothers, but rather they must regularly serve, because those partaking of the benefit are also precious believers.

False Teaching and True Wealth

You must regularly teach and encourage these things. 3. If someone teaches a different doctrine and does not go in sound doctrine with those of our Lord Jesus Messiah and in teaching that promotes godliness, 4. he has become puffed up, since he knows nothing, but has a morbid craving for controversies and disputes, out of which come envy, strife, blasphemies, evil suspicions, 5. because people have been ruined by constant irritation of the mind and have destroyed the truth for themselves, thinking *that* godliness is a means of *financial* gain. 6. But godliness with contentment is a great gain: 7. for we have brought nothing into the world, so that *as a result* we are not able to take anything out: 8. but if we have food and covering, we will content ourselves with these. 9. But those who want to be rich are falling into temptation and trials and many foolish and harmful desires, which sink people into ruin and destruction. 10. For the love of money is a root of all the evils, which because some strove for, they went astray from the faith and they pierced themselves with many sorrows.

The Good Fight of Faith

6:11. But you, O man of God, must habitually flee these things: and you must steadily pursue righteousness, godly faith, *and* patient gentle love. 12. You must constantly fight the good fight of faith, you must immediately take hold of eternal life, into which you have been called, and make the good confession before many witnesses. 13. I am commanding you before God, the One Who gives all things life, and Messiah Jesus, the One Who gave testimony, the good profession, to Pontius Pilate, 14. you *are* to keep the whole body of principles blameless, above reproach, until the appearing of our Lord Jesus Messiah, 15. which[2] in *His* own time *God* will show, the blessed and only ruler, the King of Kings and Lord of Lords, 16. the only One Who has immortality, unapproachable Light,[3] Whom no one of mankind saw and no one is able to see: to Whom be honor and sovereignty forever, amen.

6:17. You must continually command those *who are* rich in the present

---

1   (v.25) Mitsvot, see Mitsvah in Glossary.
2   (v.15) The second coming
3   (v.16) The Light that is the aura of God is spoken of here. This is a reference to Shekinah. Shekinah itself means Dwelling, and where God is, so is the Light. See Shekinah in Glossary.

age not to be proud and not to hope in riches in uncertainty, but in God, the One Who supplies richly everything for our enjoyment, 18. *and that they are* to do good

works, to be rich in good works,[1] to be generous, sharing, 19. *and in this way* to be storing up for themselves a good foundation for the coming age, so that they would really take hold of life.

6:20. O Timothy, you must now guard the deposit, the correct knowledge and pure doctrine of the gospel, turning away for yourself from the profane chatter

and contradictions of what is falsely called knowledge,[2] 21. in which some missed the mark while professing about the faith. Grace *be* with you.

---

1   (v.18) Righteousness, good deeds, mitsvot are all synonyms that fit here. See both Mitsvah and Righteousness in Glossary.

2   (V.20) Ps 118:8 "It is better to trust in the Lord than to put confidence in man."

~ 2 TIMOTHY¹ ~

Salutation

1.1. Paul, an apostle of Messiah Jesus through *the* will of God according to a promise of life in Messiah Jesus, 2. to Timothy, beloved child, grace, mercy, peace from God *the* Father and Messiah Jesus our Lord.

Loyalty to the Gospel

1:3. I am thankful to God, Whom I serve after the manner of *my* forefathers with a pure conscience, as night and day I remember you constantly in my prayers, 4. longing to see you, remembering your tears, so that I would be filled with joy, 5. remembering your sincere faith, which dwelt first with your grandmother Lois and your mother Eunice, and I have been persuaded that *it is* also in you. 6. For which reason I am reminding you to rekindle the gift of God, which is in you through the laying on of my hands. 7. For God did not give us a spirit of timidity² but of power and love and self-control. 8. Therefore do not be ashamed of the testimony of our Lord, nor me His prisoner, but you must now suffer hardships together with me to further the gospel according to *the* power of God, 9. the One Who rescues us and calls *us* to a holy calling, not according to our works but according to His own purpose and grace, because that *grace* was given to us by Messiah Jesus before eternal time,³ 10. but *only* now has been revealed by the appearing of our Savior Messiah Jesus, when He indeed broke the power of death, and brought life and immortality to light through the Good News 11. for which I was placed a herald and apostle and teacher. 12. For which reason therefore I am suffering these things: but I am not ashamed, for I know in Whom I have been believing and I have been persuaded that He is able to guard my deposit for that Day.⁴ 13. You must constantly have a standard of Christian teaching which you heard by me in faith and love that is through Messiah Jesus: 14. you must directly guard the good deposit *of that entrusted to you* through the Holy Spirit, the One Who dwells in us.

---

1   (Title) Written about 66-67 AD.
2   (v.7) This is an exhortation to move in the gifts of the Spirit as listed in 1Cor. 12.
3   (v.9) Creation
4   (v.12) Judgment Day. See Re 20:4, 11-14.

1:15. You know this, that all those in Asia deserted me, of whom are Fugelos and Hermogenes. 16. May the Lord give mercy to the household of Onesiphorus, because many times he refreshed me and was not ashamed of my chains. 17. But while I was in Rome he eagerly sought me and found *me*: 18. the Lord would give him to find mercy from *the* Lord on that Day. And what things he ministered in Ephesus you know better *than I.*

A Good Soldier of Messiah Jesus

2.1. Therefore you, my child, must constantly be strong in the grace that is in the Messiah Jesus, 2. and to what you heard from me in the presence of many witnesses. You must now put these *instructions* before faithful people who will also be qualified to teach others. 3. You must now suffer hardship *with me* as a good soldier of Messiah Jesus. 4. No one serving as a soldier is entangled in the business affairs of life, so that he could please the one who enlisted *him*. 5. And if someone would compete in athletics, he is not crowned if he would not compete by the rules. 6. It is necessary for the laboring farmer to first share the fruits. 7. You must regularly consider what I am saying: for the Lord will give you understanding in everything.

2:8. You must faithfully remember Jesus Messiah *Who* has been raised from *the* dead, from *the* seed of David, according to the gospel I *proclaim*, 9. because of which I am enduring hardship, not even shrinking from imprisonment as a criminal, but the Word of God has not been bound: 10. because of this I endure all things for the sake of the elect, so that they also will attain salvation in the Messiah Jesus with eternal glory. 11. The statement is faithful and worthy of all approval:

for if we died with *Him*, then we shall live with *Him*:
12.   If we endure, then we shall reign with *Him*:
If we will deny *Him*, then He will deny us:
13.   "If we are unbelieving, that One remains faithful,
for He is not able to deny Himself." (Nu 23:19)

An Approved Workman

2:14. You must continually recall to mind these things being charged before God, not to dispute about words, *which does* nothing beneficial, but *is* to the ruin of the listeners. 15. You must now be diligent to present yourself approved to God, a workman who has no cause to be ashamed, teaching the doctrine of the Truth correctly and directly. 16. And you must now avoid profane discussions of vain and useless matters: for they will advance ungodliness more 17. and their message will have growth like cancer. Of whom are Hymenaeus and Philetus, 18. who departed concerning the truth, saying that the resurrection[1] has already happened, and they are overturning the faith of some. 19. Nevertheless

---

1   (v.18) They were saying Jesus' second coming had taken place.

the firm foundation of God has stood, having this seal: "*The* Lord must now know those who are His," (Nu 16:5) and "Everyone who names the name of *the* Lord must depart at once from unrighteousness." (Nu 16:26) 20. And in a great house are not only gold and silver vessels but also wood and clay, and one for honor but *the* other for dishonor: 21. therefore, if someone would cleanse himself from these *profane discussions of vain and useless matters*, he will be a vessel for honor, since he has been sanctified, useful to the Master, prepared for every good work. 22. And you must steadily flee youthful desires, and you must habitually pursue righteousness, faith, love, peace, with those who call upon the Lord out of clean hearts. 23. And you must steadily avoid foolish and stupid controversies, because you know that they would beget strife: 24. and a servant[1] of *the* Lord must not be quarrelsome but gentle toward all, skillful in teaching, bearing evil without resentment, 25. in humility correcting those opposing *you*. Perhaps God would give them repentance into a knowledge of truth 26. and they would come to their senses, to *do* the will of that One, *escaping* from the snare of the devil, because they have been captured alive by him.

The Character of People in the Last Days

3.1. But you must always understand this, that troublesome times will come in *the* last days: 2. for people will be selfish, greedy, boasters, arrogant, blasphemers, disobedient to parents, ungrateful, wicked, 3. unloving, hostile, slanderous,[2] without self-control, savage, not loving good, 4. betrayers, thoughtless, being conceited, loving pleasure more than loving God, 5. having an appearance of reverence,[3] but denying the power of it: so you must continually turn away from these things. 6. For from these are those who worm their way into homes and carry away idle women who are overwhelmed with sins, being led on by various desires, 7. always learning and never being able to come into *the* knowledge of truth. 8. But just as Janus and Jambros[4] opposed Moses, so also they are opposing the truth, men depraved in their minds, worthless, unfit concerning their faith. 9. But they will not advance further: for their folly will be quite evident to all, as also happened to *Janus and Jambros*.

Last Charge to Timothy

3:10. But you have faithfully followed my teaching, in my way of life, in my way of thinking, in my faith, in my patience, in my love, in my perseverance, 11. in persecutions, in sufferings, what sort *of things* happened to me in Antioch, in Iconia, in Lystra, what persecutions I had submitted to and the Lord rescued me from all. 12. And all those who want to live in a godly manner in Messiah Jesus will be persecuted. (Jn 15:20) 13. But evil people and swindlers will go from bad

1   (v.24) Or slave, see Servant in Glossary.
2   (v.3) See Gossip/Slander in Glossary.
3   (v.5) Godliness
4   (v.8) According to tradition Janus and Jambros were the magicians in Pharaoh's court who withstood and reproduced the miracles of Moses and Aaron.

to worse, deceiving more and being deceived. 14. But you must continuously remain in what you learned and became convinced of, because you know from whom you learned, 15. and because you have known the sacred writings from childhood,[1] the things that are able to make you wise for salvation through faith in Messiah Jesus. 16. All Scripture[2] *is* God-inspired and useful for teaching, for reproof, restoration, for training in righteousness,[3] 17. so that the man of God would be able to meet all demands, since he has been equipped perfectly for every good work.[4]

4.1. I am charging *you* before God and Messiah Jesus, the One Who is going to judge *the* living and *the* dead, *at* His appearance and *in* His kingdom: 2. you must now preach the Word, you must now be ready in season out of season, you must now correct, you must now rebuke, you must now encourage, with great patience and every kind of instruction. 3. For there will be a time when sound teaching will not be listened to but they will heap up teachings according to their own desires in themselves, *what* their ears *are* itching to hear 4. and indeed they will turn their ears from the truth, and they will turn aside to myths. 5. But you must continually be sober in everything, you must now bear hardship patiently, you must now do *the* work of an evangelist, you must now fulfill your ministry.

4:6. For I am being offered up here, and the time of my departure is imminent. 7. I fought the good fight, I have completed the course, I have kept the faith: 8. finally, the crown of righteousness is being stored up for me, which the Lord, the Righteous Judge, will grant me on that Day,[5] and not only for me, but also for every one of those who have loved His appearance.[6]

Personal Instructions

4:9. You must now be diligent to come to me hastily: 10. for Demas abandoned me, because he loved the present age and he went to Thessalonica, Crescens to Galatia, Titus to Dalmatia: 11. only Luke is with me. After you pick up Mark you must right away bring *him* here with you, for he is useful to me in ministry.[7] 12. And I sent Tychikus to Ephesus. 13 When you come you must bring the cloak that I left in Troas with Carpus, and the scrolls, especially the parchments. 14. Alexander the coppersmith did much evil to me: the Lord will grant to him according to his deeds: 15. and against whom you must continually

---

1   (v.15) Timothy's grandmother Lois and mother Eunice were trained in Scripture. This training was mandatory for Jewish boys, but optional for Jewish girls in Jesus' day.
2   (v.16) The emphasis was on what is now contained in the Tanach (Old Testament), but also included the oral teachings and the inter-testament writings. See Torah in Glossary.
3   (v.16) Righteousness is action: doing and saying the right things, being just.
4   (v.17) Each of us who is committed to the Living God has already been equipped perfectly through knowledge of His Word!
5   (v.8) Judgment Day. See Re 20:4, 11-14.
6   (v.8) His walk on earth or second coming. See Coming of Messiah in Glossary.
7   (v.11) Mark had truly matured and grown into a valuable minister. See Acts 15:36-39.

guard, for he vehemently opposed our message.

4:16. In my first defense no one stood by me, but they all abandoned me: may it not be reckoned to them: 17. but the Lord stood by me and He strengthened me, so that, through me, the preaching would be completed and all the heathens would hear, so I was rescued from *the* lion's mouth. 18. The Lord will rescue me from every evil work and will save *me* for His heavenly kingdom: to Whom *be* the glory forever and ever, amen.

4:19. You must now greet Priscilla and Aquila and the household of Onesiphorus. 20. Erastos was staying in Corinth but I left Trophimus behind in Mileto because he was sick. 21. You must now be diligent to come before winter. Eubolos and Pudens and Linus and Claudia[1] and all the brothers greet you. 22. The Lord *be* with your spirit. Grace *be* with you.

---

1   (v.21) Pudens and Claudia are women. The word Brothers includes sisters as well and does not mean only men.

~ TITUS[1] ~

Salutation

1.1. Paul, a servant[2] of God, and an apostle of Jesus Messiah, of God's elect according to faith and knowledge of truth according to godliness 2. upon hope of eternal life, which God, *Who is always* truthful, promised before time began, 3. but He has revealed in their own times by preaching His Word, the care of which I was entrusted according to *the* command of God our Savior, 4. to Titus, a genuine child according to common faith, grace and peace from God *the* Father and Messiah Jesus our Savior.

Titus' Work in Crete

1:5. I left you in Crete for this purpose, so that you would correct what still remains to be set in order and you would ordain elders in every city, as I directed you, 6. if someone is blameless, husband of one wife, *has* children *who* are believers, with no charges of debauchery or *being* undisciplined. 7. For it is necessary for an elder to be above reproach as a steward of God, not self-willed, not quick tempered, not addicted to wine, not pugnacious and combative, not fond of dishonest gain, 8. but hospitable, loving what is good, self-controlled, righteous, holy, disciplined, 9. holding fast the word of faith according to the doctrine, so that he would be able to exhort with sound teaching and to convict those who speak against *it*.

1:10. For there also are many undisciplined people, idle talkers (Mt 12:36,37) and deceivers, especially those from the circumcision. 11. It is necessary to silence them, who because of dishonest gain are overturning whole houses by teaching what is not proper. 12. A certain prophet of their own said of them,

"Cretans are always liars, evil beasts, idle gluttons."
(Epimenedes, "de Oraculis")

13. This testimony is true. For which reason you must continually disprove them sharply, so that they would be sound in the faith, 14. not giving heed to Jewish

---

1   (Title) Written about 64-66 AD. This was not written from prison, see Chapter 3:12.
2   (v.1) Or slave, see Servant in Glossary.

myths or to commandments of men when they turn away from the truth. 15. All things *are* pure to the pure: but to those who have been defiled and without faith nothing *is* pure, but they and their mind and conscience have been defiled. 16. They profess to know God, but they are contradicting themselves by their works, being detestable and disobedient and unfit for every good work.

The Teaching of Sound Doctrine

2.1. But you must regularly be speaking what is proper in sound teaching. 2. Old men *are* to be temperate, serious, self-controlled, keeping true and incorrupt doctrine in faith, in love, in patience: 3. old women *are* likewise *to be* in worthy behavior, not slanderous,[1] not being slaves to much wine, teaching what is good, 4. so that they could encourage the young women to be loving *to* their husbands, loving their children, 5. self-controlled, pure, good housekeepers, being subject to their own husbands (Eph 5:1), so that the Word of God would not be blasphemed. 6. You must likewise continually exhort the younger people to be self-controlled 7. about all things, showing yourself *to be* an example of good works,[2] in teaching soundness, respectfulness, 8. a wholesome message, beyond reproach, so that the one from an opponent would be ashamed, because he does not have evil *things* to say about us. 9. *Exhort* slaves to be subject to their own masters in everything, to give satisfaction, not back talk, 10. not misappropriating for their own use, but proving complete faithfulness, character, *to be* good so that they would be a credit to the teaching of the salvation of our God in everything *they do*.

2:11. For the grace of God has appeared with salvation for all mankind, 12. training us, so that by denying ungodliness and worldly desires we would live soberly and rightly and reverently in the present age, 13. expecting the blessed hope and the appearing of the glory of our great God and our Savior Jesus Messiah, 14. Who gave Himself for us, so that He could redeem us away from every wickedness[3] and He would purify for Himself a special people, zealous of good works.[4] 15. You must continually speak these things and you must constantly exhort and refute with all gravity: *so* no one would ever look down on you.

Maintain Good Deeds

3.1. You must continually remind them to be subject to leaders, authorities, to be obedient, to be ready for every good work, 2. and not to blaspheme, to be peaceable, gentle, showing *the* greatest courtesies to everyone. 3. For we were once foolish, disobedient, being deceived, serving various desires and pleasures, while we were living in wickedness and envy, hateful, hating one another. 4. But

---

1   (v.3) See Gossip/Slander in Glossary.
2   (v.7) Mitsvot, see Mitsvah in Glossary.
3   (v.14) Or all lawlessness, which is doing without Torah, the Scriptures, teachings, and obedience.
4   (v.14) Mitsvot, see Mitsvah in Glossary.

when the goodness and loving kindness of the Savior our God appeared, 5. He saved us, but according to His mercy, not as the result of works of righteousness which we did, but through *the* washing of regeneration and of renewal by *the* Holy Spirit, 6. Whom He poured out richly upon us through Jesus Messiah our Savior, 7. so that since we have been made righteous by the grace of that One, we would become heirs according to the hope of eternal life.

3:8. The statement is faithful and worthy of all approval: and I wish you to speak confidently concerning these things, so that those who have believed in God would be intent, busying themselves on good works:[1] these things are good and profitable for mankind. 9. But you must now shun seeking foolish things and genealogies and strife and quarrels pertaining to traditions: for they are useless and vain. 10. You must continually reject a person *who* causes division, after one, then a second admonition, 11. because you know that such as that *person* has turned aside and is sinning, being self-condemned.

Personal Instructions and Greetings

3:12. When I will send Artemas or Tychikus to you, you must immediately be diligent to come to me in Nicopolis, for I have decided to spend the winter there. 13. You must now make every effort to send Zenas, the Torah scholar, and Apollos on their way, so that nothing would be lacking for them. 14. And our own *people* must also learn to be engaged in good works for the indispensable needs *of themselves and others*, so that they would not be unfruitful.

3:15. All those with me greet you. You must now greet those who love us in faith. Grace *be* with all of you.

---

1   (v.8) Notice that this exhortation to be busy with good works comes just after a verse saying that we are saved by grace. We do not do good works in order to be saved, but we do them because we have been saved. Righteous behavior is the result of being saved.

~ PHILEMON[1] ~

Salutation

1. Paul, a prisoner of Messiah Jesus, and Timothy our brother, to the esteemed Philemon, our fellow worker 2. and Apphia our sister and Archippus our fellow soldier and to the congregation[2] at your house, 3. grace and peace to you from God our Father and *the* Lord Jesus Messiah.

Philemon's Love and Faith

4. I give thanks to my God always, as I make mention of you in my prayers, 5. because I hear of your love and faith, which you have toward the Lord Jesus and for all the saints, 6. that the sharing of your faith would be working in consciousness of every good thing within us through Messiah. 7. For I had great joy and comfort in your love, because the hearts of the saints have been refreshed through you, brother.

Paul Pleads for Onesimus

8. On which account, although I have much boldness in Messiah to charge you *to do* what is due, 9. rather I urge because of love, since I am this sort of person, Paul, an old man, and now even a prisoner for Messiah Jesus: 10. I urge you concerning my child, Onesimus, whom I fathered while in chains, 11. once useless to you but now useful both to you and to me, 12. whom I sent back to you, this one is very much on my heart: 13. whom I wanted to hold fast for myself, so that he could serve me on your behalf while *I am* in prison for the gospel, 14. but I did not want to do anything without your consent, so that your good would not be as according to necessity but according to free will. 15. For perhaps because of this he was separated for a time, so that you could keep him forever, 16. no longer as a slave but more than a slave, a beloved brother, especially for me, and how much more for you, both in *the* flesh and in *the* Lord.

17. Therefore if you look upon me *as* a partner, you must now take him in as *you would* me. 18. And if he wronged or owes you anything, charge this to

---

1   (Title) Written about 61-62 AD.
2   (v.2) Although often translated "church," no Greek word meaning church is used in the NT. See Congregation in Glossary.

me. 19. I, Paul, have written in my hand, I will repay: so that I am not saying to you then that you owe *it* to me. 20. Indeed brother, let me have some benefit from you in *the* Lord: you must now refresh my heart in Messiah.

21. Since I have been convinced by your obedience, I wrote to you because I also know that you would do more than what I ask. 22. And also now prepare a room for me: for I hope that through your prayers I will graciously be given to you.

Final Greetings

23. Epaphrus, my fellow prisoner in Messiah Jesus, greets you, 24. *as do* Mark, Aristarchus, Demas, Luke, my fellow workers. 25. The grace of the Lord Jesus Messiah *be* with your spirit.

~ HEBREWS[1] ~

God Has Spoken by His Son

1.1. Long ago and in many various ways when God spoke to our fathers, *He spoke* through the prophets. 2. On *the* last of these days, He spoke to us through a Son, Whom He appointed heir of all, through Whom He also made the universe: 3. He is the radiance of the glory and representation of His nature, and carries everything[2] by the power in His word. After He made Himself purification[3] for our sins, He sat at the right hand[4] of the Majesty on high, 4. then He became so much higher *in* rank than the angels as *the* name He has inherited *is* more excellent than theirs.

The Son Superior to Angels

1:5. For of which of the angels did He say,
"You are My Son,
today I have begotten you."? (Ps 2:7)

and again,

"I will be as a father to Him,
and He will be My son."? (2Sm 7:14, 1Chr 17:13)

6. And again when He brought the Firstborn into the inhabited world, He said,

"And all *the* angels of God must now kneel before Him."

7. And indeed with reference to the angels He says,

"The One Who makes His angels spirits
and His ministers flames of fire," (Ps 104:4)

8. But to the Son,

"Your throne, God, *is* forever and ever,

---

1   (Title) Probably written before 70 AD by an unknown author with great Scriptural knowledge.
2   (v.3) The universe
3   (v.3) He made Himself purification by leading a sinless life, to qualify as the perfect sacrifice.
4   (v.3) "At the right hand" is a Hebrew idiom that speaks of power and strength, from Ex 15:6. See Right Hand in Glossary.

and the scepter *is the* righteous[1] scepter of Your
kingdom.

9. You loved righteousness and You hated iniquity:
because of this, God, Your God, did anoint You
above Your companions with *the* oil[2] of gladness." (Ps 45:6,7)

10. And,

"You, Lord, laid the foundation of the earth from the beginning,
and the heavens are *the* works of Your hands:

11. they will pass away, but You will remain,
and all will become old as a garment,

12. and You will roll them up
like a cloak,
like a garment and they will be exchanged:
but You are *always* the same
and Your years will not come to an end." (Ps 102:25-27)

13. And to which of the angels did He ever say,

"You must now sit at My right hand,[3]
until I would place your enemies as a footstool
for your feet?"[4] (Ps 110:1)

14. Are not all ministering spirits being sent in ministry for the sake of those who
are going to inherit salvation?

The Great Salvation

2.1. Because of this it is so much more necessary that we pay attention
to what we have heard, lest we would drift away. 2. For, if the message which
was spoken through angels became established, and every transgression and
disobedience took a just penalty, 3. how will we escape, if we neglect so great a
salvation, spoken through the Lord, which was taken by those who heard *from*
the beginning, *and* it was confirmed in us, 4. when God testified at the same time
in signs and even omens[5] and in various miracles and *gifts*[6] of *the* Holy Spirit in
distributions of various kinds according to His will? (1Cor 12:11)

The Pioneer of Salvation

2:5. Indeed He did not subordinate the coming inhabited world to *the*

---

1   (v.8) The word used here is euthutes, which means uprightness, equity, impartiality,
which are a description of righteousness. See Righteousness in Glossary.
2   (v.9) In the Talmud, olive oil symbolizes knowledge of Torah, which provides spiritual
illumination. Oil is also the symbol of joy, from Is 51:3, so it is called the oil of gladness.
3   (v.13) See Right Hand in Glossary.
4   (v.13) Enemies as footstool speaks of putting a foot on the necks of your enemies prior
to cutting off their heads. See Footstool in Glossary.
5   (v.4) This Greek word refers to signs in the heavens of things to come, to wonders and
miracles.
6   (v.4) The gifts of the Spirit are listed in 1Cor 12:4-11.

angels, about which we are speaking. 6. And someone somewhere testified saying,

> "What is man that You should remember him,
>> or the Son of Man that You would be concerned about Him?
> 7.   You made Him lower than angels for a little while,
>> You crowned Him in glory and honor,
> 8.   You made all things subject under His feet." (Ps 8:6,7)

For in this to make all things subject to Him, He left nothing *that was* not subject to Him. But now we do not yet see that all things have been subjected to Him: 9. but we see Jesus crowned in glory and honor since, because He suffered death, for a short time He was made less than angels so that by *the* grace of God He would taste death on behalf of all.

2:10. For indeed it was fitting for Him, by Whom all things *were made* and through Whom all things *are*, when He led many sons into glory, the Prince of their salvation *was* perfected through suffering. 11. For also the One Who sanctifies and those who are sanctified *are* all out of One: for which reason He is not ashamed to call them brothers 12. saying,

> "I report Your name to My brothers,
>> I will sing praises to You in *the* midst of *the* congregation,"
> (Ps 22:22)

13. And again,

> "I shall have confidence in Him," (Is 8:17)

and again,

> "Behold Me and the children whom God gave Me." (Is 8:18)

14. Therefore because the children had partaken of blood and flesh, then likewise He shared with them, so that through death He would make ineffective the one who had the power of death, this is the devil, 15. and He would set them free, as many as were in bondage through their lifetime because of fear of death. 16. For surely He is not concerned with helping angels, but He is concerned with *the* seed of Abraham. 17. For this reason He was obligated to become like His brothers in every way, so that He would also become a merciful and faithful High Priest in the things relating to God for the propitiation[1] for the sins of the people. 18. For because He suffered when He was tested, He is able to help those who are being tested.

Jesus Superior to Moses

3.1. For this reason, holy brothers, sharers of *the* heavenly calling, you must now consider the Apostle and High Priest of our confession, Jesus, 2.

---

1   (v.17) To be the propitiation means to be the agent through Whom forgiveness, atonement can be achieved.

because He was faithful to the One Who appointed Him, as also Moses *was faithful* in His whole house. 3. For He has been judged more worthy than Moses, as the one who built it has so much more honor *than* the house: 4. for every house is built by someone, and God *is* the One Who built everything. 5. And Moses *was* indeed faithful in His whole house as servant in affirmation of the things which were to be spoken, 6. but Messiah as Son over His *own* house: of Whom we are a house, if we would hold fast the boldness and the boasting of the hope.

A Rest for the People of God

3:7. On this account, just as the Holy Spirit says,

"Today if you would hear His voice,
8. you would not harden your hearts as in the rebellion[1]
  as in the day of testing in the wilderness,
9. where your fathers tested *Me* in trials
  and they saw My works 10. for forty years:
for this reason I was angry with that generation
and said, 'They always go astray in their hearts,
  and they did not know My ways,
11. so that I took an oath in My wrath:
  'They shall certainly not enter My rest.[2]'" (Ps 95:7-11)

3:12. You must beware, brothers, lest a heart evil with unbelief will be in some of you, causing you to fall away from *the* living God, 13. but you must continually exhort yourselves throughout each day, until the Day[3] is called, so that none of you would be hardened by sin's deceitfulness - 14. for we have become partakers of the Messiah, if indeed we would hold firm the confidence *we had in* the beginning, steadfast until *the* end - 15. as in the *Psalm* it is being spoken,

"If you would hear His voice today,
  do not harden your hearts as in the rebellion." (Ps 95:7,8)

16. For did some[4] provoke *God* after they heard? But were not all those who left from Egypt *led* by Moses? 17. And with whom was He disgusted *for* forty years? And *were they* not among the sinners whose corpses fell in the wilderness? 18. And to whom did He swear that they would not enter His rest, except to those who disobeyed? (Nu 14:1-35) 19. So we see that they were not able to enter because of unbelief.

4.1. Therefore we should fear so we would not in any way depart from a promise to enter His rest *and* any of you would seem to have been excluded. 2.

---

1 (v.8) The rebellion of Korah, Numbers Chapter 16
2 (v.11) This, and each rest referred to throughout this and the next chapter, is the eternal rest. See Rest in Glossary.
3 (v.13) Judgment Day. See Re 20:4, 11-14.
4 (v.16) This is another reference to those who joined Korah in rebellion.

For also we have been evangelized just as those: but the word of the report *of the gospel* that they heard did not benefit *them* because those who heard did not mix *it* with faith. 3. For we who have believed enter the rest, just as He has said,

> "As I swore in My wrath,
> 'They will not enter My rest,'" (Ps 95:11)

and yet the works have been *completed* since the foundation of *the* world. 4. For He has said somewhere concerning the seventh *day*[1] in this manner, "And God rested[2] on the seventh day from all His works," (Gn 2:2) 5. and again in this, "They will not enter My rest."[3] (Ps 95:11) 6. Then since some remained to enter this *rest*, then those who heard the Gospel in former times did not enter because of obstinate opposition to the Divine will, 7. again some determine a day, "Today," as when David said after such a time, just as it has been spoken before,

> "If you would hear his voice today,
> do not harden your hearts." (Ps 95:7,8)

8. For if Joshua had given them eternal rest, He would not afterward have been speaking about another day. 9. Consequently *the* Sabbath rest remains for the people of God.[4] 10. For the one who enters *God's* rest, then God brought him into rest from his works just as He from His own *labors*. 11. Therefore we should make every effort to enter that eternal rest,[5] so that no one would fall into this example *of destruction* through obstinate opposition to the Divine will.

4:12. For the Word of God is living[6] and powerful and sharper than any two-edged sword[7] and pierces until separation of *breath of* life and spirit, of joints and marrow and passing judgments on *the* thoughts and understandings of *your* heart: 13. and no creature is hidden before Him, but everything is uncovered, since it has been laid bare to His eyes, to Whom an accounting by us *is required*.

Jesus the Great High Priest

4:14. Therefore as we have a great High Priest *Who* has passed through the heavens,[8] Jesus, the Son of God, we should hold fast the confession. 15. For we do not have a High Priest not able to be sympathetic with our weaknesses, but *One Who* has been tested against all things in quite the same way *as we are but* without sin. 16. Therefore we should come to the throne of grace with boldness,

---

1   (v.4) Sabbath
2   (v.4) This is eternal rest, evidence that God created everything during the time of Gn 1.
3   (v.5) Again, eternal rest. See Rest in Glossary.
4   (v.9) The Sabbath is the seventh day, from sundown Friday until sundown Saturday, with Scriptural proscriptions.
5   (v.11) We can enter that eternal rest now, in the midst of work and turmoil, by giving every burden to Him, per Ps 55:22, but in eternal rest we will still have assignments. See Re 6:11, 14:13. See Rest in Glossary.
6   (v.12) The Greek construction puts great emphasis on "living."
7   (v.12) This is the small, personal sword.
8   (v.14) This implies that He went through all seven layers of heaven. See Heavens in Glossary.

so that we could take mercy and we would find grace in well-timed help.

5.1. For every High Priest *who* is taken from men is ordained by men for the things with regard to God, so that he would bring gifts and also offerings[1] for sins, 2. being able to deal gently with the ignorant[2] and *those* led astray, because he is himself subject to weakness 3. and because of it he is obligated, just as *he does* for the people, so also *he* offers for himself for *his* sins.[3] 4. And who does not take honor for himself, *when he is called High Priest*, but *he must* be called by God as also Aaron *was*.

5:5. Thus also the Messiah did not glorify Himself by becoming a High Priest, but as the One spoke to Him,

"You are My Son,
I have this day begotten You:" (Ps 2:7)

6. just as in another He then says,

"You *are* a priest forever
according to the order of Melchizedek,"[4] (Ps 110:4)

7. Who in the days of His flesh, in prayers and also supplications with loud crying and by having brought tears to the very One able to rescue Him from death and then He was heard because of His godliness, 8. although He was a Son, He learned obedience from that which He suffered, 9. and when He was finished He became *the* source of eternal salvation for all those who were obedient to Him. 10. Then He was designated by God, High Priest according to the order of Melchizedek.

Warning against Apostasy

5:11. Concerning this subject we have much to say but *it is* hard to explain, since you have become sluggish in your hearing. 12. For now you ought to be teachers[5] by *this* time, *but* you again need someone to teach you the fundamental principles of the words of God from the beginning and you have become needy of milk and not solid food. 13. For everyone who shares milk *is* inexperienced in the teaching about righteousness, for he is a baby: 14. but solid food is for *the* mature *saints*, those who have exercised for themselves the senses that are trained by practice for distinguishing both good and evil.[6]

6.1. On this account, let us leave the elementary message about Messiah, for the maturity *to which* we should be brought, not again laying a foundation of

---

1   (v.1) This would include first fruits, meal offerings, as well as animals that were sacrificed.
2   (v.2) The ignorant refers to sins committed unintentionally. See Sin in Glossary.
3   (v.3) See Sin and Sin, Forgiveness of in Glossary.
4   (v.6) In Hebrew this is Melki-Tsedek, meaning King of Righteousness or Righteous King.
5   (v.12) Each one of us is to grow spiritually so that we are teaching others. We all teach others by the way we live even more than by what we say. We all should also be knowledgeable enough in Scriptures to teach those who are less learned in the Word.
6   (v.14) This requires using the gifts of the Spirit, discerning of spirits, 1Cor 12:4-11.

repentance from dead works and faith in God, 2. of teaching of baptisms,[1] and of laying on of hands, and of resurrection[2] of *the* dead, and of eternal judgment. 3. And, if only God will permit, we will do this. 4. *It is* impossible for those who have once been enlightened, and have tasted the heavenly gifts[3] and have become sharers of *the* Holy Spirit 5. and have tasted *the* full measure of *the* Word of God *and* works of power of *the* coming age[4] 6. then if they fall away, to restore *them* again to repentance, because they crucify the Son of God anew for themselves and hold *Him* to contempt. 7. For *the* land that has often drunk rain *that* has come upon it and bears useful plants for those for whom it is cultivated, receives a share of *the* blessing from God: 8. but when it bears thorn plants and thistles *it is* worthless and close to cursed, for which the end is to be burned over.

6:9. But, even though we are speaking this way, we have been convinced concerning you, beloved, *you are* holding fast the better things that belong to salvation. 10. For God is not unjust to overlook your work and the love that you demonstrated in His name, when you ministered and are *still* ministering to[5] the saints. 11. But we desire each of you to make evident the same earnestness until *the* end with the full assurance of the hope, 12. so that you would not become lazy, but imitators of those who, through faith and patience, inherit the promises.

God's Sure Promise

6:13. For when God promised Abraham, since He had no one greater to swear *by*, "He swore by Himself" (Gn 22:6) 14. saying, "When I bless, I will surely bless you and when I multiply I will *surely* multiply you:" (Gn 22:17, Sir 44:21) 15. and so after he was patient he obtained the promise. 16. For men swear by the one greater *than themselves*, and with them the oath serves as confirmation beyond all doubts: 17. by which, since God resolved to show the promise more abundantly to the heirs, He guaranteed the unalterable *result* of His purpose with an oath, 18. so that through two unchangeable events, in which *it is* impossible for God to lie, we, those who have taken refuge, would have strong encouragement to take hold of the hope that is set before us: 19. which we have as an anchor of life, both firm and secure and since *the hope* enters the inner of the veil,[6] 20. where a forerunner, Jesus, entered on our behalf, Who has become forever a High Priest according to the order of Melchizedek.

---

1   (v.2) We use the English spelling of baptisma, which means immersion, in this verse. The use of the plural shows that the author was teaching the Jewish practice of immersion for purification, calling for rather frequent immersion. See Baptize in Glossary.

2   (v.2) See Resurrection in Glossary.

3   (v.4) The heavenly gifts are those referred to in Chapter 5:14, see footnote for v. 14 above.

4   (v.5) As we use the gifts we are to expect miracles, to experience the awesome power of God in our everyday lives. We will not have the fullness of the power in this age, but we are surely to taste the power. Every saint is to be trained to walk in victory and power, in order to bring into the kingdom those who do not have a relationship with God.

5   (v.10) These could be translated "when you served and are still serving.."

6   (v.19) Holy of Holies, see Sanctuary in Glossary.

The Priestly Order of Melchizedek

7.1. For this "Melchizedek, King of Salem, priest of the Most High God, the one who met Abraham when he returned from the slaughter of the kings and had blessed him, 2. with whom Abraham also divided a tithe[1] from everything," (Gn 14:17-20) first on the one hand translated "King of Righteousness" but then also "King of Salem" which is King of Peace, (Gn 14:17-20) 3. without a father, without a mother, without genealogy, having neither beginning of days nor end of life, but *Who* was made like the Son of God, remains a priest forever.

7:4. But you see how great he *was* to whom Abraham the Patriarch gave a tithe of the spoils. 5. Now indeed those of the sons of Levi, the priesthood, have a command, that they take a tithe *from* the people according to the Torah,[2] these are their brothers, who also come from the seed of Abraham: 6. but the one who does not have descent has received a tithe from Abraham and he blessed the one who had the promises. 7. And without any dispute the inferior is blessed by *the* greater one.[3] 8. So then indeed mortal men take a tithe, but there *with Melchizedek* it is testified that he lives *forever.* (Ps 110:4) 9. And so it could be said that Levi, the one who takes a tithe, has paid a tithe through Abraham: 10. for *Levi* was still in the loin of his father when Melchizedek met him.

7:11. So if perfection was *obtained* through the Levitical priesthood, for the people have received Torah through it, why then *is there* a need for a priest to be raised in the order of Melchizedek and not in the order of Aaron? 12. For when the priesthood is changed, then from necessity there is a change of Torah. 13. For over Whom it says these things, He belonged to another tribe, from which no one had officiated at the altar: 14. for *it is* clear that our Lord has descended from Judah, for which tribe Moses spoke nothing about priests. 15. And yet it is even more clear, if another priest rises according to the likeness *of* Melchizedek, 16. He was not according to *the* tradition of fleshly command but according to *the* power of endless life. 17. For it is testified that

"You are a priest forever
according to the order of Melchizedek." (Ps 110:4)

18. For certainly a preceding commandment becomes set aside because of its weakness and uselessness - 19. for legalism perfected nothing - but a better hope is introduced through which we draw near to God.

7:20. And just as *it was* not without an oath: for indeed the *Levites* became priests without an oath, 21. but then He called to Him with an oath because of this,

---

1   (v.2) See Tithe in Glossary.
2   (v.5) Torah means teaching or instruction and here refers to the first five books of the Bible. See Torah in Glossary.
3   (v.7) This is a puzzling statement because many, many Jewish prayers begin "Blessed are You.." (Baruch Atah) referring to our heavenly Father.

> "*The* Lord has sworn
> > and will not change His mind,
> You *are* a priest forever." (Ps 110:4)

22. By so much then Jesus has become a guarantee of a better covenant. 23. And there are certainly many priests who have been denied by death to remain *priests*: 24. but because He remains forever He has the permanent priesthood: 25. and He is able to save for all time those who come to God through Him, because He always lives to intercede on their behalf.

7:26. It is fitting for such a One as this *to be* a High Priest for us, holy, blameless, undefiled, *Who* has been separated from the sinners and has been raised to greater heights than the heavens, 27. Who does not need day by day, as *did* the earlier High Priests, to offer sacrifices on behalf of their own sins, then the *sacrifices* for the people: for He did this once and for all when He offered Himself. 28. For the Torah[1] ordains men, High Priests *who* have weaknesses, but the word of the oath, which *was made* after the Torah, *ordained the* Son Who has been perfected forever.

The High Priest of a New and Better Covenant

8.1. But the main thing for those who are being addressed *is that* we have such a High Priest, Who has sat down on the right hand[2] of the throne of The Majesty in the Heavens, 2. One blessed with the holy things, a minister of the saints and of the true tabernacle, which the Lord built, not man. 3. Every High Priest is appointed to bring both gifts and offerings: therefore *it was* necessary to also have something that this *High Priest* would offer *for himself*. 4. If truly now He were upon *the* earth He would not even be a priest, while those who are *priests* would offer the gifts according to Torah: 5. they are serving in a copy and in a shadow *of the tabernacle* of the heavenlies, just as Moses had been divinely commanded when he was going to erect the tabernacle, "For you see" He said, "You will make everything according to the pattern which was shown to you on the mountain:" (Ex 25:40) 6. but now He has obtained a so much more excellent service, and He is mediator of a better covenant, which has been enacted on better promises.

8:7. For if that first had been faultless, a second place would not have been sought. 8. For finding them at fault He says,

> "Behold days are coming, says *the* Lord,
> > when I will establish a new covenant upon the house of Israel,
> > and upon the house of Judah,
> 9.   not according to the covenant that I made with their fathers
> > in days when I took hold of their hand
> > to bring them out from Egypt,

---

1   (v.28) Torah means teaching or instruction. See Torah in Glossary.
2   (v.1) The Right Hand of God symbolizes the power and strength of the Incarnate One.

because they did not remain in My covenant,
>> and I neglected them, says *the* Lord:

10. because this *is* the covenant, which I will make with the house of Israel
>> after those days, says *the* Lord:

when I put My Teachings[1] into their minds for understanding
>> and I will write them[2] upon their hearts,

and I will be their God,
>> and they will be My people:

11. and each will **not** teach his neighbor
>> and each his brother saying, 'You must now know the Lord,'

because all will have known Me
>> from *the* least to *the* greatest of them,

12. because I will forgive[3] their unrighteousness
>> and I will **no longer** remember their sins." (Jr 31:31-34[4])

13. When He says "New"[5] He has made the first old: and the one that is old *is* near disappearing.[6]

The Earthly and the Heavenly Sanctuaries

9.1. Now truly the first *covenant* had both regulations for service and the earthly sanctuary. 2. Indeed a tabernacle was prepared. The first *room* in it *had* the lamp stand and the table and the bread of the presence, which *first room* is called "Holy:" 3. but after the second veil in *the* tent, the one called "Holy of Holies," 4. there was a golden altar of incense[7] and the Ark of the Covenant, which was covered entirely in gold, *and* had in it the gold jar with the manna and the rod of Aaron that budded and the tablets of the covenant, 5. and above it *two* cherubim[8] of glory *that* overshadowed the mercy seat: I will not now speak in detail about this.

9:6. And such as these indeed were the furnishings in the first tabernacle, and so the priests always entered, fulfilling the services,[9] 7. but in the second *room, the Holy of Holies*, once a year,[10] only the High Priest, not without blood, which he offered on behalf of *both* himself and the people for the sins committed

---

1   (v.10) His Teachings are from the Torah. See Torah in Glossary.
2   (v.10) Divine Instructions
3   (v.12) Literally this is "I will be merciful" which is a Hebrew idiom for "I will forgive."
4   (v.12) In Jr 31:34 the Hebrew word for sins is khatatem, meaning "their sins," referring to sins committed in error, carelessly. See Sin in Glossary.
5   (v.13) In Jeremiah the word translated new has a primary meaning of renew. See Gal 3:15-21.
6   (v.13) Some translations say something to the effect that the first covenant is made obsolete, which is not implied by Paul in Ro 9:4 and Eph 2:12. See Replacement Theology in Glossary.
7   (v.4) The altar of incense was only placed in the Holy of Holies on the Day of Atonement.
8   (v.5) Cherubim is the plural form while the singular is cherub.
9   (v.6) In the Holy Place the priest ministered to the Lord, and in the Holy of Holies on behalf of the people.
10   (v.7) On Yom Kippur, the Day of Atonement

in ignorance,[1] 8. although the Holy Spirit made this clear, the way into the Holy of Holies had not yet been revealed while the first tabernacle was still standing, 9. which *was* a symbol for the present time, according to which both gifts and sacrifices were brought which were not able to perfect *the* conscience of the worshipper, 10. *they were* only regulations of flesh on food and drink and different baptisms,[2] imposed until *the* time of the new order.

9:11. But when Messiah appeared *He was* High Priest of the things that were of a higher order through the greater and more complete tabernacle, that was not made by *human* hands, that is not of this creation, 12. and not *entering* by the blood of goats and calves, but through His own blood, He entered once into the Holy of Holies, finding eternal redemption *for us*. 13. For if the blood of goats and bulls and sprinkling *the* ashes of a heifer sanctify those who have been defiled, making their flesh clean, 14. how much more the blood of the Messiah, Who through *the* eternal Spirit presented Himself blameless as an offering to God, cleanses our conscience from dead works in service to *the* living God.

9:15. Then because of this *death* He is Mediator of a new covenant, by payment of a ransom for transgressions under the first covenant. When *His* death took place those who have been called could take the promise of the eternal inheritance. 16. For where *there is* a will, death of the testator must be announced: 17. for *since* a will *is* valid only upon death, then *it is* not valid while the one who made the will *is* still alive. 18. On this account the first was not inaugurated without blood: 19. for when every commandment was spoken by Moses to all the people according to the Torah, then he took the blood of the calves and the goats with water and red wool and hyssop and this he sprinkled *on* the scroll and all the people 20. saying, "This *is* the blood of the covenant which God commanded for you." (Ex 24:8) 21. And he sprinkled the tabernacle and all the vessels of the service with the same blood. 22. Then he cleansed every vessel by means of blood according to the Torah,[3] and without blood being shed there is no forgiveness.

Sin Put Away by Messiah's Sacrifice

9:23. So of necessity, the copies of the things in the heavens on the one hand are cleansed, but on the other hand the heavenly things *are* with better offerings than these. 24. For Messiah did not come into *the* Holies made by human hands, corresponding to the true *Holies*, but into heaven itself, now to appear in the presence of God on our behalf: 25. and not that He would offer Himself many times, as the High Priest enters the sanctuary[4] year after year with another's blood, 26. else He was needing to suffer many times from *the*

---

1   (v.7) These sins are those committed in error, without thinking. See Sin in Glossary.
2   (v.10) Immersions or baptisms for purification. See Baptize in Glossary.
3   (v.22) Torah means teaching or instruction and here refers to the first five books of the Bible. See Torah in Glossary.
4   (v.25) Holy of Holies, see Sanctuary in Glossary.

foundation of *the* world: but now He has appeared once for all time by setting aside sin through His offering. 27. And just as it is destined for people to die once, and after this, Judgment, 28. thus also, when the Messiah was offered once, He took the sin of many upon Himself. He will be seen a second *time* without any relation to sin by those waiting eagerly for Him for *their* salvation.

10.1. For the Torah[1] is a shadow of the coming good *things*, not the form of things themselves, never able to perfect those who come year by year with these offerings which they offer continually: 2. otherwise would they not have ceased being offered, after they had once been cleansed, because those who worship would not still have consciousness of sins? 3. But with these yearly reminders of sins: 4. *it is* impossible for blood of bulls and goats to *permanently* take away sin, *by a single offering.*[2]

10:5. On account of which, when He came into the world He said,

"You did not want sacrifices and offerings,
> but You did make ready a body for Me:
6. and You did not take pleasure in a whole burnt offering
> on behalf of sin. (1 Sa 15:22, Hos 6:6, Ps 51:18)
7. Then I said,
> 'Behold! I come,
> > in *the* roll of a scroll *which* has been written about Me,
> to do Your will O God.'" (Ps 40:6-8)

8. After saying first that "You did not want sacrifices and offerings and You did not delight in whole burnt offerings on behalf of sin," (Ps 40:6) which were being offered according to Torah, 9. then, He said, "Behold! I am coming to do Your will." (Ps 40:7) He takes away the first so that the second would stand, 10. in Whose will we are, since we have been sanctified through the offering, once and for all, of the body of Jesus Messiah.

10:11. And truly every priest stood day by day, serving and offering the same offerings many times, which were never able to entirely take away sin,[3] *with which we are enveloped*, 12. but this One, when He offered a sacrifice on behalf of sins, sat down continually at the right hand[4] of God, 13. from now on waiting until His enemies would be made a footstool for His feet.[5] 14. For He has perfected forever, in one offering, those who are being sanctified.

10:15. And the Holy Spirit is testifying to us: for after it He said,

---

1   (v.1) Torah means teaching or instruction. See Torah in Glossary.
2   (v.4) See Blood in Glossary.
3   (v.11) Sin will be a force on the Earth until the Messianic Age banishes Satan.
4   (v.12) The right hand is a Hebrew idiom symbolizing power and strength, from Ex 15:6. See Right Hand in Glossary.
5   (v.13) Making your enemy your footstool is a metaphor for the decisive defeat of enemies, originating in the custom of the victor placing his foot upon the neck of the conquered general or king. See Jsh 10:24. See Footstool in Glossary.

16.   "This *is* the covenant which I will make" with them
        "after these days, says *the* Lord:
     putting My Teachings[1] upon their hearts
        and I will write them upon their minds
17.   and I will **never, ever** remember their sins
        and their iniquities."[2] (Jr 31:34[3])

18. And where there is forgiveness of these *sins and iniquities*, *there is* no longer an offering concerning sins.

Exhortation and Warning

10:19. Therefore, brothers, since we have confidence to enter the Holies by the blood of Jesus, 20. a new and living way which He dedicated to us, through the veil, this is by His flesh, 21. so *we have* a great Priest in the house of God. 22. We should present ourselves with a true heart in full assurance of faith, since we have purified our hearts from a consciousness of evil, and have washed[4] the body in clean water: (Eze 36:25) 23. we should, without wavering, hold fast the confession of the hope, for the One Who promised *is* faithful, 24. and we should consider one another in provoking by love and good deeds,[5] 25. not forsaking the assembling of ourselves, as *is* custom for some, but exhorting, and so much the more as you see the Day draw near.

10:26. Indeed when we are sinning deliberately after taking the knowledge of the truth, no further offering remains concerning sins, 27. but some fearful expectation of judgment with its blazing flames appears like a living being intent on devouring God's adversaries. 28. Anyone *who* has set aside *the* Torah[6] of Moses dies without pity on *testimony* by two or three witnesses: (Dt 17:6, 19:15) 29. how much more worthy of punishment do you suppose the one will be who trod down the Son of God and who looked upon the blood of the covenant, by Whom he was sanctified, as defiled, and has insulted the Spirit of Grace? 30. For we know the One Who said,

     "Vengeance is Mine, I will repay." (Dt 32:35)

And again,

     "*The* Lord will judge His people." (Dt 32:36, Ps 135:14)

31. *It is* fearful to fall into *the* hand of *the* living God.

10:32. You must continually remember the former days, during which, when you became spiritually enlightened you endured many struggles with

---

1   (v.16) Teachings or Torah: see Torah in Glossary.
2   (v.17) Iniquities are intentional sins, a-von in Hebrew. See Sin in Glossary.
3   (v.17) The Hebrew word used for sin in v. 33 is khata-ah, referring to sins committed in error, carelessly. See Sin in Glossary.
4   (v.22) This is another way of speaking of immersion or baptism for purification.
5   (v.24) The Hebrew word for good deeds is mitsvot, with mitsvah the singular. See both Mitsvah and Righteousness in Glossary.
6   (v.28) Torah means teaching or instruction. See Torah in Glossary.

suffering, 33. sometimes in reproaches, and then afflictions, being shamed publicly, then being sharers *with others who suffered* acts such as these. 34. Indeed you also sympathized with the prisoners and you received willingly the seizing of your possessions with joy, because you knew you have a better possession and an abiding one. 35. Therefore do not cast away your confidence,[1] which has great reward. 36. For you need patience, so that after you do the will of God you would receive[2] the promise.

37.　　For yet "a little while,
　　　　　　the One Who is coming will come and not delay:" (Is 26:20)
38.　　"And My righteous one will live by faith,
　　　　and if he would withdraw,
　　　　　　My inner being will not take pleasure in him." (Hab 2:3,4)

39. But we are not of *those who* shrink back but *of those who are* faithful in preserving life.

Faith[3]

11.1. And trust is being confident of things being hoped for,[4] proof of things not seen. 2. Indeed the elders were approved by this.

11:3. By trusting we understand that the worlds were created by a spoken Word[5] of God, so that what is seen has not come out of *things* which were visible.

11:4. By trusting, Abel, contrary to Cain, bore a better offering to God, through which he was testified to be righteous, when God witnessed his gifts, and through it he is still speaking, although he died. (Gn 4:3-10) 5. By trusting, Enoch was transferred so he did not see death, and he was not found because God translated him. For before his translation, he had been attested to be pleasing to God: (Gn 5:24, Sir 44:16, En 70:1-4, Wsd 4:10) 6. and without trusting *it is* impossible to please *God*: for it is necessary *for* the one who comes to God to believe that He is, *that He does exist*, then He becomes a rewarder to those who seek Him out. 7. By trusting, Noah, when he was warned about things not yet seen, in reverence, built an ark for *the* salvation of his household, through which He condemned the world, and he became an heir of righteousness according to *his* trust. (Gn 6:13-22, 7:1)

11:8. By trusting, Abraham, when he was called, obeyed to come out to a place which he was going to take for an inheritance, and he came out not knowing where he was going. (Gn 12:1-5) 9. By trusting, he sojourned in *the* land of the

---

1　　　　(v.35) Confidence is a synonym of faith in this context.
2　　　　(v.36) The Greek word translated receive is komidzo, which means to carry off. We need to really take hold of the promise and run with it.
3　　　　(Caption) The word we normally translate "faith" meant "trust" to the NT authors. Trust is used instead of faith in this chapter, even though trust sounds strange to most of us.
4　　　　(v.1) Salvation with joy and full of confidence
5　　　　(v.3) The word used here is rhema. See Logos/Rhema in Glossary.

promise, dwelling as a stranger in tents with Isaac and Jacob, the fellow heirs of this promise: (Gn 23:4, 26:3, 35:12&27) 10. for he was waiting for the city *that* has foundations, of which God was *the* designer and builder. 11. By trusting also Sarah, herself barren, took power for conception from *Abraham's* seed even past the normal age. (Gn 17:19, 18:11-14, 21:2) Because of trust, she considered what was promised. 12. On that account then *his descendants* were begotten from one *man*, and that one had been as good as dead, *now* they *are* just as the stars of the sky in multitude and as the innumerable sands beside the shore of the sea. (Gn 15:5,6, 22:17, 32:12, Ex 32:13, Dt 1:10, Sir 44:21)

11:13. These all died while trusting, although they did not take the promises but saw them *fulfilled* from a distance and received them joyfully even while they confessed that they were strangers and sojourners on the earth. (Gn 23:4, 47:9, Ps 39:12) 14. For those who said such things as these were making clear that they were seeking *their true* native land. 15. And indeed if they were thinking of that *country* from which they had come down, they had ample time to turn back. 16. But as a matter of fact, they were striving for a better way, this is of *the* heavenly. For this reason God is not ashamed of them, (Ex 3:6, 15:4&5) *or* to have been called God by them: for He prepared a city for them.

11:17. By trusting, Abraham, when he was tested, brought Isaac and he was offering *his* only *son*, he who had received the promises, (Gn 21:1-10) 18. to whom it was spoken that "Your seed will be called by Isaac, *inherited by him*," (Gn 21:12) 19. so he considered then that God *was* able to raise *Isaac* from *the* dead, from which then, figuratively speaking, he received this. 20. By trusting then Isaac blessed Jacob and Esau concerning *what was* coming. (Gn 27:27-29, 39&40) 21. By trusting, Jacob, when he was dying, blessed each of the sons of Joseph and "He prayed *leaning* upon the top of his staff." (Gn 48:15,16) 22. By trusting, Joseph, when he was dying, remembered about the exodus of the children of Israel and he gave orders concerning his bones. (Gn 50:24,25)

11:23. By trusting, after Moses was born, he was hidden three months by his parents, because they saw a beautiful child and were not afraid of the edict of the king. 24. By trusting, after Moses became great, he denied to be called a son of Pharaoh's daughter, 25. because he chose to suffer with the people of God rather than to have a temporary *life* in *the* pleasure of sin, 26. since he considered reproach *suffered* for the anointed One a greater wealth than the treasures of Egypt: for he looked forward to the reward. (Ex 2:10-12, 15) 27. By trusting, he left Egypt although he did not fear the wrath of the king: for he was steadfast while looking at the invisible *One*. (Ex 12:21-30) 28. By trusting, he had instituted the Passover and the sprinkling of the blood, so that the destroying angel of the first-born would not touch them. 29. By trusting, they passed through the Red Sea as through dry ground, which when the Egyptians tried to do *that*, they were swallowed *by the sea*. (Ex 14:21-31) 30. By trusting, the walls of Jericho fell after they were encircled for seven days. 31. By trusting, Rahab the idolatress,[1] after she received the spies with peace, was not destroyed with those who were disobedient. (Jos 2:11,12, 6:12-25)

11:32. And yet what am I saying? For time will fail me telling about Gideon, Barak, Samson, Jephthah, David, and also Samuel and the prophets. 33. They overcame kingdoms through trusting, they worked righteousness, they obtained *the* Good News, they stopped mouths of lions, (Jdg 14:6,7, 1 Sa 17:34-36, Dn 6:1-27) 34. they quenched fire in power (Dn 3:23-25), they escaped *the* edges of swords, they were strengthened from weakness, they became strong in war, they caused armies of others to fall. 35. Women received their dead by resurrection:[2] (1Ki 17:17-24, 2Ki 4:25-37) but others were tortured, (2 Macc 6:18-7:42) rejecting deliverance, so that they would obtain a better resurrection: 36. and others took mockings and scourgings, trials, and still *others* chains and prison: (1Ki 22:26,27, 2 Chr 18:25,26, Jr 20:2, 37:15, 38:6) 37. they were stoned, (2 Chr 24:21) they were sawed in two, (Ascension of Isaiah 5:11-14) they died by being murdered with a sword, *still others* went around in sheepskin, in goat skins, being in need, experiencing persecution, being maltreated, 38. wandering about in deserts and mountains and in caves and in the holes of the earth, of whom the world was not worthy.

11:39. And these all, having been praised for their trusting, did not obtain the promise for themselves, 40. because God selected something better concerning us, so that they would not be perfected without us.

The Discipline of the Lord

12.1. We also, therefore, since we have so great a host of witnesses surrounding us, after we have put off every weight and the easily distracting sin, would ourselves, patiently steadfast, run the race that is set before us 2. fixing our eyes on the Author and Finisher of the faith, Jesus, Who, to obtain the joy set before Him, endured *the* cross,[3] having despised *the* shame *of it* He sat down at *the* right hand[4] of the throne of God. 3. For you must now consider the One Who endured such hostility as this toward Himself by the sinners, so that you would not be weary, losing heart in your inmost beings.

12:4. Thus you in your struggling with sin have not resisted to a bloody death. 5. And you have forgotten the exhortation, which speaks to you as sons,

---

1   (v.31) The word used here is porne, which could be translated harlot, but it was very common to use this term for any form of idolatry, as it is in the book of Hosea. See Dt 24:1,2;   Jr 3:6-10. See Harlot in Glossary.
2   (v.35) See Resurrection in Glossary.
3   (v.2) The cross did not become a Christian symbol until the fourth century, when the Romans stopped using the cross for executions.
4   (v.2) "At the right hand" is a Hebrew idiom that speaks of power and strength, from Ex 15:6. See Right Hand in Glossary.

> "My son, you must not ever make lightly of *the* discipline of *the* Lord
> and you must not ever lose courage by His reproving:

6.   for whom *the* Lord loves He disciplines,
> and He punishes every son whom He accepts." (Pr 3:11,12)

7. Endure discipline, God deals with you as sons. For what son *is there* whom a father does not discipline? 8. But if you are without discipline, of which you have all become sharers, then you are illegitimate and not sons. 9. Then indeed we have the fathers of our flesh and we respect *their* discipline: then will we not much more be subject to the Father of our spirits and live? 10. For indeed they were disciplining for a few days according to what seemed good to them, but He for our advantage to make *us* sharers of His holiness. 11. And indeed no discipline at the time seems to be joy but grief, but later it would yield *the* peaceful fruit of righteousness to those being trained by it.

12:12. On this account you must immediately strengthen the weakened hands and the disabled knees, 13. and you must continually make a straight path for your feet, so that the lame would not now be twisted, but rather would be immediately healed.

Warning against Rejecting God's Grace

12:14. You must continually pursue peace and holiness with all, without which no one will see the Lord, 15. seeing to it that no one fails to partake of the grace of God, *so* no root of bitterness would spring up and through it many would be defiled. 16. No one *should be* immoral or profane like Esau, who in exchange for food gave his own birthrights. (Gn 25:33,34) 17. For you know then that afterward, when he wanted to inherit the blessing, he was rejected, for he did not find a place of repentance although he searched for it with tears. (Gn 27:30-40)

12:18. For you have not approached *Mt. Sinai*, which *can* be touched and was being burned by fire and *was* in darkness and gloom and storm 19. nor by a trumpet sound or by spoken words, which when they heard they begged that no further message be given to them, 20. for they were not bearing patiently that which was commanded, "If a beast would even touch the mountain, it will be stoned:" (Ex 19:12,13) 21. and so it was a fearful spectacle. Moses said, "I am terrified" (Dt 9:19[1]) and trembling. 22. But you have come to Mount Zion and *the* city of *the* living God, heavenly Jerusalem, and thousands of angels, in festal assembly 23. and to *the* congregation[2] of *the* Firstborn, *whose names* have been written in *the* heavens and to God, judge of all, and to spirits of *the* righteous *who* have been perfected 24. and to *the* Mediator of a new covenant, Jesus, and to sprinkled blood *that* speaks a more useful *message* than Abel's.

---

1   (v.21) Dt 9:19 says Moses was afraid for the people because of the severe wrath of the Lord against them, but no Scripture says Moses was terrified to face God.

2   (v.23) Although often translated "church," no Greek word meaning church is used in the NT. See Congregation in Glossary.

12:25. See *that* you would not reject for yourselves the One Who speaks: for if those who refused to hear did not escape the warning on earth *by a man*, how much more we, if we reject the One from *the* heavens, 26. Whose voice shook the earth then, but now He promises saying, "Yet once *again* I will shake not only the earth but also heaven." (Ex 19:18, Jdg 5:4, Ps 68:8) 27. And "Yet once *again*" shows the transfer of the shakings as having been done, so that those that are not being, *and cannot be*, shaken would remain. 28. On this account we should be thankful, since we are receiving an unshakable kingdom, through which we could serve God in an acceptable manner with reverence and awe: 29. for our God *is* also a consuming fire. (Dt 4:24, 9:3, Is 33:14)

Service Well-Pleasing to God

13.1. Brotherly love[1] must continually remain. 2. You must habitually not neglect hospitality, for through this some who entertained angels were not aware *of it*. (Mt 25:35-40) 3. You must continually remember the prisoners as if you were bound yourselves, those who are being mistreated as they also are in *the* body. 4. Marriage is honorable with all and the marriage bed undefiled, for God will judge fornicators and adulterers. 5. Do not in any way love money, *but* be satisfied with your possessions. For He said, "I will **not** abandon you and I **will not ever** forsake you," (Dt 31:6, Jos 1:5) 6. so that we are confident to say,

"The Lord *is* my helper,
  and I will not be afraid,
what will man do to me?" (Ps 118:6)

13:7. You must constantly remember your leaders, who spoke the Word of God to you, whose faith you must habitually imitate by observing carefully the result of their way of life. 8. Jesus Messiah is the same yesterday and today and forever. (Ps 102:27, Mal 3:6) 9. You must stop being carried away by various and strange teachings: *it is* good for the heart to be established in grace, not in discussions *of* foods[2], which are of no benefit to those who live that way. 10. We have an altar from which those who serve in the tabernacle do not have authority to eat. 11. For *while* the blood of these animals is brought into the Holies by the High Priest to atone for sin, the bodies of these are burned outside the camp. 12. For this reason then Jesus, so that He would sanctify the people through His own blood, suffered outside the gate. 13. So we should come out to Him outside the camp *where* He bore His reproach: 14. for we do not have a permanent city, but we are diligently seeking the one *city* that is coming. 15. Through Him therefore, we should continually bring an offering of praise to God by everyone, (Ps 50:14) which is *the* fruit of lips that confess His name. (Ho 14:2) 16. But you must

---

1   (v.1) Brotherly love is broad, including unbelievers as indicated in v. 3, referring to prisoners. The word brother refers to both men and women any time it is not specifically referring to a person's natural brothers.

2   (v.9) While the primary meaning is about what is fit to eat, this also has spiritual application in that you are what you eat, that is what you read, study, watch in movies and television: is it spiritual to bring you closer to God, or is it worldly, to take you further from God?

not ever forget to do good things and *to be* generous:[1] for God takes delight in offerings such as these.

13:17. You must continually comply with your leaders and you must yield *to them*, for they keep watch over *you* as *people who* will give an account on behalf of your lives, and they could do this with joy if you do not complain: for this *complaining is* harmful to you.

13:18. You must regularly pray concerning us: for we are convinced that we have a good conscience, as we wish to behave rightly in all things. 19. And I urge *you* all the more to do this, so that I would be restored to you more quickly.

Benediction and Final Greetings

13:20. May the God of peace, the One Who led up from *the* dead the Great Shepherd of the sheep by *the* blood of an eternal covenant, our Lord Jesus, 21. make you complete in every good thing to do His will, while He makes us pleasing in His judgment through Jesus Messiah, to Whom be the glory forever and ever, amen.

13:22. And I urge you, brothers, you must constantly bear the word of encouragement, for I just wrote briefly to you. 23. You know that our brother Timothy has been released *to come to me*, with whom I shall see you, if he would come quickly.[2]

13:24. You must now greet all your leaders and all the saints. Those from Italy greet you. 25. Grace *be* with you all.

---

1   (v.16) The word translated generous means to share, that this is not speaking of donating extra money, but sharing whatever you have with someone in greater need.

2   (v.23) If he comes soon enough, he will be with me when I come to be with you.

~ JAMES[1] ~

Salutation

1.1. Jacob,[2] a servant[3] of God and of *the* Lord Jesus Messiah, greetings to the twelve tribes[4] in the Diaspora.

Faith and Wisdom

1:2. Consider *it* all joy, my brothers, when various trials light upon you, 3. knowing that the proving of your faith produces endurance. 4. And the endurance must attain its purpose, so that you would be mature and complete and not falling short in any way. 5. But if anyone of you lacks wisdom, he must continually ask from God, the One Who gives generously, without reproaching, and it will be given to him. 6. But he must always ask in faith without doubting: for the one who doubts is like the surf of the sea, being moved by the wind and blown here and there. 7. For that man must not expect to receive anything from the Lord, 8. *since he is* a double-minded man, unsettled in all his ways.

Poverty and Riches

1:9. And the humble brother must boast in his high position, 10. but the rich in his humiliation, because like a flower of *the* grass he will pass away. 11. For the sun rose with the scorching wind and dried the grass and its flower fell off and the beauty of its blossom was destroyed: and in this way the rich person will fade in his undertakings.

Trial and Temptation

1:12. Blessed *is* a man who endures temptation *or trial*, because when he becomes approved, *having stood the test*, he will take the crown of life that was being promised to those who love Him. 13. One who is tempted must not ever say that "I am being tempted by God:" for God is untemptable by evils, and He

---

1   (Title) Written about 45-48 AD.
2   (v.1) The Greek text has Iakob, which is Jacob in English. The Greek title of this book is Iakob. In Nov. 2002 a stone burial box, reported in Biblical Archeology Review, was shown in Jerusalem, inscribed "Yaakov, bar Yoseph, Akh Yeshua," which is translated "Jacob, Son of Joseph, Brother of Jesus."
3   (v.1) Or slave
4   (v.1) This letter is also to the Hebrews.

tempts no one. 14. But each is tempted by his own evil desire, being lured away and being enticed. 15. Then when desire conceives it brings forth sin, and when sin is fully formed it brings forth death.

1:16. You must not ever be deceived *about this*, my beloved brothers.[1] 17. Every good gift and every perfect gift is from above, being sent down by the Father of Lights, with Whom there is not one change or shadow variation. 18. According to His will, He brought us forth by a word of truth for us to be a kind of first fruits of His creatures.

Hearing and Doing The Word

1:19. You know, my esteemed brothers: that every person must continually be quick to hear, slow to speak, slow in anger: 20. for a man's anger does not work the righteousness of God for him. 21. On this account, as you lay aside all filth and abundance of wickedness, you must immediately take for yourselves, in humility, the implanted Word which enables *you* to save your very beings.

1:22. And you must steadily be doers of *the* Word and not only hearers, deceiving yourselves. 23. Because if someone is a hearer of *the* Word and not a doer, this one is like a man when he observes his own natural face in a mirror: 24. for he observed himself then went away, and immediately forgot what manner of person he was. 25. But the one who looked into *the* perfect Torah,[2] the one of freedom, and continues to do so, not being a forgetful hearer but being a doer of work,[3] he will be blessed,[4] *happy* in what he does.

1:26. If someone thinks he is religious but *is* not restraining his tongue, *he is* deceiving his heart *and* this religion *is* useless. 27. Religion, pure and undefiled, before our God and Father is this, to care for orphans and widows in their affliction,[5] to keep oneself spotless from the world.

Warning against Partiality

2.1. My brothers, when you show partiality you do not have the faith of our Lord, the glory of Jesus Messiah. 2. For if a man in splendid clothing with a gold ring would come into your synagogue, and also a poor *man* in filthy clothing would come in, 3. and if you would care about the *one* wearing the splendid clothing and you would say, "You sit here in a good place," and to the poor you said, "You sit there, or sit under my footstool," 4. did you not judge between them and become judges who make judgments based on evil motives?

2:5. You must now listen, my esteemed brothers: has not God chosen

---

1   (v.16) The word Brothers refers to all members of the congregation, both men and women.
2   (v.25) Torah, meaning teaching or instruction, here refers to the first five books of the Bible, brought to fulfillment by Jesus. See Torah in Glossary.
3   (v.25) See Mitsvah in Glossary. See Mt 25:35-40.
4   (v.25) The word used here is makarios, which means both blessed and happy.
5   (v.27) See Mt 25:35-40.

the poor in the world *to be* rich in faith and heirs of the kingdom which has been promised to those who love Him? 6. You dishonored the poor. Do not the rich oppress you and drag you into court? 7. Do they not blaspheme the good name that has been called upon you? 8. If you really fulfill the royal law according to the Scriptures, "You shall love your neighbor as yourself," (Lv 19:18) you do well: 9. but if you show partiality, you are working sin, being exposed as a transgressor under the Torah.[1] 10. For whoever would keep the whole Torah but would stumble in one thing, has become guilty of all.[2] 11. For the One Who said, "Do not commit adultery," also said, "Do not commit murder:" but if you do not commit adultery but do commit murder, you have become a transgressor of Torah. 12. So you must continually speak, and so you must act as *one* going to be judged through *the* law of freedom. 13. For judgment without mercy *is to be given* for the one who does not do mercy:[3] mercy, full of glad confidence, has no fear of judgment.

Faith and Works

2:14. What benefit *is it* my brothers, if someone would say he has faith, but does not have works?[4] Is *that* faith able to save him?[5] (Mt 7:21, 16:27, Jn 5:29, Ac 26:20, Ro 2:10,25-29, 1Co 3:8, Eph 2:10, 2Ti 4:14, Titus 1:16, 2:14, 3:8, et al.) 15. If a brother or sister would be poorly clothed and *is* falling short of daily food 16. and if any *of you* would say to them from your *plenty*, "You must now go in peace, be warm and be filled," but would not give them their bodily needs, what *is the* benefit? 17. So then faith, if you would not have works, is dead in itself.

2:18. But someone says, "You have faith, and I have works. You must now show me your faith without works, and I will show you my faith by means of my works." 19. You believe that God is One, you do well: the demons also believe and shudder. (Mt 8:29, Mk 1:24 & 5:7, Lk 4:34 & 8:28) 20. But are you willing to find out, O Senseless Man, that faith without works is unprofitable? 21. Was not our father Abraham vindicated by works, when he offered Isaac his son on the altar? 22. You see that his faith was working together with his works and that faith was made complete by his works, 23. also the Scripture was fulfilled saying, "And Abraham believed in God and it was reckoned to him as righteousness" (Gn 15:6) and he was called a friend of God. (2Chr 20:7, Is 41:8) 24. You must now see that a person is made righteous by means of works, and

---

1   (v.9) Torah here refers to the first five books of the Bible. See Torah in Glossary.
2   (v.10) See Sin and Sin, Forgiveness of in Glossary.
3   (v.13) The full meaning of the word translated mercy is: kindness or good will towards the miserable and afflicted, joined with a desire to relieve the afflicted. See Mt 25:35-40.
4   (v.14) Mitsvot. See Mitsvah in Glossary.
5   (v.14) The Greek construction anticipates a negative answer, faith will not be able to save him.

not only by faith.[1] 25. And likewise also Rahab the idolatress,[2] was she not made righteous by works, when she gave hospitality to the messengers and then sent *them* out another way? 26. For as the body is dead without a spirit, so also faith without works is dead.

The Tongue[3]

3.1. Not many of you *will* become teachers, my brothers, since you know that we shall take greater judgment. 2. For we all stumble in many things. If someone does not stumble in the act of speaking,[4] this is a perfect man, able to bridle his whole body. 3. And if we put bridles in the mouths of horses for them to obey us, we also guide their whole body. 4. And look at the ships, *which* are so large and are driven by a strong wind, they are guided by a very small rudder, where the helmsman wishes, 5. in the same way the tongue is also a little member and boasts great things.

Behold how small a fire sets ablaze a large forest: 6. the tongue *is* also a fire: a world of unrighteousness, the tongue, is sitting for itself among the parts of our *body*, defiling the whole person and destroying the wheel[5] of life, and is itself set on fire by Hell.[6] 7. For every species of beasts, and also of birds, and of reptiles, and even of sea creatures, is tamed and has been tamed by humans, 8. but no one is able to tame the tongue of men, unstable, evil, *and* full of deadly poison.[7] 9. With this we bless the Lord and Father and with this we curse people, those who have been made according to the likeness of God, 10. from this mouth come forth blessing and curse.[8] It ought not be, my brothers, that these things happen like this. 11. Does the well pour forth water, *both* the sweet and the bitter, from the same opening?[9] 12. Is a fig tree able, my brothers, to bear an olive or the grapevine a fig? Nor *is* bitter water *able* to make sweet.

The Wisdom from Above

3:13. Who is wise and learned among you? He must constantly show by

---

1　　　(v.24) Although we are made righteous by faith, righteousness is action, that is, doing for others. See Mt 7:21-23.

2　　　(v.25) This could be translated harlot, but more likely meant idolatress, since that term was used to refer to any sin, as in Hosea. See Harlot in Glossary.

3　　　(Caption) Pr 21:23 "Whoever guards his mouth and his tongue keeps his soul from troubles." and Ps 12:3 "The Lord shall cut off all flattering lips, and the tongue that speaks arrogant things;" Ps 34:13. "Keep your tongue from evil, and your lips from speaking guile." Ps 141:3 "Set a guard, O Lord to my mouth; keep watch over the door of my lips."

4　　　(v.2) This is not just public speaking, but also every day conversation. See Mt 12:36, 37. See Gossip/Slander in Glossary.

5　　　(v.6) Machinery

6　　　(v.6) The Greek word is Gehenna. See Gehenna in Glossary.

7　　　(v.8) Mark 7:15 quoted Jesus saying, "..the things which go out from a person are the things that defile him." Mt 15:11 is a similar passage.

8　　　(v.10) Pr 18:21 says "Death and life are in the power of the tongue: and they that love it shall eat its fruit."

9　　　(v.11) The Greek construction anticipates a negative response. What we speak under stress reveals our true spiritual condition.

good conduct his works of wisdom in humility. 14. But if you have bitter jealousy and strife in your heart, do not boast against and do not tell lies against the truth. 15. This *wisdom* is not wisdom coming down from above, but *is* earthly, worldly, proceeding from an evil spirit. 16. For where *there is* jealousy and strife, from that place *is* disorder and every worthless, wicked deed. 17. But the wisdom from above is indeed first pure, then peaceable, kind, obedient, full of mercy and of good fruits, unwavering, without hypocrisy. 18. And the fruit of righteousness is sown in peace by those who make peace. (Is 32:17, Mt 5:9)

Friendship with the World

4.1. From where is *the source of* strife and from where is *the source of* fighting among you? *Is it* not from this source, from your desire for pleasures that are warring in your natures? 2. You desire but you have not, you kill and strive after and you are not able to attain, you fight and make war, you have not because you ask not, 3. you ask and you do not take because you ask for yourselves in error, so that you could squander in your pleasures. 4. Adulterous people, do you not know that love of the world is enmity with God? Whoever desires to be a friend of the world makes himself an enemy of God. 5. You think it to no purpose the Scripture says, "The Spirit that settled in us longs for *us* with envy," (Ex 20:5) 6. but He gives greater grace. On this account He says,

"God opposes *the* proud,
but He gives grace to *the* humble." (Pr 3:34)

7. Therefore *if* you would be subject to God, you should resist the devil and he will flee for his life from you, 8. draw near to God and He will draw near to you. Cleanse *your* hands, *you* sinners, and purify *your* hearts, *you* double-minded! 9. You must now feel afflicted and miserable and weep and cry! Let your laughter turn into grief and joy into dejection! 10. *If* you would humble yourselves before *the* Lord, then He will lift you up. (Mt 23:12, Luke 14:11, 18:14)

Judging a Brother

4:11. You must not ever speak evil[1] of one another, brothers. The one who speaks evil of a brother or judges his brother is speaking against Torah[2] and is judging Torah: if you judge Torah, you are not a doer, but a judge of Torah. 12. There is *only* One Torah-giver and Judge Who is able to save or to destroy: but who are you to judge your neighbor?

Warning against Boasting

4:13. Come now! Those who say, "Today or tomorrow we shall go into this city and we shall work there a year and we shall carry on business and we shall make a profit:" 14. yet you do not understand what your life will be

---

1   (v.11) See Gossip/Slander in Glossary.
2   (v.11) Torah, meaning teaching or instruction, here refers to the Old Testament. See Torah in Glossary.

tomorrow: for you are vapor, appearing briefly, then also being made invisible. 15. Instead you ought to say, "If the Lord wills and we will live, then we will do this or that." 16. But now you boast in your arrogance: all boasting such as this is evil. 17. So then *someone* who knows that he should do good but does not do *it*, it is sin for Him.

Warning to the Rich

5.1. Come now! *You* rich people, you will weep, crying aloud over the miseries that are coming upon you. 2. Your wealth has decayed and your garments have become moth eaten. 3. Your gold and silver have become covered with rust and their corrosion will be testimony against you and will consume your flesh as fire. You stored up *treasure* for *the* last days.[1] 4. See! The wages of the workers, of those who reap your fields, what was stolen by you calls out, and the cries of those who reaped have come into the ears of *the* Lord of Hosts.[2] 5. You have lived a life of merriment upon the earth and you have lived luxuriously, you have nourished your hearts for a day of slaughter, 6. you have condemned, you have murdered the righteous one, he offers you no resistance.

Patience and Prayer

5:7. Therefore you must now have patience, brothers, until the coming of the Lord. See, the farmer expects the valuable fruit from the earth, when he has patience over it until it has received early rain and late rain. 8. You too must now be patient, you must strengthen your hearts, because the coming of the Lord has drawn near:[3] 9. do not murmur, brothers, against one another so that you would not be judged: behold the Judge has been standing before the doors. 10. You must take *as* an example, brothers, the suffering and the patience of the prophets, those who spoke in the name of *the* Lord. 11. Behold we consider blessed those who hold out: you have heard of the patience *of* Job and you have seen the Lord's *reward*, the end *of Job's trial*, because the Lord is sympathetic and compassionate.

5:12. But above all things, my brothers, do not swear either by heaven or by earth or any other oath: but with you it must be a "Definitely yes!" or a "Definitely no!"[4] so that you would not fall under judgment. (Lv 19:12, Nu 30:2, Dt 23:21,22, Ecc 5:4, Ps 76:11, Mt 5:33-37)

5:13. Whoever suffers misfortune among you must continually pray: whoever cheers up must steadfastly sing Psalms: 14. whoever is sick among you,

---

1   (v.3) The way you have lived counts. From the time you made Him the Lord of your life, what you have done and said determines your reward (Re 20:12).
2   (v.4) Some translations say Lord Sabaoth, which is the Greek spelling of the Hebrew word for Hosts. See Lord of Hosts in Glossary.
3   (v.8) See Coming of Messiah in Glossary.
4   (v.12) The absolute dependability of your word should make an oath unnecessary. See Double Yes in Glossary.

must summon the elders of the congregation[1] and they must pray over him, after they anoint him with olive oil[2] in the name of the Lord. 15. And the prayer of faith will save the ill and the Lord will raise him: and if he had committed sin, it will be forgiven for him. 16. Therefore you must continually confess[3] your sins for yourselves with one another and you must continually pray for yourselves on behalf of one another so that you would be healed. *The* plea of a righteous person is very powerful, working effectively. 17. Elijah was a man with the same nature as us, and he prayed fervently *for it* not to rain and it did not rain on the earth for three years and six months: 18. then he prayed again, and heaven gave rain and the earth produced its crops.

5:19. My brothers, if any among you would be deceived from the truth and someone would turn him around *bringing him back to the Lord*, 20. he must know that the one who converts a sinner from his way of error has rescued his life out from death and covered a multitude of sins.[4]

---

1   (v.14) Although often translated "church," no Greek word meaning church is used in the NT. See Congregation in Glossary.

2   (v.14) In the Talmud, olive oil symbolizes knowledge of Torah, which provides spiritual illumination. Oil is also the symbol of joy, from Is 51:3, so it is called the oil of gladness.

3   (v.16) This does not mean to repeatedly confess the same old sin, because once the sin has been forgiven it is gone! It never happened! See Jeremiah 31:33. See Sin and Sin, Forgiveness of in Glossary.

4   (v.20) Received a pardon from God, speaking of the new convert.

~ 1 PETER[1] ~

Salutation

1.1. Peter, an apostle of Jesus Messiah to *the* chosen sojourners of *the* Diaspora,[2] of Pontus, Galatia, Cappadocia,[3] Asia, and Bithynia, 2. according to Father God's foreknowledge *of us* in holiness by *the* Spirit in obedience and sprinkling of *the* blood of Jesus Messiah, may grace and peace increase in you.

A Living Hope

1:3. God and Father of our Lord Jesus Messiah *be* praised, the One Who has begotten us anew[4] according to His great mercy into living hope through *the* resurrection[5] from *the* dead of Jesus Messiah, 4. into an incorruptible pure and unfading inheritance, *which* has been kept in *the* heavens for you, 5. those who are guarded by *the* power of God through faith into salvation, ready to be revealed in *the* last time. 6. In which you must continually rejoice, even if it must be for a short time now, *you* are grieved in various trials, 7. so that the testing of your faith *will be* more valuable than gold, which perishes even though it is tested by fire, *and your faith* would be found in praise and glory and honor at *the* revelation of Jesus Messiah: 8. Whom you love, although you have not seen *Him*, in Whom now, not seeing but *still* believing, you are rejoicing with unspeakable and glorious joy 9. carrying off for yourselves the goal of your faith, salvation of *your* very beings.

1:10. Concerning which salvation prophets, those who prophesied about the grace in you, sought out and inquired carefully, 11. searching for what or what sort of time the Spirit of Messiah testified beforehand *predicting* the sufferings of Messiah and of the glories after these *sufferings*. 12. To whom it would be revealed that they were not caring for themselves with these things but for you, which now would be disclosed to you through the Good News, by means of *the* Holy Spirit, Who was sent from heaven, into which things *even* angels are

---

1   (Title) Written about 65 AD.
2   (v.1) This too, along with Hebrews and James, is addressed to the Jewish people scattered by persecution to the various regions of the Greek and Roman empires.
3   (v.1) Cappadocia is referred to as Gammadim in Eze 27:11.
4   (v.3) Caused us to be born again
5   (v.3) See Resurrection in Glossary.

desiring to look carefully.

A Call to Holy Living

1:13. On this account, you, when you have girded up the loins of your minds, perfectly calm and collected in spirit, must immediately hope upon that grace which is brought to you by *the* revelation of Jesus Messiah. 14. As children of obedience, not being molded in ignorance by your former desires 15. but just as the One Who called you *is* holy, so now you must be holy in all *your* conduct, 16. because it has been written that "You will be holy because I AM[1] holy." (Lv 11:44,45, 19:2, 20:7)

1:17. And if you call upon *Him as the* Father, the One Who judges impartially according to the work of each, you must live the time of your sojourning in reverent fear, 18. knowing that you have been redeemed, not with corruptible things *like* silver or gold from futile living handed down from your fathers 19. but by *the* precious blood of Messiah, as of *the* unblemished spotless Lamb, 20. because He was indeed known before the foundation of *the* world, but has been revealed for the last of times for your sakes, 21. those Who believe through Him in God, the One Who raised Him from *the* dead and gave glory to Him. Therefore your faith and hope are in God.

1:22. Since you have purified your inner beings by your obedience to the truth in genuine brotherly love, you must now earnestly, constantly love one another out of clean hearts 23. because you *all* have been born again, not from a perishable seed but imperishable, through *the* Word of *the* living and forever enduring God. 24. For

"All flesh *is* like grass
    and all *flesh* glory like a flower of grass:
the grass withers
    and the flower falls:
25.   but the Word of *the* Lord remains forever." (Is 40:6-8)

And this is the Good News message that was proclaimed to you.

The Living Stone and the Holy Nation

2.1. Therefore, having put off all malice and all guile and hypocrisy and envy and all evil speech,[2] 2. you must now long for the unadulterated spiritual milk as a newborn baby, so that by it you would be grown up into salvation, 3. since you have tasted that the Lord is good. 4. As you have come to Him, *the* Living Stone, Who on the one hand has been rejected *declared useless* by men, but on the other hand chosen, honored by God, 5. then you must, like living stones, be continually built up *into* a spiritual house for a holy priesthood, to offer

---

1   (v.16) The great I AM, ani in Hebrew in the verses referenced here: See Anokhi in Glossary.
2   (v.1) See Gossip/Slander in Glossary.

a spiritual offering acceptable to God through Jesus Messiah. 6. On this account it contains in Scripture,

> "Behold I place in Zion a stone
> > a valuable, chosen *corner*stone,
> and the one who believes in Him would **not** be put to shame." (Is 28:16[1])

7. Therefore for you who believe, *He is* precious, but with *the* disbelieving *He is*

> "A stone that the builders rejected,
> > This one became *the* cornerstone" (Ps 118:22)

8. and

> "a stone of stumbling
> > and a rock causing them to fall in sin:" (Is 8:14)

those who stumble in the Word *do so* because they disobey *it*, for which they also were appointed.

2:9. But you *are* "a chosen race,[2] a royal priesthood, a holy nation, a people that has become God's property, so that you would proclaim the manifestation of divine power" (Is 43:20, Ex 19:6) of the One Who called you out of darkness into His marvelous light:

10.   "those once not a people
> > but now a people of God,
> those who had not received mercy[3]
> > but who now have received mercy." (Ho 2:23)

Live as Servants of God

2:11. Beloved, I urge *you* as strangers and sojourners to abstain from *the* desires of the flesh that are warring against your very beings: 12. so have your good way of life among the heathens, *as a living example to them*, so that, while they will speak evil of you as of evildoers, when they observe your good deeds[4] *then* they would glorify God on *the* Day of visitation.[5]

2:13. You must now be subordinate to every human institution in creation for the sake of the Lord, whether to a king as in authority, 14. or to governors who are sent by him for punishment of evildoers and *for* praise of *those who* do good: 15. because so is the will of God that by doing good *you* muzzle the ignorant talk

---

1   (v.6) While often translated shame from the Greek text, the Hebrew text refers to a period of time. A 12th Century rabbi wrote "He will remain steadfast in his faith however long realization may be delayed." See Is 28:16 in Glossary.
2   (v.9) Family
3   (v.10) Mercy is a Hebrew idiom for Forgiveness.
4   (v.12) Mitsvot, see Mitsvah in Glossary.
5   (v.12) Judgment Day. See Re 20:4, 11-14.

of foolish people, 16. as free *people* and, since you have freedom, *do* not *use it* as a pretext for evil things, but as servants[1] of God. 17. You must now honor all *people*, you must constantly love the brotherhood, you must continually fear God, honor the king.

The Example of Messiah's Suffering

2:18. You house slaves must be subject to your masters in every respect, not only to the good and gentle, but also to the unjust. 19. For this *is* grace, if, through consciousness of God, someone bears patiently some grief of unjust sufferings. 20. For what kind of credit *is there* if *you are* sinning and you will endure being beaten? But if when you are doing good, and then you will endure suffering, this brings God's favor. 21. For you were called into this, because Messiah also suffered on your behalf, leaving an example behind for you so that you could follow in His footsteps,

22.　"Who did not sin
　　　　and no deceit was found in His mouth," (Is 53:9)

23. Who, when He was reviled did not revile in return, while suffering He was not threatening, but He gave *Himself* over to the One Who judges righteously: 24. Who took away our sins Himself by means of His body on the tree, so that by dying to our sins we could live in righteousness, (Is 53:4,12) by Whose wound you were healed. (Is 53:5) 25. For you were being led astray, like sheep, but you have now been returned by *the* Shepherd and overseer of your lives. (Is 53:6, Eze 34:5,6)

Wives and Husbands

3.1. Likewise[2] let the wives be in subjection to their own husbands, so that even if some *husbands* are disobeying in the Word, through the way of life of the wives they will have been gained without a word, 2. because they watched your pure way of life in reverent fear, 3. for whom *your beauty* must not be the external things, by the braiding of hair and wearing gold or putting on adorned clothes 4. but the secret person of the heart, in the imperishable *quality* of the gentle and quiet spirit, which is of surpassing value before God. 5. For so also in former times the holy wives, those who hoped in God, were putting themselves in order by being subject to their own husbands, 6. as Sarah obeyed Abraham, calling him lord, of whom you have become daughters by doing good and not being afraid and not at all in terror.

3:7. Likewise husbands, because you live together, you know *your wife* as the weaker feminine vessel. By showing honor *to her*,[3] as also to fellow heirs

---

1　　　(v.16) Or slaves, see Servant in Glossary.
2　　　(v.1) The word "likewise" refers to 2:13, 18 and 3:7, making this the third group being instructed.
3　　　(v.7) This is a parallel to Paul's statement in Col 3:19 for husbands to love their wives and in Eph 5:1 to be subject one to another.

of *the* grace of life, your prayers would not be hindered.

Suffering for Righteousness' Sake

3:8. Finally, all *believers be* united in spirit, like-minded, loving brothers,[1] compassionate, humble, 9. not paying back evil for evil, or reproach against reproach, but on the contrary blessing because you have been called into this, so that you would inherit a blessing.

10.	For "The one who wants to love life
	and to see good days
	must immediately stop his tongue from evil
	and not speak deceitfully,
11.	but he must at once turn away from evil and do good,
	he must immediately seek and pursue peace:
12.	because *the* eyes of *the* Lord *are* upon *the* righteous
	and His ears for their appeal,
	but *the* face of *the* Lord *is* against *those who* do wickedness."
	(Ps 34:12-16)

3:13. And who is the one who will harm you if you would be eager for moral goodness? 14. But even if you might suffer because of righteousness, *you are* blessed. And you should not be afraid of them and you should not let yourselves be intimidated, 15. but you must now hold *our* Lord the Messiah in reverence in your hearts, always prepared with a reply for every one who questions your report about the hope within you, 16. but with gentleness and respect, because you have a clear conscience, so that while you are being spoken evil of, those who revile you would be put to shame by your good way of life in Messiah. 17. *It is* better to suffer for doing good, if he might want the will of God, rather than for doing wrong.[2] 18. Because Messiah also once suffered concerning sin, *the* righteous One on behalf of *the* unjust, so that He could bring you to God when He did indeed die in *the* flesh, but then was made alive by *the* Spirit: 19. with Whom[3] also, when He went, He preached to those spirits in prison, 20. *to those* formerly disobedient. While the patience of God was eagerly awaiting, in *the* days of Noah an ark was being built for which a few, that *is* eight lives, were rescued through water. 21. And now baptism,[4] which is a fulfillment of the type, saves you, not in removal of dirt from flesh, but an appeal for a clear conscience toward God, through *the* resurrection[5] of Jesus Messiah, 22. Who went into heaven *and* is on *the* right hand of God, with angels and authorities and powers being subject to Him.

---

1   (v.8) This means to love not only all believers, but to love your neighbor as yourself.
2   (v.17) This is a rabbinic teaching. See Suffering in Glossary.
3   (v.19) The Holy Spirit
4   (v.21) This is the Greek word baptisma, which means immersion. See Baptize in Glossary.
5   (v.21) See Resurrection in Glossary.

Good Stewards of God's Grace

4.1. Therefore since Messiah suffered in *the* flesh, then you must now arm yourselves with *the* same thought, that the One Who suffered in *His* flesh has stopped sin 2. with mankind not to *live* any longer in desires but *for* the remaining time to live in *the* will of God in *the* flesh. 3. For sufficient time has passed for you to be doing what the heathens like to do, as they go in licentiousness, lusts, drunkenness, carousing, drinking bouts, and lawless idolatries. 4. In which they are astonished at your not running together *with them* in this flood of debauchery, so they revile *you*. 5. They will render an account to the One ready to judge *the* living and *the* dead. 6. For this reason the Good News was proclaimed to *the* dead,[1] so that they could be judged in *the* flesh according to men but they could live in *the* spirit according to God.

4:7. But the end of all things has come near. Therefore you must now be serious and exercise self-restraint to help you pray: 8. above all things having constant love among yourselves, because love hides a multitude of sins (Pr 10:12). 9. So be hospitable to one another without complaining, 10. just as each took a gift for himself, ministering this as good stewards of a diversified grace of God. 11. If someone speaks, *let it be* as words and admonitions of God: if someone serves, as from strength which God supplies, so that in all things God would be glorified through Jesus Messiah, to Whom be the glory and the power for ever and ever, amen.

Suffering as a Christian

4:12. Beloved, you must not ever be surprised at the burning[2] within you, *which* is for a trial in you as *if* a strange *thing were* happening in you, 13. but rather in so far as you are sharing in the sufferings of Messiah, rejoice, so that also in the revelation of His glory you would shout for joy. 14. If you are reproached because of *the* name of Messiah, *you are* blessed, because the Spirit of the glory, even the *Spirit* of God, rests[3] upon you. 15. For none of you must suffer as a murderer or a thief or evildoer or as a spy: 16. but if as a Christian, he must not be ashamed, but he must glorify God in this name.[4] 17. Because the time to begin the judgment of the house of God *is at hand*: and if with us first, what *is* the end of those who are disobedient to the Good News of God?

18.   And "If the righteous is scarcely saved,
        how will the godless and sinner appear?" (Pr 11:31)

19. So also those who suffer according to the will of God must entrust their lives to the faithful Creator while doing good.

---

1   (v.6) See Jn 5:25.
2   (v.12) Fiery ordeal, painful test, refining fire
3   (v.14) This rest is temporary, referring both to our sojourn on earth and the possibility of losing that rest.
4   (v.16) This name refers first to a Christian, then to the name of the Lord. We are to glorify His name, not profane it, by the way we live, no matter what the circumstances.

Tending the Flock of God

5.1. Therefore I, the fellow elder and witness of the sufferings of the Messiah, as well as a sharer of the glory to be revealed, urge elders among you: 2. you must continually shepherd the flock of God among you, not overseeing by compulsion but voluntarily according to God, and not in fondness of dishonest gain but willingly, 3. and not as lording it over your charges, but becoming patterns for the flock: 4. and when the Chief Shepherd is revealed you will receive the unfading crown of glory.

5:5. Likewise, young men, you must always be subject to elders: and with one another you must continually clothe yourselves *with* humility, because

"God is opposed to *the* arrogant,
but gives grace to *the* humble."[1] (Pr 3:34)

5:6. Therefore you must now be humble under the powerful hand of God, so that He could lift you up in time, 7. immediately casting your every care upon Him, because He cares about you. (Ps 55:22)

5:8. You must now be sober, you must now be watchful. Your adversary, the devil, walks like a roaring lion seeking someone to devour: 9. whom you must immediately resist, strong in faith, since you know *that* the same sufferings are laid upon the brotherhood throughout the world. 10. But the God of every grace, the One Who called you into His eternal glory by means of Messiah Jesus, after you have suffered a short time, will Himself put in order, will establish, will strengthen, will lay the foundation. 11. To Him be the power forever, amen.

Final Greetings

5:12. Through Silas,[2] the faithful brother, as I consider, I wrote to you briefly, urging and bearing witness that this is the true grace of God, in which you must now stand. 13. The fellow elect in Babylon and my son Mark greet you. 14. You must now greet one another with a kiss of *agape* love. Peace to all you who *are* in Messiah.

---

1   (v.5) Humble is a metaphor for the faithful remnant. See Humble in glossary.
2   (v.12) Silas was Peter's scribe for this letter. Silas did not act as scribe for 2 Peter.

~ 2 PETER[1] ~

Salutation

1.1. Simon[2] Peter, servant and apostle of Jesus Messiah, to those who have received a like precious faith with us by divine allotment through *the* righteousness of our God and Savior, Jesus Messiah, 2. may grace and peace be multiplied to you through knowledge of the *only* God and of Jesus our Lord.

The Christian's Call and Election

1:3. As everything of His divine power has been bestowed upon us for life and godliness, through the knowledge of the One Who called us by His own glory and power, 4. through Whom the precious and very great promises have been bestowed upon us, so that through them you would become sharers of *the* divine nature, escaping from the depravity in the world because of *its* desire *for forbidden things*. 5. And for this very reason, by having made every effort, you must immediately show by your deeds[3] the moral goodness in your faith, and knowledge in your moral goodness, 6. and self-control with knowledge, and patience with self-control, and godliness with patience, 7. and your brotherly love with godliness, and love for brothers and sisters in the faith. 8. For as these things are present and multiply in you, they do not make you useless or fruitless in the knowledge of our Lord Jesus Messiah: 9. for *the one* in whom these things are not present is blind, shortsighted, *who* long ago forgot the cleansing of his sins. 10. For this reason, brothers, you must now be more diligent, *for* your calling and election to be made secure: for when you do these things you would **never**, ever, stumble. 11. For thus the entrance into the eternal kingdom of our Lord and Savior Jesus Messiah will be richly supplied to you.

1:12. On this account, I am always going to remind you about these things, although you have known and have been established in the present truth. 13. And I consider what is right, as long as I am in this tabernacle, to arouse you

---

1   (Title) Written about 66-67 AD.
2   (v.1) The Greek word written here as Simon is identical to the Greek word written as Simeon in Lk 2:25. Early English translators wrote Simeon in Luke and Simon for Peter's name and the difference has stuck. See Names in Glossary.
3   (v.5) Mitsvot, see Jas 2:14-26. See Mitsvah in Glossary.

as I remind you, 14. since I know that the removal of my tabernacle[1] is coming soon, as also our Lord Jesus Messiah has made clear to me, 15. and I will indeed always be zealous to have you to recall these things to mind after my death.

Messiah's Glory and the Prophetic Word

1:16. For we did not make known to you in craftily devised myths, but because we were eye witnesses of that majesty we followed in the power and coming of our Lord Jesus Messiah. 17. For then He took honor and glory from Father God when such a unique voice announced to Him by the Majestic Glory, "This is My Son, My Beloved, with Whom I take delight," (Mt 17:5, Mk 9:7, Lk 9:35) 18. and we heard this voice as it was brought out from heaven while we were with Him on the holy mountain. 19. And we have the more certain prophetic word, in which you will do well, if you pay attention, as with a lamp shining in a dark place, until that Day[2] would dawn and *the* Morning Star would rise in your hearts, 20. if you understand this first, that no prophecy of Scripture happens by the *prophet's* own interpretation: 21. for a prophecy was never brought by *the* will of a person, but people[3] spoke from God, while they were being carried along by *the* Holy Spirit.

False Prophets and Teachers

2.1. But false prophets were also among the people, as even false teachers will be among you, who will bring destruction by *their* opinions, even denying the Master, the One Who has purchased them. Although they quickly bring utter destruction on themselves, 2. many will then follow in their unbridled lusts, because of which the way of the truth will be blasphemed,[4] 3. and they will use you for *their* gain with made up messages in their greedy desire to have more, for whom the judgment has for a long time not been idle and their destruction is on its way.

2:4. For if God did not spare angels when they sinned, but, after He held *them* in pits of darkness in Tartarus,[5] He gave *them* over, guarding *them* until judgment. 5. Nor did He spare *the* ancient world, but when He brought a flood on an ungodly world He guarded Noah, a preacher of righteousness, and seven others. 6. Again with *the* cities of Sodom and Gomorrah, when He reduced *them* to ashes in destruction He condemned *them* as He made *them* an example for *those who were* going to be ungodly, 7. and He rescued righteous Lot, when he was tormented by the way of life of the lawless in sensuality: 8. for *that* righteous man, as he lived among them day after day, was tormented, a righteous being,

---

1   (v.14) This tabernacle is Peter's body.
2   (v.19) Judgment Day. See Re 20:4, 11-14.
3   (v.21) The Greek word translated person or people is anthropos, meaning man or mankind, but in the Hebrew idiom, person or people would be more appropriate.
4   (v.2) Their immoral behavior will bring shame on the congregation.
5   (v.4) Tartarus is the parallel from Greek mythology to Sheol or Gehenna in Hebrew, where the wicked dead are sent.

in seeing and hearing unrighteous[1] works: 9. *the* Lord knows how to rescue *the* godly from trial, and to keep unjust *ones*[2] for a day of judgment when they *will* be punished, 10. and *the* most *punished* of all *will be* those who go after defiling lust and despise authority.

Daring, arrogant they do not tremble at *the* glorious angelic beings, blaspheming *even angels*, 11. whereupon angels, although they are greater *than people* in strength and power, do not bear blasphemous judgment from *the* Lord against them. 12. But these who have been born to be captured and killed as irrational natural animals, when they revile *things* in which they are ignorant, they will be destroyed in their corruption 13. suffering hurt as the reward of unrighteousness. *They are* thinking of pleasure, reveling by day, spots and blemishes carousing in their deceitfulness, feasting together with you, 14. having eyes full of adulterous and unceasing sins, having lured unstable souls, a heart *that* has been trained, having covetousness, people worthy of a curse: 15. they were deceived, when they left the right way behind, *and* followed in the way of Balaam the *son of* Beor, who loved *the* reward of *his* wickedness 16. but he was rebuked for his own evil doing: a dumb beast *that* spoke in a man's voice restrained the madness of the prophet. (Nu 22:28)

2:17. These *men* are waterless wells, and mists being driven by hurricanes, in which the gloom of darkness has been kept. 18. For speaking haughty emptiness, they lure those just now escaping, with licentious desires of flesh, those who live in error, 19. promising freedom to them, while they are slaves beginning *their* corruption: for in this he has been enslaved to whatever he had succumbed. 20. For if, after escaping the defilement of the world, with knowledge of our Lord and Savior Jesus Messiah, and again entangling with these who are defeated, their last *state* has become worse for them than the first. 21. For it would be better for them not to have known the way of righteousness than if they had known, to turn back from *the* holy commandment after it was delivered to them. 22. The true proverb happened to them,

"As a dog returned to its own vomit," (Pr 26:11)

and,

"After a hog was washed, *it was* wallowing in mud."

The Promise of the Lord's Coming

3.1. Now beloved, I am writing this second letter[3] to you in which I am stirring up the pure understanding by way of a reminder 2. to recall the words spoken before by the holy prophets and the command of our Lord and Savior through your apostles. 3. Since you know this first, that mockers will come to

---

1   (v.8) The word translated unrighteous refers to intentional sin. See Sin in Glossary.
2   (v.9) The word translated unjust *ones* refers to sin committed with the intention of anger-ing God. See Sin in Glossary.
3   (v.1) From this we infer that Peter wrote this letter to the same people as in 1 Peter.

you with their mocking in the last days when they indulge their physical nature in their own desires that defile 4. and asking, "Where is the promise of His coming?" For our fathers slept from *the time of the Promise*, thus everything remains as it was from *the* beginning of creation. 5. For they willfully forget that long ago *the* heavens were *created*, then earth *came* out from water, then through water, being held together by the Word of God, 6. through which the world, when it was inundated by water, was destroyed: 7. but now the heavens and the earth are reserved by the same Word, being kept for fire on *the* Day of Judgment and *the* destruction of the ungodly people.

3:8. But this one thing must not escape your notice, beloved, that one day with the Lord *is* as a thousand years and a thousand years as one day. (Ps 90:4) 9. *The* Lord does not tarry with His promise, as some consider slowness, but He is patient with you, not wanting any to be destroyed but all to come to repentance. 10. But *the* Day of the Lord will come like a thief, on which *Day* the sky[1] will pass away with a roar and the elements from which all things are made will be destroyed, being burned up, and *the* earth and the deeds *of all* on it will be laid bare[2] in this *Day*. 11. Thus, while everything is being destroyed in this manner, it is necessary for you to be in holy conduct and pieties, 12. awaiting and hastening the coming of the Day of God, because of which *the* flaming heavens[3] will be destroyed and heavenly bodies will be destroyed, being dissolved by the heat. 13. But now we are looking for a new sky and a new earth according to His promise, in which righteousness dwells. (Is 65:17, 66:22, Re 21:1)

3:14. For which reason, beloved, since you expect these things you must now make every effort to be found spotless and blameless in Him in peace 15. and you must always consider the patience of our Lord *for* salvation, just as also our beloved brother Paul wrote to you, according to the wisdom given to him, 16. as also in all *his* letters when he speaks in them about these things, in which some things are hard to understand, in which the unlearned and unstable people are twisting *them* as *they* also *do* the rest of *the* Scriptures to their own destruction. 17. Therefore you, beloved, since you know beforehand, must habitually guard, so that you would not lose your own steadfastness, being carried away in the error of the lawless, 18. but you must continually increase in grace and in knowledge of our Lord and Savior Jesus Messiah. To Him *be* the glory both now and to *the* eternal Day. Amen

---

1   (v.10) The sky and the earth, meaning the solar system, will be consumed, but not the universe. See Re 21:1.
2   (v.10) Literally Found, meaning exposed, judged
3   (v,12) This could be the entire solar system, but not the whole universe.

~ 1 JOHN[1] ~

The Word of Life

1.1. The One Who was from *the* beginning, Whom we have heard, Whom we have seen with our eyes, Whom we looked upon and our hands touched concerning the *very* Word of Life - 2. and the life was revealed, and we saw and we are bearing testimony and we are reporting to you the Eternal Life, Who was with the Father and was revealed to us - 3. Whom we have seen and we have heard, we are reporting also to you, so that you too would have fellowship with us. And our fellowship indeed *is* with our Father and His Son Jesus Messiah. 4. And we are writing these things so that our joy would be made full.

God is Light[2]

1:5. And this is the message, which we have heard from Him and are making known to you, that God is light and there is no darkness at all in Him. 6. If we would say that we have fellowship with Him and we would walk in darkness, we are lying and we are not practicing the truth: 7. but if we walk in the light as He is in the light, we have fellowship with one another and the blood of Jesus His Son cleanses us from every sin. 8. If we say that we do not have sin, we deceive ourselves and the truth is not in us. 9. If we confess our sins,[3] He is faithful and righteous, so that He would forgive our sins and He would cleanse us from all unrighteousness. 10. If we say that we have not sinned, we make Him a liar and His Word is not in us.

Messiah Our Advocate

2.1. My little children, I write these things to you so that you would not sin. But if anyone does sin, we have an advocate with the Father, Jesus Messiah, *the* righteous: 2. and He is *the* means by which our sins are forgiven, not concerning ours only but also on behalf of the whole world. 3. And by this we know that we have known Him, if we keep His commandments.[4] 4. The one who says, "I have known Him," and does not keep His commandments, is a liar

---

1   (Title) Written about 85-90 AD.
2   (Caption) Light had for a long time been known as a representation of the Living God.
3   (v.9) See Sin, Forgiveness of in Glossary
4   (v.4) To John His commandments refers to all those in the Tanach, the OT.

and the truth is not in him: 5. but whoever keeps His Word, truly the love of God would have been completed in him, because we know that we are in Him. 6. The one who says he remains in Him is obligated to walk *the* same *walk* just as that One walked.

The New Commandment

2:7. Beloved, I am not writing a new commandment to you but an old commandment, which you had from *the* beginning: the old commandment is the message that you heard. 8. Moreover, I am writing a new commandment to you, which is true in Him and in you, because the darkness is passing away and the true light is already shining.[1] 9. The one who says he is in the light but hates his brother is in the darkness until now. 10. The one who loves his brother remains in the light and offense is not in him: 11. but the one who hates his brother is in the darkness and he is walking in darkness and does not know where he is going, because the darkness has blinded his eyes.

12.   I write to you, little children,
            because your sins have been forgiven because of His name.
13.   I write to you, fathers,
            because you have known Him from the beginning.
        I write to you, young people,
            because you have overcome the evil one.
14.   I have written to you, children,
            because you know the Father.
        I have written to you, fathers,
            because you have known Him from the beginning.
        I have written to you, young people,
            because you are strong
            and the Word of God remains in you
                and you have overcome the evil one.

2:15. Do not love the world or the things in the world. If someone loves the world, the love of the Father is not in him: 16. because everything in the world, the lust of the flesh and the lust of the eyes and pride in one's position and possessions, is not from the Father but is from the world. 17. And the world and its lust pass away, but the one who does the will of God remains forever.

The Anti-Messiah

2:18. Children, it is *the* last hour, and just as you heard that anti-Messiah is coming, even now many anti-Messiahs have come, from which we know that this is *the* last hour.[2] 19. They went out from us but were not *really* of us: for

---

1   (v.8) The message has now been revealed by the Light that Jesus gave to the commandments.
2   (v.18) A number of verses show that Jesus and the disciples felt they were living in the end times. See Coming of Messiah in Glossary.

if they had been of us, then they would have remained with us: but so that they would be revealed because they all are not of us. 20. And you have an anointing[1] from the Holy One as you all know. 21. I did not write to you because you do not know the truth but because you do know it and because every lie is not from the truth. 22. Who is a liar, except the one who denies for himself *by saying* that Jesus is not the Messiah? This one is the anti-Messiah, the one who denies the Father and the Son. 23. Everyone who denies the Son does not have the Father, the one who confesses the Son also has the Father. 24. What you heard from *the* beginning must continually remain in you. If what you heard from *the* beginning would remain in you, then you will remain in the Son and in the Father. 25. And this is the promise, which He promised to us, eternal life.

2:26. I wrote these things to you about those who deceive you. 27. And *about* the anointing *of the Holy Spirit*, which you took from Him, which remains in you, and you do not need someone to teach you, but as this anointing for the gifts of the Spirit (1Cor 12:4-11) teaches you about all things (Jr 31:34) and is true and is not a lie, so just as He taught you, remain in Him.

2:28-3:10   **Children of God** "How great is the love"

2:28. And now, little children, remain in Him, so that if He would be revealed we would have boldness and we would not be shamed by Him at His coming. 29. If you know that He is righteous, you also know that everyone who does righteousness would have been begotten by Him. 3.1. You must now see what manner of love the Father has given to us so that we could be called children of God, and we are. Because of this the world does not know us, because it has not known Him. 2. Beloved, now we are children of God. But it has not yet been revealed what we shall be. We know that if He would be revealed, we shall be like Him, because we shall see Him for ourselves just as He is. 3. And everyone who has this hope in Him purifies himself, just as that One is pure.

3:4. Everyone who commits a sin then is doing a lawless deed, for sin is lawlessness.[2] 5. And you know that He was revealed, so that He would take our sins, and sin is not in Him. 6. Everyone who remains in Him does not sin: everyone who is sinning has neither seen Him nor known Him. 7. Little children, you must not be deceived by anyone: the one who does righteousness is righteous, just as that One is righteous: 8. the one who continues sinning is from the devil, because the devil has been sinning from *the* beginning. The Son of God was revealed for this, so that He would destroy the works of the devil. 9. No one who has been begotten from God continues sinning, because His seed remains in him, and he is not able to sin, because he has been born of God. 10. The children of God and the children of the devil are made known by this: everyone who does not

---

1   (v.20) Gifts of the Holy Spirit
2   (v.3) Lawlessness could also be translated "without Torah."

do righteousness, and the one who does not love his brother, is not from God.[1]

Love One Another

3:11. For this is the message that you heard from *the* beginning, that we should love one another, 12. not as Cain, who was from evil, and slew his brother: and for what reason did he slay him? Because his works were evil and his brother's righteous. 13. And do not marvel, brothers, if the world hates you. 14. We know that we have passed over out of death into life, because we love our brothers: the one who does not love remains in death. 15. Everyone who hates his brother is a murderer, and you know that no murderer has eternal life abiding in him. 16. By this we know His love, because that One did lay down His life on our behalf: and we are obligated to lay down our lives on behalf of our brothers. 17. But whoever would have the resources of the world and would see his brother when he has need and would shut his heart of mercies and compassion from him, how does the love of God remain in him? (Dt 15:7,8) 18. Little children, we should not love just in word or speech but in deed and in truth. (Jas 2:15,16)

Confidence before God

3:19. And we will know by this that we are of the truth and we will tranquilize, *bring peace to* our hearts before Him, 20. that if our hearts would accuse *us*, that God is greater than our hearts and He knows all things. 21. Beloved, if our hearts do not condemn *us*, we have confidence before God 22. and we receive from Him whatever we would ask, because we are keeping His commandments and we are doing what *is* pleasing before Him. 23. And this is His commandment, that we would believe in the name of His Son, Jesus Messiah, and we would love one another, just as He gave *the* commandment to us. 24. And the one who keeps His commandments remains in Him and He in him: and by this we know that He remains in us, by the Spirit Whom He gave to us.

The Spirit of God and the Spirit of Anti-Messiah

4.1. Beloved, do not believe every spirit but you must continually try the spirits *to see* if they are from God, because many false prophets have come out into the world. 2. You can know the Spirit of God by this: every spirit that declares that Jesus Messiah has come in *the* flesh is from God, 3. and every spirit that does not acknowledge Jesus is not from God: and this is the anti-Messiah, the one that you have heard is coming, and now he is already in the world. 4. You are from God, little children, and you have overcome them, because the One Who *is* in you is greater than the one who *is* in the world. 5. These are from the world, because of this they are speaking from the world and the world listens to them. 6. We are from God; the one who knows God listens to us, who is not from God does not listen to us. By this we know the spirit of truth and the spirit of error.

---

1   (v.10) See v. 18

God is Love

4:7. Beloved, we should love one another, because love is out of God, and everyone who loves has been begotten of God and does know the *only* God. 8. The one who does not love *his brother¹* does not know God, because God is love. 9. The love of God was revealed to us by this, that God sent His only Son into the world so that we could live through Him. 10. Love is *expressed* by this, not because we have loved God but because He loved us and sent His Son *to be* an atonement on behalf of our sins. 11. Beloved, if God loved us this way, then we are obligated to love one another. 12. No one has ever looked upon God.² If we would love one another, God dwells in us and His love has been made complete in us.

4:13. By this we know that we abide in Him and He in us, because He has given us of His Spirit. 14. And we have looked upon and we bear witness that the Father sent His Son *to be* Savior of the world. 15. Whoever would confess that Jesus is the Son of God, God remains in him and he in God. 16. And we have known and we have believed the love that God has for us.

God is love, and the one who dwells in love dwells in God and God lives in him. 17. By this, love has been made complete among us, so that we would have fearless confidence in the Day of Judgment, because just as that One is, we ourselves are *like Him* in this world. 18. There is no fear in love but complete love casts fear outside, because fear has *to do with* punishment, and the one who fears has not been made complete in love. 19. We can love, because He loved us first. 20. If someone would say, "I love God" and he would hate his brother, he is a liar: for the one who does not love his brother whom he has seen, is not able to love God Whom he has not seen. 21. And we have this commandment from Him, that the one who loves God would also love his brother.

Faith is Victory over the World

5.1. Everyone who believes that Jesus is the Messiah has been born of God, and everyone who loves the One Who begot also loves the one who has been born of Him. 2. We know that we love the children of God by this, when we would love God and we would carry out His commandments.³ 3. For this is the love of God, that we would keep, *do*, His commandments, and His commandments are not burdensome. 4. Because everyone who has been born of God overcomes the world: and this is the victory overcoming the world, *this* faith of ours. 5. And who is the one who overcomes the world except the one who believes that Jesus is the Son of God?

---

1   (v.8) Brother is used in the broadest sense, like neighbor in Lv 19:18.
2   (v.12) The next sentence of this verse tells us that people should see God in us, as each of us loves his neighbor.
3   (v.2) Our behavior must change, as Jas 2:14-17.

The Witness concerning the Son

5:6. This is the One Who has come through water[1] and blood,[2] Jesus Messiah, not by water only but by the water and by the blood: and the Spirit is the One Who bears witness, because the Spirit is the truth. 7. There are three who bear testimony, 8. the Spirit and the water and the blood, and the three are in the One. 9. If we take the testimony of people, the testimony of God is greater: because this is the testimony of God, that He has testified concerning His Son.[3] 10. The one who believes in the Son of God has the testimony in himself, the one who does not believe in God has made Him a liar, because he has not believed in the testimony that God has borne concerning His Son. 11. And this is the testimony, that God gave us eternal life, and this life is by means of His Son. 12. The one who has the Son has *eternal* life: the one who does not have the Son of God does not have *eternal* life.

Knowledge of Eternal Life

5:13. I have written these things to you who believe in the name of the Son of God so that you would know that you have eternal life. 14. And this is the confidence that we have with Him, that if we would ask anything according to His will, He hears us. 15. And if we know that He hears us, whatever we would ask, we know that we have the requests that we have asked from Him.

5:16. If someone would see his brother committing a sin not to death, if he will ask then He will give life to him, to those who do not sin to death. There is a sin to death: I am not saying that he should ask concerning that. 17. Every unrighteousness is sin, but there is sin not to death.[4]

5:18. We know that everyone who has been begotten from God does not sin, but the one who has been begotten from God keeps himself *by observing the commandments* and the evil one does not take hold of him. 19. We know that we are of God and the whole world lies in the power of the evil one. 20. And we know that the Son of God has come and He has given us understanding so that we would know the Genuine One, and we are in the Genuine One, by means of His Son Jesus Messiah. This One is the true God and eternal life. 21. Little children, you must now keep yourselves from the false gods.[5]

---

1 (v.6) Water refers to at least three things: amniotic fluid of His birth, baptism, and also to Torah, for which water is a metaphor, from Is 55:1 and Ex 14:22.
2 (v.6) This is the blood of our covenant. The life is in the blood, Gn 9:4.
3 (v.9) There are two ways by which the Father testified about Jesus: in Jn 5:36 Jesus says "the works which I do testify.." and several times the Father Himself spoke, such as at Jesus' baptism and at His transfiguration.
4 (v.17) Jesus identifies food as one example of a sin not unto death, Mt 15:11, Mk 7:15.
5 (v.21) False gods, idols, are a very real threat to each of us, tempting us to seek material things and to focus on distractions such as sports. Sports are not evil, but it is wrong to focus on sports more than on God.

~ 2 JOHN[1] ~

Salutation

1. The elder to the chosen lady[2] and her children, whom I love in truth, and not only I, but all those who know the truth, 2. because the truth which remains in us will be with us forever. 3. Grace, mercy, peace will be with us from God *the* Father and from Jesus Messiah, the Son of the Father in truth and in love.

Truth and Love

4. I rejoice greatly because I found your children walking in truth, just as we were commanded by the Father. 5. And now I ask you, lady, not as writing a new commandment to you, but which we have had from the beginning, that we would love one another. 6. And love is this, that we would walk according to His commandments: the commandment is this, just as you heard from *the* beginning, that you should walk in this, *love.* 7. Because many deceivers have come out in the world, those who do not confess that Jesus Messiah has come in *the* flesh: this *person* is the deceiver and the anti-Messiah. 8. You must watch out for yourselves, that you would not lose what we all worked for, but that you would receive a full reward. 9. Everyone who goes further than is right or proper and does not remain in the teaching of the Messiah does not have God: the one who remains in the teaching, this one has both the Father and the Son. 10. If someone comes to you and does not bring this teaching, do not take him into *your* house and do not speak to greet him: 11. for the one who is speaking to greet him is sharing in his evil works.

Final Greetings

12. Since I have many things to write to you I was not wanting *to speak* through paper[3] and ink, but I was hoping to come to you and to speak face to face, so that our joy would be full. 13. The children of your preeminent sister[4] greet you.

---

1   (Title) Written after 96 AD.
2   (v.1) Lady could be a certain person or this could be a general letter to one or more congregations. Since the Greek word ekklesia, translated congregation, is a feminine noun, lady could be a reference to a congregation.
3   (v.12) The Greek word here is xartou, referring to a sheet of paper made from papyrus. The ink is black, made with lamp-black and gum.
4   (v.13) This could be a sibling or another congregation.

~ 3 JOHN[1] ~

Salutation

1. The elder to the esteemed Gaius, whom I love in truth.

2. Beloved, I pray *that* concerning everything, for you to do well and to be in good health, just as your inner being is well. 3. For I rejoiced greatly when the brothers came and testified about your *living* in the truth, how you are walking in truth. 4. I have no greater joy than this, *when* I hear that my children are walking in the truth.

Cooperation and Opposition

5. Beloved, you are doing faithfully. Whatever you would do *be* faithful among the brothers,[2] even *when they are* strangers. 6. They have testified of your love in front of *the* congregation,[3] *and* you will do well if you send them forward in a manner worthy of God: 7. for they came out for the sake of the Name, not taking anything from the heathens. 8. Therefore we ought to support such as these, so that we would become fellow workers in the truth.

9. I wrote something to the congregation: but the one of them who desires to be first, Diotrephes, does not accept our authority. 10. Because of this, if I should come, I will bring up what he is doing when he slanders us with evil words, and, not being content with that, neither does he accept the *visiting* brothers, but he keeps back those who want *to welcome them* and throws *them* out of the congregation.

11. Beloved, you must not ever imitate evil but *imitate* good. The one who does good things is from God: the one who does evil has not seen God. 12. Demetrius has been spoken well of by all and by this truth: and also we testify, and you know that our testimony is true.

Final Greetings

13. I have many things to write to you but I do not want to write to you

---

1   (Title) Written after 96 AD.
2   (v.5) Every reference like this to the brothers refers to all believers.
3   (v.6) Although often translated "church," no Greek word meaning church is used in the NT. See Congregation in Glossary.

through pen[1] and ink: 14. but I hope to see you presently, and we will speak face to face. 15. Peace to you. Our friends *here* greet you. You must greet our friends *there* by name.

---

1   (v.13) This is the Greek word kalamou, meaning reed pen. Different color inks were often used, but in this case melanos means black ink, made with lamp-black and gum.

~ JUDE[1] ~

Salutation

1. Judas, a servant of Jesus Messiah, brother of Jacob,

To those who have been loved by Father God and who have been kept, called by Jesus Messiah: 2. may mercy and peace and love be multiplied in you.

Judgment on False Teachers

3. Dear ones, while I was making every effort to write to you concerning our common salvation, I had a need to write to you urging *you* to fight for the faith once handed down to the saints. 4. For certain men did sneak in stealthily, those who long ago were written for this condemnation, ungodly, because they changed the grace of our God into licentiousness, and denied Jesus Messiah our only Master and Lord.

5. And I wish to remind you, that you all know that the Lord has saved people once for all from the land of Egypt *but* the second *time* He destroyed those who did not believe, (Nu 14:29,30) 6. and those angels who did not keep themselves *from the* beginning, but who deserted their own dwelling places,[2] He has kept *those angels* in eternal chains in darkness for judgment on *the* great Day.[3] 7. Again, *take* Sodom and Gomorrah and the cities around them, which indulged in immorality and went after other flesh, *in immorality*, as they *continue to* undergo *the* punishment of eternal fire they are exhibited as a *horrible* example, *a warning to others*.

8. Likewise also in fact these dreamers are defiling flesh and they are rejecting great authority, *the One Who possesses dominion*, and they are blaspheming glorious angelic beings. 9. And Michael the archangel, when he argued about the body of Moses as he was disputing with the devil, did not dare to pronounce curses in judgment but said, "May the Lord rebuke you." (Assumption of Moses) 10. But these *people* who indeed do not understand what they are cursing, but what things they understand by nature, *using bodily senses* like

---

1   (Title) Written about 66-67 AD.
2   (v.6) They not only left heaven when they followed Satan, but they also left their sanctuaries, which were their sanctified bodies.
3   (v.6) Judgment Day. See Re 20:4, 11-14.

animals, are destroyed by these things. 11. Woe to them, because they have gone the way of Cain and they abandoned themselves for a reward in the deception of Balaam. (Nu 22:7, 31:16) And they were destroyed in the rebellion of Korah. (Nu 16:19-35) 12. These, the ones who feast together fearlessly in your affections, are those hidden reefs *waiting to wreck a ship*, taking care of themselves, *not the flock*, waterless clouds being carried away by winds, late autumn trees without fruit, being uprooted, twice dead, 13. wild waves of *the* sea casting up their own shameful deeds like foam, wandering stars for whom the gloom of darkness has been reserved forever.

14. But then *the* seventh from Adam, Enoch, prophesied to the *people* saying, "Behold! *The* Lord has come with His holy ten thousands (En 60:8, Dt 33:2, Zch 14:5) 15. to execute judgment upon all, even every living being," (En 1:9) concerning all their ungodly deeds which sinners committed and concerning all the harsh *words* which ungodly sinners spoke against him. 16. These *people* are murmurers, faultfinders who go according to their own desires, and their mouth speaks hypocrisy, as they flatter for the sake of *gaining* an advantage.

Warnings and Exhortations

17. But you, beloved, must now keep in mind the words that were spoken earlier by the apostles of our Lord Jesus Messiah 18. because they were saying to you "In the last time there will be mockers who go *the way* of the ungodly according to their own desires." 19. These are those *people* who divide; *they have* a physical *sensuous nature*, since they do not have *the* Spirit. 20. But you, beloved, as you build yourselves up in your most holy faith, praying in *the* Holy Spirit, 21. you must continually keep yourselves in the love of God, anticipating the mercy of our Lord Jesus Messiah for[1] eternal life. 22. And you must indeed habitually show mercy on those who doubt, 23. but save others, as you snatch them from fire, and on others have mercy in fear, hating even the tunic that has been stained by the flesh.

Benediction

24. Now to the One Who is able to keep you without stumbling and to stand before His glory blameless in extreme joy, 25. to *the* only God, our Savior through our Lord Jesus Messiah, *be* glory, majesty, strength, and power before every age, both now and forever, amen.

---

1   (v.21) Or in

~ REVELATION[1] ~

Introduction and Salutation

1.1. A revelation by Jesus Messiah which God gave Him to show His servants things that must happen soon, (Dn 2:28,29,45) and He made known, when He sent by His messenger to His servant John, 2. who testified what he saw, the Word of God and the testimony of Jesus Messiah.[2] 3. Blessed *is* the one who reads and *are* those who hear[3] the words of the prophecy and keep the things that have been written in it, for the time is near.

1:4. John, to the seven congregations[4] which *are* in Asia: grace and peace to you from the One Who is, and Who was, and the One Who is coming, (Ex 3:14, Is 41:4) and from the Seven Spirits which *are* before His throne 5. and from Jesus Messiah, the Faithful Witness, Firstborn from the dead (Ps 89:27) and the ruler of the kings of the earth.

To the One Who loves us and has loosed us from our sins (Ps 130:8, Is 40:2) by His blood, 6. and made us a kingdom, priests[5] to His God and Father, (Ex 19:6, Is 61:6) to Him *be* the glory and the power forever and ever. Amen.

1:7. "Behold He is coming with the clouds," (Dn 7:13)
   "and every eye will see Him
even they who had pierced Him,
   and all the tribes of the earth will mourn on account of Him."
   (Zch 12:10,12,14)

Yes indeed, amen.

1:8. "I AM the Alef and the Tav,[6] says the Lord God, the One Who is and

---

1   (Title) Written about 89-96 AD. See Book Order in Glossary for insight to interpreting John.
2   (v.2) See Testimony of Jesus in Glossary.
3   (v.3) The one who reads is the one who takes the only copy of a scroll and reads it to the congregation.
4   (v.4) Although often translated "church," no Greek word meaning church is used in the NT. See Congregation in Glossary.
5   (v.6) There will be one kingdom, only One King, and all its citizens will be priests.
6   (v.8) Alef is the first letter in the Hebrew alphabet, tav is the last. Together alef and tav make a word that is placed in front of the direct object of the verb. See Alef in Glossary.

Who was and Who is coming, (Ex 3:14, Is 41:4) the Lord of Hosts."[1]

A Vision of Messiah

1:9. I, John, your brother and partner in affliction and in kingdom and in patient expectation in Jesus, I was on the island called Patmos because of the Word of God and the testimony of Jesus. 10. I was in *the* Spirit on the Lord's Day[2] and I heard behind me a loud voice like a trumpet 11. saying, "You must write in a book[3] what you see and you must send *it* to the seven congregations, in Ephesus and in Smyrna and in Pergama and in Thyatira and in Sardis and in Philadelphia and in Laodicea."

1:12. And I turned to see the voice that was speaking with me, and when I turned I saw seven golden lamp stands 13. and in *the* middle of the lamp-stands *I saw someone* like a Son of Man (Dn 7:13) clothed to His feet and girded at the chest with a golden belt. (Eze 9:2, Dn 10:5) 14. And His head and hair *were* white as wool, white as snow, (Dn 7:9) and His eyes as flame of fire (Gn 49:12) 15. and His feet like a metal more precious than gold[4] (Dn 10:6) as heated thoroughly in a furnace and His voice as a sound of many waters, (Eze 1:24, 43:2) 16. and *Who* had in His right hand seven stars and *there was* going out from His mouth a large sharp two-edged sword[5] (Is 49:2) and His face *was* as the sun shines in its power *at noon*.

1:17. And when I saw Him, I fell toward His feet as dead, and He placed His right hand upon me saying "Do not fear: I AM[6] the First and the Last (Is 44:6, 48:12) 18. and the One Who is living. And I died, but look! I am living forever and I have the keys of death and Hades. 19. Therefore, you must write what you have seen and what is happening and what is going to happen after these things. (Is 48:6, Dn 2:28,29,45) 20. The mystery of the seven stars which you saw in My right hand and the seven golden lamp stands: the seven stars are messengers[7] of the seven congregations and the seven lamp stands are the seven congregations.[8]"

---

1   (v.8) Coming with His angels on Judgment Day

2   (v.10) This is the Sabbath, from Friday sundown to Saturday sundown. See Sabbath in Glossary.

3   (v.11) These letters were written on papyrus, made in sheets ranging in size from six by nine to twelve by fifteen inches. The sheets were pasted together, end to end, in rolls of twenty sheets. The rolls were vertical, not horizontal, and rolled from left to right, then unrolled from the right for Greek and Latin, which read from left to right. The Greek word biblos, generally translated book or scroll, means pith, referring to the pith of the papyrus planFt.

4   (v.15) This is commonly translated burnished bronze, but the Greek word refers to a metal even more precious than gold. See 2:18.

5   (v.16) This large, broad sword, often used by barbarians, required a great deal of strength to use.

6   (v.17) The verses referenced use the Hebrew word ani for I AM. See Anokhi in Glossary.

7   (v.20) Each church member is to be like each of these messengers, a light in the darkness, whose light is to be seen by those in darkness. Although not perfect, each one of us is to be a good example to others.

8   (v.20) Each congregation is to be like these lamp stands, which represent the Holy Spirit and the Torah, empowering each member to shine like a beacon, filled with the Spirit and the Word

Revelation

The Message to Ephesus

2.1. "To the messenger of the congregation[1] in Ephesus you must now write:

'The One Who holds the seven stars in His right hand, the One Who walks among the seven golden lamp stands, says these things: 2. I know your works and toil and your patience and that you are not able to bear evil, and you tested those who say they are apostles and they are not and you found them false: 3. and you have patience and you endured because of My name and you have not wearied. 4. Nevertheless I have against you that you left your first love. 5. Therefore you must remember from where you have fallen and you must now repent and you must do the works *you did* at first: and if not, I am coming to you and I will remove your lamp stand from its place, if you would not repent. 6. But you have this, that you hate the works of the Nicolaitans,[2] which I also hate. (Ps 139:21) 7. The one who has ears must now listen to what the Spirit is saying to the congregations. To the one who conquers,[3] I will give him *permission* to eat from the tree of life, (Gn 2:8, Eze 28:13, 31:8,9) which is in the Paradise of God.'"

The Message to Smyrna

2:8. "And to the messenger of the congregation in Smyrna you must write:

'The First and the Last, (Is 44:6, 48:12) Who died then was restored to life, says these things: 9. I know your affliction and poverty, but you are rich, and *I know* the slander of those who say they are Jewish, and they are nothing but a synagogue of Satan.[4] 10. And you must not fear what you are going to suffer. Behold the devil is going to cast you into prison so that you would be tested and you will have distress ten days. (Dn 1:12,14) You must be faithful until death, and I will give you the crown of life. 11. The one who has ears must now listen to what the Spirit is saying to the congregations. The one who conquers cannot be injured by the second death.'"

The Message to Pergamum

2:12. "And to the messenger of the congregation in Pergama[5] you must write:

---

of God.
1   (v.1, v.8, v.12, et al) Although often translated "church," no Greek word meaning church is used in the NT. See Congregation in Glossary.
2   (v.6) Nicolaitans taught compromise with the world system, materialism and tolerance of immorality.
3   (v.7) Overcomer is the traditional translation, but it really means to be victorious, to conquer, so as you read the letters to the cities whenever you see overcomer, think conqueror!
4   (v.9) See Satan in Glossary.
5   (v.12) Pergama was the city where the process was later developed for making fine parchment, which in the fourth and fifth centuries AD replaced papyrus as the choice for written documents. The word parchment is derived from the name Pergama.

'The One Who has the large sharp two-edged sword is saying these things: (Is 49:2) 13. I know where you live, where the throne of Satan *is*, and you are holding fast My name. You did not even deny My faith in the days of Antipas,[1] My faithful witness who was killed in your sight, where Satan dwells. 14. But I have against you a few things because you have *some* there who hold the teaching of Balaam, who taught Balak to put a stumbling block in front of the children of Israel, to eat meat offered to idols and to practice idolatry.[2] 15. In this way then you have likewise held the teaching of the Nicolaitans. 16. Therefore you must now repent: and if not, I am coming to you quickly and I will fight with them with the great sword[3] of My mouth. 17. The one who has ears must now listen to what the Spirit is saying to the congregations. To the one who conquers,[4] I will give the manna which has been concealed (Ps 78:24) and I will give him a white amulet, and a new name (Is 62:2, 65:15) written upon the amulet which no one knows except the one who takes *it*.'"

The Message to Thyatira

2:18. "And to the messenger of the congregation in Thyatira you must write:

'The Son of God says these things, the One Who has His eyes like flames of fire and His feet like a metal more precious than gold:[5] (Dn 10:6) 19. I know your works and love and faith and service and your patience, and your last works *are* more than your first. 20. But I have against you that you do not hinder the woman Jezebel, the one who calls herself a prophet and she is teaching and deceiving My servants so they commit fornication[6] (1Ki 16:31, 2Ki 9:22) and eat meat offered to idols. (Nu 25:1,2) 21. And I gave her time so that she could repent, but she does not want to repent from her idolatry. 22. Behold I am casting her and those who commit adultery with her into a bed in great torment, unless they would repent from her deeds. 23. And I will put her children to death in *eternal* death. And all the congregations will know that I AM the One Who examines minds and hearts, (Ps 7:9, Pr 24:12, Jr 11:20, 17:10) and I will give to each one of you according to your deeds. (Ps 62:12, Pr 24:12, Jr 17:10) 24. And I say to you, to the rest of those in Thyatira, those who do not hold this teaching,

---

1 (v.13) This Antipas was a Christian martyr in Pergama, no kin to Herod Antipas.

2 (v.14) Or practice immorality. See Nu 31:16 & 25:1,2.

3 (v.16) This large, broad sword, often used by barbarians, required a great deal of strength to use. It is the most powerful personal weapon, and here in coming from His mouth it defeats our enemies as He fights for us. The Word of God is the most powerful personal weapon we can use, if we know the Word and have faith.

4 (v.17) Overcomer is the traditional translation, but the Greek really means to be victorious, to conquer, so as you read the letters to the cities in other translations whenever you see overcomer, think conqueror!

5 (v.18) This is the same word for a metal more precious than gold, used in Re. 1:15.

6 (v.20) This refers to any sin and definitely includes greed -- putting your desires before the needs of others.

who did not know the depths of Satan[1] as they were speaking *it*: I am not placing another burden upon you, 25. nevertheless you must hold what you do have until whenever I would come. 26. And the one who conquers and the one who keeps My works until *the* end,

> "I will give him authority over the heathens
> 27. and he will shepherd them with an iron rod
> *and shatter them* as the vessels made of clay shatter,"

(Ps 2:8,9, Ps Sol 17:23,24)

28. just as I have taken *this power* from My Father, so will I give him the Morning Star. 29. He who has ears must now listen to what the Spirit is saying to the congregations.'"

The Message to Sardis

3.1. "And you must write to the messenger of the congregation in Sardis:

'The One Who has the Seven Spirits of God and the seven stars says these things: I know your deeds *and* that you have a reputation, that of life, but you are dead. 2. You must become watchful and you must strengthen the rest who are about to die, for I have not found your works to have been completed before My God.[2] 3. Therefore you must remember what you have received and heard and you must continually pay attention to it and you must at once repent. But if you would not be watchful, I will come as a thief, and you will **not** know what sort of time I will come upon you. 4. But you have a few people in Sardis who did not stain their garments, and they will walk with Me in white, because they are worthy. 5. The one who conquers[3] will be clothed in this way, in white garments,[4] and I will **not** wipe out his name from the Book of Life (Ex 32:32,33, Ps 69:28, Dn 12:1) and I will confess his name before My Father and before His angels. 6. The one who has ears must now listen to what the Spirit is saying to the congregations.'"

The Message to Philadelphia

3:7. "And to the messenger of the congregation in Philadelphia you must write:

> 'The Holy One, the True One, says these things,
> "the One Who has the key of David,
> the One Who opens and no one will shut
> and closes and no one opens:" (Is 22:22, Job 12:14)

---

1   (v.24) See Satan in Glossary.
2   (v.2) You have not done those things you ought to have done. Jas 2:14-24
3   (v.5) Overcomer is the traditional translation, but it really means to be victorious, to conquer, so as you read the letters to the cities whenever you see overcomer, think conqueror!
4   (v.5) White garments represent being in a state of spiritual preparedness, from Ecc 9:8, "Let your garments be always white; and let your head lack no ointment."

432

8. I know your deeds. Behold! I have caused a door to open in front of you and no one is able to shut it. For you have little power but you kept My word and you did not deny My Name. 9. Behold! I am causing to come forth from the assembly of Satan[1] those who say they are Jewish, but they are not, they are lying. Watch! I will make them so that they will come and fall down to pay homage before your feet (Is 45:14, 49:23, 60:14) and they will know that I have loved you. (Is 43:4) 10. Because you observed My lesson of patient endurance, I will protect you from the time of the testing, which is about to come upon the whole inhabited world, to try those who dwell upon the earth. 11. I am coming quickly: you must steadily hold what you have, so that no one could take your crown. 12. The one who conquers, I will make him a pillar in the sanctuary of My God and he would **not** go outside *the sanctuary* and I will write upon him the name of My God and the name of the city (Ez 48:35[2]) of My God, the new Jerusalem, the one which descends from heaven from My God, and *will also write* My new name. (Is 62:2, 65:15) 13. The one who has ears must now listen to what the Spirit is saying to the congregations.'"

The Message to Laodicea

3:14. "And to the messenger of the congregation in Laodicea you must write:

'He, the Amen, the Faithful and True Witness, the Beginning of the Creation of God, (Pr 8:22) says these things: 15. I know your deeds, that you are neither cold nor hot. I wish[3] you were cold or hot. 16. Because you are lukewarm in this way and neither hot nor cold,[4] I am going to spew you out of my mouth. 17. Because you say "I am rich and I have become wealthy[5] (Ho 12:8) and I do not need anything," but you do not know that you are the wretched and miserable and poor and blind and naked, 18. I am advising you to buy gold from Me *which* has been burned by fire so that you would be rich, and so that you would be clothed in white garments[6] and the disgrace of your nakedness would not be revealed, and to rub in an ointment on your eyes so that you could see. 19. Whom I love I do correct and I discipline: (Pr 3:12) therefore you must be earnest and you must now repent. 20. Behold! I have been standing at the door and I am knocking:[7] if someone would hear My voice and would open the door, then I will

---

1   (v.9) See Satan in Glossary.
2   (v.12) Adonai Shama, The Lord is There
3   (v.15) This verb, translated wish, means that even though He wishes you were cold or hot, He knows you will not become either, but will stay lukewarm.
4   (v.16) Many churches are filled with Sunday Christians, who come on Sunday, but leave all thoughts of God in the church when they head for home. There are pastors who preach 'feel good' messages and never challenge or lift their flocks. All of us should be enthusiastic for the Lord and show by the way we live that we know He is with us all day, every day.
5   (v.17) I did it myself.
6   (v.18) White garments represent being in a state of spiritual preparedness, from Ecc 9:8, "Let your garments be always white; and let your head lack no ointment."
7   (v.20) He is still standing and knocking today!

enter to him and I will dine with him and he with Me. 21. The one who conquers I will give him permission to sit with Me on My throne, as I also conquered and sat with My Father on His throne.[1] 22. The one who has ears must now listen to what the Spirit is saying to the congregations.'"

The Heavenly Worship

4.1. After these things I looked, and there was a door *that* was opened in heaven, and the first voice which I heard speaking with me *was* like a trumpet saying, "You must come up here, (Ex 19:20,24) and I will show you what must happen (Dn 2:28,29,45) after these things." 2. I immediately was in *the* Spirit, and there was a throne standing in heaven, and *One* seated upon the throne, (1Ki 22:19, 2Chr 18:18, Ps 47:8, Is 6:1, Eze 1:26,27, Sir 1:8) 3. and the One Who was seated had an appearance like a jasper and sardius stone. And a rainbow, like an emerald in appearance, surrounded the throne. (Eze 1:26-28) 4. And all around the throne *were* twenty-four thrones, and upon the thrones twenty-four elders sitting (Is 24:23) clothed in white garments and with gold crowns on their heads. 5. And lightnings and voices and thunders (Ex 19:16, Eze 1:13) were going out from the throne, and in front of the throne seven lamps of fire *were* burning, (Eze 1:13, Zch 4:2) which are the seven Spirits of God, 6. and in front of the throne as a sea of glass like crystal. (Eze 1:22)

And in *the* middle of the throne and around the throne were four living creatures full of eyes before and behind. 7. And the first living creature *was* like a lion, and the second living creature like a calf, and the third living creature having a face like a man, and the fourth living creature like a flying eagle. (Eze 1:5-10, 10:14) 8. And the four living creatures, each one of them having six wings, (Is 6:2) all around and within[2] they were full of eyes, (Eze 1:18, 10:12) and they do not have rest[3] day and night saying,

"Holy, holy, holy,
Lord God of Hosts,[4] (Is 6:3)
Who was and Who is and Who is coming." (Ex 3:14)

9. And whenever the living creatures give glory and honor and thanksgiving to the One Who sits on the throne, (1Ki 22:19, 2Chr 18:18, Ps 47:8, Is 6:1, Eze 1:26,27, Sir 1:8) to the One Who lives forever and ever, (Dn 4:34, 6:26, 12:7) 10. the twenty-four elders fall down before the One Who sits upon the throne and they worship the One Who lives forever and ever and they cast their crowns before the throne saying,

11.   "Worthy are You, our Lord and our God

---

1   (v.21) This is an awesome verse. Think about it. See Re 22:1.
2   (v.8) Under their wings
3   (v.8) The word for rest means a short break. Not needing sleep, they praise continuously.
4   (v.8) Other translations say Almighty, but Hosts is appropriate. See Is 6:3. See Lord of Hosts in Glossary.

to receive glory and honor and power,
because You did create all things
and by Your will they indeed were created."

The Scroll and the Lamb

5.1. And I saw in the right hand of the One Who sits upon the throne (1Ki 22:19, 2Chr 18:18, Ps 47:8, Is 6:1, Eze 1:26,27, Sir 1:8) a scroll *that* had been written within and on the back,[1] (Is 29:11, Eze 2:9,10) *and* had been sealed with seven seals. 2. And I saw a strong angel proclaiming in a loud voice, "Who is worthy to break its seals and to open the scroll?" 3. And no one in heaven and no one on earth and no one under the earth was able to open the scroll and to see it. 4. And I was weeping copiously, because no one was found worthy to open the scroll and to see it. 5. And one of the elders said to me, "Stop weeping! Look! He was victorious, the Lion of the Tribe of Judah, (Gn 49:9,10) the Root of David, (Is 11:1) so He can open the scroll and its seven seals."

5:6. And I also saw in *the* midst of the throne[2] the four living creatures and in *the* midst of the elders a Lamb standing as having been slain, (Is 53:7) having seven horns and seven eyes (Zch 4:10) which are the seven Spirits of God that were sent into all the earth. (Is 11:1,2) 7. And He came and took *the scroll* from the right hand of the One Who sits on the throne. 8. And when He took the scroll, the four living creatures and the twenty-four elders fell before the Lamb, each having a harp and a gold bowl filled with burning incense, which are the prayers of the saints, (Ps 141:2) 9. and they were singing a new song saying,

"Worthy are You to take the scroll
and to open its seals,
because You were slain and You purchased *mankind* for God by means of
Your blood from every tribe and tongue and people and nation
10. and You made them a kingdom and priests for our God,
(Ex 19:6, Is 61:6)
and they will reign upon the earth."

5:11. And I looked, and I heard a sound of many angels surrounding the throne and the living creatures and the elders, and the number of them was ten thousand of ten thousands and a thousand of thousands[3] (Dn 7:10, En 14:22) 12. saying in a loud voice,

"Worthy is the Lamb that was slain to take
the power and wealth and wisdom and strength
and honor and glory and blessing." (1Chr 29:11, Is 53:7)

1　　(v.1) This is a reference to a papyrus roll, called an opisthograph.
2　　(v.6) Throne is sometimes a metaphor referring to the authority of the Ruler of the Universe or here it may be a semi-circle, with the four living creatures partially enclosed. It could also be that the throne is surrounded by the four living creatures, the elders, and the Lamb.
3　　(v.11) Many millions

13. And every living thing that *is* in the sky and on the earth and under the earth and in the sea and I heard them all saying,

> "To the One Who sits upon the throne and to the Lamb
> blessing and honor and glory and power
> forever and ever."

14. And the four living creatures were saying, "Amen." And the elders fell down and worshipped.

The Seals

6.1. And I looked when the Lamb opened **one of the seven seals**, then I heard one of the four living creatures saying in a voice like thunder, "You must come." 2. And I looked, and there was a white horse, (Zch 1:8, 6:3,6) and the one who sat upon it had a bow, and a crown was given to him and he came out conquering, so he could overcome *every enemy*.

6:3. And when He opened the **second seal**, I heard the second living creature saying, "You must come." 4. And another horse came out, red, (Zch 1:8, 6:2) and to the one who sat upon it, it was given to him to take peace from the earth so that they will slay one another and a great small sword[1] was given to him.

6:5. And when He opened the **third seal**, I heard the third living creature saying, "You must come." And I looked, and there was a black horse, (Zch 6:2,6) and the one who sat upon it had a balance *scale* in his hand. 6. And I heard like a voice among the four living creatures saying, "A quart of wheat for a denarius[2] and three quarts of barley for a denarius, and do not harm the olive oil and the wine."

6:7. And when He opened the **fourth seal**, I heard *the* voice of the fourth living creature saying, "You must come." 8. And I looked and there was a pale horse, like the pallor of a sickly person, and the one who sat upon it *was* named Death, and Hades was following in company with him and authority was given to them over a fourth of the earth to kill with a broad sword[3] and with famine and with death, and by beasts of the earth. (Jr 14:12, 15:3, Eze 5:12,17, 14:21, 33:27)

6:9. And when He opened the **fifth seal**, I saw under the altar the lives[4] of those slain because of the Word of God and because of the testimony which they had. 10. And a loud voice cried out saying, "How long, the Holy and True Lord, are You not judging and exonerating our blood from those who live upon the

---

1   (v.4) This is a large model of the small personal sword and could have resembled a saber.
2   (v.6) A day's pay
3   (v.8) This is the large, broad sword.
4   (v.9) Breaths or force of life

earth?" (Dt 32:43, 2Ki 9:7, Ps 79:10) 11. And a white robe[1] was given to each of them and it was told to them that they will rest[2] yet a little time, until *the number of* their fellow servants[3] and their brothers would be completed, (Ro 11:25) those who are going to be killed as also they *had been*. (Rev 20:4)

6:12. And I looked when He opened the **sixth seal**, and there was a great earthquake and the sun became black like sackcloth made of hair and the whole moon became like blood (Jl 2:31) 13. and the stars of the sky fell to the earth, as the fig tree shaken by a strong wind casts its summer figs, (Is 13:10, Eze 32:7,8, Jl 2:10, 3:15) 14. and the sky was separated like a scroll rolling up (Is 34:4) and every mountain and island was moved out of its place. 15. And the kings of the earth and the great men and the military leaders and the rich and the powerful and every slave and *the* free people hid themselves in caves and in the rocks of the mountains (Is 2:10,19,21, Jr 4:29) 16. and they were saying to the mountains and to the rocks, "You must fall on us and you must hide us (Ho 10:8) from the face of the One Who sits upon the throne and from the wrath of the Lamb, 17. because the great Day of Their wrath has come, and who is able to stand?" (Jl 2:11, Na 1:6, Mal 3:2)

The 144,000 of Israel Sealed

7.1. After these things I saw four angels standing upon the four corners of the earth, holding the four winds (Jr 49:36, Eze 37:9, Dn 7:2, Zch 6:5) of the earth so that the wind could not blow upon the earth and not upon the sea nor even upon any tree. 2. And I saw another angel going up from *the* east, having a seal of *the* living God, and in a loud voice he cried out to the four angels to whom it was given to destroy the earth and the sea 3. saying, "Do not harm the earth or the sea or the trees, until we could seal the servants of our God upon their foreheads.[4] (Eze 9:4, Re 9:4, 14:1, 22:4) 4. Then I heard the number of those who had been sealed, a hundred forty-four thousand, that they had been sealed from every tribe[5] of *the* children of Israel:

5.   having been sealed from *the* tribe of Judah twelve thousand,

 from *the* tribe of Reuben twelve thousand,

 from *the* tribe of Gad twelve thousand,

6.   from *the* tribe of Asher twelve thousand,

 from *the* tribe of Naftali twelve thousand,

 from *the* tribe of Manasseh twelve thousand,

---

1   (v.11) White garments represent being in a state of spiritual preparedness, from Ecc 9:8, "Let your garments be always white; and let your head lack no ointment."
2   (v.11) This is the short break as the attached phrase makes clear. See Rest in Glossary.
3   (v.11) The references to servants in Revelation could also be translated slaves. See Servant in Glossary.
4   (v.3) According to John's style of writing "Emet" (Truth) is the name that will be sealed on the foreheads. See John in Book Order in Glossary.
5   (v.4) The tribe of Dn is missing from this list.

7.   from *the* tribe of Simon twelve thousand,

       from *the* tribe of Levi twelve thousand,

       from *the* tribe of Issachar twelve thousand,

8.   from *the* tribe of Zebulun twelve thousand,

       from *the* tribe of Joseph twelve thousand,

       from *the* tribe of Benjamin twelve thousand having been sealed.

The Multitude from Every Nation

7:9. After these things I looked, and there was an enormous crowd, which no one was able to number, from all nations and tribes and peoples and languages, standing before the throne and before the Lamb, *who* had been clothed with white robes[1] and *they had* date palms in their hands, 10. and they were crying out in a loud voice saying,

> "Our salvation *is* with our God, the One Who sits upon the throne, and with the Lamb."
>   (1Ki 22:19, 2Chr 18:18, Ps 47:8, Is 6:1, Eze 1:26,27, Sir 1:8)

11. And all the angels and the elders and the four living creatures stood around the throne and they fell upon their faces before the throne and they worshipped God 12. saying,

> "Amen, praise and glory and wisdom and thanksgiving and honor and power and strength to our God forever and ever: amen."

7:13. And one of the elders answered, saying to me, "Who are these clothed in white robes and where did they come from?" 14. And I said to him, "My lord, you know." Then he said to me, "These are those who came out of the great affliction (Dn 12:1) and they washed their robes and they made them white in the blood of the Lamb. (Gn 49:11)

15.   'Because of this they are before the throne of God
                and they are serving Him day and night in His sanctuary,
                and the One Who sits upon the throne will spread His
                tabernacle over them.
16.   They will not hunger any longer and they will thirst no more
                and no longer will the sun and scorching heat
                fall upon them,' (Is 49:10)
17.   because the Lamb at the center of the throne is shepherding them
                (Ps 23:1, Eze 34:23)
                and He will guide them to fountains of waters of life,
                (Ps 23:2, Is 49:10, Jr 2:13)
        and God will wipe away every tear from their eyes." (Is 25:8)

---

1   (v.9) White garments represent being in a state of spiritual preparedness, from Ecc 9:8, "Let your garments be always white; and let your head lack no ointment."

The Seventh Seal and the Golden Censer

8.1. And when He opened the **seventh seal**, there was silence in heaven for about half an hour. 2. And I saw the seven angels who stood before God, and seven trumpets were given to them.

8:3. And another angel came and stood by the altar of incense, *he* had a golden censer and much incense was given to him, so that he could present the prayers of all the saints upon the golden altar which *is* before the throne. (Ps 141:2, Ex 30:1-3) 4. And the smoke of the incense ascended from the angel's hand with the prayers of the saints to the presence of God. 5. And the angel took the censer and filled it up from the coals of the altar (Lv 16:12)[1] and cast *them* to the earth, and there were thunders and sounds and lightnings and an earthquake. (Ex 19:16-19)

The Trumpets

8:6. And the seven angels who had the seven trumpets prepared themselves so that they could sound them.

8:7. And the **first trumpeted**: and there was hail and fire mixed in blood and it was cast to the earth, and a third of the earth was consumed by fire and a third of the trees were consumed by fire and all green grass was consumed by fire. (Ex 9:23-25, Eze 38:22, Wsd 16:22)

8:8. Then the **second** angel **trumpeted**: and *something* like a great fiery mountain was cast burning into the sea, and a third of the sea became blood. (Ex 7:20,21) 9. And a third of the creatures in the sea that had life died and a third of the ships were destroyed.

8:10. And the **third** angel **trumpeted**: then a great star fell from heaven, burning like a lamp and it fell upon the third of the rivers and upon the springs of the waters, 11. and the name of the star was called Apsinthos.[2] A third of the waters were made into apsinthos and many people died from the waters that were made bitter. (Jr 9:15)

8:12. Then the **fourth** angel **trumpeted**: and a third of the sun was struck and a third of the moon and a third of the stars, so that a third of them would be dark and a third of a day could not be made visible and the night likewise. (Is 13:10, Eze 32:7,8, Jl 2:10, 3:15)

8:13. Then I looked and I heard one eagle flying in the middle of the sky, saying in a loud voice, "Woe, woe, woe, *to* those who live on the earth, *because* of the remaining sounds of the trumpet which are about to be sounded by the three angels."

9.1. Then the **fifth** angel **trumpeted**: and I saw a star that had fallen out

---

1   (v.5) This is speaking of the Day of Atonement.
2   (v.11) Wormwood, absinth, bitter

from heaven to the earth,[1] then the key of the pit of the abyss was given to *the star* 2. and it opened the pit of the abyss and smoke rose from the pit like smoke of a great furnace, (Gn 19:28, Ex 19:18) and the sun and the air were darkened by the smoke from the pit. 3. And locusts came out from the smoke to the earth, (Ex 10:12,15, Wsd 16:9) and authority was given to them as the scorpions have authority[2] over the earth. 4. And it was said to them that they could not injure the grass of the earth nor any green *thing* and not any tree, only the people who do not have the seal of God on their foreheads. (Eze 9:4, Re 7:3, 14:1, 22:4) 5. And it was given to them that they could not kill them, but that they would be tormented *for* five months, and their torment *will be* like a torment of a scorpion when it would sting someone. 6. And in those days people will seek death but they will **not** find it, and they will desire to die but death flees from them. (Job 3:21, Jr 8:3, Ho 10:8)

9:7. And the appearance of the locusts *was* like horses when they had been prepared for battle, (Jl 2:4,5) and upon their heads *were* crowns like gold, and their faces *were* like faces of men, 8. and they had hair like women's hair, and their teeth were like lions' *teeth*, (Jl 1:6) 9. and they had breastplates like iron breastplates, and the sound of their wings like a sound of many chariot horses running in battle, (Jl 2:5) 10. and they had tails like scorpions and stings, and in their tails *was* their power to injure people *for* five months. 11. they had for their king the angel of the abyss, *whose* name in Hebrew *is* Abaddon,[3] and in the Greek it has *the* name Apollyon.

9:12. The **one woe** has passed. Behold! Two woes are still coming after these things.

9:13. And the **sixth** angel **trumpeted**: and I heard one voice from the four horns of the golden altar that *is* in front of God, 14. saying to the sixth angel, the one who had the trumpet, "You must release by the great river Euphrates the four angels who have been bound." 15. And the four angels who were prepared for the hour and day and month and year were released, so that they could kill the third of mankind. 16. And the number of the cavalry troops *was* twenty thousand of tens of thousands, I heard their number. 17. And then I saw the horses in my sight and those who sat upon them, having fiery breast-plates also dark blue and sulfurous, and the heads of the horses like lions' heads, and fire and smoke and sulfur were going out from their mouths. 18. And a third of mankind was killed by these three plagues, by means of the fire and the smoke and the sulfur going out from their mouths. 19. For the power of the horses was in their mouths and in their tails, for their tails were like snakes, having heads and they injure with them.

9:20. And the rest of mankind, those not killed by these three plagues,

---

1   (v.1) Satan. See Is 14:12 and Lk 10:18.
2   (v.3) Power
3   (v.11) Destruction, Hell

did not repent from the deeds of their hands, so they would not *any longer* be paying homage to the demons and idols of gold and silver and brass and copper and wood, (Dt 32:17) which things are not able to see or to hear or to walk, (Ps 115:4-7, 135:15-17, Dn 5:23) 21. and they did not repent from their murders nor from their witchcraft[1] nor from their idolatry[2] nor from their thefts.

The Angel and the Little Scroll

10.1. Then I saw another mighty angel descending from heaven clothed in a cloud, and a rainbow upon his head and his face like the sun and his feet like pillars of fire, 2. and having in his hand a little scroll *that* had been opened. And he placed his right foot upon the sea, and the left upon the ground, 3. and he cried out in a loud voice as a lion roars. And when he cried out, the seven thunders spoke their own voices. 4. And when the seven thunders spoke I was going to write, then I heard a voice from heaven saying, "You must seal what the seven thunders were speaking, and do not write these things."[3] (Dn 8:26, 12:4,9) 5. And the angel, whom I saw standing upon the sea and upon the earth,

raised his right hand to the sky
6.   and he swore by the One Who lives forever and ever,
(Dt 32:40, Dn 12:7)

Who created the sky[4] and the things in it and the earth and the things on it and the sea and the things in it, (Gn 14:19,22, Ex 20:11, Ne 9:6, Ps 146:6) that there shall be no more delay, 7. but in the days of the voice of the seventh angel, when he would be going to blow the trumpet, then the mystery of God was fulfilled as He brought the Good News by His servants the prophets. (Dn 9:6,10, Am 3:7, Zch 1:6)

10:8. And the voice from heaven which I again heard *was* speaking with me and saying, "You must go. You must take the opened scroll in the hand of the angel, the one who stands upon the sea and upon the earth." 9. And I went to the angel telling him to give the little scroll to me. And he said to me, "You must take *it* and you must devour it, and it will make your stomach bitter, but in your mouth it will be sweet as honey." (Eze 2:8, 3:1-3) 10. Then I took the little scroll from the hand of the angel and I devoured it, and in my mouth it was sweet as honey but when I ate it, it became bitter in my stomach. (Eze 2:8, 3:1-3) 11. Then they said to me, "It is necessary for you to prophesy again to many peoples and nations and languages and kings." (Jr 1:10, 25:30, Dn 3:4, 7:14)

---

1   (v.21) The Greek word translated witchcraft is pharmakon, referring to the use of drugs to cause visions and messages from spirits. See Sorcery in Glossary.
2   (v.21) Or immorality
3   (v.4) This and Re. 11:2 refer to the same time period, from 70 AD to 1967 when Israel was scattered and did not have authority over Jerusalem. From 1948 to 1967 Jordan controlled half of the city, including the temple mount.
4   (v.6) Or heaven

The Two Witnesses

11.1. And a reed like a rod was given to me, *the angel* saying, "You must rise and you must measure the sanctuary of God and the altar and *count* those who worship at it." (Eze 40:3, Zch 2:1,2) 2. And you must exclude the court outside the sanctuary[1] and do not measure this outside, because it has been given to the heathens, and they will tread upon the holy city forty-two months. (Ps 79:1, Is 63:18, Zch 12:3) 3. And I will give My two witnesses *power*, and they will prophesy one thousand two hundred sixty days clothed in sackcloth. 4. These are the two olive trees and the two lamp stands that are standing before the Lord of the Earth. (Zch 4:3,11-14[2]) 5. If anyone determines to injure them fire goes out from their mouth and devours their enemies: *yes*, if someone would purpose to injure them, it is necessary for him to be killed in this way. (2Sm 22:9, 2Ki 1:10, Ps 97:3, Jr 5:14) 6. These have the authority to close the sky so that rain would not fall the days of their prophecy, (1Ki 17:1) and they have authority upon the waters to turn them into blood, (Ex 7:17,19,20) and to strike the earth with every plague (1Sm 4:8) as often as they would want. 7. And when they finish their testimony, the beast that ascends from the abyss (Dn 7:3) will make war with them, and will overcome them (Dn 7:7,21) and he will kill them. 8. And their corpses *will be* upon the streets of the great city, which is called spiritually Sodom and Egypt, where also their Lord was crucified. 9. And they from the people and tribes and languages and nations will see their corpses three and a half days and they will not allow their corpses to be placed in a tomb. 10. And those who dwell upon the earth will rejoice over them and they will be happy and they will send gifts to one another, because these two prophets tormented those who dwell upon the earth. 11. And after the three and a half days *the* breath of life from God entered them, and they stood upon their feet, (Eze 37:5) and great fear fell upon those who saw them. 12. Then *the two* heard a loud voice from heaven saying to them, "You must ascend to this place." Then they ascended into heaven (2Ki 2:11) in the cloud, and their enemies watched them. 13. And in that hour there was a great earthquake, and a tenth of the city fell and seven thousand named of mankind were killed in the earthquake and the rest *of the people* became terrified and gave glory to the God of heaven. (Eze 38:19,20)

11:14. The **second woe** has passed. Behold the third woe[3] is coming quickly.

The Seventh Trumpet

11:15. Then the **seventh** angel **trumpeted**: and there was a loud voice in

---

1   (v.2) The outer court welcomed heathens and others who had not dealt with sin. The sanctuary is only for priests, and only those who have dealt with sin. See Sanctuary in Glossary.
2   (v.4) Zch 4:14 refers to the "two anointed ones" who are Joshua and Zerubbabel in the literal, restored second temple, but the sages say these will be Moses and Aaron or David and Aaron to represent the restoration of the kingdom and the priesthood.
3   (v.14) This is the only mention of the third woe. Could the destruction of Babylon in Re 18:10, 15, & 19 be the third woe?

heaven saying,

> "The kingdom of the World of our Lord
> and of His Messiah has come,
> and He will reign forever and ever."
> (Ex 15:18, Ps 10:16, 22:28, Dn 2:44, 7:14, Ob 21, Zch 14:9)

16. Then the twenty-four elders who were sitting upon their thrones fell upon their faces before the throne of God and they paid homage to God 17. saying,

> "We give thanks to You, Lord God of Hosts,
> Who is and Who was,
> Because You have taken Your great power
> and You have come to reign.

18.   And the heathens were enraged, (Ps 2:1, 46:6)
> and *now* Your wrath has come
> and the appointed time of the dead to be judged
> and to give the reward to Your servants the prophets
> (Dn 9:6,10, Am 3:7, Zch 1:6)
> and to the saints and to those who fear Your name,
> *both* the small and the great, (Ps 115:13)
> and to destroy those who destroy the earth."

19. Then the sanctuary of God, the one in heaven, opened and the ark of His covenant (1Ki 8:1,6, 2Chr 5:7) was seen in His sanctuary, and there were lightnings and voices and thunders and an earthquake (Ex 19:16, Est 1:1, Eze 1:13) and a violent hailstorm. (Ex 9:24)

The Woman and the Dragon

12.1. And a great miracle was seen in heaven, a woman clothed with the sun, and the moon beneath her feet and upon her head a crown of twelve stars, 2. and *she* was pregnant, and she cried out in labor and was distressed to give birth. (Is 66:7, Mic 4:10) 3. And another miracle was seen in heaven, and there was a great red *like fire* dragon[1] *which* had seven heads and ten horns (Dn 7:7) and seven crowns upon its heads, 4. and its tail was dragging a third of the stars of the sky and it cast them to the earth. (Dn 8:10) And the dragon stood before the woman, the one about to give birth, so that when her child would be born he could devour *the child*. 5. And she bore a son, (Is 7:14, 66:7) a male child, *the one* who is going to shepherd all the heathens with an iron rod. (Ps 2:9) And her child was caught away to God and to His throne. 6. And the woman fled into the desert, where she has a place there *that* was prepared by God, so that they could feed her there one thousand two hundred sixty days.

---

1   (v.3) The dragon is the giant, earth-girdling serpent-fish called Leviathan. Some say it symbolizes the great world powers, such as ancient Rome in Dn 7:7 and others as Egypt. See Is 27:1, Re 12:9.

12:7. And there was a war in heaven, Michael (Dn 10:13,21, 12:1) and his angels made war with the dragon. And the dragon and his angels battled, 8. but he was not strong enough and a place for them was still not found in heaven. 9. And the great dragon, the old serpent, the one called Devil and Satan,[1] the one who deceived the entire inhabited world, was cast to the earth, (Is 14:12) and his angels were cast with him. 10. And I heard a loud voice in heaven saying,

"Now has come the salvation and the power
and the kingdom of our God
and the authority of His Messiah,
because the accuser of our brothers has been thrown *down*,
the one who had accused them before our God
day and night. (Job 1:9-11, Zch 3:1)
11. And they overcame him because of the blood of the Lamb
and because of the word of their testimony
and they did not love their life *even* to the enduring of death itself.
12. Because of this you, the heavens and those who dwell in them,
must constantly rejoice.
Woe to the earth and the sea,
because the devil has come down to you
having great wrath,
since he has known that he has little time."

12:13. And when the dragon saw that he was thrown to the earth, he pursued the woman who gave birth to the male child. 14. And the two wings of the great eagle were given to the woman,[2] so that she could fly into the desert to her place, where she was fed there a time and times and a half time, (Dn 7:25, 12:7) away from *the* presence of the serpent. 15. And the serpent spewed water like a river from its mouth behind the woman, so that it could make her *be* swept away by a stream, drowned in the waters. 16. Then the earth helped the woman and the earth opened its mouth and swallowed the river that the dragon cast from its mouth. 17. And the dragon was angered on account of the woman and left to make war with the rest of her seed, of those who keep the commandments of God and have the testimony of Jesus.[3] (Dn 7:7,21) 18. Then he stood upon the sand of the sea.

The Two Beasts

13.1. Then I saw a beast rising from the sea, (Dn 7:3) *which* had ten horns and seven heads and upon its horns ten crowns and slanderous names[4] upon its heads. 2. And the beast that I saw was like a leopard and its feet like a bear and

1   (v.9) See Satan in Glossary.
2   (v.14) This is a parallel to Ex 19:4 when God said He bore the children of Israel on the wings of eagles when He brought them out of Egypt.
3   (v.17) See Testimony of Jesus in Glossary.
4   (v.1) There are ancient texts that have name, singular, so scholars are not sure whether this is more than one slanderous name or the same name on every head.

its mouth like a lion's mouth. (Dn 7:4-6) And the dragon gave to it its power and its throne and great authority. 3. And one of its heads *was* as if it had been slain in death, then its fatal wound was healed. And the whole earth was astonished and followed the beast 4. and they paid homage[1] to the dragon, because he gave his authority to the beast and they paid homage to the beast saying, "Who *is* like the beast and who is able to war against him?"

13:5. And the power of speech was given to him, speaking loud and blasphemous *things*, (Dn 7:8,20,25, 11:36) and authority was given to him to do *miracles*[2] *during* forty-two months. 6. And his mouth opened in blasphemies to God to revile His name and His tabernacle, those who live in His tabernacle in heaven. 7. Then it was given to him to make war with the saints and to overcome them, (Dn 7:7,21) and authority was given to him over every tribe and people and language and nation. 8. And all those who live on the earth will pay homage to him, whose name is not written (Ex 32:32,33, Ps 7:10, 69:28) in the Lamb's Book of Life, *the book* of the One Who has been slain from *the* foundation of *the* universe. (Is 53:7)

13:9. If someone has an ear he must now listen.
10.   "If someone *is to go* into captivity,
            he is taken into captivity:
if someone *is* to be killed by means of a sword
            he is killed by a sword." (Jr 15:2, 43:11)
Here is the patience and the faith of the saints.

13:11. Then I saw another beast rising from the earth, and he had two horns like a lamb and he was speaking, *roaring*, like a dragon. 12. And he carried out all the authority of the first beast before him, and he caused the earth and those dwelling in it to bow down and pay homage to the first beast, whose fatal wound was healed. 13. And he performed great miracles, so that he would make fire descend from the sky to the earth before mankind, (1Ki 18:24-39) 14. and he deceived those who lived on the earth by the miracles which were given to him to do in the sight of the beast, saying for those who lived on the earth to make an image to the beast (Dt 13:2-4) that had the wound from the small sword, but still lived. 15. And it was given to him to give a spirit to the image of the beast, so that the image of the beast could also speak and could cause as many of those that would not pay homage to the image of the beast, that they would be killed. (Dn 3:5,6) 16. And he forces everyone, the small and the great, and the rich and the poor, and the free and the slaves, so that he could give them a mark upon their right hand or upon their forehead 17. and so that no one would be able to buy or to sell except the one who had the mark, the name of the beast, or the number of its name. 18. Here is the wisdom. The one who has understanding must count

---

1   (v.4) Fall down on their knees, touching their foreheads to the ground. See Pay Homage in Glossary.
2   (v.5) The beast will even have authority to change times, affecting natural laws, Dn 7:25.

the number of the beast, for it is a number of mankind, and its number is six hundred sixty-six.

The Song of the 144,000

14.1. Then I looked and there was the Lamb standing upon Mount Zion and with Him one hundred forty-four thousand having His name and His Father's name written upon their foreheads.[1] (Eze 9:4,[2] Re 7:3, 9:4, 22:4) 2. Then I heard a sound from heaven like a sound of many waters (Eze 1:24, 43:2) and like a clap of great thunder, and the sound which I heard *was* like harpists playing on their harps. 3. And they were singing a new song (Ps 33:3, 40:3, 96:1, 98:1, 144:9, 149:1, Is 42:10) before the throne and before the four living creatures and the elders, and no one was able to learn the song except the one hundred forty-four thousand, those who had been purchased from the earth. 4. These are those who had not been stained with women, for they were virgins, these are those who follow the Lamb wherever He would go. They were purchased from mankind, first fruits to God and to the Lamb, 5. and a lie was not found in their mouth (Ps 32:2, Is 53:9, Zph 3:13), they are without blemish.

The Messages of the Three Angels

14:6. And I saw another angel flying in mid-sky, having everlasting Good News to proclaim to those who are dwelling temporarily, *sojourning*, upon the earth, and for every nation and tribe and language and people, 7. saying in a loud voice, "You must now fear God and you must now give glory to Him, because the hour of His judgment has come, and you must immediately pay homage[3] to the One Who made heaven and earth and sea and fountains of waters." (Ex 20:11, Ps 148:5)

14:8. And another, a second angel, followed saying, "She has fallen, she has fallen! Babylon the Great, by whom all the heathens had been given to drink from the wine of the wrath of her idolatry.[4]" (Is 21:9, Jr 51:7,8)

14:9. Then another, a third angel, followed them saying in a loud voice, "If someone pays homage to the beast and his image and takes his mark on his forehead or upon his hand, 10. then he will drink from the wine of the wrath of God which has been poured undiluted in the cup of His wrath (Ps 75:8, Is 51:17,22, Jr 25:15) and he will be tortured in fire and sulfur before holy angels and before the Lamb. (Gn 19:24, Ps 11:6, Eze 38:22, 3Macc 2:5) 11. And the smoke of their tormenting *fire* ascends forever, (Is 34:10) and those who pay homage to the beast and his image do not have rest[5] day or night, even if someone *just* takes the mark of his name. 12. Here is the *need for* patient endurance by the

---

1　　(v.1) The name on the foreheads will be "Emet". See John in Book Order in Glossary.
2　　(v.1) Eze 9:4-6 says to mark the saints, strike the sinners, and to begin at the sanctuary.
3　　(v.7) Fall down on their knees, touching their foreheads to the ground.
4　　(v.8) All forms of idolatry, see Harlot in Glossary.
5　　(v.11) The Greek word for rest here refers to a short break, like a coffee break. In their torment they will not have even a moment's rest.

saints, those who keep the commandments of God and their faith in Jesus."

14:13. Then I heard a voice from heaven saying, "You must now write: 'Blessed are the dead, those who die in *the* Lord from now on.'" "Indeed," says the Spirit, "that they will rest[1] from their labors, for their works are following in company with them."

The Harvest of the Earth

14:14. Then I looked, and there was a white cloud, and sitting upon the cloud like a Son of Man, (Dn 7:13) *Who* had a gold crown on His head and a sharp sickle in His hand. 15. Then another angel came out of the sanctuary crying in a loud voice to the One Who was sitting on the cloud, "You must now send your sickle and you must now reap, because the time to reap has come, because the harvest of the earth has withered."[2] (Jl 3:13; 4:13 in Tanakh) 16. Then the One Who was sitting on the cloud threw His sickle forcefully over the earth and the earth was harvested.

14:17. Then another angel, *who* also had a sharp sickle, came out of the sanctuary, the one in heaven. 18. And *still* another angel, who had authority over fire, came out from the altar, and he called in a loud voice to the one who had the sharp sickle saying, "You must now send your sharp sickle and you must at once gather in the bunches of grapes of the vine of the earth, because its grapes have ripened." 19. Then the angel threw his sickle forcefully to the earth and he gathered in the vine[3] of the earth and he cast *it* into the great winepress of the wrath of God.[4] 20. And the wine press was trod outside the city and blood came out from the wine press as far as the bridles of the horses for one thousand six hundred stadia.[5] (Is 63:3, Lm 1:15)

The Angels with the Last Plagues

15.1. Then I saw another great and marvelous miracle in heaven, seven angels having seven final plagues, (Lv 26:21) because with them the wrath of God is completed.

15:2. And I saw like a glassy sea *that* had been mixed with fire, and those who overcame the beast and his image and the number of his name *were* standing upon the glassy sea with harps of God. 3. And they were singing the song of Moses, the servant of God, and the song of the Lamb saying, (Ex 15:1)

---

1   (v.13) This is just a short break from their labors -- those in heaven will be busy. See Rest in Glossary.

2   (v.15) God has been patient. See 2Peter 3:9.

3   (v.19) The vine is used to represent numerous things, but there are two kinds of vines: Holy and strange. Strange represents Sodom, the evils with which the wrath of God is dealing in this passage.

4   (v.19) The winepress of the wrath of God is from Jl 4:13, while Jl 4:2 says the nations will gather at the Valley of Jehoshaphat, the Valley of God's Judgment, from v.12. This valley is about twelve miles south of Jerusalem.

5   (v.20) About 180 miles. See Re. 16:16

"Great and wonderful *are* Your deeds, (Ex 15:11, Ps 92:5, 111:2, 139:14)
>   Lord God of Hosts:[1]
righteous and true *are* Your ways, (Dt 32:4, Ps 145:17)
>   O King of the nations:[2] (Jr 10:10, Theodotion, Tob 13:7, En 9:4)
4.   who would **not** fear You, Lord,
>   and will not glorify Your name? (Jr 10:6,7)
because only *You are* undefiled by sin,
>   because all the nations will come
>   and bow down to pay homage before You,
>   (Ps 86:9, Mal 1:11)
because Your righteous deeds have been revealed."

15:5. Then after these things I looked, and the sanctuary of the tabernacle of the testimony in heaven opened, (Ex 38:21, 40:34) 6. and seven angels, holding the seven plagues, came out from the sanctuary clothed in pure brilliant linen, and gold belts had been fastened about their chests. 7. And one of the four living creatures gave to the seven angels seven golden vials filled with the wrath of God, the One Who lives forever and ever. (Ps 75:8, Is 51:17,22, Jr 25:15) 8. And the sanctuary was filled with smoke from the glory of God and from His power, (Ex 40:34, 1Ki 8:10,11, 2Chr 5:13,14, Is 6:4, Eze 44:4) and no one was able to enter the sanctuary until the seven plagues of the seven angels were completed.

The Bowls of God's Wrath

16.1. Then I heard a loud voice from the sanctuary (Is 66:6) saying to the seven angels, "You must go and pour out upon the earth the seven vials of the wrath of God." (Ps 69:24, Jr 10:25, Eze 22:31, Zph 3:8)

16:2. Then the **first** came and poured his **vial** to the earth, and vile and evil sores came upon mankind, those who had the mark of the beast, those who bowed down to his image. (Ex 9:10, Dt 28:35)

16:3. Then the **second** *angel* poured out his **vial** into the sea, and it became like *the* blood of a dead *man*, and every living being of the things in the sea died. (Ex 7:17-21)

16:4. Then the **third** poured out his **vial** into the rivers and the fountains of the waters, and they became blood. (Ex 7:19-24, Ps 78:44) 5. And I heard the angel of the waters saying,

"You are righteous, the One Who is and Who was, the Undefiled,
>   because You have judged these things,
6.   because they poured out *the* blood of saints and prophets (Ps 79:3)
>   and You have given them blood to drink, (Is 49:26)
which they deserve."

---

1   (v.3) This could also be translated Almighty, but see Lord of Hosts in Glossary.
2   (v.3) Or King of the heathens

7. Then I heard the altar saying,

> "Indeed, Lord God of Hosts,[1]
>> Your judgments *are* true and righteous." (Ps 16:9, 119:137)

16:8. Then the **fourth** poured out his **vial** upon the sun, and it was given to it to scorch mankind with fire. 9. And mankind was burned *by* a great heat and they blasphemed the name of God, the One Who had authority over these plagues, but they did not repent to give Him glory.

16:10. Then the **fifth** poured out his **vial** upon the throne of the beast, and its kingdom became darkened, (Ex 10:21, Is 8:22) and they chewed their tongues from the pain, 11. yet they blasphemed the God of heaven because of their pain and because of their sores but they did not repent from their deeds.

16:12. Then the **sixth** poured out his **vial** upon the great river Euphrates and its water dried up, (Is 11:15, 44:27, Jr 50:38, 51:36) so that the way of the kings from the east could be prepared. 13. And I saw three unclean spirits like frogs *come* from the mouth of the dragon and from the mouth of the beast and from the mouth of the false prophet: 14. for spirits of demons were performing miracles, which were going out over the kingdoms of the whole inhabited world to gather them into the war of the great Day of the God of the Hosts. (Mt 25:31) 15. "Behold I am coming as a thief. Blessed is the one who is awake and keeps his garments *ready*, so that he would not walk naked[2] and they would see his shame." 16. And He gathered them into the place called in Hebrew Har Megiddo.[3] (Jdg 5:19, 2Ki 9:27, 23:29, Zch 12:11)

16:17. Then the **seventh** poured out his **vial** upon the air and a loud voice came out of the sanctuary (Is 66:6) from the throne saying, "It is finished." 18. And there were lightnings and sounds and thunders and there was a violent earthquake, such as had not happened since mankind came upon the earth, so powerful an earthquake as this. (Dn 12:1) 19. Then the great city was *split* in three parts and the cities of the heathens fell. And Babylon the great was remembered before God, to give to her the cup of the wine of the wrath of His punishment. (Ps 75:8, Is 51:17,22, Jr 25:15) 20. Then every island fled and mountains were not found. 21. And great hail as heavy as talents[4] came down from the sky on mankind, and mankind blasphemed God because of the plague of the hail, because this plague is exceedingly great.

The Great Harlot and the Beast

17.1. Then one of the seven angels who had the seven vials came and spoke with me saying, "Come here, I will show you the judgment of the great

---

1   (v.7) This could also be translated Almighty, but see Lord of Hosts in Glossary.
2   (v.15) In the Hebrew idiom, to be in a loincloth, underwear, was to be naked.
3   (v.16) The Greek term is Harmageddon, usually written Armageddon, over 40 miles north of Jerusalem.
4   (v.20) A talent weighs about seventy-five pounds.

harlot who sits upon many waters,[1] (Jr 51:13) 2. with whom the kings of the earth did fornicate and those who dwell on the earth did become drunk from the wine of her idolatry."[2] (Is 23:17, Jr 51:7) 3. and he carried me away in *the* spirit into *the* wilderness. And I saw a woman sitting upon a scarlet beast, full of blasphemous names, *which* had seven heads and ten horns. 4. And the woman was clothed *in* purple and scarlet and adorned with gold and precious stones and pearls, (Eze 28:13) having in her hand a gold cup filled with detestable and unclean things of her idolatry[3] 5. and a name had been written upon her forehead, "Mystery, Babylon the Great, the Mother of the Fornications and of the Detestable Things of the Earth." 6. And I saw the woman drunk from the blood of the saints and from the blood of those testifying about Jesus.

And I marveled, seeing her with great amazement. 7. And the angel said to me, "Why were you astonished? I will tell you the mystery of the woman and the beast which is carrying her, the one that has the seven heads and the ten horns. 8. The beast you saw which was *earlier* and is not *any longer* then it is going to ascend from the abyss (Dn 7:3) and go into destruction. Then those who dwell upon the earth, whose names are not written in the Book of Life (Ex 32:32,33, Ps 69:28, Dn 12:1) from *the* foundation of *the* world, will be amazed, when they see the beast, because it was and it is not and it will be present. (Dn 7:3) 9. Here is *the need* for a mind that has wisdom. The seven heads are seven mountains, where the woman is staying on them. And the *seven heads* are seven kings: 10. five fell, one is, the other has not yet come, and when he would come, it is necessary for him to remain *only* a little while. 11. And the beast who was and who is not, even he himself is *the* eighth *king* and is from the seven, and he is going into destruction. 12. And the ten horns (Dn 7:24) that you saw are ten kings, who did not yet take a kingdom, but they take authority as kings for one hour with the beast. 13. These have one purpose and they impart their power and authority to the beast. 14. These will make war against the Lamb but the Lamb will conquer them, because He is Lord of Lords and King of Kings (Dt 10:17, Dn 2:47, 2Macc 13:4, 3Macc 5:35, En 9:4) and those with Him *are* called and chosen and faithful.

17:15. Then he said to me, "The waters which you saw, on which the harlot is seated, are people and crowds and nations and languages. 16. Then the ten horns which you saw and the beast, these will hate the harlot and will make her desolate and naked and devour her flesh and will burn her in fire. (Lv 21:9) 17. For God gave into their hearts to do His purpose and to make one judgment[4] and to give their kingdom to the beast until the words of God will be fulfilled. 18. And the woman whom you saw is the great city, the one which reigns over

---

1   (v.1) Many waters can be used as a symbol for an enormous crowd of people, as in v. 15 and Re. 19:6.
2   (v.2) Or immorality, see Harlot in Glossary.
3   (v.4) Or immorality
4   (v.17) To be in unity

the kings of the earth."

The Fall of Babylon

18.1. After these things I saw another angel, *who* had great authority, descending from heaven, and the earth was given light[1] by his glory. 2. And he cried out in a strong voice saying,

> "She has fallen, Babylon the Great has fallen, (Is 21:9, Jr 51:8)
> > and she has become a dwelling place of demons
> and a prison of every unclean spirit
> > and a prison of every unclean bird
> > and a prison of every unclean and hated beast,[2]
> > (Is 13:21, 34:11, Jr 50:39, Bar 4:35)

3.
> because all the nations have drunk from the wine
> > of the passion of her idolatry[3] (Is 23:17, Jr 51:7)
> and the kings of the earth committed adultery with her
> > and the merchants of the earth became
> > > wealthy from the power of her excessive wealth."

18:4. Then I heard another voice from heaven saying,
> "My people, you must immediately come out from her
> > (Is 48:20, 52:11, Jr 50:8, 51:6,9,45)
> > so that you would not share her sins,
> and so that you would not take any
> > of her plagues,

5.
> because her sins reached as far as heaven (Gn 18:20,21, Jr 51:9)
> > and God remembered her crimes.

6.
> You must now reward her as she also rewarded (Ps 137:8, Jr 50:15,29)
> > and you must immediately pay back double *to her* according
> > > to her deeds.
> > In the cup in which she mixed you must now
> > > mix double to her,

7.
> who did glorify herself and live sensually,
> > You must now give so much torment and mourning to her.
> Because in her heart she says that
> > 'I sit as Queen
> and I am not a widow
> > and I will **never** see mourning.'

8.
> Because of this her plagues will come in one Day,
> > death and mourning and famine,
> and she will be burned up in fire, (Lv 21:9)

---

1   (v.1) This refers both to the light of glory and to the light of understanding.
2   (v.2) This last line of v. 2 was dropped by a number of ancient manuscripts, but included by the 4th Ed. UBS Greek text.
3   (v.3) Or immorality, see Harlot in Glossary.

because the Lord God Almighty *is* the One
Who is judging her." (Is 47:7-9, Jr 50:34)

18:9. Then the kings of the earth, those who committed adultery[1] with her and lived luxuriously *with her*, will weep and mourn, when they see the smoke of her burning, (Eze 26:16, 27:30-35) 10. standing from afar because of fear of her torment, saying,

"Oh! It can't be![2] The great city,
Babylon the powerful city,
because your judgment came in one hour." (Eze 26:17, Dn 4:30)

18:11. And the merchants of the earth were weeping and mourning over her, because no one is buying their cargo any longer, (Eze 27:36) 12. cargo of gold and silver and precious stones and pearls and fine linen and purple cloth and silk and scarlet, and every vessel of citron wood and every ivory vessel and every vessel of very precious wood and copper and iron and marble, 13. and cinnamon and amomum[3] and incense and perfume and frankincense and wine and olive oil and fine flour and wheat and cattle and sheep, and horses and carriages and slaves,[4] and lives of men. (Eze 27:12,13,22)

14.   And the ripe fruits from your craving for life's forbidden things
have been taken away from you,
and all the luxuries and brilliance
have been lost, *taken* from you
and **no longer** will they find these things.

15. Their merchants who became rich from her will stand from afar because of the fear of her torment, crying and mourning, (Eze 27:36) 16. saying,

"Oh! It can't be![5] The great city,
the one clothed in fine linen
and purple and scarlet
and adorned in gold
and precious stone and pearl," (Eze 28:13)

17. because in one hour so much wealth was laid waste.

And every pilot and everyone who sails along the coast and sailors and as many as *are* working the sea stood from afar (Eze 27:27-29) 18. and they were crying out while they were watching the smoke of her burning saying, "What *other city* is like the great city?" 19. And they were throwing dirt on their heads

---

1   (v.9) Any form of idolatry, see Harlot in Glossary.
2   (v.10) Literally the text has, "Woe, woe," which is a gasp of horror, doubled for emphasis.
3   (v.13) Indian spice
4   (v.13) This Greek word is literally "bodies," referring to slaves in the Greek and Roman sense. See Slaves in Glossary.
5   (v.10, v. 16 & v.19) Literally the text has, "Woe, woe," which is a gasp of horror, doubled for emphasis, here translated "Oh, it can't be!" Could this be the third woe of Re 11:14?

and they were crying out weeping and mourning saying,

> "Oh! It can't be! The great city,
>> in which all those who had ships in the sea
>> had gained great wealth from her expensive things,
> that in one hour she was laid waste." (Eze 27:30-34)

20.   Heaven, and saints and apostles and prophets,
>> you must perpetually rejoice in her,
> because God condemned her judgment of you. *He has vindicated you.*

18:21. And one strong angel brought a stone like a great millstone and cast it forcefully into the sea saying,

> "Like this, the great city Babylon
>> will be cast in violence
>> and it would **never** again be found. (Jr 51:63,64, Eze 26:21)

22.   Then *the* sound of harpists and musicians
>> and flute players and trumpeters
>> will **never** again be heard in you, (Is 24:8, Eze 26:13)

> and **no** craftsman of any skill
>> will **ever** again be found in you,
> and a sound of a millstone will **never** again be heard in you,

23.   And a light of a lamp
>> will **never** again be visible in you
> and a voice of a bridegroom and a bride
>> will **never** again be heard in you, (Jr 7:34, 16:9, 25:10)
> because your merchants were the great men of the earth, (Is 23:8)
>> because all the heathens were deceived by your sorcery,[1]
>> (Is 47:9)

24.   and in her was found *the* blood of prophets and of saints
>> and all those who had been slain upon the earth."
>> (Jr 51:49, Eze 24:7)

19.1. After these things I heard like a great sound of an enormous crowd in heaven saying,

> "Hallelujah: (Tob 13:18)
> the salvation and the glory and the power of our God!

2.   For His judgments *are* true and righteous:
>> (Ps 19:9, 119:137)
> because He has judged the great harlot

---

1   (v.23) The Greek word translated sorcery is pharmakeia, referring to the use of drugs. See Sorcery in Glossary.

who was corrupting the earth with her fornication,
and He did avenge the blood of His servants
out of her hand." (Dt 32:43, 2Ki 9:7, Ps 79:10)

3. And they said a second time,

"Hallelujah:
and her smoke rises forever and ever." (Is 34:10)

4. Then the twenty-four elders and the four living creatures fell and worshipped God, the One Who sits upon the throne, (1Ki 22:19, 2Chr 18:18, Ps 47:8, Is 6:1, Eze 1:26,27, Sir 1:8) saying,
"Amen Hallelujah,"

The Marriage Supper of the Lamb

19:5. And a voice came out from the throne saying,

"You, all His servants, and those who fear Him,
the least and the greatest, (Ps 115:13)
must continually sing praises
in honor of our God." (Ps 22:23, 134:1, 135:1)

6. And I heard a noise like an enormous crowd even like *the* sound of many waterfalls (Eze 1:24, 43:2) and like a sound of strong thunders saying,

"Hallelujah, because *the* Lord our God, the Lord of Hosts,[1] has come
to reign. (Ex 15:18, Ps 22:28, 93:1, 99:1, Dn 7:14, Zch 14:9)
7.   Let us rejoice and be glad
and we will give Him the glory,
because the marriage festival of the Lamb has come
and His wife has prepared herself[2]
8.   and it was given to her that she would be clothed
in brilliant pure fine linen:
for the fine linen is the righteous deeds[3] of the saints." (Is 61:10)

19:9. Then he said to me, "You must now write: 'Blessed are those who have been called to the wedding[4] supper of the Lamb.'" And he said to me, "These are the true words of God." 10. Then I fell before his feet to pay homage to him. And he said to me, "Stop! Don't do that: I am a fellow servant with you and your brothers who have the testimony of Jesus: you must now pay homage to God. For the testimony of Jesus is the Spirit of Prophecy."[5]

---

1   (v.6) This could also be translated Almighty, but see Lord of Hosts in Glossary.
2   (v.7) The bride having to prepare herself means that individually and collectively each one of us must prepare for the supper. Each of us must do the things in Mt 25:35-40. See Mt 7:21.
3   (v.8) There is no robe for the person who has not done righteous deeds. See Mitsvah in Glossary.
4   (v.9) See Wedding in Glossary.
5   (v.10) See Testimony of Jesus in Glossary.

The Rider on the White Horse

19:11. Then I saw heaven opened, (Eze 1:1) and there was a white horse (Zch 1:8) and the One Who sits on it, called Faithful and True, and He judges in righteousness (Ps 96:13, Is 11:4) and He makes war. 12. And His eyes are like a flame of fire, (Dn 10:6) and upon His head many crowns. He has a name written which no one knows except Himself, 13. and is clothed in a garment dyed in blood, (Gn 49:11, Is 63:1-3) and His name has been called the Word of God. 14. And the troops in heaven[1] were following Him on white horses, being clothed in pure fine white linen.[2] 15. And a large sharp sword[3] was going out of His mouth, (Is 49:2) so that with it He could slaughter the heathens, and He will shepherd them with an iron rod, (Ps 2:9) and He treads the wine press (Is 63:3, Lm 1:15, Jl 3:13) of the wine of the burning wrath of the God of Hosts, 16. and He has upon His garment, even over His thigh[4] a name *that* has been written: "King of Kings and Lord of Lords."[5] (Dt 10:17, Dn 2:47, 2Macc 13:4, 3Macc 5:35, En 9:4)

19:17. Then I saw one angel standing in the sun and he cried out in a loud voice saying to all the birds flying in *the* sky,[6] "Come, you must gather for the great supper of God 18. so that you could eat *the* flesh of kings and flesh of commanders of thousands and flesh of mighty men and flesh of horses and of those who sit upon them and flesh of all both freeborn and slaves, both small and great." (Eze 39:17-20) 19. And I saw the beast and the kings of the earth and their soldiers gathering to make war with the One Who was sitting on the horse and with His army. (Ps 2:2, Mt 25:31) 20. Then the beast was seized and with him the false prophet, the one who did the miracles in front of him, by which he deceived those who took the mark of the beast and those who paid homage to his image: the two were cast alive into the lake of fire which was burning in brimstone. (Is 30:33) 21. Then the rest were killed with the sword[7] which was coming out from the mouth of the One Who was sitting upon the horse, and all the birds were fed from their flesh. (Eze 39:17,20)

The Thousand Years

20.1. Then I saw an angel descending from heaven, who had the key of the abyss and a large chain in his hand. 2. And he arrested the dragon, the old serpent, who is *the* Devil and Satan,[8] then he bound him for a thousand years

---

1   (v.14) These are the angels of the Lord of Hosts.

2   (v.14) White garments represent being in a state of spiritual preparedness, from Ecc 9:8, "Let your garments be always white; and let your head lack no ointment."

3   (v.15) This is the large, broad, two-edged sword that only the strongest could handle.

4   (v.16) The name is written on the garment that covers His thigh.

5   (v.16) Verses 13-19 have these references: Re 2:17, Is 63:1-3, Jn 1:1,14, Is 49:2, Re 1:16, 2:12,16, Ps 2:9, Re 12:5, Is 63:3, Lm 1:15, Jl 3:13, Re 14:20, Am 3:13, 4:13, Re 1:8, 4:8, 11:17, 15:3, 16:7,14, 19:6, 21:22, Dt 10:17, Dn 2:47, 2Macc 13:4, 3Macc 5:35, En 9:4, 1Tim 6:15, Re 17:14, Ez 39:17-20, Ps 2:2.

6   (v.17) The Greek has mid-sky, referring to high flying birds, such as eagles.

7   (v.21) The great large sword that only the strongest could use.

8   (v. 2 & v.7) See Satan in Glossary.

3. and cast him into the abyss and shut and sealed *the abyss* above him, so that he could not deceive the heathens any longer until the thousand years would be completed. After these things it is necessary for him to be loosed for a short time.

20:4. Then I saw thrones and *those that* sat upon them and judgment was given to them, (Dn 7:9,22,27) and *I saw* the lives of those who had been beheaded because of the testimony of Jesus[1] and because of the Word of God and who did not worship the beast or his image and did not take the mark upon their foreheads or upon their hands. (Re 6:9-11) Then they became alive again and reigned with the Messiah one thousand years. 5. The rest of the dead did not become alive again until the thousand years were completed. This is the first resurrection.[2] 6. Blessed and holy *is* the one who has a part in the first resurrection: the second death has no power to destroy them: but they will be priests of God and of the Messiah and they will reign with Him (Ex 19:6, Is 61:6) the thousand years.[3]

The Defeat of Satan[4]

20:7. Then when the thousand years are completed, Satan will be loosed from his prison 8. and he will come out to deceive the heathens who are in the four corners of the earth, (Eze 7:2) Gog and Magog, (Eze 38:2) to gather them for the war, whose number is as the sand of the sea. 9. And they went up upon the breadth of the earth and they surrounded the army of the saints and the beloved city, and fire descended from the sky and consumed them. (2Ki 1:10, Eze 38:22, 39:6) 10. Then the devil, the one who was deceiving them, was thrown violently into the lake of fire and brimstone (Is 30:33, Gn 19:24, Ps 11:6, Eze 38:22, 3Macc 2:5) in which place also the beast and the false prophet *had been cast*, and they will be tormented day and night forever and ever.

The Judgment at the Great White Throne

20:11. Then I saw a great white throne and the One Who sits upon it, from Whose presence the earth (Ps 114:3,7) and the sky fled and a place was not found for them. 12. Then I saw the dead, the great and the small, standing before the throne. And scrolls were opened, and another scroll was opened, which is of life, (Ex 32:32,33, Ps 69:28, Dn 12:1) and the dead were judged according to their deeds, (Ps 28:4, 62:12, Pr 24:12, Is 59:18, Jr 17:10) by what had been written in the scrolls. (Dn 7:9,10) 13. Then the sea gave up the dead that *were* in it and death and Hades gave up the dead, those in them, and each was judged according to his works. 14. Then Death and Hades were thrown violently into the lake of fire. This is the second death, the lake of fire. 15. And if someone

---

1   (v.4) See Testimony of Jesus in Glossary.
2   (v.5) See Resurrection in Glossary.
3   (v.6) This is generally understood to be one thousand, but this word, xilia, was also used in a general sense, referring to a very large number.
4   (Caption) See Satan in Glossary.

was not found written in the Book of Life, he was cast into the lake of fire. (Is 30:33)

The New Sky and the New Earth

21.1. Then I saw a new sky[1] and a new Earth. (Is 65:17, 66:22) For the first sky and the first Earth passed away, *fading from sight*, and the sea was no longer. 2. Then I saw the holy city, (Is 52:1) new[2] Jerusalem, descending from heaven, from God, prepared like a bride when she was adorned for her husband. (Is 61:10) 3. Then I heard a loud voice from the throne saying, "Behold the dwelling of God with mankind, and He will dwell with them and they will be His people, and God Himself, *Emanuel*, will be with them, their God, (Lv 26:11,12, 2Chr 6:18, Eze 37:27, Zch 2:10) 4. and He will wipe away every tear from their eyes and death will no longer be, there will be neither mourning nor crying or pain, because the first things went away." (Is 25:8, 35:10, 65:19)

21:5. Then the One Who sits on the throne said, "Behold I am making all things new," then He said, "You must now write, because these words are faithful and true." 6. Then He said to me, "It has been done! I AM[3] the Alef and the Tav,[4] the Beginning and the End. (Is 44:6, 48:12) I will give freely from the fountain of the water of life to the one who thirsts. (Is 55:1) 7. The one who conquers will inherit these things and I will be God to him and he will be a son to Me. (2Sm 7:14) 8. But for the cowardly, *those of little faith, the* unbelieving, abominable, murderers, immoral, sorcerers,[5] idolaters, and all the liars their part *is* in the lake that burns fire and sulfur, (Is 30:33, Gn 19:24, Ps 11:6, Eze 38:22, 3Macc 2:5) this is the second death."

The New Jerusalem

21:9. Then one of the seven angels, of those who have the seven vials full of the seven last plagues, came and spoke with me saying, "You must come, I will show you the bride, the wife of the Lamb." 10. Then he took me away in *the* spirit to a great and high mountain, and he showed me the holy city, Jerusalem, (Eze 40:2) descending out of the sky from God, 11. having the glory of God, her radiance like a precious stone as a crystal jasper stone. (Is 60:1,2,19) 12. Having a great and high wall, *which* has twelve gates and upon the gates twelve angels and names *that* have been written upon *the gates*, which are the names of the twelve tribes of *the* Children of Israel: (Ex 28:21) 13. on *the* east three gates and

---

1   (v.1) This could also be translated Heaven, but Heaven is eternal. The planet Earth and even the Solar System may well pass away, but the Universe will remain. See 2Peter 3:10.
2   (v.2) From the Hebrew usage this could be renewed. This also applies to Re. 3:12 & 21:5.
3   (v.6) The great I AM, ani in Hebrew in the verses referenced here: See Anokhi in Glossary.
4   (v.6) Alef is the first letter of the Hebrew alphabet, tav is the last. They spell a word that is placed in front of the direct object of a verb. See Alef in Glossary.
5   (v.8) The Greek word translated sorcerers is pharmakois, referring to people who prepare drugs to cause visions or messages from spirits. See Sorcery in Glossary.

on *the* north three gates and on *the* south three gates and on *the* west three gates. (Eze 48:30-35) 14. And the wall of the city had twelve foundations and upon them twelve names of the twelve apostles of the Lamb.

21:15. And the one who was speaking with me had a golden measuring rod, so that he could measure the city and its gates and its wall. 16. And the city is lying square with its length as great as the width. And he measured the city with the reed to twelve thousand stadia,[1] the length and the breadth and its height are equal. 17. Then he measured its wall one hundred forty-four forearms of a man,[2] a measure men use, which the angel was using. (Eze 48:16:17) 18. And the material of its wall was jasper and the city pure gold like pure *transparent* glass. 19. The foundations of the wall of the city were adorned with every precious stone: (Is 54:11,12) the first foundation jasper, the second sapphire, the third chalcedony, the fourth emerald, 20. the fifth sardonyx, the sixth sardius, the seventh chrysolite, the eighth beryl, the ninth topaz, the tenth chrysoprase, the eleventh hyacinth, the twelfth amethyst, 21. and the twelve gates *were* twelve pearls, in the midst of each one of the gates was *a door made* out of one pearl. And the wide street of the city *was* pure gold like translucent glass.

21:22. And I did not see a sanctuary in it for the Lord God of Hosts[3] and the Lamb are its sanctuary. 23. And the city has no need of the sun nor of the moon, that they would give light to *the city*, for the glory of God, and the light of the Lamb, did illuminate it. (Is 60:19,20) 24. And the multitudes will walk by its light, (Is 60:3, Ps Sol 17:34) and the kings of the earth will bring their glory into it, 25. and its gates would **never** be shut *all* day, for there will not be night there, (Is 60:11, Zch 14:7) 26. and they will bring the glory and the honor of the nations into it. (Ps 72:10,11, Ps Sol 17:34) 27. And **no** unclean thing and **no** one doing a detestable *thing* or *telling* a lie could enter it, (Is 52:1) only those whose *names* have been written in the Scroll of Life of the Lamb. (Ex 32:32, Ps 69:28, Dn 12:1)

22.1. Then *the angel* showed me a river of water of life, bright as crystal, going out from the throne[4] of God and the Lamb.[5] (Eze 47:1, Jl 3:18, Zch 14:8) 2. In *the* middle of its street, also on each side of the river, *is* a tree of life making twelve fruit, yielding its fruit each month, and the leaves of the tree *are used* for *the* healing of the multitudes.[6] (Gn 2:9, 3:22, Eze 47:12) 3. And there will no

---

1   (v.16) One thousand five hundred miles

2   (v.17) The forearm is a cubit and 144 equal 216 feet.

3   (v.22) This could also be translated Almighty, but see Lord of Hosts in Glossary.

4   (v.1) There is one throne because God and the Lamb are One, Jn 10:30.

5   (v.1) See Re 3:21.

6   (v.2) Some say this must be translated nations, not multitudes or heathens because the former things such as sickness have passed away. If sickness has passed away, then other evils, such as national pride and prejudices, would also have passed away. The leaves take away the results of every evil thing that has come against any person or group. In the same way that a person who has been healed of polio still has the crippling effect, those who have been healed from various evils carry the scars. The leaves of the trees will remove even the scars. See Tree of Life in

longer be anything there *that is* cursed. And the throne of God and of the Lamb will be in it, and His servants will serve Him 4. and they will see His face, (Ps 17:15, 42:2) and His name *will be* upon their foreheads.[1] (Eze 9:4, Re 7:3, 9:4, 14:1) 5. And there will no longer be night and they will not need *the* light of a lamp or *the* light of *the* sun, (Zch 14:7) because the Lord God will give light upon them, and *those whose names are written in the Lamb's Book of Life* will reign[2] forever and ever. (Is 60:19,20, Dn 7:18,27)

The Coming of Messiah

22:6. Then he said to me, "These words *are* faithful and true, and the Lord God of the spirits of the prophets sent His angel to show to His servants what must happen in a short time." (Dn 2:28,29,45) 7. "So behold! I am coming quickly. Blessed is the one who keeps the words of the prophecy in this scroll."

22:8. And I am John, the one who heard and saw these things. And when I heard and I saw, I fell to pay homage before the feet of the angel, the one who showed me these things. 9. But he said to me, "Stop! I am a fellow servant of yours and of your brothers the prophets and those who keep the words of this scroll: you must now pay homage to God." 10. And he said to me, "Do not seal the words of prophecy in this scroll, for the time is near. (Dn 12:4) 11. Let the one who does wrong still do wrong and the one who is filthy still be filthy and let the righteous still do righteousness and let the holy still be holy."

22:12. "Behold! I am coming quickly, and My reward *is* with Me (Is 40:10, 62:11), to reward to each one according to his deeds.[3] (Ps 28:4, 62:12, Pr 24:12, Is 59:18, Jr 17:10) 13. I am the Alef and the Tav,[4] the First and the Last, the Beginning and the End. (Is 44:6, 48:12)

22:14. "Blessed are those who are washing their robes, so that He will give them permission to use the tree of life[5] (Gn 2:9, 3:22, Eze 47:12) and they could enter the gates of the city. 15. And outside *will be* the dogs and the sorcerers[6] and the immoral and the murderers and the idolaters and everyone loving and doing falsehoods.

22:16. "I, Jesus, did send My messenger to testify these things to you for the congregations.[7] I AM the Root and the Offspring of David, (Is 11:1,10)

Glossary.
1   (v.4) The name of God will be "Emet" (Truth) according to the Zohar. See John in Book Order in Glossary.
2   (v.5) The saints will reign as priests in one kingdom, as in Re. 1:6.
3   (v.12) Mitsvot. See Mitsvah in Glossary.
4   (v.13) Alef is the first letter in the Hebrew alphabet, tav is the last. Together they make a word that is placed in front of the direct object of the verb. See Alef in Glossary.
5   (v.14) See Tree of Life in Glossary.
6   (v.15) The Greek word translated sorcerers is pharmakoi, which refers to people devoted to using drugs to cause visions or messages from spirits. See Sorcery in Glossary.
7   (v.16) Although often translated "church," no Greek word meaning church is used in the NT. See Congregation in Glossary.

the Bright Morning Star. (Nu 24:17) 17. And the Spirit and the bride are saying, 'You must come.' And the one who hears must now say, 'You must come.' And the one who thirsts must come faithfully, the one who wants must now take *the* water[1] of life as a free gift." (Ex 14:22, Is 55:1)

22:18. I am testifying to everyone who hears the words of the prophecy in this scroll: if someone would add to these things, God will add to him the plagues that have been written in this scroll, 19. and if someone would cancel from the words of the scroll of this prophecy, God will cancel his part in the tree of life and the holy city, of those things that have been written in this scroll. (Dt 4:2, 12:32)

22:20. The One Who testifies these things says, "Indeed, I am coming quickly." Amen, You must come, Lord Jesus.

22:21. The grace of the Lord Jesus *be* with all *of you.*

---

1   (v.17) Water is a metaphor for the Torah, based on Ex 14:22 & Is 55:1.

~ GLOSSARY ~

Section I

Section I is general, Section II lists an English name with its original Hebrew name.

Adultery   The verses from John 7:53b-8:11 were added to the New Testament in the fifth century and teach a valuable lesson, which is that we are not to be quick to condemn others, but each of us must know and do what is right. The textual scholars determined that these verses were added by examining ancient manuscripts rather than by criticizing content, but here the content too tells us the person who wrote these verses was not familiar with Jewish Scripture and practice. If you catch someone in adultery, you have to catch two because one person cannot commit adultery: Yet only the woman was brought to be stoned. That was the practice of the societies of the ancient world, except for Judaism. In all the other societies, except for a few that were matriarchal, the wife was a chattel, a possession of the husband, so if she was caught in adultery it was a crime against her husband and he could punish her any way he wished. She was just like any other possession, to be treated like furniture or a slave. Adultery to those societies was not sin. It was a crime against the husband. Only in Judaism was adultery a sin against God. Because it was a sin against God both participants were to be stoned -- it was not a lesser sin for one than for the other. Leviticus 20:10 and Deuteronomy 22:22 say "If a man is found lying with a woman married to a husband, then they shall both of them die, both the man who lay with the woman, and the woman; so shall you put away evil from Israel."

Although the verses, John 7:53b-8:11, were added long after the Scriptures were written, we need to keep the basic message of the addition, that we are to love the sinner, but hate the sin. It is more important for each of us to focus on his own shortcomings rather than on the shortcomings of others.

461

Agapao is an ancient Greek verb used well over one hundred times in the NT. Its meaning in Classic Greek was to welcome, entertain, and, in reference to things, to be content. In first century Israel the meaning was love, as in "love your neighbor" in Matthew 5:43. Other forms of agapao are: agape, a noun meaning love; agapemai, a noun indicating the object of love; agapenor, meaning loving manliness, manly, used to refer to heroes; agapesis, a noun meaning affection; agapetikos, a noun meaning affectionate; and agapetos, an adjective meaning worthy of love, beloved, esteemed.

Of the above only the verb agapao, the noun agape, and the adjective agapetos are used in the Greek New Testament. The feminine noun agape uses case endings that are not used in any classic Greek literature. Case endings on Greek nouns and adjectives varied depending on how the word was used in a sentence.

Agape apparently was in common usage by the Hellenists for several centuries before Jesus' birth because it is used more than a dozen times in the Septuagint, the 250 BC Greek translation of the Hebrew Scriptures. At least four forms: the feminine agape, a neuter agape, agapesis, and agapao, are used in the Septuagint. The feminine agape is used in the Septuagint in 2 Samuel 13:15, Ecclesiastes 9:1 & 6, and Song of Songs 2:4, 5, 7, 3:5, 10, 5:8, 7:6, 8:4, 6, 7. Since the word agape is used by every New Testament author except Mark and is used about one hundred fifteen times in the New Testament, it must have been common throughout the Roman world, wherever the Epistles were sent. Koine Greek was the common language of the Roman Empire, not being replaced by Latin until the third and fourth centuries AD. The people spoke Greek in Rome, Corinth, Galatia, Ephesus, Philippi, Colossae, Thessalonika, and the various cities written to by the authors of Hebrews, Peter, Jude, and John.

Phileo, a synonym of agapao, is used only twenty-four times in the New Testament. It is used in John 5:20 and 16:27 of God loving Jesus and of His loving us. It is used to speak of Jesus' love for us in John 11:3. 11:36, 20:2, and Revelation 3:19. Phileo is used in the Septuagint in similar proportion as in the New Testament.

Alef is used in this translation instead of the Greek letter Alpha. Alef is the first letter of the Hebrew alphabet. Tav, the last letter of the Hebrew alphabet, is used instead of omega because Hebrew was the first language of the apostles and was widely used in Jesus' day as is evident from archeological finds, including the Dead Sea Scrolls. All teaching of Scripture was in Hebrew, as was every service in a synagogue or the temple. Any other language was considered to profane those buildings and the people inside. The alef and tav spell a word, et, which is placed in front of the direct object of a verb to show the object of the action. For more on this see John under Book Order.

Anokhi   is a very powerful Hebrew word translated "I AM." The basic word translated "I AM" is Ani. Adding the syllable "khi" makes the word a very definite, deliberate action. God uses Anokhi fourteen times in the Hebrew Scriptures, while He uses Ani hundreds of times. Some examples of Anokhi are: Your Shield, Genesis 15:1; With You, Genesis 25:24, 28:15; God of Your Fathers, Genesis 46:3, Exodus 3:6; Brought You Out of Egypt, Exodus 20:2, Deuteronomy 5:6; He Who Blots Out Your Transgressions and Will Not Remember Your Sins, Isaiah 43:25, and Who Makes All Things, Isaiah 44:24. For each of the above God says "I AM" and does so with great and intense purpose. Read the above verses and remember that God put extra emphasis in each of them, and that He has determined to be your shield, to be with you, and to forget your transgressions and not remember your sins. See Sins, forgiveness of in this Glossary.

Anokhi is referenced three times in New Testament writing: Matthew 22:32, Mark 12:26, and Acts 7:32. These all refer to the same verse in the Hebrew Scriptures, Exodus 3:6, "And he said, I AM the God of your father, the God of Abraham, the God of Isaac, and the God of Jacob. And Moses hid his face; for he was afraid to look upon God."

Apostle   is the English spelling of the Greek word used to describe someone who is sent. There was a position in the ancient synagogues for someone who was sent from that synagogue to another or to authorities in Jerusalem or to some school in order to get the correct interpretation of a Scripture or point of oral law. The Hebrew name of this office is Shelakhim, meaning the "ones sent." Shelakhim is plural. The apostles in the New Testament were sent from Jerusalem to outlying areas to bring correct interpretation to early Christian congregations. Some of these apostles were promoting themselves and not focusing on the Jerusalem agenda. Paul referred to them in 2 Corinthians 3:1 as using letters of recommendation to get invitations. Since Corinth was a wealthy city, those seeking large offerings would have coveted ministry there. Paul also referred to false apostles in 2 Corinthians 11:12. "But what I am doing, and I will keep on doing, so that I will cut off the opportunity of those who want opportunity, so that in whom they are boasting they would have been found just like us. 13. For such false apostles as these are deceitful workers disguising themselves as apostles of Messiah. 14. And no wonder: for Satan disguises himself as an angel of light. (Is 14:12) 15. Therefore it is not great if his, Satan's, servants also are disguised as servants of righteousness: whose end will be according to their works." Today we still have ministers who do not report to anyone, but each of us needs to be accountable to some organization or board so we do not go off in error like those Paul wrote about.

The first century apostles did not have organizations other than the council in Jerusalem; they simply went out, with more than one going to the same synagogues. In the first century there were no churches, just synagogues and home congregations, even if a congregation was all non-Jewish. While there was not a formal organization, there was order. Notice that Paul reported to Jacob and the council in Jerusalem, as in Acts 15 and Acts 21:23. The false apostles were those who answered to no one. We still have rebels today, those who report only to God Himself. Just what Phoebe's responsibilities were is not clear, but Paul refers to her in Romans 16:1 as being from Cencrae, the sister city of Corinth, and being set over others, even himself.

The Latin word for apostle is missionare, meaning to send, which gives us a better handle on the role of the apostle. Missionaries are those who are sent to take the Gospel message to new peoples. We generally have missionary organizations to supervise missionary activity, whether denominational or some separate organization. Some of these organizations are very tightly run, while others are more open, like first century Jerusalem. Our Western minds require organizations with managers and organization charts, but that is not what the Middle Eastern mind requires, so it is not what Paul and other NT authors understood the word translated Apostle to mean.

Baptize is the English spelling of the Greek word, baptidzo, which means to immerse. The Jewish people had practiced immersion for purification after repentance, or being defiled, for more than 1,000 years before the birth of Jesus. The Jewish people call this immersion a mikveh. All the people that John's and Jesus' disciples baptized were thoroughly familiar with immersion, which we call baptism. We do not see baptism in Christian translations of the Old Testament because the Hebrew word that could appropriately be translated baptize is translated with some other word. Often our Christian translators, as in Leviticus 16:4 NIV, say "..so he must bathe himself.." The word translated bathe is rakhats, meaning immerse, which is the same meaning as the Greek word baptidzo.

As in modern Judaism, most baptisms in the NT were self-immersion. John and the disciples who baptized by the Jordan River would stand on the bank preaching, then as people became repentant, they would wade into the river and immerse, with the one preaching still standing on the bank. The same would be true of Peter's messages at the temple in Acts 2:14-42. After Peter's call to repentance the three thousand saved could have immersed in about twenty minutes because there were so many immersion pools under Solomon's Porch at the temple.

Certainly many in the NT were baptized by others, as Philip baptized the eunuch in Acts 8:38. When this was done, the person doing the baptizing placed a hand on the head of the one being baptized to hold him under water, forcing a struggle to come out of the water as a reminder of the dying to self and the new birth, paralleling a newborn baby's struggle in birth.

Each synagogue in Jesus' day had one or more ritual baths, baptismal pools, for immersion. These were to be filled with "living water" from a stream or even roof cisterns to catch rainwater. In John 2:6 we see stone jugs used to carry the water of purification to the immersion pool. Stone jars were used because stone did not become ritually unclean. Metal and glass containers became unclean, but could be cleansed. Pottery vessels that became unclean had to be destroyed.

Most Christians are baptized just one time, but Judaism calls for baptism whenever someone has become defiled by contact with a dead body, or blood, or even when going someplace defined as unclean, such as entering the governor's residence in John 18:28. Immersion was called for to prepare for the Sabbath (see Preparation Day elsewhere in this Glossary). Paul immersed as part of his purification in Acts 21:26.

Some denominations now immerse, as did the first century church, while others sprinkle. The early churches always immersed, but in later centuries some began to pour water over someone being baptized, then still later some of those churches began to sprinkle the one being baptized. Sprinkling was made official at the Council of Ravenna in 1311 AD.

Blood   of Bulls and Goats did take away sin. Hebrews 9:13,14 say "For if the blood of goats and bulls and sprinkling the ashes of a heifer <u>sanctify those who have been defiled, making their flesh clean</u>, 14. how much more the blood of the Messiah, Who through the eternal Spirit presented Himself as an offering to God, cleanses our conscience from dead works in service to the living God." The following statement is made ten times just in the book of Leviticus "..and the priest shall make atonement for him with the ram of the guilt offering, and it shall be forgiven him." (Leviticus 5:16b) In Jesus' day books were very expensive, so people memorized worthwhile writings. For Jewish children that meant memorizing Scripture. When a child was five years old the father would start teaching, giving a section to memorize every day. The book they started with was Leviticus; the book of purity, holiness, so every New Testament author and those receiving the letters Hebrews, James, and Peter had as children memorized the verses referred to above. We can deduce from that the author's emphasis in the tenth chapter of Hebrews is on the permanence of Jesus' sacrifice, that He had only to offer His blood one time for all mankind. "For the Torah is a shadow of the coming good things, not the form of things themselves, never able to perfect those who come year by year with these offerings which they offer continually: otherwise would they not have ceased being offered, after they had once been cleansed, because those who worship would not still have consciousness of sins? But with these yearly reminders of sins: it is impossible for blood of bulls and goats to permanently take away sin, by a single offering." (Hebrews 10:1-4)

From ancient times rabbis used wine to express covenant, with wine representing blood.

Book Order   The traditional book order is used in The Power New Testament, but try reading through in a different order. The Gospels have a natural progression based on principles established by rabbis. These principles provide a progression from the simplest, most easily understood, to the most mystical of the books. They give us insight to the writers as well as to the writings by taking us inside the authors and by giving us a natural progression in the proper book order. Each author came from a different background and it is helpful to know something about the author's perspective. The four styles are listed here and we suggest reading through the Gospels in this order.

Author Description

Mark: Rabbi Hillel wrote seven laws, called <u>P'shat,</u> for the average layman. Peshat means simple. This is the style of the Mishnah studied by modern Judaism today. Mark, in this style, is very basic, factual, getting right to the meat, not presenting background information like Luke and Matthew. In Scriptural interpretation this is the literal reading. Rabbi Hillel formulated these principles late in the first century BC at the age of seventeen. He was from Galilee and was teaching during Jesus' lifetime. Many of the teachings of Jesus were similar to Rabbi Hillel's, whose yeshiva in Galilee continued after his death.

Luke: Rabbi Ishmael wrote the thirteen laws called <u>Remez</u> (Hint), for the aristocracy, the professional class. This is the style of the Gemara, using many technical terms, in Luke's case medical terms. There are more healings, not just more technical terms in Luke than in any other Gospel. There are more allusions and more incidents or events in Luke, but there is less detail in any one incident than in Matthew. Compare the Beatitudes and the Lord's Prayer to see this.

This style concentrates on facts. Peshat and Remez combined are called Talmud.

Matthew: Rabbi Gallil wrote the thirty-two laws called D'rush (Thresh) or homily for the ethical teaching. It is also called LeMelekh (To the King) because it is aimed at the royalty, the Levitical leaders. There are more ethical details in Matthew than in any other Gospel, which is typical of this style known as Midrash (From the Threshing). Again, compare the Beatitudes and the Lord's Prayer with those passages in Luke. This style presents a chronology, rather than a genealogy of Joseph, to establish the appropriate time for the birth of the Messiah. For another view of this genealogy, see Genealogy of Jesus in this Glossary.

John: Rabbi Ben Yohai wrote the forty-two laws called Sohd (The Secret Level), for only the most learned Jewish scholars. Those who reach this level are called Kabbalists because Kabbal (Receive) means they have received the secret level of interpretation. The forty-two laws are also called Kabbal and Zohar (Radiance). R. Ben Yohai taught these laws in his yeshiva starting late in the first century, but they were not written until the second century. Typical of this style is John's use of similes and metaphors, with Jesus as the Way, the Truth, and the Light, the Word, the Bread and the Blood, the Good Shepherd and the Resurrection and the Life. One of the teachings in the Zohar is that the mark on the foreheads of the faithful ones (Ezek 9:4) is EMET, meaning TRUTH as the name of God. The first letter of EMET is Alef; the last letter is Tav so the teaching says that the faithful ones are those who have kept Torah from Alef to Tav.

The underlined names of these four levels form an acronym PaR'DeS, meaning orchard, and in Modern Hebrew PaR'DeS is the name by which these four methods of Bible study are known. Orchard is significant because the Word of God is an orchard from which we can harvest fruit in every season. It is also significant because there is more than one way to interpret any verse. One example we can look at is Hebrews 11:5 referring to Enoch's being translated, which is a possible reading of Genesis 5:24. In this case the simple primary meaning is that Enoch died, but "threshing" the word brings out another meaning, that of his being translated. Both interpretations are correct, the first being from the Peshat, the second from the Derush style. There are many examples in each Gospel tying each one to the style listed above, so try reading the Gospels in this order, which really does add to our understanding of Scripture.

The order of the Epistles can also be changed. Try reading the Epistles based on more probable chronological order. The major change is to follow Acts with 1st Thessalonians, 2nd Thessalonians, 1st Corinthians, 2nd Corinthians, Romans, then Galatians, etc. This puts Paul's teachings in a different perspective. Reading James before Hebrews also provides insight.

Books in New Testament times were generally on scrolls, although a book form was also common. This book form, called Codex, consisted of large pages of either parchment or papyrus being stitched together. The letters were large because the reed pen used and the rough surface of either parchment or papyrus required a heavy hand. The letters were about an inch high, so you can imagine how bulky even a small book would have been. For example, the book of Matthew would have been about thirty feet long. Since copies had to be made by hand by skilled scribes and since both papyrus and parchment were expensive, few people had many books. Many in Israel were literate and had some books of the Bible, but for the most part they relied on memorization. Even though books are no longer prohibitively expensive the Jewish people still memorize Scripture. In 1995 a school in Israel was shown on TV, with the Rabbi saying that every ten year old in that school had memorized the entire Tanach, the Old Testament, and could discuss any passage, relating it to other passages. Our Jewish brothers still use memorization far, far more than we do.

C The letter C was not in either the Greek or the Hebrew alphabet. It was introduced in the Latin language, so when you see a letter C in a name, you know that that word was copied from a Latin text. Actually, Wycliffe made the first English translation of the Bible from the Latin Vulgate manuscripts that were the standard texts of the Roman Church. Thessalonika, Makedonia, and Kefa are examples of the Greek spelling.

Census was to be taken according to Scripture, so only men able to go forth to war were counted, even at the feeding of the 5,000 and the 4,000. Numbers 1:3 is the defining verse so only men older than twenty, but not over fifty, were to be counted. Women, children, aged, and handicapped were not to be counted, restrictions not applying to the Roman census.

Cephas is the Latin spelling of an Aramaic word for rock. The word for rock is Kefa, which is used in John 1:42, 1 Corinthians 1:12, 3:22, 9:5, 15:5, and Galatians 1:18, 2:9, 11, & 14. This is evidence that the apostles called Peter by the Aramaic name given to him by Jesus and that the apostles did not normally speak Greek. That Hebrew was widely spoken in Israel in Jesus' day has been substantiated by recent archeological finds. The Hebrew word for rock is kaf which is used well over 100 times in the Hebrew Scriptures, most often with its basic meaning as sole of the foot or palm of the hand, but not with the meaning of rock. Kaf is simply a rock, small enough to be lifted in one hand. Three other Hebrew words speak of God or Messiah as a Rock. They are tsor, referring to a sheer rock cliff; sali, referring to a huge rocky cliff; and even (pronounced eh-ven) speaking of a cut stone as used in construction, particularly the corner stone.

Chapter and Verse Numbers　　were added long after the NT was written. Bishop Stephen Langton added the chapter numbers around the year 1205. His text was the Latin Vulgate, but his divisions were applied to both the Hebrew and the Greek texts. Robert Estienne, a printer who used the pen name Stephanus, added the verse numbers with his 4th Edition of a Greek text printed in 1551. The Greek text in use at that time contained many additions and some other changes from the early texts, so chapter and verse numbers are sometimes quite out of place. Acts Chapters 22 and 23 are examples of chapter numbers out of place. See Manuscripts in this Glossary.

Christ　　　　is the English spelling of the Greek word Xristos. The meaning of Xristos is Messiah or Anointed One, so this translation uses Messiah.

Cleanse　　　　How could Jesus cleanse a leper by touching him? Numbers 19:22 says "Whatever the unclean person touches shall be unclean; and anyone who touches it shall be unclean until evening." A leper lived outside town because anything or anyone he touched would be unclean, yet Jesus cleansed the leper by touching him. An excerpt from the Jewish Midrash, Song of Songs Rabbah 1:19, is interesting: "Just as water purifies man from ritual uncleanness, as it says, And I will sprinkle clean water upon you, and ye shall be clean (Ezek. 36:25), So the Torah cleanses an unclean man of his uncleanness, as it says, The words of the Lord are pure words (Ps. 12:7). Just as water cleanses the body, as it says, He shall bathe himself in water (Lev. 16:15), so the Torah cleanses the body, as it says, Thy word is purifying to the uttermost (Ps. 119:140). Just as water covers the nakedness of the sea, as it says, As the waters cover the sea (Isaiah 11:9), so the Torah covers the nakedness of Israel, as it says, Love covereth all transgressions (Proverbs 10:12)."

Jesus is the Living Word, the Living Torah, John 1:14, "The Word became flesh and lived among us.." As the Living Torah He thus cleanses everyone He touches.

Coming of Messiah　　We see many signs that lead us to believe that Jesus could return any day now. Many of us remember "88 Reasons.." why Jesus would return in 1988, which had very scientifically set a given day in September of that year for His return. An engineer who had spent his life savings and many hours in research to establish the time wrote that book. There are several "End Times" ministries who feel that His return is just a few years away. There certainly are many signs today that Jesus mentioned in Matthew 24. In verse 36, "But no one knows about that Day and hour, and neither do the angels of the heavens nor the Son, except the Father only." While the word translated hour is commonly translated hour, it can also be translated as follows: a certain definite time or season fixed by natural law, such as winter, spring, etc., any definite time, point of time, or moment, or a fit or opportune time.

Just a few years ago much End Time talk related to the millennium, when our calendar turned the year 2,000. Some of the leaders of the Roman church said the same things that we heard in the 1990's as the world approached the year 1,000. However, Jesus used the Jewish calendar, which in the year 2000 was in the year 5760, not 6000. The New Year 5760 began on September 10, 1999, at sundown. Our calendar based roughly on the year of Jesus' birth was not used until somewhat later, although except for the year, the calendar we use today was decreed in 46 BC by Julius Caesar, using the plan of the Egyptian astronomer Sosigenes. A side note is that England used March 25th as the New Year until 1752. The point is that it takes considerable rounding off to make our year 2,000 a true millennium.

It is also useful to look at some of Jesus' statements about His return. Read all of Matthew 24, and then note verses 36, 42-44, which say, "36. But no one knows about that day and appointed time or hour, and neither do the angels of the heavens or the Son, except the Father only. 42. Therefore you must steadily be watchful, because you do not know what sort of day your Lord is coming. 43. But you know it, that if the house owner had known what sort of watch when the thief was coming, he would have been watchful and would not have allowed his house to be broken into. 44. Because of this then you must always be prepared, because in this you must not continually think of the time the Son of Man is coming." This is really a definitive command: we are to be about His business, feeding the hungry, caring for those less fortunate, and not to be focused on His return, but on Him.

Mark 13:32 states, "But concerning that day and the hour no one knows, not even the angels in heaven and not the Son, only the Father. 33. You must watch out! You must continually be alert: for you do not know when the time is." In Luke 12:40 He says, "..the Son of Man is coming in a time you do not think He is coming." Then He talks of the coming Kingdom of God in 17:20-37. Verse 20 includes "The kingdom of God does not come by means of, or in company with, close observation." Watching for Him will not speed up His coming. If anything can speed up His coming, it would be feeding the hungry, housing the homeless, and so on as listed in Matthew 25:35-40.

Matthew 10:23 "And when they would persecute you in this city, you must flee to another: for truly I say to you, you would not finish the cities of Israel until the Son of Man would come." 24:32 "Truly I say to you that this generation would not pass until all these things would happen." Since these words were written in the first century each generation has had advocates that THIS is the generation that will see His coming. Paul believed He was coming soon as we can see in his remark, "And I say this, brothers, the time is short:" talking about not getting married, in 1 Corinthians 7:29.

Matthew 24:45 "Who then is the faithful and wise servant whom the owner appointed over his household servants to give them food in due season? 46. Blessed is that servant who when his master comes will find him doing this: 47. truly I say to you that he will place him over all his possessions. 48. but if that evil servant would say in his heart, 'My lord lingers,' 49. and he would begin to beat his fellow servants, and he would eat and he would drink with the drunkards, 50. the master of that servant will come in a day in which he does not expect and in a moment that he does not know, 51. and he will punish him severely and his lot will place him with the hypocrites: there will be weeping and gnashing of teeth in that place."

In Luke 9:27, Jesus says "But I say to you truly, there are some of those who are standing in this place who will not taste death until they would see the kingdom of God." This is evidence of Jesus' statement in Mark 13:32 that no one but the Father knows.

John wrote in 1 John 2:18, "Children, it is the last hour, and just as you heard that anti-Messiah is coming, even now many anti-Messiahs have come, from which we know that this is the last hour."

Clearly, we need to be taught about the end times, but just as clearly, we need to focus on the task at hand, to raise up mature believers and to evangelize, to feed the poor, and bring deliverance to the world. Each generation is to believe the time is at hand as Jacob (James) wrote in James 5:8 "You too must now be patient, you must strengthen your hearts, because the coming of the Lord has drawn near."

What is written here is not in any way to be thought of as putting down those who are teaching about the soon coming of the Messiah. They are being obedient to their call and are keeping many occupied as good servants as well as bringing many converts to the Lord. Then too, He might come tonight!

Congregation is the appropriate translation of the Greek word Ekklasia, meaning "a gathering of citizens called out from their homes into some public place; an assembly." (New Thayer Greek-English Lexicon) This is a group called for some particular purpose, such as a political meeting or social occasion. For Christians it meant to gather for worship or teaching.

No Greek word meaning Church is used in the Greek NT. The other Greek word sometimes translated Church, in James 2:2, is Sunagoga, now written synagogue in English. Sunagoga means a gathering of people, an assembly. Church is not an appropriate translation of either word because that in our minds refers to an organization or to a building, while both Greek words, Ekklasia and Sunagoga, refer to people, but not to buildings or organizations. The people are far more important than the organization or the building. Therefore in The Power NT Ekklasia is always translated congregation, and Sunagoga is translated synagogue or gathering. Since the authors of the NT did not use a word for Church, the word Church does not appear in this volume.

Conjunctions are used very frequently, much more than would be considered reasonable in modern English. This is according to the pattern established in the Hebrew Scriptures, which the Rabbis say is to verify the connection from one action or statement to another. So be sure that "and," "but," "then," were used intentionally. The sentences are very long because Greek sentences are long. Even though the New Testament was written without punctuation the editors have added punctuation appropriately. This translation shortened sentences by inserting a period in place of a conjunction as little as possible because the long, sometimes awkward sentences contribute to the flow of Scripture.

Daily Bread from the Lord's Prayer is not clear. The word often translated daily is epiousion, which is found only in Matthew 6:11 and Luke 11:3 and not in any other ancient documents. Since it was not part of the Koine Greek vocabulary, the scholars have had to determine the meaning from the components of epiousion. They are not unanimous, but the consensus is that it means enough food and other necessities to last a day or so.

Dates given for the writing of each book are commonly accepted but not universally accepted. There are scholars who put dates for writing these books from the second through the fourth centuries. To me the many Hebrew idioms and Jewish customs woven throughout the NT are evidence that every author was Jewish, which would not have been the case if it were written later than the first century.

Day Days began at sundown. The night hours were divided into watches, with the first watch extending from sundown until midnight. The second watch was from midnight until 3:00 AM, and the third from 3:00 AM to 6:00 AM. Matthew 14:25 and Mark 6:48 use the Roman time of the fourth watch, since the Romans divided the night into four equal parts, from 6:00 PM to 6:00 AM. Late in the day and evening meant between 3:00 PM and 6:00 PM.

Death   is spoken of with two idioms, one being "is not" in Matthew 2:18 and Revelation 17:8 & 11. This idiom is used rarely in the Tanach as well, in just Genesis 5:24 and Jeremiah 31:15. The other idiom for death is used very frequently and that is to "sleep" as in John 11:11-16 with Lazarus. When this mortal body dies we are only sleeping until He comes for us. Acts 7:60 tells us that Stephen slept after the religious people stoned him. Psalm 17:15 "And I -- in righteousness I shall behold Your face: upon awakening I will be sated by Your image." Awakening refers to the hereafter. Song of Songs 7:9, speaking of the sleeper, is used by the Rabbis as one of a number of verses speaking of resurrection. Another idiom, not appearing in the NT, is used in Isaiah 58:8, saying, "Then your light will burst out like the dawn and your healing will speedily sprout; your righteous deed will precede you and the glory of the Lord will gather you in." To be gathered in is to enter eternal life.

Dekapolis   is a Greek word meaning Ten Cities. These ten cities were set apart after Pompey conquered Israel in 63 BC. Nine of these are east of the Jordan, between Galilee to the north and the Dead Sea to the south. The tenth is Beit Sh'an, an important Israeli city today, a few miles west of the Jordan, south of the Lake of Galilee. These ten were declared "Free Cities" by Rome, a great honor for each of the cities.

Disciples   refers to all those who traveled with Jesus or who believed in Him whether or not they were able to travel with Him. The twelve apostles had a great deal of company much of the time, including both women and men. The replacement for Judas Iscariot came from this group that traveled with Him. Sometimes the twelve were referred to as Disciples, sometimes as Apostles. See Mark 4:10, 14:12 & 17, Luke 6:13-16, 8:1-3, 19:37.

Division   of Abijah is given in 1 Chronicles 24:1. "And these are the divisions of the sons of Aaron. The sons of Aaron: Nadab, and Abihu, Eleazar, and Ithamar. 2. And Nadab and Abihu died before their father, and had no children; therefore Eleazar and Ithamar performed the priest's duties. 3. And David and Zadok of the sons of Eleazar, and Ahimelech of the sons of Ithamar, organized them according to their duties in their service. 4. And there were more chief men found of the sons of Eleazar than of the sons of Ithamar; and thus were they organized. Among the sons of Eleazar there were sixteen heads of fathers' houses, and eight among the sons of Ithamar for the houses of their fathers. 5. Thus were they organized by lot, one sort with another; for the officers of the sanctuary, and the officers of God, were of the sons of Eleazar, and of the sons of Ithamar." The sixteen heads from Eleazar and the eight from Ithamar made twenty-four divisions, so each division served in the temple one week at a time, with two times of service each year. Zechariah, of the Division of Abijah, which had the eighth lot, most likely served in June and December, although that could vary some. That would have the birth of John the Baptist in March-April or Sept.-Oct. Since Jesus was born six months after John, His birth would also have been March-April or Sept.-Oct. The wild card is the Hebrew leap year because there are fifty-one weeks in the lunar year of the Jewish calendar, three divisions served a third time each year, and four additional divisions served in leap years. Since this system of leap years was initiated in the fourth century AD, we do not know with certainty the dates of the first century. See Jewish Calendar in this Glossary.

Donkey   as used by Jesus for His Triumphal Entry, recorded in Matthew 21:1-11, Mark 11:1-11, Luke 19:28-38, and John 12:12-19, is significant beyond the reference in Zechariah 9:9. See *** toward the end of this article. The first reference to this is in Genesis 49:10-12. "The scepter shall not depart from Judah nor a scholar from among his descendants until Shiloh arrives and his will be an assemblage of nations. He will tie his donkey to the vine; to the vine branch his donkey's foal; he will launder his garments in wine and his robe in the blood of grapes. Red eyed from wine, and white toothed from milk." The Stone Edition Chumash, a volume with the Torah readings, the Haftorah, and Rabbinic commentary, is the source of the above translation and the following commentary. The italicized names are acknowledged Torah scholars.

"The scepter shall not depart from Judah. The privilege of providing Israel's sovereign ruler - symbolized by the royal scepter - shall not pass from the House of Judah (Onkelos). This blessing did not take effect immediately, however, for the first Jewish king was Saul, a Benjamite. However, Jacob's blessing applied uninterruptedly from the time that the monarchy went to David, and it continued even after the demise of the royalty, for after the destruction of the Second Temple, the Exhilarchs, or heads of the Babylonian exile, were appointed from the tribe of Judah (Rashi). As to present times and before the time of David, when kings did not come from Judah, Gur Aryeh explains as follows: Jacob's blessings applied only when there would be a legally constituted king. The times of Saul and judges were temporary aberrations. Similarly, the current exile, too, will be followed by a return of the Davidic dynasty, proving that Jacob's blessing remains in force.

"Nor a scholar, i.e., an allusion to Hillel's descendants, the Nesi'im, or Princes in Eretz Yisrael, whose greatness in Torah was enhanced by their descent from the royal line of Judah (Talmud, Sanhedrin 5a).

"Until Shiloh arrives. Onkelos, followed by Rashi, (two great scholars, Onkelos 2nd century, Rashi 11th century) renders: until the Messiah comes, to whom the word Shiloh is a composite of the words Sh' loh a gift to him, a reference to the King Messiah, to whom all nations will bring gifts. This verse is a primary Torah source for the belief that the Messiah will come, and the rabbis always referred to it in the Middle Ages, when they were forced to debate with clerics of other religions.

"The word until does not mean that Judah's ascendancy will end with the coming of Messiah. To the contrary, the sense of the verse is that once Messiah begins to reign, Judah's blessing of kingship will become fully realized and go to an even higher plateau (Sh'lah). At that time, all the nations will assemble to acknowledge his greatness and pay homage to him.

"11-12. Though Jacob could not reveal the "End" to his sons, he did provide them with tiny glimpses of the Messianic era (Abarbanel). Judah's district will be productive and flow with wine like a fountain. So lush will his vineyards be that a farmer will tie his donkey to a single vine, for it will produce as many grapes as a donkey can carry (Rashi, Rashbam). The passage continues hyperbolically with more illustrations of the productivity of Judah's land.

*** "Messiah is associated with a donkey rather than a horse ready for battle, because he is depicted not as a warrior but as a man of peace who represents prosperity; thus the simile of the vineyard. His wars will be won by God, not through force of arms (Sforno)."

The three verses from Genesis 49 are truly rich. Notice the reference in verse 11 to Messiah washing His garments in wine and His robe in the blood of grapes. Revelation 7:14 tells of the 144,000 who washed their robes and they made them white in the blood of the Lamb. It is obvious in reading the above that God blinded our Jewish brothers for a season. They see so much, but have been given a blind spot to hold the door open for the heathens. See Romans 11:8, 25-27, Deuteronomy 29:4, and Isaiah 29:10.

Double Names as when Jesus said, "Martha, Martha" make a Hebrew idiom of some force. This is punctuated "Martha. Martha!" to indicate the forcefulness that it is a stern attention getter. Someone saying, "Lord.

Lord!" would certainly not be stern, but would be making a strong plea. This idiom is still used in modern conversational Hebrew.

Double Negative   in Greek is the opposite of the double negative in English, in which doubling the negative cancels the negative. In Greek doubling the negative strengthens the negative. Where they are doubled in this text, bold type is used to show the emphasis.

Double Yes or No   means "Definitely Yes!" or "Definitely No!" This idiom is still in use in modern conversational Hebrew.

Dwelling Places   in John 14:2 is not speaking of a building, but of a place for each of us to fit into the heavenly organization, operation. The word translated dwelling places, mon-ai, has a primary meaning of staying, tarrying, abiding. Used only in John 14:2 and 23, Jesus says He is making a ministry for each of us in the heavenly plan, an assignment for each one. We will not have houses in heaven that resemble our earthly homes, that we go to when we are off duty, to rest and play games. Our physical bodies need food and sleep to recharge, but our spirits are recharged as we worship and study His Word. In the hereafter our spirits will not need sleep or food -- although we may be able to eat (Revelation 19:7), food will not be a necessity. It is also possible the marriage supper will have spiritual food, not natural food.

First Fruits   of the three harvest festivals are joyful celebrations, filled with thanksgiving. The quantities of produce brought were not specified, and were never a great quantity; a basket carried a family's offering, although a king brought a basket that required two to carry. Deuteronomy 26:2 tells us the offering should be brought in a basket. Deuteronomy 26:1. "And it shall be, when you come in to the land which the Lord your God gives you for an inheritance, and possess it, and live in it; 2. That you shall take of the first of all the fruit of the earth, which you shall bring of your land that the Lord your God gives you, and shall put it in a basket, and shall go to the place which the Lord your God shall choose to place his name there. 3. And you shall go to the priest who shall be in those days, and say to him, I declare this day to the Lord your God, that I have come to the country that the Lord swore to our fathers to give us. 4. And the priest shall take the basket from your hand, and set it down before the altar of the Lord your God."

The offering was presented as described in Deuteronomy 26:2, then the one presenting would make this statement from Deuteronomy 26:5. "And you shall speak and say before the Lord your God, 'A wandering Aramean was my father, and he went down into Egypt, and sojourned there with a few, and became there a nation, great, mighty, and populous; 6. And the

Egyptians dealt ill with us, and afflicted us, and laid upon us hard slavery; 7. And when we cried to the Lord God of our fathers, the Lord heard our voice, and looked on our affliction, and our labor, and our oppression; 8. And the Lord brought us out of Egypt with a mighty hand, and with an outstretched arm, and with great awesomeness, and with signs, and with wonders; 9. And he has brought us to this place, and has given us this land, a land that flows with milk and honey. 10. And now, behold, I have brought the first fruits of the land, which you, O Lord, have given me.' And you shall set it before the Lord your God, and worship before the Lord your God; 11. And you shall rejoice in every good thing which the Lord your God has given to you, and to your house, you, and the Levite, and the stranger who is among you." The quotation in verses 5-10 was repeated by each one bringing a First Fruits offering to the temple.

The produce offered at First Fruits are defined in Deuteronomy 8:8. "A land of wheat, barley, vines (grapes), fig trees, and pomegranates; a land of olive oil, and date-honey." These were the only crops offered for First Fruits. During the Feast of Unleavened Bread barley was the crop that was being harvested, so that is what would have been brought, although someone who had not been able to come to the previous First Fruits could bring that offering at the next First Fruits. This modest offering from just a few crops expresses commitment to God and thanksgiving to Him for His provision. First Fruits offerings were in addition to the tithe, which was offered separately.

Fish Nets   The Greek word for net in Matthew 13:47 is Sag'ene, referring to the large net used in commercial fishing, which was done at night. For weights this net used round stones, each stone having a hole drilled through the middle, resembling a doughnut or bagel. The stones were usually flint, which is very hard and how the holes were drilled is not known. Thousands of these 2,000 – 2,500 year old stones have been found around the lake we call Galilee. Sag'ene is used only once in the NT, but there are other references to this net, referred to by the Greek word diktuon, which is a generic reference to nets, not specifying the type of net used. The twenty-first chapter of John describes the use of a large net used at night that would have been a sag'ene, because only the commercial net could have held 153 fish. Mark 1 and Luke 5 also have descriptions of nets, but those cannot be identified with certainty as to type.

The other type of net was used by one person for daytime fishing and was round, about twenty feet in diameter. It had lead weights. This type was used until the middle of the last century when nylon nets replaced it. It is not directly referred to in the NT, but probably was used by some of the NT fishermen, either in Mark or Luke. A man named Mendel Nun, a Galilean fisherman, has for years studied the fishing on Galilee. He believes that the nets described in Luke 5 are the small casting nets, so while it cannot be proven from the Greek text the net used could well have been the smaller net. A net twenty feet in diameter can hold quite a few fish.

Footstool is a tough place for an enemy to be. "The Lord says to my Lord, 'Sit at my right hand, until I make your enemies your footstool.'" (Ps 110:1) Jesus cited this verse in Luke 20:43. The full meaning of making your enemies your footstool is "..Joshua called for all the men of war who went with him, 'Come near, and put your feet upon the necks of these kings.' And they came near, and put their feet upon their necks. And Joshua said to them, 'Fear not, nor be dismayed, be strong and of good courage: for thus shall the Lord do to all your enemies against whom you fight.' And afterwards Joshua smote them, and slew them, and hanged them on five trees:" (Josh 10:24) When he smote them he cut off their heads, completely removing the enemy - the meaning of "make your enemies your footstool." God put everything under Jesus' feet, and Jesus gave us all authority. We are obligated to put the spiritual enemies under our feet.

Future Tense is frequently translated as a command of God. The Ten Commandments are in the future tense and some say that is because once we have made a commitment to God that our behavior will change and we will do those things that our Heavenly Father tells us to do and we will no longer do those things He tells us not to do. It is too bad that people committed to God have not been perfected so that would be absolutely true. Nevertheless, thinking positively, throughout this translation commandments in the future tense are usually translated in the future tense.

Gehenna is the Greek spelling of the Hebrew term, Ge Hinnom, for valley of Hinnom, the place outside Jerusalem where garbage, trash, dead animals, and even executed criminals were disposed of. Fires continually burned to get rid of the trash and also the bodies. Worms lived in whatever had not been consumed by the fires. The smoke, fires, and worms were a constant reminder to the residents and visitors to Jerusalem of the description of Sheol, so Gehenna was used as a synonym for Sheol. From early in the history of Israel this valley was used for human sacrifices, offerings of babies to the heathen god, Moloch. Joshua 15:8 is the earliest reference, then Joshua 18:16, 2 Chronicles 28:3, and Jeremiah 7:32, 19:2,6, 32:35. 2 Kings 23:10 uses the full name of the valley, Valley of the Sons of Hinnom. Hinnom means wailing, lamentation.

The Talmud varies some from some traditional Christian views of hell. Regarding Gehenna Talmud Mas. Nedarim 8b says, "There is no Gehinnom in the world to come, but the Holy One, blessed be He, will draw forth the sun from its sheath: the righteous shall be healed, and the wicked shall be judged and punished thereby." A footnote on Gehenna says, "Gehinnom (Gehenna) as an equivalent of hell, purgatory, takes its name from the place where children were once sacrificed to Moloch, viz., ge ben Hinnom, the valley of the son of Hinnom, to the south of Jerusalem (Josh. XV, 8; 11 Kings XXIII, 10; Jer. VII, 32-32; XIX, 6. 13-14)." Note that in the Talmud purgatory is the same as hell, not a temporary holding place.

Genealogy of Jesus   Because the genealogies of Matthew and Luke are different, we need to study them closely. There is no basis for saying that one Gospel gives the genealogy of Mary. Mary is named in Matthew 1:16, where she is identified as Jesus' mother, but not in any way named in the lineage of Jesus. Even more compelling, the tribal inheritance could not have come through the mother, only through the father.

"The New Testament Its Background and Message," by Thomas D. Lea, has the following: Some scholars "explain the difference by referring to the practice of Levirate marriage. The early Christian leader Africanus (c. A.D. 220) suggested that Eli (Luke 3:24) died childless and that Jacob (Matthew 1:15-16), who had the same mother but a different father, married the widow of Eli and fathered Joseph. If we follow this view, Matthew's Gospel provides Joseph's genealogy through his actual father Jacob, and Luke's Gospel provides Joseph's genealogy through his legal father Eli."

Another view from the book says, "J. G. Machen suggested that Matthew named the legal descendants of David, those men who were the official line of succession to the throne. Luke, in turn, listed the descendants of David in that branch of the Davidic family to which Joseph, Mary's husband, belonged. This view assumes that Jacob, the father of Joseph in Matthew, died without offspring, and the line of succession then passed to the descendants of Heli."

The genealogies of the Gospels list Joseph as Jesus' actual father. If, as we believe, Jesus was born of a virgin, that He is in truth God Incarnate, then Joseph was not His father. Matthew 1:18 and Luke 1:35 identify the Spirit of the Lord God as His father. What is Jesus' tribe?

Gentile   is a word that is not used in The Power New Testament because the Greek word often translated gentile means heathen. Gentile is actually the English spelling of the Latin word for heathen, so other translators have for centuries chosen the politically correct term, gentile, instead of what the authors wrote, heathen. The Latin word was used because the earliest English translations were made from the Latin Vulgate text. Those early translators chose not to translate the Latin word gentilis, instead just spelling the word in English.

God Incarnate   If we can truly grasp that Jesus is God Incarnate, we will see Him in a new and astonishing way. While a high percentage of Christians say that Jesus is God Incarnate, few realize the depth of meaning in this phrase. In 1779, John Newton wrote: "Incarnate God! The soul that knows thy name's mysterious power shall dwell in undisturbed repose, nor fear the trying hour."

How important today to see Jesus with all present, past and future Authority and Power! The Incarnate God! What should this mean to every Christian? The word 'incarnate' means 'to put into concrete form, to embody in flesh, especially human flesh,' and is a foundational belief of Christianity. Yet few have understood the vast scope of our God Incarnate. Can we lift this truth from dusty doctrinal archives and see Him touching our very lives in His unfathomable-mind-blowing Reality? Can we see Jehovah God exploding myth and mystery, expounding and expanding the embodiment of Eternal Life in human form with infallible integrity?

The Incarnate God wants to reveal Himself in all His fullness to us from this surprising and miraculous perspective, so that we stand strong in the faith and victory of our Great God, the Lord YHVH, King of the Universe.

Jesus walked the Earth for thirty-three years and spent His last three and a half years teaching and laying hands on people, bringing healing and deliverance to thousands. His ministry brought credence to the account of His Divine Conception and birth. He taught about His being One with the Father, in John 10:31 and other verses.

The Holy Spirit of the Lord roams over all the Earth continuously so He can show Himself strong on our behalf. We see the Spirit of the Lord in all that Jesus did while His Incarnate form was walking the Earth. This is the same Spirit that was given to mankind on Shavuot ten days after the ascension of Jesus. This was described by Jesus in John 14:25. I have spoken these things to you while staying with you: 26. but the Comforter, the Holy Spirit, Whom the Father will send in My Name, that One will teach you all things and will remind you of everything which I Myself said to you. Jeremiah spoke of this in Jeremiah 31:30. Behold, the days come, says the Lord, that I will make a new covenant with the house of Israel, and with the house of Judah; 31. Not according to the covenant that I made with their fathers in the day that I took them by the hand to bring them out of the land of Egypt; My covenant which they broke, although I was their master, says the Lord;

32. But this shall be the covenant that I will make with the house of Israel; After those days, says the Lord, I will put My Torah in their inward parts,

and write it in their hearts; and will be their God, and they shall be My people. 33. And they shall teach no more every man his neighbor, and every man his brother, saying, Know the Lord; for they shall all know Me, from the least of them to the greatest of them, says the Lord; for I will forgive their iniquity, and I will no longer remember their sin. 34. Thus says the Lord, who gives the sun for a light by day, and the fixed order of the moon and of the stars for a light by night, which divides the sea when its waves roar; The Lord of hosts is his name.

God's Incarnate form, Jesus, after His ascension, made the way for the Lord to send His Spirit to each person, to all mankind, one person individually and simultaneously to all mankind. At His baptism, immersion, as reported in John 1:29-34, we see The next day he saw Jesus coming toward him and he said, "Behold the Lamb of God, the One Who takes away the sin of the world. 30. This is concerning Whom I said, 'A man is coming after me Who was before me, because He is more prominent than I.' 31. And I had not known Him, but, so that He would be revealed to Israel through this, I came baptizing in water." 32. And John testified, saying that "I had seen the Spirit descending from heaven as a dove and it was staying on Him. 33. And I would not have known Him, but the One Who sent me to baptize in water, that One said to me 'Upon whomever you would see the Spirit descending and remaining upon Him, He is the One Who baptizes in the Holy Spirit.' 34. And I saw and I had borne witness that this One is the Son of God." The Spirit came upon Him, covering Him, immersing Him. This same experience, the covering and immersing of the Spirit, was given to 120 close followers ten days after His ascension from the Mount of Olives in Jerusalem, and even to us in modern times. This Spirit makes available to each one of us the power that we see in Jesus' ministry. No one person has yet achieved the yielding to His will, dying to self, so that he would do all the things that Jesus did. We see many miracles and healings in our services and in miracle services all over the world, but no one has yet walked as Jesus did. We are all to strive for that dying to self so each one can replicate Jesus' ministry.

Several names are used for both God the Father and for Jesus. One that stands out is I AM. The name I AM is used almost 100 times in just the books Genesis through Deuteronomy and Jesus used I AM about 40 times, referring to Himself. An example is Matthew 14:27 And Jesus spoke to them at once saying, "You must be courageous! I AM! Stop being afraid!"

Some other shared names are: Help, 2 Samuel 10:11 And he said, If the Arameans are too strong for me, then you shall help me; but if the Ammonites are too strong for you, then I will come to Help you. The word translated Help is Lishua (LYshua), using Jesus' name, Y'shua. The letter L is the prefix, to. God is referred to as My Help in Exodus 18:4 And the name of the other was Eliezer; for the God of my father, said he, was My Help, and saved me from the sword of Pharaoh; This Hebrew word is B'ezri. Another two are King of Kings and Lord of Lords, Revelation 19:6 and He has upon His garment, even over His thigh a name that has been written: "King of Kings and Lord of Lords." Paul refers to God as King of Kings and Lord of Lords in 1 Timothy 6:15 which in His own time God will show, the blessed and only ruler, the King of Kings and Lord of Lords, 16. the only One Who has immortality, unapproachable Light, Whom no one of mankind saw and no one is able to see: to Whom be honor and sovereignty forever, amen. Savior refers to Jesus in Philippians 3:20 For our citizenship is in the heavens, out from which then we have received for ourselves a Savior, Lord Jesus Messiah, and God is referred to as Savior in Hosea 13:4 And I am the Lord your God from the land of Egypt, and you know no god but Me; for there is no Savior beside Me. God's power is evident in each aspect of His nature: Holy Spirit in Spirit of Might, Isaiah 11:2, Jesus as Mighty God in Isaiah 9:5, and The King of the Universe in Isaiah 1:21 as Might of Israel.

We are to be a kingdom of priests, stated in Exodus 19:6. And you shall be to me a kingdom of priests, and a holy nation. What the Lord told Moses for the Israelites Jesus brought for the apostles to take to all mankind. Jesus was sent to teach the Jewish people as He instructed the apostles in Matthew 10:5. Jesus sent these twelve, after He commanded them, saying, "On the way do not go to the heathens and do not enter a Samaritan city: 6. but you must rather go regularly to the lost sheep of the house of Israel." It was after His ascension that the Lord instructed Peter to go to the heathens as well as the house of Israel. Peter was sent to the home of Cornelius, a Roman officer in Caesarea, and said this in Acts 10:34. Then when Peter opened his mouth he said, "In truth I understand that God does not show partiality, (Dt 10:17, 2Chr 19:7, Mk 12:14) 35. but in every nation the one who fears Him and works righteousness is acceptable to Him.

God came in bodily form to show by example the way each of us is to live and to minister. The Holy Spirit that abides in each of us is the same Spirit that walked in Jesus. We have but to yield ourselves to the Lord, dying to self so the God Who resides in us is free to act.

So there is one throne, One God. Jesus at the right hand does not indicate a second throne, but uses a Hebrew idiom, that of the right hand speaking of power when in Psalm 110:1. A Psalm of David. The Lord says to my master, Sit at my right hand, until I make your enemies your footstool. Jesus walked as the right hand of the Lord, John 10:38. but if I am doing the works, even if you would not believe in Me, believe in the works, so that you would know and you would continue knowing that the Father is in Me and I am in the Father. John 14:10. Do you not believe that I am in the Father and the Father is in Me? The words, which I speak to you, I am not speaking from Myself, but the Father Who lives in Me does His works.

Even now He does those works using our bodies. He in us is seen in John 14:15. If you love Me, you will keep My commandments: (Wisdom 6:18) 16. and I will ask the Father and, so that He would be with you forever, He will give you another Comforter, 17. the Spirit of Truth, Whom the world is not able to accept, because it does not see and does not know Him: you know Him, because He remains beside you and will be inside you. This One Who is inside us is the Spirit of the Living God, the King of the Universe, enabling us to do miraculous things and to live in victory, no matter what our circumstances.

Two words, one Hebrew, one Greek have been misunderstood. These are Y-Sh-A in Hebrew and Sodzo in Greek. Y-Sh-A has a primary meaning "to deliver" with "to save" as secondary. Sodzo means "to save," but has "to deliver" as a secondary meaning. Deliverance makes a person whole, eliminating the evil effects of illness, rejection, abuse, addiction, and a host of other ploys of the devil. As a kingdom of priests we are to walk in the anointing that Jesus showed us, bringing wholeness to each individual who seeks it.

Jesus did not come to establish a new religion. The new religion was established in a later century by men who did not know the God of Abraham, Isaac, and Jacob – their Jewish roots. Jesus came, as God Incarnate, to demonstrate God's love for all humanity. The Holy Spirit was given to us at the first Shavuot after His ascension to enable us to take God's love to all humanity. He taught that we should live by the spirit regarding Scripture; that we need to obey Scripture, but not make extensive rules to define His commands. In Mark 7:14. And again after He summoned the crowd He was saying to them, "You must all listen to Me and understand. 15. There is nothing outside of a person that goes into him that is able to defile him, but the things which go out from a person are the things that defile him." (Ro 14:17, 1Jn 5:17) 17. And when He entered the house from the crowd, His disciples were asking Him about the parable. 18. And He said to them, "Are you too without understanding? Do you not perceive that everything from the outside, which goes into a person, is not able to defile him 19. because it is not going into his heart but into his stomach, after the stomach cleanses all the food, then it goes out into the latrine?" 20. And He was saying, "That going out from a person defiles him. 21. For the evil purposes within go out from the hearts of people, immoralities, stealing, murder, 22. adultery, covetousness, evil, deceit, sensuality, stinginess, blasphemy, pride, foolishness: 23. all these evils within go out and defile the person." Therefore the dietary teachings are not crucial for salvation, but He is teaching us about foods for our own health and safety. In the 5th chapter of John we read about the man who was healed, with Jesus instructing him to get up and carry his pallet on a Sabbath, when Scripture says not to carry a burden. The instructions not to carry burdens are in Jeremiah and Nehemiah in passages about buying and selling, so Jesus gave us an idea of what constitutes a burden. We are to be in constant contact with Him to obey the spirit of His teachings, not regulations written by denominational leaders.

The Incarnate God was essential for at least three things: one was to teach us how to understand His teachings, as illustrated above; another to release His faithful ones to evangelize the world; and a third to give believers authority over evil spirits. See Matthew 10:1 and 28:18 for examples He kept the non-evangelical believers, the Jewish people to preserve Scripture and Jewish roots because He knew that the heathens who came into the church would take us off on a tangent of incorrect doctrines. An example of those is the widely accepted concept of the Trinity taught by many Biblical scholars. To see the Godhead consisting of three elements is correct. There is the One Who spoke to create the universe, that some call the Godhead, with the Incarnate body called Jesus and the Holy Spirit for the Earth. These three are One, there are not three persons as in official doctrines of several denominations. God is One and has many attributes. The Trinity is not to be the object of our worship, but His Oneness is. Jesus on the cross was God on the cross. The Lord on the throne in Isaiah 6:1 is God/Jesus/Holy Spirit. This verse is interesting because it is almost universally translated, "In the year that king Uzziah died I saw also the Lord sitting upon a throne, high and lifted up, and His train filled the temple." The word translated "temple" also means palace, which is where the throne would be. There is no throne in the tabernacle as seen by Moses, when Moses was shown the heavenly tabernacle, so he could have the earthly tabernacle built as a copy. His train filled the throne room of the palace, where the King of the Universe reigns. His Spirit sat on the mercy seat of the Holy of Holies.

God has appeared on earth more than once in His Incarnate form. In Genesis 18 He came to Abraham. In Genesis 32:25 Jacob wrestled all night with a man (ish) who was most likely Jesus. Ish also means husband and Jesus is THE Bridegroom. Exodus 24:9. Then Moshe and Aharon, Nadav, and Avihu, and seventy of the elders of Yisrael went up. 10. And they saw the God of Yisrael: and there was under His feet as it were a paved work of brilliant sapphire, and as it were the body of heaven in its clearness.[1] 11. And He did not lay His hand upon the nobles of the children of Yisrael:

---

1   (v.10) They all saw the King of the Universe!

also they saw God, then they ate and drank Exodus 33:10 says that the Lord spoke to Moses face to face, and the people rose up and worshipped, every man in his tent door. 11. And the Lord spoke to Moses face to face, as a man speaks to his friend... In Exodus 34:6 the Lord passed by Moses on the mountain, with Moses seeing His back, but not His face. In 1 Samuel 3:10. And YHVH came, and stood, and called as at other times, Sh'muel, Sh'muel... In 1 Kings 22 we have we the prophet Michayahu saying, 19. And he said, Hear you therefore the word of the Lord; I saw the Lord sitting on his throne, and all the host of heaven standing by him on his right hand and on his left. Hoshea 7:7 Thus He showed me: and, behold, YHVH stood on a wall made by a plumb-line, with a plumb-line in His hand.

God's coming appearance is told in Zechariah 14:1-5 Behold, the Day of YHVH is coming and booty from you shall be divided in your presence. 2. For I will gather all the heathens against Jerusalem in battle and the city shall be taken and the houses rifled and the women ravished, and half the city shall go into captivity and the rest of the people shall not be cut off from the city. 3. Then YHVH shall go forth and fight against those heathens, like when He fought in the day of battle. 4. And His, YHVH's, feet shall stand in that day upon the Mount of Olives, which is before Jerusalem on the east, and the Mount of Olives shall split in the middle toward the east and toward the west and there shall be a very great valley, and half of the mountain shall remove toward the north and half of it toward the south. 5. And you shall flee to the valley of the mountains, for the valley of the mountains shall reach to Azal. Yes, you shall flee, like you fled from before the earthquake in the days of Uzziah king of Judah and YHVH my God shall come and all the saints with you. Most translations use the Lord to translate YHVH, the personal name of God, but this is the King of the Universe Himself Who comes in this passage!

To carry the oneness of God one step farther, we must consider the God of Abraham, Isaac, and Jacob. The One God is the Almighty Whom the Jewish people worship. Their failure to recognize His Incarnate form does not negate their relationship with Him – especially because He has caused insensibility to come upon them. Ro 11.1. Therefore I ask, did not God reject His people? May it not be! For also I myself am an Isreali, from the seed of Abraham, tribe of Benjamin. 2. God did not reject His people whom He knew beforehand. Or do you not know with Elijah what the Scripture says, as he intercedes with God with reference to Israel? 3. Lord, "They killed Your prophets, they tore down Your altars, and only I was left and they are seeking my life." (1Ki 19:10,14) 4. But what does the divine statement say to him? "I reserved seven thousand men for Myself, who did not bend a knee to Baal." (1Ki 19:18) 5. Then, just as also in the present time, a remnant has come into being according to the election of grace: 6. and if by grace, it is no longer by means of works, because, if it were, grace would no longer be grace. 7. Then what? What Israel is seeking, this it did not obtain, but the election did obtain: and the rest grew callous, 8. just as it has been written,

> "God gave them a spirit of stupor,
> their eyes to not see
> and their ears to not hear,
> until this very day." (Dt 29:4, Is 29:10, see also Is 6:10a)

God gave them a spirit of stupor so they could not recognize the Incarnate God, but He did not rescind His covenants. Ro 11:25. For I do not want you to be ignorant, brothers, of this mystery, lest you become conceited, because dulled perception in part has come upon Israel until the fullness of the heathens would come in (Lk 21:24) 26. and in this way all Israel will be saved, just as it has been written,

> "The One Who rescues will come out of Zion,
> He will banish ungodliness from Jacob.
> 27. and this is the covenant for them with Me,
> when I would take away their sins." (Is 59:20,21)

Christians assume YHVH and Jesus are two different Beings, especially as Father and Son. This has led to a basic conflict with Judaism, which says, God is One, and Christianity referring to the Trinity of Father, Son, and Holy Spirit. The Apostles Creed talks about three persons. While the elements of the Trinity are in Scripture, with references to the Holy Spirit as roaming to and fro over all the earth (2Chron. 16:9), the Trinity is an oversimplification of our unfathomable, awesome God.

The Holy Spirit is called the Comforter in John 14:15, but YHVH says I AM your Comforter in Isaiah 51:12. The Spirit of God is within us (John 17:23). YHVH Goes Before us and is our Rear Guard, all at same time.

God is complex with some attributes man has credited to Jesus that are God Himself. Look at these shared names: God Incarnate, Jesus, and YHVH are known as Savior, Deliverer, Husband or Bridegroom, I AM, Help, Y'shua, King of Kings, Lord of Lords, Redeemer, With you, Messiah.

The last named is the most significant, when YHVH touches down on the Mount of Olives in Zech. 14:3,4, to begin His reign as King over all the earth. YHVH and Jesus are One and the same.

Truly, the Lord is our God, the Lord is One.

Gossip/Slander   We will be judged by every idle word, as Jesus spoke in Matthew 12:36 "and I say to you that every idle word which men will speak will be paid back with regard to his account on Judgment Day: 37. for you will be justified because of your words, and you will be condemned because of your words." (Psalm 51:4, Proverbs 6:2, 21:3)

James 3:6. "The tongue is also a fire: the world of unrighteousness, the tongue, is sitting for itself among the parts of our body, defiling the whole body and destroying the wheel of life and being set on fire by Gehenna. 7. For every species of beasts, and also of birds, and of reptiles, and even of sea creatures, is tamed and has been tamed by humans, 8. but no one is able to tame the tongue of men, unstable, evil, full of deadly poison. 9. With this we bless the Lord and Father and with this we curse men,.."

Paul wrote similar admonitions in Romans 1:29,30, 2 Corinthians 12:20, Colossians 3:8, and 2 Timothy 3:1-5. The Jewish teachers had known since the earliest times that the tongue was a great problem for most people.

One source of this knowledge is Leviticus 14, which in English is only about cleansing a leper, but in Hebrew has an obvious, strong spiritual meaning. This is because the Hebrew word for leper, M'tsora is pronounced the same as two words, M'tso ra. The two words mean, "finding evil" so from the earliest days the Jewish people knew the reference to gossip and slander. In fact the whole portion on cleansing the leper relates to gossip and slander. The offering of the two birds (v. 4) represents the twittering and chirping of the gossiper and slanderer. One of the birds is killed, then not offered on the altar, but it is buried, as gossip and slander should be buried. The second bird is set free, representing the repentant sinner, forgiven by God, given another chance, and released to go and sin no more.

The crimson thread and hyssop brought with the birds (v. 4) are also significant. The red dye for the thread is made from an insect and represents the penitent's newfound humility. Hyssop is a low bush, also symbolizing humility.

The root causes of this sin come from pride, which breeds contempt for others that lets them talk about others callously, and jealousy. The hair of the head, beard, and eyebrows are shaved (v. 9) because these are symbols of pride. The beard also frames the mouth that spoke the gossip and slander. The eyebrows represent the base trait of jealousy, as someone looking with envy.

Rabbis say that Joseph had a problem with this, based on Genesis 37:2, which says "These are the chronicles of Jacob: Joseph, at the age of seventeen, was a shepherd with his brothers by the flock, but he was a youth with the sons of Bilhah and the sons of Zilpah, his father's wives; and Joseph would bring evil reports about them to his father." Bringing evil reports showed the wrong motive, when his goal apparently was to curry favor with Jacob, not to change the brothers' behavior.

Our tongues do sin and we too should remember to walk in repentance every day of the year, guarding every word, because "no one is able to tame the tongue of men." Keep in mind Matthew 12:37, that we will be condemned by our words.

Hallel means praise and refers to the Seder Haggadah after the meal is eaten. During the Hallel Psalms 113-118 are sung, so these Psalms are called Hallel. They are also sung each week in the home during a mini-Seder welcoming the Sabbath on Friday evening.

Hanukkah is the Feast of Dedication in Hebrew and its history is very interesting. It is referred to one time in Scripture. "At that time it was the Feast of Dedication in Jerusalem, it was winter, and Jesus was walking in the temple, on Solomon's Porch." (John 10:22,23)

Around 170 BC the Greeks under Antiochus IV Epiphanes desecrated the temple by sacrificing a pig at the altar. Antiochus tried to eliminate Judaism, not so much by killing the Jews as by forbidding the practice of Judaism. Reading Torah was forbidden, along with circumcision, honoring the Sabbath, etc. In 167 BC a priest by the name of Mattityahu Hasmonea started guerrilla warfare along with his sons and a few followers. What they did in the hill country of Judea and Samaria was so amazing that books on their exploits are still studied by modern guerrilla fighters. Early in the war Judas Hasmonea took over after his father's death and he is the one who came up with the legendary tactics. His motto was "Mi Camokha Ba Elim Adona'y," from Exodus 15:11. The translation is: "Who is Like You, Oh Lord, Among the Mighty." The initials of those words spell Maccabee, which is the name that was later applied to Judas and his followers. Although spelled differently in Hebrew, the Hebrew word for hammer sounds like maccabee. Therefore he was called "The Hammer," which in Hebrew is Maccabeus, so the books of Maccabees in the Apocrypha were written about their successful wars. In 164 BC they took over the temple. This was the first war fought over a principle, religious freedom, and was the first successful guerrilla war, paralleling our American Revolution, also fought over principle, using guerrilla tactics.

They needed to repair and dedicate the temple right away. Dedication is an eight-day process that requires the use of sanctified oil for the lamp stand in the Holy Place, the first room of the sanctuary. They could only find a one-day supply of oil, but rather than wait eight days to sanctify more, they began the temple sanctification process with the one-day supply. The Lord through a creative miracle made that one-day's supply last the full eight days. For this reason Hanukkah is also called the Festival of Lights.

Harlot fornicator, immoral are common translations of the Greek word porneia. While this is the primary meaning of the word, it is used to speak of any idolatry, as in Hosea 1:2. See John 8:41, Revelation 2:21. Another example is Rahab, not necessarily a harlot, but certainly an idolater in pre-Israeli Jericho.

The verses of Isaiah 23:15-18 tie luxurious living to harlotry, with verse 18 putting wealth in its proper perspective. V.15. "And it shall come to pass in that day, that Tyre shall be forgotten seventy years, according to the days of one king; after the end of seventy years it shall be Tyre as in the harlot's song. 16. Take a lyre, go about the city, you harlot that has been forgotten; make sweet melody, sing many songs, that you may be remembered. 17. And it shall come to pass after the end of seventy years, that the Lord will visit Tyre, and she shall turn to her hire, and shall play the harlot with all the kingdoms of the world upon the face of the earth. 18. And her merchandise and her hire shall be holiness to the Lord; it shall not be treasured nor laid up; for her merchandise shall be for those who dwell before the Lord, to eat sufficiently, and for fine clothing."

Jeremiah 3:9 says "..with the frivolity of her (Israel's) adultery she brought guilt upon the land, because she committed adultery with stone and wood [idols]." In the call to repentance of Jeremiah 4:3,4 the commentary in the Artscroll Tanach (OT) says "..Jews must circumcise their hearts, (Deuteronomy 10:16, Jeremiah 9:25) i.e., remove the impediments to total commitment to God's will, lest sinful thoughts ruin the efficacy of their supplications." Rashi wrote that commentary in the eleventh century. See Wealth elsewhere in this Glossary.

Harmony of the Gospels is very real, but as you read the Lord's Prayer or the Beatitudes in both Matthew and Luke or parables in any of the Gospels, remember that Jesus would have taught any given message more than once. He was teaching principles that did not require word-for-word repetition, so when you notice differences make notes to see where and to whom each teaching was given. The Sermon on the Mount is a good example. In Matthew 5 Jesus went up on a mountain to teach. In the parallel passage beginning with Luke 6:17 Jesus went down and stood on a flat place to teach, so we know that these are two distinct messages, not a differing report of the same message.

Havdalah is the name of the service at the beginning of the day after the Sabbath. Havdalah means separation in Hebrew. One hour after sundown ends the Sabbath, there is a service at the synagogue to make the transition back to the secular workday. The one-hour delay is to be absolutely certain that the Sabbath is over, no fudging allowed. Some congregations make that a two-hour delay. This separation between holy and profane is discussed in the Zohar, Vayikra Section III, "we should say at the close of Sabbath, 'who divideth between holy and profane', the separation consisting in the fact that holiness is something apart, and the rest issue from it."

After the Havdalah service money can be discussed and used because the worshippers have returned from their separation with God to the secular, work-a-day world. It was after a Havdalah service that Paul instructed the Corinthians (1 Corinthians 16:2) to set aside their money. The Havdalah service is also the reason Paul spoke so late in Troas, when Eutuchus fell out the window (Acts 20:7). Acts 20:6 tells us that Paul and those with him left Philipi after the Feast of Unleavened Bread, so allowing for the travel time, from Philippi to Troas, of five days, this was likely sometime from mid April to early May. That would put sunset at 7:00 PM or later, so the Havdalah service would have started sometime after 9:00 PM. Allowing time for the service and the meal it could have been 11:00 PM when Paul began to speak, making it easy for him to go on past midnight.

Heavenly Hosts   also called Lord of Hosts or Lord Sabaoth, is Tsvaot in Hebrew, as in 2 Kings 6:17. This is the army commanded by the Lord of Hosts. When the Hebrew Scriptures were translated into Greek, the Septuagint, Tsvaot was translated by the Greek word Pantokrator. This translation of the Greek translates Pantokrator as Hosts because that is most likely the meaning to its Jewish authors. The Greek spelling of Tsvaot, Sabaoth, shows up twice in the New Testament, in Romans 9:29 and James 5:4.

Heavens   is always plural in Hebrew, with seven levels of heaven noted in Scripture. The names are: Vilon, Rakia, Shechakim, Zevul, Maon, Machon, and Aravot.

Vilon is "That stretches out the heavens as a curtain (Vilon), and spreads them out as a tent to dwell in." (Isaiah 40:22) Vilon retires in the morning and comes out in the evening, and renews the work of creation daily. Vilon is the entire universe, going beyond what we can see with telescopes. Vilon is the word for curtain used in the Talmud, but a synonym, doq, pronounced like coke, is the word used in Isaiah 40:22.

Rakia is where "God set them in the firmament (Rakia) of the heavens." (Genesis 1:17) This is a reference to the stars, sun, moon, and planets: outer space where the various heavenly bodies move in their prescribed orbits and/or maintain relationships in constellations, solar systems, galaxies, etc. Rakia is the part of the heavens that can be seen.

Shechakim is from "He commanded the skies (Shechakim) above and opened the doors of heaven; and He rained down manna upon them to eat." (Psalm 78:23) This is where the millstones are located that grind manna for the righteous. His Word is still miraculously feeding us. Shechakim is the atmosphere.

Zevul is the location for "I have surely built you a house of habitation (Zevul), a place for you to dwell in forever." (I Kings 8:13) This is the location of celestial Jerusalem and the temple with the heavenly altar where Michael offers a sacrifice. How do we know that Zevul is this place? Because, "Look down from heaven and behold from the habitation (Zevul) of Your holiness and Your glory." (Isaiah 63:15)

Maon is where "The Lord will command His loving kindness in the daytime and in the night his song shall be with Me." (Psalm 42:8) This is where His ministering angels stay, singing in the night. We know that this is heaven because of "Look down from your holy habitation (Maon) from heaven." (Deuteronomy 26:15)

Machon is the location of the storehouses of snow, rain, hail, whirlwinds, storms, etc. "The Lord shall open unto you His good treasure..." (Deuteronomy 28:12) We know that this is heaven because "Hear in heaven, the habitation (Machon) of Your dwelling..." (I Kings 8:39)

Aravot is that in which are righteousness, judgment, and charity, the storehouses of life, of peace and of blessing, the spirits of the righteous, with which the Lord will hereafter revive the dead. Those living here include the Ophannim, Seraphim, holy Chayyot, the ministering angels, the Throne of Glory, and the King of the Universe. "Cast up a highway for Him Who rides upon the clouds (Aravot); His name is Yah." (Psalm 68:4) The storehouse of life contains the force of life for all those yet to be born because when God finished creation (Genesis 2:1) He had made everything that would ever be -- including your descendants. The spirits of the righteous are the dead who are sleeping with their fathers.

Notice that the first three represent the universe, the visible night sky and sun, and the atmosphere. These are natural, physical things even when beyond the range of telescopes.

Each of the other four levels is both physical and spiritual. Three levels are translated Habitation, but that is not the clue we need. Three levels are populated: Zevul, with the celestial Jerusalem; Maon, with bands of ministering angels; and Aravot, with various heavenly beings, the Throne, and the spirits of the saints. That is probably the level Paul referred to, the third of the populated levels, in 2 Corinthians 12:2.

Hebraisms   are those elements of Hebrew grammar and vocabulary that show up in the Greek text. It is interesting that the writings of Luke contain the most Hebraisms in the New Testament. One of the Hebraisms he used is to speak of going "from Judea to Caesarea." He is the only New Testament author to write of going from Judea to Caesarea, and that at a time when Caesarea was the capital of Judea. The Rabbis considered it profane to think of any city other than Jerusalem as the capital and any alien government was also profane. The expression "from Judea to Caesarea" was only used by Rabbis.

Hellenists   There are several references to Hellenists in the New Testament so it is important to understand who they were.

Hellenists came into being shortly after Alexander the Great overran Israel on his way to Egypt in 332 BC. He was not a ruthless dictator in the countries he conquered but gave each country a great deal of autonomy. What he wanted was taxes and trade, so he had to leave only a relatively small number of troops to maintain their allegiance. Each country had religious freedom, so Israel might not have been greatly affected except that many of its citizens were taken with Greek culture. They liked the affluence, the theater, the games - various aspects of Greek life that were introduced to Israel by the new society.

Those most affected by this were the rich and the powerful. They started to speak Greek instead of Hebrew and to go to the Greek theater and games instead of to synagogue or the temple. They came to be called "Tsadeek" which means Righteous. The Greek spelling of Tsadeek is Sadducee when written in English letters. These people were the Hellenists, only nominally Jewish although they viewed themselves as righteous. In the 20th century people who acted as they did with their conquerors were called collaborators. The High Priests came from the Hellenists and in Jesus' day they were appointed by Pontius Pilate. The Sadducees were very strict in enforcing laws, while the Pharisees were more merciful.

Opposing the Hellenists were the Hasidim, or Pious, also referred to as Lifrot, meaning Broke Away. These included the top students in the yeshivas (schools) who were also known as rabbis. The Hasidim later became known as Parush, meaning self-denying, dissident, seceder, seclusive, sanctimonious. The Greek spelling of Parush is Pharisee when written with English letters. The division and animosity between Pharisees and Sadducees was strong, even though both were represented on the Sanhedrin. How close to the surface this animosity was can be seen Acts 23:6-10. As a point of information, the present group of Hasidim is not related to the ancient, but rose in Eastern Europe in the 18th century.

The Greek successors to Alexander became very oppressive and in 168 BC desecrated the temple and forbade the reading of the Torah and the honoring of the Sabbath. Some Pious under the leadership of a priestly family, named Hasmonea, who had remained loyal to Judaism, rebelled and won. See Hanukkah in Glossary. However in just a few years they were again under Greek Seleucid domination until 64 BC when Rome took over at the invitation of Herod Hyrcanus II. Although they were descendants of Aaron they continued to rule and never appointed someone from another tribe to be king. Eventually the Hasmoneans became corrupt and compromised, said by some rabbis to be the result of their not being from the tribe of Judah. This is because Jacob said to Judah in Genesis 49:10 "The scepter shall not depart from between his (Judah's) feet..", meaning that the scepter, the sign of kingship, would always belong to the tribe of Judah.

Herod the Great was a son of the Hasmonean prince Hyrcanus II, also called Antipater, who was military governor of Idumea (Edom). Herod was so extraordinarily successful at courting Roman favor that he was the first to be called "King of the Jews" and his descendants became the puppet rulers for Rome throughout the 1st century. Herod the Great reigned from 37BC-4 BC.

Since the Sadducees were Hellenists, they are referred to frequently in the New Testament. The Hellenists are also seen in Acts 6:1, 9:29, 11:20, and 21:37. This puts into perspective John 11:50 when Caiaphas said "and you do not consider that it profits you that one man should die on behalf of the people so then the whole nation would not be lost." The coming of Messiah would have totally destroyed the world of the Hellenist rulers in Israel. Remember that the High Priest was appointed by Pontius Pilate and he only appointed politically powerful Hellenists.

The friction between the Hellenists and the Pharisees ran deep and can even be seen in the fledgling church in Acts 6:1-6, with the Hellenists complaining that the congregational leaders were overlooking the needs of the Hellenists.

The Hanukkah feast celebrates the victory of the Parush over the Greek forces that were backed by the Hellenists. This was a victory for those who chose to align themselves with the teachings of God over those who aligned themselves with appeasement and tolerance of pagan beliefs. This parallels today's spiritual battle in the US and the world of those loyal to God's teachings vs. those who tolerate all manner of evil, accepting homosexuality as another "life style" and abortion as "choice." They encourage teaching occult and false religions in our public schools, but forbid the teaching and practice of Christianity, all in the name of "multi-culturalism." This battle will not be won with the weapons of war, but will be won in the hearts of Americans as revival takes root.

Hosanna   is the English spelling of Hoshea-na, meaning Deliver Us Now! This comes from the same Hebrew root as Yeshua, the Hebrew name of Jesus. The ending, "na," is something we do not have a translation for, in English, a demanding "NOW!" that is not rude or impertinent. It is properly translated "Please!" or "I pray you!" or "Behold!" and always needs the exclamation point to convey the urgency. The shouting of "Hoshea-na" at Jesus' triumphal entrance in Jerusalem with the waving of palm fronds and branches were traditionally done on the sixth day of the Feast of Succot, welcoming the reigning Messiah to assume the throne in Jerusalem. All those shouting "Hoshea-na!" knew this and believed Jesus was the Messiah Who had come to claim His throne, then and there. See Matthew 21:8,9, Mark 11:8,9, Luke 19:37,38, and John 12:13.

Humble   when used collectively, referring to a group, represents the faithful remnant as seen in 1 Kings 19:18. Rabbi David Kimkhi, 12th & 13th century scholar, wrote that the Hebrew Scriptures frequently use Humble to "denote the faithful minority in Israel who remained staunch throughout the national trials and did not yield to the pressure of the nations among whom they were scattered." This remnant is referred to in 1 Kings 19:18 when God spoke of the 7,000 who had not bowed a knee to Baal. There are about two dozen verses with this reference, but they are hidden in most English translations because the Hebrew word, Anav, is translated by different English words, as poor, meek, or lowly, in addition to humble. Some of the verses where anav refers to the remnant are: "He guides the humble in judgment; and he teaches the humble his way." (Psalm 25:9) "But the humble shall inherit the earth; and shall delight themselves in the abundance of peace." (Psalm 37:11) "When God arose to judgment, to save all the humble of the earth. Selah." (Psalm 76:9) "Surely he scorns the scorners; but he gives grace to the humble." (Proverbs 3:34) "The humble also shall increase their joy in the Lord, and the poorest among men shall rejoice in the Holy One of Israel." (Isaiah 29:19) "The spirit of the Lord God is upon me; because the Lord has anointed me to announce good news to the humble; he has sent me to bind up the broken hearted, to proclaim liberty to the captives, and the opening of the prison to those who are bound;" (Isaiah 61:1) "Seek the Lord, all you humble of the earth, who have performed his judgment; seek righteousness, seek humility; it may be that you shall be hidden in the day of the Lord's anger." (Zephaniah 2:3)

In past years humble and meek may have been synonyms, but in modern English humble denotes a lack of pride, while meek speaks of low self-esteem, lacking confidence.

Ignored Commandments   There are some commandments that are not appropriate for today. The most prominent of these concern animal sacrifices. The Jewish people stopped making animal sacrifices when the temple was destroyed and the Jewish people were deported to other countries in 70 AD. Deuteronomy 12:14 commands Israel to offer sacrifices in just one place: "But only in the place which the Lord shall choose in one of your tribes, there you shall offer your burnt offerings, and there you shall do all that I command you." The place chosen by God is in Jerusalem on what is now called the Temple Mount. There are some in Judaism who are preparing to resume sacrifices in the Third Temple, but others say animal sacrifices are no longer appropriate. This is in reference to verses such as Hosea 6:6 "I desire kindness, not sacrifice; and knowledge of God more than burnt offerings." Other verses saying something similar are 1 Samuel 15:22, Psalms 81:18, 90:7, and Isaiah 1:11.

Paul includes circumcision with commands that are no longer to be adhered to. Romans 2:28. "For the Jewish person is not the one to be plainly recognized by what he wears, his prayer shawl, and neither is circumcision just openly in the flesh, 29. but one is Jewish inwardly, and circumcised in his heart in spirit, not letter, whose praise is not from people but from God." He wrote in Galatians 5:2, referring to heathen converts, "Behold, I, Paul, say to you that if you would be circumcised, Messiah will profit you nothing. 3. And I am testifying again to every circumcised man that he is obligated to do the whole tradition." Paul did not come up with this on his own, but knew his Scriptures: Deuteronomy 10:16. "Circumcise therefore the foreskin of your heart, and be no more stiff-necked." Jeremiah 4:4 "Circumcise yourselves unto the Lord – remove the barriers of you hearts" Jeremiah 9:25. "Egypt, and Judah, and Edom, and the Ammonites, and Moab, and all who dwell in the wilderness; for all these nations are uncircumcised, and all of the house of Israel are uncircumcised in the heart."

In regard to all the commandments, we are to give our hearts to the Lord, to walk in repentance, and speak through our actions, by the way we live to give evidence that we have an ongoing relationship with the God of Abraham, Isaac, and Jacob.

Isaiah 28:16   is quoted in Romans 9:33, 10:11, and 1Peter 2:6. The last sentence of verse 16 is often translated similarly to the Greek rending, "and the one who believes upon Him will not be put to shame." The NIV has "..the one who trusts will never be dismayed." The Hebrew is stronger and deeper than that. "..the one who believes will not make haste." The word translated 'one who believes' or 'one who trusts' is ma'amin, which has a root meaning that speaks of both training and loyalty or faithfulness. There is a difference between just believing and being loyal through hard times. James 2:19 says, "You believe that God is One, you do well: the demons also believe and shudder." The demons know God and His power, but are not obedient and faithful to Him.

The two words translated "dismayed" or "make haste" are more difficult, but refer to something not done quickly. The twelfth century rabbi, Ibn Ezra, wrote, "He (the faithful one) will remain steadfast in his faith however long realization may be delayed." Each of us must understand that when the Lord has given us a vision for ministry, that the timing is His, not ours, and we need to hold strong in faith while He brings all things in His timing. If we get ahead of His timing the ministry becomes our ministry, not His. That ministry may have financial success but will not have spiritual success. When He gives any of us the vision for a ministry there may be years of preparation before we are to begin.

What to us seems to be a delay may be something the Lord is doing in us. Paul wrote in Philippians 4:11-13: "Not that I am talking on account of a great need, for I learned to be content with what things I have. And I know how to submit myself to want, and I know how to be abundant: in everything and in all things I have learned the secret, both how to be filled and how to be needy and how to be affluent and how to suffer want: I have strength to overcome all things in the One Who strengthens me." Psalm 105 says: v. 17 "...Joseph was sold as a slave." Then verse 19 says: "Until the time that His word came to pass, the decree of the Lord had purified him." (Artscroll Tanach) This refers to the time Joseph spent in slavery and in prison. The word translated purified comes from a root which means to refine, purify, test, or burn. The time spent waiting for the Lord's timing has a purpose, whether to purify the minister or to prepare other elements, a true refining process. We need to be like Paul, content in this season of lack. The lack can be money, as Paul wrote about, or it may be in ministry. Each of us has a ministry, with or without ordination. Remember, each of us is a priest. We are a "... kingdom, priests to His God and Father.." (Revelation 1:6). It is important to be obedient; to wait contentedly, to keep the faith and grow spiritually while He works His will in us.

There are many promises in His Word for Israel and for end times, but we cannot put our timetables on them. If you listen to tapes made ten or more years ago about end times, or read end time books written at least that long ago, you will see that the speakers/authors did not have a handle on God's timing. There are many prophecies for Israel today that we hold in faith, even though they may not be fulfilled in my lifetime. They will be fulfilled in His timing. The eleventh chapter of Hebrews dwells on this theme.

Italics	are words that have been added to the translation to make smoother reading or to complete a statement. Many times the verbs is, are, were, etc. are inserted because Hebrew does not use a verb of being, so the Hebrew speaking authors of the NT did not use them.

Jacob	is the name used in this translation wherever the Greek name Iakob appears in the text. English Bibles and Bibles translated to another language from those English Bibles are the only ones not spelling Iakob in their language. Tradition has other English translations using James, but this translation uses the English spelling of Iakob.

Jesus	is the English spelling of the Greek Iesous. The J came into Old English from the German language and was used for the English spelling of names from the Latin. Wycliffe made the earliest English translation, from the Latin Vulgate. The German language pronounces the "J" as a "Y" which is why the German Jesus would be pronounced the same as the Greek Iesous and Latin Iesus. His Hebrew name was Yeshua, the Galilean pronunciation of Yeshu. The root word of Yeshu is YShA, a verb meaning save, deliver from. Since Greek has no "sh" sound, that was changed to s in Iesous. The final s in Greek is there for what is called the declension of the noun, and in the first use in the New Testament of the name Jesus, in Matthew 1:1, Jesus is spelled Iesou in Greek, as close as Greek can come to Yeshua. In the November-December 2002 issue of Biblical Archeology Review there was a report of a burial box found in Jerusalem, bearing the inscription "Jacob, son of Joseph, brother of Jesus." The burial box, made of stone, has been authenticated as a first century burial box. This is the first object known to refer directly to Jesus.

Yeshu is very interesting because it was a common enough name that it has been found at several archeological digs. There is a noun, Yeshuah, pronounced the same as His Galilean Yeshua, that is used about seventy-five times in the Old Testament, and is translated Victories, Welfare, Health, Saving Health, Deliverance, Salvation, and is transliterated in New Testament Greek as Hosanna. Hosanna means Deliverance Now! Or, Salvation Now! The people were actually shouting "Yeshuah-na!" or "Hoshea-na!" from the same Hebrew root. The Na suffix is a demanding "Now" or "Please!" that would be rude to our Western minds. The meaning of Yeshuah is deliverance more than salvation and where hosanna is used in Matthew 21:9, 15, Mark 11:9,10, and John 12:13, as Jesus rides the donkey into Jerusalem, the people were looking for deliverance from the Roman conquerors. They viewed Jesus as the Messiah Who had come to sit on the throne in Jerusalem and restore Israel to full independence. That was on the mind of each one who called Him "Son of David" as Bartimaeus did in Mark 10:47.

Jewish Calendar   Our New Testament authors and Jesus Himself went by the Jewish calendar, which still times the spiritual lives of our Jewish friends and neighbors. It is one of those things that we need to know more about and to teach in our churches so we can return to the appointed seasons of the Lord.

The Jewish calendar is based on the phases of the moon, meaning that the beginning of each month coincides with the appearance of the new moon.

In the fourth century AD, Hillel II established a fixed calendar based on mathematical and astronomical calculations. This calendar, still in use, standardized the length of months and the addition of months over the course of a nineteen-year cycle, so that the lunar calendar realigns with the solar years. Adar II is added in the 3rd, 6th, 8th, 11th, 14th, 17th and 19th years of the cycle. The current cycle began in Jewish year 5758 (the year that began October 2, 1997). Before this schedule was set the leap year was determined each year by examining the barley crop on the first of Adar. If the crop was not going to be ready to harvest in two weeks, then the second month of Adar was called for, because the barley harvest was needed for the First Fruits of Unleavened Bread. Also the spring equinox always fell in the month Adar.

In addition, <u>Yom Kippur</u> should not fall adjacent to <u>Shabbat</u> because this would cause difficulties in coordinating the fast with Shabbat, and <u>Hoshanah Rabba,</u> the seventh day of Sukkot, should not fall on Saturday because it would interfere with the holiday's observances. The adjustment is made by adding a day to the month of Kheshvan (or Heshvan) or subtracting a day from the month of Kislev of the previous year.

In the leap years, since there are two months Adar, Purim is celebrated in Second Adar to keep its proper perspective four weeks before Passover. Purim as a feast exposes persecution with Haman representing those trying to destroy the Jewish people. Esther 9:24. "Because Haman the son of Hammedatha, the Agagite, the enemy of all the Jews, had plotted against the Jews to destroy them, and had cast Pur, that is, the lot, to consume them, and to destroy them;" At Purim the Book of Esther is read to recount God's miraculous works that saved the Jewish people from certain death.

Purim is similar to Passover because both holidays celebrate the miraculous deliverance of the Jewish people. At the Passover meal the story of the Exodus is told (ordered in Ex 13:8), reminding all of the deliverance from Egyptian bondage and of the call of God upon their lives, with the giving of the Torah. The destination of the Exodus was the Promised Land. The purpose of the Exodus, the goal, was the creation of the Kingdom of

Priests (Ex 19:6, Is 61:6), the Holy People (Ex 19:10, Le 20:24, 26:12, Dt 7:6, 14:2,21, 28:9).

The New Year of the Jewish calendar begins on the first of the month Tishrei, the seventh month, which comes sometime in late August to mid September. It is called Rosh HaShannah, meaning New Year, but the Scriptural name of the Holy Day is the Day of Remembrance. This is the anniversary of the creation of the world and the day that is set aside to remember all that God has done for each one of us. It is a call to repentance in preparation for Yom Kippur, the Day of Atonement. Even though the year begins six months earlier with Tishrei, the months are counted from Nisan, because when God spoke to Moses commanding the Passover and Exodus He said "This month shall be the beginning of months: it shall be the first month of the year to you. Speak to all the congregation of Israel, saying 'On the tenth day of this month they shall take to them every man a lamb, according to the house of their fathers, a lamb for a house:..'" (Exodus 12:3)

The natural assumption is that this means the first of Nisan is New Year's Day. Not so. Who are we to question God? Until 1752 England and its colonies celebrated the New Year on March 25th.

Kingdom   speaks of several things. It is difficult to put kingdom references into the neat pigeonholes with which we are so comfortable. One use of the kingdom is to refer to God Himself as in "But you must continually seek first the kingdom of God and His righteousness, then all these things will be provided for you." in Matthew 6:33 and "But if I am casting out demons by a finger of God, then the kingdom of God has come upon you." in Luke 11:20. Then we have in the same vein "But if I cast out demons by the Spirit of God, then the kingdom of God has come upon you." (Matthew 12:28) This means that all who have the Spirit of the Living God should expect deliverance from demonic influence, whether sickness or the evil spirits that oppressed the Gadarene demoniac.

Another use refers to the Eternal Kingdom, "I say to you that many will come from east and west and will recline with Abraham, Isaac, and Jacob in the kingdom of the heavens." (Matthew 8:11) "And Jesus said to them, 'Truly I say to you that you who follow Me in the restoration of all things, when the Son of Man would sit upon the throne of His glory, then you will be seated upon twelve thrones judging the twelve tribes of Israel.'" (Dan 7:9,10) This is in Matthew 19:28, also referring to the Eternal Kingdom.

Acts 1:6 has a clear reference that some were looking for the Messianic Reign, when an Israeli king would sit on the throne, saying "Therefore indeed those who came asked Him saying, 'Lord, in this time are You restoring the kingdom in Israel?' 7. But He said to them, 'It is not for you to know the times or seasons which the Father set by His own authority, 8. but you will take power when the Holy Spirit comes upon you and you will be My witnesses in Jerusalem and in all Judea and Samaria and to the end of the earth.'"

Mark 4:11 says "To you has been given the mystery of the Kingdom of God." The kingdom means more than one thing, so each time it is used we are to meditate to discern the appropriate meaning.

The late Chief Rabbi of the British Empire, J. H. Hertz, wrote "Peace is no negative concept and is not the equivalent of inactivity. Whether for the individual or for society it is that harmonious co-operation of all human forces towards ethical and spiritual ends which men call the Kingdom of God. The Prophets longed for a Messianic peace that should pervade the universe, and include all men, all peoples - that should include also the beasts of the field; Isaiah 11:6-10."

Korban   is an offering to God. Korban is the Greek spelling of a Hebrew word: Korban has no meaning in Greek. Often translated sacrifice, which is very inappropriate, the actual meaning comes from a Hebrew verb meaning to come near. The purpose of the offering is to bring the one making the offering closer to God, to elevate the person to a higher spiritual plane. This is the opposite of sacrifice. It is no sacrifice to present a gift to the Lord, and the giver receives a blessing in return. We sometimes sing of making a 'sacrifice of praise,' but there is no sacrifice of praise in Scripture. It is never a sacrifice to praise God. There is a sacrifice of joy (Psalm 27:6), to be joyful in a time of grief, and a sacrifice of thanksgiving (Psalm 107:22), offering thanks at a time of loss.

Your offering must be presented in the right attitude because the Lord loves a cheerful giver, 2 Corinthians 9:7. Whenever you are making an offering to God, whether tithes or free will offerings, whether through your church, giving to missionaries, feeding the poor, or ministering to prisoners (Matthew 25:35-40, Isaiah 61:1) you are being blessed by God. He is raising you to a higher spiritual plane. This principle is presented in the Hebrew of the first chapter of Leviticus describing the burnt offerings and meal offerings. The offering can be for atonement of sin or a free will offering, but the benefit is the same, the giver rises to a new level of relationship with the Lord.

Legalism   is man's way of defining Scripture. The motivation for this is good -- so that everyone will understand and agree on the boundaries that are vague in Scripture. This defining can then become the focus instead of studying the Scriptures and that is where man goes astray, because we are to keep our focus on God, not our own rules. This focus on rules can lead people to look for loopholes, rather than seek the Lord to see what

Focus on God not rules

the Spirit wants. An example of this is the Sabbath, where much of the Church has neglected the Scriptural prohibitions, saying the prohibitions are not important or that every day is a Sabbath -- an impossibility if you refer to the very nature of Sabbath, which is to be a day of rest, time with the Lord. Jesus never did anything on a Sabbath that is prohibited in Scripture, but legalism had come in and He was criticized for doing things that well-intentioned men had defined for clarity and consistency. See Sabbath elsewhere in Glossary.

Leprosy in Scripture is not like the disease known by that name today. The Hebrew word 'Tsara-at' is translated into Greek by the word 'Lepra' which is the source of our word leprosy, but the Scriptural rash and contagion are not the same as the symptoms of the disease now called leprosy. Leprosy is perhaps the least contagious of all contagious diseases and is today generally treated on an outpatient basis. The Biblical disease translated leprosy was obviously very contagious, as are a number of skin rashes still with us. See Gossip/Slander in this Glossary.

Life as in John 10:10 refers both to life on Earth and in the hereafter. Jewish commentators, in reading Psalm 34:13. "Who is the man who desires life, and loves many days, that he may see good? 14. Keep your tongue from evil, and your lips from speaking guile. 15. Depart from evil, and do good; seek peace, and pursue it." say "life" refers to the World to Come, and "days" refers to man's years in this world, which are only days by comparison to the eternal life of the next world. Then Moses describes how to have the abundant life in Deuteronomy 30:15. "See, I have set before you this day life and good, and death and evil; 16. In that I command you this day to love the Lord your God, to walk in his ways, and to keep his commandments and his statutes and his judgments, that you may live and multiply; and the Lord your God shall bless you in the land which you are entering to possess." These verses speak of the dual life, having a rewarding life in the here and now, but looking forward to the ultimate goal of eternal life with our heavenly Father. Many people have rewarding lives without having an abundance of material goods. Jesus says in Luke 12:15. "And He said to them, 'You must continually understand and guard yourselves from all covetousness, because someone's life is not abundant from his possessions.'" Then He adds in Luke 14:33. "So in this way every one of you who does not renounce all his own possessions is not able to be My disciple." Live every day to the fullest, knowing that doing His perfect will is the greatest reward of all, both in the here and the hereafter.

[handwritten margin notes: life / world / to come / days / man's years / in this world]

Location of the Feeding of the Five Thousand is identified in Luke 9:10 as being near Beit-Tsaida. There are two towns by that name, one between Capernaum and Tiberias, on the west side of the lake. The other Beit-Tsaida was across the lake, at the northeast corner. That would be about seven miles north and east from Capernaum, but nearly diagonally across the lake from Tiberias.

Rowing from east to west, going to Capernaum from the northeast Beit-Tsaida would be against the strong winds as described in the Gospels, as Jesus walked on the water (John 6:19) to catch up to them. Those strong winds blew them off course so they landed at Gennesaret (Mark 6:53) instead of the western Bethsaida (Mark 6:45). Gennesaret is a plain of good farm land adjacent to Capernaum on the northeast.

Logos/Rhema   Logos is sometimes thought of as word in the context of a statement or maybe even the entire Bible, while Rhema is thought of as a specific word or verse. Actually the two are synonyms and the emphasis in Greek is on the sound as the word is spoken. This relationship is seen in the translation of the Septuagint, where rhema is used for ilat, meaning word or speech, and peh, meaning mouth or speech. Logos in the Septuagint is used for daber (da-bear), meaning word, and omer, meaning say, and milah, meaning word or speech.

Both words are often more appropriately translated message, statement, teaching, or something similar, so when you see the phrase "word of the Lord" and word is not capitalized, message, statement, or teaching could be an appropriate translation. John 5:38 and 5:47 are good examples. In 5:38 logos is translated message and in v. 47 rhema is translated teachings, both words referring to all that Jesus had taught to that time. In some cases it is not clear whether the author was referring to a message about the Lord or about Scripture.

Lord of Hosts   is the translation of the Greek word Pantokrator. In secular Greek this meant something closer to "almighty" and was used to refer to Hermes or some other false god. The Jewish translators of the Septuagint, the translation from Hebrew to Greek around 250 BC, translated Tsvaot as Pantokrator. Tsvaot means Hosts, referring to the Lord of Hosts, so this translation translates Pantokrator as Hosts. The heavenly hosts make up the army of angelic beings, as seen by the servant of Elisha at Dothan in 2 Kings 6:15-17. Revelation 4:8, quoting Isaiah 6:3, uses Pantokrator to translate Tsvaot in the Hebrew text. Rabbis consider El Shaddai (Almighty God) to be a synonym of Tsvaot. See Romans 9:29, James 5:4, Revelation 1:8, 4:8, 11:17, 15:3, 16:7,14, 19:6,15, 21:22.

Lord's Prayer   This is the prayer Jesus taught His disciples in Matthew 6:9-13. Some say that this should not be called the Lord's Prayer, but the Disciples' Prayer, because it is what Jesus instructed His disciples to pray.

It is appropriate to call it the Lord's because He taught this prayer, but then whatever the prayer is called should not be our concern, but that we do pray this and do pray it with the positive thrust that Jesus taught.

"Our Father," This is an immediate statement of our relationship with the King of the Universe, at once bringing to mind His love and concern for us and our submission to Him, as a small child should be submitted to his father. The Pharisees frequently started their prayers with "Our Father" (Avinu in Hebrew) and cited Hosea 11:1 as the Scriptural basis for that. That verse starts "When Israel was a child I loved him." In Isaiah 63:16 and other verses He is called "Our Father." When they began a prayer with that they went on,

"Who art in the heavens," recognizes His role as Creator and King of the Universe. We need in every prayer to acknowledge Him, to praise Him, to give Him all the glory. Prayers of the Pharisees used this phrase, which is Sh'ba shamayim in Hebrew. Psalm 115:16 says, "As for the heavens, the heavens are the Lord's, but the earth He has given to mankind."

"Your name must immediately be made holy" is a command for us, those who are praying, not just to refrain from profaning His name, but for us to do those things that make His name holy during this day. In Is 29:23 God tells us "sanctify My name." We sanctify His name by what we do. This is not an option, but every word we speak and every single thing we do must glorify the King of the Universe.

"Your kingdom must now come:" is a call for the reigning Messiah to begin His rule on earth. Jesus said that we are to know that the kingdom has come upon us when He casts out demons by a finger of God. (Lk 11:20) He also said "..the kingdom of God is within you." (Lk 17:21) Therefore this is another command for us to be aggressive about living in the kingdom of God right here, right now. That does not mean that this is all we will ever see of the kingdom, but He is telling us to believe that we have the authority He has given us, and He is telling us to use that authority. We have barely grasped the principles of spiritual warfare and have a long way to go to live as the overcomers that we should be. This agrees with Jewish thought as Rabbi Ben-Yehuda wrote August 11, 2000, "We cannot accept the lowest common denominator, for it hits rock bottom. We are challenged and called to achieve a world that is loftier and more spiritual, to rise and to raise, to elevate and establish His kingdom, right here, right now. Nothing less will do - nothing less will insure our survival."

"Your will must immediately be done, also on earth as in heaven." Who is here at this time to do His will? Is it not each one of us? This is not an appeal for the Lord to do things for us, but for us to be motivated to do absolutely everything that He would want us to do. We are His agents on earth, the ones through whom He works. Once again we are not asking this of God, but stating to Him that we have to be determined to do all we can to walk in His perfect will. It is up to each one of us to be all we can, in every relationship, in every way.

This first half of the prayer is entirely for us to do. Each of these lines is an individual, not a corporate responsibility, so Jesus gave us this prayer to strengthen each believer. As you do these things, incorporating the worship and the doing of His will into your personal walk with God, you lay the ground work for the Lord to be able to do the things that are to be done on your behalf in the second half of the prayer.

"You must immediately give to us (the) bread necessary today for our existence." The word translated "necessary for our existence" seems to have been coined by the early evangelists and in Scripture is used only here and in Luke 11. Some scholars translate it "daily," others "tomorrow" and others as "necessary for our existence." But the real thrust of this request is the command, a statement of our covenant relationship with our heavenly Father, coming as a small child to say, "Daddy, you have to.." Jesus was teaching us to speak boldly with our heavenly Father, the King of the Universe. See Daily Bread in this Glossary.

"You must immediately forgive our sins as we have already completed forgiving everyone of every little thing each has done to me." This accurately brings out that we cannot ask God to forgive our very real sins until we first forgive everyone of every little thing that has irritated us. This is an individual requirement, even though it is written in the plural. No one can do this for someone else. Each believer must forgive everyone of every little thing and of every big thing. Once we have finished totally forgiving everyone of everything, then we are to ask boldly that all our sins will be forgiven.

"And do not lead us into temptation, but You must continually rescue us from the evil one." The word translated lead means to bring or to carry in. The word translated temptation means test, trial, or temptation. When we go through difficult times we often think that God is testing us, and sometimes He is. A test is for the one being tested to prove to himself that he can do what is required. God already knows what he will do. Many times though He has given us an assignment, because we have been called into service, not into rest and relaxation. We complain about our circumstances when we should be charged up like Green Berets on being given a tough assignment. We need to be as thoroughly trained for spiritual warfare as a Green Beret or Special Forces soldier is for modern warfare. God does not tempt us, but He does test us, as Jesus tested Philip when He asked Philip where he could buy bread to feed the crowd. (John

6:6) Not to abort an assignment or wheedle our way out of a test, but to get out of a true satanic attack, we are to address God in the imperative, saying, "You must rescue me from the evil one!"

In the Lord's Prayer Jesus taught us to first of all acknowledge the Father as the Creator, the King of the Universe, the One to Whom we owe everything and to Whom we submit everything we have. When that is done we are to express our need in the same way a two year old addresses a parent, saying, "You have to do this for me!" He does supply all our needs, including deliverance from all evil spirits, sickness, poverty, relationships with others, virtually every need. While this prayer is in the plural "we," it brings out the need for individual relationship. No one can make up for your lack of faith or lack of asking. Jesus said, "And I say to you, You must continually ask and it will be given to you, you must continually seek and you will find, you must continually knock and it will be opened to you: for everyone who asks takes and the one who seeks finds and for the one who knocks it will be opened. And which of you if a son will ask his father for a fish will he then give him a serpent instead of a fish? Or also, if he will ask for an egg, will he give a scorpion to him? If therefore you, who are evil yourselves, know how to give good gifts to your children, how much more the Father from heaven will give the Holy Spirit to those who ask Him." (Luke 11:9-13) This is one example of this principle that is in each Gospel. However, we should not judge the faith of another saint when we see a saint fail in some way, or call him unspiritual because of a failure to overcome. Remember that neither Ezekiel nor his wife had shown sin or lack of faith when the Lord took her.

Note that this prayer in Matthew is included in His Sermon on the Mount, given to a large crowd. The prayer He taught in Luke 11:1-4 was given in a private place just to the twelve, so the two prayers would not be identical.

Manuscript   The text used for this translation is the 4th Revised Edition of Greek manuscripts edited by Barbara Aland, Kurt Aland, Johannes Karavidopoulos, Carlo M. Martini, and Bruce M. Metzger, published by the United Bible Society. This group used the methods of Textual Criticism to determine the versions closest to the original, first century manuscript. The methods of Scriptural Textual Criticism are similar to traditional methods used to determine the proper texts of the ancient secular classics.

We like to think that the New Testament has been preserved exactly as it was originally written, every word perfectly preserved. However, this is not the case since we do not have even one fragment of an original document. What we do have though is about 5,000 documents, some the complete NT, others fragments, with some dating to the second century. This massive volume of literature confirms all the facts of Jesus' life and ministry and the basic tenets of Christianity, even though there are numerous differences in the various manuscripts.

The differences are there for several reasons. First of all, the authors of the NT did not realize that they were writing Scripture, and neither did the first century readers. To all in the first century, Scripture was what Christians call the Old Testament and our Jewish brothers call the Tanach. The first NT books to be copied were not copied by professional scribes, but by anointed people who simply wanted to share some really good news with a friend or associate. From second and third century fragments we know that they did not feel compelled to make exact copies and they felt free to insert explanatory notes. They harmonized the Gospels in places and added explanations.

A spoken language evolves, as we know from reading Shakespeare and historical documents by the founding fathers of the United States. As the common Greek spoken in the early centuries of the Christian era evolved, the copiers of what later became Scripture made changes that would make the language more contemporary, so it would be more easily understood.

Even after the NT was canonized in the fourth century, the monks who copied manuscripts added quite a bit, in explanations, in words to smooth out a reading, and in adding passages such as the woman caught in adultery (John 7:53b-8:12). The monks were less demanding of accuracy than professional copiers and Jewish scribes, so some mistakes were made, but the greatest numbers of changes were additions. The important thing is that these changes did not alter the basic gospel message. One way to look at it is to examine the thirty or so different English translations that we have today. Each one has its merit. No one translation completely captures all that the Holy Spirit put in those Scriptures.

Jewish scribes set the standard for copying accuracy. They applied Masorah, meaning tradition, in their copying and were called Masoretes. They were responsible for memorizing the sounds of the words since vowels have never been written in Torah scrolls and were not commonly written in other Hebrew documents until the eighth century, although they were developed centuries earlier. The Masoretes counted every letter on each line and every use of a word on each line and in each passage. The oldest Masoretic text that is known today is from the tenth century, located in a St. Petersburg, Russia, library, with Jewish scholars now having access to it. When the book of Isaiah from St Petersburg is compared with the Dead Sea Scrolls there are only a few letters that have been changed. The scrolls used in today's synagogues are hand copied, without vowels, to the same standards used by the ancient copiers. One mistake on a scroll and the scroll is destroyed. Printed Jewish Bibles, Tanachs, do have the vowels added.

In contrast to the reverence that the Jewish copiers have for Scripture, look what an expert on the ancient manuscripts found in a monastery just over one hundred fifty years ago. The expert's name was Tischendorf and, in 1849, he was walking down a hallway in St. Catherine's Monastery in the Sinai Peninsula when a monk coming in the opposite direction passed him. Tischendorf noticed that the monk was carrying an armload of manuscripts and recognized that the writing was very old script. He was curious and wanted to see the text so he stopped the monk and asked to look at it. The monk agreed and said he was taking it to burn it. Can you imagine that? That manuscript happens to be the oldest nearly complete text of the New Testament that we have. It is called the Aleph and is now in a library in London, England. We have to wonder how many priceless manuscripts were destroyed in a similar disregard for their value.

If you have noticed that chapter and verse numbers sometimes seem out of place, it is because a Bishop Stephen Langton added the chapter numbers around 1205, and a printer named Robert Estienne, who used the pen name Stephanus, added the verse numbers in 1550. The editors of the various texts added punctuation much later. The manuscripts had many additions, which kept growing through the years. See Chapter and Verse in this Glossary.

Also there was no standard manuscript before the invention of the printing press. What they had were several "families" of manuscripts and the family with the most additions was the Byzantine, the manuscripts used by Bishop Langton and Robert Estienne.

While we like to think that the Scriptures are unchanged from the 1st century, this is simply not the case. My feeling is that the closer we can get to the original texts, the more revealed truths we will have. There is power that is lost in trying to make a smooth reading, aggravated by various translators' not appreciating spiritual warfare, healing, deliverance, etc. As stated previously every translation of Scripture has its merit.

Matthew 28:19   in the Greek text contains a reference to Father, Son, and Holy Spirit. There is considerable evidence that this phrase was added at the Nicean Council in 325 AD. Several early Christian theologians, who had seen the complete book of Matthew, attested that the early copies of Matthew did not contain the phrase. Eusebius was one of those and even though he believed in the Trinity, he wrote that the phrase, "baptizing in the name of the Father and of the Son and of the Holy Ghost" was not in the early texts. Today there are only two copies of Matthew earlier than the 4th C and the last page of each of those was destroyed.

William R. Conner, Litt.D. writes, "While no manuscript of the first three centuries is in existence, we do have the writings of at least two men who did actually possess, or had access to manuscripts much earlier than our earliest now in existence. These bring forward evidence from the following, either to direct quotation from their writings, or indirectly through the writings of their contemporaries, viz. Eusebius of Caesarea, the unknown author of De Rebaptismate, Origen, Clement of Alexandria, Justin Martyr, Macedonius, Eunomius and Aphraates." Dr. Connor's discussion of these covers twenty-one pages so it is not included here, but the evidence he cites is overwhelming that the original Matthew 28:19 did not include the phrase "baptizing them in the name of the Father and of the Son and of the Holy Ghost." For that reason the phrase does not appear in the text of this translation.

Memorization of Scripture   is needed to read the scrolls in the synagogues. Any boy or man who has had his Bar Mitsvah and every girl or woman who has her Bat Mitsvah can be called upon to read from the synagogue Torah scroll at any service. While Modern Hebrew Bibles have vowels added, the synagogue scrolls do not have vowels, so those who read have to memorize the vowels. Before Jesus' time the Torah scholars had determined that it was not proper to quote Scripture without looking at the scroll because the one quoting could make a mistake, and the people who made this policy had memorized all Scripture. For that reason the Scripture references cited in the New Testament are not absolutely consistent. What was important was to convey the meaning of the Scripture but to be clear that it was not a quote. A good example of not quoting word for word is in Revelation 13:10, using Jeremiah 15:2. Revelation 13:10.

> "If someone leads others into captivity,
> he himself is taken into captivity:
> if someone is to be killed by means of a sword
> he is killed by a sword." (Referring to Jr 15:2b)

Jeremiah 15:2b is

> "Those destined for death, to death;
> those for the sword, to the sword;
> those for starvation, to starvation;
> those for captivity, to captivity." NIV

See Hebrews 3:7,8a & 3:15 for another example of this.

Mitsvah   the plural is mitsvot, meaning religious and moral obligations. These obligations include obeying all commandments, statutes, ordinances, observances, teachings and testimonies. Rabbi Eliezer Ben-Yehuda wrote "The Hebrew word 'Mitzvah' - which has no exact translation, and is rendered in different contexts as 'good deed,' 'law' or 'command,' can also be taken to mean 'duty' or 'obligation' - a concept which becomes the key to Jewish law."

The expression in the Greek is normally translated either good deeds or good works, but can include righteousness, because doing righteousness is a common usage. Charitable giving, as in Matthew 6:2, in the Hebrew language is either Tsedekah or Mitsvah. Tsedekah is from the root tsadak, to do right, to be just, and specifically refers to charitable giving. Our salvation is not the result of our works, but it is the cause of our works. You are not made righteous by your works, but do good works because you are righteous. Mitsvot are evidence that you have been made righteous by faith (Genesis 15:6). Good deeds are the evidence of our relationship with God. Jesus said, "You will recognize people by their fruit." (Matthew 7:16) Paul said, defending himself in Acts 26:19. "For which reason, King Agrippa, I have not been disobedient to the heavenly vision 20. but first to those in Damascus and then in Jerusalem, and in every region of Judea and to the heathens, bringing a call to repent and to turn back to God, doing works worthy of repentance." Works worthy of repentance are also called mitsvot or righteousness. See Mt 7:21, 16:27, Lk 3:8, Jn 5:29, Ac 26:20, Ro 2:10,13, 1Co3:8, Eph 2:10, 2Ti 4:14, Ti 1:16, 2:14, 3:8, Heb 10:24, Jas 2:14-26, 2Pe 1:5, 3:10 1Jn 2:4, 3:16-18,22, 5:2,3, Rev 2:5, 19:8, 20:12,13, 22:12. See Righteousness in this Glossary.

Names   are not written consistently in English, so this translation uses the traditional English names, which came from Latin more than Greek, and not from Hebrew. For the Hebrew names, see Section II in this Glossary. Peter is a good example of what has happened to names. He is introduced to us in Matthew 4:18 as Simon Peter, with the Greek work word Simon. In 2 Peter 1:1 it is written Sumeon, as is the witness at Jesus' presentation at the temple in Luke 2:25. Several others are also spelled Sumeon in the Greek. The only time Sumeon is written Simon in English is in 2 Peter 1:1.

In John 1:42, and then five times by Paul, Peter is called Kefas in Greek. Kefa is a Hebrew/Aramaic word for rock. In English that became Cephas because that is the Latin spelling. Any name with the letter "C" in it came from Latin, because neither Hebrew nor Greek has the letter "C."

Mary is another name taken from Latin since the Greek is Mariam and the Hebrew is Miryam.

Throughout Scripture it is difficult to make sense of the English names, especially from Hebrew, as one glance of the listing in Section II will show. Traditional names are used here because correct English spelling of the Hebrew and Greek names in too many cases are very different from what we are used to and could be confusing to many readers.

Negative Hebrew Imperative   represented in the Greek text by the Greek imperative, usually translated here by "Stop doing.." or "You must not do.." is a very strong statement. When you see those statements in this translation do not think that these are an exaggeration. The Hebrew spoken by the NT authors uses a negative imperative that is very strong. Implicit in both statements is "Do not dare to even think about doing.!"

New Covenant   referred to by Jesus in Luke 22:20, is from Jeremiah 31:31-35.[1] v.31. "Behold, the days come, says the Lord, that I will make (cut) a new covenant with the house of Israel, and with the house of Judah; 32. Not according to the covenant that I made (cut) with their fathers in the day that I took them by the hand to bring them out of the land of Egypt; my covenant which they broke, although I was their master, says the Lord; 33. But this shall be the covenant that I will make (cut) with the house of Israel; After those days, says the Lord, I will put my Torah in their inward parts, and write it in their hearts; and will be their God, and they shall be my people. 34. And they shall teach no more every man his neighbor, and every man his brother, saying, Know the Lord; for they shall all know me, from the least of them to the greatest of them, says the Lord; for I will forgive their iniquity, and I will no longer remember their sin. 35. Thus says the Lord, who gives the sun for a light by day, and the fixed order of the moon and of the stars for a light by night, which divides the sea when its waves roar; The Lord of hosts is his name."

Paul in Romans 9:4 and Ephesians 2:12 refers to covenants, plural. Both the Greek word and the Hebrew word translated New have the basic meaning of Renew, so this is really a renewal of the previous covenants plus the addition of a new blessing. The underlined words are the new points given in this covenant. As those under this covenant read and study Scripture, God will put the tenets into their spirits and reveal hidden meanings. This will change our behavior, bringing true knowledge of Him. What a blessing that He no longer remembers our sin. Satan does keep a record of our sins and wants to remind us of past sins, but do not let Satan put you into that trap. God's record says that that sin never happened, so believe Him. See Sin, Forgiveness of in this Glossary.

Passover   is the name of the celebration of the release of the children of Israel from Egyptian bondage. It is celebrated with a feast called Seder, the subject of another article in this Glossary. Jesus, the disciples, and every author of the New Testament celebrated Passover. In the year 196 AD the celebration of Passover was replaced with the worship of Ishtar,

---

1   In the Hebrew text of Jeremiah 31 these are verses 30-34.

the Babylonian fertility goddess. The name Ishtar is written in Greek as Istar because there is no "sh" sound in the Greek language. Istar became Easter when translated from the Greek into English. The celebration of Ishtar brought with it eggs and rabbits, symbols of reproduction. This was done to separate from Jewish roots and to make it easier for heathens to become Christian by letting them retain the pagan customs.

Pay Homage is the translation of Proskuneo, which is frequently translated worship. The meaning is to get on one knee and touch the forehead to the ground at the feet of someone of royal rank. Jesus was frequently greeted this way. Often it is not clear whether to translate it pay homage or worship, so here the standard was to use pay homage if it was a greeting, whether to Jesus or someone else. When John greeted the angel this way in Revelation 19:10, the angel told him to get up. A place where worship is the obvious meaning is John 4:20 "..our fathers worshipped on this mountain."

Pentecost the Greek word for fifty, is the Greek name for the Feast of Shavuot, or weeks. This celebrates the wheat harvest and at two days is the shortest major feast. The major feasts are Unleavened Bread, Shavuot, and Succot, each one celebrating a First Fruits. The names Pentecost and Shavuot come from the command to count the time from the First Fruits during the Feast of Unleavened Bread to this First Fruits. Shavuot is the Hebrew word for weeks, for the seven weeks plus one day for the time from the First Fruits of Unleavened Bread to the next First Fruits. That time is called counting the Omer, which is the day after the seventh week, or fifty days. See Leviticus 23:15. See Shavuot elsewhere in this Glossary.

Peter is the English spelling of the masculine form of the Greek word petra. The feminine form, petra, means rock. See Cephas.

Placement of a name in a listing of two or more names is significant. The most important name was placed first. Thus the placing of Priscilla before Aquila signified greater respect for her.

Prayer Shawl is given in Numbers 15:37-41 where Moses is told, "Speak to the children of Israel, and bid them that they make them fringes in the corners of their garments throughout the generations, and that they put upon the fringe of each corner a thread of blue: and it shall be to you as a fringe, that you may look upon it, and remember all the commandments of the Lord, and do them: and that you may remember, and do all My commandments, and be holy to your God. I am the Lord your God, Who brought you out of the land of Egypt, to be your God: I am the Lord your God." The fringes, called tsitsit in Hebrew, kraspedon in Greek, were placed on the corners of the outer garment, which was larger than the current prayer shawl and looked like a poncho with tsitsit. This was like a sheet with a hole in the middle for the head. The front piece was tied behind the back, and then the back was lapped over and tied in front. This is the seamless garment in John 19:23. Recent archeological digs have found a number of these from Biblical times.

The garment now made to these specifications is the talit, also spelled tallit, called a prayer shawl in English. There two sizes, one a little larger than a man's scarf, the other about twice as wide as the smaller. The purpose for it is for everyone, including the wearer, to look at the corner fringe and remember all the commandments of the Lord. Rabbis centuries ago made a list of 613 commandments, including the promises of God, so in Jesus' day people would see all the power of God in that fringe, called tsitsit in Hebrew, when the prayer shawl was worn by an anointed man of God. That is why the woman with the bloody issue reached for the fringe in Matthew 9:20 and Luke 8:44 and why many sought to touch the tsitsit of His talit in Matthew 14:36 and Mark 6:56. We know this is the tsitsit because the Jewish translators who translated the Hebrew Scriptures into Greek used the Greek word kraspedon for tsitsit and kraspedon is used in the Gospels where tsitsit would be appropriate.

Jesus used the prayer shawl in Mark 5:41, the raising of Jairus' daughter. We know that Jesus was wearing a talit at the time because of the reference to it regarding the woman with the bloody issue, after Jesus and Jairus had started on the way to Jairus' home. At Jairus' home Jesus took the girl's hand and said "Talitha coum!" This is Hebrew for "Talit rise!" The verse goes on and says "..translated means 'maid arise'" (KJV) and "my child get up." (NIV) The Greek word translated maid or child is talitha, the Greek spelling of talit. Coum is the Hebrew word for rise, or get up. Some Greek texts say coumi, the feminine form, which is the correct word for this verse, since talitha is a feminine noun. There is an Aramaic word similar to talitha that was taken for talitha. That is talyetha, which means young woman. That would require the misspelling of talyetha instead of talitha in all the manuscripts. We know that His use of the talit in this miracle and His speaking to the talit would have been appropriate and would have been understood by those with Him. In that case He would have placed His prayer shawl over the girl, then spoken to the prayer shawl. There is another Aramaic word that some say is the correct word for this verse. It is taly'tah, meaning lamb. This would have Jesus address her as "Lambkin" a not unreasonable assumption. Coumi would also be the correct verb because it is the same in Aramaic and Hebrew. My personal feeling is that Jesus would have been speaking Hebrew, so I will stick with the talit, which is the closest word to the Greek spelling.

Prayer shawl making required Rabbinic training which Paul, Priscilla, and Aquila had. (Acts 18:2,3) The Greek word skenopoioi, translated prayer shawl makers or tent makers, is not found anywhere else in Scripture or secular Greek writing. Perhaps Luke coined the word or possibly skenopoioi was used by Jewish people when speaking of making prayer shawls. Jewish men referred to the prayer shawl as a tent or prayer closet because it was placed over the head to shield the eyes while praying.

The Greek Lexicon by Bauer Arndt and Gingrich devotes nearly an entire column to skenopoioi. Bauer does not identify the trade, but says that it was of a technical nature and it would not have been in making ordinary tents, leather working, or erecting tents, possibilities suggested by other scholars. The technical training that we know all three had was rabbinic training, which was required to make another item referred to as a tent. That is the prayer shawl, which when it was pulled over the head to shield the eyes while praying, was called a tent or prayer closet. Making prayer shawls is an occupation that Paul could have pursued in any metropolitan area without having to haul various tools and supplies as he traveled. While Bauer leaves the trade an open question, prayer shawl making stands out as the most likely single prospect.

A prayer shawl reference not often recognized is in Matthew 25:35 "For I was hungry and you gave Me to eat, I was thirsty and you gave Me to drink, I was a stranger and you took Me in, 36. and I was poorly clothed and you clothed Me," The Greek word for "you clothed" is peribaleo, referring to putting on the outer garment, which would have been the prayer shawl of a Jewish man. The fact that it was just the outer garment to be put on shows that the person had not been naked, as some translations say, but the stranger was poorly clothed. The fact that it was a prayer shawl indicates that the person who gave the garment ministered to the spiritual needs of the stranger while meeting the material needs.

Another reference to the prayer shawl is in 1Corinthians 11:15. This Greek word, peribolaiou, means wrapper or covering in reference to a garment. The NIV translates it as covering. Deuteronomy 22:12 says "You shall make twisted cords upon the four corners of your covering, wherewith you cover yourself." The twisted cords are the tsitsit of the prayer shawl. The word translated covering is k'sootkha, and simply means "your covering." There are no alternative meanings for k'soo(t) (the kha suffix is the pronoun "your"). In the Septuagint peribalou is the word used to translate k'soo(t) in Deuteronomy 22:12. Paul was clearly saying that women were given long hair instead of a prayer shawl. The word k'soot-ho, meaninig "his covering" is used in Exodus 22:26. There it shows the use of this large garment as a blanket.

Preparation Day refers to the things that must be done in the daylight hours leading to the Sabbath, which begins at sundown. This is mentioned in Matthew 27:62, Mark 15:42, Luke 23:54, and John 18:28 & 19:14, 31, 42. Some say there is a conflict in dates between the Synoptic Gospels of Matthew, Mark, and Luke, and the Gospel of John because the Synoptic Gospels describe the Last Supper, calling it a Seder, but John does not call it a Seder. Although John does not call it a Seder, his 13th chapter describes the Last Supper. The confusion comes because the text in John refers to Preparation Day, the day before the weekly Sabbath, but the text also refers to eating the Seder and to Passover. Since Passover is not a Sabbath, immersion is not required.

Modern Judaism celebrates Passover on the 15th of Nisan, the first day of the Feast of Unleavened Bread. To have Passover on the 15th requires translating the Hebrew word for dusk as afternoon in Leviticus 23. However, dusk is after sundown, not before sundown. Both Exodus 12:6 and Leviticus 23:5 use the same expression for dusk, "bain harba'im." This expression refers to the time between light and darkness, which is twilight or dusk, the time between sunset and darkness. 1 Chronicles 33:3 says, "They journeyed from Ramses in the first month, on the fifteenth day of the first month: -- on the day after the Pesakh-offering." The Pesakh-offering is the Passover lamb that had to be eaten the evening of its sacrifice, the fourteenth of Aviv or Nisan. Thus we can surmise that in Jesus' day Passover was celebrated at the eve of Preparation Day and the change for eating the Seder to the first day of Unleavened Bread was made sometime later. Exodus 12:18, Numbers 28:16-18, and Joshua 5:10 say the Pesakh is eaten on the fourteenth.

The fact is that the Passover is not a Sabbath, unless it happens to fall on the weekly Sabbath. The Scripture says in Leviticus 23: 5. "In the fourteenth day of the first month at evening is the Lord's Passover. 6. And on the fifteenth day of the same month is the Feast of Unleavened Bread to the Lord; seven days you must eat unleavened bread. 7. In the first day of Unleavened Bread you shall have a holy gathering; you shall do no labor in it. 8. But you shall offer an offering made by fire to the Lord seven days; in the seventh day is a holy gathering; you shall do no labor in it."

The Sabbaths of the Feast of Unleavened Bread are the first day, which is the day after Passover, and the last day. Feast day Sabbaths, except for Yom Kippur, are not full Sabbaths, but only prohibitions of doing your normal work. The Hebrew text in Leviticus calls the weekly Sabbath, "Shabbat Shabbaton," translated as "complete rest" in some texts. Work in feasts is "M'labet Avodah" referring to whatever is done for a living. Cooking in the home is permitted on a feast day. Mark 15:42 and Luke

23:54 clearly show the regular weekly Sabbath. Mark 15:42. "And now when it became evening, since it was the day of preparation, that is the day before a Sabbath," Luke 23:54 "And it was the day of preparation for it was approaching the Sabbath." John also ties preparation day to the Sabbath, 19:31. "Then the Jewish people, since it was preparation day, so that the bodies would not remain on the cross on the Sabbath, for it was to be a great day of that Sabbath, they were asking Pilate that the soldiers would break their legs so they could remove the bodies." These are all speaking of the full Sabbath that does require preparation, especially the mikveh, which is immersion for purification, also called sanctification. In Jesus' day all observant Jewish men immersed as preparation for the Sabbath. Some time later the mikveh started being used to prepare for feast days as well as the Sabbath.

Besides the mikveh, the Talmud speaks of food preparation for the Sabbath because food to be eaten on the Sabbath had to be prepared before sundown brought the Sabbath. Food eaten on Passover was to be prepared on that day, per Exodus 12:16. "And in the first day there shall be a holy convocation, and in the seventh day there shall be a holy convocation to you; no kind of work shall be done in them, save that which every man must eat, only that may be done by you." From this verse we know that the day before Passover and the day before the first day of Unleavened Bread were not preparation days. Preparation was for the weekly Shabbat.

The Seder was to be prepared after sundown on Nissan 14, then eaten that same night. Exodus 12:6. "And you shall keep it up until the fourteenth day of the same month; and the whole assembly of the congregation of Israel shall kill it in the evening." 8. "And they shall eat the meat in that night, roast with fire, and unleavened bread; and with bitter herbs they shall eat it." 10. "And you shall let nothing of it remain until the morning; and that which remains of it until the morning you shall burn with fire. 11. And thus shall you eat it; with your loins girded, your shoes on your feet, and your staff in your hand; and you shall eat it in haste; it is the Lord's Passover." There was not a day of preparation.

John's text refers twice to the Seder, in 18:28. "Then they led Jesus from Caiaphas to the praetorium: it was early: but they did not enter the praetorium, so that they would not be defiled, but could eat the Seder." and in 19:14. "And it was preparation day for Passover, it was about the sixth hour. And he said to the Jewish people, 'Behold your king.'" The preparation to be done was immersion for purification, which we call baptism. This was to de done during daylight hours, for the Sabbath that would begin at sundown. Since those at the home of Caiaphas were there during darkness, if this were Preparation Day, they would not yet have immersed, so the phrase "but could eat the Seder" is incorrect. Either the

Seder had already been eaten or it was too early to have immersed for purification. The Passover would be eaten at the beginning of Preparation Day, so the meal that Jesus and the disciples had eaten was the Passover Seder. Later that day during daylight hours each one would go to one of the pools for immersion. The temple had many pools under Solomon's Porch and many of the hundreds of synagogues in Jerusalem would have had immersion pools to accommodate the thousands coming for the Feast.

John describes a meal in Chapter 13:21-30 when Jesus washed the feet of the disciples before reclining to eat. This meal must have been the Seder. For that to be the case the references to the Seder in John 18:28 "but could eat the Seder" and Passover in 19:14 "for Passover" would have to be later additions to the text, the copier who added those words assuming that Passover was a Sabbath, and not knowing that Preparation Day required immersion during daylight but before the Sabbath began at sundown. Whoever added those words also did not understand that the Seder was eaten in the home and that entering the Praetorium would not prevent anyone from eating the Seder with his family, but would prevent a priest from performing his Sabbath duties in the temple. Matthew, Mark, and Luke are all clear that Jesus was crucified on Preparation Day, in the daylight hours following the Seder.

As much as we would like to think that every word in the NT was written by the 1st century author, such is not the case. Early copiers were sending Good News to a friend, not knowing that what they were copying would later be Scripture. There was no need for professional copying, which had exacting standards. An additional problem was that Koine Greek was a group of dialects based on the Greek language, but with regional variations. A traveler from Greece who found a believer in Syria, when copying his friend's notes would not just feel free, but would feel obligated to change Syrian Koine to Greek Koine.

Look at English, the language common to both US and England, with fewer differences than the various 1st century Koine dialects.

US	England
Hood of car	Bonnet
Trunk of car	Boot
Sedan	Saloon
Napkin	Serviette
Diaper	Napkin
Men's suspenders	Braces
Women's garters	Suspenders

You can see that Koine Greek would have had its differences, too, as it was used in various regions. In the first century there was considerably less communication among various communities than today with our mass media.

Even after the 2nd century changes in the manuscripts were made continually until the first Greek texts were printed in the 16th century. The NT as it was copied was never subjected to the standards of the Hebrew Massoretic text, copied by Jewish scribes, or of classic literature, which was copied by professional copiers. Most of the changes in the NT were additions, added with the intention of bringing clarity, but there were also mistakes in copying and misspelling. Since NT copiers were not Jewish, many of the additions showed a lack of knowledge of Jewish Scripture and Jewish customs, such as with the woman caught in adultery. Whoever inserted that passage, John 7:53b-8:11, did not know that each person, both man and woman, caught in adultery was to be punished. (Leviticus 20:10, Deuteronomy 22:22) These additions still leave the basic Gospel message intact, but the closer we can get to the original text the better off we will be. See Adultery and Manuscript in this Glossary about additions to the New Testament.

Preparation Day is subject to some confusion. Mark 15:42, Luke 23:54, and John 19:31 properly record that the preparation was for the Sabbath. Mark and Luke record that it was after the Seder. John records that Preparation Day came after the Last Supper in John Chapter 13, although John does not refer to that meal as the Seder. There is no conflict in Mark, Luke, and John, except we have to see that apparently the words "but could eat the Seder" in John 18:28 and "for Passover" in John 19:14 were added sometime later by a copier who was not familiar with Jewish customs.

The timing of the Seder on Thursday evening, then His arrest, trial, and crucifixion during the daylight hours, with His burial before sundown Friday, has Jesus entombed before the Sabbath started. Sundown Friday is the start of the second day, the regular Sabbath, which that year also was the first day of the Feast of Unleavend Bread. Sundown Saturday starts the third day, which happened to be First Fruits that year. This had Jesus in the tomb for two nights and parts of three days. His resurrection coming by sunup of the third day goes with the following verses, which say "the third day:" Matthew 16:21, 17:23, 20:19, 27:64, Luke 9:22, 18:33, 24:7,46. Only Matthew 12:40 quoting Jonah 1:17 says "three days and three nights." The other eight references to His resurrection say "the third day." Since we have no manuscripts from the first century we cannot know these things for a certainty, but this is a likely scenario. If Jesus had been in the tomb for three nights, He would have been resurrected on the fourth day.

This chart puts the timing in perspective:

Date	Happenings	Chronology
Nissan 14		
Thursday sundown	Start of Passover Seder Jesus' Arrest Trial	1st Day
Next morning	Crucifixion	
Afternoon	Preparation Day, preparing for weekly Sabbath Burial	
Nissan 15		
Friday sundown;	Weekly Sabbath Day Unleavened Bread, 1st Day Jesus in tomb entire day	2nd Day
Nissan 16		
Saturday sundown;	First Fruits	3rd Day
During night	Resurrection	

An interesting point is that the Jewish sages said long ago that the resurrection of the righteous would take place during the Feast of Unleavened Bread, just as we see here with Jesus.

Prophets   in the Jewish Bible refers to the Books of Joshua, Judges, 1 Samuel, 2 Samuel, 1 Kings, 2 Kings, Isaiah, Jeremiah, Ezekiel, then the Twelve Prophets. The Book of Daniel is placed with the group of books called The Writings. The Jewish Bible is called The Tanach, an acrostic of the names of the three sections, Torah, Neviim (Prophets), and Ch'tuvim (Writings). The last books of the Writings are 1 & 2 Chronicles, which were the last books of the Tanach to be written.

Proselyte   is an interesting word because it is translated as convert, and has even come into modern English as a verb, to proselytize, meaning to make converts. The meaning in Greek is different: residence as a stranger, with the related verb meaning to live in a place as a stranger. A convert would live there as a member of the community, not as a stranger. Modern Judaism uses proselyte according to the original Greek meaning, referring to righteous proselytes as those who love God, love Torah, love Israel, and love the Jewish people, but do not convert. Thus many evangelical Christians would qualify as proselytes to Judaism. The Power New Testament translates proselyte as convert, but we need to be curious about what Luke and Matthew had in mind when they used the word. Proselyte is used in Matthew 23:15, Acts 2:10, 6:5, and 13:43.

Reclining to eat   was the standard practice and was a symbol of their being free, not slaves as in Egypt. At the Last Supper as at every Seder they reclined and they reclined at the various meals described in the Gospels. Sometimes there is no mention of the meal because when it was written that they reclined, the meal was understood. The couches they reclined on were angled at the table, so each only took up a small space at the table, not the full length of a couch. The person who reclined in front of someone was spoken of as reclining or leaning on the bosom, or chest, or, more commonly, the lap of that person, as John was at the Last Seder, John 13:23 & 25. To be in Abraham's bosom meant to have the place of honor at a banquet. Luke 16:23 tells of Lazarus in Abraham's bosom, referring to his being a partaker of the same state of bliss as Abraham in Paradise.

Replacement Theology   is the term used for the doctrine saying that the Church has replaced Israel as God's chosen people, that the Church is now Israel in Old Testament prophecies. One of the prime NT verses used for that theory is Hebrews 8:13, which is sometimes translated as saying the OT, old covenant, has been made obsolete. If, as many scholars believe, the book of Hebrews was written before 70 AD, obsolete could not have been what the author had in mind. The first time the idea that the new covenant replaced its predecessors was put forth was in the middle of the second century AD by Marcion, who was a heretic. Therefore if the author meant to say obsolete, the book of Hebrews could have been written no earlier than the middle of the second century. There are scholars who date the letter from that time.

Another reason for thinking that the author of Hebrews did not believe the old covenant, or Old Testament, was obsolete, is the use of so many OT references. The author would have restricted OT verses to those that made the case for saying that the OT was now obsolete. The number of Biblical references and the familiarity with priestly duties indicate the author was Jewish and the reference to Timothy (Hebrews 13:23) indicates it was written in the first century.

No NT author suggested in any way that the OT was obsolete, and neither did Jesus. Jesus is quoted in John 10:16 as saying, "But I also have sheep which are not from this sheepfold: and it is necessary for Me to lead those and they will hear My voice, and they will become one flock, one shepherd." Jesus was speaking to the Jewish people referring to the heathens as the other flock. Paul wrote in Romans 11:17. "But if some of the branches were broken off, and you, since you are a wild olive, were yourself grafted into them, then you would be a participant for yourself of the richness of the root of the olive tree. 18. Stop boasting of the branches: but, if you do boast, you do not support the root, but the root supports you. 19. Therefore you will say, 'Branches were broken off so that I could be grafted in.' 20. Just so: they were broken off by unbelief, but you have stood by faith. Do not be proud, but you must continually fear for yourself: 21. for if God did not spare the natural branches, neither in any way will He spare you. 22. You must now see the goodness and severity of God: on the one hand severity upon those who fell, but on the other hand goodness of God upon you, if you would remain in the goodness, otherwise you would be cut off. 23. And even these, if they would not remain in unbelief, they will be grafted in: for God is able to graft them in again. 24. For if you were cut off from the naturally wild olive tree and contrary to nature you were grafted into the cultivated olive tree, how much more will these natural branches be grafted into their own cultivated olive tree." He goes on to say in verse 26 that "..all Israel will be saved." See Matthew 5:17,18, John 11:52, Ephesians 2:14-16, Isaiah 44:5.

If we are grafted in, then we are part of the original covenants God made with Abraham and the successive covenants made through the centuries.

Rest   There are three Greek words translated rest. One, epanapauomai, means to lean upon, to trust in something and is used only twice in the NT, in Lk 10:6 and Ro 2:17. The other two are used much more often, but there is a major difference between the two.

Katapausis is the permanent rest of the eternal kingdom, used in Hebrews 3:11,18, 4:1,3,5,10, & 11. It is also used in Acts 7:49, in reference to the eternal kingdom. Katapauo is the verb form and is used in Hebrews 4:4,8, & 10. It is also used one other time, in Acts 14:18 regarding restraining a crowd. In Revelation 6:11 we see this temporary rest which is evidence that we will have duties even in our eternal rest. That is because in eternal rest we will not have any evil influences to harass us as we go about His business.

Anapausis is a temporary rest, like a coffee break at work. This is the type of rest we are to have in this life to keep us from getting stressed. This rest is what we find in Matthew 11:29, 12:43, Luke 11:24, and Revelation 4:8 & 14:11. The verb anapauo is used in Matthew 11:28 when Jesus says, "I will give you rest." For all of us are to take breaks, to be sure we do not overextend ourselves to our physical and, especially, spiritual detriment. If you are too busy to spend time with God you need to change your priorities so you do not break communication with God and become stressed. Anapauo is used another eleven times in the New Testament, Matthew 26:45, Mark 6:31, 14:41, Luke 12:19, 1Corinthians 16:18, 2Corinthians 7:13, Philemon 7 & 20, and Revelation 6:11, 14:13.

In 1&2Corinthians and Philemon it is translated refresh or refreshed. The use of anapauo in Revelation is interesting because it indicates that we will have work to do, that the rest promised in both those verses is temporary. When we enter God's eternal rest we will still have assignments.

Resurrected Body Scripture cites a number of people resurrected from the dead, but only one of these, Jesus, is resurrected to eternal life. Elijah and Elisha raised the dead, as did Jesus on numerous occasions, then Peter raised Tabitha and Paul raised Euticus. All of those who were raised simply returned to their human, earthly, mortal bodies. Since none is mentioned later in Scripture and apparently none is still alive, it is probably safe to believe that all have perished. Those resurrected bodies did not have any unusual qualities, other than returning to life after being dead.

Our bodies after resurrection to eternal life will be remarkably different. We should expect them to be like Jesus was after His resurrection. What we know of Him and what is in Ezekiel 37:4 tell much about bodies resurrected to eternal life. Ezekiel 37:4 says: "And he said to me, Prophesy over these bones, and say to them, O you dry bones, hear the word of the Lord." What we do not see in the English is that the phrase, "say to them" does not refer to the bones, but to the people. We know it refers to people because of the Hebrew word translated "them." That word is masculine, while the word for bones is feminine, so that the Lord's instruction to Ezekiel means to a Jewish, Hebrew speaking, reader "And He said to me, 'Prophesy over, or in the direction of, these bones, and say to them, the people, O you dry bones, hear the word of the Lord.'" The word translated over can also be translated on, upon, above, towards. Instead of saying, 'over these bones,' it could just as well be toward, or in the direction of, these bones.

Now, look at the verses in the New Testament describing Jesus after His resurrection:

John 20:2. "Then she ran and came to Simon Peter and to the other disciple whom Jesus loved and she said to them, 'They took our Lord from the tomb and we do not know where they put Him.'" This is also in v. 13. We know His earthly body was missing from the tomb.

His body could assume a different look, so that He would not be recognized. In v. 14. "After she said these things she turned to those behind and saw Jesus standing but had not recognized that it was Jesus." This shows that His resurrected body could look different from His earthly body. 15. "Jesus said to her, 'Ma'am, why are you crying? Whom are you seeking?' Because she thought that He was the gardener she said to Him, 'Sir, if you removed Him, you must tell me where you carried Him and I will take Him.' 16. Jesus said to her, 'Mary.' After she turned to that One she said to Him in Hebrew, 'Rabbi,' which means Teacher." This shows that at will He could make Himself recognizable. 17. "Jesus said to her 'Stop touching Me, for I have not yet ascended to the Father: you must go to My brothers and you must say to them, "I am ascending to My Father and your Father and My God and your God.""

v. 19. ".. after the doors were shut where the disciples were because of fear of the Jewish leaders, Jesus came and stood in their midst and said to them, 'Peace be with you.' 20. And after He said this He showed them His hands and His side. Then the disciples rejoiced, because they had seen the Lord." His resurrected body could go through walls or closed doors, apparently not having bones.

v. 27. "Then He said to Thomas, 'Put your finger here and see My hands and you must reach out your hand and you must put it into My side, and stop being faithless but have faith.'" The resurrected body had the apearance and feel of flesh, yet could still go through walls or become invisible.

Now see what Luke has: 24:3. "but when they entered they did not find the body of the Lord Jesus. 15. And it was, while they were speaking and discussing these things that Jesus Himself, having approached, was going with them, 16. but their eyes were being hindered so they did not recognize Him. 23. and when they did not find His body, they came saying then that in a vision they saw angels, who were saying 'He is alive.' 24. Then some of those with us left for the tomb and also found thus just as the women said, but they did not see Him. 25. But He said to them, 'O foolish and slow in heart to believe on all that the prophets were saying: 26. and was it not necessary for the Messiah to suffer these things, then to enter His glory?' 27. And beginning with Moses and with all the Prophets He explained to them with all the writings concerning Himself."

v. 30. "And it happened while He reclined with them, when He took the bread He praised God and after He broke it He gave it to them, 31. and their eyes were opened and they recognized Him: then He became invisible for them."

His resurrected body could be visible or invisible. If visible, it could take different appearances so that at His will, He could be recognized or not. He ate with the disciples, as in Luke 24:41 & 42. While His body could show the holes in His hands and side, in what appeared to be human flesh, it could also look quite different, being flesh without the holes in His hands. He could walk through walls, indicating that His resurrected body has neither flesh nor bone. Then why did His body disappear from the tomb? Will our resurrected bodies also disappear from their tombs, or wherever those who are alive happen to be at the time of the resurrection?

Paul discussed the resurrected body in 1 Corinthians 15. Beginning with verse 35, "But some will say, 'How are the dead raised?' And 'What sort of body is coming?' 36. Foolishness! What you are sowing does not live unless it would die first: (John 12:24) 37. then what you are sowing, you do not sow what will be the body, but a naked seed. Perhaps it will turn out to be wheat or some of the other grains: 38. but God would give it a body just as He wished, and to each of the seeds its own body. 39. But not all flesh is the same, but there is one kind of flesh for people, and another kind of flesh for domestic animals, and another flesh for birds, and another for fishes: 40. then there are heavenly bodies, and earthly bodies: another of the splendor of the heavenlies, but another of the earthlies. 41. With another kind of splendor for the sun, and another kind of splendor for the moon, and another splendor for the stars: for star differs from star in splendor.

15:42. "So also the resurrection of the dead. It is sown in corruption, it is raised incorruptible: 43. it is sown in dishonor, it is raised in magnificence: it is sown in weakness, it is raised in power: 44. a <u>body is sown fleshly, it is raised a spiritual body. If there is a fleshly body, there is also a spiritual.</u> 45. And so it has been written, 'The first man was Adam in living life,' (Gn 2:7) the last Adam has become a life-giving spirit. 46. But the spiritual was not first but the physical, then the spiritual. 47. The first man is from dust of the earth, the second man out of heaven. 48. What sort of earthly man, and such as these earthly ones, and what sort of the heavenly One, then such as these born of the heavenly nature: 49. and just as we bore constantly the image of the earthly, we shall bear constantly also the image of the heavenly One." According to verse 44 the spiritual body is different from the physical.

Resurrection was not a strange idea to the people of Israel in Jesus' day. In John 11:24 Martha says to Jesus that she knows her brother will be resurrected in the resurrection on the last day, which is Judgment Day. From this we know that it was common knowledge that eventually everyone will be resurrected and that the resurrection will be for Judgment.

The basis for this belief comes from numerous Old Testament verses. One of the verses the rabbis use to speak of resurrection is Numbers 18:28 which speaking of the tithe says "..you shall give it to Aaron the priest.." This is clearly a reference to paying the tithe after they enter the Promised Land, but Aaron did not even live to see the Promised Land, let alone receive a tithe there. The way he could receive the tithe then would be because he has been resurrected.

Deuteronomy 11:9 refers to "..your days in the land, which the Lord swore to your fathers to give to them.." Again this could only happen because they had been resurrected.

Deuteronomy 31:16 says "And the Lord said to Moses, Behold, you shall sleep with your fathers; and this people will rise up." There are many Scriptural references to the dead as sleeping. This is why Jesus said "I am the God of Abraham and the God of Isaac and the God of Jacob: He is not the God of the dead but the living." (Matthew 22:32)

Isaiah put it straight out there when he said "The dead men of your people shall live, my dead body shall arise. Awake and sing, you that dwell in dust: for your dew is as the dew on herbs, and the earth shall cast out the shades of the dead." (Isaiah 26:19)

The most beautiful reference to resurrection is more subtle. Job 1:2 & 3 say "And there were born to him seven sons and three daughters. His possessions also were seven thousand sheep, and three thousand camels, and five hundred yoke of oxen, and five hundred she donkeys, and very many servants: so that this man was the greatest of all the men of the east." Job 42:12 & 13 say "So the Lord blessed the latter end of Job more than his beginning: for he had fourteen thousand sheep, and six thousand camels, and a thousand yoke of oxen, and a thousand she donkeys. He also had seven sons and three daughters." If Job was given twice the flocks and herds after his ordeal, why did the Lord give him the same number of children that he had before the ordeal? The answer has to be that in the hereafter Job does have twice the children, fourteen sons and six daughters. That is a great comfort to all those who have lost children in this life. My wife had a miscarriage about a year after our second son was born. We know that we will be with that child some day. As David said, "I shall go to him, but he will not come back to me." (2 Samuel 12:23)

Jesus referred to resurrection in Matthew 22:31. "And concerning the resurrection of the dead did you not read what was spoken to you by God saying, 32. 'I AM the God of Abraham and the God of Isaac and the God of Jacob?' (Ex 3:6,15,16) He is not the God of the dead but the living." This is also reported in Mark 12:27 and Luke 20:38

Resurrection is the reason why Jesus spoke numerous times about entering life when he was referring to the time after this body dies. He said "And if your hand causes you to sin, you must immediately cut it off and cast it from you: it is better for you to enter life maimed than having two hands or two feet to have been cast into the eternal fire." (Matthew 18:8 & 9)

Right Hand is very significant as a Hebrew idiom, having two different meanings. In one it symbolizes power and strength, from Exodus 15:6 "Your right hand, O Lord, is glorious in power; your right hand, O Lord, has dashed in pieces the enemy." In the other it represents salvation, from Psalm 20:6 "Now I know that the Lord saves his anointed; he will answer

him from his holy heaven with the saving strength of his right hand."
From this it is said that the left hand represents calamity and judgment.
Jesus is the right hand of God and is still His power here on Earth, now
just as much as when He walked the Earth in His flesh, as also His Saving
Power has been here from the time of His resurrection and will be forever
more.

Hand has additional meaning, from Zechariah 8:9 & 13, "Thus said the
Lord of Hosts; Let your hands be strong, you who hear these days these
words from the mouths of the prophets, which were [were spoken] on the
day that the foundation was laid for the Temple of the Lord, the Lord of
Hosts -- the Sanctuary -- to be built." The expression "Let your hands be
strong" is also used in verse 13. In those verses "hand" is a metaphor for
"resolve or determination."

Righteousness   We are made righteous by faith and grace, but
righteousness is action. The word righteousness is the noun form of the
Hebrew root Tsedek. Tsedek and the Greek verb Dikaio both mean to do
right, to be just. They are verbs that require action by the subject of the
verb. When we are made righteous by our faith our behavior has to change.
If it does not, see what John says: 1John 2:3. "And by this we know that
we have known Him, if we keep His commandments. 4. The one who
says that 'I have known Him,' and does not keep His commandments, is a
liar and the truth is not in him: 5. but whoever keeps His Word, truly the
love of God would have been completed in him, because we know that we
are in Him. 6. The one who says he remains in Him is obligated to walk
the same walk just as that One walked."

There are many times in the New Testament that we have references like
Acts 16:31 "..You must believe at once in the Lord Jesus and you and
your household will be saved." To Paul, Luke, and all NT authors, the
word "believe" required action, as in Acts 26:19. "For which reason, King
Agrippa, I have not been disobedient to the heavenly vision 20. but first
to those in Damascus and then in Jerusalem, and in every region of Judea
and to the heathens, bringing a call to repent and to turn back to God,
doing works worthy of repentance."

This change in behavior comes from above, as evidenced by Paul's
reference to "the gift of righteousness" in Romans 5:17 and 6:18. There is
a lot each one can do to be a better person, but we can do so much more
when faith and commitment to God bring us the gift of righteousness.

Paul says in 1Corinthians 6:9. "Or do you not know that the unrighteous
will not inherit the kingdom of God? Stop being deceived: neither
fornicators nor idolaters nor adulterers nor effeminate nor homosexuals
10. nor thieves nor covetous people, nor drunkards, nor abusive people,

nor swindlers will inherit the kingdom of God."

We need to know that in the Jewish mind Believe requires the change in behavior that John was talking about in the verses quoted above. See Mitsvah in this Glossary. See James 2:14.

Righteousness and Holiness are the foundation of relationships for all of humanity. Each of us has a relationship with God, with other people, even with animals. We are to do right, to be just in every endeavor, and we are to keep ourselves pure. Our heavenly Father said "For I am the Lord that brings you out of the land of Egypt, to be your God; you shall therefore be holy, for I am holy." (Leviticus 11:45) Although none of us will be perfected while in this earthly body, each of us must strive to do right and to keep pure. God knows none of us is perfect, but He also knows our hearts and sees our faith and the blood of the Lamb. So long as we acknowledge Him, do right, and keep ourselves pure, we know that we have eternal life.

Sabbath Shabbat in Hebrew, can have different meanings when it is plural. The plural is Shabbatot in Hebrew and can refer to a feast day Shabbat. The feast day Shabbat does not have the prohibition of all work. On those days it is permissible to cook and do chores, but not to go to a regular job.

The plural can also mean that something happened regularly on the Sabbath, as when Jesus taught in the synagogues on the Sabbaths. When the plural is used it is not always clear which meaning to apply. For instance in Mark 2:23 the disciples were plucking grain on a particular day but the Pharisees called that to Jesus' attention using the plural, Sabbaths. This could have been Shavuot, which is the time of the grain harvest. This would not have been against the Scriptural admonitions in Leviticus 23, but just against the Pharisees' code. In the Sabbath year it was permissible to pick a day's need, but not to harvest.

It is important to remember that for all the Jewish people the day started at sundown. The Sabbath starts at sundown one day and ends at sundown the following day. One hour, sometimes two hours after sundown ending a Sabbath there is a service called Havdalah which returns the congregation to the secular world from the holy day that is completely dedicated to the Lord. After this service money can be discussed and handled, but during the Sabbath money cannot be used or discussed. The Havdalah is still used in the synagogue. This is the service in Acts 20:7-12 when Paul talked past midnight. Since this service starts two hours after sundown, on June 22nd the Havdalah might not start until 11:00 PM. The rule of thumb for beginning the service is for it to be dark enough to see three stars in the sky. I Corinthians 16:2 is another reference to the Havdalah, dealing with money. While there is no mention of the Havdalah in Matthew 8:16 there is a reference to the end of the Sabbath where it says that when it became evening they brought the sick and the lame.

There is nothing in the New Testament to indicate that the Sabbath was changed from the Jewish day of Friday sundown to Saturday sundown. Understanding the Havdalah is key to proper interpretation of the New Testament.

Jesus was criticized for doing things that the Pharisees and others said should not be done on the Sabbath, but He never did anything on a Sabbath that is prohibited in Scripture. The fourth commandment, given in Exodus 20:8, says to keep the Sabbath holy and to do no work on it. This prohibition against work was taken by the Pharisees and others to include healing in the definition of work, but to heal on the Sabbath is not prohibited in Scripture. Jeremiah 17:21 includes the admonition "Take heed to yourselves, and bear no burden on the Sabbath day, nor bring it in by the gates of Jerusalem; 22. Do not carry a burden out of your houses on the Sabbath day, nor do you any work, but sanctify the Sabbath day, as I commanded your fathers." Jesus gave some indication of what constitutes a large load in John 5:10,11 when He told the lame man to carry his pallet. Carrying things at some point becomes work, which is forbidden. Some legalists have defined "burden" as something as small as a handkerchief. We are not to set arbitrary rules to define such things, but go by the spirit. The purpose for not carrying burdens on the Sabbath is related to buying and selling, but obviously work enters the equation because a large load is definitely work. Each of these definitions is to be an individual decision, made in an attitude of prayer. Scriptures giving the prohibitions for the Sabbath are: Exodus 20:8-11, 16:29, 35:3, Jeremiah 17:21, Nehemiah 10:32, 13:15.

"If you restrain your foot because it is the Sabbath; refrain from accomplishing your own needs on My holy day; if you proclaim the Sabbath 'a delight,' and the holy [day] of the Lord 'honored,' and you honor it by not engaging in your own affairs, from seeking your own needs or discussing the forbidden -- then you will delight in the Lord, and I will mount you astride the heights of the world; I will provide you the heritage of your forefather Jacob, for the mouth of the Lord has spoken." (Isaiah 58:13, 14)

Sanctuary is the name of that part of the Temple and also the Tabernacle that was set apart for the Lord God. It consisted of two rooms, the first being the Holy Place. The Holy Place held the lamp stand, the table of the Bread of the Presence and the Incense Altar. This was where the priests ministered to the Lord. To enter the Holy Place the priest needed to be sanctified first. Any priest entering the Holy Place who had not already dealt with sin would have been struck dead at the doorway.

The second, or inner room was called the Holy of Holies or the Most Holy Place. The Holy of Holies held only the Ark of the Covenant except on Yom Kippur, the Day of Atonement, when the Altar of Incense was placed in it. Only the High Priest could enter and he could only enter on Yom Kippur. In this room the High Priest interceded for the people, for the Lord God to forgive their sins and his sins.

The temple had an outer court where sinners, even heathens, were welcome and an inner court, which had the altar where people would deal with sin. Only a priest could enter the Sanctuary and then only after he had dealt with sin, by making the appropriate offerings, washing, and wearing the holy garments. Washing or immersing is what we call baptism.

When Jesus said "Tear down this temple and I will rebuild it in three days, speaking of His body," in John 2:19-21, He did not say "temple" but He said "sanctuary." Most translators say temple, but sanctuary is correct. The Greek word is naos, meaning sanctuary. The word for temple is hieron. No one can deny that Jesus' body was without sin and was holy.

We too have bodies that are sanctified by the blood of the Lamb, so our bodies are called sanctuaries. We are not to be like the temple or tabernacle, with an area where sin is welcome. This is why Paul wrote that our bodies are sanctuaries of the Holy Spirit in I Corinthians 3:16, 17, 6:19, and 2 Corinthians 6:16, and John was told to exclude the outer court when he measured the sanctuary. (Revelation 11:2) Psalm 119:48 "and I will lift my hands to Your commandments.." The rabbinic commentary on that says that lifting your hands means to practice, do, His commandments. Psalm 134:2 repeats that theme.

2 Peter 1:14 uses the metaphor for our temporary bodies, the tabernacle or tent, which is temporary. Our sanctuaries are spiritual bodies that are permanent.

An interesting point is that in the Gospels and Acts there are many references to the temple, but after those books the word hieron, for temple, is only used one time. That is in I Corinthians 9:13 in a reference to the temple in Jerusalem. So, from the book of Romans on, now you know that with one exception wherever you see the word temple in another translation the author was actually talking about the sanctuary. Now you also know that your body is a sanctuary, requiring you to walk in repentance every day, because sin must be dealt with prior to entering the sanctuary.

Satan   The Hebrew language has two spellings for Satan, samech-tet-nun and sin-tet-nun. The latter is the one used in Scripture, in Numbers 22:22,32, 1Samuel 29:4, 2Samuel 19:22, 1Kings 5:4, 11:14,23,25, 1Chronicles 21:1, Job 1:6,7,8,9,12, 2:1,2,3,4,6,7, Psalm 109:6, and Zechariah 3:1,2. The former, which does not appear in Scripture, means slander, slanderer, accuser. The latter means adversary, archenemy, foe, devil, the Evil One, and hinderer, accuser. The verb form means to hate, denounce, condemn, speak against and is used several times in Scripture. The difference between these words is not great, but it is significant that Scripture uses the stronger word because it includes, but is not limited to, accusing, but goes far beyond that in actively pursuing evil ends.

Creatures, including the dragon and serpent of Revelation 12:9, symbolize the results of Satan's endeavors. In Isaiah 27:1 those symbols are called Leviathan, referring to the evils of the modern world. The Stone Edition Tanach comments, "Leviathan, the giant, earth-girdling serpent-fish, symbolizes the great world powers. Isaiah uses the death of the Leviathan to allude to the eventual downfall of all the enemies of Israel (Radak). The Three descriptions -- bar-like, twisting, in the sea -- allude to the different natures of the world powers (Rashi)." See Isaiah 27:1.

Sea of Galilee is the phrase we are used to. However it is a lake, a body of fresh water that supplies most of Israel's drinking water, about 15 miles long by 7 miles wide. The Greek word thalassa is translated sea in the traditional English translations. Thalassa was used by the Jewish translators of the Septuagint, from Hebrew to Greek, to translate lake. In the New Testament the lake is referred to by four names, Galilee, Kinneret, Tiberias, and Genesseret.

Seder is the name of the Passover meal. This meal may be called a feast but it really is a modest, but ample, meal, frequently featuring roast chicken and not the overeating we associate with Thanksgiving dinners. Seder means order and is a reminder of the Passover meal eaten in Egypt at the deliverance of the chosen people from bondage as Egyptian slaves. To start the Seder a cup of wine is raised and a blessing recited to sanctify the table so it can serve as the altar for the evening's service. This cup is called the Kiddush, which means Sanctification and is seen in Luke 22:17. The blessing over the meal is referred to in Luke 22:19 when Jesus raised the bread. Each blessing He said started "Blessed are You O Lord our God King of the Universe.." The blessing over the bread continued with: "Who brings forth bread from the earth." Bread in this context means everything we need.

Before eating, the story of the Exodus is told, then after the meal songs are sung, glorifying God and blessing Israel. Included in these songs are the Hallel, Psalms 113-118. The Seder closes with a cup of wine for Elijah, coming to announce the coming of Messiah. A mini-Seder is held in every Orthodox Jewish home every Friday evening to welcome the Sabbath.

Exodus 6:6,7 set the pattern for the Seder, each cup representing a promise in those verses. These are referred to as the "Four expressions of Redemption:"

Cup 1. "I will bring you out from under the burdens of the Egyptians." This is the promise to remove the children of Israel from their bondage. This first cup of wine is called the Kiddush, meaning the sanctification. Since the Seder is a family gathering, the Kiddush sanctifies the family table so the table can serve as the family's altar for the evening's celebration. This was the cup that Jesus drank in Luke 22:17 and the blessing He said as He gave thanks was "Blessed are You, Lord our God, King of the Universe, Who creates the fruit of the vine." This is the same blessing said in the Kiddush today in Jewish homes and synagogues around the world.

Cup 2. "and I will deliver you out of their bondage.." tells of the exit from Egypt, from the slavery. Some translations say "I will save.." but deliverance is the primary meaning of the Hebrew and for Christians this is an interesting parallel that should be in the walk of each of us. As each receives the promise to be taken out of bondage and receives salvation by faith, the next step should be deliverance from all that bondage. Very few churches come through with deliverance, with the result that church after church is filled with the walking wounded. This is a cup that we surely need. This cup is drunk during the meal and represents our walk at this time.

Cup 3. "and I will redeem you with an outstretched arm, and with great judgments:" Redemption came to Israel when they walked through the Red Sea. The only redeemer in Hebrew is the kinsman redeemer, the one who pays the price to redeem his kin. This is the cup that Jesus drank in Luke 22:20 when He said that this was the New Covenant in His blood.

Cup 4. A separate cup is filled, reserved for Elijah, then this verse is read: "and I will take you to Me for a people, and I will be to you a God: and you shall know that I am the Lord your God, Who brings you out from under the burdens of Egypt." This represents the crossing of the Jordan into the Promised Land, and spiritually, the crossing into eternal life. It is called the cup of Elijah and is poured, but not drunk. It can only be drunk after Elijah comes, heralding the return of Messiah and the beginning of the Messianic reign. Could this have been the cup in Luke 22:20? Some rabbis have taught that there are five cups, by inserting one after the third cup, but before the cup of Elijah. The cup of Elijah announces the Messianic reign, but we have not yet had the Messianic reign bringing peace to all mankind, so we cannot yet drink the cup of Elijah.

When you take COMMUNION remember these cups and remember what the Lord has done for you. This puts Paul's admonition in 1 Corinthians 11:17-26 in perspective. Verse 17. "But when I give these instructions I do not praise you, because you come together, not for the better but for the worse. 18. For indeed to begin with when you gather in a congregation I hear there are divisions among you and I believe it in part. 19. For it is necessary there should even be dissension among you, so that also the proved ones would become revealed to you. 20. Therefore when you come together for this it is not the Lord's supper you eat: 21. for each takes his own supper to eat beforehand, and indeed one is hungry and another is drunk. 22. Do you not have homes in which to eat and to drink? Or do you despise the congregation of God, and do you shame those who do not have enough? What could I say to you? Shall I praise you? I do not praise you in this.

11:23. "Now I received from the Lord, which I also gave over to you, that the Lord Jesus, on the night in which He was betrayed, took bread 24. and after He gave thanks He broke it and said, 'This is My body being given on your behalf: you must regularly do this in remembrance of Me.' 25. Likewise also the cup after supper saying, 'This cup is the New Covenant by means of My blood: you must continually do this, as often as you would drink it, in remembrance of Me.' 26. For as often as you would eat this bread and you would drink the cup, you are proclaiming publicly the death of the Lord until He would come." We need to come in humility with repentant hearts, truly seeking to be better in the coming days than we have been so far.

Septuagint is the name given to the translation of the Hebrew Scriptures into Greek in Alexandria, Egypt, around 250 BC. This translation was ordered by Ptolemy Philadelphus who reigned from 284-247 BC. He called seventy, or perhaps seventy-two, scholars from the ten tribes in Jerusalem to do the work in Alexandria. These scholars would not have included scribes because all scribes were from the tribe of Levi, not the ten tribes. Also, few scribes were among the Hellenists, the Greek speaking Jewish people.

The name of the Greek text, Septuagint, is the Latin word for seventy. The Septuagint translation opened the Scriptures to nominal Jewish people who did not attend synagogue, as well as to non-Jewish populations of the civilized world, but its value to us lies in which Greek words those Hellenists used to translate the Hebrew into Greek. This gives real insight into the meanings of various Greek words used by the New Testament authors, because for the most part they learned Greek from the Hellenists. Until this century, translators of the Greek text relied heavily on classic Greek and non-ecclesiastical Greek writings to determine the meanings of the Greek text. Using the meanings from the Septuagint, rather than the classics, gives meanings more in tune with the Hebrew Scriptures. See Hellenists elsewhere in Glossary.

Servant is a correct translation of three Greek words, diakonos, oiketays, and doulos. These three are worlds apart because diakonos is also translated minister and deacon while doulos and oiketays are also translated slave, or bondservant. An oiketays was a bondservant who worked only as a household servant; a maid, cook, nurse, butler, or some similar job. A bondservant is a person who has been purchased or contracted for a specific time or job. In the late 1800's it was common for people in Europe to agree to work for a U.S. company for a specified time in payment for their passage to the U.S. A believer is to be a bondservant for the Lord in the sense that we are obligated totally to Him, because our Redeemer purchased us with His blood. He is more than an employer because he has each of us under contract. This is different from slavery because we have free will and can break the contract if we desire. Paul's letters to the Romans and to Titus, James' letter, 2 Peter, and Jude start by referring to the author as a doulos, a bondservant, of God or Jesus. The relationship to people is as a diakonos. In several places this translation uses servant/minister to convey this point. A minister is ordained to serve people as Jesus came to serve, not to be served. The Greek word diakonos is the equivalent of the Hebrew word, shoret, which also means servant or minister, but usually translated minister. In 1 Kings 19:21 Elisha ministers to or serves Elijah.

Under Torah the references to slaves are overwhelmingly to bondservants. Slaves in Greek and Roman law were possessions, like furniture, that an owner could treat however he wanted. Killing a slave was not a crime. In Jewish law, Scripture, the slaves were bondservants, who had to be set free if they were injured. "If a man shall strike the eye of his slave or the eye of his maidservant and destroy it, he shall set him free in return for his eye. And if he knocks out the tooth of his slave or the tooth of his maidservant, he shall set him free in return for his tooth." (Exodus 21:26 & 27) He also had to be given a bonus to make a new beginning. "Beware that there be not a thought in your wicked heart, saying, The seventh year, the year of release, is at hand; and your eye be evil against your poor brother, and you give him nothing; and he cry to the Lord against you, and it be sin to you." (Deuteronomy 15:9 & 10) When you see references to slaves in the Old Testament, that passage is most often speaking of bondservant. The only OT reference to slavery is in Ezekiel 27:13 where the phrase "nefesh adam" is used, commonly translated "human souls" or "human lives." In the NT the only reference to Greek and Roman slavery is in Revelation 18:13 where the Greek word somata is used of the merchants weeping over the loss of their wealth with the destruction of Babylon. That is speaking of bodies as possessions, which was the case with slavery, not only in Greece and Rome, but even in the United States, and it was not the slavery of Scripture.

Shavuot is the second First Fruits of the growing season. It is one of the three feasts men are commanded to attend. The date varies from year to year because the lunar calendar does not have fixed months. The month begins with the new moon and lasts twenty-nine or thirty days. Shavuot comes seven weeks plus one day after the First Fruits of Unleavened Bread. That is a total of fifty days, so Christians often refer to this as Pentecost, the Greek word for fifty. While Shavuot, which comes at the time of the wheat harvest, is not named in the Gospels, there are two passages that could refer to it. These are Luke 6:2 when the disciples pick grain on a Sabbath and John 5:1 when Jesus goes to an unnamed feast.

Shavuot, pronounced Sha-VOO-ote, celebrates the wheat harvest. See First Fruits elsewhere in this Glossary. Leviticus 23:15. "And you shall count from the next day after the Sabbath, from the day that you brought the sheaf of the wave offering; seven Sabbaths shall be complete; 16. To the next day after the seventh Sabbath shall you count fifty days; and you shall offer a new meal offering to the Lord. 17. You shall bring out of your habitations two wave loaves of two tenth deals; they shall be of fine flour; they shall be baked with leaven; they are the first fruits to the Lord. 18. And you shall offer with the bread seven lambs without blemish of the first year, and one young bull, and two rams; they shall be for a burnt offering to the Lord, with their meal offering, and their drink offerings, an offering made by fire, of sweet savor to the Lord. 19. Then you shall sacrifice one kid of the goats for a sin offering, and two lambs of the first year for a sacrifice of peace offerings. 20. And the priest shall wave them with the bread of the first fruits for a wave offering before the Lord with the two lambs; they shall be holy to the Lord for the priest. 21. And you shall proclaim on the same day, that it may be a holy gathering to you; you shall do no labor in it; it shall be a statute forever in all your dwellings throughout your generations. 22. And when you reap the harvest of your land, you shall not make clean riddance up to the corners of your field when you reap, nor shall you gather any gleaning of your harvest; you shall leave them to the poor, and to the stranger; I am the Lord your God."

This commandment to leave the corners and not to glean is the only commandment in Leviticus 23 that deals with something other than these special days. The reason for this command is that this reminds the farmer that the crop is not his, but the Lord's.

Counting the days between them ties the two First Fruits together, just as Jesus ties His resurrection, ascension, and the giving of the baptism of the Holy Spirit at the Feast of Weeks, called Pentecost by many Christians.

Exodus 19:1 tells us that in the third month, the month of Shavuot, the people were at Sinai. The rest of the chapter tells how He gave the Torah to His people there. For this reason Weeks, Shavuot, also celebrates the giving of Torah. The emphasis on Torah brings to mind the statement "..You shall have no other gods before Me." This means we must leave all our idols behind, which is hard to do in this materialistic, Nicolaiton, Humanist, pleasure-filled age. Old habits die hard, seen with the children of Israel in the wilderness, and in our focus on material things instead of doing the things Jesus brings out in Matthew 25:35. "For I was hungry and you gave Me to eat, I was thirsty and you gave Me to drink, I was a stranger and you took Me in, 36. and I was poorly clothed and you clothed Me, I was sick and you visited Me, I was in prison and you came to Me."

Because in Exodus 19:8 all the people answering said, "All that the Lord has spoken we will do.." and this was on Shavuot; this day is likened to a wedding, tying His people permanently to Him.

Shavuot is important for Christians because it ties deliverance and salvation celebrated at Passover with Jesus' crucifixion, to His resurrection on First Fruits of Unleavened Bread, His ascension forty days later, then, ten days after that, His sending the baptism of the Holy Spirit on the first Fruits of Shavuot. This gives us the power to live victorious lives, so we can witness to all non-believers by the way we live.

The time of waiting for the Baptism of the Holy Spirit parallels the Counting of the Omer, from the First Fruits of Unleavened Bread to the First Fruits of Shavuot. Just as the farmers could not use the wheat crop until the offering of the loaves, so also Jesus, the Bread of Life, had to ascend before the rest of the grain, His disciples could take the Holy Spirit and be used in such awesome power. After their baptism in the second chapter of Acts they healed the sick, delivered the oppressed, and raised the dead.

Shekinah is a word that is not used in Scripture, but it is significant. It comes from the Hebrew root, sh-k-n, meaning to dwell. Shekinah is used by the Rabbis to speak of the presence of God, which is automatically accompanied by brilliant light so His presence is associated with the light that now is associated with Shekinah. Called The Divine Presence, Shekinah as a feminine noun speaks of God's feminine attributes of mercy and love.

A related word is mishkan, meaning tabernacle, most often used for the tabernacle of Moses, but sometimes translated "dwelling places" and very few times referring to David's tabernacle.

Shofar   One Greek word was used to translate both shofar and trumpet. The shofar is used to call to repentance and many think that the feast referred to as the Day of Memorial in Leviticus 23:24 will be Judgment Day, which is a call to repentance. We call this the Feast of Trumpets, but the Hebrew Scripture has neither the word feast nor the word trumpet. The shofar is the instrument used. The Power New Testament in 1 Corinthians 15:52 and 1 Thessalonians 4:16 translates this word, salpiggi, as shofar. Most other translations say trumpet, but from the context of resurrection, the shofar would be used because resurrection is for judgment. The rabbis say resurrection takes place during the Feast of Unleavened Bread. Whether it takes place during Unleavened Bread or the Day of Memorial, resurrection will probably be called by a shofar. If Paul, in 2 Corinthians 5:10, meant trumpet the reference would be to the Feast of Booths (Tabernacles) calling for the celebration of the eternal kingdom.

Sin   is spoken about in the Old Testament with six different Hebrew words. The first three are general, speaking of any wickedness or evil.

Avel, meaning wickedness, injustice, wrong

Rasha, wicked, cruel, evil

Zadon, wickedness, evil, insolence, malice

These last three involve intent, which is how God classifies sin.

Avon, translated Iniquity, Avah is the root word of avon, simply meaning "to sin," and which is used in Scripture for Intentional Sin.

Fesha, translated Willful Sin. Fesha comes from the root pesha, which means to sin or to rebel. Pesha is used to describe sin committed with the Intention of Angering God.

Khata-ah, translated Error. Khata is the root for khata-ah and means to sin, transgress, or miss. Khata-ah is used in Scripture for Unintentional Sin, sin that is committed in carelessness.

We can better understand how these words regarding sin were used by Jewish translators of Exodus 34:7 into Greek. See both Hellenists and Septuagint elsewhere in this Glossary.

A-von = Greek anomia; iniquity or workers of iniquity.

Fesha = Greek adikia; injustice, unrighteousness, or wickedness.

Khata-ah = Greek amartia; failure, fault, sin

In the NT amartia is the most frequently used of those three words.

A fourth Greek word comes from a Hebrew idiom for sin and is used only three times in the NT: astokheo. The literal meaning is to miss the mark, which is a Hebrew expression for sin. Stokhos means target, mark. Astokheo is used only in 1 Timothy 1:6, 6:21, and 2 Timothy 2:18.

Man tends to rate sins, with some more serious than others. The closest God comes to rating sins is in Proverbs 6:16. (K) "There are six things which the Lord hates, seven which are an abomination to him; 17. An arrogant look, a lying tongue, and hands that shed innocent blood, 18. A heart that plots wicked plans, feet that swiftly run to evil. 19. A false witness who speaks lies, and he who sows discord among brothers."

Note that pride and arrogance, then lying are listed even before murder. God's rating system is by intent, not the specific sin.

Sin, Forgiveness of   While many Hebrew Scriptures proclaim forgiveness of sins, there is an order, a formula to obtaining forgiveness.

1. Forgiveness of others   There is one precondition, without which no amount of repentance can bring forgiveness. That is the sinner must forgive everyone of every little thing before God will accept the sinner's repentant heart. Jesus taught in the Lord's Prayer, "You must right now forgive our sins for us, in the same manner as we have completed forgiving everyone of everything, big and little, against us:" (Matthew 6:12) Verses 14 and 15 then continue this theme, "14. For if you would forgive all other people their transgressions, your heavenly Father will also forgive you: 15. but if you would not forgive all other people, neither will your Father forgive your sins." Mark 11:25 and Colossians 3:13 reaffirm this principle.

2. Forgive yourself   As you forgive others be sure to include yourself among those you forgive, to remember God's great miracle of erasing your sin. You cannot make things right with God until you make things right with everyone, and until you make things right with yourself. Do not beat yourself over past mistakes, but forgive yourself. It is not possible for you to give your love to other people if you do not love yourself. A parent who does not love himself or herself is not able to give love to spouse or children. Forgive yourself and love yourself, then, with repentance, all of God's love and forgiveness can flow through you.

3. Seek forgiveness from others   Jesus says "And I say to you that everyone who is angry with his brother will be guilty in the judgment. And whoever would say to his brother 'Empty-headed,' that one is guilty to the Sanhedrin: whoever would say, 'Stupid' is guilty in the Gehenna of the fire. 23. If therefore you would present your gift at the altar and there you would remember that your brother has something against you, 24. you must right away leave your gift there in front of the altar and go. You must first become reconciled with your brother, and then, after you come

back, present your gift." (Matthew 5:22-24) The Talmud makes clear the need to seek forgiveness of those sins committed unintentionally. It also makes clear that the sinner must make things right with the offended party before going to God. See Gossip/Slander elsewhere in this Glossary.

In seeking forgiveness from someone you are automatically confessing to that person. "And if your brother sins against you, you must go, you must show him the error between you and him alone. If he listens to you, you have gained your brother: (Lv 19:17) 16. but if he would not listen, you must take with you yet one or two, so that 'by a mouth of two or three witnesses every word would stand:' (Dt 19:35) 17. and if he refuses to listen to them, you must speak at once to the congregation: then if he refuses to listen to the congregation, he must be to you even as the heathen and the tax collector." (Matthew 18:15-17)

Confessing to a third party is not called for aside from the above sequence. Confessing to a group is not called for unless that group is the injured party. "Therefore you must continually confess your sins for yourselves with one another and you must continually pray for yourselves on behalf of one another so that you would be healed. The plea of a righteous person is very powerful, working effectively." (James 5:16) Confession here is to the injured party. This verse has been misunderstood, but Jacob was not talking about public confession, nor was he talking about confessing the same sin over and over.

4. Repent "'Therefore I will judge you, O house of Israel, everyone according to his ways,' says the Lord God. 'Repent, and turn yourselves from all your transgressions; so that iniquity shall not be your ruin.'" (Ezekiel 18:30) The Bible frequently uses the word return to express repentance, as "Come, and let us return to the Lord; for he has torn, and he will heal us; he has struck, and he will bind us up." (Hosea 6:1) Return is appropriate because repentance requires action, much more than just regretting something. Without action, a change in behavior, there is not true repentance. The sinner must resolve not to repeat the mistake. Read Psalm 51 for a model prayer of repentance.

5. Forgiveness from God There are three verses that clearly state God's position. Exodus says, "Preserver of Kindness for thousands of generations, Forgiver of Iniquity (avon), Willful Sin (fesha), and Error (khata-ah), and Who Cleanses.." (Exodus 34:7) Isaiah wrote, "I, only I am He Who wipes away your willful sins (fesha) for My sake, and I shall not recall your sins (khata-ah)." (Isaiah 43:25) Jeremiah wrote, "They will no longer teach – each man his fellow, each man his brother – saying 'Know the Lord! For all of them will know Me, from their smallest to their greatest – the word of the Lord – when I will forgive their iniquity (avon) and will no longer recall their sin (khata-ah)." (Jeremiah 31:34)

6. Clean slate From the following verses we see that with repentance all sins are forgiven, even those committed with the intention of angering God. All forgiven sins are then deleted from God's computer. "The soul that sins (khata-ah) shall die. The son shall not bear the iniquity (avon) of the father, neither shall the father bear the iniquity (avon) of the son; the righteousness of the righteous shall be upon him, and the wickedness (rasha) of the wicked (rasha) shall be upon him. 21. But if the wicked man (rasha) will turn from all his sins that he has committed, and keep all my statutes, and do that which is lawful and right, he shall surely live, he shall not die. 22. None of his transgressions (fesha) that he has committed shall be remembered against him; in his righteousness that he has done he shall live." (Ezekiel 20b-22) So Ezekiel removes all doubt about remembering sins, even those that are not mentioned in other verses about remembering. Our merciful heavenly Father forgives and forgets. Our All-Knowing Father is not forgetful, but He deletes forgiven sin from His computer. Ezekiel 33:11 says, "Say to them: 'As I live – the word of the Lord God – [I swear] that I do not desire the death of the wicked one, but rather the wicked one's return from his way, that he may live. Repent; repent from your evil ways! Why should you die, O House of Israel?'"

A rabbi wrote many years ago, that the greatest miracle of all happens when a sinner repents; because then God takes that person back in time to when the sin was committed – only this time the person does not commit the sin. Therefore the sin was never committed. So each of us needs to know that any remorse over past sin is not from God, but from the Accuser. Satan is the one who wants you to wallow in guilt. God says that any repented sin was never committed. Accept God's forgiveness, knowing that you are never again to dwell on that past mistake. The miracle of that sin's being erased is the greatest of all miracles.

Sin, National   National sin is a problem for Israel that crops up throughout history from the book of Numbers on. Ezekiel 34 is dedicated to this theme, with the shepherds representing the leaders of Israel. National sin does have individuals who are set apart for God, as the Lord spoke in 1 Kings 19:18, when God spoke to Elijah, after Elijah complained to God that he was alone in worshipping God. "Yet I will leave seven thousand in Israel, all the knees that have not bowed to the Baal, and every mouth that has not kissed him." Even though the nation was doomed, the saints were not. In the exiles of the Northern Kingdom, then later the people of Judea, the good were punished with exile along with the idolaters, but God placed the blame on the leaders, as expressed in Ezekiel 34 and other passages.

In our democratic society, the elected leaders and the bureaucrats will bear punishment, but with a democracy all eligible voters bear responsibility.

Saints will be saved, but will go through hardship, as did the Godly people of the times of exile, whether they were taken out of the country or left behind. Those left behind were the poor, the laborers and servants of the new hierarchy. The United States is now on the fence between righteousness and wickedness. All eligible voters have a share in whether our leaders at every level of government steer us toward the holy or toward the profane. Will we be a Godly nation? Will we have a society that adheres to God's Word? Will we care for the poor, the widow, the sick? Will we encourage or discourage abortion? Will we encourage or discourage homosexuality? Will we permit the teaching of God's Word in schools? Will we continue the current political correctness where the teaching of witchcraft in our schools is more acceptable than prayer or Bible clubs?

In standing by Israel the United States could be in line for a great blessing. It is time for every believer to persist in prayer and to actively work for the godliness of this nation. The alternative is not pretty.

Son of David/Son of Joseph   We normally think of Jesus as the Son of David the king. Certainly there are many Scripture references to the Son of David as being on the throne. Those watching the entry of Jesus on Palm Sunday are all looking toward the expected soon Messianic reign of the Son of David. However, those who called on the Son of David for healing, such as Bartimaeus in Mark, were calling another Son of David, the Shepherd. In John 10:11 Jesus says, "I am the Good Shepherd" and in John 21:16 tells Peter to tend the flock. What is it that a shepherd does? His task is to keep his flock together, to see that they are nurtured, wounds and illnesses treated, properly fed, watered, sheltered, protected from any enemies. To do this he takes them from one pasture to another in the appropriate season and to ensure that they have shelter whenever that is called for. He shears them in proper season, both selling and using the wool and the milk while preserving the flock.

The rabbis tell us that there is also a Son of Joseph as a Messianic figure. The Son of Joseph is representative of the farmer because of Joseph's dream of the sheaves in Genesis 37:6&7. The seven years of plenty are also representative of this. The rabbis say that the enmity toward him by his brothers is from the brothers' call to shepherding contrasted with Joseph's call as a farmer. The two careers speak of two different ways of life, as we know from many tales of the ranchers and the farmers in old west of the US.

While the shepherd maintains the status quo, the farmer is out to transform the land, from grasslands, woods, and swamps into land that produces crops, returning up to one hundred fold on his labor and seed. The labor is intense and includes eleven tasks forbidden on the Sabbath. These are sowing, plowing, reaping, gathering, threshing, winnowing, sorting, grinding, sifting, kneading, and baking. Of the shepherd's duties only shearing and processing wool or milk are forbidden for the Sabbath.

With his transformation of the land, the Son of Joseph brings material blessings, while the Son of David, also known as Judah, guards the past. In Ezekiel 37:15-17 we have the two sticks, one representing Judah and the other Ephraim, being joined together. Since David is a son of Judah and Ephraim a son of Joseph, the elements are there for the merger of all believers, both Jewish and Christian, all segments of Judaism and Christianity coming together in a Messianic celebration.

It is interesting that the rabbis say that neither Judah nor Joseph can prevail alone. The two brothers need each other because a world of Josephs would lose sight of the old in its pursuit of the new, and a world of only Judahs could trap Judaism in a web of irrelevances.

Another expression of two Messiahs is with the terms "suffering Messiah" and "reigning Messiah." Jesus suffered in His first coming, but will reign on His next appearance. We can see both Judah and Joseph in His ministry, with many references to shepherding and many to being transformed. Examples of being transformed include the parables of the sower and statements such as "You will know them by their fruit." (Matthew 7:16) Paul also referred to our transformation in Romans 12:2 "..by the renovation of your mind." When Jesus reigns it seems that His reign will be more like Joseph's as the Prime Minister under the King of the Universe. Another similarity to Joseph is His physical absence from us for a season. The current Church is more under David than Joseph, being maintained more than transformed. Satanic forces still have power, much of it conceded by the Church, since very few teach and minister deliverance and spiritual warfare. Messiah's reign will be without Satan while he is bound for a thousand years (Revelation 20:2). Only then, without Satanic influences, will people be totally transformed and be able to be all that they can be. In that sense the current status is more like the Davidic reign and the Messianic reign will be more like the reign of Joseph. By that we can readily see that Jesus is both Son of David and Son of Joseph, whether 2,000 years ago or in His reign. What do you think?

Sorcery is described by three Greek words: pharmakeia, pharmakeus, and pharmakos. Pharmakeuw is the verb that means to administer drugs for the purpose of inducing spells, with visions and messages from spirits. Two nouns come from this verb: pharmakeia, used in Galatians 5:20, Revelation 9:21 & 18:23, is the form that refers to the sorcery, while pharmakeus, used in Revelation 21:8, is the form that refers to the person who either prepares the drugs or uses them. Pharmakos, used in Revelation 22:15, refers to one who is devoted to this use of drugs. From these we have compelling proof that what is now euphemistically called "recreational drug use" is sinful.

Numerous verses tell us that drunkenness is sinful and three, Luke 21:34, Romans 13:13, and Galatians 5:21 tell us that any intoxicant is wrong. The Greek word used in those verses is methai, which is nearly always translated drunkenness. Methai literally means intoxicant, so in the three verses mentioned here the reference is to any intoxicant, not just alcohol. Intoxication from any source is a sin and is to be avoided completely.

Sowing and Reaping   Paul wrote in 2 Corinthians 9:6. "And this, the one who sows sparingly will also reap sparingly, and the one who sows bountifully will also reap bountifully. 7. Each just as he chose in his heart, not reluctantly or from compulsion: for God loves a cheerful giver, 8. And God is able to abound all grace in you, so that in all things always having sufficiency you would abound in every good work, 9. just as it has been written,

'He scattered, he gave to the poor,

   his righteousness remains forever.' (Ps 112:9)

10. But the One Who supplies seed to the sower also provides bread for food and He will increase your seed and will increase the yield of your righteousness."

Paul is speaking of sowing money into the congregation in Jerusalem, and this principle applies to all giving to ministries and charities. We often use this symbol of sowing for financial gifts, but we sow much more than money as we go about our business every day. In all sowing we need to be careful what we sow, where we sow, and how much we sow. Seed should not be wasted by sowing too much or too little, or by sowing on ground that will not give a return.

While finances are an obvious application of the metaphor of sowing, the primary seed we sow is not money, but action – that is, the things we do and say throughout each day. A teaching by R. Eleazar holds, "Greater is he who performs charity than [he who offers] all the sacrifices, for it is said, To do charity and justice is more acceptable to the Lord than sacrifice." (Proverb 21:3)

"He further stated, 'Practice of Kindness is greater than charity, for it is said, "Sow to yourselves according to your charity, but reap according to your loving kindness;" (Hosea 10:12) if a man sows, it is doubtful whether he will eat [the harvest] or not, but when a man reaps, he will certainly eat. R. Eleazar further stated, 'The reward of charity depends entirely upon the extent of the kindness in it, for it is said, "Sow to yourselves according to charity, but reap according to the kindness."

"Our Rabbis taught, In three respects is Practice of Kindness superior to charity: charity can be done only with one's money, but Practice of Kindness can be done with one's person and one's money. Charity can be given only to the poor, Practice of Kindness both to the rich and the poor. Charity can be given to the living only, Practice of Kindness can be done both to the living and to the dead (by speaking well of the person or tending the grave)."

"R. Eleazar further stated, He who executes charity and justice is regarded as though he had filled all the world with kindness, for it is said, He loves charity and justice, the earth is full of the loving kindness of the Lord. (Psalm 33:5)

"They are worthy, in His sight, because they 'sow above all waters', that is to say, they sow 'according to righteousness' (Hosea 10:12), for of him who sows according to righteousness it is said: 'For thy mercy is great above ('al) the heavens'" (Psalm 108:5). (The quotes in the four paragraphs above are from The Talmud of the Judaic Classics Library)

We need to remember that we are sowing with every word we speak, everything we do. A missed opportunity is a seed not sown.

Succot   is frequently called the Feast of Tabernacles. A better English translation would be Feast of Booths, which is the meaning of the title in Hebrew. This feast celebrates the fall harvest, with the third First Fruits of the growing season. (See First Fruits just after Unleavened Bread.) During Succot, the first day and the eighth day, (Shemini Atseret, see John 7:37) are Sabbaths. During this feast each family builds a succah, or booth, outside the home, a flimsy structure of palm branches that provides shade, but not much else. A good rain will come right through the roof and walls. The family eats all its meals in the succah and the men are supposed to sleep in it. It is to be a room for visitors, even strangers, to come in and share stories and meals.

The sixth day of Succot is a cry for salvation, "Hoshea na rabah" "Save us now! Let us increase!" This is a time for repentance, necessary for salvation, and a reminder of Yom Kippur, which was just eleven days ago. On this day during the second temple period (Jesus' day), there was a procession through the streets of Jerusalem, singing Hoshea na! from Psalm 118:25. Hoshea na, written in Greek as Hosanna, means Save us! Now!! Some might say that this could have been the date of Jesus' triumphal entry, but the date is not what is most important. The critical point is that all those at Jesus' triumphal entry knew about this practice and the full meaning of it.

The day after the end of the feast is a one-day post-Biblical celebration honoring the completion of the reading of the Torah and the beginning of the new round of reading Torah, Simchat Torah (Joy of the Torah). Today in Jerusalem many combine Simchat Torah with Shemini Atseret, celebrating both on the last day of Succot.

Suffering as in 1 Peter 3:17 "It is better to suffer for doing good, if he might want the will of God, rather than doing evil. 18. Because Messiah also once suffered concerning sin, the righteous One on behalf of the unjust, so that He could bring you to God when He died on the one hand in the flesh, but then was made alive by the Spirit:" Jesus said we would be persecuted. (John 15:20) The Rabbis say "Whosoever does not persecute them that persecute him, whosoever takes an offense in silence, he who does good for its own sake, he who is cheerful under his sufferings - they are the friends of God: and of them Scripture says, 'They that love Him shall be as the sun, when he goes forth in his might.'" This is based on Judges 5:31 "..as the sun when he goes forth in his might."

Take/Receive Greek words with a basic meaning of take are often translated receive and there is a big difference between the two. Our Western mind-sets seem to make us want to say receive when the New Testament authors wrote take. This translation uses take more often than most translations, but there are places where receive is used. One place where take is important is in John 20:22. "And after He said this He breathed upon them and said to them, 'You must immediately take the Holy Spirit: 23. whomever you would forgive, their sins have been forgiven for them, whomever you would retain their sins have been retained.'" The Baptism of the Holy Spirit is to be sought after and taken. It is not a passive, automatic gift.

Testimony of Jesus The key verse is Revelation 19: 10. "Then I fell before his feet to pay homage to him. And he said to me, 'Stop! Don't do that: I am a fellow servant with you and your brothers who have the testimony of Jesus: you must now pay homage to God. For the testimony of Jesus is the Spirit of Prophecy.'" The testimony means two different things.

One is that we are to testify about Him. We certainly are to testify about Him in both word and deed. We are to show our family, friends, neighbors, co-workers, and everyone we meet that we are different, set apart from the world. We are to show by the way we live that we are committed wholeheartedly to the Lord.

The second and deeper meaning speaks of Jesus as the Word of God, as in John 1:1 "In the beginning was the Word, and the Word was with God, and the Word was God." Revelation 1:2, 9, and 20:4 use the expression "the Word of God and the testimony of Jesus," using a Hebrew form of repetition to emphasize the statement, in effect saying "He is Scripture." Psalm 119:2 has "Praiseworthy are those who guard His testimonies, they serve Him wholeheartedly." Jewish Commentary says that "His testimonies" "refers to the Torah and mitzvot, which bear testimony to God's relationship to Israel." Those who serve Him wholeheartedly know His Scripture and do His mitzvot, which are His commandments. The phrase, "His testimonies," is used ten times in the Tanach (OT). John recorded in Revelation 19:10 "Then I fell before his feet to pay homage to him (the angel). And he said to me, 'Stop! Don't do that: I am a fellow servant with you and your brothers who have the testimony of Jesus: you must now pay homage to God. For the testimony of Jesus is the Spirit of Prophecy.'"

Spirit of Prophecy is action, putting God's Word to work and turning His commandments into deeds. Doing His commandments is the Spirit of Prophecy; that is, the goal, the fulfilling of all prophecy, as His people are doing all that He has commanded, bringing His perfect will into being so that all He has spoken has come to pass. We are to be so committed to knowing His Word and to doing His will, that we move in perfect synchronization with Him, just as His Incarnate Body, Jesus, did while He walked the earth. Spirit of Prophecy is a term used by Torah scholars from ancient times, so John would have understood the meaning when the messenger spoke this to him. Rabbinic commentary lists many examples of people being led by the Spirit of Prophecy, with a few examples here:

- The 70 elders to help Moses carry the load in the wilderness
- The ten spies to the valley of Eshcol to get the grapes that they brought back
- Rahab to instruct the two spies that their pursuers would turn back in 3 days
- Ruth to the field of Boaz

The Testimony of Jesus is the very Spirit of Prophecy. Each of us has been given the gift of prophecy and each of us is to live by that, to be so in tune with the perfect will of God that we follow the examples cited above to bring His perfect will here to earth. Romans 13:14. "but you will become so possessed of the mind of the Lord Jesus Messiah that you will resemble Him and you must not be concerned for desires of the flesh." To be possessed of or to have the mind of the Lord is to have your spirit so in tune with the Lord that you understand what He means, what He would have you do. That is also the primary meaning of 1 Corinthians 2:16. See Lord's Prayer in this Glossary.

This commentary on the Testimony of Jesus was written by June Rice, author of inspirational books: "The Hebrew references all had one thing in common. In each instance cited, they relate to His Consummate Plan for the Ages. Each event moves, and is prompted, according to Prophetic Time, so there are actually two Time Lines here, the natural and Prophetic Time (personal prophecy included) because both move along according to and with God's Prophetic Time, with increasing frequency, like labor pains coming faster, toward the final crowning of that particular birth.

"The testimony of Jesus is Himself reigning now in us, and ultimately on the new earth. This shows me why we need one another, and why the move of the saints is so critical. In each of your Hebrew references cited in OT it had to do with others; such as the 70 elders (government of God) the ten spies getting the grapes (this can refer to the abundance of the final harvest, but not all are willing to step out in faith for it) or Ruth going to the field of Boaz that resulted in the birth of Jesus, a daring new thing, and also bore witness to the new man birthed from both Gentile and Jew which should be the new pattern birthed in the Church, which is also quite startling."

Tithe   Matthew 23:23. "Woe to you, hypocrite scribes and Pharisees, because you tithe the mint and the dill and the cumin but you have canceled the more important things of the Torah, justice and mercy and faith: but it was necessary to do these things but not to cancel those things." Jesus said it is necessary to tithe so we all accept the principle of the tithe. Abraham tithed, then later it was commanded in Leviticus 27:30, reinforced in Numbers 18:21-28, and Deuteronomy 12:6-17 and 26:12. It is further endorsed in 2 Chronicles, Nehemiah, Ezekiel, Amos, and Malachi. Tithing is mentioned six times in the New Testament, but not one time is there any suggestion that tithing is not required.

Deuteronomy 14:28. "At the end of three years you shall bring forth all the tithe of your produce in that year, and shall lay it up inside your gates; 29. And the Levite, because he has no part nor inheritance with you, and the stranger, and the orphan, and the widow, who are inside your gates, shall come, and shall eat and be satisfied; that the Lord your God may bless you in all the work of your hand which you do."

Deuteronomy 26:12. "When you have finished tithing all the tithes of your produce the third year, which is the year of tithing, and have given it to the Levite, the stranger, the orphan, and the widow, that they may eat inside your gates, and be filled; 13. Then you shall say before the Lord your God, I have brought away the hallowed things out of my house, and also have given them to the Levite, and to the stranger, to the orphan, and to the widow, according to all your commandments which you have commanded me; I have not transgressed your commandments, nor have I forgotten them;"

The statement of Deuteronomy 14:28 "At the end of three years you shall bring forth all the tithe of your produce in that year.." is confusing because it might lead some to think that it is an accumulation of three years' tithe. What is to be brought is the tithe of that year, the third year.

Tithing in Israel was to operate in a seven-year cycle:

First year to the local priest (if there is one) and the local Levites.

Second year to the priest in Jerusalem. This tithe was to feed the tither and his household while in Jerusalem for the feast, but the remainder went to the priest. If the tither was wealthy and could afford to pay for his party's meals in Jerusalem, he was still to eat something symbolic from his tithe, such as one olive.

Third year to the Levite and the poor, according to Deuteronomy 14:29. "And the Levite, because he has no part nor inheritance with you, and the stranger, and the orphan, and the widow, who are inside your gates, shall come, and shall eat and be satisfied; that the Lord your God may bless you in all the work of your hand which you do." This is called the Tithe of the Poor.

A second set of three years is identical to the above.

Seventh year, no tithes because that is the Sabbath year and no crops were raised.

Numbers 18:26. "Thus speak to the Levites, and say to them, When you take of the people of Israel the tithes which I have given you from them for your inheritance, then you shall offer up an offering of it for the Lord, a tenth part of the tithe. 27. And this your offering shall be reckoned to you, as though it were the grain of the threshing floor, and as the fullness of the wine press. 28. Thus you also shall offer an offering to the Lord of all your tithes, which you receive from the people of Israel; and you shall give from it the Lord's gift to Aaron the priest."

The Hebrew word for tithe is M'ASER, which is the word for ten, ASER, pronounced ah'sair', plus the prefix, M. The M prefix indicates a projection of the noun, so in the case of the tithe that tells us that the tithe is to be given freely, cheerfully, that the tithe is no big deal - here is more for the Lord's work. Giving beyond the tithe is summarized by Nehemiah.

Nehemiah 10:33. "Also we made ordinances for us, to charge ourselves yearly with the (1) third part of a shekel for the service of the house of our God; 34. (2) For the bread of display, and (3) for the continual meal offering, and (4) for the continual burnt offering, (5) of the sabbaths, (6) of the new moons, (7) for the appointed feasts, and (8) for the holy things, and (9) for the sin offerings to make an atonement for Israel, and (10) for all the work of the house of our God. 35. And we cast lots among the priests, the Levites, and the people, (11) for the wood offering, to bring it into the house of our God, after the houses of our fathers, at appointed times year by year, to burn upon the altar of the Lord our God, as it is written in the Torah; 36. And to bring the (12) first fruits of our ground, and the first fruits of all fruit of every tree, year by year, to the house of the Lord; 37. Also the (13) first born of our sons, and (14) of our cattle, as it is written in the Torah, and (15) the firstlings of our herds and of our flocks; and to bring to the house of our God, to the priests who minister in the house of our God; 38. And that we should bring the (16) first fruits of our dough, and (17) our offerings, and the (18) fruit of all kinds of trees, of wine and of oil, to the priests, to the chambers of the house of our God; and the tithes of our ground to the Levites, for they, the Levites receive the tithes in all the cities of our tillage. 39. And the priest, the son of Aaron, shall be with the Levites, when the Levites take tithes; and the Levites shall bring up the tithe of the tithes to the house of our God, to the chambers, into the treasure house. 40. For the people of Israel and the Levites shall bring the offering of the grain, of the new wine, and the oil, to the chambers where the utensils of the sanctuary are, and the priests who minister, and the gatekeepers, and the singers; and we will not forsake the house of our God."

Some of these offerings are rather small, like first fruits, which are brought in a basket by each worshiper. Others are considerable, like the firstborn son, redeemed for five shekels (the third of a shekel was worth 2 drachmas, two days pay in Jesus' day, from Matthew 17:24, so 5 shekels equaled 30 days wages), based on Numbers 18:15, 16. It is obvious that God intends for us to make frequent offerings and to be generous in our giving. As David said, "All things come of thee, and of thine own have we given Thee." (1 Chronicles 29:14)

We are to give such offerings as thanksgiving, peace, and vow whenever something is a special blessing to us. The wood offering is interesting because it was by lot and even the priest, who had no land, was eligible. By lot was fair in an agricultural society in which almost everyone had wood lots from which to cut the wood, but today if this were carried out it would have to be an assessment for utilities – hopefully not by lot.

The goal for each congregation should be to return to God's Word regarding giving. We should not be legalistic, but be open to the Holy Spirit to be guided so that our stewardship would line up with His will. We know that more of the tithe should be going for missions, to ministry workers, and to feeding and caring for the poor. To restructure any church's finances will take time and sacrifice. The beginning is to understand God's principles - His teachings - and to know that changes need to come. Many pastors and many ministry workers are grossly underpaid. As believers put these truths in their spirits, to tithe and then go well beyond the tithe as Nehemiah wrote. As boards and pastors understand God's plan for distribution of church funds, finances will accomplish all that God has ordained for them.

Torah

The word Torah appears over two hundred times in the Old Testament, and the word Nomos over two hundred times in the Greek New Testament. Nomos is the word that was used by the translators of the Septuagint to translate the Hebrew word Torah into Greek. Our Christian translators to the best of my knowledge always translate both Torah and Nomos as Law, even though that is not the meaning for either the Hebrew or the Greek.

Torah means teaching or instruction, not law. Please make a conscious effort to erase what you have heard about "LAW" in Biblical teachings. In the Jewish Bible the first five books are referred to as Torah, but that name is sometimes loosely applied to all Scripture and even the rabbinical teachings. The emphasis is on the teachings in Genesis through Deuteronomy so that we can live the kind of lives that God wants us to live.

The Greek word Nomos refers to anything that has been established and can mean law, but would more accurately be translated Torah most of the time in the New Testament. That it can mean either teaching or law seems baffling to us, but there is a valid reason.

Rabbi Eliezer Ben-Yehuda wrote, "Jewish religious law is based upon morality, and deals with every aspect of human life. A Jew's contemplations, abstractions, reflections, intentions, private conduct, even when they have no social consequences — all are included, for in our religious law one is always seen as standing under God's watchful eye. In our creed, all law is an attempt to make us better servants of the Lord - and since the world is His - we must act in concert with the needs of this world. God acts in grace out of love for His world - can we, dare we do anything less?

"Thus, the law is concerned not with protecting society, nor even with defending the rights of people, but rather with the basic question of what is a person's duty. The Hebrew word 'Mitzvah' - which has no exact translation, and is rendered in different contexts as 'good deed,' 'law' or 'command,' can also be taken to mean 'duty' or 'obligation' - a concept which becomes the key to Jewish law. So Jewish law concerns itself not with what is 'legal,' but with what it is that God wants us to do, what is our duty. The Torah judge does not sit on the bench as an inquisitor, nor as a symbol of governmental powers, he sits on his tribunal as a teacher, as

548

one to whom has been given the privilege of interpreting in human terms God's will and God's word.

"Another characteristic of Jewish law is that it is community-oriented. While the origin of Jewish law is in the Torah, its details come from the Mishna and the Gemara - texts that were written and edited outside of Eretz Yisrael, after the Jewish homeland had been destroyed, and the Jewish people no longer had any sovereignty or independence. The great code of Maimonides in the twelfth century, and the code of Juda Caro in the sixteenth century, were produced on 'foreign' soil, where this law, mitsvot, became the only guardian of Jewish integrity. In a chaotic world deprived of order and civility, the Jews had an established code that allowed them to travel and to conduct business - which made possible their survival. Mitsvot also kept the Jews united in all their far-flung lands of exile. East and West, North and South were united in respect of Mitsvot.

"The Jewish legal system functioned without any coercion; it could not exercise any physical or penal sanctions. There were no prisons alongside the academies or the synagogues where the Jewish tribunal would convene. There were neither policemen nor bailiffs prepared to carry out the orders of the court. The judge sat completely disarmed. He had nothing, not any powers -- except for the reverence of Torah and the conscience of the people. Jewish law addressed itself to developing the character of a people, to refining individuals as human personalities, to replacing the lack of external force with the presence of inner sanctity. The law was obeyed not because there were jails, but because a people inwardly accepted it and its decisions. Consequently, its decisions and decrees were carried out with a fidelity and dispatch that no penal system ever inspired. Further, I believe that the law was obeyed because the people realized and accepted that it was righteous, humane, considerate, and motivated by love of God and total surrender of vanity and self-interest to the principles of His teaching of the inviolate nature of Tzedek - true teaching of God's justice."

The Christian concept of LAW is not at all close to the meaning of Torah, so please mark your Bibles, changing the word law to Torah.

There are several commonly used metaphors for Torah in Scripture. Water is one, based on Isaiah 55:1 "Ho, every one who thirsts, come to the waters, and he who has no money; come, buy, and eat; come, buy wine and milk without money and without price." and on Exodus 14:22 "And the people of Israel went into the midst of the sea upon the dry ground; and the waters were a wall to them on their right hand, and on their left." This gives added meaning to many verses such as Ephesians 5:26 "so that He, Jesus, would sanctify his wife (congregation), making her pure by washing with the Word of the Torah."

Another metaphor for Torah is light, based on Proverbs 6:23 "For a commandment is a lamp and the Torah is light; and reproving discipline is the way of life." The Talmud says that knowledge of Torah brings spiritual illumination. Torah lights our path, showing us the way to go, our spiritual illumination. A third metaphor is olive oil, from Isaiah 51:3, with oil as the source of illumination and also the source of joy. It is called the Oil of Gladness.

Paul wrote in 1 Corinthians 6.1 "Does someone of you dare having a lawsuit with another, to be judged by the unrighteous and not by the saints? 2. Or do you not know that the saints will judge the world? (Daniel 7:22, Wisdom 3:8) And if the world is to be judged by you, are you not competent in trivial cases? 3. Do you not know that we will judge angels, let alone ordinary matters? 4. Indeed if you are having lawsuits over ordinary matters, do you appoint as judges men who have no standing in the congregation? 5. I am saying this to shame you. So, is not one among you wise? Who will be able to judge between one and his brother? 6. But is brother judged with brother and this by unbelievers? 7. Surely now then these are an utter loss for you that you are having lawsuits with one another. Why not rather be wronged? Why not rather be defrauded?"

In ancient Israel both criminal and civil law were handled in the synagogue and the temple. Paul was telling the early church to follow that example, that Christians had no business going before the heathen courts, but were to resolve their differences within the body of believers. Each first century synagogue had an appointed judge, whose primary qualifications were knowledge of Torah and application of those principles in the lives of the members. The Torah was their legal code, their guide for every legal decision, based on the 613 commandments in the first five books of the Bible. Although the commands had been known for some time, it was not until the 3rd century AD that the count of 613 was first written. Rabbi Simlai gets credit for that, with 248 positive and 365 negative commands.

We have not understood some of these passages. Most of the 613 commandments deal with personal relationships and many deal with the spoken word. Thus it was not a surprise to His listeners when Jesus said "And I say to you that everyone who is angry with his brother will be guilty in the judgment. And whoever would say to his brother 'Empty-headed,' that one is guilty to the Sanhedrin: whoever would say, 'Stupid' is guilty in the Gehenna of the fire." (Matthew 5:22) There was a local Sanhedrin in each community as well as the Sanhedrin in Jerusalem. Each one was a council of elders that served to determine local matters according to Torah.

The Rabbis had long before Jesus' day determined that the references such as "an eye for an eye" and a "tooth for a tooth" (Exodus 21:24) were not to be taken literally. They said this because the basic premise was that God is just, and if a one-eyed man knocked out the eye of someone with two eyes, then to take the second eye from the other man would make him blind. This would not be just. If a toothless man knocked out someone else's tooth then he would escape punishment. This would not be justice. Therefore these and other scriptures were used as the base for establishing monetary punishment - fines.

This use of Torah for legal decisions is why Jewish writers sometimes refer to Torah as Law. This is a whole different context from the mind-sets that we have acquired from our Christian teachings. Remember, Torah means teaching or instruction, so substitute the word Torah for law as you read different translations.

Tree of Life   in Revelation 22:2 is the same kind of tree named in Genesis 2:9, 3:22, and Ezekiel 47:12. Revelation 22:2 "In the middle of its street, also on each side of the river, is a tree of life making twelve fruit, yielding its fruit each month, and the leaves of the tree are used for the healing of the multitudes." The leaves have healing power, which is strange, so perhaps a tea will be made from the leaves. Most translators use the word nations instead of multitudes, but this healing is for people, not nations. Only when the people are healed will the nations be at peace. After Satan is thrown into the Lake of Fire he will no longer afflict people with diseases, or rejection, greed, pride, or any other of the myriad evils that he is now using against people. The problems of nations, whether they are poverty, ignorance, pride, hatred, jealousy, or whatever, are a result of Satan's attacks on individuals. The national psyche is the result of spirits common to an area. After Satan is dispatched and no longer able to afflict mankind, the results of his earlier attacks will need to be healed. Blind eyes and deaf ears will need to be opened, crippled people to be made whole, mentally ill to be set free, and every bit of pride, prejudice, and hatred will have to be removed. When that has been done the peace of the Lord will have free reign on the entire Earth and we shall all live in the Kingdom of God.

In Judaism "Tree of Life" is one of the symbols of Torah.

Trials   "A trial has not taken you except what is common to mankind: but God is faithful Who will not permit you to be tested beyond what you are able, and therefore He will then in the test make you to be able to patiently bear the way out." (I Corinthians 10:13) While some translations of this verse talk about escape or the Lord providing a way out, this is the literal translation. As much as we would like an escape, most of us know that escape has not been typical of our Christian experience. We all have seasons that have been uncomfortable or even downright painful, but God has always enabled us to endure the way out. It is a process, a process of maturing in the Lord, as we learn to stand in faith and pursue the things of God. A trial is a heavenly test that forces a person to choose between God's will and his own nature or understanding of what is right. By standing in faith we serve as witnesses to the world of His power working through us. God knows how you will respond before the test begins.

Remember "And he called the name of the place Massa and Meriva, because of the strife of the children of Israel, and because they tempted the Lord, saying, 'Is the Lord among us, or not?' Then came Amelek and fought with Israel in Refedim.." (Exodus 17:7, 8) Two major things happened here that we need to avoid: first, the people questioned the presence of the Lord. The second is the coming of Amelek. If you question the presence of the Lord, you can be sure that Amelek will come on the heels of the question. "Remember what Amelek did to you by the way, when you were come out of Mitzrayim (Egypt): how he met you by the way, and smote the hindmost of you, all that were feeble in your rear, when you were faint and weary: and he feared not God." (Deuteronomy 25:17,18) Satan will attack you where you are weakest, and you will cry, "Why are You not here, Lord?" which will invite more trouble: a cycle we all want to avoid.

Keep your faith level high, bearing in mind at all times that "..He (God) Himself has said, I will not in any way fail you nor give you up nor leave you without support. [I will] not, [I will] not, [I will] not in any degree leave you helpless, nor forsake nor let [you] down, [relax My hold on you]. - Assuredly not!" (Hebrews 13:5 Amp) In the Greek language repeated use of a negative strengthens the statement, so the author of Hebrews is saying God will not in any way ever, under any circumstances, leave you or forsake you for even a moment. A rabbi wrote centuries ago "A just God does not impose trials that are beyond the capacity of the individual - God tests only the righteous people who will do His will, not the wicked who will disobey." (Nahmanides, 13th Century)

"..because the wrestling is not with blood and flesh, but with the rulers, with the powers, with the world rulers of the darkness, with the spiritual (powers) of the wickedness in the heavens." (Ephesians 6:12) "Through every prayer and entreaty, praying in every time in the Spirit, and being alert in Him, by means of every perseverance and entreaty concerning all the saints." (Ephesians 6:18) "Have not I commanded you? Be strong and of a good courage; be not afraid, neither be dismayed: for the Lord your God is with you wherever you go." (Joshua 1:9)

Keep your faith level high. Know that there will be seasons when you are being challenged and stretched. But be absolutely certain that the Lord your God is with you wherever you go, that He will never abandon you or forsake you. Never, never say "Is God among us or not?" You can be sure that He is with you and that He will make you to be able to endure, to patiently bear the way out.

Unleavened Bread   This feast begins on Nissan 15, the day after Passover. The symbol of Unleavened Bread is matzah bread, which is made without yeast. Matzah is eaten throughout the entire seven days of the Feast of Unleavened Bread.

Today Passover and Unleavened Bread combined are often just called Passover. The emphasis of this feast is on freedom from bondage, the release from Egyptian bondage for the purpose of worshipping God.

The Rabbis teach that resurrection for judgment takes place during the Feast of Unleavened Bread. Jesus was resurrected during Unleavened Bread, on First Fruits. Please note that Judgment Day takes place several months later, on Rosh HaShannah, the Day of Memorial.

Wealth   is neutral to our salvation. It is neither evil nor good of itself, but it is a great factor in many lives. Paul wrote to Timothy (1 Timothy 6:10) that "..love of money is a root of all the evils.." so it is not the money itself that is evil, but loving money can certainly cause evil. Greed is the enemy. Many who are wealthy have put their faith in wealth and not in the Lord. Many have acquired or retained inherited wealth because money was their god. You do not need to have money to love money, so there are many poor who have money as their god.

The kingdom of God here on earth benefits from the wealth of those who are not greedy and who give generously to God's work, but not everyone is to be wealthy. We should all be prosperous enough to have respectable housing and the other necessities of life, but we should not expect more than that simply because we are believers. Jesus said "You must continually see and guard yourselves from all covetousness, because someone's life is not abundant from his possessions." (Luke 12:15) Paul wrote to the Philippians (4:11) that he had "..learned to be content with what things I have."

The story of the Rich Ruler in Luke 18:18-23 tells about a young man to whom his possessions were more important than the kingdom of God. Jesus saw that quality in him so He told the man to sell all his possessions, give the money to the poor, and then follow Him. We all have to view our possessions, no matter how small or how great, as less important than the kingdom of God. See Harlot elsewhere in this Glossary.

Wedding   The wedding in Jesus' day began with an agreement between the bride and groom, like engagement today. At the time of this agreement a document, called a Ketubah, which was a formal document, was signed. The Ketubah included a price to be paid for the bride. At that time the couple was considered to be married, even though the marriage was not consummated. The groom then prepared a place, usually on family property, for the couple and when his father approved of the apartment or house, the son would come for his bride and the wedding ceremony would take place. Neither the bride nor groom knew when the father would say it was good enough, so they both needed to be ready as the finishing was about done. Then the groom would go for the bride, often at night, and she would have to be ready.

The guests too would be notified at the last minute. The party began with the ceremony, and then the party lasted a whole week. Immediately after the ceremony, the bride and groom retired to the place he had prepared, then the friend, best man, of the groom stood by the door. When the marriage had been consummated, the groom would shout in his joy and the friend of the groom would relay the good news to the guests.

Yod and Vav are the two smallest letters in the Hebrew alphabet. In Matthew 5:18 the text says "For truly I say to you: until the sky and the earth would pass away, not one yod or one vav could pass away from the Torah, until everything would come to pass." Luke 16:17 is similar but lists only the vav. We know that every Rabbi taught in the Hebrew language from the earliest days in Israel all the way up to modern times. The Hebrew language was preserved because Scripture was in Hebrew and Hebrew was and still is the language of the synagogue. Jesus would have used the Hebrew letter yod, which was recorded in Greek using the comparable Greek letter, iota.

The Hebrew letter vav has no comparable Greek letter since there is no "v" sound in Greek. Both Matthew and Luke overcame the problem with the Greek word keraia, which some say refers to decoration of the Torah manuscript, but it actually means little horn or little hook. The Hebrew word vav, the name of the letter, means hook, so this is how we know that Jesus was speaking of the letter vav. It is not likely to refer to decoration because the Dead Sea Torah scrolls, dating from the days of Jesus, show that scrolls of that era were not decorated. Besides being the two smallest letters in the Hebrew alphabet the yod and the vav are also called soft letters because under some circumstances either letter can be left out of a word and the word would still be spelled correctly. So Jesus was saying that even the letters that can properly be left out of a word would not be omitted from the Torah as long as the Earth exists. We need to learn more about the Torah, the first five books of the Bible.

Yoke is mentioned by Jesus "Come to Me all those who work and are burdened, and I will give you rest. 29. You must immediately take My yoke upon you and you must now learn from Me, because I am gentle and humble in My heart, and you will find rest in your lives: 30. for My yoke is pleasant and My burden is insignificant." A yoke is a heavy wooden frame for harnessing together a pair of oxen or other draft animals. The rabbis teach that the Lord's yoke means total commitment, total surrender to His perfect will for your life. All your idols must be destroyed - there can be no pride, no love for possessions, fame, sports, or any other thing that could interfere with His plan for your life. Having nice things and enjoying some sporting event are not evil, but neither are they to interfere with the Lord's plan for your life. He will provide for all your needs. This does not necessitate a vow of poverty because He does take good care of His saints.

The yoke has other significance since it is made for two. For the vast majority of us that means a spouse fills the other side, but for some the Lord is the spouse. What is significant about the yoke is that each animal must pull its own weight. Often in ministry one has had the pride to feel he or she could go it alone, that the spouse was the provider or the cheerleader, or some other non-involved position. In this metaphor Jesus was saying that each couple is yoked, that if each is not pulling his own weight the ministry would not achieve all that could be done. We need to understand that God instituted marriage when He built Eve. He made Eve equal to Adam and adequate for any task assigned to Adam, based on the word translated meet in Gen. 2:18, KJV. The NIV translates it suitable, which is much closer to the Hebrew meaning. A couple is to act as one, but with each one carrying his load - they are not to be identical, but complementary.

The yoke can refer to any two joined together in any endeavor. As Paul said not to be unequally yoked referring to marriage with an unbeliever, so also any ministry or business yoking must be in line with God's perfect will.

The yoke belongs to the owner of the oxen, not the oxen. Each animal must be in total submission to the driver's will, obeying every command. If one animal is spirited and continually presses ahead it will wear itself out, but not go any faster than the mate. It's pressing will also tire the driver, who continually is pulling back on the reins. Obedience is the desired character.

The word for Rest in Matthew 11:28 & 29 means a temporary rest. It is a break, like a coffee break at work, or a brief respite from battle. Whenever possible, army units at the front are pulled back every few days so the soldiers can rest and clean up. They are not far from the battle, but are back far enough to get good food, sleep, clean their weapons, and prepare to go back into battle. This temporary rest is what Jesus is talking about here. A different Greek word is used for the permanent rest in His kingdom, spoken about in Hebrews, Chapters 3 & 4.

The yoke of the Lord is pleasant. The word translated pleasant is used seven times in the New Testament and this is only place the KJV translated it as easy. It is a word that always means something good and is sometimes used in talking about food. Pleasant is appropriate in this case regarding His yoke. We know from experience that doing His ministry may not always be easy, but it is pleasant. We are acquainted with missionaries who live under what anyone in this country would consider difficult conditions, but they love where they are and they are uncomfortable in the US because of all the materialism and pleasure seeking.

There is a prayer, called the Sh'ma, said three times each day by observant Jewish people. This is from Deuteronomy 6:4, "Hear O Israel, the Lord is our God, the Lord is one. And you shall love the Lord your God with all your heart and mind, with all your being, and with all your might." (Amp.) The rabbis refer to this as "acceptance of the yoke of heaven."

The burden of the Lord is so light it is insignificant. The Greek word translated light in Matthew 11:30 indicates the burden is so light that its weight cannot be detected. When the weight seems heavy it must mean that something is out of line, as when Jesus told Paul he was kicking against the goad, the cattle prod. Paul had been busy with his ministry, not His ministry.

Yom Kippur and Day of Memorial are not named in the NT, but there is a definite reference to Yom Kippur, the Day of Atonement. That Day is referred to in Acts 27:9, where it is called the Fast. Yom Kippur comes five days after the Day of Memorial, which most Christians call Feast of Trumpets. However, the Hebrew does not mention either a feast or a trumpet for this day. This is a call to repentance, which calls for a shofar, not a trumpet. The day spoken about in Matthew 24:31, Acts 27:9, 1 Corinthians 15:52, and 1 Thessalonians 4:16 with the phrase "last trumpet" is probably during the Feast of Unleavened Bread and not the Day of Memorial, also known as Rosh Hashanah.

Section II
Hebrew Names

The Biblical names we use today were first written in English nearly a thousand years ago, taken from the Latin Vulgate texts then in widespread use. The English alphabet frequently used the "J" from the German alphabet for the "I" giving us Jesus instead of Iesous, the Greek and Latin spellings. The German J is pronounced as Y, the same as the I in Latin or Greek. Other names on this list are radically different from the Hebrew for similar reasons, because they were filtered through Latin and/or Greek.

Note: the Hebrew ch or kh is pronounced as an H with a slight guttural

English	Hebrew
Abiathar	Avyatar
Abiud	Avichud (ch pronounced with a very faint guttural "H")
Abraham	Avraham
Akeldama	Chakal D'ma
Alpheus	Chalfai (every "Ch" pronounced as above)
Amminadab	Amminadav
Amos	Amotz
Anna (see Hannah)	Chanah
Ananias	Chananyah
Annas	Anan
Arimathea	Ramatayim
Armageddon	(See Harmageddon)
Babylon	Bavel
Barabbas	Bar-Abba
Barnabas	Bar-Nabba
Barsabbas	Bar-Sabba
Bartholomew	Bar-Talmai

Glossary

English	Hebrew
Bartimaeus	Bar-Timai
Beelzebul, Beelzebub	Baal-Zibbul
Bethany	Beit-Anyah, meaning house of sighing or lamenting
Bethesda	Beit-Hesed, meaning House of Mercy
Bethlehem	Beit-Lechem, meaning house of bread
Bethphage	Beit-Pagey
Bethsaida	Beit-Tsaidah
Bethzatha	Beit-Zata
Balaam	Bil'am
Belial	B'liya'al
Benjamin	Binyamin
Caiaphas	Kayafa
Cain	Kayin
Cainan	Keinan
Cana	Kanah
Canaan	Kanaan
Capernaum	Kafer Nachum, meaning Pleasant Village
Cherub (sing.)	K'ruv
Cherubim (plural)	K'ruvim
Clopas	Klofah
Eber, Heber	Ever
Egypt	Mitzrayim
Eli	Heli
Eliezer, Lazarus	El'azar
Elijah	Eliyahu
Elizabeth	Elisheva
Emmaus	Ammaus
Enoch	Chanoch
Enos	Enosh
Ephraim	Efrayim
Esli	Chesli
Eve	Chavah
Fringe on corner of Prayer Shawl	Tsitsit
Gabriel	Gavriel

English	Hebrew
Gehenna, Hell	Gey Hinnom
Gethsemane	Gat Sh'manim
Gideon	Gid'on
Gomorrah	Amora
Hamor, Emmor	Chamor
Hannah	Chanah
Haran	Charan
Harmaggedon	Har Meggido, meaning Mount Meggido (The correct English spelling of the Greek word is Harmaggedon.)
Hezron, Esron	Chetzron
Issachar	Yissass'khar
Isaac	Yitzchak
Jacob	Ya'akov
Jaffa, Joppa	Yafo
Jairus	Ya'ir
Jared	Yered
Jeconiah, Jehoiachin	Y'khanyahu
Jehoshophat	Y'hoshofat
Jericho	Yericho
Jerusalem	Yerushalayim
Jesus, Jose	Yeshua
Jeremiah	Yirmeyahu
Jesse	Yishae
Joanna	Yochannah
Joey	Yosi, nickname for Yosef
Joel	Yoel
John	Yochannan
Jonah	Yonah
Jordan	Yarden
Joseph	Yosef
Joshua	Y'hoshua
Jotham	Yotam
Judah, Judea, Judas	Y'hudah
Julius	Iulio
Korah	Korach
Isaiah	Yeshayahu

English	Hebrew
Iscariot	K'riot
Levi	L'vi
Manasseh	M'nasheh
Martha	Marta
Mary	Miryam in Hebrew, Mariam in Greek, Maria in Latin
Matthew	Mattityahu
Manaen	Menachem
Methuselah, Mathusala	Metushelach
Michael	Mikha'el
Midian	Midyan
Moses	Moshe
Nahor	Nachor
Nashon, Nasson	Nachson
Nagge	Naggai
Nahum	Nachum
Nain	Naim
Naphtali	Naftali
Nathan	Natan
Nazarenes	Natsratim
Nazareth	Natseret
Nicodemus	Nakdimon
Noah	Noach
Obed	Oved
Passover	Pesach
Pentecost	Shavuot, Feast of Weeks
Perez	Perets
Peter	Kefa, meaning rock. Spelled Kefa in Greek, Cephas in Latin.
Pharisee	Parush, P'rushim (plural)
Prayer Shawl	Tallit, Tallitot (plural)
Psalms	Tehillim, meaning Praises
Rahab	Rachav
Ram, Aram	Ram
Rebecca	Rivkah
Rehoboam	Rechavam

English	Hebrew
Rephan	Reifan
Reuben	Re'uven
Rhesa	Reisha
Ruth	Rut
Sabbath	Shabbat
Sabbaths, Weeks	Shabbatot
Sadducees	Ts'dukim
Salem	Shalem
Salome	Shlomit
Samaria	Shomron
Samson	Shimshon
Samuel	Shmuel
Sapphira	Shappirah
Satan	Satan, meaning Adversary, Arch Enemy
Saul	Sha'ul
S'dom	Sodom
Seder	Pesach Meal, the Last Supper
Semein	Shimi
Seth	Shet
Shealtiel	Sh'altiel
Sheol, Hell	Sh'ol
Silas	Sila
Siloam	Shiloach
Simon	Shim'on
Simeon	Shim'on
Solomon	Shlomo
Susanna	Shoshanah
Sychar	Sh'khem
Tabitha, Dorcas	Tavita
Terah	Terach
Thaddeus	Taddai
Thomas	T'oma
Timaeus	Timai
Torah	Torah, meaning Teaching, Instruction: Name of First Five Books of the Bible
Tyre	Tsor

Glossary

English	Hebrew
Unleavened Bread	Matzah
Uriah	Uriyah
Uzziah	Uziyahu
Vav	Vav, 2nd smallest Hebrew Letter
Village	Kafer
English	Hebrew
Yeshiva	Yeshiva (Talmudic College)
Yod	Yod, smallest letter in the Hebrew alphabet
English	Hebrew
Zacchaeus	Zakkai
Zadok	Tsadok
Zarephath	Tsarfat
Zebbedee	Zavdai
Zerah, Zara, Zarah	Zerach
Zerubbabel	Zerubavel
Zion	Tsion
Zebulun, Zebulon	Z'vulun
Zechariah	Z'kharyah

~ APPENDIX ~

LISTING OF APOCHRYPHAL REFERENCES AND ALLUSIONS

Book	Abrev.	Verses	NT Verses
Ascension of Isaiah		5:11-14	Heb 11:37
Assumption of Moses			Jude 9
Baruch	Bar	4:7	1Cor 10:20
		4:35	Rev 18:2
Enoch	En	1:2	1Pet 1:12
		1:9	Jude 14,15
		9:4	Rev 15:3, 17:14, 19:16
		14:22	Rev 5:11
		25:5	Rev 15:3
		27:3	Rev 15:3
		46:3	Col 2:3
		51:2	Lk 21:28
		60:8	Jude 14
		63:10	Lk 16:9
		69:27	Jn 5:22
		70:1-4	Heb 11:5
1 Esdras		1:32 (LXX)	Mt 1:11
Judith		11:19	Mt 9:36, Mk. 6:34
		16:17	Jas 5:3
1Maccabees	1Macc	1:54	Mt24:15,Mk.13:14
		2:60	2Tim 4:17
		3:45,51	Lk 21:24
		4:59	Jn 10:22
		6:7	Mt 24:15
2Maccabees	2Macc	3:26	Lk 24:4
		6:18-7:42	Heb 11:35

Book	Abrev.	Verses	NT Verses
2Maccabees (cont'd)	2Macc	13:4	1Tim 6:15
			Rev 17:14, 19:16
3Maccabees	3Macc	2:5	Rev14:10, 20:10, 21:8
		5:35	1Tim 6:15
			Rev 17:14, 19:16
4Maccabees	4Macc	2:5	Rev 7:7
		7:19	Mt 22:32
Psalm of Solomon	Ps Sol	5:4	Lk 11:21,22
		5:9-11 (LXX)	Mt 6:26
		7:6	Jn 1:14
		17:23, 24	Rev 2:26, 27
		17:34	Rev 21:24, 26
Sirach	Sir	1:8	Rev4:2,9,10,5:1,5:7,
			5:13, 6:16, 7:10, 15,
			9:4, 21:5
		1:10	1Cor 2:9
		5:3	1Thes 4:6
		5:11	Jas 1:19
		11:19	Lk 12:19, 20
		15:11-13	Jas 1:13
		16:14	Ro 2:6
		23:1	Mt 6:13
		23:4	1Pet 1:17
		25:23	Heb 12:12
		27:6	Mt 7:16
		28:2	Mt 6:12
		28:18	Lk 23:24
		29:11	Mt 6:20, Lk 18:22
		33:1	Mt 6:13
		35:19	Mt 16:27
		37:28	1Cor 6:12
		38:18	2Cor 7:10
		44:16	Heb 11:5
		44:21	Gal 3:8, Heb 6:14,
			11:12
		48:10	Lk 1:17

Book	Abrev.	Verses	NT Verses
Susanna	Sus	46 Theodotion	Mt 27:24
Tobit	Tob	4:6 (LXX)	Jn 3:21
		5:15	Mt 20:2
		7:17	Mt 11:25
		11:9	Lk 15:20
		13:7, 11	Rev 15:3
		13:18	Rev 19:1
		14:4	Mt 23:38
		14:5	Lk 21:24
Wisdom	Wsd	2:11	Ro 9:31
		2:18-20	Mt 27:43
		2:23	1Cor 11:7
		3:8	1Cor 6:2
		4:10	Heb 11:5
		5:5	Ac 20:32, 26:18
		5:22	Lk 21:25
		6:18	Jn 14:15
		7:1	Ac 10:26
		7:7	Eph 1:17
		9:1	Jn 1:3
		9:16	Jn 3:12
		12:12	Ro 9:20
		12:13, 14	Ac 5:30
		14:3	1Pet 1:17
		15:3	Jn 17:3
		15:7	Ro 9:21
		16:9	Ro 9:3
		16:13	Mt 16:18
		16:22	Rev 8:7
		18:1	Ac 9:7, 22:9

Other Writings:

Aratus, Paenomena 5   Ac 17:28

Epimenides, de Oracalis Ac 17:28, Ti 1:12

Menander, Thais (218)   1Cor 15:33